A History of Psychology in Autobiography

in Autobiography

VOLUME VIII

A History of Psychology in Autobiography

VOLUME VIII

Edited by Gardner Lindzey

STANFORD UNIVERSITY PRESS   1989

Stanford, California

Stanford University Press, Stanford, California

© 1989 by the Board of Trustees
of the Leland Stanford Junior University

Printed in the United States of America

LC 30-20129
ISBN 0-8047-1492-4

Photograph on p. 2 courtesy of the
Oskaloosa Independent

To KENNETH MACCORQUODALE

A close friend and former colleague whose dignity,
quality of mind, taste, and talent
were immediately recognized by all who knew him

Preface

I begin with a slight diversion—a brief history of the histories. This series now spans almost 60 years. It comprises eight volumes and has involved five publishers and three editors. My participation began when, on a casual visit to Harvard in the early 1960's, I found myself in the basement of Memorial Hall chatting with a long-time and admired friend, Gary Boring. During our conversation I asked Gary whether he would be willing to participate in a revival of the autobiography series. With a good deal of initial ambivalence, he agreed to participate in the venture "if you do all the work." By the time I had returned to my office at the University of Minnesota shortly thereafter, I found two of Gary's famous postcards—typed by him and with the initial postcard (not necessarily the first to arrive) continuing on to the second. These messages were full of reflections and suggestions for next steps and made clear that, as I had known, I would not "do all the work."

We agreed to move the series from the defunct Clark University Press, which had published the first four volumes in the series, to Appleton-Century-Crofts. At the time, I had joined Richard M. (Mike) Elliot and Kenneth MacCorquodale as co-editor of the Century Psychology Series. It seemed to me to represent the ultimate in stability, continuity, and quality for all publishers of significant psychological works. Indeed, my friend Gordon Ierardi had invited me to become an editor for Wiley (a serious competitor in quality), but I declined because Gordon did not want to commit to a "series" and I looked upon Appleton-Century-Crofts as providing more continuity and being less dependent than Wiley upon the charm and talent of a single person. Things change—particularly in the publishing world—and while the second volume in which I was implicated was in press, Appleton-Century-Crofts was swallowed by Prentice-Hall. That orphaned volume was put out of print almost as it saw the light of day. When preparation of Volume VII began, I happily moved it to W. H. Freeman, where I was now a co-editor (with Richard C. Atkinson and Richard F. Thompson), working with a psychology editor (W. Hayward "Buck" Rogers) who was an old friend. Freeman had developed from a San Francisco base and had a very strong set of psychological volumes. Omitting all of the interesting details, I will say only that W. H. Freeman was acquired by Gerard Piel and *Scientific American* and ultimately moved to New York with a good many personnel changes.

By this time (1984) I was convinced that, at least for the sake of continuity, the series properly belonged with a university press, and for many reasons the appropriate choice seemed to be Stanford University Press. With Stanford's long history of excellence in academic psychology and a willingness and interest on the part of friends and colleagues at the university and the Press, it seemed likely that the future of the series could be guaranteed. I do hope this will prove to be the case, and I am certainly relieved that the American Psychological Association's Board of Directors rebuffed the offer that Gary and I made many years ago to have the APA sponsor the series. Although the intimacy and scope of my relationships with the APA have waxed and waned over the past 30 years, it has generally been on a downward trajectory, and I would not be pleased to deal with the current APA on the details of this volume. In all, our current publishing arrangement promises to be productive and congenial for all concerned.

Now, about this book. It was prepared with the active collaboration of an Advisory Committee composed of Anne Anastasi, Richard C. Atkinson, Frank A. Beach (deceased), Kenneth E. Clark, R. J. Herrnstein, Ernest R. Hilgard, David E. Leary, Kenneth MacCorquodale (deceased), Roger W. Russell, Robert R. Sears, Richard F. Thompson, Leona E. Tyler, and Seymour Wapner. After the usual compilation of lists of names made up of past candidates for previous volumes, nominations from committee members, and lists of psychologists who had received major awards or honors, we went through a process of rating, ranking, and eventually inviting. The process was begun in June 1983, and the volume went to press in September 1988. As in the past, we had virtually no declinations but a significant number of delinquencies.

In my biased judgment, this is the most interesting set of accounts that has yet appeared in the series. It includes several of the most gifted writers that psychology has (or has had); it includes our first joint autobiography; and although the contributors are less balanced in nationality and gender than we wished, our three women contributors exceed the number in any previous volume. Bärbel Inhelder's contribution provides a delightful and essential report on her own work and much of what has transpired in Geneva since Piaget's autobiography was published in this series more than 30 years ago.

By now we have a fascinating set of perspectives on Harvard and its Department of Psychology and Social Relations. In previous volumes Gordon Allport, E. G. Boring, H. A. Murray, B. F. Skinner, and S. S. Stevens provided quite different views of the old Department of Psychology and the formation of the new Department of Social Relations. Roger Brown and George Miller offer another perspective, not exactly from the bottom up, but certainly from different time periods and roles. Various others, among them Leo Hurvich, provide further insights into the complex interactions involving Memorial, Emerson, and William James halls. We also have had an array of Stanford contributions, including Lewis Terman, Robert R. Sears, Ernest R. Hilgard, and Quinn McNemar. These papers, when added to Eleanor Maccoby's, Roger Barker's, William Estes's, and Lee Cronbach's, give us an illuminating array of views of a department that for many years has had one of the strongest graduate psychology programs in the world. The contributions of William Estes, George Miller, and Carl Pfaffmann provide differing views of the interesting intersection between psychology and the Rockefeller Institute and University. We need only Neal Miller's autobiography to round out this picture. These and comparable sets of overlapping accounts are rich material for historians of psychology as well as fascinating reminiscences for those of us who have known and interacted with some or all of these distinguished psychologists.

Preparation of this volume would not have been possible without the skillful interventions (editorial, motivational, and organizational) of Muriel Bell, Joyce McDonald, and Ellen F. Smith. Facilities indispensable to the enterprise were generously provided by the Center for Advanced Study in the Behavioral Sciences.

Center for Advanced Study in the Behavioral Sciences   G.L.
Stanford, California

Contents

A History of Psychology in Autobiography

VOLUME VIII

Roger M. Barker

Roger G. Barker

For most of my career in psychology, I have been a naturalist, investigating relations between persons, environments, and behavior as they occur, without input from me as investigator. My task in this autobiography, as I see it, is to carry on in the same way with respect to my traits as a person, the situations of my life, and my behavior as a psychologist. This confronts me with a problem. I have always made sure that the variables I have dealt with were independently and objectively appraised. In the present case, however, I alone am the observer, appraiser, and reporter of my personality, my environments, and my behavior. Are less independence and objectivity possible? As I look back on my life, will it be more than a TAT card from which I construct a self-satisfying story, omitting and altering parts in accordance with my conscious and unconscious motives? Although I cannot avoid selective and distorted perception and memory, on reviewing my life, I discover extended periods dominated by distinctive and verifiable environmental conditions and personal characteristics. By focusing on these salient epochs, I hope to reduce the projection effect. I emphasize the early epochs because it appears to this amateur personologist that the child in my case has been father of the man and the successive environments, the mothers. The middle years are presented briefly. They have been dealt with extensively in another publication (Barker, 1979a).

Hoofed to Plover?

I was born in Macksburg, Iowa, on March 31, 1903. My family moved to Plover when I was a few months old; it was here I lived the first seven years of my life. Plover at this time consisted of approximately 30 families living in detached houses scattered over 60 acres of land along four streets. It was a real town, not a crossroads. It had a grain elevator, railroad station, restaurant, tavern, general store (which my father managed), drug store, bank, barbershop, harness shop, lumber yard, telephone exchange, doctor's office, school, two churches, creamery, Masonic Lodge, blacksmith shop, and hotel. The town was the principal trading center for an area of about 50 square miles with approximately 150 farms. The land was very productive, but times were hard. There were foreclosures and tax sales; there was the County Poor Farm. In Plover and district, small-scale free enterprise was unrestrained; there were winners ("Capital!") and losers ("Too bad"). There was no big brother. A kind of defiant freedom reigned. Mary Henderson, my first grade teacher, was on target when she taught me my first patriotic song.

> There was a little man with a big bass drum.
> Boom! Boom! Boom!
> Who knows when a war may come.
> Boom! Boom! Boom!
> I'm not at all frightened, you understand,
> But if I'm called to fight for my land,
> I want to be able to play in the band.
> Boom! Boom! Boom!

During the Plover years, I was on the frail side. The accepted family lore is that I cried continuously during my first six months because of feeding difficulties. Burly farmers, customers in the store, would sometimes blare forth for all to hear, "Guy, send that boy of yours out to the farm. I'll put some meat on his bones and make a man of him." And I was shy. A picture taken when I was about four years old tells the story. A traveling photographer with his big camera, tripod, and black shroud came to take the children's picture. Posed on the porch before the big bay window with my sister, 14 months older, I found the hidden, crouching man and the big eye looking at me too much—I retreated into the house despite vigorous protests by my mother and sister. The result was a picture of my exuberant, smiling sister, center stage, with me in the upper right background peeping through the curtains of the window. This picture might be appropriately titled "Portrait of a Field Psychologist as a Young Child."

We had a horse and buggy, cow, chickens, apple trees, a walnut grove, a superior privy with three seats of different heights and sizes of apertures. By the time my sister, Lucile, and I could travel by foot, we ranged over most of the town. We knew most of the inhabitants by name, and we had considerable information and opinions about them. The general store, which dealt in the full range of available consumer goods from yard goods and shoes to cheese and spice, was the most heavily populated of the town's settings. It was owned by our grandfather and managed by our father, so Lucile and I had easy access to Plover's Crystal Palace. My memories of the delights of Plover are almost endless. But traces of negative experiences remain, and two of them may be of prescient significance. Both involved public humiliation. Our father was an enthusiastic player of parlor games. When I, about three years old, refused to play blindman's buff at a neighbor's party and seemed to sulk, he picked me up and gave me a smart spank on my bottom to find I had wet my pants. The double public embarrassment of wetting my pants and being spanked is still with me. The other occasion was at the "children's program," an important church gala in Plover; individuals and classes sang, gave recitations, and presented skits. The church sanctuary was always packed. My recitation on this occasion was:

> Some little boys are very shy
> To speak a piece they will not try,
> But as for me, I do not fear
> To speak before the people here,
> For they are all my friends, I know,
> So now I'm through,
> I'll bow and go.

I did nobly, I am told, up to "For they are all my friends," when the sight of the multitude of their faces before me crushed me and I fled from the stage. The applause was tremendous. This humiliating experience is not only prominent in my memory, it is regularly recounted by family members.

These are the most unpleasant memories of my life in Plover; there are very few others. The pleasures are dominant: swinging on the marvelous swing from a high limb on the elm tree; riding Santa Anna, the burro, who patiently accommodated many children on his short back and neck; going for buttermilk with a pail when the creamery whistle blew signaling that churning was complete (unpasteurized milk, of course); getting eggs from the nests hidden in the mangers and the haymow; going for rides in the surrey pulled by unreliable Old Glory who would sometimes, to our great excitement (almost pleasure), balk and lie down in the shafts. I shall stop here not knowing how long the list might be.

So Plover, Iowa, and Roger Barker linked up to produce a belle époque for the boy. Did it have consequences for his career in psychology? Students of imprinting and homing may have ideas about its bearing on the fact that 37 years later I returned to a Plover in Kansas and engaged in 25 years of research in the town, living there during this time and continuing to do so after retirement. The sheep farmers of Yorkshire, with whom I became acquainted in the course of the research, have ideas also; they have the answer, in fact. Yorkshire sheep cannot be moved from the moor where they are born and raised. If moved, they return to the home moor over long distances. When a moor is sold, the sheep are as much a part of the transfer as the grass, heather, and bracken rooted to it. The sheep are said to be "hoofed" to the moor. According to these Yorkshire experts, I was "hoofed" to the likes of Plover and my fate in this respect was sealed during my first seven years.

A Regular Fellow

My family consisted of mother, father, and five children when we left Plover. My parents were both offspring of homesteaders who had settled in Iowa in the 1850's and 1860's, but who by 1903 had left their farms and become small business and political figures in neighboring towns. When I knew my grandparents, they had retired to California.

In the summer of 1910 I was suddenly removed from the secure, warm womb of Plover to the precarious, impartial world of Des Moines. During the next seven years, I lived in nine houses, eight neighborhoods, four towns, two countries; I attended five schools and four churches; I encountered the vicissitudes of rural, town, and urban life and of the lower-middle and lower-upper social classes. I was regularly confronted with new situations that were potentially hazardous yet at the same time potentially beneficent; consequently, I experienced unpredictable disasters and lucky breaks. The balance of pluses and minuses suited me. I was a puny, shy seven-year-old at the beginning of this epoch and a sturdy, confident, neo-adolescent at the end. The annals of these years are brief, but they were not simple for me or my family.

Our move to Des Moines was a step up financially and socially, and the ascent continued for the five years we lived in the city. We started in a slate-colored, six-room house on Harrison Avenue, not far from the East Side (the other side of the tracks), and ended in a balconied, lawned, twelve-room house on 30th Street, not far from Grand Avenue (the upper uppers and our father's boss lived there). We started with Old Glory and the surrey and ended with a 1909 Pierce Arrow automobile on the reinforced floor of the barn.

Our father was a middle-level executive in a small national insurance company. In the spring of 1915 he lost his job as the result of a "hostile takeover" of the firm. What do 42-year-old parents with five children do in such a case? These parents hitched the Pierce Arrow to a four-wheeled trailer loaded with camping gear (with my new bicycle on top) and drove the Lincoln Highway to the Panama-Pacific International Exposition in San Francisco. There were 30 miles of paved road between Des Moines and Placerville, California. The summer of 1915 was the wettest for years in Iowa and Nebraska; the trailer had narrow carriage wheels with hard rubber tires that cut to the bottom of every mudhole. The trip took six weeks; on a good day we might make 75 miles. We visited the fair, staying with my father's parents in Palo Alto.

We moved to Escondido in Southern California for the winter, living with my mother's sister in a big house that had belonged to their parents. Our father "looked around for an opening" during the winter, but finding nothing, opted for farming in Canada near Provost, Alberta, on land he had purchased in 1909 as a speculative investment. The family followed in the late spring and were plunged, without preparation, into a pioneer life: a homesteader's shack, a wood-burning cook stove, water from a well via bucket and rope, horse power (our nearest neighbor used oxen), a Democrat (light, one-horse wagon with two double seats for trips to town, six miles distant), and thrashers (sixteen men to bed and feed for the better part of a week). The 1916 crop was excellent, so we returned to Palo Alto for the school year, renting a house near our grandparents. The family fortunes were reviving. Here is a sample from my memory film clips of events that boosted and battered me into shape during these years.

PUBLIC HUMILIATION IN FOREST AVENUE THIRD GRADE

New boy, Roger, eager for approval, knows the eight-times-table perfectly, so in the test he writes in bold figures down the center of the half-page provided. Miss Delahoyd, the teacher, corrects the papers while the class does "quiet seat work." The boy is startled by Miss D's piercing voice. "Roger, come to the front of the class." Although stunned, the boy manages. "Face the class, Roger, and hold up your paper for all to see." He does. "What is wrong with Roger's paper, class?" No reply. "Irma, what did Roger do wrong? What mistake did he make?" Irma: "He wrote on the whole page." Teacher, "That is correct; a times-table should use only a corner of the page. Show Roger your paper, Irma." A disaster. The boy hugs the floor back to his seat and joins the losers at recess in their hymn:

Old lady Delahoyd
Sitting on a fence
Trying to make a dollar
Out of fifteen cents.

ALLEY LIFE ON HARRISON AVENUE

Boy quickly learns from the Alley Tribe the trade of collecting bottles for sale to the junk man. To be profitable, this business requires retrieving bottles from the back stoops of houses and back rooms of stores. There are tribal ceremonies such as the one under the overhanging roof at the rear of Mrs. Pry's Notion Store. Members gather and sing as loudly as possible:

I went down town
To buy a penny drum
I knocked at the door
And nobody come.
So I picked up a brick
And slung it at the glass
And along came a devil
A sliding on his ass.

Then they vamoose in all directions.

ANXIETY IN THE FOURTH GRADE, KIRKWOOD SCHOOL

Boy is doing seat work, but glances occasionally at a metal grating on the front wall near the ceiling. He has been told it is part of the ventilating system, but he has his suspicions. He thinks it is really a spy hole for Mr. Perk, the principal, and that behind it is a kind of catwalk along which Mr. Perk strides, checking on the goings-on in the room. Mr. Perk is very quiet, but occasionally his shadow can clearly be seen as he passes. The boy has a good view; he sits at the center desk of the front row; he sits there because the teacher can't decide if he belongs in the "A" group on the right or the "B" group on the left.

READING

The boy checks out a library book for the first time. It is from the newly established circulating shelf at Kirkwood school. It is called *The Wizard of Oz*. As he lugs it home he finds it to be very big, thick, heavy; this so discourages him he returns it next day without opening it. It is easier to listen to his father read almost every evening from such writers as Thornton W. Burgess, James Whitcomb Riley, Eleanor H. Porter, Frances Hodgson Burnett, Robert Louis Stevenson, and Harold Bell Wright. In good weather, all the children in the family often meet their father at the street car stop with the latest book, which he reads as they walk the block home.

CAMPFIRES AND HUNTING

The boy's evening job on the trip west is to gather firewood for the supper cooking. Wood is often scarce, but there is usually sagebrush—and jackrabbits. He always takes the ".22" rifle in his search for wood (a ".22 long" will kill a rabbit). On several occasions he comes back triumphantly with game. Rabbits are good eating, especially since, without refrigeration, other fresh meat is an infrequent luxury.

A SCHOOL SUCCESS

The question before the seventh and eighth grade of the Escondido Primary school is how to "point off" the decimals in the answer to a division problem involving decimals. Mr. Judd, the teacher (and school principal): "Roger, will you come to the front of the room and tell the rule?" The boy complies with alacrity: "When dividing with decimals, point off as many places in the quotient as those in the dividend exceed those in the divisor." The boy is surprised; he does not know why he knows the answer or how Mr. Judd seems to know that he knows. This is the only grade school success he can remember.

BUFFALO SKULLS

On the unbroken prairie near Provost a few buffalo skulls remain from the once great herds. The boy diligently searches for them and makes a pile of a score or more before the shack. He is very proud.

ATHLETE FOR A DAY

On the first day of the boy's attendance at the junior high school in Palo Alto there is a free-throw basketball contest. Boy reluctantly joins the line of contestants; he has never thrown a basketball. He comes to the throw line; he hefts the ball and is surprised by its great weight. He throws—a good one. Another good one. Still another basket. On and on, he can't understand it. He is a machine, . . . 13, 14, . . . 24 hits out of 25. The boy is famous for an hour, his only sports-connected achievement.

THE BOY SCOUT

The boy joins the Palo Alto Scout Troop; he is a Tenderfoot. He "sells" Victory Bonds (to his grandfather) and wins a bronze medal. The troop goes on a weekend camping trip in the Coast Range mountains. The boys are surprised and excited to find a Girl Scout camp on the next ridge. It requires some careful scouting to spy them out. Some scouts report success: "We saw their boobies." The boy isn't so successful; in fact, he isn't sure what he is looking for. On returning Sunday evening, the boys are let off the flatbed truck at the town center. The boy races home through the cool evening air and deserted streets; he feels his time has come.

Did my seven-year journey through Des Moines, California, and Alberta presage my life in psychology? I find no sign of things to come, no pushes, no preparation. But in the eyes of my family and other associates, I had improved. At fourteen, I was fully acceptable to my father as a son. I had changed from a spindly, timid child to become, in my own eyes, a regular fellow who could make it on my own. In no way did this point me toward psychology, but it remained with me during the next disastrous period and, I believe, helped to pull me through.

Down for the Count

A few weeks after my exhilarating return from the Boy Scout camp, my family was awakened by my cries of terror. I was having a nightmare. I had a high fever. Terrors and high fever continued for some time without a diagnosis or precise treatment. The fever was lowered by a new drug from Germany that the doctor used with considerable misgiving because the side effects were unknown. It was called aspirin. When the diagnosis of osteomyelitis was finally made, the prognosis given my parents was not encouraging and proved to be correct. For seven years I was an invalid, usually with a low fever, often with a discharging sinus from knee, hip, elbow, or back. All treatments were ineffective, including two surgical interventions at the Mayo Clinic and bed rest in a sanatorium. As the mainline doctors gave up we turned to folk remedies, nostrums, and mind and spiritual cures. It was while taking the "milk diet" cure recommended by Bernarr Macfadden, publisher of the journal *Physical Culture* and later of "yellow" tabloid newspapers, that I began to improve and slowly became symptom-free. In fact, there had been remissions before; I had been able to attend school for intervals amounting to about three school semesters.

During this period the family's fortunes were downhill. We lived in or near Provost, Alberta, most of the time. After the good wheat crop of 1916 there was a succession of poor crops that, year by year, reduced my father's resources until he was forced to give up farming and sell his land. We moved permanently to Palo Alto.

One source of the family's financial troubles was the continual drain of my medical expenses and special education (as a residential student at Alberta College at Edmonton). Nothing was ever said to me about this; the expenses were accepted without question. But I knew I was a burden, and I was ashamed. I was ashamed for six years: ashamed of the financial burden on my family; ashamed of letting my father down (from a regular fellow, I had become a weak sister); ashamed of the trouble I caused my mother (I took the place in her cares and worries of my Down's syndrome sister who had died); ashamed of my idleness and lack of achievement (the continual low fever and the time required for treatment interfered with any persistent endeavor).

When I seek for the influence this epoch of life had upon my career in psychology, the evidence is all negative: poor education (meager science and mathematics, no foreign language); no strong interests; low self-confidence (when I did attend school, I was three or four years older than my schoolmates, yet I was generally behind scholastically and socially). It is true that my breadth of experience was greatly expanded: I had experienced deep despair and great pain; I had explored a number of philosophies of life. But in some ways, these deeper experiences put me into conflict with my peers as I emerged from my lost adolescence. On the one hand, I felt greatly inferior to them and was, in fact, inadequate on their turf; on the other hand, I knew more about life in other situations, about real life as I saw it—so, in this respect, I felt superior. I was simultaneously diffident and self-assured, deferential and condescending. It was not a comfortable experience or a solid base for resuming my education and eventually a career. In these respects, 1917–24 appeared to be lost years. As it turned out, however, a secret agenda was being prepared that became of crucial importance for my life in psychology.

College Days

I was lucky that in 1924 elitism had not yet afflicted higher education. I had no high school transcript; only a letter from the pastor of the First Baptist Church of Palo Alto to the president of the University of Redlands was required to gain admission as a freshman. A year later, I had only to bicycle from our house in Palo Alto to Stanford University on registration day, present my record from Redlands (a fair one), pay $75 tuition, select the courses I wished to take, and I was a Stanford student.

The watchword of Stanford's first president, David Starr Jordan, was

"the winds of freedom blow." Fortunately some of this spirit still prevailed in 1925, so I could begin to get my bearings in the academic world
at my own pace. I could explore with few restrictions, and missteps were
not dangerous. I could not escape, however, the oppressive race for grades.
I came to the university from my years of isolation with some convictions
that were out of joint with the time and place and that did not help my
grades. One was that not all things in life are of equal importance, that
some classes do not deserve the work required for a good grade. I worked
hard at genetics, which was important to me, and received an A; I listened
in geology, a side issue, and received a C. Another conviction: what is in
the head is important, not what is on the exam papers. So I did not take
notes; I wrote brief accounts of what I had learned at the end of each day.

When it became time to declare a major field of study I drifted into
psychology because it seemed to open many doors to a future life: "doing
good" via clinical or educational psychology, getting rich if applied in
business, becoming a scholar in experimental or theoretical psychology.

As a Stanford undergraduate, I began to recover from my initial defi-
cits of education, motivation, and self-confidence. But it was a particular
change in my environment that gave me a future.

Right Support

Louise Dawes Shedd entered my life in 1927. We were more-or-less engaged in the spring of 1928 when we both received B.A. degrees, and we
were married in 1930. What has this to do with my career in psychology?
Much indeed.

My family had been devoted to me and had showered me with evidence
of their love and high regard, but I could not accept this as unbiased evidence of my standing in the larger world. They had invested too much in
my welfare to admit any doubt of their judgment. Stanford University
had been noncommittal; I had been tolerated with only a few signs of approval (B.A. "With Distinction," not "Great Distinction"). The Psychology Department and my peers voted "judgment deferred." So when the
independent voice of a stranger not implicated in my past spoke up clearly
and pronounced me worthy, I listened and began to believe it. She was
intelligent (Phi Beta Kappa, B.A. "With Great Distinction"), and she
moved in the university's ruling circles (president of her living group).
When she stamped me with approval some others, too, took notice. One
of these was Lewis M. Terman, chairman of the Psychology Department.

Much of Terman's life in psychology was devoted to studies of gifted persons, and he gave special heed to those who came to his attention. Louise was one. Terman was a friend and champion of the president of the university, Ray Lyman Wilbur, who strongly backed his research, some of which, such as his studies of marriage, were sensitive in those times. So, when Terman discovered that Louise Dawes Shedd was not only an able student, but also the niece of Ray Wilbur, the halo effect became operative, and I became more than "that student Barker"; I became Roger Barker, the friend of his friend's brilliant niece. Such are the influences that shape careers, even in science.

From her childhood Louise had aspired to be a teacher, and she prepared to teach biology (M.A. 1929). During the first six years of our marriage, she taught in a high school near Stanford and was our main financial support. During this time, and for the next ten years when our three children were young, she became more interested in people than in biological specimens; she took classes (testing, counseling, remedial reading) and part-time jobs (teaching and counseling at all levels from nursery school to college) preparing for dealing with people. In 1947 she joined me as co-investigator in a field study of child and adult behavior.

In the Rebekah Lodge of Oskaloosa there is the position of Right Support of the Noble Grand. Since 1927, when Louise Dawes Shedd validated me as a worthy person to myself and to my associates she has been Right Support of my career in psychology, and in the later years Co-Noble Grand. She has been a sustaining environmental force.

Becoming a Psychologist

The school year 1928–29 was a beautiful one for Louise and me. She worked toward her M.A. in biology, and I, toward mine in psychology. The laboratories were in adjacent buildings. She was studying the protozoan *Busaria truncatella*, which thrived in the long grass of the wet swales of the nearby Coast Range mountains, and she required help in collecting specimens. Who, but I?

In the spring, we were able to announce our engagement and the good fortune that she had been hired to teach biology in an Oakland, California, high school and that I had been admitted as a graduate student in neighboring University of California, Berkeley, with a teaching assistantship. Oh blessed prospects!

Then came a double whammy. During the summer, symptoms of my old enemy appeared. I could not accept them; I denied them; I kept them from Louise. But the infection was obdurate, and by September I was on my back with my father as nurse (my mother was ill and away for treatment; his projects had not thrived; he had time). I was scarcely able to form the letters, to write the words, to compose the sentences to convey the news to Edward Tolman that I could not start my work at the University of California. I received a kind, regretful reply.

The basic questions in my mind were: Will Louise stand by me? Should I let her? I cannot remember that this was ever openly discussed between us. She was caught up in her new job. She came to see me on weekends in the hot upstairs room where I was bedfast. She told me of her exhilarating experiences. Time did pass. In the spring of 1929 I was able to get out to Stanford, and the department accepted me as a graduate student. I have presented in another publication (Barker, 1979a) some details of how Stanford and later the University of Iowa undertook to mold me into a psychologist, so here I shall deal with basic features.

Stanford University

Stanford cast me in three roles in the five years I was under its direction: student, apprentice, and participant observer. The effectiveness of these assignments in shaping me into the psychologist I became was, I believe, in the order given, least to most effective.

The student program of classes, seminars, reading lists, and so forth, got me through the examinations making me eligible for the lifetime brand of Ph.D., but much of what I put down in the exam paper was becoming obsolete as I wrote. However, the student program did provide a fairly solid base for the continually changing structure of psychological knowledge I was to build for myself. I say "fairly solid" because most of the staff of the Psychology Department were devoted to research; teaching was secondary and was, therefore, allotted a small portion of their limited resources of time and energy. This was not negligence, but a matter of policy; they did not think didactic teaching was of great importance. Preoccupation with research not only diminished the quality of classroom exposition but also contributed to the omission of enduring problems of psychology. Research scientists, and I am one, are necessarily preoccupied with details of obtaining and analyzing data. This limits perspective; they teach what is on their minds—the nuts and bolts of their investigation—not principles and theories or the implications of their projects for basic issues.

The apprenticeship program at Stanford was another matter; consequences of my thesis research under the aegis of Walter R. Miles and of my post-doctoral work with Calvin P. Stone are still with me. Miles was in tune with the department ethos in one respect; he let the winds of freedom blow to an extreme degree. He was entranced by instrumentation of all sorts (some called them gadgets). When I began with him, he was working on finger mazes, and I fell in with the project by devising two new finger mazes for studying human learning (Barker, 1931a, 1931b). Miles was impressed by my mazes and told me to "do something with them," which I did for my master's thesis (Barker, 1931c). When, two years later, Miles signed it, he was starting the Later Maturity Study, a pioneer investigation of changes in old age. He had a research assistantship available, which I badly needed. I chose to study "ability to do fatiguing muscular work in the elderly" for my doctoral dissertation. I devised an apparatus for measuring changes in the rate at which air is pumped into a spirometer with a hand-held bulb. The rate of input was graphically recorded on a revolving drum. Miles liked the apparatus and told me to go ahead; I did, and in about eighteen months turned in my thesis, which he approved (Barker, 1934). Other assistants used the same subjects for studies in learning, memory, reaction time, comprehension, etc. A vast amount of data was assembled for what gave promise of being a landmark volume.

When we finished, Miles was preparing to move to Yale, and the theses and supporting data were packed into strong trunks and departed with him. We all looked forward to seeing the publication in a year, two years, maybe three; we hoped it would forward our careers in psychology. It has now been 53 years, and neither I nor any of the other assistants with whom I have been in touch know what happened to our data or the pioneer volume.

I learned a nuts-and-bolts lesson from Miles that was very important to me later. The Later Maturity Study required a sample of subjects unbiased along many social-cultural dimensions. To accomplish this, Miles spent almost all his time on community activities and was very successful in getting subjects. When I planned field work, fifteen years later, this experience guided me in devoting sufficient resources to this respect of the research.

I worked with Calvin P. Stone almost full time for two-and-a-half years. When I received my degree, there were no jobs, and Stone, providentially, kept me on his research budget as a research assistant. These

were my most valuable years at Stanford. Stone's research dealt with relations between sexual maturity, behavior, and physical development in
animals (rats) and humans. My subsequent research career has been influenced by my experiences in Stone's laboratory; some of the consequences
were surprising and long delayed, but their origins are clear.

One of these is a continuing concern with the influence of the environment on behavior. This is surprising in view of Stone's intention to investigate the effects on somatic and behavioral development of hormones
involved in sexual maturation. We discovered that girls who reach the
menarche at an early age have more mature physiques and more mature
interests, attitudes, and social behavior than girls of the same chronological ages who reach the menarche five or six years later (Stone and Barker,
1937a, 1937b). A clear case of hormonal control of both somatic and behavioral development? Stone and I had made the measurements of the
girls' physiques, and we knew that nine-year-olds who are past the menarche are no longer "little girls," that they present quite different social
stimuli to themselves and others than their immature age mates. Could it
be that the social environments of the mature girls instigate more mature
social behavior? This was the origin of the question about the environment that has dominated my research in psychology ever since.

As a participant observer, I found the "role models" displayed before
me by the Stanford faculty to be congenial; without doubt, I have taken
the three most productive staff members as exemplars. Lewis M. Terman,
Edward K. Strong, and Calvin P. Stone were similar in these respects:
they were not brilliant, yet their accomplishments are valued by science;
they were narrow in their concerns, they focused their research efforts on
one or a very few problems; they worked hard, as if their motto was
"dogged does it."

University of Iowa

The University of Iowa means Kurt Lewin to me. I first met him in
1932 when he was a visiting professor at Stanford. I did not attend his
class, but I visited it occasionally and knew the reaction of the students.
The class was noteworthy for his use of the English language, for his tolerance, vitality, even gaiety, while firmly maintaining his own views, and
for his ideas that were sui generis to Stanford students. We could find no
places for valence, psychological force, inner-personal regions, lifespace,
motoric, levels of irreality, and so forth, in the house of psychology we had

built for ourselves from Boring, Gesell, Lashley, Spearman, Thorndike, Woodworth, and other notables of the 1930's. Lewin left Stanford a popular person but without having aroused interest in his views.

This was true of me, too, until the spring of 1935 when Terman asked me if I was interested in a fellowship to work with Lewin at the University of Iowa Child Welfare Station. Lewin? Child welfare? My expertise was with old people, rats, and adolescent girls. A single year's appointment? But Louise and I were at the end of our hope. Two years post-doc and no job in sight. No choice really.

My real introduction to Lewin and his psychology was traumatic. When we arrived in Iowa City, he was at work completing *Principles of Topological Psychology* (Lewin, 1936), and beginning *The Conceptual Representation and Measurement of Psychological Force* (Lewin, 1938). I immediately joined the routine already established. Tamara Dembo and Herbert F. Wright, the other assistants, met each morning with Lewin to go over what he had written the day before. The text would be read and then the comments and arguments would begin, everything from the exposition to the ideas was on the table. Tamara was an old hand with Lewinian methods and concepts; she had done a thesis with him. Herbert was a recent student of Donald K. Adams at Duke University; Adams had studied with Lewin in Berlin. The issues under discussion were not novel to the other assistants, but I was a raw recruit thrown into a series of battles in progress. The issues in contention, the rules and material of the engagements, and the fervor displayed were a revelation to me. At Stanford, disagreements were sometimes sharp, but they were usually over technical issues: reliability, significance of differences, instrumentation; more information would often solve these issues. Thinking aloud in public about such things as logical inconsistencies, deviation from theories, definitions of concepts was new to me. I was not properly introduced to Lewinian psychology as a system in comparison with other systems; I was thrown into its midst, and Stanford had provided me with no theoretical ballast to steady me. Although I did not gain a detached, scholarly comprehension of the place of Kurt Lewin's theories within the total array of psychological theories, particulars of his methods, concepts, and attitudes toward science have become crucial ingredients of the total mix from which my contributions have emerged.

The watchword at Stanford was "work hard." Lewin's axiom was "think hard." He would say to us, his assistants, "We must think more about this; think about other possibilities." We did this for hours at a time at morning sessions. From this thinking I winnowed five ideas that have been crucial to me ever since.

1. *Molar action.* Lewin's definition of molar action in terms of a person's needs, goals, and paths between the person and the goal (Lewin, 1938) is the basis of our studies of the structure of the stream of behavior.

2. *The person behaves.* Lewin's basic idea—that an individual's behavior is determined by multiple person-environment systems so interdependent that they function as a single dynamic unit (Lewin, 1936)—has implication for research methods as well as for personality theory. It means that measurements of single behavior systems cannot usually be made. Whereas a mechanic can remove a part of an engine, such as a spark plug, and test it "by itself," a psychologist cannot do this with an IQ, a dream, a hand grasp. I had not learned this lesson when I worked with Miles. I assumed the preciseness with which I measured "ability to do fatiguing muscular work" conferred precision on the findings. In fact, many systems were involved (muscles, motivation, joints, attention, and anxiety), but I made no effort to evaluate them separately. Handling this problem by independent measures of systems involved and weighting the contribution of each was not possible, as is often the case. It was not possible, either, in the research on frustration and regression that Dembo and I did with Lewin (Barker, Dembo, and Lewin, 1941). Our focus in the research, on the basis of theory, was the intellectual level of the children's activities. We could have made valid and reliable ratings of this, and we could have quickly analyzed the numerical ratings, as I had done in the Later Maturity study. Fortunately Lewin directed us to a more primitive, more time-consuming, but less restrictive method—the universally employed narrative account. It enabled us to consider not only evidence of intellectual level, but also evidence of tension and time perspective, both of which proved to be factors in the intellectual regression. This early experience encouraged me later to use narrative accounts as the primary method in major research. It is a mystery why psychologists avoid a coding system that has been used, tested, and improved over epochs of time. When the narrative record is used by a skilled observer with facility in language, it is extraordinarily effective for describing multiple attributes of behavior and the immediate situation.

3. *Unity of dynamic systems.* Lewin's theory of dynamic unity, including criteria for determining degrees of unity (Lewin, 1941), provides the basis for identifying the environmental unit we have used in our studies.

4. *Overlapping situations.* Lewin dealt with adolescent and minority behavior in terms of overlapping situations (Lewin, 1939); we have extended this to physically disabled persons.

5. *Psychological environment (E$_\psi$) and ecological environment (E$_\epsilon$).* Lewin was greatly concerned with the relation between "the totality of facts which determine the behavior of the individual" (Lewin, 1936, p. 12) that he represented as the *lifespace*, whose processes are completely determined by psychological laws, and "the physical and social facts which obey non-psychological laws," (p. 75) and occur at the boundary of the lifespace. He emphasized how greatly the latter can change the former, how, for example, a rainstorm can completely change the best laid plan. But he also emphasized that effects across this boundary cannot be predicted, because psychological and nonpsychological laws are incommensurate. The psychology of fear of storms and the meteorology of storms have nothing in common. He thought relations across the boundary between psychological and nonpsychological events are forever an empirical matter with only probabilistic predictions possible. Egon Brunswik, who was also concerned with this problem, agreed with this conclusion (Brunswik, 1955).

When, years later, environment-behavior relations became of central importance to me, my research findings led me to modify Lewin's views in two respects. I found not only that the nonpsychological environment affects the lifespace at the boundary, but also that the distal environment has consequences. I came to agree with Brunswik, who said, "Psychology . . . must be concerned with the texture of the environment as it extends in depth away from the common boundary" (Brunswik, 1957, p. 5). I call this environment the ecological environment (E$_\epsilon$) and the environmental part of the lifespace the psychological environment (E$_\psi$). (The latter term, E$_\psi$, replaces the term psychological habitat used in earlier publications to clarify linguistically a difficult conceptual distinction.) I also found that not all relations among the E$_\epsilon$ and E$_\psi$ are probabilistic; precise, lawful predictions can be made from some aspects of the E$_\epsilon$ to some aspects of the E$_\psi$ and behavior (Barker, 1960, 1968, 1987).

New ideas and attitudes were not the only benefits Iowa bestowed upon me and Louise. The Iowa Child Welfare Research Station and the Topology Meetings (discussion conferences Lewin sponsored at other schools) were all stops on the more-or-less underground, nonestablishment railroad of psychological ideas and methods. There I first met people who have become esteemed colleagues, warm friends, and valued acquaintances of the 47 ensuing years.

Trial and Error

In the decade following my fellowship at Iowa, I was affiliated with five universities for intervals of one to three and one-half years.

Harvard

In the 1930's Lewin was known as a child psychologist, eminent enough for Harvard University to call on him as a consultant: Lewin recommended me to teach their first undergraduate course in child psychology. Louise and I and Celia, our 16-month-old daughter, arrived in Cambridge in September 1937 and were immediately enveloped by new situations. Many were exhilarating, some were tense and vexatious, and almost all were strenuous. The pattern of life was strange in important respects. I had never taught a college class, so the prospect of inaugurating both my teaching career and an innovation in Harvard's teaching program was not relaxing. My unease was increased by my appointment as an instructor, a position without status or a future at Harvard. Instructors were a class apart from both the graduate students (an elite and powerful minority) and the faculty (still more elite and powerful); instructors were transients with a half-life of one, two, or (at most) three years. Then, it was up (for a negligible proportion) or out. Instructors ran scared. I was set apart further by my geophysical location in the Harvard Psychological Clinic, situated a block and a half from Emerson Hall, headquarters of the department. Unfortunately, Henry A. Murray, the clinic director, was on leave, so the clinic was on idle throttle for the year. It was a fine place to work on my class preparations, on the manuscript of *Frustration and Regression*, and on an experiment in the resolution of conflict (Barker, 1942a, 1946). Little of Harvard's uniqueness penetrated the clinic in the year 1937–38. I did have one regular excursion outside the clinic: I was hired, I understood, to teach child psychology at Harvard, but the small print said I would repeat the lecture each day at Radcliffe. As it turned out, the class schedule required me to "repeat" the class to women at Radcliffe *before* I gave it to Harvard men. As I huffed and puffed the 10-minute trek between the classes, I remembered with incredulity some family history that told of my grandmother being a regular student in classes with men at the University of Iowa in 1867.

As the year passed, it became increasingly clear to Louise and me that we should move on; that another year or two would not increase the benefits we were receiving. At the end of the year I had demonstrated my ability to teach sophisticated college students (there was no foot shuffling in my class and sufficient applause at the end, but the student publication evaluating the college offerings warned that my course had "too much statistics and not enough Freud"); I had done some research and writing; I had reaped the prestige value of a Harvard connection; I had begun to marshal my own resources; for the first time I was not a student or an apprentice. Our son Jonathan had his auspicious beginning in Boston. Now seemed the time to get to a place where I could do my own thing with some security of tenure.

There were some raised eyebrows when I informed the staff that I would be going to the University of Illinois, College of Education, as an assistant professor the next year. The only comment, "We think there would be no difficulty in placing you in another year."

Illinois and Chicago

At the University of Illinois in Champaign-Urbana, I was able to get my own life in psychology under way. Despite a heavy teaching schedule, there were favorable conditions for research initiatives and professional advancement.

Subjects were available from the university-connected school, so it was easy to return to a problem that first arose in Stone's laboratory, the environmental significance of physique in adolescence. Louise and I investigated the social situations of pre- and post-menarcheal girls and found that parents and teachers exert more pressure and provide more opportunities for mature behavior by physically mature girls than by their immature age-mates (Barker, Wright, Meyerson, and Gonick, 1946, pp. 27–41). I extended this line of research to the environmental significance of crippling (pp. 85–111).

Observations incidental to one of my more burdensome teaching duties were one source of my long-continued studies of community-wide environmental influences. My teaching included Saturday classes in child psychology in state teachers colleges located 35 to 200 miles from the university. The weekly trips by automobile or railroad took me through many small towns similar to Plover. Moving rapidly through the towns from sparsely inhabited country on one side to almost deserted regions on the other, I began to see them as cages with walls of open space that were almost impenetrable to children. I began to wonder, "What goes on in those cages? What are the living conditions and behavior of the children? Can towns such as these be used by child psychologists in the way students of animal behavior use wildlife refuges?" These wonderments were encouraged by two concurrent experiences.

During my second year at Illinois, I had a partial leave of absence to attend a year-long seminar in child development at the University of Chicago under the auspices of Daniel A. Prescott. I was relieved of my campus classes but continued teaching in the state colleges. Members of the newly formed Society for Research in Child Development were brought to the seminar to share the latest developments with the dozen or so resident members. This benefited me greatly by strengthening my rather meager background in child psychology. I was impressed by the fact that almost all scientific knowledge of children's behavior came from laboratories and clinics under conditions created by the investigators. We were given almost no information about the everyday living conditions and behavior of children. I noted that this was quite different from the information possessed by an agronomist with whom I became acquainted at the university. He could tell me about the growth and yields, the soils and nutriments of grain and grasses on the university's famous experimental plots, on farm fields, and even on the few remnants of the native prairie. I would have been embarrassed if he had asked me about the environmental conditions and child behavior yield of the homes, schools, and wild ranges of the streets of the towns. These experiences began to coalesce as a plan for research. Seven years passed before it took form and was underway.

The Child Development Seminar had other important consequences for me. It introduced me to ideas and attitudes that have been of lasting importance to me, and it introduced me to people who have become professional and personal friends, such as Ralph Tyler, Ernest (Jack) Hilgard, Herbert and Lois Stolz, and Nevitt Sanford. I became convinced that the ideas and information presented at the seminar should be more widely distributed. This inspired me to recruit two Iowa colleagues, Herbert Wright and Jacob S. Kounin, to cooperate in preparing the book, *Child Behavior and Development* (1943). It consisted of 35 research studies nominated by members of the Society for Research in Child Development as being the most important. The reports were prepared by the investigators themselves. The book had quite a wide distribution for a specialized publication, and it has some historical value as an indication of the state of the discipline in the 1930's.

Illinois and Chicago were good for us. Louise operated a nursery school in Urbana and taught remedial reading in Chicago's Central Y.M.C.A. College. The university administration was more than cooperative, it was indulgent: it gave me time off for the Chicago seminar; it paid my salary when I was ill with my old complaint and off duty; and it allowed me to teach small classes in my home when I was convalescing. My greatest obligation and appreciation is to Jack Kounin, who added my heavy teaching duties to his own when I was severely ill.

Still there were shortcomings. I was completely shut off and, to some degree, estranged from the psychology establishment. In the ordinary course of my duties I met no one from the Psychology Department. At Harvard I was not comfortable with the elite, and at Illinois I was uncomfortable with the plebs. I felt superior to my associates (and, at the same time, guilty), and I am sure they knew it. This became so salient I wrote a paper about the relations between psychologists and educators in an effort to understand (and relieve?) my unease (Barker, 1942b). In the fourth year an administrative policy added greatly to my unhappiness. The dean announced a change in policy whereby the small classes I taught would be consolidated into a single large class with attendance required. I was greatly distressed by both the policy and the way it was done without any consultation. Finally, there was the central Illinois weather. The best corn-growing weather is not the best weather for bone ailments. By the spring of 1942, it was clear to Louise and me that we should leave Illinois, if possible. I wrote to Terman, and by summer we were on our way back to Stanford. I was to be acting associate professor for the duration of the war.

Stanford Again

We were invigorated to be back on our old stomping ground where the sun was dependable and the winds of freedom still blew to some degree. But the war had imposed great changes. Stanford was no longer a community of scholars and learners; it was a waiting room filled with transients, both staff (like me) and students (the majority were women recruited to keep the university afloat during the war). For me, personally and professionally, there were both minuses and pluses. Although the teaching loads were heavy, including short intensive courses for military personnel, my career in psychology was furthered by the wartime environment. The staff shortage enabled me to attract some excellent graduate students (my first). Paul Mussen, Lee Meyerson, and I went to work on a problem that had had its origins at Stanford, namely, the environmental significance of physique, in this case disabled physique. I had begun working on this at Illinois as a purely scientific problem, and now the war enhanced its practical importance. Quinn McNemar, now my colleague on the staff (formerly my colleague as a graduate student), knew of our research and brought it to the attention of the Social Science Research Council, which was interested in a publication surveying current knowledge of the psychological aspects of physical disability that would be of value for the great task of rehabilitating the war injured. Funding arrangements were made, and I fell to with enthusiasm. The monograph, *Adjustment to Physical Handicap and Illness* (Barker, Wright, Meyerson, and Gonick, 1946) was published in 1946 and revised in 1953. It was a general survey of scientific aspects of physical disability and appeared at the beginning of a great surge of interest that has continued to become an important specialty in the profession. I recruited Beatrice A. Wright and Lee Meyerson to contribute chapters and Tamara Dembo as a consultant. Since then they have been wheelhorses of the specialty called rehabilitation psychology. I am immoderately proud of having had a hand in bringing them into the field.

My personal adjustment, especially my self-regard, was greatly improved by my wartime experience. My desire to be of some use to the national emergency despite my physical inadequacies was satisfied to an important degree by the heavy teaching load and by work on the monograph. The latter was especially gratifying, for I was, at last, retrieving something of value from my long years of illness. I was able to go forward on it with energy because I thought those years gave me the competence beyond most others who could have undertaken the task. At last, the secret agenda of my lost adolescent years was in operation. Louise, too, led a full, rich life during these years. She returned to the school where she had taught biology seven years earlier, this time as a counselor for truant children and their families. Our third child, Lucy, was born in May 1943.

But the environment in which we were living so comfortably and productively was changing. After three years, the regular staff was coming back from the war; R.G.B., the acting associate professor, was about to be bumped by the tenured associate professor. What to do? Letters went out and visits were made. Stanford was not unique; most colleges and universities were in a postwar shock; they were unable to act. Jack Hilgard, the returning chairman, was eager to continue the child development program we had started on a shoestring (we had established a nursery school); he made valiant efforts to find financing for another regular position, but the lead time for arranging new programs is long. So, in the autumn of 1945 it was announced that, without a miracle, I would be released by Stanford at the end of the spring term. I was out of a job as my father had been at about the same age. My intimate knowledge of his experience increased my anxiety.

But miracles do happen. On a job-seeking trip to Los Angeles in the summer, I had met President Wallace Atwood of Clark University. It was a get-acquainted meeting; no position was sought or offered. I dropped Clark University from my list of possibilities as the only opening there was the endowed position of G. Stanley Hall Professor. Then, in late autumn, came a letter asking if I was interested in that position. Was I! So, Louise and I and three children arrived in Worcester, Massachusetts, in January 1946.

Clark University

Clark was in transition. President Atwood was about to retire; the Psychology Department was low in staff and graduate students; there was an interim chairman. We settled in the satellite town of West Boylston, where we could probe the possibility of studying the everyday lives of the children. We found that West Boylston was not a community, but a political entity, a township; there was no town center. As the only academics in our neighborhood of old families and young executives, we were isolated (no playmates for our children). But all was not grim: Kurt and Gerti Lewin were within an hour's drive; Fritz and Grace Heider were only a little further; David Shakow and some of his associates at Worcester State Hospital were congenial and supportive; there were two promising graduate students, Chris Argyris and Howard Perlmutter. We were all set to ride out a poor stretch of road; it would surely improve. During 1946, I completed the manuscript and proof for the disability monograph, and I prepared an application for research funds to the newly-established National Institute of Mental Health for a field study of the everyday lives of the children of a single small town. No town was identified; to find one would be part of the research.

In the early spring of 1947 I received a telephone call from Dean Paul Lawson of the University of Kansas; he was in Boston. Could he come to Worcester to talk with me? "Surely, glad to see you." Dean Lawson? Have I met him? University of Kansas? Louise and I met the dean that evening in a downtown cafe. His story: psychology at the University of Kansas is on hard times. J. F. Brown is ill and will not be returning; the chairman, W. H. Wheeler, has resigned; only two regular staff members are left. The university has decided to give strong support for the revival of psychology. Are you interested? A deciding factor: can I carry out the research I am committed to? I outlined the project. The dean: "I know the exact place; I have been there many times. Its name is Oskaloosa." After two trips to Lawrence and recruiting, prospectively, Fritz and Grace Heider from Smith College and my former colleague at Iowa, Herbert Wright, from Northwestern University, the deal was struck.

Meeting of Minds

By the end of my three-year stint as chair of the University of Kansas Department of Psychology, the regular staff consisted of Herbert Wright, Fritz and Grace Heider, Martin Scheerer, Alfred Baldwin, Erik and Beatrice Wright, Anthony Smith (the only hold-over), and me. We fulfilled my idea of what a department should be: scholars with sufficiently similar orientation to important problems, theories, and methods to make communication possible and profitable; teachers and a curriculum with a coherent, but not narrowly partisan point of view. I was no supporter of eclecticism within a research and teaching group. As for research, it seemed to me to defeat the value of the group if there were not clear connections between the undertakings of the members. As for the teaching, I thought we could not expect a grab bag of courses that the experts themselves could not fit together to provide students with a useful body of knowledge and procedures. The members of our group were of what was then known as an organismic persuasion. This was in line with a long tradition at Kansas both in psychology (W. H. Wheeler, J. F. Brown, F. T. Perkins) and biology (G. E. Coghill). We were all set for a congenial, productive Golden Age of our kind of psychology.

But it was not to be. We were defeated by a kind of tragedy of the commons. When we arrived, the University's enrollment was about 5,000 students. These numbers soon doubled, then tripled. New staff had to be secured quickly; it was impossible to maintain a single point of view. Students in other departments wanted specialized and practical courses. The pleasant refectory we had planned and initiated with its savory, nutritious menu was overrun by the hordes and was transformed into a long-line cafeteria (with a number of excellent dishes).

After three years, it became clear that I could not handle the three jobs of administrator, teacher, and research psychologist at a location 20 miles from the university. It was not difficult to choose which job to drop. Alfred Baldwin became chair.

Field Station

From Plover, Iowa, to Clark University in 1946, my life was an encounter with imposed ecological environments, some beneficent, others uncongenial. Plover (beneficent) was thrust upon me by parental actions; Clark (uncongenial), by university policies. Now, in 1947, I was to create an ecological environment to my own specifications, the Midwest Psychological Field Station in Oskaloosa, Kansas. The details of the station's program were developed in cooperation with Herbert Wright, who gave it his enthusiastic and creative support.

The field station was a place (suite of rooms); a program (agenda of action); and operators (staff); located in Oskaloosa, a town of 715 inhabitants, a county seat, and a trading center for farmers. The program of the field station included a purpose, policies, and methods. The purpose was to describe the living conditions (both E_e and E_{ψ}) and behavior of the children of the town; this was soon changed to include the adults, for it became obvious that adults are a principal part of the children's environments. We also extended the field work beyond Oskaloosa to nearby towns and, in 1954, to Leyburn, North Yorkshire, England, where we engaged in cross-national studies for ten years.

A guiding policy was to leave the environments of the towns unaltered by the staff and their methods. This required establishing the field station as an authentic setting of the town with a permanent resident staff who participated in the ongoing affairs of the town but did not initiate them. To avoid misunderstanding and mistrust, all programs, methods, and findings were made public; there were no secret agendas.

The policy had clear implications for methods. It required a break with the common practice of studying "subjects," who, according to both Webster and psychological scientists, are "under the authority, dominance, control, or influence of someone." The someone in the case of psychological science is the investigator using experiments, tests, and interviews. Our policy demanded methods for studying free-ranging persons, "not subject to the will" of the investigators; we were to become transducers of human behavior and environment. In the beginning, we thought of placing staff members as unbiased sensors at random locations about the town to observe and record the behavior and situation of each child within range. This, however, would destroy the ongoing course of behavior as the child moved in and out of the range of the sensor; so, we had the sensor move with the child, producing a narrative record of the kind Dembo and I made in the frustration experiment in Iowa. The observer's narrative proceeded *pari passu* with the child's actions and situations; it preserved the sequentiality of behavioral and environmental events.

Armed with this purpose, policy, and method, we set out to stake our claim for field station rights in Oskaloosa. Herbert presented our case to editor John Roberts of the *Oskaloosa Independent*, to lawyer and state Senator James Swoyer, to Reverends Drew Hammond and Willard Thompson of the Methodist and Presbyterian churches, and to Superintendent Walter Meyers of the school. I spoke to the Rotary Club, and we talked with the people in the West Side Cafe and Simon's Service Station. Responses were favorable, summed up best, perhaps, by a local political figure, "If it's for the good of children and doesn't raise taxes, I'm for it."

So in the autumn of 1947 Herbert and Lorene and their two children settled in the town; the next spring Louise and I and three children, and Phil and Maxine Schoggen (research assistants) and baby followed. We put down roots. Our children went to the schools; we joined the churches of denominations with which we had long been associated elsewhere; we marketed and purchased home furnishings locally; Lorene was invited and joined the Women's Study Club; and Louise began calling on all families with children, explaining our purpose and methods. A frequent viewpoint was expressed explicitly by one mother, "So you'll be watching us, but remember, we'll be watching you." By autumn of 1948 we had "proven up" on our field station claim with a resident staff of the Barkers, the Wrights, the Schoggens, and later, beginning in 1961, Paul and Natalie Gump. The Barkers remained for 25 years; the Wrights, for seven years, when they left to initiate research on the lives of children in cities and towns (Wright, 1969); the Schoggens stayed for nine years overall, with an interruption; and the Gumps for the duration of the station. Two or three graduate students usually lived in the town.

We immediately began making day-long specimen records which we analyzed in a variety of ways (Barker and Wright, 1951, 1955; Barker, 1963a; Wright, 1967). This provided information about the behavior and everyday living conditions, the psychological environments (E_ψ) of individual children. A major achievement, due largely to the dedication and insights of Herbert, was the reliable identification of discrete units of action that we called behavior episodes (Wright, 1967). They are grounded in Lewin's theory of molar action, and they reveal the basic structure of the stream of behavior.

As we went about the town observing and recording the behavior of children one at a time, we soon noted that behavior is as distinctive of places as it is of persons—more so, in fact. The difference between Music Class and School Playground with respect to the behavior of Raymond and Tom was much greater than the difference between the behavior of the boys in either place. We could predict behavior better from places than from people. We also noted that behavior in places is more stable than the people; the distinctive patterns of behavior in Music Class and School Playground continued year after year with little change, whereas the participants changed regularly. We began to see that people are replaceable parts of places. Finally we found places to be as distinctive for people as for behavior. Only old men and women gathered at the Congregate Meals location, and there were only young boys and a single adult at the Cub Scout meeting. At first we thought this was a matter of individual choice, that people with similar needs gathered at places with appropriate sources of satisfaction. But we soon found that places themselves sort and select occupants regardless of their wishes. Only children with 50 cents in hand (in 1985) could enter the Merry-Go-Round place, and children six years of age were required to be in Music Class. After a few months of working on specimen records, these observations overcame our bias, as psychologists, for individuals; we could no longer ignore what our eyes told us, namely, that behavior comes not only as the behavior of particular persons, but also as the behavior of particular places. Thereafter, we devoted most of our attention to places. We called them *behavior settings* and the behavior within them, *extraindividual behavior*.

School Playground and Music Class are behavior settings; they, and all the other behavior settings, are discrete entities of the ecological environment (E_e). They consist of distinctive standing patterns of human and nonhuman actions and structures within precise space-time boundaries; homeostatic controls and forces select the human and nonhuman components, regulate their activities, and produce a high degree of interdependence among the parts; they maintain the operation of each setting at a semistable equilibrium. Behavior settings are eco-behavior phenomena for which psychological theories are inadequate; overarching concepts linking persons, their psychological environments (PE_ψ), and the ecological environment (E_e) are required. So it is not surprising that psychologists have not been comfortable with behavior settings. We have proposed a beginning toward an eco-behavioral science (Barker, 1965, 1968, 1969, 1987), one that goes a step beyond Lewin's belief that derivations about behavior can be made only via psychological concepts (Lewin, 1936; 1943). We predicted, and verified the prediction, that behavior in settings with fewer than the optimal number of inhabitants ("undermanned" settings) differ in specified ways from behavior in settings with the optimal number of inhabitants (Barker, 1960; Barker and Gump, 1964; Wicker, Kirmeyer, Hanson, and Alexander, 1976). The theory rests upon the ideas of Egon Brunswik for organism-environment relations in general (Brunswik, 1955); upon Kurt Lewin for the distinction between the psychological and the ecological environments (Lewin, 1936) and for criteria for identifying behavior settings on the basis of degree of unity (Lewin, 1941); upon Fritz Heider for fundamental properties of elements and patterns of elements (Heider, 1959); and upon W. R. Ashby for cybernetic concepts and methods for dealing with relations between parts and wholes (Ashby, 1956).

Empirical investigation discovered that behavior settings blanket the public regions of towns. In the year from September 1963 to August 1964, there were 884 behavior settings in Oskaloosa and 758 in Leyburn (Barker and Schoggen, 1973, p. 57). One or more of these settings was the ecological environment (E_e) of every molar action occurring outside the homes of the towns; all individual psychological environments (E_ψ) involved in these actions occurred within and were shaped by the towns' behavior settings. For these reasons, many aspects of the living conditions a town provides its inhabitants can be assessed in terms of the properties of its behavior settings. The total ecological environment of Oskaloosa relative to that of Leyburn was 95 percent as extensive (p. 57); 93 percent as varied (p. 66); and produced 125 percent as much behavior per inhabitant (p. 264). If only the settings of the towns that produced educational activities are considered, that is, the towns' educational environments, Oskaloosa was 116 percent as extensive as Leyburn (p. 102); 86 percent as varied (p. 103); and generated 236 percent as much behavior per inhabitant (p. 285). These data are obtained without subjects, that is, without observing or interviewing particular persons about their behavior. For a discussion of behavioral research without subjects, see Barker 1987.

Behavior settings are of concern to both students of individual behavior and students of institutions, communities, and societies. For the former, two issues are prominent. First, what psychological mechanisms insure that people conform to the characteristic standing behavior patterns of the settings they enter? Why do the inhabitants of Pat's supermarket engage only in supermarket behavior and not in playground behavior (a fine place for hide-and-seek) or worship service behavior (hymn singing)? Second, what motives and abilities are needed to enter, to alter, and to create behavior settings, and how can they be nurtured? Why did John Fox succeed in establishing and operating the setting, Fox Auto Repair Garage, soon after Richard King's garage had failed? How could King have been helped? (Wicker, 1987)

Behavior settings are constituent parts of institutions, communities, and societies; these wholes can be precisely described and changes charted in terms of behavior settings (Barker, 1987). Changes come via the establishment, the alteration, and the termination of behavior settings. In 1972 the Oskaloosa settings of Wayside Restaurant, High School German Class, and Saddle Club Rodeo were established; the setting Public Library was altered by an increase in its availability (hours open) from 15 to 30 hours per week; and Wolf's Law Office, Women's Study Club, and Midwest Psychological Field Station were terminated. Thus did the town change as a place to live. It is important to discover the sources of these beginnings, alterations, and endings, for it is largely they that increase, alter, and decrease communities and institutions as environments for people (Barker, 1979b; Bechtel, 1977; Fox, 1985; Fox and Ghosh, 1981; Fox and Miles, 1986; Gump, 1980, 1982, 1987; Kaminski, in press; Kounin and Sherman, 1979; Oxley and Barrera, 1984; Schoggen and Schoggen, 1984; Wicker, 1979, 1981, 1987; Willems and Halstead, 1978; Wright, 1969).

I would like to end this account of the field station by acknowledging by name those who supported it. Unfortunately, this is not possible, for crucial persons are unknown. Who brought Barker to Dean Lawson's attention, and who encouraged the dean to sponsor a way-out research program? Who in Carnegie Corporation went to bat for the funds for the research in Leyburn? Who in Oskaloosa silenced the one known critic of the station? (We were fingered as communists; it was alleged that our ancient IBM punch-card sorter sifted secret information we received via the radio antenna on our home.) We know nothing of the identity of the many people who constituted the invisible but essential infrastructure of the station. Furthermore, although the authors of theses and publications issuing from the station are given in Barker and Associates (1978) and the sources of funds for particular investigations are given in the relevant publications, the complete roster of known sponsors and collaborators is too long to report here. It includes Mr. and Mrs. Gary Grant who opened their home at 7 A.M. on a cold winter day for the first of the seven observers who would make a 14-hour specimen record of three-year-old Tony; it includes Margaret Mead and high school students whom she instructed in the fieldwork they would do in area high schools; it includes volunteer informants who reported attendance in behavior settings. A psychological field station is not a laboratory with an underwriter (or two), an investigator (or two, three, or four), and X number of subjects; it is a community/university/agency-wide undertaking with known and unknown participants.

Yesterday or Tomorrow?

When my family lived in Des Moines, an occasional treat was "going to the Vaudeville Show" on a Saturday afternoon. It was always broad daylight when we entered the theater, and surprisingly and somewhat bewilderingly, pitch dark when we emerged. The first time my four-year-old sister was included in the adventure into the wondrous world of acrobats, ventriloquists, trained animals, clowns, and moving pictures, she looked about in astonishment when we came out into the streetlighted city and said, "What is it, yesterday or tomorrow?"

Many who adventure into the unfamiliar Eco-Behavioral Show of behavior settings, behavior episodes, action patterns, authority systems, territorial range, urbs, and the like emerge with the same question. I hear both answers, but I listen most happily to those whose response, on balance, is "tomorrow."

Selected Publications by Roger G. Barker

(1931a). The stepping-stone maze: A directly visible space problem apparatus. *Journal of General Psychology, 5,* 280–285.
(1931b). Factors influencing transfer between finger mazes. *Journal of General Psychology, 6,* 115–131.

(1931c). A temporal finger maze. *American Journal of Psychology, 43,* 634–636.

(1934). *The relation of age of human adults to some aspects of the ability to do fatiguing muscular work.* Unpublished doctoral dissertation, Stanford University, Stanford, CA.

(with C. P. Stone) (1937a). Aspects of personality and intelligence in post-menarcheal and pre-menarcheal girls of the same chronological ages. *Journal of Comparative Psychology, 23,* 439–455.

(with C. P. Stone) (1937b). On the relationship between menarcheal age and certain measurements of physique in girls of the ages 9 to 16 years. *Human Biology, 9,* 1–23.

(with T. Dembo & K. Lewin) (1941). Frustration and regression: An experiment with young children. *University of Iowa Studies in Child Welfare, 18,* 1–314.

(1942a). An experimental study of the resolution of conflict by children. In Q. McNemar & M. A. Merrill (Eds.), *Studies in personality* (pp. 13–34). New York: McGraw-Hill.

(1942b). Difficulties of communication between educators and psychologists. *Journal of Educational Psychology, 5,* 280–285.

(with J. S. Kounin & H. F. Wright) (1943). *Child behavior and development.* New York: McGraw-Hill.

(1946). An experimental study of the relationship between certainty of choice and the relative valence of the alternatives. *Journal of Personality, 15,* 41–52.

(with B. A. Wright, L. Meyerson, & M. R. Gonick) (1946). *Adjustment to physical handicap and illness: A survey of the social psychology of physique and disability.* New York: Social Science Research Council (Bulletin 55).

(with H. F. Wright) (1951). *One boy's day.* New York: Harper & Row. (Reprinted 1966. Hamden, CT: Shoestring Press.)

(with H. F. Wright) (1955). *Midwest and its children.* Evanston, IL: Row, Peterson.

(1960). Ecology and motivation. In M. R. Jones (Ed.), *Nebraska Symposium on Motivation* (pp. 1–50). Lincoln, NE: University of Nebraska Press.

(Ed.) (1963a). *The stream of behavior.* New York: Appleton-Century-Crofts.

(1963b). On the nature of the environment. *Journal of Social Issues, 19,* 17–38.

(with P. V. Gump) (1964). *Big school, small school.* Stanford, CA: Stanford University Press.

(1965). Explorations in ecological psychology. *American Psychologist, 20,* 1–14.

(1968). *Ecological psychology: Concepts and methods for studying the environment of human behavior.* Stanford, CA: Stanford University Press.

(1969). Wanted: An eco-behavioral science. In E. P. Willems & H. L. Raush (Eds.), *Naturalistic viewpoints in psychological research* (pp. 31–43). New York: Holt, Rinehart, & Winston.

(with P. Schoggen) (1973). *Qualities of community life.* San Francisco: Jossey-Bass.

(with Associates) (1978). *Habitats, environments, and human behavior.* San Francisco: Jossey-Bass.

(1979a). Settings of a professional lifetime. *Journal of Personality and Social Psychology, 37,* 2137–2157.

(1979b). The influence of the frontier environment on behavior. In J. D. Steffen (Ed.), *The American West* (pp. 61–93). Oklahoma City: University of Oklahoma Press.

(1987). Prospecting in environmental psychology. In D. Stokols & I. Altman (Eds.), *Handbook of environmental psychology* (Vol. 2, pp. 1413–1432). New York: Wiley.

Other Publications Cited

Ashby, W. R. (1956). *An introduction to cybernetics.* New York: Wiley.

Bechtel, R. (1977). *Enclosing behavior.* Stroudsburg, PA: Dowden, Hutchinson, & Ross.

Brunswik, E. (1955). The conceptual framework of psychology. *International Encyclopedia of Unified Science, 1,* 656–750.

Brunswik, E. (1957). Scope and aspects of the cognitive problem. In H. Gruber, R. Jessor, & K. Hammond (Eds.), *Cognition: The Colorado Symposium* (pp. 5–31). Cambridge, MA: Harvard University Press.

Fox, K. (1985). *Social system accounts.* Dordrecht, The Netherlands: D. Reidel.

Fox, K., & Ghosh, S. K. (1981). A behavior setting approach to social accounts combining concepts and data from ecological psychology, economics, and studies of time use. In F.T. Juster & K.C. Land (Eds.), *Social accounting systems: Essays on the state of the art* (pp. 131–217). New York: Academic Press.

Fox, K., & Miles, D. G. (Eds.). (1986). *System economics: Concepts, models, and multidisciplinary perspectives.* Ames, IA: Iowa State University Press.

Gump, P. V. (1980). The school as a social situation. *Annual Review of Psychology, 31,* 553–582.

Gump, P. V. (1982). School settings and their keeping. In D. Duke (Ed.), *Helping teachers manage classrooms* (pp. 98–114). Alexandria, VA: Association for Supervision and Curriculum Development.

Gump, P. V. (1987). School and classroom environments. In D. Stokols & I. Altman (Eds.), *Handbook of environmental psychology* (Vol. 1, pp. 691–732). New York: Wiley.

Heider, F. (1959). On perception, event structure, and the psychological environment. *Psychological Issues, 1*(3) (entire issue).

Kaminski, G. (in press). The relevance of ecologically oriented conceptualizations for theory building in environment and behavior research. In G. T. Moore & E. H. Zube (Eds.), *Advances in environment, behavior, and design: Theory, research, and practice* (Vol. 2). New York: Plenum.

Kounin, J. S., & Sherman, L. W. (1979). School environments as behavior settings. *Theory into Practice, 13,* 141–151.

Lewin, K. (1936). *Principles of topological psychology,* New York: McGraw-Hill.

Lewin, K. (1938). The conceptual representation and measurement of psychological force. *Duke University Contributions to Psychological Theory,* no. 4, *1,* 1–247.

Lewin, K. (1939). Field theory and experiment in social psychology. *American Journal of Sociology, 44,* 868–897.

Lewin, K. (1941). Analysis of the concepts of whole, differentiation, and unity. *University of Iowa Studies in Child Welfare*, *18*, 226–261.

Lewin, K. (1943). Defining the "field at a given time." *Psychological Review*, *50*, 292–310.

Oxley, D., & Barrera, M., Jr. (1984). Undermanning theory and the workplace: Implications of setting size for job satisfaction and social support. *Environment and Behavior*, *16*, 211–234.

Schoggen, P., & Schoggen, M. (1984). Some emerging common themes in environment-behavior research. *Peabody Journal of Education*, *61*(3), 36–51.

Wicker, A. W. (1979). *An introduction to ecological psychology*. Monterey, CA: Brooks/Cole.

Wicker, A. W. (1981). Nature and assessment of behavior settings: Recent contributions from the ecological perspective. In P. McReynolds (Ed.), *Advances in psychological assessment* (Vol. 5, pp. 22–61). San Francisco: Jossey-Bass.

Wicker, A. W. (1987). Behavior settings reconsidered: Temporal stages, resources, internal dynamics, content. In D. Stokols & I. Altman (Eds.), *Handbook of environmental psychology* (Vol. 1, pp. 613–653). New York: Wiley.

Wicker, A. W., Kirmeyer, S. L., Hanson, L., & Alexander, D. (1976). Effects of manning levels on subjective experiences, performance, and verbal interaction in groups. *Organizational Behavior and Human Performance*, *17*, 251–274.

Willems, E. P., & Halstead, L. S. (1978). An eco-behavioral approach to health care. In R. G. Barker and Associates (Eds.), *Habitats, environments, and human behavior* (pp. 169–189). San Francisco: Jossey-Bass.

Wright, H. F. (1967). *Recording and analyzing child behavior*. New York: Harper & Row.

Wright, H. F. (1969). *Children's behavior in communities differing in size*, Parts 1, 2, 3, and Supplement (Report to NIMH). Lawrence, KS: University of Kansas.

Roger Brown

There is no man who differs more from another than he does from himself at another time.—PASCAL

Me

When Roger Brown comes out of the closet, the time for courage must be past. So I thought in 1984. But a Supreme Court opinion and a Justice Department ruling in 1986 showed how extreme was the new hostility rooted in AIDS and that almost stopped me from writing this autobiography at all. What I would not do is write a life story with sexuality censored out, but the confessional form had certainly lost its appeal. With the project stalled in the summer of 1986, I read recent truthful biographies of John Maynard Keynes (Skidelsky, 1986) and E. M. Forster (Furbank, 1977) and thought how intolerable it was that even such small beer as myself should be tempted to keep the secret that had made psychological nonsense of all but the most recent biographies of these two. Intolerable, but not surprising. Not surprising, because while we always hope social morality will progress, there is no progress of this kind in history. Nevertheless, nothing forces one positively to impede progress. So, braced for cold water and with eyes closed, here goes.

But after all what is there to confess, since I am certainly not gay? "Gay" is the name of a rarefied state of consciousness attainable only by those born after 1960 or so, and I was born in 1925. Gay, you see, is not the same as homosexual. I learned the distinction a few years ago, overhearing it explained to an Israeli man by a qualified young American. During an opera intermission we had run into an all-male group of middle-aged judges and lawyers and other professional gentlemen and exchanged firm handshakes and smiles not too glittering, and the Israeli whispered: "But what are they? Are they gay?" The young American explained: "No, they are not gay, they are ho-mo-sexuals." In the United States between 1950 and the mid-1980's, it was no serious handicap in a professional career to be homosexual so long as you were "discreet"—which meant compartmentalizing your various social selves somewhat more sharply than most people do. With luck the worst that would be said of you in your hearing or written where you could read it was: "He's a very private person." If, however, you were unlucky or simply indiscreet, you could be imprisoned or possibly shamed into suicide as was Alan Turing of "Turing's Test" in the 1950's (Hodges, 1983).

Because it may be educational for some, I offer the following facts. I have never had sex with any of my students, nor even made a pass, and I have lived with the same man since graduate school, some 35 years ago. However, when younger, I was sometimes promiscuous in the ways that gay men and homosexuals are, or used to be. I think it is true that men having sex with men tend to be much more promiscuous than women with women and even somewhat more so than boys and girls together. Everyone sometimes separates love from sex without doing any harm. To be unable ever to connect love and sex is pitiable. The rest is either nonsense or hypocrisy.

My parents were born in London, Ontario, but moved to Detroit and became American citizens. In age they were about 20 years apart, and my father had had a first wife who died. From that marriage I had two older half brothers and from my parents one slightly older full brother. For several years in Detroit my father and the four brothers, plus two sons of the eldest brother, all lived together. My mother was then the sole woman, and that made the competition to become her favorite a tough fight, but I won. Some think that winning this particular contest makes one a long-term loser in just the way that they would judge me a loser, but I don't agree.

My childhood cannot be dismissed with a quip though I wish it could, because I do not want to experience again those old passions. I understand that a full disclosure might interest a few readers, but I am not sure that I would like their motives, and besides I am not getting paid for this. For my own peace of mind I intend to keep the facts minimal and the tone light. The trouble is that with this particular material I am not fully in control.

We can clear the stage of my two older half brothers and their wives and children and grandchildren. They are all fine people, and I am proud of them, but they are not part of my childhood nucleus, which contained only my mother and father and my slightly older full brother, Don. My mother and father are still very much alive in me, though they died over

20 years ago. They are occasionally in my dreams—crystallized as they appeared to me in their old age and not as they appeared to me in my childhood. My mother appears more often, and one theme has been recurrent. It seems that she is not dead at all, but that I have in some incomprehensible way mislaid her or forgotten her or just failed to call and I cannot find her number and it is terrible to imagine her state of mind. That is because I was not there when she died, at the end of a summer when I had been traveling and constantly telephoning from various remote places and trying to keep her spirits up when she had had two coronaries and saying what a good time we would have when I got home. I did get home in time and stayed a week. The next morning Don called my office and said: "Grandma's gone" (when there are grandchildren in a family it often happens that everyone adopts their terms of reference).

My father was a traveling salesman, and when I was born in 1925, a very successful one. What company was it, I wonder, that he was so proud to represent and used to bless for its magnanimity until they let him go in the first year of the Great Depression. When he came home from being "on the road," he brought presents, and we were excited and happy to see him. He was a handsome man, a great talker, who charmed the women. He had had to leave school after the third grade, but he became the "corner poet" on the editorial page of a Michigan newspaper. Late in his life (he lived to be 85) he decided he would write his autobiography, but when he had typed one half-page, that seemed to be it. He may already have had the beginning of Parkinson's disease at that time. It pains me that my brother and I made fun of his autobiography.

My mother had gone to nursing school but she quit before finishing—to marry my father—and did not work as a nurse until the Depression. She had a very beautiful face—loving, intelligent, without vanity, and increasingly spiritual as she grew older. She was always a great reader, going through three library books a week even though that entailed doing the dishes with her book propped up in front of her. She took out a library card in the same spirit that other parents enroll a son at birth in their favorite prep school. That card and her example did more to make my intellectual life possible than any other such advantage I ever enjoyed.

What chiefly distinguished my parents from Don and me was luck. Theirs was bad. Don and I, just at the right time, had the G. I. Bill to send us to college and graduate school, and we looked for our first jobs in the prosperous 1950's. My parents had, at just the wrong time, the 1930's Depression, which knocked them out of the middle class and into the Detroit factories—when they could find work at all. The Depression did not have this effect on their brothers and sisters, whose incomes were more secure, and I remember prosperous uncles and aunts who kindly sent us picture postcards from Florida in the winter, invited us to their cottages in the summer, and at Christmas gave richer gifts than we could return. For years my parents balanced accounts with humility. However, later on they took some satisfaction in voting for Franklin Roosevelt and joining labor unions and created in me a lifelong identification with the underdog— economic, social, and sexual.

In my family our hearts ached for one another's relative deprivation, not our own, and those years left me with a longing to make it up to my parents for all that they had missed. Since I had only a very small salary and no savings in the year that both died, I was never able to afford much, but we did get to Florida (Miami Beach) several times, and we thought it was terrific!

During World War II, my brother was in the Army in England, and I was in the Navy—first at the University of Michigan in the V-12 program, later at midshipmen's school at Columbia and still later in the Pacific. It was no part of my plan in joining the Navy ever to go to sea; when we were interviewed at commissioning time as to our duty preferences, I asked: "What's the longest school you've got?" It was Japanese Language School in Colorado, and I said: "Put me down for that." A mistake. In a class of about 1,000 I was the only one to be sent directly to sea. We read our assignments from a bulletin board and opposite my name it said "USS *Wichita*." "What school is that?" I asked my smugly smiling division commander. He was a salty dog who had earned his lieutenancy as a professor of economics at Columbia.

As it turned out, I had mistaken my own best interests. Because I hated the Navy ashore, I assumed I would like it still less in its proper element at sea, but in fact I was crazy about shipboard life. By the time I caught up with the *Wichita*, it was at the Battle of Okinawa, and the war shortly ended. I put in thousands of tranquil nautical miles reading the Random House edition of the complete Greek drama and also John Watson's *Behaviorism* (1930). It was Watson who inspired me to study psychology, but it was the Greek drama and its resonance in my own life that prepared me to think later on, and still, that Sigmund Freud was the greatest of psychologists, the one who knew where the vital action is.

Because my tie with my parents was very strong, I felt keenly their lone-liness and worry with both sons at war and tried to make it up to them by writing long letters several times a week. I strained to bridge the distance between us by putting them in possession of my state of mind. These pa-pers were never graded or corrected, but I think all that practice without feedback taught me more about writing than all the English courses I ever had. The habit of transforming experience into narrative actually became too strong, and I remember when I first noticed that. The *Wichita* was the first American ship to go into Nagasaki harbor—a historic occasion, you might say—and there I was on the foredeck, so busy trying to find good metaphors to convey the look of atomic devastation that I was feel-ing nothing at all. I was not having any experience worth capturing. After that I held back the words until I had apprehended the things.

And what about sex? No experience whatsoever. In and out of San Francisco, up and down the Yangtze River, I saw no evil and did no evil. Incredible as it must seem to young people today, my first encounter did not occur until I was out of the navy, back in school at Michigan, and 21 years old. By which age my kind of experience was still not legal. How-ever, I knew which sex turned me on and had known from as early an age as I could remember, as do most people (Bell and Weinberg, 1978; Bell, Weinberg, and Hammersmith, 1981). I also had always known that my orientation had come out wrong and so, with John Watson's help, I in-vented behavior modification. I "tossed off" (as the British cheerily say) while scrutinizing pictures of naked women, and I tried to induce vom-iting (finger down the throat) when I thought of men. It did not change me at all, even as it has never deeply changed anyone (Brown, 1986a).

While we are on the subject: "What about the ontogenesis of your ori-entation, Ensign Brown? Were you not, in point of fact, a mother's boy?" Indeed I was. I loved that woman with a fierce spiritual intensity that has never burned out, and she loved me back. My father, not jealous I think, used to say: "If anything happens to one of you, I don't know how I will ever console the other." When I took my doctorate, both Harvard and Michigan offered me instructorships, and when I chose Harvard, I know my parents wished they had encouraged me to be one degree less ambi-tious. In choosing Harvard, I had no intention of giving up my parents; the first year I moved them and our cat into an apartment in Somerville, but I was too busy, and they were not happy. One day they came with me to tea at a housemaster's, and they thought all that sterling silver and

Brahminism would surely draw me away from them, but it never did. I went home several times a year, as long as they lived. Harvard's glamour could not prevail over a really well-developed Oedipus Complex.

In using Freud's term, do I mean to admit that my love for my mother caused my "negative resolution"? I thought so for a time but without any rancor for my mother; I figured she was worth it, and no one ever wants to change an orientation, because it feels natural (Bell and Weinberg, 1978; Bell, Weinberg, and Hammersmith, 1981). However, by now I have had intimate talks with scores of friends, homosexual, heterosexual, and bisexual, and my conclusion is that feeling closer to mother than to father is not related at all to adult sexual orientation. That is also the conclusion of the Kinsey Institute survey studies that I have cited here. Still, I think Freud alone captures the real passions of the family drama. He was absolutely right about the phenomenology of it all and right in relating childhood sexuality to dreams, art, and religion, but orientations I would guess are prenatally, though not necessarily genetically, determined (Brown, 1986a).

In a way both Don and I did somewhat compensate our parents for their years of tight budgets and terror of any unbudgeted expense—even something trifling going wrong with the car—and especially their loss of status with their own brothers and sisters. Don took a master's degree in what was called "industrial psychology"; for a while that only got him a modest job with a tacky neighborhood department store. However, he was smart and hardworking, and he soon was hired by one of the major department store chains in the country, where he rapidly became a top executive. The greatest gift he gave my parents was a good-tempered daughter-in-law and, above all, *grandchildren*. When I was teaching at MIT but was nominated for a professorship at Harvard and waiting for Harvard's Robert White to call and tell me how the *ad hoc* committee had come out, my father and mother were waiting by the phone in Detroit deeply identified with my wish to be chosen. I remember my mother saying, "You are the only person I have ever known who got out of life what he wanted most." That probably was true of me then, but how had I come to such an odd state?

Some will think that a strong wish to become a Harvard professor needs no explanation in view of Harvard's great reputation. However, in my family in Detroit we were outside the range of that reputation and had scarcely heard of Harvard. Wayne State University in Detroit seemed the only possible college to aim for when Don and I were in high school; the

University of Michigan was the most glamorous school we knew of; but unattainable before the G. I. Bill, and the most exciting school in the country, because of the educational experiments of President Robert Maynard Hutchins, was, of course, the University of Chicago.

It is true that, by the time I took my doctorate at Michigan, I had at least heard that Harvard was much esteemed in the effete East, and I have implied that I chose Harvard over Michigan for reasons of "o'erleaping" ambition. That *is* what I led my parents and almost everybody else to think, but it is not the truth. I chose Harvard because I was deeply in love with a fellow graduate student; for reasons too complicated and too personal to relate, going to Harvard seemed the right move at that time in a plan to stay together for life. I was so ignorant of Harvard's way of doing things that I assumed, when I first traveled there to be "looked over" in 1951, that I would be expected to go by train, and I worried about giving a talk after sitting up all night. Just in time Gordon Allport let me know that Harvard could afford an airplane ticket. So it does take some explaining that ten years later in 1961 a Harvard professorship had become "what I most wanted in life." Even odder is the fact that Donald Marquis, a member of the *ad hoc* committee, told President Pusey, "He really belongs at Harvard."

It was the library card that started it all. I read everything—from the *Penrod* books and *Lad, a Dog*, to, eventually, such Himalayas as *War and Peace* and *Crime and Punishment*. Thousands of comic books too. God alone knows how much I understood; I certainly recall very little, and that little is highly fortuitous. Of Booth Tarkington's *Penrod* I remember reading a representation of Penrod's thoughts on his twelfth birthday on my twelfth birthday, and the reason I remember is that I vowed never to forget how deeply false the representation was. Philip Roth's *Portnoy's Complaint* is closer to adolescence as I knew it. From much reading I think one acquires not just a vocabulary but a good sense of when one word is right and other words close in meaning are not. It is the lack of that sense that causes most of the errors in English composition which teachers can spot and label "awkward" or "usage" but cannot really do anything to correct. From much reading too one learns about other worlds, including some you would rather live in than, say, Detroit, Michigan.

To enter other worlds that attracted me you had to know about things that I was not learning in school or at home—for instance philosophy, art, and classical music. I went about learning them in a cold-blooded, totally

Philistine way. With respect to music the behavior described in books that I could not match was identification of compositions. Therefore I started a file of 3×5 cards writing the name of every piece I heard on the radio and trying to anticipate titles before they were announced. I got to be quite good at recognizing all classical compositions up to five minutes long. The reason my competence was limited to works of short duration was that the only classical music on the radio in those years in Detroit was the J. L. Hudson Company's "Minute Parade" from 8 A.M. to 9 A.M., and that program took no chances on overstraining its listeners. Having mastered classical music of up to five minutes' duration, I can tell you that I was not altogether pleased to learn of the existence of fellows like Wagner, Mahler, and Bruckner.

Recognition, we know, gives a little pleasure but not a lot. Music soon gave me a lot and has done so all my life. The first piece to yield emotion beyond the small thrill of recognition, the first piece to make my heart pump was, as its file card read, "The Toreador Song from Act II of *Carmen* by Georges Bizet (pronounced Zhorj Beezay)."

My culture-mongering was not in imitation of my parents, and they did not exactly encourage it, because they did not really see the use of it. However, when I began to live some of the time in an exalted world of music, I wanted the people I loved to be there with me and so I would turn up the volume on the Metropolitan Opera broadcasts, trying to blast my way through to them but never succeeding. It was done in much the same spirit that Harvard and Radcliffe students in the spring turn up the volume on their stereos and throw open the windows on the Yard trying to convert the world to Bach or to Stevie Wonder. It is a need that Walkman does not satisfy, a need to have others with you in your moments of transcendence.

Over the elevators in William James Hall at Harvard there is inscribed a text from William James, selected by Gordon Allport and E. G. Boring, that is not especially pithy but is true: "The community stagnates without the impulse of the individual. The impulse dies away without the sympathy of the community." When I graduated from grade school, I had still no community to share the impulse that pointed the way that I would go, but at Edwin Denby High on the east side of Detroit I found my Bloomsbury set, my Cambridge Apostles. Not Forster and Keynes and Virginia Woolf and Lytton Strachey and Clive Bell but Phil and David and Marilyn and Jane and Sam. Between Bloomsbury and the Denby set there is not only an analogy but also a historical connection that none of us knew

Roger Brown 45

of. They had read and admired what we read, Ibsen and Shaw and Wells and Sophocles and Plato and Tolstoy and Jane Austen and everybody, but we also read and indeed loved the former Apostles, especially Forster, and their like-minded contemporaries and such modern echoes as Eugene O'Neill, Sinclair Lewis, and Noel Coward. Bloomsbury had created a constellation of values that we recreated not in imitation of them but partly because of the imprint they left on literature.

Forster has said (Furbank, 1977) that at King's College, Cambridge, there were only two sets, the included and the excluded, and that he belonged to the excluded, who were uncertain about their clothes and spent their time in coffee-drinking and argument rather than champagne breakfasts and race meets. The Denby Apostles were also excluded— from big band music and dates and team sports. The Cambridge Apostles, while excluded from the hearty set, were themselves a very select coterie, valuing philosophical argument, if the tone were light, and close friendship and radical social views, and so we were at Denby; and while we did not star at athletics or get elected "Best Looking" or class president, we ran the school paper and the drama club and debate and got elected "Wittiest" and "Most Intelligent."

The members of the first Bloomsbury and its university auxiliary, the Apostles, had numerous internecine love affairs, often homosexual, and could talk straight about sexuality, including many matters that would have devastated Victorian and Edwardian England and that were never openly introduced into the literature they published. The Denby Bloomsburyites, much younger, had exactly no sex life at all and could not talk about sex except in wild outrageous jokes. Bloomsbury₁ had a suicide and a schizophrenic and several bisexuals and homosexuals and so did Bloomsbury₂. Some would say these things were evidence of psychopathology, but I just take them as signs of more than ordinarily intense inner lives and alienation from the dominant materialistic culture.

In high school everything was embryonic, and with graduation we dispersed and only learned about individual outcomes indirectly and at long intervals. The friend who became schizophrenic was Sam. He stopped off for an hour in Ann Arbor, connecting with a train for Chicago, and looked me up, though it must have been four years or more since we had met and I had not thought about either Sam or our high school set for a very long time. We talked a little clumsily for a few minutes about what seemed to me a very remote past, and then Sam said: "You know I saw you last week in Chicago." I had not been in Chicago last week and only once, ever, several years ago. "I saw you all." Who all? Why David and Marilyn and Phil and Jane. The phrase "pseudo-community" floated through my mind as Sam went on to say how his high school set had been spying on him and tormenting him all through his graduate studies at Chicago. I had about twenty more minutes with him before he would board his train, and I just kept saying: "Promise me you will go to the university psychiatrist and tell him just what you have told me."

What Sam said to me was not all delusion. We had not been in Chicago and had not seen one another, except Phil and I, who both went to Michigan and have been lifelong friends. But that intense community did powerful things, both good and bad, to all of us. It gave all of us our only real high school educations because, except for a few courses in math, the curriculum was an intellectual void. For me it validated a set of interests and confirmed my right to be an intellectual of some sort.

There is not enough mystery in this story as I am reporting it or inventing it. Actually everything was totally mysterious, but I cannot help spinning explanations. What could be more mysterious than my becoming an opera fan? When I was a boy, no one in my family had ever been to an opera, and I made my start with file cards and the Minute Parade. Some years later Jerome Bruner and George Miller got me invited to what was probably the first-ever Conference on Thinking, which was held at Cambridge with Sir Frederick Bartlett as host. I enjoyed it very much— but not nearly so much as my first performances at Wagner's Bayreuth, which is where I headed as soon as the conference ended. When I wrote *Words and Things* in 1957, I had Italian operas on the phonograph the whole time and had my only brush with the uncanny when someone wrote that parts of the book had a Donizettian lilt. Now, many years later, I have seen opera in all the famous houses all over the world and probably know more about the subject than anyone except—a few friends of the same age and sexual orientation.

There was some kind of strange affinity between nineteenth-century European opera and American male homosexuals in the 1940's and 1950's. How do I know? I have looked at a lot of audiences. In Germany and Italy, where opera is indigenous and conventional, there seems to be either no link with homosexuality or a much attenuated one. Gay men today are not notably attracted to opera. They have, I think, the same distribution of tastes as their straight counterparts—from Renaissance and baroque to hard rock and disco. But opera audiences in the United States three decades ago seemed to be very disproportionately homosexual. The first time I went to Miami, I went into a seedy pet shop looking to buy a live alligator for a young nephew, and the clerk, a weedy high school boy, was listening to a Met broadcast of *La Forza del Destino*. I said, "Milanov is a wonderful singer, isn't she?" and he looked up in wonderment as if meeting his first fellow Martian on this alien planet. To speak of opera at all was as good as a confession, and most straight people also knew that.

But opera of the kind in question is called "grand opera" by people who never listen to it, and in the grandeur may lie the explanation. This exotic and irrational entertainment is also glamorous, with its diamond horseshoes and crystal chandeliers and formal dress and foreign tongues. Surely it satisfied a yearning in that boy in Miami for something more than sawdust and pet iguanas, but I do not think glamour is the main thing. You could read about the glamour in Miami or Detroit, but you certainly were not exposed to any. The only performances of any kind that we ever saw in those days were put on by the San Carlo Opera, a traveling troupe that visited Detroit once a year. The relevant dimension of those performances is epitomized by an *Otello* that I saw with Phil. As the curtain rose on the throne room scene the hungry eye beheld what was recognizably a gold-painted kitchen chair. Phil whispered: "Christ, what splendor!"

I think the answer lies in the music and not the trappings. In 1978 I did some experiments on emotional meanings in music which were published in a report of a conference on education and music (Brown, 1981) and are not known to many psychologists. For these experiments tapes were created of twelve short musical passages such that six pairs had been judged to be approximately synonymous emotionally though unlike in surface form. I picked the pairs and made the tapes, and the question was how well subjects would match my pairings. One pair consisted of the opening phrases of the song *La Mattinata* (morning) and the start of Haydn's quartet called *The Lark*. As surface forms, one selection was vocal and the other a string quartet, but both, I thought, expressed a kind of spring-morning buoyancy.

The main thing the experiments demonstrated was that subjects whose musical knowledge and tastes were like mine (roughly nineteenth-century romantic) made the same matches I made. Subjects with little knowledge of any kind of "classical" music paired selections that had the same surface features: a soprano aria with a soprano aria, a symphonic allegro with another symphonic allegro, etc. Subjects with a lot of musical knowledge—composers and graduates in music theory—did not make the pairings I made, but in matching selections they did agree quite well with one another. The general point seemed to be that individuals who heard the same things "in" music, who extracted the same meanings "from" music, always turned out to have a shared background of musical experience and knowledge and were in that sense a community. In this respect the various kinds of music are like so many languages mutually intelligible for members of the same community but not across communities.

In making the tapes I learned something additional, to my own satisfaction which is, however, not susceptible of proof. It turned out to be extremely difficult to match anything from nineteenth-century opera with anything outside such opera. It seemed as if opera drew on a class of emotional meanings peculiar to itself. While the meanings are indefinitely various, very few of them exactly match anything expressed in either the instrumental or the song literature, let alone anything in the mellow dance music that preceded rock. Operatic emotions are more extreme and more extrovert. The words one thinks of are *hatred, jealousy, rapture, vengeance, exaltation, triumph*, and *despair*. There is not much serenity, good cheer, resignation, or calm sadness. My notion is that in the years of suppression, not just of sex but also of feelings, operatic music expressed what we felt. Underneath the tight control we were screaming arias at one another and at all the world.

It is necessary to add that opera is a competitive sport, a sport in which the relevant muscle is invisible and very small. This is obvious enough in the tense hush that falls whenever the tenor or soprano approaches an extra-high hurdle and the explosion of applause that rewards successful negotiation of the trial, though the applause is usually held back until the number ends. Performing artists are like athletes rather than creative artists in that they experience big highs and big lows in public, rather than private, and riding that roller coaster with your star is the excitement of fanhood.

In addition to reading fiction and philosophy, writing short stories, plays, and poems, and gorging myself on music, I also looked at painting and sculpture. Literature and music took hold, but the visual arts never did. I learned to identify the styles of many artists but cannot today even pick out a tasteful lamp. My natural affinities are for music and language, and they are equally strong, but except for the few experiments described above, I have done no psychological research on music, whereas psycholinguistics has been my research life. For psychology to become seriously interested in either music or language, it was necessary to relinquish the faith of the 1940's—that the laws of behavior would be completely general across species and "content," so why not study the undemanding white rat? For psychology to get anywhere with the content-specific operations of the human mind, it is necessary for the researcher to have serious knowledge of the content subject, and that means studying either music theory or linguistics. Since I had never learned to read music or to play an instrument, music theory was totally out of my reach when I was studying psychology, and I could not have worked in psychomusicology even if it had existed then. However, linguistics was not only accessible but deeply congenial and from the first filled my mind with research ideas. The first lecture I ever heard on linguistics—it was on the phoneme—was given by Charles Fries at Michigan. It was my first postdoctoral year, and I was a bit bored with the ancient questions of psychology and doubtful of my ability to help solve them. But the science of linguistics pulled me together as a person, combining as it does philosophy, literature, and the good linguistic intuitions that come of much reading.

As a graduate student at Michigan, I was in the experimental program and was for several years one of the teachers of the experimental laboratory course—along with John Swets and Donald Lauer. In that course I discovered a way of working that fully engrossed me and caused the hours to fly, and it has been a principal pleasure ever since. I have an almost Talmudic taste for poring over data, for hands-on solitary contact unmediated by machine, involving no human interaction, uncommitted to particular statistical analyses—involving nothing but the free exercise of the principles of induction. In the years 1962–72 I practically turned myself into an induction machine, analyzing and re-analyzing the speech of three small children. This was the longest continuous stretch, but I have always worked this way.

Mine is a laborious, low-tech, minimally mathematical research style. I would hardly make a canon of it, but I also make no apology for it. Of course, absorption in data is an anodyne—I have always been able to use a good pain killer, but so can everyone. Mathematics and machines used to be sex-typed interests, and in lesser degree (never forget Turing and Keynes) they were also typed by sexual orientation, typed by interest, not ability. I can remember that my various intelligence test scores from grade school on were always at about the same level in the quantitative area as in the verbal, and I was always very surprised, because I was much less interested in numbers than in words and did not really feel that numbers were for me. The strength of my research method is that it aims at understanding, not at *p* values, and understanding is the more demanding test. The method is I think responsible for the good record of replicability of all the work I have done from phonetic symbolism (Brown, Black, and Horowitz, 1955) through the fine detail of English in the first stages of acquisition (Brown, 1973) to implicit causality in verbs (Brown and Fish, 1983).

The department at Michigan let me do a lot of teaching, including four or five lecture courses. They let me do this, I suspect, in the same spirit that Tom Sawyer allowed his friends to help whitewash the fence, but I did not mind, because teaching was a pleasure, especially teaching of fairly exact subject matter. The passion to communicate that I felt so strongly in connection with my parents during the war was not peculiar to them or to that time. Somewhere along the line I developed a knack for finding telling examples and for dramatic structure. Teaching, especially lecturing, is more difficult for me now than it used to be, and I do it less well, but I, at least, do not lose much, because the central pleasure is communication; writing for an imagined readership is at least as satisfying as speaking to a real audience.

There is one last thing to be said about my research style. It has always started with some phenomenon and only later become theoretical. Like Stanley Milgram and Solomon Asch, I have tended to pick some mystery and poke it and prod it and turn it all round in an effort to figure it out. My phenomena have not been socially consequential things such as obedience and conformity but, sometimes, wayside curiosities like the tip-of-the-tongue state and the flashbulb memory state and, always, the most mysterious phenomenon of all—acquisition of a first language. The non-obvious but real similarity in research style of Asch, Milgram, and myself is, I think, the reason why we were always great appreciators of one another's work. For myself, though probably not for Asch or Milgram, the phenomenon-centered style has a component of avoidance as well as a component of attraction. Theory is in the center ring, and to operate in the center ring you need a combative temperament, and I have never been combative.

While no one seems to recommend a phenomenon-centered approach to research, it can be argued that its record is at least as good in psychology as that of theory-centered work. You can teach social psychology today and never mention cognitive dissonance, but no one leaves out Asch's conformity experiments or Milgram's obedience experiments. You can teach learning and never mention Hull's (1943) hypothetico-deductive theory, but the phenomena of classical conditioning and instrumental learning continue to be essential.

My intellectual history is peculiar in that it was largely a matter of finding a congenial content area and a satisfying way of working. Language turned out to be the area, and informal but exhaustive induction the method. Neither of these was a free or deliberate choice; both were determined by characteristics that can be traced to childhood and beyond. It is not that I lack interest in ideas; ideas are what I like best, but I have been interested in too many for my history to be represented as a single continuous line. I have, I am afraid, hopped around in the field of language like a robin trying to detect significant movement beneath the turf, and, no, it has not always been worms. It is curious to me how untransferable my modest creativity is. I have taught social psychology for more than thirty years and written two textbooks on the subject, and I love the stuff, but I do not get good ideas for social psychological research.

Two ideas have had rather long though discontinuous runs in my work and the work of my students. One is the very familiar linguistic relativity hypothesis of B. L. Whorf. The paper Eric Lenneberg and I wrote (1954) on color naming and color recognition started things off on a relativistic note, but Eleanor Rosch and Donald Olivier in several brilliant studies (e.g., Heider [Rosch] and Olivier, 1972) in this country and among the Dani of New Guinea proved to the satisfaction of all that color perception is a species universal. The first test of linguistic relativity really adequate to the theories was Alfred Bloom's (1981) book on language and thinking in China and the West, and the results seemed strongly to favor relativity. However, Terry Kit-fong Au (1983) in experiments with Chinese subjects in Hong Kong found strong evidence against one portion of Bloom's position: the claim that for linguistic reasons counterfactual reasoning is more difficult for speakers of Chinese than for speakers of English. For the G. Stanley Hall Centennial volume (Brown, 1986b) I reviewed the 30-year-long (with many interruptions) story of language-and-thought research and concluded that while we all had ventured forth expecting to find evidence of linguistic relativity, we had all come up against cognitive universality. The many discoveries made along the way demonstrate the heuristic value of a striking idea, and who knows whether linguistic relativity may not yet prove to be true.

A second theoretical idea was more continuously pursued and more rapidly disconfirmed. It was the idea that the order of acquisition of English-language constructions would be predictable from their order of cumulative derivational complexity as computed from generative grammars. Brown and Hanlon (1970) and Brown (1973) found lots of confirming evidence, but Maratsos (1983 and elsewhere) disproved the thesis in the general case. Once again, however, something very important to know was incidentally discovered. Brown and Hanlon (1970) found strong evidence that the two most obvious forms of positive and negative reinforcement were not selectively used by parents in responding to the syntactic well-formedness of the utterances of their offspring and so could not possibly explain the learning of syntax.

In 1952 I left Michigan and went to Harvard, and that was the end of me. Not exactly; personal life did go on but was less deeply felt and seems, including the work described above, to have been the spinning out of consequences largely foreordained. From 1952 on I worked as a professional psychologist, and I view the professional psychologist, especially the public aspect of him, with a certain objectivity for which the third person seems more appropriate than the first.

Him

In 1952–53, Brown became an instructor at Harvard, joined Jerome Bruner's cognition research project, and was assigned to teach the undergraduate courses in social psychology and in the psychology of language. From 1953 to 1957, he was an assistant professor at Harvard and head tutor (a job that involved administering aspects of the undergraduate program). This was an intellectually exciting time for Brown, because the category-attribute-strategy line of thought developed in the cognition project suggested many interesting experiments to do in the psychology of language. Jerome Bruner, then as now, had the gift of providing great intellectual stimulus, but also the rarer gift of giving his colleagues the strong sense that psychological problems of great antiquity were on the verge of solution that afternoon by the group there assembled.

In 1957 Harvard let Brown go as it lets most of its assistant professors go, and as he had assumed it would do—though privately hoping not. He suspects today that he did the administrative work of the head tutor so that Harvard would at least feel a twinge of guilt over its ingratitude. He wrote *Words and Things* on a final sabbatical half-year and in 1957 was appointed associate professor of social psychology at the Massachusetts Institute of Technology and professor in 1960. There he taught social psychology, the psychology of language, theories of personality, psychology for industrial executives, and just about anything he liked. He found the MIT students as stimulating as the Harvard students and, to his surprise, more interested in the supposedly soft topics of psychology than the well-developed scientific topics. They thought of psychology as a needed holiday from calculus and chemistry, and were not about to be cheated out of Freud and ESP and race relations by an overdose of psychophysics. Brown saw quite a lot of Noam Chomsky and Morris Halle and began to learn generative transformational grammar.

While always interested in taking a flyer on pronouns of address or questions of literary style (these with the collaboration of Albert Gilman of the Boston University English Department), Brown's research increasingly became concentrated on the child's acquisition of its first language. Having done a number of experiments on very limited aspects of this process, he conceived a desire to study the whole process, naturalistically, on a level of detail that meant working with just a very few children.

Returning to Harvard as a professor of social psychology in 1962, Brown also obtained National Institute of Mental Health support for a five-year study of three children, the three called in the literature Adam, Eve, and Sarah. The work chiefly consisted of the collection, transcription, and linguistic analysis of large samples of spontaneous conversation between mother and child at home. In the first year of the project, there was a concurrent weekly seminar to discuss the children's protocols. When he recalls the membership of that seminar, Brown realizes how exceptional a year it was: Ursula Bellugi, Colin Fraser, Courtney Cazden, Jean Berko Gleason, David McNeill, Dan Slobin, Sam Anderson, Richard Cromer, and Gordon Finley.

Brown's *Social Psychology* was finished in 1965. He knew that it made a combination of topics that was distinctly eccentric for social psychology, including two interminable chapters on language, which most teachers who adopted the book have surely skipped. He knew too that there was much "unscientific" use of anecdote and introspection but could not see why a text in social psychology should look like a text in chemistry or physics. The one principle he followed was to write only on things that seriously interested him; he also tried to find a level of detail that could engage interest. He thought it very decent of the Free Press to publish *Social Psychology* at all. The success of the book with both teachers and students was both a great surprise and a gratification to him. In 1981 the 1965 *Social Psychology* became an official "Citation Classic," largely because of the analysis in the book of the risky shift, which became a popular research topic. Until 1986 the unrevised first edition was still in print.

The National Institute of Child Health and Human Development generously extended support of the study of Adam, Eve, and Sarah from five to ten years. Brown had not foreseen the labor involved in a detailed study of the linguistic development of even three children. The first round of analysis, which took some years, comprised the writing of five extensively annotated grammars for each child at evenly spaced developmental points. The grammars had to be indeterminate at many points; there is never enough material to settle everything. The result was fifteen manuscripts, all 50 pages or more in length, which Brown estimated about half a dozen people in the world combined the interest, the knowledge, and the patience to read; nay, not so many as half a dozen. He decided the whole venture had been a vast fishing expedition. It did leave him knowing what things something reliable could be written about and what things one might as well remain silent about. And so he began again—a work intended to be in two volumes. The first volume, *A First Language: The Early Stages*, was published by the Harvard University Press in 1973.

Of *A First Language* Brown says it does not explain how the acquisition of language is possible. But it did establish some empirical generalizations that have held up very well in subsequent research. In 1982 *A First Language* became a "Citation Classic" and in 1988 is in print and still frequently cited.

The planned second volume of *A First Language*, which was to cover *The Later Stages*, was never written. People used to ask about it, but after several years that became embarrassing, and developmental psycholinguists came to assume it never would appear. Why has it not? Data collection had been completed in 1973 and so had data description in the form of unpublished grammars. Brown had an unhappy sabbatical year in which he worked hard on *The Later Stages* but finally had to admit defeat. The detailed analyses of presumptive Stages III, IV, and V did not yield up any strong generalizations comparable to those of the early stages, and he could see no value in publishing the possibly quite idiosyncratic details available in the unpublished grammars. In addition, linguistic theory was evolving rapidly, and Brown, never quick at learning new formalisms, could hardly keep up. Finally, the international data base of acquisition studies had grown apace, and it seemed that only a prodigious polyglot, which Brown never was, could hope to think productively on a "human species level" about acquisition. Brown gave up on *The Later*

Stages and also regretfully decided that the time was now past when he
could effectively initiate research on first language acquisition. However,
gifted students like Jill de Villiers, Helen Tager Flusberg, and Kenji Hakuta kept coming along and initiating on their own.

By 1985 Dan Slobin and his associates had accomplished what seemed
impossible ten years earlier: acquisition studies for eleven languages (published in two volumes) and the findings from all effectively integrated. But
then, Dan Slobin *is* a prodigious polyglot. Michael Maratsos (1983) and
Steven Pinker (1984), both very gifted at learning formalisms, are up-to-
date on linguistic theory and cognitive psychology and have proposed acquisition theories (different theories) that are more explicit and detailed
than one expected to see in this decade. And the protocols of Adam, Eve,
and Sarah have been entered into the Child Language Data Exchange
System directed by Brian MacWhinney and Catherine Snow and are
available to all. It is not easy nowadays to understand events on the frontier of developmental psycholinguistics, but it is clear that the field has an
advancing frontier and not just a new shuffle.

In 1967–70 Roger Brown served as chairman of the Department of Social Relations at Harvard, the last chairman of that department as it happened, because many things came together in those years to cause the sociologists to set up their own independent department and all the varieties
of psychologists to come together as the Department of Psychology and
Social Relations. As chairman of Social Relations in the late 1960's, Brown
had a number of "confrontations," as they used to be called, with angry
students over issues now difficult to remember because they were never
over the only real issue, which was the war in Vietnam. On that one real
issue there was almost no student-faculty disagreement in Social Relations, but members continued to fight little substitute wars with one another over courses and curriculum and other such nonsense. From these
confrontations Brown remembers only one event—his single shining
hour. Hundreds of students had gathered in Harvard's largest auditorium
to wave flags and stamp feet over some policy the chairman was bound,
by his office, to defend. First came a really abusive harangue to which
Brown replied. "I think," he said, "that I make a very unlikely Fascist Pig."
Everyone had to admit he did, and there was a relaxing laugh that briefly
broke the spell of that Theater of the Absurd.

In 1974 Brown published, with his colleague Richard Herrnstein, *Psychology*, which is an introductory textbook with a difference. The book
was developed out of the authors' collaboration in teaching the introduc-

tory course and is more searching and more difficult than the average text. *Psychology* was praised by most reviewers but adopted by very few teachers. The fact that American teachers of psychology did not assign the book meant that students in the United States did not read it, and that was a great disappointment to the authors. They find some consolation in the fact that the German translation is widely used in Europe.

In the early 1980's Roger Brown had some very enjoyable research experiences in divers areas. In May and June of 1978 he did about a dozen experiments on emotional meanings in music. The experiments did not favorably impress the music educators who created the occasion for the work. They would have preferred a generative transformational grammar of music theory, but Brown was not about to "dash the hopes" of a perfect springtime with anything so glum.

"Flashbulb Memories," done in collaboration with James Kulik, is a paper that Brown groups with "The Tip of the Tongue Phenomenon" as cases in which phenomenon-centered studies yielded surprising knowledge. "The Psychological Causality Implicit in Language," done with Deborah Fish, felt unique in that it was not just a study but a discovery. No one, they thought, had ever realized that interpersonal verbs (*admire*, *like*, *charm*) allocated causality in lawful ways to their logical arguments. It seemed a discovery and not just a study, because it represented new knowledge, even if that knowledge was not terribly consequential. When Brown and Fish learned that the knowledge was not, in fact, entirely new but had been partially anticipated by Catherine Garvey and Alfonso Caramazza, it did not matter, because they had already had the thrill of feeling themselves to be discoverers.

At the start of his sabbatical year in 1983 Brown began a large undertaking. The success of the 1965 *Social Psychology* and his continuing fascination with the subject matter made him want to try again. He had been teaching the course every year and had worked out ways of presenting about half the content a text must necessarily cover. The sabbatical would provide the unbroken stretch of time needed. But what should such a book be like? Brown knew he had no choice. He could only write one kind of book: selective in content, essayistic and argumentative in style, long-winded by comparison with most texts. In fact, it would have to be an entirely new book, continuous with the first on a deep level, but with many new topics and issues and all new sentences.

What, when it was finished, could such a book be called? One would like to carry over the good will the first edition had won, and so there was good reason to say *Social Psychology, 2d ed*. But *2d ed*. did not convey the fact that this was an entirely new book. To say "completely revised" would be laughable since any decent text not completely revised after twenty years would be inconceivable. What about *Social Psychology The Second Edition* with every word in the title on the same level, nothing subordinate and nothing superordinate? *Social Psychology* for the things preserved— the style of writing, the deep questions that do not go away, the haunting experiments that are timeless—and *Second Edition* for the new book that it is, the fresh presentation of everything, the recently emerged social issues.

In January 1986, the book was published and the suspense—for Brown—was killing. Could a book of this kind succeed today? A rather difficult book, a book that needed to be studied, a book that did not just list findings but developed arguments.

In 1988 it is clear that the book is not a success. It has its admirers but has not been widely adopted and so not been widely read. Since this has not killed him, Brown supposes it has made him stronger.

Me Again

Harvard is a noble place, but none I think do there embrace. None of the senior faculty anyway. The university is a lot like the Metropolitan Opera. As institutions each is the best of its kind in the country, and each as an institution stands for humane values. One must be proud of such an association. The strength of Harvard is, as President Bok has often said, its faculty, and the strength of the Metropolitan is its artists. But star faculty like star singers are an overtrained, nervy lot, very attentive to their prerogatives. However, my immediate senior colleagues have always been amiable to me, and I do not underestimate that accomplishment on their part.

Junior faculty do often become close friends, companions in adversity. Better friends at Harvard than at Yale. It appears that a zero-opportunity structure is a more comfortable environment than a structure of some small opportunity. Most of my best friends among psychologists I met first as junior faculty.

It is with graduate students that professors have their easiest friendships and I have been notably lucky there. In April 1985 at the Hampshire House in Boston, eighteen of my former students, those in psycholinguistics, gave me a wonderful warm birthday party and presented me with papers for a festschrift, which Frank Kessel edited and which was published in 1988 by Erlbaum. Like an old lady telling her beads I recite their illustrious names: Jean Berko-Gleason, Dan Slobin, Ursula Bellugi, Courtney Cazden, Richard Cromer, Eleanor Rosch, Eric Wanner, Michael Maratsos, Melissa Bowerman, Howard Gardner, Ellen Winner, Jill De Villiers, Kenji Hakuta, Helen Tager-Flusberg, David Rubin, Lerita Coleman, Steven Pinker, and Laura Petitto.

How have I come to be blessed with so exceptional a succession of students? Time and place had a lot to do with it. Psycholinguistics has been and is a profound subject, a deep and serious subject, with, nevertheless, an aspect of playfulness, and Harvard is a place that attracts students who respond to this combination of qualities. The teacher's role has been an easy one; to nod encouragement at the better ideas and withhold it for the worser. For these students I have had more than nods to dispense or withhold; I have had strong affection. The affection is no credit to me. Anyone not determined to deny all frivolous things any role in science would notice that these graduate students were quite unusually attractive persons.

Psycholinguistics has never been institutionalized at Harvard. There has never been a degree program or any power of appointment or even a fixed set of requirements. The graduate students who worked with me took degrees in experimental psychology, or social, or developmental; none has a Ph.D. in psycholinguistics. Looking back, I count that as an advantage. It is mainly responsible, I think, for their intellectual spacing. A well-defined topic in psychology, even so broad and difficult a topic as the acquisition of language, seems able to support only a small number of first-rate careers. Eighteen doctoral students doing psycholinguistics at one university might well find themselves "stacked up," after 30 years, in a holding pattern over one or two American professorships. But the present eighteen with their interests in sign language, artistic language, developmental variation, universals of development, language and thought, and bilingualism live in neighboring but not disputed territories. The necessity for each one in his or her training to be something more than a psycholinguist, to do something else in a major way, has, I think, inclined them to discover connections and invent new things.

Of my closest friends, my second family, only a few are psycholinguists. Mary, Lois, Sharon, Rebecca, Camille, Carolyn, Betty, Don, Jim, Bonnie, Sarah, George, Burr, Anastasia, Kaye, Marianne, Phil, Dorothy, Jane, Michael, and John (who kindly typed this manuscript) are teachers, artists, writers, musicians, librarians, and psychiatrists. At the center is the fine scholar who has shared his life with me.

Roger Brown was President of the New England Psychological Association in 1965–66 and of the Division of Personality and Social Psychology of the APA in the same year. In 1971–72 he served as President of the Eastern Psychological Association. He is a Fellow of the American Academy of Arts and Sciences. In 1969 the University of Michigan gave him its "Outstanding Achievement Award," and in 1970 York University, England, gave him the honorary degree "Doctor of the University." In 1971 Brown received the Distinguished Scientific Achievement Award of the American Psychological Association, and in 1972 he was elected to the National Academy of Sciences. In 1973 he was awarded the G. Stanley Hall Prize in Developmental Psychology of the American Psychological Association. In 1980 Bucknell University made him an honorary D.Sci., and in 1983 Northwestern University did the same. In 1980 Brown gave the Katz-Newcomb Lecture in Social Psychology at the University of Michigan, and in 1985 he was awarded the international prize of the Fondation Fyssen in Paris.

Selected Publications by Roger Brown

(with E. H. Lenneberg) (1954). A study in language and cognition. *Journal of Abnormal and Social Psychology*, 49, 454–462.

(with A. H. Black & A. E. Horowitz) (1955). Phonetic symbolism in natural languages. *Journal of Abnormal and Social Psychology*, 50, 388–393.

(1958). *Words and things*. New York: Free Press.

(with A. Gilman) (1960). The pronouns of power and solidarity. In T. Sebeok (Ed.), *Aspects of style in language* (pp. 253–276). Cambridge, MA: MIT Press.

(1965). *Social psychology*. New York: Free Press.

(with A. Gilman) (1966). Personality and style in Concord. In M. Simon & T. H. Parsons (Eds.), *Transcendentalism and its legacy* (pp. 87–122). Ann Arbor: University of Michigan Press.

(with C. Hanlon) (1970). Derivational complexity and order of acquisition in child speech. In R. Hayes (Ed.), *Cognition and the development of language* (pp. 11–53). New York: Wiley.

(1973). *A first language: The early stages*. Cambridge, MA: Harvard University Press.

(with R. Herrnstein) (1974). *Psychology*. Boston: Little, Brown.
(with J. Kulik) (1977). Flashbulb memories. *Cognition*, 5(1), 73–99.
(1981). Music and language. In *Documentary report of the Ann Arbor Symposium*
(pp. 233–264). Reston, VA: Music Educators National Conference.
(with D. Fish) (1983). The psychological causality implicit in language. *Cognition*,
14, 237–273.
(1986a). *Social psychology the second edition*. New York: Free Press.
(1986b). Linguistic relativity. In S. H. Hulse & B. F. Green, Jr. (Eds.), *One hundred
years of psychological research in America* (pp. 241–276). Baltimore: Johns Hopkins University Press.
(with D. McNeill) (1966). The "tip of the tongue" phenomenon. *Journal of Verbal
Learning and Verbal Behavior*, 5, 325–337.

Other Publications Cited

Au, T. K. (1983). Chinese and English counterfactuals: The Sapir-Whorf hy-
pothesis revisited. *Cognition*, *15*, 155–187.
Bell, A. P., & Weinberg, M. S. (1978). *Homosexualities*. New York: Simon & Schus-
ter.
Bell, A. P., Weinberg, M. S. & Hammersmith, S. F. (1981). *Sexual Preference*.
Bloomington, IN: Indiana University Press.
Bloom, A. H. (1981). *The linguistic shaping of thought: A study in the impact of lan-
guage on thinking in China and the West*. Hillsdale, NJ: Erlbaum.
Furbank, P. N. (1977). *E. M. Forster: A life*. New York: Harcourt, Brace, Jovan-
ovich.
Heider, E. R. & Olivier, D. C. (1972). The structure of color space in naming and
memory for two languages. *Cognitive Psychology*, *3*, 337–354.
Hodges, A. (1983). *Alan Turing: The enigma*. New York: Simon and Schuster.
Hull, C. L. (1943). *Principles of behavior*. New York: Appleton-Century-Crofts.
Kessel, F. S. (Ed.) (1988). *The development of language and language researchers:
Essays in honor of Roger Brown*. Hillsdale, NJ: Erlbaum.
Maratsos, M. (1983). Some current issues in the study of the acquisition of gram-
mar. In J. H. Flavell & E. M. Markman (Eds.), *Cognitive Development* (pp. 706–
787). Vol. 3 of P. H. Massen (Ed.), *Handbook of child psychology*, 4th ed. New
York: Wiley.
Pinker, S. (1984). *Language learnability and language development*. Cambridge,
MA: Harvard University Press.
Skidelsky, R. (1986). *John Maynard Keynes: Hopes betrayed, 1883–1920*. New York:
Viking.
Slobin, D. (Ed.) (1985). *The crosslinguistic study of language acquisition, Vols. 1–2*.
Hillsdale, NJ: Erlbaum.
Watson, J. B. (1930). *Behaviorism*. New York: Norton.
Whorf, B. L. (1956). *Language, thought and reality: Selected writings of Benjamin
Lee Whorf*. (J. B. Carroll, Ed.) Cambridge, MA: MIT Press.

Lee Cronbach

Lee J. Cronbach

Psychology caught me early. I was born in 1916, just before Lewis Terman's disciples fanned out to spread the gospel of mental testing. One, Blanche Cummings, became school psychologist in my hometown, Fresno, and she tried the Stanford-Binet on me in 1921. Ms. Cummings arranged newspaper publicity for my test score, used me as a subject for Binet demonstrations, and enrolled me with Terman as "gifted." The story Cummings spread centered on an IQ of 200, and that was the mirror held up for me as a child. But Terman's staff—as I learned only a few years ago—rejected that first test as invalid and used as data a plausible lower figure from a second test. ("Dr. Terman" became a fixture in family conversation. In later years, his responses to my letters moved from generalized encouragement to specific advice on educational plans and, in time, to generous but not uncritical comment on professional writings.)

My mother evidently was eager that I start school. So, a month after my first test and prior to my fifth birthday, Ms. Cummings arranged for my midyear enrollment in the upper second grade. In fifth grade my eccentric teacher, being retired against her will, made the grand year-end gesture of double promoting everyone in her class, on the grounds that pupils learned twice as much from her as from other teachers. School officials let a few of the double promotions stand. Hence I finished high school at age fourteen (and college at eighteen).

My parents met in Fresno, having migrated from mid-America around 1910. My mother, a superior student in high school, had lacked resources to continue her education and moved to California in part because of poor health; she returned to full strength only when I was in my teens. Over many years she pushed me toward achievement and recognition (sometimes meretricious), and pushed others to advance me. My father, or-

I thank Goldine Gleser, J. Thomas Hastings, and R. E. Snow for checking parts of my draft against their recollections.

phaned, had left school after eight years. In Fresno he sold silk and other dress goods; in time, he became a "buyer" with twice-a-year train trips to New York and complimentary tickets for Broadway shows (Eddie Cantor!). His capital was the trust expressed by repeat customers from all round the San Joaquin Valley. At home he was a quiet source of support. I recall when, by digging out of the library facts about the Liberty Bell, I won a contest promoting a local concert by Sousa's band and then learned that the concert had been sold out. My father took my disappointment seriously enough to talk us past the doorman.

Religion played little part. My father was Jewish; I went to a Sabbath school, and my parents went to the temple on occasion. My mother was raised a "Campbellite" (Disciples of Christ), and after a cross-town move about age twelve, I attended a nearby Presbyterian Sunday school. As a child I knew of Passover and of a nonreligious Christmas.

Social life was minimal. My father got out to the Elks Club on Sundays to play cards, but I cannot recall my parents' entertaining another couple. I had neighborhood playmates and later went to city playgrounds; indeed, there was a good deal of adult-sponsored recreation, including a stamp club and a chess club. Until around age sixteen, my relations with classmates were distant at best.

I was a debater from eighth grade through college, never better than third-string. In college my social relations became normal enough for me to be lampooned beside others in a school paper. I recall a line of doggerel about me as debater: "Little Lee, boldly demanding 'By *whose* authority?'" The style of debate then was to have ready, on 3-by-5 cards, dozens of quotations from notables that could be pulled forth to counter what an opponent might say. I recall having defined, somewhere in those years, my goal in life as Being An Authority.

Specifically, child of an era of Gilbert "chemistry sets" and Slosson's *Creative Chemistry*, I would be a chemist; so at Fresno State College I took the straight dose of chemistry, physics, math, and German. When lack of money precluded junior-year transfer to Berkeley, I shifted to the broader program for a Fresno State degree. Encountering *Henry IV*, *Marbury vs. Madison*, and such, I started a liberal education I would not have appreciated earlier. My English teachers encouraged me to the point of inviting me to join would-be poets and novelists in the Writers' Club. I completed majors in math and chemistry. Later years were to prove that I comprehended the math; little of chemistry stuck, beyond appreciation of using a surface to express the yield of a reaction as a function of parameters.

First Encounters with Research

My awareness of Terman had attracted me to psychology as a high school elective, but psychology came at the hour for solid geometry; I substituted sociology. Every student was to investigate something (a demand I did not encounter in physical science until my fifth year of college). I measured the space newspapers gave to each category of crime. As a college junior taking "tests and measurements," I was entranced by the Thurstone-Chave monograph (1929) on measuring attitudes, and my term project was construction of a Thurstone scale. I especially admired Thurstone's inventive use of mathematics to sharpen the central construct and ferret out equivocal items; the virtue of rigorous engineering analysis of psychological measuring devices became fixed in my mind.

Fresno State being a teachers' college, I had to take history of American education. A report on the tryout of some curricular improvement reached the professor. Liking it, and knowing that I had done public speaking, he requested me to tell the class about it. Because I detested the course and because the report had poor evidence for its claims, my talk was a science major's scornful dissection. The class loved it. Strolling back with me toward his office, the professor had no direct comment. Instead he asked, "Have you ever considered a career in educational research?" "Is there such a thing?" I asked in all seriousness. His suggestion, coming just as I realized that chemistry had lost its appeal, pointed me toward my career. (Incidentally, by virtue of a bequest he made, the professor's portrait looks down on me when I use the Stanford psychology library, and a chair is named for him, which Gordon Bower occupies.)

I needed to become employable fast. High school teaching being the surest option, I went to Berkeley for a credential; I could work on a masters in education at the same time. Berkeley provided two fine experiences. Student teaching provided lasting inspiration. University High had a remarkable faculty and, as a "progressive" high school, was working closely with developmental psychologists. Second, courses required for mathematics teaching introduced me to the writings of Hilbert and Klein, hence to how model building preconditions the mathematical conclusions I had hitherto thought of as "truths." As for the rest, Herbert Conrad's statistics course didn't go far, but it was a delight to watch him bring along students who had no mathematical qualifications and wanted none. My adviser Luther Gilbert was helpful, but his interest in the psychology of spelling was too specific for me. I never forgave Berkeley for requiring me to complete an undergraduate education major as a preliminary to the M.A. program; some of those courses demonstrated the worst that detractors have said about education professors. I remain grateful to Gilbert for advising me to shift to Chicago for the doctorate.

Fresno High School hired me to teach, more because my mother was then president of the city PTA than because no teacher who had reached age twenty could be found. I taught mathematics for two and a half years (and chemistry briefly) and was adviser (highly participant) to the school paper. (I had written for Fresno State's *Collegian* in my senior year and then did editorial work on *The Daily Californian*—a happy arena for bringing verbal skills to a peak, "being part of things," and, at long last, relating to peers.) My colleagues were tolerant of my instructional innovations—for example, my demonstrating musical intervals on a sonometer to add interest to Euclid's Book on Proportions. Though I made many bad judgments, on the whole I got along well with students—and also, with some spare cash and a college down the street, began to date.

My only course ever from a Department of Psychology (save for Psych 1) was Warner Brown's course on motivation at Berkeley, during the summer of 1938. My attentions were elsewhere. A few weeks after meeting Helen Claresta Bower, I was buying an engagement ring, with the ecstatic understanding that she would follow me to Chicago and become a doctoral student's wife. Her father being an astronomy Ph.D. and former college teacher, she knew something of what she was getting into. The formative highlight of her life had been the job of caring for triplets, at their home in Berkeley and during a summer at Mesa Verde where their father was a park official. She would be pleased to cheer me on in my career if I would do as much for her projected—and, in the event, highly gratifying—career as mother. Triplets not having been made part of the contract, the births of our five children spread from 1941 to 1956.

Thanks largely to Sidney Pressey, educational psychologists were then concerned with technical terms as a stumbling block for pupils. For a master's thesis I studied understanding of vocabulary in algebra. Dewey's *How We Think* showed me that "knowing the meaning of a word" is not all-or-none; multiple discriminations are required to match a word accurately to possible referents. Hence, a teacher needs to know how words are misunderstood by pupils. Each of my miniature tests had five yes-no items on recognizing, for example, a *coefficient*. This enabled me to list words the pupil could apply properly and to tabulate how the students' ideas departed from the textbook's concept. Later, I devoted a longer test to one concept. Each item described a relationship between quantities and asked whether the word "function" applied to it. From disagreements among responses of mathematics teachers, I identified twelve features of their concepts (Cronbach, 1943b). Although each teacher's concept of "function" existed, it did not "exist in some amount" (to recall a Thorndikean cliché). It existed in the pattern of criteria the teacher applied.

Doctoral Training

Educational psychology had been planted at the University of Chicago by C. H. Judd and F. N. Freeman, both trained in Leipzig. The strong empirical tradition was now led by Judd's student Guy Buswell (with whom Gilbert had studied). In the summer of 1937 I poked a toe in the water. Buswell's course in laboratory methods (finger mazes, kymographs, memory drums) required a term paper on a research method. Having filmed eye movements under Gilbert, I chose to trace the history of the technique. I quailed only briefly upon finding that the key sources were in German; after all, my freshman advisor had signaled that Science is International when he put German on my study list. The history started with flakes of white pigment on corneas and photographic plates dropped past a slit; I had a fine compulsive time assembling it. My triumph was undercut when, just before my deadline, I discovered a British publication in which Madeleine Vernon said everything I had to say; even so, the term paper helped win me a fellowship.

In 1938 I entered full-time work toward the Ph.D. in education. Feeling driven to complete my degree and return to a payroll, I moved so fast that Chicago had little chance to educate me. I was so centered on "meeting requirements" that, for example, it never occurred to me to elect courses with L. L. Thurstone in another department. I rushed at qualifying examinations a month after arrival; my marginal pass entitled me to start dissertation research and cleared the way for marriage. I profited that year from Karl Holzinger in statistics, from an evaluation seminar with Ralph Tyler (who had succeeded Judd as chairman), and from miscellaneous assisting roles. When Tyler set out to stimulate his faculty, he assigned me to extract items reflecting their "behavioral objectives" from them (for a master's comprehensive exam). I barely escaped from that presumptuous undertaking with a whole skin.

Back in 1907 Judd and Cowling had had children inspect a nonsense squiggle, draw it, inspect again, draw again, and so on. The shortcomings of the reproductions led them to broad conclusions about information processing that were still being cited. For a dissertation I proposed a replication that, to shorten the span of inference, would film eye fixations. The finished study (Cronbach, 1941) led to no large insight, though it touched on styles and on encoding; someone else might have made it a starting point for some of today's studies of cognition. I had originally hoped to complete my straightforward study within the year, but became discontented with my accuracy in measuring the films and revised my schedule.

The needed financial support came from a mind-stretching assistantship with the Eight-Year Study (Smith and Tyler, 1943). Tyler had brought to Chicago the staff that was monitoring 30 "progressive" high schools (including the one at Berkeley). The schools sought to develop social attitudes, personality, and ability to solve problems in each subject area; they tried to view the student "as a whole." Such goals, a part of my thinking from Berkeley days, became an ideology through my work with Tyler's group.

I was the desk-bound analyst who saw all the test scores and prepared statistics for the file while the senior staff, specialists within curricular areas, visited schools to help teachers and counselors interpret scores. Among the dozen seniors were Hilda Taba (social studies), George Sheviakov (personal development), and Bruno Bettelheim (visual arts). Asked to suggest methods for scoring Bettelheim's brilliantly clinical art-appreciation test and for summarizing the 21-score profile of Sheviakov's inventory, I was launched as all-purpose methodologist. In such large enterprises the schedule of field work precludes intensive analysis of data and reflection. Puzzles I stored up carried the seed of several studies I did later.

The Pullman Years

A whimsical god or goddess made me instructor in psychology in 1940. Washington State College was so isolated in Pullman that each department had to nominate faculty appointees on the basis of paper credentials. In June the President took the departments' lists and circled the country, interviewing wherever he stopped. Reaching Chicago, his last stop before home, he was shocked to realize that he had failed to interview the nominees for the vacancy in psychology. Responding to his desperation, the university placement office pulled my name from the file. Despite my ignorance of mainstream psychology, I was interested, because I wanted to get back to teaching and to the West. The interview revealed that the appointee was to conduct a reading clinic for college students, which made me even less credible as applicant. My director, Professor Buswell, operated such a clinic, I explained, but my training was along other lines. "But you know what he does there, do you not? Surely you have visited the clinic?" I had. I got the job.

In the first year I taught introductory, social, child, applied, and industrial psychology, and operated the reading clinic. (Carl Erickson, trained by C. E. Seashore, covered experimental and abnormal.) The extension division asked me to carry on a course in sex education my predecessor had offered in Spokane. I didn't know anything about that either, but while reading across the library shelves preparing for courses, I might as well spend time in the locked cage! After two years in the stacks, I knew much of the psychological literature from 1900 to 1942. I proved to be inventive in remedial reading and by the second year had a practicum course for seniors and graduate students. Not only did I enjoy the students at Pullman, but Helen and I found ourselves at home in the social community of young faculty.

Psychology was within the School of Education. Its dean had been a G. Stanley Hall Ph.D., and its measurement specialist, C. W. Stone, had done a famous piece of work under Thorndike in 1906. A certain mustiness blew away when the new dean brought aboard in January 1941 turned out to be an active figure in educational measurement, J. Murray Lee. He was delighted to have a faculty member who shared his interests and energy, and my opportunities were unlimited. His first proposal was that I offer for the 1941 summer session a course with the avant-garde title "Evaluation."

At various times in Pullman, I managed academic classification for an Air Force training detachment, helped survey a school system, directed students in rendering testing service to a veterans' guidance clinic, and published dozens of scattered papers. As needed for particular studies, I invented what I later recognized to be Pearson's intraclass correlation and a Monte Carlo technique suited to a small IBM tabulator; my knowledge of the statistical literature was never great enough to inhibit intuition and invention. Fortunately, the papers banged out by the fastest typewriter in the West were quickly lost from view.

One Sunday in 1941 I was listening to the New York Philharmonic broadcast while tabulating what high school students had written for me about "What war would mean," when the radio told of Pearl Harbor. Dean Lee set up a press conference on my findings and advice to schools, and encouraged me in a wider, more structured survey. Then Herbert Conrad, encountered at a professional meeting, asked if I might prepare something for the *Applied Psychology Monographs* he was initiating. My report (1943a) was modest as science, but in practical aim the project was a close cousin to today's effort to understand and reduce youngsters' anxieties about the nuclear threat.

In 1945 Timothy Leary, back from a clinical post as Army noncom, came to Pullman, his wife's hometown. He was in remission that year from his anti-Establishment life course, and we worked cordially. As he completed a master's degree under my direction, he taught me about clinical test interpretation, particularly of the Rorschach and Wechsler. That year Dean Lee turned over the "Mental Measurements" course to me, and I was so discontented with available textbooks that I started at once on *Essentials of Psychological Testing* (1949a). By then I had some experience with clinical testing, vocational guidance, educational diagnosis, achievement and attitude testing, and personnel psychology. My experience with individual intelligence tests was of particularly long standing.

An Interlude as Military Psychologist

From early 1944 to the end of the war, I was research psychologist at the Navy's sonar school in San Diego, part of a tiny civilian group under Adelbert Ford. After doing routine validation of selection tests, I was shifted to training projects. I developed a course on echo-ranging (topside) sonar, then one on underwater listening for submariners. In a specially equipped classroom the trainee listened to a recording, pressed a button upon detecting a significant sound, then pressed others to indicate his interpretation. Responses from all the stations were traced onto paper before the instructor, so that he could correct and clarify. For the second project, the student station had 100 buttons. At the controls the instructor could see instantly that a certain student had pressed, say, 77 (meaning "I hear snapping shrimp" and suggesting shoals). I observed the class while each trial lesson was run, then dashed off with an armload of tracings to tabulate response times and errors. Identifying a type of confusion for which exercises were needed, I would go to the recording studio, select suitable sound specimens from the library, and have technicians dub them into a lesson for trial next day. When the class moved out I had a few days to rearrange all the material, being free to decide on distribution of time, on difficulty of exercises, and on visual adjuncts. (Pictures of the sound envelope, plotted electronically, proved particularly useful.) A complete course, a manual, and a set of tests resulted. Here, if ever, were perfect conditions for instructional research: unambiguous goals, replicable lessons, objective and detailed evidence of student progress and perplexities, and perfect communication between the evaluator and the person charged with improving the instruction. Also, not to be overlooked, close association with intelligent and observant instructors.

I did a bit of psychophysical research after experienced submarine listeners asserted that they could detect whether a ship topside was closing or opening the range. I verified the claim, established that the cues were transients in the sounds from bow-on ships, and, finally, developed lessons for training others to notice those subtle cues.

Now, about the sub I sank. A training sub followed a dreary routine. It cruised at periscope depth while one echo-ranging vessel after another made a run and sheered off as the range neared a still-safe 300 yards. To set up a position for recording bow-on, we civilians wrote special orders which the squadron commander signed: on this day attack ships would hold on course and the *submarine* would turn away. The sub captain took aboard our recording team and found space for us, but did not read the orders, assuming them to be those of every other repetitious day. When his periscope showed the first attacker about to plow through us, he ordered a crash dive that cost the boat its buoyancy and threatened to go on forever. My colleague and I pasted ourselves to the control-room bulkhead while the desperate crew forced the boat to an up-angle such that the screws could thrust us to where the leaks stopped.

Chicago, Urbana, Stanford

The University of Chicago educated me at last when I returned as Assistant Professor of Education in 1946. Bill Henry and Annaliese Korner provided seminars on projective tests; the Thurstones invited the psychometric community to their home for evening talks (it is Thelma's pastries I still remember); Max Corey had weekly meetings on instructional design; and Herb Thelen invited me to meet regularly with a team dissecting social processes in classroom discourse. I developed a Thematic Apperception Test for Teachers; Frances Dillon, working with it and me, showed how student teachers' expectations about their professional role reflected their life histories and personality. I devised methods for evaluating Carolyn Tryon's training of teachers in child study and provided statistical backup for the monumental project of Kenneth Eells and Allison Davis on "social class bias" in mental tests (Eells et al., 1951). Tyler handed me the course "Introduction to Educational Psychology," which he had shaped around teachers' tasks that psychology should illuminate. My syllabus followed his lead but added developmental emphases; that was the genesis of my successful textbook in educational psychology (1954).

Five minutes with Joseph Schwab had a profound influence. Tyler took command of "Education as a Field of Study," a course mandated for doctoral students, and wished to apply the Hutchins-Adler "Great Books" model to readings from Aristotle, Dewey, Spencer, and a few nonphilosophers. The sections would be taught by Tyler and five assistant professors. Schwab (a veteran instructor in Hutchins's program) was to limit the damage from our incompetence by conducting us through each week's assignment. An uphill battle: philosophy was alien to the department's "a fact is a fact" tradition in which we assistant professors had been reared. In some context Schwab remarked that biologists have to *decide* what to count as a species—and I was at sea. Surely, I thought, species are marked off by natural law, and biologists have only to cut along the dotted lines. Schwab was acute enough to catch my flicker of surprise and force home the idea of scientist as construer rather than as discoverer of categories the Creator had in mind. That conversation, blended with my early reading of Dewey and Hilbert and later tutoring from Paul Meehl, resonates in my thinking to this day.

I had offered a paper (Cronbach, 1946) to my first APA convention and recall heeding someone's warning that the audience would be demanding. I crammed twenty minutes with evidence that response biases (such as acquiescent yea-saying and evasive resort to "cannot say") affect test scores, and also analyzed their influence on validity. "This kind of paper APA programs need more of"; that generous comment from the session chairman rewarded me beyond my dreams, because the chairman was Thurstone. After this time I reined in my journalist's delight in filling pages and tried to give my publications scope and significance. It is worth noting that the APA paper grew out of my detecting one response bias in a Navy pitch test, another in a minor follow-up of my vocabulary test, and a third in an attitude scale of the Eight-Year Study. This was the first of many instances where bits of inquiry, superficially unrelated and perhaps trivial in themselves, coalesced.

I settled into a style that became both the main strength and main weakness of my scholarly production. My interests being wide, I avoided specialization narrower than "measurement and individual differences." I knew even then that research on instruction, in particular, becomes appropriately rich and informative when it concentrates on a few students or on circumscribed subject matter; my study of algebra vocabulary, the sonar work, and case studies of students I was making showed the merit of close-up inquiry. But apart from wartime urgency I was unwilling to tie myself to sustained work in a content area, and this is a chief reason for my lack of contribution to instructional psychology and for my being a measurement specialist who did next-to-no measuring.

I collected some sets of data at Chicago, and for many more years would think of myself as an observing scientist. In retrospect, I realize that even in 1946–48 I was relying on graduate students and colleagues for most of the data that fueled my thinking. Increasingly I found satisfaction in secondary analysis and critical synthesis. Digging into the logic of a published investigation or reworking filed data, I often reached conclusions beyond or better than those originally reached. Weaving strands into a tapestry was what I enjoyed, not spinning the thread. My desire for broadly relevant insights has always conflicted with my conviction that intimate acquaintance informs an investigator of the true complexity of behavior. I settled for developing methods useful to numerous primary investigators and adopting a style of writing in which specific examples carry much of my message.

The University of Illinois, bracing for a leap to prominence after the war, had been appointing research professors, R. B. Cattell and O. H. Mowrer among them. Positions in the Bureau of Educational Research and Service carrying comparable resources and expectations were offered to Nate Gage and me in 1948. Highly important for me was the desire expressed by the senior faculty that we generate fresh perspectives relevant to education through comparatively basic research, and not restrict ourselves to short-run "practical" questions of educators. This charge departed radically from the tradition of educational research bureaus in state universities.

Champaign-Urbana was an attractive place for a family. Helen found a niche in a cooperative nursery school, and in time was called to be director of religious education for the local Unitarian church. The high point of her assignment was a Lake Geneva, Wisconsin, workshop with Pete Seeger's singing as fringe benefit. I, having found the intellectual stimulation of Chicago something of an overdose, welcomed the less vibrant collegiality of Urbana. I worked up from substitute to regular in the faculty bowling league and sometimes joined a gang of would-be poker players; in Chicago, there would have been seminars on those nights. I must acknowledge, however, that my sociability always remained far below the norm; I would much rather read than engage in small talk.

Professionally I worked most closely with Tom Hastings (who not only was Buswell-Tyler trained but had, for *his* master's thesis, developed algebra vocabulary tests that ran rings round mine). Hastings liked to work with teachers on local problems, whereas I was seeking more general knowledge; so our students developed magnificent hybrid vigor. With our overlapping interests, Gage and I agreed that he would concentrate on teacher characteristics and behavior and move away from psychometrics, while I would do the opposite. Still, we collaborated from time to time over 25 years. Students associated with J. McV. Hunt, C. E. Osgood, and like innovators brought me provocative questions. In 1948 Chicago had offered tenure in Education and Psychology, and my Illinois appointment took that form after Lyle Lanier became head of Psychology. After Henry Kaiser, Lloyd Humphreys, Ledyard Tucker, and others joined the faculty, the Illinois measurement program had few rivals.

An upheaval in the 1940's had left the College of Education with an exaggerated commitment to faculty control. A trivial curricular proposal could set off a dozen caucuses and formal meetings; the school was a hothouse for the skills of academic politics. Suddenly I, who could not have been elected ratcatcher as an adolescent, had a following. I was chosen for responsibilities in the College and University and then in national organizations (and moved on to a professor's kind of international diplomacy). I cherished teamwork on scholarly projects and was an energetic committee member and chair; but a brief trial taught me to steer clear of administrative posts. Administrators must find fulfillment vicariously, through what they enable others to accomplish. That was not for me.

In the early 1960's more and more of my time was going to faculty governance, leading faculty seminars, and guiding institutional research within the university; worthwhile, but not a rut to tread for two more decades. My flow of enthusiastic ideas for research seemed to be drying up, and retreat from the privileges of a research professorship seemed proper. The pull of California had always been strong, and at this time Robert Sears, as head of Psychology at Stanford, made a first move to recruit me. After Sears shifted to a deanship, the central administration took up the courtship as part of a plan to build Stanford's professional schools.

I asked for a joint appointment in Education and Psychology, as distinct from nonparticipant "courtesy" membership in Psychology. Although the high-ranking administrator dealing with me quickly agreed, he evidently forgot the stipulation and certainly neglected to put the appointment before the Department of Psychology. The School of Education was offered my services and the money to pay me. The minutes show that its faculty (where I did have friends) voted acceptance *provided that* this would not delay the appointments they really wanted to make. Fortunately, when H. Thomas James became dean I found a central role in the thrust that was to make Stanford's School of Education preeminent in training for educational research. The appointment in Psychology I did not, could not, get; whether the contretemps was a judgment on me or was fallout from unrelated events will never be known. More interaction with Psychology faculty and students would have affected my development and research, I feel sure. (Years later, after some faculty turnover, Psychology did offer the joint appointment; by then I was heavily committed elsewhere and declined.)

The remaining chronology can be brief. In the 1970's slow moving commitments created a logjam, and my activities began to seem like "work." In the end, seven books appeared between 1977 and 1984 (counting some committee projects). I retired from teaching in 1980, partly to finish certain books and partly because teaching, suffering from my increasing remoteness from classrooms, psychologists, and testmakers, had lost its zest. From such contacts my earlier teaching had gained a sense of proportion, and examples that enlivened even mathematical test theory. Now, only the fraction of my teaching having to do with evaluation and policy was enriched by recent contacts with practitioners.

Consultant and Committeeman

A "marginal man" gets exceptional stimulation and opportunities for service. Statisticians viewed me as a psychologist who understood some of their language. To clinical and social psychologists, I was a statistician who appreciated their work. Educationists saw me as an established scientist. Natural and social scientists who became interested in improving education looked to me for expertise regarding instruction or student characteristics. In most working groups, whether as consultant or leader, I as intellectual outlier was the member who learned most.

I was immersed in APA affairs for seven years. Proper testing and proper claims for tests loomed large in the code of ethics APA was close to adopting in 1950. Explicit standards for technical characteristics would be needed to apply the code. The Board of Directors, apparently believing that nothing was required beyond writing out an existing consensus, appointed a youthful committee of specialists. I was chair, presumably because a paper on research into the Rorschach and my textbook on testing had displayed respect for both critical and imaginative approaches.

The committee developing the ethical standards had proposed an "APA seal of approval" for tests, but our committee rejected this. A test excellent for one purpose is unsuited for others. We approached standard-setting cautiously, fearing to choke off innovation. We came to focus not on the absolute quality of a test but on the producer's obligation to assist professionals to judge how well it can meet particular needs. Our report of 1954 recognized the diversity of tests and tried to avoid perfectionism. The Standards were successful enough to evolve (American Educational Research Association and others, 1985) and to be cited by the Supreme Court in connection with employment testing.

The first energetic year of the Test Standards committee impressed the Board of Directors enough that they named me chair of the Publications Board. I defended publication policies before the Council, and it put me on the Board of Directors when a vacancy occurred. Election as APA President, which followed in 1955, continued a pattern; persons known for commitment to a rigorous but person-centered psychology were favored by the voters of those years. The directors had a busy time coping with growth and change. My individual role consisted mostly in encouraging Roger Russell to leave his London professorship to become executive officer and thereafter providing him a sympathetic ear. My offices in other associations were similarly uneventful.

Consultancies—as short-term employee, task-force member, or sporadic visitor—appealed to my appetite for new experience. They paid off with examples for my teaching and writing, anomalies from which methodological studies grew, and awareness of how topics that interested me appeared to persons from other corners of psychology, other disciplines, and other cultures.

Vivian Edmiston (later Todd), a Tyler alumna, was in Japan in 1947 as educational specialist at Occupation headquarters; she nominated me to help plan a Japanese college-entrance test. My credentials for the task were flimsy, but my few weeks in Tokyo (plus a brief trip to the Kansai) brought much aesthetic pleasure, a sharper awareness of the politics of testing, and a pleasant relationship with the project assistant Tadashi Hidano. Years later, having become a senior educational psychologist, he encouraged Hiroshi Azuma to take a doctorate with me. Azuma became a collaborator, and then mentor during my 1967 Fulbright year at the University of Tokyo, where Hidano was senior professor.

Other important collaborators also entered my life through consultancies. Fred Fiedler was assistant in the Kelly-Fiske project (Kelly and Fiske, 1951) on selection of clinical psychologists when I joined discussions of its analyses. Goldine Gleser was teamed with DuBois and Loevinger on an Air Force measurement project (see Loevinger, DuBois, and Gleser, 1953) when my comments on Loevinger's psychometric theory brought me an invitation to consult.* And a conference I organized for the Social Science Research Council began my association with Dick Snow. On these, more later.

I was lucky enough in 1955 to be engaged as liaison scientist at the Office of Naval Research (ONR) in London. For 13 months I was to go anywhere—well, as far as West Berlin and Helsinki—and facilitate exchange of research information. I need not detail a travelogue essentially like the one Frank Geldard described in Volume 7 of this series. It was a great family year, starting with a crossing on SS *United States* and including an Easter motor trip as far as Rome.

My predecessors having been sensory psychologists, I looked into social, educational, and differential psychology. I wished especially to learn "how Europeans thought" in these matters. My first chance came when the captain at ONR-London called me in for a reprimand: I had been on board ten days and hadn't yet made a trip! A Yale physicist-philosopher had just paid a call on the captain; *he* had come over for a psychology meeting, and It Was My Duty to attend. The Society for Psychical Research, unhappy over being a front-page staple of British tabloids, was keeping this international conference under cover. But Gardner Murphy was in their good graces, he happened to be in my debt, and he would get me in if I promised to keep a low profile. So the Navy ran off the prescribed ten copies of orders sending me to Cambridge for a day. Throughout the meeting—except for sound preaching on methodology from Murphy—the participants solemnly exchanged ghost stories. That was my introduction to *Geisteswissenschaft*. The Yale professor, who had been invited so he could evaluate the seriousness of the SPR commitment to science, closed the meeting by lauding the caliber of the reports. As the year proceeded, I

---

*In Snow and Wiley (in press) I have described several projects, ideas, and experiences related to technical psychometrics and data analysis. Although these include my most substantial and effortful lines of research, to avoid duplication I give them little space here. The superscript [1] is used to mark topics covered more fully in that other essay.

encountered more substantial humanistic psychology and came to appreciate its possibilities.

I appreciated the varied and interesting work in laboratories emerging from World War II disruption and was able to put investigators with similar interests in touch with each other. It was particularly pleasing in subsequent years to promote the development of many persons by nominating them for visiting appointments or other support. But I failed notably to appreciate some of the important Continental research. In Copenhagen I must have been the first American to learn of the Rasch model now prominent in psychometrics; I dismissed it because its assumption of homogeneous test items ran counter to my experience and preferences.[1] Visiting Geneva, I perceived no large difference between the recent work of Piaget's group and his books of the 1920's that Americans had found unpersuasive; yet in the 1960's that work on numerical and spatial concepts, translated, inspired American educators and entered significantly into my own thinking and writing. (In my defense: it was genetic epistemology that preoccupied Piaget at the time I visited, and these ideas have remained abstruse.)

Especially satisfying—for what I gave and for what I got—was advising the National Institute of Mental Health (NIMH) on research grants, first as member of the Mental Health Study Section, then (after my return from London) as chair of a new Behavioral Sciences Study Section. Every hour brought its own brisk seminar on a hot research topic; proposals ranged over a dozen disciplines and over medical, educational, family, and community applications. Typically, at least two members were experts on any grant request put before us, and they found aspects to disagree about; they had to educate the rest of us to the point where we could vote intelligently. How much I could learn will be obvious if I refer only to comparative and physiological psychology. Harry Harlow and Don Lindsley represented that field at one time, John Lacey and Eliot Stellar at another. Equally instructive were the visits to applicants and grantees that the Institute encouraged. Fairly typical was a trip to Kansas, where I looked into William Young's study of hormones and animal behavior, the field station Roger and Louise Barker set up to study community influences on child development, and various projects at the Menninger Clinic. Not so typical: a visit to the ethologist Margaret Altmann, who, at sunrise on a lake beside the Tetons, acted out for me the courtship ritual of the male elk.

Educational reform came to a boil after Sputnik, the reformers being professors of science and mathematics who wanted to remain independent of professors of education. Some of them, however, hoped that *psychologists* would help them get the results they intended. Jerry Bruner's Woods Hole Conference was important as a symbolic meeting of psychologists with chemists, mathematicians, and the like who headed curriculum projects. Some of the funds having come from the U.S. Office of Education, educationists were included; but most of them were shoved to the periphery while the central group hammered out the subsequently influential thesis that structural understanding is a chief aim of instruction (Bruner, 1961). Bärbel Inhelder and I were allies of Bruner; significantly, the report lists us as representing psychology, though we both held appointments in education faculties.

The Social Science Research Council undertook to stimulate research relevant to educators' concerns, and communication of scholars' insights to educational reformers. I chaired their Committee on Learning and the Educational Process from 1961 to 1966; the other members were Richard C. Atkinson, Eleanor Gibson, Evan Kieslar, and Judson Shaplin. Our most significant undertaking was summer postdoctoral institutes. The one at Stanford in 1964 was offered to Americans, but a substantial fraction of the second group (1965) was recruited abroad. The young foreign scholars were so impressive that we next organized a conference in Stockholm, followed by similar meetings at Nancy, Munich, and Bangkok. The UNESCO Institute for Education (Hamburg) replaced SSRC as administrative sponsor, and I served for a time on its board. Typically, about five instructors were selected, lively current topics listed, and about 35 applicants selected (who came more or less equally from educational projects and basic psychological research). My role was largest as instructor (Stanford 1965 and Bangkok); I was also codirector of three conferences. The conferences were particularly valuable for reinforcing the research ideal in education and building a network of young leaders. Some members later joined into teams, some redirected their research careers. Marcia Guttentag is a striking example; discussions of evaluation ignited her enthusiasm, and she went on to prominence and leadership, founding the Evaluation Research Society ten years later.

Methodology for Studies of Persons and Groups

My scholarly work must be discussed topically rather than chronologically, as I pursued interests simultaneously and discontinuously. Methodological and substantive lines entwine, because studies changed character as they developed, usually in a methodological direction. From the time I encountered Thurstone and Chave, I was intensely interested in the logic of questioning people and capturing their characteristics in numerical form. As soon as I had data to inspect, I kept finding that methods of measuring and summarizing introduced artifacts—relationships that had nothing to do with the persons measured and everything to do with choices the inquirer had made. Furthermore, these choices often buried important relationships. I became insistent that analytic methods should be matched to substantive ideas, not chosen on criteria of convenience, familiarity, or statistical stylishness.

Personality and Social Psychology

My substantive studies of personality and related social psychology were limited, but I had much to say about method in those fields. For a study connecting Rorschach response styles of doctoral students with their research styles, my assistant was George DeVos. DeVos provided qualitative descriptions of students' problem-solving approaches that I wished to validate objectively. My method (Cronbach, 1947) gained notoriety when assigned as a topic for successive American Board examinations to certify clinical psychologists. Unfortunately, the rigorous method demanded more than the clinical work-ups could deliver. (Henry and Farley [1959], applying the method to Thematic Apperception Test interpretations, appraised them as having validity "better than chance.") My constructive self still avows that DeVos's portrayals contained much truth, though the style congenial to the person was not mirrored directly in behavior. And my anal-retentive self avows that descriptive interpretations (including those made nowadays by computers) should be checked by methods like mine.

When I moved to Illinois, my intention was to probe further into styles of learning, problem solving, and problem definition—a theme of the studies of Rorschach, response bias, and eye movements. This work did not progress, partly because I was looking on styles as traits or habits, and had no handle on the situational determiners of response.

Many psychologists were attempting to improve Rorschach interpretation and to gain respect for it by statistical research. My first paper from Illinois was a research review highlighting errors that arose when conventional statistics were applied to this unconventional test, and suggesting more appropriate procedures (Cronbach, 1949b). When my suggestions were adopted, consistent positive findings did not ensue; my sympathetic formulation of the validity questions that had to be faced probably greased the skids for the decline of projective testing.

Like many others, I was impressed by the phenomenalist retort to behaviorism: perceptions of persons and situations, not stimuli as such, regulate behavior. William Stephenson's "Q" correlation, which summarized the similarity of two multivariate profiles, seemed to be an appropriate way to compare a clinician's impression of a client's self-concept with the client's own statement, or a teacher's perception of class attitudes with the statements of class members. Fred Fiedler, who had been studying clinicians in much this way, joined me in a study of leaders that ONR supported. Before long, the Air Force, interested in bomber crews, had added to our funds and our tasks. By agreement, Fiedler pursued substantive fieldwork while I took a close look at possible analyses. When the initial methodological inquiry was finished, I turned the project over to Fiedler, for whom it began a lifelong inquiry into leadership styles.

These studies were not as remote from education as they might seem. The work spun off striking hypotheses about the importance of teachers' expectations regarding their students in general—"stereotypes" and "implicit personality theories"—and demonstrated that "adapting to individual differences" (a much-recommended policy) can easily become counterproductive because of error in sizing up individuals. It is strange that such substantive propositions could be generated by reasoning that was primarily mathematical, but I have had that happy experience several times.

Goldine Gleser and I found that Q discarded important information that a Euclidean distance measure retained. Experience with that method led to a subtler proposal resembling analysis of variance, which separates four or more components worthy of interpretation. Trials of this in students' dissertations showed that all indices of similarity lose sight of the nature and direction of dissimilarities. The data, I came to think, ought almost always to be interpreted dimension by dimension, and not aggregated across factors (Cronbach, 1958).[1] Perhaps we should have seen that early on; but premature enthusiasms, false leads, and partial solutions are the usual route toward my best interpretation.

Generalizability and Validity of Measurements

The theory of measurement error as laid down by Spearman and by Brown early in the century remained the core of psychometrics for a long time. The first intimations of an upheaval came when Kuder and Richardson (1937) derived formulas that estimated reliability coefficients from item statistics. Kuder and Richardson were at Chicago when I enrolled, and one of my tasks was to apply their formulas to tests of the Eight-Year Study. Many results were puzzling—an occasional negative reliability coefficient, for example—and other investigators quickly began to show that no test was likely to fit certain assumptions Kuder and Richardson had implicitly, unwittingly made. Still, the questionably grounded Formula 20 seemed to work pretty well, and in time it was derived from plausible assumptions. One of the earliest steps, taken by a Chicago colleague Cyril Hoyt, was derivation of an equivalent formula from Fisher's newly prominent analysis of variance.

I did small studies on aspects of reliability theory I was curious about and wrote papers to clarify basic concepts. Mathematically trained persons take pains to tie conclusions tightly to assumptions, but in test theory and data analysis choosing the assumptions is equally critical. A coding that omits something important or introduces a limiting assumption may give a poor answer to the real-world question with which mathematical help is wanted. Criticizing test theory thus becomes a matter of comparing what the mathematician assumes with what the psychologist can reasonably believe about people's responses. I treated reliability this way in a 1951 paper centered on Hoyt's version of the KR20 Formula (relabeled "Coefficient Alpha").[1]

With respect to validation, I worked on specific procedures and on a conception of the process in the large. I never succeeded, however, in integrating two lines of development: a utilitarian, short-term analysis of personnel decisions and an intellectualization, rooted in philosophy of science, that looks through the eyes of eternity (Cronbach, 1987).

I was consulting at the Naval Electronics Laboratory regarding sonar training in 1949 when J. C. R. Licklider came by to lecture to their psychoacousticians on Claude Shannon's information theory. As I listened my mind popped with analogies: a test is a system for encoding information; true score and error have the properties of signal and noise; a multiscore profile or a diagnostic workup is a message with low redundancy (great bandwidth) whereas a narrow, homogeneous test maximizes redundancy. Shannon demonstrated a trade-off: redundant messages are transmitted with great fidelity, at the price of less information delivered. Traditional psychometrics, seeking fidelity for each single score, overlooked this. I had a dazzling vision of a psychometric theory, unified round Shannon's mathematics and applicable to single scores, profiles, and the notably wideband clinical descriptions.

For thinking about tests the information *metaphor* proved more useful than Shannon's mathematical model, and Gleser and I were led to a utility model as a replacement.[1] This theory (Cronbach and Gleser, 1957), which builds on earlier conclusions of our consultant Hubert Brogden, has a continuing influence in personnel psychology. The theory did produce ideas about multiscore tests, but these went unused. Personnel psychologists liked the idea of translating selection data into utility terms ("the dollar criterion") but found that hard to accomplish; procedures for that purpose are still being advanced and disputed. It is not surprising, then, that more complex ideas about military classification, guidance, and clinical assessment remain in limbo. There were ramifications outside the personnel field to which I shall return.

At this time the Committee on Test Standards was formulating guidelines on validation. The traditional approach of linking the test to a criterion measure—for example, linking an employment test to a later rating of job performance—presented no major issue. Distinct from criterion validity was the "content validity" of (for example) an American history test; this was equally easy for the committee to discuss. What was difficult was explaining how to validate measures of motivational and cognitive variables, and indicators of categories of mental illness. Aware of defense mechanisms and response biases, we could not accept content analysis as validating a questionnaire or observation procedure that purported to measure, say, latent hostility. Nor can one point to any kind of behavioral observation or clinical judgment sufficiently valid to be accepted as "criterion" for such a variable. Paul Meehl, working with colleagues in philosophy of science at Minnesota and using fellow committee members as a sounding board, made the case that the required validation process is an integration of reasoning and direct observation like that by which (said the philosophers) physical scientists can justify a theoretical interpretation of an observed variable. "Construct validation" has remained central to the Test Standards and may have influenced psychologists' research strategy more generally. My personal contribution was minor, but as committee chair I collaborated on the paper that fully set forth the idea; a coin toss that Meehl insisted on put my name first (Cronbach and Meehl, 1955).

By 1956 I had come to think that my empirical studies were far from memorable and that I was serving primarily as a teacher of my professional peers. My textbooks were shaping their fields, and my most cited papers were helping specialists broaden themselves—helping clinicians to do quantitative research, for example. Perhaps this perception was not immodest, but the undertaking it inspired surely was. With Gleser's help, I would produce a handbook on measurement. The handbook would tell persons attacking problems in social science, education, and psychology how to get help from mathematical systems for transforming the flow of behavior and events into quantitative conclusions. Also, it would suggest how to construct mathematical systems suited to that use. In time, some of the chapters required by the plan did get written and were used in seminars.

At the very outset, however, we found that even the overfamiliar terrain of reliability was not well enough understood to be the base for explicating how to think. We scaled our ambition back to clarifying that one topic. A tortuous path carried us to the theory of generalizability (Cronbach, Gleser, Rajaratnam, and Nanda, 1972).[1] The theory is a highly flexible system of analysis that, unlike classical theory, distinguishes types of error of observation. It rests on the postwar development of the "random model" variant of Fisherian analysis of variance; our investigation began just when this powerful tool became ripe for use. By 1961 we had worked out the mathematical structure for the univariate case; our main activity in the following ten years was learning to handle the complications in each fresh body of data. Many workers are extending generalizability theory today, among them our former associate Jean Cardinet.

The Interaction Paradigm

Mental testers from Binet onward had been mostly interested in identifying what level of education (removal from school? a slow section? acceleration?) was suitable for each pupil. Looking at the value of tests for decision making, Gleser and I came to see these "placement" decisions as distinctive, and as missing from psychometric theory. By specifying placement formally, we showed that choosing option A rather than B for pupils with high scores is valid only if high scorers have, on average, their best outcomes in A. The reverse has to be true for low scorers, to justify assigning them to B. In statistical terms, the regression lines have to cross; there must be an interaction of aptitude and treatment, an "ATI." The same principle applies to choice among clinical treatments.

At the time our book (Cronbach and Gleser, 1957) went to press, I had an APA Presidential address to prepare. The personnel-decision theory provided a fresh angle on the divisions within the profession, a theme recurrent in addresses of my predecessors. Our theorem on placement implies that much test use of clinicians, counselors, and educators can be validated empirically only by calculating regressions within treatments. An experimental contrast is required; the pertinent question cannot be answered by the traditional analysis correlating test with criterion within one group. Nor is it enough to compare outcome means across treatments, as experimenters traditionally have done. In the presence of interaction, the comparison of means neglects regression information having scientific and practical interest. Psychology, then, will be richer if experimental and correlational psychology are wedded; that union will beget knowledge of individual differences in response to treatments (Cronbach, 1957).

For a decade I was occupied with other matters. Then Snow, whose work included an exceptional demonstration of ATI (Snow, Tiffin, and Seibert, 1965), joined a research center at Stanford, and we obtained funds to pursue the theme. Information on ATI lay buried within numerous reports. Often, investigators had reported data that allowed comparison of regressions but had not made the comparison. By compiling the information, particularly from instructional research, Snow and I hoped to frame tentative generalizations and make a start toward a theory. We allowed three years for the reviewing and for a few experiments of our own; ten years were required, because we had repeatedly to rethink the problem (Cronbach and Snow, 1977).

Searching for instructive published evidence was not a wholly successful strategy. Studies were scattered over many topics and lacked power, and many of them, including those we initiated, had not been based on adequate hypotheses about the intellectual processes used by learners. Reviewers were sympathetic to us, if not to our sources: "Cronbach and Snow ingeniously extract useful conclusions from . . . a large experimental literature that is *not* of uniformly high quality. . . . Hercules only had to clean the stables of King Augeas. Cronbach and Snow sifted through the accumulation" (Rothkopf, 1978).

We found plenty of interaction effects, but few coherent ones. Where several studies did bear on much the same question, findings were usually discordant. Almost no ATI effects were confirmed by multiple studies. We had expected to find, for example, that some types of instruction capitalize on verbal ability, some on spatial ability, and so on across the Thurstonian spectrum. The evidence was negative. A spatial pretest, for example, may or may not predict outcomes from instruction filled with diagrams. The most consistent interactions were those of general abilities. In particular, students with superior intellectual development seem to profit from instruction that places on them considerable responsibility for organizing and interpreting. Conversely, below-average students tend to profit most from tightly structured lessons.

Our hindsights seem important for instructional research. For one thing, studies of the usual size, if analyzed correctly, leave great statistical uncertainty. In studies of classrooms, it is numbers of classes and not numbers of students that generate statistical power.[1] We also found that educational psychologists typically assessed brief instructional treatments. Trials probably should be lengthy, however, because students encountering an unfamiliar style of lesson have to develop new strategies of study to make the most of it. Another of our topics was the decades-long debate about the relation of rate of learning to measured mental ability. We sided with Robert Thorndike (1966): the correlation can be changed from positive to negative simply by altering the scale on which learning is measured. We added that learning is multidimensional. Many developments proceed side by side, at different rates.

As in 1957, in 1974 I found myself with an APA address to prepare— this time in response to a pleasantly surprising award "for scientific contributions." I made it a sequel, carrying the theme of 1957 to a higher power (Cronbach, 1975a). A Baconian search for first-order interactions is no more sensible a strategy than the empirical searches limited to main effects that I had criticized. Human events reflect innumerable interactions among planned and unplanned features of situations, so subtler observation of the interplay between person characteristics and situational variables is needed. Where once I had called for teaming experimental and correlational methods to pin down more general and hence more lasting truths, I now proposed greater reliance on rich descriptions, recognizing that a social-science "conclusion" is only a record of an event at a moment in history.

Measurement and Public Policy

Issues in Testing

In Tyler's view of educational testing, what matters most is the consequences it has in actions of students and teachers and in operations of the system. Tests determine how teachers and students direct their efforts. That was the starting point of Tyler's appraisal of progressive schools. Among other experiences, participating (with Tyler) in the Davis-Eells study of possible social-class bias in tests sensitized me to the role of ability tests in sorting youngsters. This concern for the effects of testing on the system and on youngsters' life chances was expressed mostly in my textbooks, until the late 1960's.

I participated then in planning the National Assessment of Educational Progress and served for some years on the committee providing technical direction. It was a delight to work with the incomparable John Tukey, and the activity produced stimulating questions for my classes. I doubt that I made any special contribution save when, in an early session, I drew attention to the technical device of matrix sampling, devised for quite another purpose. That sampling design would present different questions to different students, allowing many more topics to be surveyed. With so many questions in play, no one can coach for the test, and the research is unlikely to distort day-to-day instructional decisions of the teachers surveyed.

During the civil rights struggle, controversy over test bias rose to a fury that contrasted utterly with the apathetic response to Allison Davis's earlier challenge. I shall not repeat here my evaluation (1975b) of the disputes, beyond recalling that those resisting the new egalitarianism seemed unrealistically to separate questions that science would settle from questions open to political contention. I was drawn in to comment on Arthur Jensen's provocative article (1969), but avoided most invitations to play games of the mass media. Instead, I undertook a scholarly study of the interplay between tests and society. At the Center for Advanced Study in the Behavioral Sciences at Stanford in 1971–72 I read relevant history, philosophy, and sociology. My attempts to trace conflicting conceptions of "fairness" and their implications did not jell. I also read court cases on test use and thought of trying to serve as expert witness. My few discussions with lawyers came to nothing, probably because I was interested in keeping both sides of an argument in perspective and not in making a case for plaintiff or defendant.

A California program mandated an annual achievement test for pupils in selected grades, with the hope that making each school's average scores public would goad educators to try harder. A legislator wishing to make more of that program enlisted me as chair of a committee of measurement specialists drawn from school districts and universities. A number of our proposals were written into law, but proposals to lower the key of the program were coolly received.

All this was excellent preparation for joining the Committee on Ability Testing of the National Research Council. The committee included economists, legal scholars, other social scientists, and experimental psychologists, plus a few testing specialists. Strenuous contention coalesced finally in a comprehensive statement on what tests can contribute and on the consequences of certain misuses (Wigdor and Garner, 1982). I consider the report wise, but, rendered bloodless for the sake of unanimity, it made no best-seller list.

Program Evaluation

From Florence Nightingale on, social reformers have looked to scientific inquiry for help. Not all well-intended innovations are effective, hence both conservatives and progressives call for evaluation. Public interest in evaluation fluctuates, but from 1960 to 1980 it was a major activity of psychologists. Clarifying the function of program evaluation and the choices to be made in evaluation planning became my last major undertaking. Perhaps it was destined; recall that my career started with a critique of an evaluation as a college junior. The coincidence of Tyler's arrival at Chicago and mine was certainly fateful.

Tyler adopted the term "evaluation" to challenge the common practice, after 1920, of judging school systems on the basis of standard tests of knowledge and skill. Teachers should be planning their instruction to fit their pupils and community, not matching it to content chosen by remote authorities. Followers of Dewey were concerned with students' independent thinking and sense of purpose, as well as with knowledge and skills. Tyler and his associates used their novel tests of student development primarily to stimulate teachers to reconsider their teaching, and most of Tyler's apprentices made careers in direct work with teachers. I took a different route, partly because working clinically with one set of teachers after another seemed repetitious, hence unappealing.

The sonar project was productive, but the training program was quickly rendered obsolete by changes in sonar technology. This heightened my awareness that evaluators write on sand. A bit later, my students and I asked pupils to recall what they had taken away from particular instructional films. We found strong indications that the films were ineffective and should be redesigned, and for a time I considered pointing my career in that direction; but other interests won out. The tests of teachers' perceptions and attitudes devised in 1947 for Carolyn Tryon's project were my last dip into evaluation for many years, save for reviewing some evaluation plans submitted to NIMH.

As the post-Sputnik curriculum projects reached the tryout stage, the

National Science Foundation, as sponsor, began to press for evidence on their effectiveness. The staff asked a professional from the testing industry to describe to project directors what evaluation should be and, knowing me from Woods Hole, invited me as discussant. Their speaker covered the accepted wisdom: detachment on the evaluator's part, objective measurement, test content matched to the curriculum, conformity to statistical standards . . . The prescription fitted an evaluator serving as scorekeeper, tallying up after the teams had finished and left for home. But I spoke up for the more constructive assignment of providing feedback on students' accomplishments and difficulties week by week, not delaying inquiry until the final examination; most of the conventional prescription was wrong for that kind of evaluation. I was, obviously, extending Tyler's view beyond the local teacher, using evaluation to reshape a course of study that would be widely distributed. (The published version of my remarks [1964] had some influence on evaluation practice, and became famous when philosopher Michael Scriven [1967] wrote a forceful, widely read rejoinder defending "summative" evaluation against my "formative" preference.) Continuing its pressure in 1963, NSF had Tom Hastings and me conduct a ten-day workshop for representatives of the projects. The meeting succeeded, perhaps chiefly because it enabled project representatives to exchange experiences.

Upon moving to Stanford, I developed an evaluation course in which each student planned an evaluation. Though the projects brought many realistic, painful dilemmas to the students' attention, I was not content with training limited to imagined fieldwork. Asked in 1972 to evaluate Stanford's nascent undergraduate program in Values, Technology, and Society, I was delighted by the training opportunity it offered. Over three years, a student team visited classes, interviewed professors, devised questionnaires for VTS students, and made formal and informal reports. Because the courses were offered outside departmental structures by faculty volunteers, and because the usual VTS student elected only one or two of the courses, almost no one save the evaluators had a comprehensive picture. The team's internal discussions centered less on the facts than on what report, with what slant or tone, would be most constructive. The political side of evaluation, much neglected in the previous scientistic literature, came alive.

Students from many specialties within the School of Education, including science education, curriculum theory, philosophy, statistics, and administration, had been attracted to the VTS project. Some also came from the Department of Communication. It was apparent that each specialty could be valuable in thinking through a particular evaluation. Learning incidentally that a dozen of my colleagues were engaged in evaluation projects, I organized a seminar for faculty and a few advanced students that went well enough to suggest launching a collaborative training program. Russell Sage Foundation supported us as a study group to think through issues and pursue field work likely to illuminate them. This gave a social and financial base for the training. Among the colleagues who shouldered the burden, I mention particularly Stephen Weiner, trained in administration and policy, who became codirector.

We had a great time capitalizing on our mix of specialties, chiefly in small teams. We dealt with plans, or data collection, or analyses related to control of violence in schools, a test for plastic surgeons, a national comparison of reading methods, a statewide testing program, a postdoctoral institute for marine biologists, and continuing education for lawyers. With sustained argument in a multidisciplinary group, we could integrate and deepen ideas that many others were beginning to offer, producing a theory of evaluation as a function in a political system. Scientific technique and dispassionate reporting are not sufficient to steer the polity to more judicious accommodations (Ambron, Cronbach, et al., 1980). As editor of the volume I assigned myself to a sabbatical year of reading at the London School of Economics and in the British Museum, to expand our draft with material from older political and social thought.

I continued to argue for formative evaluation, notably by formalizing my lectures with a syllabus. A classic chapter on research in education by Donald Campbell and Julian Stanley (1963) had emphasized the conclusiveness of experiments with equivalent groups. Students reading that had come away with little or no sympathy for naturalistic, qualitative studies or for less strongly structured quantitative studies. I admired many ideas in the chapter, but argued that every design feature trades off one good against another. The lectures might not have become a book if Campbell had not produced a new chapter, now with Thomas Cook as collaborator; again admirable, but inspired by visions of a slowly evolving basic science. There is good feeling between Cook and Campbell and me, and we agree on many aspects of methodology; but their chapter and their later book (Cook and Campbell, 1979) seem insensitive to the dilemmas of time-bound policy studies. My writing task became exciting with these strong colleagues to push against.

I am pleased with *Designing Evaluations of Educational and Social Programs* (1982) as a guide to practical social inquiry. Only in the rarest of circumstances can such research end with a technological fix. Continued monitoring has to check on local modifications or departures from plan, and to warn when altered conditions make it wise to change the plan. Determination of what works best on the average ought to be supplemented with whatever can be learned about situational factors that moderate effects. Since time and money are limited, precision of measurement and of within-treatment means can only be purchased by reducing diversity of variables, settings, and treatment realizations. Narrative reports on the local history of an intervention may not be "scientific," but they can be essential for reading truth into the bottom line of the statistical report.

If interactions regulate most of human thought, feeling, and action, any regularities not closely linked to physiology are likely to be conditional on the immediate situation and on the participants' histories. I am therefore ambivalent about psychologists' quest for lawlike propositions. Of course I favor "scientific method" in psychology. Any precaution that makes observation and inference more reproducible is valuable, provided that—here glimpse the cloven hoof!—the controls do not so restrict the events observed or the facts recorded as to denature the subject matter (Cronbach, 1986). Psychological findings are contextual, and investigators should note as much of context and process as they can. The best experimental scientists, including psychologists, have always done that; but textbook advice on doing research stresses blind testing of propositions, preferably under sterile conditions, rather than open-eyed learning from whatever happens or can be caused to happen. Though propositional knowledge is elusive and evanescent, I am optimistic about the power of systematic inquiry to generate ever-better questions with which to analyze human development and social arrangements.

Selected Publications by Lee J. Cronbach

(1941). Individual differences in learning to reproduce forms: A study in attention. *American Journal of Psychology*, *54*, 197–222.

(1943a). Exploring the wartime morale of high school youth. *Applied Psychology Monographs*, No. 1.

(1943b). What the word 'function' means to algebra teachers. *Mathematics Teacher*, *36*, 212–218.

(1946). Response sets and test validity. *Educational and Psychological Measurement, 6,* 475–494.

(1947). A validation design for qualitative studies of personality. *Journal of Consulting Psychology, 12,* 365–374.

(1949a). *Essentials of psychological testing.* New York: Harper & Row. (2nd ed., 1960; 3rd ed., 1970; 4th ed., 1984)

(1949b). Statistical methods applied to Rorschach scores: A review. *Psychological Bulletin, 46,* 393–429.

(1951). Coefficient Alpha and the internal structure of tests. *Psychometrika, 16,* 297–334.

(1954). *Educational psychology.* New York: Harcourt Brace & World. (2nd ed., 1963; 3rd ed., 1977)

(with P. E. Meehl) (1955). Construct validity in psychological tests. *Psychological Bulletin, 52,* 281–303.

(1957). The two disciplines of scientific psychology. *American Psychologist, 12,* 671–684.

(with G. C. Gleser) (1957). *Psychological tests and personnel decisions.* Urbana, IL: University of Illinois Press. (2nd ed., 1965)

(1958). Proposals leading to analytic treatment of social perception scores. In R. Tagiuri and L. Petrullo (Eds.), *Person perception and interpersonal behavior* (pp. 353–379). Stanford, CA: Stanford University Press.

(1964). Evaluation for course improvement. In R. W. Heath (Ed.), *New curricula* (pp. 231–248). New York: Harper & Row.

(1975a). Beyond the two disciplines of scientific psychology. *American Psychologist, 30,* 116–127.

(1975b). Five decades of public controversy over mental testing. *American Psychologist, 30,* 1–14.

(with G. C. Gleser, H. Nanda, & N. Rajaratnam) (1972). *The dependability of behavioral measurements: Theory of generalizability for scores and profiles.* New York: Wiley.

(with R. E. Snow) (1977). *Aptitudes and instructional methods: A handbook for research on aptitude-treatment interactions.* New York: Irvington.

(with S. R. Ambron, S. M. Dornbusch, R. D. Hess, R. C. Hornik, D. C. Phillips, D. F. Walker, & S. S. Weiner) (1980). *Toward reform of program evaluation.* San Francisco: Jossey-Bass.

(with the assistance of Karen Shapiro) (1982). *Designing evaluations of educational and social programs.* San Francisco: Jossey-Bass.

(1986). Social inquiry for Earthlings. In D. W. Fiske & R. Shweder (Eds.), *Metatheory of social science* (pp. 83–107). Chicago: University of Chicago Press.

(1987). Five perspectives on validity argument. In H. Wainer & H. I. Braun (Eds.), *Test validity* (pp. 3–18). Hillsdale, NJ: Erlbaum.

Other Publications Cited

American Educational Research Association, American Psychological Association, and National Council for Measurement in Education. (1985). *Standards for educational and psychological testing*. Washington, DC: American Psychological Association.

Brown, W. (1910). Some experimental results in the correlation of mental abilities. *British Journal of Psychology, 3*, 296–322.

Bruner, J. S. (1961). *The process of education*. Cambridge, MA: Harvard University Press.

Campbell, D. T., & Stanley, J. C. (1963). Experimental and quasi-experimental designs for research on teaching. In N. L. Gage (Ed.), *Handbook of research on teaching* (pp. 171 246). Chicago: Rand-McNally.

Cook, T. D., & Campbell, D. T. (1979). *Quasi-experimentation: Design and analysis issues for field settings*. Chicago: Rand-McNally.

Eells, K., Davis, A., Havighurst, R. J., Herrick, V. E., & Tyler, R. (1951). *Intelligence and cultural differences*. Chicago: University of Chicago Press.

Henry, W. E., & Farley, J. (1959). The validity of the Thematic Apperception Test in the study of adolescent personality. *Psychological Monographs, 73*, No. 17.

Jensen, A. R. (1969). How much can we boost IQ and scholastic achievement? *Harvard Educational Review, 39*, 1–23.

Judd, C. H., & Cowling, D. J. (1907). Studies in perceptual development. *Psychological Monographs, 8*, No. 34, 349–369.

Kelley, E. L., & Fiske, D. W. (1951). *The prediction of performance in clinical psychology*. Ann Arbor: University of Michigan Press.

Kuder, G. F., & Richardson, M. W. (1937). The theory of the estimation of test reliability. *Psychometrika, 2*, 151–160.

Loevinger, J., DuBois, P. H., & Gleser, G. C. (1953). Maximizing the discriminating power of a test. *Psychometrika, 18*, 309–317.

Rothkopf, E. Z. (1978). The sound of one hand plowing. *Contemporary Psychology, 23*, 707–708.

Scriven, M. (1967). The methodology of evaluation. In R. Stake et al. (Eds.), *Perspectives on curriculum evaluation* (pp. 39–83). Chicago: Rand-McNally.

Smith, E. R., & Tyler, R. W. (1943). *Appraising and recording student progress*. New York: Harper.

Snow, R. E., Tiffin, J., & Seibert, W. F. (1965). Individual differences and instructional film effects. *Journal of Educational Psychology, 56*, 315–326.

Snow, R. E., & Wiley, D. E. (Eds.). (in press). *Straight thinking: A volume in honor of Lee J. Cronbach*. Hillsdale, NJ: Erlbaum.

Spearman, C. (1910). Correlation calculated with faulty data. *British Journal of Psychology, 3*, 271–295.

Thorndike, R. L. (1966). Intellectual status and intellectual growth. *Journal of Educational Psychology, 51*, 121–127.

Thurstone, L. L., & Chave, E. J. (1929). *The measurement of attitude*. Chicago: University of Chicago Press.

Wigdor, A. K., & Garner, W. R. (1982). *Ability testing: Uses, consequences, and controversies*. Washington, DC: National Academy Press.

William K. Estes

Why did I become a scientist, rather than an accountant, an engineer, or a news editor, and why a psychologist, rather than a physicist, biologist, or astronomer? I think the answers lie in a combination of broad social forces and local accidents.

I was born in Minneapolis, Minnesota, on June 17, 1919, shortly after my father, George Downs Estes, was mustered out of military service. His early ambition to become a physician had been unrealized because he could not afford the necessary lengthy education, so he had settled for dentistry. Both he and my mother, Mona Kaye Estes, had their hearts set on my becoming a physician in his place, an ambition that influenced my education even though it ultimately went unfulfilled. Two younger sisters, Mary and Alice, of whom I have always been very fond, completed our family. My very early childhood was uneventful, and I remember it as happy enough until the financial crash and the beginning of the Great Depression in 1929. The effects of the Depression on our family life were crippling as we plummeted from affluence to near poverty. We managed to keep our home, but were constantly in debt, and conflict steadily mounted between the family's ambitions, in particular for my projected medical education, and lack of the means to finance them.

A major factor in my own life was the widespread unemployment that persisted nationwide from my mid-childhood into my college years. I needed to work, but steady work could rarely be found. I went through the gamut of peddling magazines door-to-door, delivering newspapers, and shoveling the always adequate supplies of snow during long Minnesota winters. I liked school well enough, more so as I grew older, and whiled away the long summers doing neighborhood odd jobs and walking or bicycling several miles each way to the Minneapolis Public Library, where I omnivorously devoured literature, history, and science, the distribution shifting steadily toward science as I went through my teens.

Getting high grades in school was an unpopular thing for boys to do in my neighborhood, and I succeeded fairly well at avoiding them through grade school, but by the time I entered high school and encountered truly fascinating subjects such as foreign languages and solid geometry I was no longer able to keep my grade average down to the socially desirable minimum. On graduation from high school I was awarded a choice of several scholarships for continuing education. One, a prize scholarship to the University of Chicago, I yearned to accept, but there seemed no possibility of financing the costs not covered by the scholarship. Thus I settled for the University of Minnesota, starting in the fall of 1937, as a streetcar commuter. That was actually no great hardship, for the university proved to have an excellent faculty, and its students were drawn heavily from an outstanding public school system, so I had no complaints about the level of intellectual stimulation.

The family finances did not recover much from the trough of the Depression, however, and unemployment persisted, so I found myself washing dishes nights in a cafe to cover the modest costs of university attendance (tuition $20 per quarter and commuting at 5¢ per trip). I started as a premedical student, which entailed a good sampling of science courses, but because it was apparent that financing medical school would be impractical, my thoughts turned toward the possibility of a scientific career—though with little idea of how one got started or how a scientist earned a living.

Some answers came to hand by accident. During my second year at the university I had taken an introductory psychology laboratory course and on arriving home after the final examination discovered I had left my glasses in the classroom. The next day I made my way to the office of the instructor, a genial young faculty member named Kenneth Baker, and was quickly reunited with my glasses; but also the instructor asked me to sit down and chat a while. It seems that even my characteristic reserve in class had not kept the quality of my lab work from making its way to his attention. He wondered whether I had thought about going on ultimately to graduate school and opened my eyes to the remarkable possibility that one could be paid for going to graduate school by merely contributing occasional pleasant work as a teaching assistant. The idea had enormous appeal. I was only a sophomore, but some calculations suggested that if I took the maximum possible loads I might finish undergraduate work in another year, perhaps even expanding a bit of research on which I had gotten started for a summa thesis. All went as calculated, and I received my B.A. from Minnesota, summa and all, in June 1940.

In the course of reading the works of the eminent psychologists of the 1930's, I had developed an interest in going to Berkeley for my graduate work where I might be able to work with the great neo-behaviorist Edward C. Tolman. However, I was maneuvered out of that scheme in a manner somewhat reminiscent of the way professional athletes are "traded." The department chairman, Richard M. Elliott, who was also my undergraduate adviser, was trying hard to keep a highly visible young faculty member, B. F. Skinner, at Minnesota, in spite of a shortage of graduate students with research drives that might be commensurate with Skinner's pace. Thus Professor Elliott (loftily waving away my recollections of his earlier advice to beware of concentrating in a single school) would not hear of recommending me to Berkeley, and I stayed at Minnesota for another three years, receiving my Ph.D. in 1943 just in time to have it packed away before being called into military service.

The proximal causes of my choosing psychology among the sciences seem fairly clear, but to explain my imprinting on science in general I think we have to look back to my earlier childhood. One of the consequences of the Depression was that, although my father had quite scholarly inclinations, there were few books in our home, and I found little at hand to go on to after a fifth reading of *The Three Musketeers*. Much of our single bookcase was taken up by one of my father's prized possessions, a full set of *The Decline and Fall of the Roman Empire*, which, however, was too densely printed and lacking in graphics to have much appeal for a young boy. There was, though, a four-volume set of Thomson's *Outline of Science*, scarcely intended as child's fare but nonetheless lavishly illustrated with spectacular plates of spiral galaxies, the sun's corona, and the like. Starting with the pictures and then working my way into the text, I was captivated with the achievements of the great classical scientists and had begun to set my sights on astronomy at an age when most of my classmates were thinking in terms of becoming fire chiefs or fighter pilots.

Before high school age I was trying a companion volume in the same small scientific collection, Eddington's *Nature of the Physical World*. The opening passages of that volume, explaining that the solid objects around us and the ground beneath our feet are largely empty space, struck me as fantasy. However, when I brought my incredulity to my father, he soon convinced me that I was selling Sir Arthur short, and there followed lengthy discussions of Bohr's model of the atom, the nature of transmission of electricity via the motion of electrons through conductors, and the thinking underlying the interpretation of the red shift in the spectra of the galaxies as an indication of an expanding universe.

On one point, though, Father was firm—the idea of becoming an astronomer or any kind of "pure" scientist was wholly impractical. Science could make a fine hobby, but I should keep my sights on a solid (and paying) profession like medicine. However, a potentially unpleasant conflict between my steadily growing interests in science and family pressure toward a profession was ultimately resolved mainly by economic forces beyond our control.

Beyond having much to do with my choice of life work, the Depression and the attendant shortage of employment had a profound effect on my personal life style. In particular, I developed a morbid fear of unemployment, extending from concern over not getting a job to anxiety over the prospect of even a half day without something specific to do. The problem was solved fairly well as long as I could stay in school—I simply went to school all year through college and graduate years—and on my entering the Army, the problem disappeared for a while since there were no threats of vacations during wartime. However, because of the Army's discharge policies, I spent nearly a year and a half overseas after the war ended, and empty days became an acute problem, mitigated only by boxes of mathematics texts shipped to me by my wife. For over a year I must have averaged more than half of each day working through problems in calculus, differential equations, number theory, and probability. Aside from the advantages for my mental health, those exercises went a good way toward making up for the scanty mathematics education I had unwisely settled for in college and left me well prepared to continue rounding out my background via auditing of graduate courses in mathematics during my early faculty years at Indiana. When asked just what I could not have done in research without this preparation in mathematics, I find it hard to give specific answers. Nonetheless, I am convinced that the effort was a worthwhile investment, for one can scarcely have too broad or deep a background for the continuing learning-to-learn that is the essence of practicing and teaching science.

Academic Itinerary

An account of my scientific and professional career may be easier to follow if I start with an overall map of the institutional settings in which I worked during succeeding periods. I served on the faculty of Indiana University from 1946 to 1962, Stanford University from 1962 to 1968, The Rockefeller University from 1968 to 1979, and Harvard University from 1979 to the present.

In view of my unemployment phobia, it is well that I have never had to seek an academic position. My first job literally sought me out, and thereafter continuity proved not to be a problem. The abrupt end of World War II in August 1945 found me on duty as a medical administrative officer in an Army hospital in the Philippines, and, along with many others, I soon had my hopes of a speedy return home chilled by the news that disassembling a vast military operation was not going to happen overnight and many officers might expect two to three years of additional duty. I continued through that fall and winter on miscellaneous assignments that did not draw heavily on my academic background (among them a stint as commandant of a prisoner-of-war camp).

In the summer of 1946, however, two events occurred that brightened my prospects. First, I learned that the flood of veterans entitled to government-funded college educations was generating an unprecedented demand for new university faculty. As a consequence, the armed services were prepared to give immediate release to officers who could show that they had teaching positions waiting for them in American colleges or universities. It didn't seem that I was in very good position to enter the competition for teaching positions at such long distance, but the problem was solved when a position found me. A letter from B. F. Skinner, who had assumed the chairmanship of the Department of Psychology at Indiana University, offered me an appointment as instructor in psychology if I could report for duty in time to begin teaching that fall. I hastened to accept, and though the official wheels did not grind fast enough to deliver me to the campus by the beginning of the fall term, I did make it by Thanksgiving, and found myself almost immediately taking over some introductory experimental psychology classes from overburdened fellow instructors who had been keeping the overflow of students occupied somehow until more help could arrive.

Conditions were not the easiest for either me or the students, since the department had no stock of laboratory apparatus, and publishers, foundering under an unprecedented volume of orders, were far behind in supplying textbooks. To the distress of the students, I kept them busy with elementary statistics while I drew on what I could recall from fortunately varied experiences in the experimental psychology laboratories at Minnesota to begin to produce some lectures and laboratory projects that actually included a little psychology. By the time spring term arrived with a new batch of students, the courses were pretty well under control, and I could begin diverting some energy into starting on research of my own that I had been dreaming about since leaving graduate school more than three years before.

The small Hoosier community in which Indiana University was nestled did not seem terribly prepossessing when my wife and I first encountered it after a drive down from Chicago on a bleak November day. The town of Bloomington, remote from major transportation routes and surrounded by untillable rocky farmland, depended for its existence mainly on the neighboring limestone quarries and the university, whose expansion the townspeople nonetheless bitterly resented at every step. However, when the time came to move away some sixteen years later, we found that we were leaving the town as well as the campus with real regret. The university, in contrast to the town, was booming with vitality as it grew almost overnight from an encapsulated small campus of some 5,000 students into a truly major university with ten, then fifteen, then twenty thousand students and with departments and schools of international renown. The early postwar influx of students and faculty, ourselves included, were accommodated at first in hastily converted Army barracks with many of the classes held in quonset huts—the lecturers straining to be heard above the noise of the builders, who also were moving in en masse.

In the Psychology Department, as no doubt in much of the university, it was an exciting time. Skinner's growing reputation and prestige were effective in recruiting a flow of able graduate students and new young faculty, so he left a major imprint on the department, even though he was only physically present for a short time before leaving for Harvard. I found many congenial spirits among the other new faculty. With Jim Dinsmoor, I developed an advanced experimental psychology course that was taken by every graduate student in the department, experimental, clinical, or otherwise, for nearly fifteen years. With Don Lauer, I mounted a project for studying probability learning in the rat under truly distributed conditions of a single trial a day (infants born in either of our families at the beginning of an experiment would be walking by the end). With Cletus Burke and Arnold Binder and a group of graduate students (among others, Mike Cole, Morton Friedman, Dick Millward, Peter Polson), I developed a precursor of the now standard computer-controlled laboratory for studying human information processing. There was no computer in ours, of course, but we did have an IBM punch wired up to transmit information from cards punched with stimulus programs to display devices and accept return data on response frequencies and reaction times.

By the mid-1950's my own teaching and research activities, like those of the department and the university at large, had passed through their growing pains into a phase of relative stability, and, though in no way dissatisfied with life at Indiana, I was ready to consider something new when invitations began to come in from the outside. The most intriguing of those came in fairly rapid succession, beginning just before 1960, from Yale, Pennsylvania, and Stanford. After a period of some uncertainty, I settled on Stanford, and we moved there in the summer of 1962. Major factors in the decision were my plans with Patrick Suppes for expansion of Stanford's Institute for Mathematical Studies in the Behavioral Sciences and the prospects of collaborating with Suppes, Richard C. Atkinson, and Gordon Bower in establishing a graduate program in mathematical psychology. The latter must certainly be termed a success, its list of graduates including such now well-known names in the field as William Batchelder, Robert Bjork, Guy Groen, Steven Link, David Rumelhart, Richard Shiffrin, James Townsend, Kenneth Wexler, Jack Yellott, and Joseph Young.

Given that all went as well as expected at Stanford, why did I leave after six years? One consideration, perhaps relatively minor, was again concern over the possibility of unemployment, now in the sense of retirement. I was not yet close to Stanford's retirement age of 65, but I could see it looming ahead and also had to witness the rather unhappy sight of able professors becoming lame ducks in their early sixties. The Rockefeller University offered much more liberal retirement options and also was well known to provide time and financial support for individual research of professors on a scale beyond that of any other American university. The major factor, though, was the vision put forward by the president of Rockefeller, Detlev Bronk, of developing an ambitious new program in behavioral science, grounded in the biological science tradition of the university and preparing to make contributions in the long term to the solution of human problems in the university's urban setting.

Bronk had shown that he meant business by recruiting such luminaries as Carl Pfaffmann, Neal E. Miller, and George A. Miller, and the enthusiasm he and they had for the task envisioned captured my imagination to the extent that in the fall of 1968 we were moving eastward again and facing a quite different life-style in New York City. The prospects of a

massively expanding behavioral science program were curtailed by the retirement of President Bronk soon after I arrived and then a nationwide
economic recession. However, the environment for research and highly
individualized graduate teaching was as advertised, and my research and
research-related activities flourished during the next decade in a way that
I don't think would have been possible in a more traditional academic setting.

I had no expectation that I would ever leave Rockefeller, but in response
to an increasingly tight financial bind, the outlook of the university began
to change, so that by the late 1970's it was no longer the same in spirit as
the institution I had joined with such enthusiasm ten years earlier. The
administration decided that its financial problems could be solved by dis-
pensing with what it regarded as some of the more peripheral programs
(those furthest from molecular biology). The enforced departure of an illustrious group of philosophers and the threat of a similar fate for the experimental physicists gave rise, however, to a nationally publicized im-
broglio, so it became apparent that the campaign would have to be one of
attrition.

There were no more firings of professors at Rockefeller, but the word
filtered down that in a number of areas, among them behavioral science,
vacancies would no longer be filled, and the prospects of continuing dim-
inution of university support led to departures of my principal colleagues
in experimental-cognitive psychology, George Miller, Michael Cole, and
Douglas Medin. With these losses not to be replaced, it became apparent
that we could no longer continue a graduate program in my area, a prospect that I found hard to face. News of such developments moves fast in
academic circles, and I soon had the heart-warming experience of receiving assurances from a number of psychology departments across the
country that I would be welcome there if ready to leave Rockefeller. Harvard seemed to offer most with regard to prospects for continuing to develop my specialty, so it was there we moved in the fall of 1979 and there
that this chapter was finished as Harvard celebrated its 350th birthday in
1986.

Some Milestones in Research

Presumably, an invitation to contribute an autobiographical sketch to
this distinguished series is based on one's published research output, so I
can most naturally begin an account of my research career with a selection

of publications that might have provided my credentials. It is interesting to note that on scanning through the cumulative list, I find that the papers that have had the greatest visibility via citation counts and tangible influence on subsequent work, my own and others, are also, in most cases, the ones that I judge to be most creative in terms of new ideas.

1. My paper with Skinner (Estes and Skinner, 1941) introduced the technique of the "conditioned emotional response" (CER) that supplanted the Pavlovian paradigm, at least for many American investigators, as the method of choice for tracing quantitative properties of conditioning. Beyond the method developed, the study is notable in my mind as the first overt manifestation of my gradually accelerating efforts to bring together ideas of memory and conditioning (though Skinner would never have allowed the term "memory" to appear under his imprint!). Immediate follow-ups were my studies of punishment (Estes, 1944) and several investigations of anticipation of rewarding events, all aimed toward decomposing operant or instrumental conditioning into constituent processes and pointing, in the longer term, toward my theoretical and experimental analyses of reinforcement in human learning (beginning with Estes, 1969) and my more formal theoretical articles on memory and conditioning (beginning with Estes, 1973).

2. Perhaps my single most influential contribution was "Toward a Statistical Theory of Learning" (Estes, 1950), which marked my first overt step into formal theorizing. Beyond the influence of this paper in the field, the theoretical ideas developed therein led directly to my treatment of probability learning (Estes, 1954; Estes and Straughan, 1954), models for spontaneous recovery from extinction and spacing effects in learning (Estes, 1955a, 1955b), the interpretation of drive in terms of stimulus variables (Estes, 1958), and the unified treatment of component and pattern models for learning in a Markovian framework (Estes, 1959).

3. My "new mental chemistry" article (Estes, 1960) marked the beginning of a shift in outlook from that of stimulus-response learning theory to the conceptual framework of information processing. It introduced a new emphasis on the need for breaking with tradition in the analysis of human learning data and influenced not only my own subsequent work on human learning but that of a number of others who were responsible for a wave of researches and simple models involving all-or-none effects (for example, Bower, 1961; Restle, 1962; Trabasso and Bower, 1968).

4. The break with the traditional framework was completed with the appearance of my first research paper in the information processing tra-

dition, which introduced the detection method of distinguishing effects of perception and memory in tachistoscopic recognition (Estes and Taylor, 1964). In this paper and its immediate followups, there appeared my first theoretical employment of inferred internal cognitive operations and a body of theory leading to later substantial studies on letter and word recognition (Estes, 1975) and interactive perceptual channels in letter recognition (Estes, 1972b, 1982a).

5. The title of "An Associative Basis for Coding and Organization in Memory" (Estes, 1972a) points up both the continuity with earlier work on learning theory and the appearance of concepts that would have been unthinkable, or at least inexpressible, in the earlier tradition. One set of ideas had to do with a "perturbation model" for short-term memory, somewhat akin to then current conceptions of reverberatory circuits in neurophysiological models. The other principal component was a hierarchical associative network, including both excitatory and inhibitory associative linkages, for the interpretation of memory for order and chronology in long-term memory. The two components have had quite different continuations. The former led directly into a lengthy series of researches on short-term memory for order and position, and is currently being extended into a more general model for information loss during retention. The second component, much in tune with the ideas of the time, has been generally influential in shaping more specific models developed by myself and others for letter and word recognition and semantic memory, but still requires much more development, especially with regard to the interactions of excitatory and inhibitory associations.

6. "Learning Theory and Intelligence" (Estes, 1974) is the only one of my major papers that does not include original research contributions; it was, however, a timely effort aimed toward bringing together the intellectual traditions of learning theory and intelligence research.

7. I will enter "Array Models for Category Learning" (Estes, 1986) as my final landmark item. This article documents the continuing viability of ideas and methods germinated in mathematical learning theory, and at the same time exhibits a "hybrid vigor" contributed by inputs from the newer traditions of cognitive science and artificial intelligence.

Toward a Statistical Theory of Learning

Though I have little confidence in my memory for details of events that occurred decades ago, I would like to set down as well as I can the origins of my first major theoretical paper. The two aspects of the paper that were to have an impact were the method and the central theoretical ideas.

The essentials of the method were to set down one's assumptions about a theoretical interpretation in quantitative form and deduce both implications that could be tested by observation and interrelationships between this bit of theory and others. This method was by no means unprecedented in psychology, a somewhat tenuous thematic thread being traceable back at least to Helmholtz, but it had not yet entered in any important way into the study of learning and memory. I was familiar enough with this kind of quantitative theorizing in physics, but might not on my own have made the leap from physics to psychology. However, the basis for the transition had been laid down for me in the work of Selig Hecht, which fell into my receptive hands while I was still an undergraduate. Though Hecht's work had to do with photoreceptor processes in vision, it provided a model of what I would like to do, in turn, for the psychology of learning and memory.

The theoretical notions in my statistical approach to learning theory are traceable to diverse origins. Beginning in undergraduate days, I had been intrigued with the problem of somehow bringing together the theoretical approach of Skinner, with whom I conducted my own early research, and that of Edwin R. Guthrie, whom I never met, but whose writings I had followed as closely as any of his own students could have. Both of these scientists seemed similarly astute at analyzing behavioral situations and detecting important relationships that others had missed, yet they came out with sharply disparate theoretical systems. Why so? A key fact seemed to me that whereas for Skinner variability of behavior under constant experimental conditions was generally treated as a kind of noise to be minimized so far as possible by experimental control, for Guthrie it represented an important aspect of the learning process, which could not be analyzed away without losing a major source of explanations of the properties of learning. Nothing tangible came of those observations, however, until memories of them revived a number of years later in a context where they could interact with my own behavioral observations.

At Indiana right after the war, Norman Guttman, then a graduate student, and I constructed an apparatus for studying operant conditioning as a function of varied concentrations of rewarding agents (such as sucrose or saccharine) in solution. The design was joint, but the construction was largely accomplished by Norman since my skill at manipulating symbols on paper has always been a good deal better than that of manipulating solid materials on the workbench. Once the apparatus was constructed, we started a new series of studies that led to Norman's Ph.D. dissertation and a number of his major publications, and on my part to a number of experiments that never got published and a much larger volume of observations of animals in the conditioning situation that did prove to bear some fruit.

During long hours of waiting for animals to progress from initial contact with food reward in the apparatus to a relatively constant rate of bar pressing for a given concentration of reward, I was most impressed by the fact that the transitions were rarely smooth and orderly, a more typical result being a period of essentially no progress followed by an almost instantaneous rise to a near maximal response rate. It seemed to me that I could generally anticipate when an animal was about to make the break by observing how closely its pattern of movements in the apparatus following the ingestion of a reward left it in the same position and exposed to the same cues as when the rewarded response had been initiated. Speed of learning seemed to depend critically on the degree to which the pattern of cues that led to a rewarded response was reinstated at the time of the next opportunity for a response.

At some point it occurred to me that the situation seemed to have features in common with a multimolecular chemical reaction. The importance of that thought was not that it put any specific usable model into my hands, but that it suggested the need to try mentally to filter out the details of the experimental situation and imagine an idealized experiment in which some aspects of the organism's learning apparatus and some aspects of the environment jointly formed an interacting system whose dynamics might be captured by the same kind of mathematical formalism that served for molecular reactions in the biochemistry of vision. In the model that emerged, the conception of learning was not a process of strengthening of bonds or connections as in Thorndike, but rather a process of classifying and reclassifying elements of information from the environment with respect to their significance as predictors of the outcomes of choices among responses.

It is of interest to try to explain why my statistical approach to learning theory proved more influential than related earlier works, for example, those of Thurstone (1930), and Gulliksen and Wolfe (1938a, 1938b), which may well have seemed similarly promising when they appeared. As had been the case with my most illustrious predecessor in quantitative learning theory, Clark L. Hull, my first major theoretical article included many ideas that seemed urgently to call for further development, and I proceeded with considerable momentum to the task of working them out in the laboratory as well as on the blackboard. But still more important, I think, were the contributions of a large number of other young psychologists who had both the background in science and mathematics and the interest, sparked by the controversies revolving around the learning theories of Guthrie, Hull, and Tolman, to be ready to participate in a new enterprise. The first wave of these comprised students at Indiana, among them Richard C. Atkinson, Edith Neimark, Max Schoeffler, and Solomon Weinstock, all of whom were soon to make major independent contributions. The second wave gathered force as my paper, filtering into departmental libraries around the country, struck resonant chords in an astonishing number of bright young minds, the result being notable contributions to the developing body of theory by such individuals as Gordon Bower, Walter Kintsch, David LaBerge, William Prokasy, and Frank Restle, en route to the highly visible and influential research careers that ensued as each developed his distinctive approach to learning and cognitive theory.

The Zeitgeist of the 1950's

Perhaps almost as important as the specific contributions of various individuals to the growth of statistical learning theory was a confluence of factors conducive to a new look in learning theory and mathematical psychology in the early 1950's. People of vision in a number of funding agencies, notably the Social Science Research Council, the Ford Foundation, the Carnegie Corporation, and the Office of Naval Research, were eager to promote the spread of mathematical thinking in social and psychological sciences, and at least on the psychological side, a number of young investigators just entering on their research careers had keen interest in taking advantage of the opportunities afforded. The situation was most propitious for the advancement of learning and cognitive theory, but the interactions of investigators with agencies that produced the actual advances had more the random character of the processes in my learning model than of the unfolding of any orderly plan. I will recount some of the early developments as well as I can recall them.

In the early 1940's, B. F. Skinner and Fred Keller initiated a series of informal conferences on operant conditioning ("experimental analysis of behavior" in Skinner's terms), and the 1949 session convened some time in the spring or summer at Columbia, including among the conferees Conrad Mueller, William Schoenfeld, William Verplanck, and myself. Mueller and Verplanck were psychophysicists by training, in the quantitative tradition of Clarence Graham, and Schoenfeld and I were "operant conditioners," but we found we had in common a feeling that the learning theories of the time presented a motley array of overlapping formulations that sorely needed some housecleaning in the form of careful comparative analysis by individuals other than the originators of the theories. This common thought gave way quickly to the suggestion that something might actually be done along those lines, and our next step was to recruit via correspondence several other young investigators whom we thought might share our outlook—Sigmund Koch, Paul Meehl, and Kenneth MacCorquodale—and prepare a proposal for a summer conference. Remarkably, the proposal, guided by the friendly hand of Albert Poffenberger, a very senior experimental psychologist at Columbia, was almost instantly approved for funding by the Carnegie Corporation. The seminar was held in the summer of 1950, and led to the published volume *Modern Learning Theory* (Estes et al., 1954), which carried out after a fashion the comparative analysis we had projected.

Concurrently, on another track, so to speak, a young physicist, Robert R. Bush, had come to Harvard for retooling in the social sciences and was working with the already eminent statistician Frederick Mosteller when a preprint of my article on statistical learning theory found its way into his hands. Bush and Mosteller quickly realized that the mathematical functions they were using to handle some adaptive effects of drug dosages were identical in form to some expressions in my learning model, and that they had in effect been developing a potential model for learning while dealing with entirely different material. The word got around quickly, and they and I (together with Cletus Burke, an associate at Indiana) were invited to report on our current work at the meeting of the Institute of Mathematical Statistics.

Bush and I hit it off from the start, and before the meeting was over the seed of an idea was germinating for a conference on new approaches to mathematical models of learning. The four of us present at the meeting invited George A. Miller and David Zeaman to join us in a proposal for a summer-long workshop. Once again, the proposal went to the Social Science Research Council, and once again the favorable response was almost instantaneous, so the workshop was held in the summer of 1951 on the Tufts University campus with the six initiators augmented by the participation of William J. McGill, then a graduate student, who came nominally as an assistant to Miller, but before July passed into August was recognized by all of us as a seventh full-scale contributor.

Of the many workshops and seminars I have attended, this one was marked by the most intense and sustained concentration of intellectual effort. So far as we knew, it was a once-in-a-lifetime opportunity to be supported for two months for no purpose other than to work on the theoretical problems closest to our hearts with no distractions and generous opportunities for consultation with the most able of our peers. A typical day comprised seven to eight hours of work on theoretical problems by individuals on scratch pads or pairs of collaborators at the blackboard, broken by a session of an hour or so at which one of us presented some segment of current work for the always critical and often constructive reaction of the others.

Very early this interplay brought out the initially disturbing finding that there was a serious flaw in the method used both by Bush and Mosteller and by me in deriving predicted learning curves from our models. The gist of the difficulty was that in some instances the predicted mean learning curves we were generating could be shown to represent neither the actually predicted course of learning for any individual nor even the average of a group. So far as it affected current work in progress, the problem quickly yielded to a fierce mobilization of intellectual effort, and in the course of solving the immediate problem we all gained a much deeper understanding of the properties of general classes of mathematical operators that are and can be used to represent learning processes.

One of my own principal accomplishments of the summer was negative, in a sense. I had been intrigued since undergraduate days with Edwin R. Guthrie's interpretation of reward and punishment in terms of contiguity principles. Guthrie's argument was, in essentials, that whatever responses a learner makes in a situation become associated with the currently effective cues, each new association between cue and response supplanting any previous association between the same cue and other responses. The function of reward and punishment was simply to determine when the learner's interaction with a given situation would terminate, the last response occurring remaining associated with the currently effective cues. My discovery was that this "postremity principle," when rigorously formulated, did not yield the effects claimed for it and could not serve as a sufficient basis for the effects of reward or punishment. The proof was genuinely difficult, and since it seemed likely that few psychologists outside of the circle gathered at Tufts that summer would ever be both able and willing to study the proof, I never published it. One of the tangible results in my own work only appeared nearly twenty years later when I returned to the problem of the interpretation of reward from a quite different standpoint (Estes, 1969).

Beyond these incidents, the summer was for me mainly an investment in the future. I was cheerfully permitted to pick the brains of my talented fellow conferees, which I did unreservedly, and I carried away a harvest of tips for finding routes through the pitfalls of formal modeling that could not have been matched by years of courses or textbook study. As an added bonus, Bob Bush and I started on what was to be an extremely fruitful professional collaboration, which led most directly to our jointly edited summarization of the first decade of the new mathematical psychology (Bush and Estes, 1959) and more indirectly had a good bit to do with the continuation of workshops and teaching seminars in mathematical social science and the founding of the *Journal of Mathematical Psychology*.

At the end of the workshop, Bush and I decided to work together the next summer in Cambridge, but before summer came we were both invited to take part in a seminar on decision processes being organized by Clyde Coombs and Robert Thrall, a pioneering mathematical psychologist and a psychological mathematician, respectively. The summer of 1952 found Bush and me together again in a new setting, RAND Corporation in Santa Monica, California, interacting mainly with applied mathematicians and social scientists schooled in statistical decision and econometric theory, among them Leo Goodman, Jacob Marschak, Roy Radner, Gerard Debreu, Herbert Simon, Allen Newell, and again the ubiquitous Fred Mosteller.

I must have been overawed on being called on to present some of my current quantitative work to such a dazzling array of mathematical talent, but I did so and was astonished at the interest it evoked. The subject was my first application of statistical learning theory to human subject data. A prediction from my model was that learners in an uncertain situation should come to match their response probabilities to the probabilities of events they were trying to predict, a phenomenon quickly dubbed "probability matching." There was no problem with the derivations, but the applied mathematicians and decision theorists were surprised and in a sense indignant that human learners should exhibit behavior quite out of line with what they should be doing on the basis of the optimal choice rules of statistical decision theory. This reaction had both unfortunate and fortunate consequences. On the former side, there ensued a wave of research on "matching versus maximizing" of choice-reward probabilities that, though fertile at first in generating useful new findings, eventually turned into a somewhat unprofitable bypath. On the positive side was the initiation of long-term friendships and professional associations with many of the participants and a sparking of my interest in problems of decision theory that has persisted down to the present. Following 1952, there was a temporary letup in the stream of summer seminars, probably fortunate for my research since some time would inevitably be needed for the heady input of intellectual stimulation to be translated into intellectual output.

The Indiana-Stanford Circuit

Research during the next few years was helped along no little by a faculty fellowship from the Social Science Research Council that gave me a full half of each year free of teaching. The high points of that period that I recall are a broad-scale attack on human probability learning, in collaboration with James Straughan and Cletus Burke, among others, and the theoretical work leading to my 1955 *Psychological Review* articles on spacing effects in learning. I was due for a sabbatical year in 1955–56 and, when the year approached, was surprised with an invitation to spend the period at the newly established Center for Advanced Study in the Behavioral Sciences in Stanford, California, during its first full year of operation. The Center proved an exhilarating place to be, with a diversely talented group of scholars free to follow their interests individually or collectively as they wished under the benign direction of the first director of the center, Ralph Tyler.

Upon my first arrival on the Center grounds I was greeted by two slightly younger psychologists of quantitative orientation, Frank Restle, a recent Stanford Ph.D., and Joseph Bennett from Michigan, with the words "we've been looking for you." It seems that they had already met Patrick Suppes, a philosopher on the Stanford faculty, who was interested in learning about the new mathematical learning theories, and they wanted to get a research seminar started almost before our bags were unpacked. The seminar was indeed started without delay and ran throughout the year, providing a stable core for our otherwise varied and relatively unstructured activities, and its fruits continued to mature long beyond our year at the Center. Suppes turned out to be the only person I have ever been able to collaborate with on theoretical work. His background in logic and formal models complemented mine in biology and experimental psychology of learning, and his quick mind kept me literally as well as figuratively on my feet as we worked in tandem at the blackboard on problems in the formalization of learning theory.

During my usually solitary mornings in my study at the Center, I carried through almost completely the task of embedding statistical learning models in the framework of Markov theory (Estes, 1959), a task in which I took a good deal of intellectual pleasure. Afternoons were often broken by seminars; beyond the one in learning theory, I enjoyed one on stochastic processes that Howard Raiffa and I promoted (and cotutored when we proved to be a bit ahead of our fellow students) and one or more on the theory of games and decision making. The gap between morning and afternoon was usually taken up with leisurely walks over the adjacent green hills with Frank Restle, Davis Howes, Joe Bennett (till his untimely death), and Martin Shubik, mostly talking theory—what else? And as the Center's fellows began to disperse toward the end of Friday afternoon each week, those in the north bank of studies generally collected for a while at Gardner Lindzey's end for a chat about the more general state of psychology and the world.

My accelerating collaboration with Pat Suppes scarcely missed a beat at the end of the year at the Center. He paid me a visit at Indiana during the next academic year and then worked out a scheme for me to come to Stanford the following summer for full-time theoretical work, primarily on our collaborative effort, in the Applied Mathematics and Statistics Laboratory, where as it turned out, I spent every summer for the next six or seven years till I finally joined the Stanford faculty. Each spring the family, my wife and I and our two boys, packed up our station wagon with a summer supply of household appurtenances and headed west. How my wife managed, I don't know in retrospect (renting our Indiana house, securing housing near Stanford, mastering the logistics of a different house every summer, and reclaiming our home from its summer occupants in time for the start of a new school year)—but she did. In fact, I think all our memories of those trips are pleasant, in spite of a few catastrophes (ranging from the occasion when both boys got measles en route to the almost routine failures of our generally frail automobiles). We varied our paths on the route between Indiana and California widely and in time became midwestern experts on the national parks of the American West.

The continuing collaboration with Suppes led most directly to our published work on the foundations of learning models and less directly to a number of fruitful byproducts. Some outstanding graduate students who had done work with me at Indiana went on to postdoctorals with Suppes at Stanford, resulting in such outputs as a ground-breaking volume on models for two-person interactions (Suppes and Atkinson, 1960) and a major study of second language learning (Crothers and Suppes, 1967). Also, the Stanford locale, with activities centering around Kenneth Arrow and his associates, as well as Suppes and myself, became the locus for annual summer gatherings of mathematical psychologists and social scientists from across the country.

One of the most active foci was a group with common interests in mathematical theories of learning and choice that included Bush and Mosteller, Duncan Luce, and Sidney Siegel among the regulars. Often some of us were involved in Social Science Research Council summer workshops on mathematics and social science, which brought in junior people in various capacities and attracted such notable visitors as John von Neumann and Oscar Morgenstern. These gatherings provided ready cross fertilization of the various theoretical strains, furthered by lively discussions of matters that would have seemed arcane to most outsiders—"expected operators" in probabilistic models, the mathematics of all-or-none acquisition in concept identification, the implications of Luce's choice axiom for nonlinear learning models.

The level of activity peaked, as I remember, in 1957 when Bush and I secured support for a workshop that brought in a number of rising young stars, including David LaBerge and Gordon Bower. Bower, still a graduate student at Yale, came with his pockets full of projects already started that were to lead to influential publications, and he and I were started on what proved to be one of the most interesting and fruitful intellectual interactions that I have had with anyone in psychology, continuing via summer meetings and correspondence until the 1960's, when we both, then professors at Stanford, found ourselves so saturated with the load of graduate students to look after that we rarely saw each other except for the famous "Friday seminars."

Erosion of the Stimulus-Response Framework

The development of a scientific theory characteristically entails a seemingly unending sequence of choices and decision points produced by interactions of the theory with observations or with other theories. The choices are determined not only by immediately available evidence, but by the philosophical outlook of the theorist. A line of demarcation between outlooks that runs through all sciences, from physics to psychology, separates two views that I shall refer to for brevity as *operationism* and *constructivism*.

Operationism became a household word in science after its vigorous explication in Bridgman's *Logic of Modern Physics* (1928), but it also characterizes the philosophy of Heisenberg, a founder of quantum mechanics, and predecessors who set themselves the goal of expressing all scientific laws in terms of relationships among entities that could be directly observed or measured. This view was first given a vigorous formal expression in psychology by S. S. Stevens (1939), following which it was taken up enthusiastically by B. F. Skinner, who, together with many followers, has been the most visible and forceful exponent of the operationist view in psychology down to the present.

By constructivism I refer to a systematic effort to build representations of observable phenomena in terms of inferred, and often abstract, underlying entities and processes, an approach exemplified by the work of Bohr and Einstein in physics, Clark L. Hull among the early learning theorists, and the cognitive scientists on the current psychological scene.

As a student, I almost wholly bought, with much enthusiasm, the arguments of Bridgman and Stevens, and their influence can be seen in the operationist flavor of my early papers published with Skinner or based on work that I did in his laboratory. Nonetheless, there were signs of ambivalence in my outlook almost from the start. The idea that learning could be interpreted in terms of transitions among inferred internal states of the organism, analogous to states of physical systems, had much appeal for me. My use of the concept of an internal state to interpret an animal's learned anticipation of a traumatic event was mostly edited out of the paper presenting work on that problem that I did with Skinner, but it became more conspicuous a few years later in follow-up studies I carried out on anticipation of rewarding events (e.g., Estes, 1943). Even at the end of my first decade as a psychological investigator, I expressed sympathy for a basically stimulus-response descriptive framework in my first formal theoretical paper. However, in the model presented, I (inconsistently) represented the effects of learning in terms of categorizations of inferred abstract "memory elements," the assumptions being only indirectly testable by the derivation of predicted action tendencies.

The ambivalence did not wear off quickly. I found much appeal in the framework of Bush and Mosteller (1951), in which learning was represented wholly in terms of changes in probabilities of observable responses, and I was pleased to note that under some circumstances empirical laws of learning derivable from my developing theory could be expressed in the form of Bush and Mosteller's mathematical operators on response probabilities. At the same time, I was developing an account of temporal spacing effects in learning and retention in terms of the inferred fluctuations in the states of ensembles of memory elements (Estes, 1955a, 1955b). I began to wonder whether, in general, learning models could be expressed in either the operationist or constructionist mode at the will of the investigator and, specifically, whether all of the predictions from statistical models of learning could be expressed in the form of Bush and Mosteller's operators on response probabilities.

The mathematical methods I had acquired while working in the strictly scientific tradition did not offer any obvious way of trying for a formal answer to the question, but the happy accident of my becoming acquainted with the philosopher Suppes at the Center in 1955 brought a new perspective based on the potentialities of logical analysis of formal systems, and our collaborative work that ensued led to substantial clarification. We were able to show that even within the domain of learning theory, given reasonable criteria of feasibility, the answer is negative—implications of statistical models can be expressed in the operator form, and therefore in the language of stimulus-response learning theory, only under limited and specifiable conditions. Also, it became clear that it makes little sense to think of any sharp line of demarcation between the operationist and the constructivist approaches, since we could demonstrate that some familiar stimulus-response laws are derivable as limiting special cases of more general laws that are expressible only in terms of more abstract concepts.

Through the 1950's, the theorists who gathered summers at Stanford to develop and debate their theories (first the continuous operator models of learning and choice, then the all-or-none state models that in turn shaded into models of memory organization) all were in tune with the times in that the models were of the "black box" character—predictions of output (behavior) in response to input (informative stimuli or feedback) being interpreted on the basis of abstract properties of a mechanism inside. Only a few years later, the zeitgeist had shifted, and many of the same theorists were formulating theories couched in terms of cognitive operations on mental representations of the external world—scans or

searches of memory buffers or collections of images of perceived events
and the like.

This rather dramatic transition most assuredly did not result from any
decisive experiments that refuted "black box" theories, or any new findings expressible only in representational and information processing terminology. What, then, does account for the transition? One contributing
factor was certainly the work of Edward Feigenbaum, Earl Hunt, Allen
Newell, and Herbert Simon on computer simulations of human mental
processes and the formulation of models in terms of information-
processing concepts, all presented and discussed in the Stanford setting
during the 1960's. One of the first psychologists to pick up those ideas and
apply them in a direct and systematic way to the interpretation of memory
was Richard C. Atkinson, my colleague and one of my closest associates
during my years on the Stanford faculty beginning in 1962. During our
morning coffee breaks and the more structured Friday afternoon seminars in Ventura Hall, I followed with lively interest the evolving thinking
of Dick Atkinson and his students on information-processing models for
memory that led to the now justly famous model of Atkinson and Shiffrin
(1968). I found the information-processing vocabulary quite congenial to
the expression of my own results on reinforcement in human learning,
and it evidently led me to be favorably disposed to a more thoroughly cognitive approach when I, quite accidentally, first stumbled into work in visual processing.

The background of my first work in visual processing was a continuing
interest in discrimination learning, and, in particular, a theoretical problem that had bothered me and my associates for a long time. The question
at issue was how individuals can discriminate perfectly between stimuli
that contain elements in common. It would seem that if attention were not
directed to all of the aspects of each stimulus on each trial, sometimes only
aspects common to two stimuli to be discriminated would be sampled and
thus discrimination would be imperfect. One answer that had been proposed by a number of theorists (Bower, 1959; Estes, 1960b; Restle, 1961)
was that response to a stimulus is the result of a process of implicit search,
or "vicarious trial and error," that has the effect of filtering out overlapping, or invalid, cues and leading to response based on unique, or valid,
cues. One test of this idea, it seemed to me, would be to constrain the individual to respond to a very brief stimulus exposure, which would not
allow time for the search process.

In preparation for the desired experiments, I collaborated with Nicholas Pappas, an engineer in Menlo Park who had started a small instrument firm, in working out a plan for a tachistoscopic device that would yield the desired stimulus control. Once the apparatus was constructed, I wanted to become familiar with its properties before starting an experiment, and, together with an assistant, Henry A. Taylor, Jr., I obtained data on some subjects who simply viewed brief exposures of random displays of printed letters and reported what they could perceive. Rough plots of number of letters perceived as function of size of display struck a resonant chord in memory, for I had seen very similar functions in a monograph by George Sperling (1960).

Retrieving Sperling's article, I was impressed by the closeness with which we had reproduced his empirical functions and, further, I became fascinated with the theoretical question that had motivated much of Sperling's study—namely, why does the number of letters reported reach an asymptote of about four or five when subjects uniformly have the impression that they can briefly see many more letters in a display? Sperling's answer, in essence, was that some of the letters initially registered in the visual system might be lost from short term memory before they could be reported—a hypothesis that was confirmed by results obtained with his *partial report* procedure. However, it seemed to me that the somewhat higher asymptotes reached by subjects with Sperling's procedure still were not high enough to satisfy one that problems of memory capacity had been eliminated. I wondered whether the memory problem could not be eliminated entirely by asking subjects, rather than reporting all of the letters seen, simply to report whether or not some predesignated target letter was present anywhere in the display. That technique worked out much as expected and quickly became one of the standard methods for exploring tachistoscopic perception relatively independently of problems of memory capacity.

One of the consequences was that I became so intrigued with the potentialities of exploring the early stages of visual letter recognition with the detection technique that I never got back to the discrimination problem that had started me on this trip. At a theoretical level, it did not seem convenient, if possible at all, to describe the kind of data generated by tachistoscopic methods in stimulus-response terms, but they did lend themselves in a most natural way to such concepts as the scanning of a fading memory trace of a visual image, an important constituent of Sperling's interpretation of his partial report data, and I was led to formulate and then initiate extended experimental testing of a model for this scanning process. Branching out from the specific line of work associated with the detection method, I began to find a good deal of attraction in a level of theorizing in which concepts are formulated in terms of information and information processing rather than stimuli and responses and their connections.

I have spoken of erosion of the stimulus-response framework, but perhaps subordination would be a better term. The fact that stimulus-response terminology is not widely popular in this period of widening influence of cognitive psychology should not be taken to obscure the time-tested value, and indeed necessity, of close analysis and description of many behavioral situations in stimulus-response terms, especially situations involving animal learning or formation of skills and habits in human beings. Cognitive psychologists ignore at their peril such securely founded principles as stimulus-response compatibility, which cannot be sensibly formulated in purely cognitive terms.

On the other hand, some of the goals enthusiastically embraced by behaviorally oriented psychologists during the period of peak influence of the classical behavior theorists no longer seem attainable. In particular, the idea that all significant regularities in learning and behavior can be captured by stimulus-response laws no longer seems viable. In many situations, both in and out of the laboratory, the interpretation, as distinguished from sheer description, of behavior must turn on the information an individual is extracting from environmental inputs and reflecting in present or future behaviors, rather than on the immediate responses evoked by those inputs. What we have seen over several decades is a parallel development of theory at behavioral and informational levels of description, with some interaction but with real integration mostly left for the future. I think now that ultimate integration is inevitable and that progress toward that desirable end is only delayed by the parochialism often seen on the sides of both behavioral and cognitive psychologists.

In the realm of theory, mixtures of vocabularies rather than pure strains seem to be the rule, in my work as well as that of others. My research in learning theory from the 1940's down to the present would generally be categorized, I am sure, as falling in the tradition of association theory, broadly conceived. At first I thought in terms of stimulus-response associations, later more abstract notions of associations among mental representations of events, and hierarchical organizations of both association and memory traces. But from the mid-1960's to the present, much of my work in cognitive psychology has led to models formulated in terms of information flow through the mental processing system and cognitive operations (memory scanning, mental comparisons, decision making) on the information.

This theoretical dualism is not peculiar to my thinking but is characteristic of many current theorists in cognitive science. In the work of Posner (1978) on mental chronometry, for example, interpretations in terms of sequences of cognitive operations run side by side with those in terms of the spread of activation in hypothetical networks. The same is true of the work of Anderson (1983) and Shiffrin and his associates (Shiffrin and Schneider, 1977; Raaijmakers and Shiffrin, 1981). Nonetheless, it is bothersome, at least in introspective moments, to find oneself working concurrently with two sets of theoretical concepts that lend themselves to quite different kinds of intuitions about cognitive functioning and so far have not been satisfactorily related to one another in any formal framework.

What should we expect of the foreseeable future, the continued coexistence of the vocabularies of cognitive operations and associative networks or some kind of decision between them? I think the former is more likely, for at least two important reasons. One is that each of these vocabularies is especially amenable to particular kinds of intuitions that are important in the analysis of cognitive functioning. The other is that theoretical progress seems to come mainly, not by the amalgamation of verbalizable concepts, but rather by development of deeper and more abstract models that can be talked about with different vocabularies when one examines them from different perspectives, just as is true of the organisms they represent.

On the Role of Models

Before concluding this sketch of the overall shifts in my theoretical outlook over a couple of decades, I would like to comment on what I see to be the role of an inclination toward mathematical thinking and the development of formal models. It seems to me that psychologists attempting to proceed from observations to theories, even more than investigators in biology or the natural sciences, are handicapped by a pervasive tendency to interpret their observations and constrain their theories in terms of a semiscientific vocabulary (motivation, emotion, fear, attitude, recollection . . .) acquired outside of scientific settings as a part of our natural language. We may replace a particular term fairly readily (a fact widely recognized by those who lament the psychologist's penchant for jargon), but we do not so readily change our basic ways of categorizing the behavior of other people or animals or the kinds of mental processes we infer to lie behind the behavior. When we formulate a mathematical model (or more recently a computer model) for a situation, however, the form of the model tends to be directed by the actual form of the data we are dealing with rather than by our linguistic habits and categories. Thus it is not an infrequent experience to formulate a model for a collection of experiments to the point that it has some predictive power, and in the course of the development to speak of elements of the model in terms of the same vocabulary we habitually use with regard to the corresponding empirical situation (response tendency, stimulus variability, subjective probability, stimulus-response association, observing response). Then we may find that the properties of the model do not actually demand such descriptions and that the salient relationships captured in the model call for quite different interpretations.

Although, unhappily, mathematical approaches in science are often regarded as excessively narrow and confining, I think that view can be maintained only by the uninitiated or the inexperienced. More often, mathematical thinking enables one to escape from the constraints of natural language habits and to see relationships between empirical domains that might never be perceived at the level of sheer observation and qualitative description. At any rate this aspect of the relationship between mathematical and scientific thinking has been conspicuous in my own experience and will be apparent in the papers cited that enable one to trace the development of some theoretical ideas and viewpoints over several decades of investigative activity.

On Doing Research

If any lessons are to be drawn from my experiences for the student of experimental psychology, they may lie in the small degree to which the various streams of research represent the outcome of looking for a problem or of translating textbook knowledge into experimental designs. The origins, rather, have nearly always had an almost accidental character. In many instances some casual observation or a reaction to a published study has led first to informal exploration of a phenomenon in the laboratory and then the flourishing of a line of work catalyzed by personal contacts with students and professional colleagues. In other cases, increasingly frequent over the years, meditating on a theoretical question or examining implications of a model has led directly into an experiment. I am by no means inclined to deprecate the importance of careful statistical design. However, in basic research, I think its useful role materializes only following a preliminary stage in which one develops an intuitive grasp of the phenomenon under study.

It is easy to see why it is so hard for students to learn from books how to do research. Knowledge of method is important, but counts for little except when complemented by alertness to the potential implications of apparently simple observations, considerable obstinacy in staying with one's intuitions even through long periods of slim payoff, and luck in brushing shoulders at the right time with stimulating associates. I am grateful for having had more than my share of luck in this sense.

The Other Side of the Coin

In trying to give a reasonably coherent account of a research career, I have left out the more personal aspects of my life. I can't do justice to the importance of these, but neither can I conclude without some explicit mention of people in two categories.

Family

I was married in 1942 to Katherine C. Walker, then a fellow graduate student at the University of Minnesota. Kay received her Ph.D. in 1945 and has both taught and published research in psychology, even though family responsibilities made it difficult for her to manage more than intermittent periods of academic employment. Beyond her companionship through the peaks and troughs of personal and professional fortunes over more than four decades, Kay has supported my academic and scientific career in more ways than I can mention. Certain images come vividly to mind. One of the earliest goes back to our first years at Indiana when Kay, busy looking after two very young children in our small home, got a phone call to the effect that an exceedingly eminent visitor to the department would be in town overnight but with no provision having been made for his entertainment. Could she instantaneously produce a dinner party? She could and did. Few individual occasions have been as memorble, but I could not possibly count the number of students, colleagues, and visitors Kay has entertained in our various homes across the country over the years. Kay has contributed a good deal to my publications as a constant critic and, on occasion, a skillful indexer, and has provided many kinds of assistance during my periods of journal editing.

Our sons, George and Gregory, were born in 1947 and 1949. Both boys proved scientifically inclined, and both turned more toward industry than academia, George finding his niche as a software specialist with A.T.&T. and Greg as a quality control chemist in government laboratories. Some of the most reliable bright spots in our off-duty calendar now are holiday and summer visits with George's son, Rhey, our only grandchild, born in 1977. It is a bit early to guess whether Rhey's addiction to my Macintosh computer signifies anything about his likely future interests.

Students

Interaction with the many students who have worked with me, both during and following our formal associations, has been one of the most rewarding aspects of my academic life. Few of them have been specifically mentioned in this sketch, because even a list would be formidable, and any account of what they did as students and what they are doing now would take me far beyond allowable bounds. Fortunately, it was possible to do a little better in an autobiographical chapter I prepared a few years ago with a somewhat different orientation (Estes, 1982b). For many years one of the most enjoyable events of the fall academic season has been the now traditional dinner during the Psychonomic Society meetings with a group of my former students together with some of their and my close associates. Usually these are happily casual, but on one occasion (in Denver in 1975) a burst of enterprise on the part of Dick Atkinson and Harry Madison expanded it into a gala affair along the lines of the fabled Gridiron Club dinners, ostensibly to celebrate the twenty-fifth anniversary of "Toward a Statistical Theory of Learning." I was glad that I had had the prescience to write the article back in 1950.

Selected Publications by William K. Estes

(A complete bibliography through 1981 may be found in Estes, 1982b.)

(with B. F. Skinner) (1941). Some quantitative properties of anxiety. *Journal of Experimental Psychology, 29*, 390–400.

(1943). Discriminative conditioning: 1. A discriminative property of conditioned anticipation. *Journal of Experimental Psychology, 32*, 150–155.

(1944). An experimental study of punishment. *Psychological Monographs, 57* (3, Whole No. 263).

(1950). Toward a statistical theory of learning. *Psychological Review,* 57, 94–107.

(1954). Individual behavior in uncertain situations: An interpretation in terms of statistical association theory. In R. M. Thrall, C. H. Coombs, & R. L. Davis (Eds.), *Decision processes* (pp. 127–137). New York: Wiley.

(with S. Koch, K. MacCorquodale, P. E. Meehl, C. G. Mueller, Jr., W. N. Schoenfeld, & W. S. Verplanck) (1954). *Modern learning theory.* New York: Appleton-Century-Crofts.

(with J. H. Straughan) (1954). Analysis of a verbal conditioning situation in terms of statistical learning theory. *Journal of Experimental Psychology,* 47, 225–234.

(with H. A. Taylor) (1954). A detection method and probabilistic models for assessing information processing from brief visual displays. *Proceedings of the National Academy of Sciences,* 52, 446–454.

(1955a). Statistical theory of spontaneous recovery and regression. *Psychological Review,* 62, 145–154.

(1955b). Statistical theory of distributional phenomena in learning. *Psychological Review,* 62, 369–677.

(1958). Stimulus-response theory of drive. In M. R. Jones (Ed.), *Nebraska symposium on motivation* (pp. 35–69). Lincoln, NE: University of Nebraska Press.

(1959). Component and pattern models with Markovian interpretations. In R. R. Bush & W. K. Estes (Eds.), *Studies in mathematical learning theory* (pp. 9–52). Stanford, CA: Stanford University Press.

(with R. R. Bush) (1959). *Studies in mathematical learning theory.* Stanford, CA: Stanford University Press.

(1960a). Learning theory and the new "mental chemistry." *Psychological Review,* 67, 207–223.

(1960b). A random-walk model for choice behavior. In K. J. Arrow, S. Karlin, & P. Suppes (Eds.), *Mathematical methods in the social sciences, 1959* (pp. 265–276). Stanford, CA: Stanford University Press.

(1969). Reinforcement in human learning. In J. Tapp (Ed.), *Reinforcement and behavior* (pp. 63–94). New York: Academic Press.

(1972a). An associative basis for coding and organization in memory. In A. W. Melton & E. Martin (Eds.), *Coding processes in human memory* (pp. 161–190). Washington, DC: Winston.

(1972b). Interactions of signal and background variables in visual processing. *Perception and Psychophysics,* 12, 278–286.

(1973). Memory and conditioning. In F. J. McGuigan & D. B. Lumsden (Eds.), *Contemporary approaches to conditioning and learning* (pp. 265–286). Washington, DC: Winston.

(1974). Learning theory and intelligence. *American Psychologist,* 29, 740–749.

(1975). The locus of inferential and perceptual processes in letter identification. *Journal of Experimental Psychology: General,* 104, 122–145.

(1982a). Similarity-related channel interactions in visual processing. *Journal of Experimental Psychology: Human Perception and Performance,* 8, 353–382.

(1982b). *Models of learning, memory, and choice: Selected papers.* New York: Praeger.

(1986). Array models for category learning. *Cognitive psychology,* 18, 500–549.

124 *William K. Estes*

Other Publications Cited

Anderson, J. R. (1983). *The architecture of cognition*. Cambridge, MA: Harvard University Press.

Atkinson, R. C., & Shiffrin, R. M. (1968). Human memory: A proposed system and its control processes. In K. W. Spence & J. T. Spence (Eds.), *The psychology of learning and motivation: Advances in research and theory* (vol. 2, pp. 89–195). New York: Academic Press.

Bower, G. H. (1959). Choice-point behavior. In R. R. Bush & W. K. Estes (Eds.), *Studies in mathematical learning theory* (pp. 109–124). Stanford, CA: Stanford University Press.

Bower, G. H. (1961). Application of a model to paired-associate learning. *Psychometrika, 26*, 225–280.

Bridgman, P. W. (1927). *The logic of modern physics*. New York: Macmillan.

Bush, R. R., & Mosteller, F. (1951). A mathematical model for simple learning. *Psychological Review, 58*, 313–323.

Crothers, E., Suppes, P. (1967). *Experiments in second language learning*. New York: Academic Press.

Gulliksen, H., & Wolfle, D. L. (1938a). A theory of learning and transfer: 1. *Psychometrika, 3*, 127–149.

Gulliksen, H., & Wolfle, D. L. (1938b). A theory of learning and transfer: 2. *Psychometrika, 3*, 225–251.

Posner, M. I. (1978). *Chronometric explorations of mind*. Hillsdale, NJ: Erlbaum.

Raaijmakers, J. G. W., & Shiffrin, R. M. (1981). Search of associative memory. *Psychological Review, 88*, 93–134.

Restle, F. (1961). *Psychology of judgment and choice: A theoretical essay*. New York: Wiley.

Restle, F. (1962). The selection of strategies in cue learning. *Psychological Review, 59*, 329–343.

Shiffrin, R. M., & Schneider, W. (1977). Toward a unitary model for selective attention, memory scanning, and visual search. In S. Dornic (Ed.), *Attention and performance, VI* (pp. 413–449). Hillsdale, NJ: Erlbaum.

Sperling, G. (1960). The information available in brief visual presentations. *Psychological Monographs, 74* (11, Whole No. 498).

Stevens, S. S. (1939). Psychology and the science of science. *Psychological Bulletin, 36*, 221–263.

Suppes, P., and Atkinson, R. C. (1960). *Markov learning models for multiperson interactions*. Stanford, CA: Stanford University Press.

Thurstone, L. L. (1930). The learning function. *Journal of General Psychology, 3*, 469–493.

Trabasso, T., & Bower, G. H. (1968). *Attention in learning: Theory and research*. New York: Wiley.

Fritz Heider

Fritz Heider

I was born in Vienna, Austria, in 1896 and when I was half a year old my parents moved to the city of Graz, the capital of the province of Styria. My father was an architect and worked for the Styrian government. This job was very much to his taste, for he was a man of hobbies that he enjoyed as he did his work, and it allowed him time for them, especially painting and sketching.

I remember some early incidents from my life and can often place them from the house that we were living in when they occurred. I must have been about two years old when I had a flash of insight about having a *self*, about being a person. I was sitting on a little footstool in a sort of nook formed by the doors between two rooms. My father was reading to my older brother, and I felt left out, frustrated. I remember the awareness that it was *I* who was frustrated, and this discovery of the self made it an exciting experience.

When I reached the age of six, I started learning the ABCs. I loved all the interesting things that could be done with numbers and figures. What impressed me most was the simple fact of writing. That one could put a description of something that had happened down on paper, that one could carry that piece of paper around like any other "thing," that even another person could read it—all this seemed very wonderful. And the greatest miracle of all was that one could even make a piece of paper hold events that had never happened— that were just adventures of fantasy.

I also acquired very early—maybe when I was seven—a familiarity with painting and sketching. Both my mother and father painted and drew, and most of my relatives painted as a hobby. It seemed to me as natural to play around with pencil and paint as to learn to walk.

As a small child I was said to have been a highly extroverted chatterbox, laughing and talking all the time. Later I became a silent person, introverted and shy, at the same time reaching out to find others with whom I could really talk. This change was probably a normal development of adolescence, but may also have been a delayed effect of the loss of vision in one eye when I investigated the workings of a cap pistol at the age of ten, and also of the gap between my very democratically oriented home and the more authoritarian school life of the day. It was then that I acquired the habit of introspection, though its beginnings had certainly arisen earlier. I was always watching and evaluating my thoughts, feelings, and attitudes, all fascinating objects of the inner world. The pleasure in writing never left me, and I acquired the habit of having a notebook into which I could record whatever came into my mind. I still have the notebooks from those days, and reading them brings back those pre–World War I years as nothing else could. They are not systematic diaries, but a mixture of notes about events, trips, observations of myself and others, and also fantastic little stories.

Since this account deals with the development of my ideas related to psychology, I will mention a theory about happiness that I recorded when I was thirteen or fourteen years old. This theory implied that happiness and unhappiness in a person's life are sooner or later balanced or equalized. One is somehow rewarded for unhappiness and will always have to pay for happy times.

It was during my school years, maybe around 1913, that I first was aware of the word *gestalt*. It was used by my father in the sense of a regular geometrical form. Because of his interest in painting and drawing, he thought a lot about visual experience, and like all German-speaking people of his day he was familiar with Goethe's ideas, some of which come close to what was later to be known as gestalt psychology. I have a sheet of paper on which he drew figures made up of dots and straight lines that seem almost to have come from one of Wertheimer's papers on unit formation. Later, when I heard more about the gestalt idea in university lectures on the psychology of perception, I had the feeling of an especially intense relationship with it.

As I look back on my life as it developed during these years, I cannot help feeling that the direction of my later interests was fully prepared during that time. There was already the concern with problems of perception growing out of my interest in sketching and a continuing preoccupation with ideas about people and their interactions that was to become intensified during the hard years of the war. And this included a growing attempt to theorize and to try to solve personal problems by working toward a conceptual understanding of them, which in a way was related to an early interest in geography. I loved maps and could easily see myself as a future geographer. Always, then and later, it gave me great pleasure to survey whatever region I was in and understand how its parts were related. Whenever I was in a strange city, I bought a map and climbed to the highest point that I could find, often a church tower, to try to get an idea of the topography of the region.

As I look back, I believe that this desire to clarify the geographical setting showed later my need to make theories. I always wanted to understand the relations between ideas. And now, when I read experimental papers, I want to place their results and find out how they fit into what I think of as the map of psychology. I am uncomfortable when I cannot relate them to other landmarks.

I passed the final examinations of the state school early in the summer of 1914 and had to decide what to do next. I was an introverted and unhappy person, leading something of the life of a hermit. The idea of becoming a geographer had faded, though the interest in geography remained with me. I played with the idea of becoming a writer and later of becoming a painter, but my father discouraged the idea of either writing or painting as a career. "Do not treat the muses as cows to be milked," he said and suggested that I follow his career of architecture, which provided a living and also left time for one's private interests. I enrolled in the technical school in Graz.

In the meantime, World War I had begun in August. I tried to enlist but was rejected because of the injury to my left eye. My brother, my cousins, my school classmates were all in the service, and I felt that I was missing out on the experience that the rest of my generation were having. And I soon began to feel that architecture was not the right thing for me. I had spent most of the first semester making meticulous drawings of classical columns and was utterly bored. I tried law, but it began with a heavy dose of memorizing Roman law, and I was never good at memorizing. I proposed to my father that I just go to the university without a definite study plan—there were so many interesting courses that I would like to attend. My father agreed, but reminded me that eventually I would have to earn my living. It was settled that I would attend the university for four years and then study some kind of agriculture. I might raise pigs on the family land near Graz.

I attended a variety of lectures at Graz from premedical courses to philosophy and art history, and after the custom of students of that day spent time at other universities. I studied zoology at Innsbruck with my Uncle

Karl, who taught there, and psychology at Munich with the Bühlers, child psychology with Karl Bühler and experimental methods with Charlotte Bühler.

When I returned to Graz, I began to concentrate on philosophy. Alexius Meinong was certainly the teacher who had the greatest influence on my thinking. He had a commanding presence in spite of his short stature and always gave the impression of being a well-organized person with extraordinary intelligence. The central feature of his philosophy and psychology was the idea that he took over from his teacher Franz Brentano, which may be designated as "intentionality" or "symbolic representation." I seem to have more or less forgotten his distinction between the content and the object of ideas, and all the rest of his treatment of intention. I don't think I ever had a real feeling for its importance. If I try to go back to the impression I had at the time of Meinong's philosophy, I would say that it seemed cold and lifeless, a chilly marble temple constructed by a man with a complicated brain but no heart. There is another aspect of his thinking that comes out when he deals with the more concrete questions of *probability* and *value*, and with the commonsense versions of these ideas. I must have learned a lot from his reflections on these problems.

Another important figure of the Graz Institute was the Italian Vittorio Benussi, a former student of Meinong. He was an elegant-looking, lean person with a finely chiseled and melancholy face and a dry, skeptical smile. He worked mostly in a darkened room where he had a cot, along with his apparatus, and he often spent the night as well as the day there. He did not give many courses because his health was not good.

Benussi came from Trieste, which at that time belonged to Austria, and he spoke German with an Italian accent. He probably had the strong Italian, anti-Austrian sentiments of his native city and felt himself an outsider in Graz. At the end of the First World War he became an Italian citizen and professor at Padua. He had made a respected place for himself in Austrian and German psychology and may not immediately have received the same recognition among Italian psychologists, though today he is certainly an important figure for them. He died when he was not quite 50 years old, a marginal man who stood between two cultures. He was one of the first to make experiments in the field of gestalt perception. The Berlin group used some of his demonstrations in their treatment of gestalt principles, though their theoretical approaches were somewhat different.

As I attended the university, friendships with fellow students began to change the color of my life, though a genuine interest in psychological observation and speculation remained. Perhaps this interest was especially strong in me because it helped me deal with my remaining shyness. In spite of the fact that I had given up my hermit life, I often still felt that the pressure of other people was overpowering. I tried to describe this peculiar influence exerted by people to myself: when one enters a room he gets a general impression of it, of its size and the brightness of the illumination, the color of the walls and the kinds of furniture. But all this is usually outweighed by reactions to the presence or absence of people, and if there are people whether they are familiar persons or strangers, whether they are people we like or not, and in what relation we stand to them. What is it that makes persons so unique in their influence on our feelings about the environment? Much of this would appear in my book *The Psychology of Interpersonal Relations* (1958).

These thoughts concerned me very much during the last years of the war. My mother had died in the influenza epidemic of 1918. My brother was still in the army, but relatives were often with us. Food was scarce, the house cold, and in the evening we all sat around a single oil lamp that gave just enough light for us to read and write. A general atmosphere of animosity and resentment developed, and every so often one of us would lose his temper at something another happened to do. I hated the mutual accusations and bickering and tried to stay out of it, falling back on my old standby, namely to observe what was going on, recording and analyzing what I observed. In thinking about what I saw, I often exaggerated what came to seem typical of these anger situations, and I tried to find general concepts and general causal connections. To phrase it in terms that I learned a few years later from Kurt Lewin, I was trying to get hold of genotypical underlying concepts, not just surface manifestations. I believe that many of my later ideas about interpersonal events and person perception were applied in this study, though certainly in embryonic form, and that it was a big step in building the background of what I would come to.

In the meantime, I noticed that one after another of my contemporaries at the university had begun work on dissertations, and I decided that I might as well. I went to Meinong and told him that I would like to work on something related to perception. He referred me to one of his books, in translation *About the Empirical Basis of our Knowledge* (1906). I worked through a cold winter on the problems Meinong dealt with. Fortunately there was a piece of forest land that belonged to the house where we lived. I worked every morning in my unheated room, well covered with thick

coats and gloves, writing what was to be my dissertation, then went out
with an ax and cut a small tree down to warm the house a little.

In the thesis I tried to solve the puzzles that Meinong posed in his book,
among them one that deals with a simple causal theory of perception.
This theory contends that we can see an object because it causes the processes that affect our eyes. In arguing against this theory Meinong asked
the following question: "When I look at a house on which the sun is shining why do I say 'I see the house'? Why do I not say, 'I see the sun' since
it is, after all, the rays of the sun that cause the process?"

Thinking about this question led me to consider broader aspects of the
causal structure and of transmission of information. A guiding thought
of the thesis concerns the difference between things (including persons as
environmental objects) and the mediation that transmits the information
about things to our sense organs. Solid objects are made up of parts that
are, to a large extent, dependent on each other. If I pull on one part of a
chair the other parts will follow. The mediation, on the other hand, con-
sists of part events that are largely independent of each other. Insofar as
the parts of the medium are tied together, are dependent on each other,
the medium loses some of the possibility of transmitting messages.

I would like to mention that Bertrand Russell dealt with similar problems in his book *Human Knowledge* (1948), and he also starts with the
question of why we say we see the object and not the sun when we look
at something that is illumined by the sun. He also answers the question
in terms of causal structure and information transmission, and he comes
to formulations that are very similar to mine.

Early in 1920 my thesis was accepted, and after a final examination I
received my degree. The time had come for me to keep my promise to my
father and prepare myself to earn my living. I planned to begin a course
in agriculture the next fall. But in the meantime the provincial government asked the university for someone to help establish a bureau for vocational guidance, and my name was suggested. I never returned to the
study of agriculture. I enjoyed devising tests and giving them to boys of
ten or eleven who decided to enter apprenticeships, but the postwar infla-
tion made the fate of the bureau insecure, and I was getting glowing reports of life in Berlin from a cousin who was living there with her father,
a zoologist at the university. I knew that I could stay with them, and I
solved the immediate financial problem of living there by asking my father whether I might have some rare books that he had collected during
his bachelor days and that now lay gathering dust in the attic.

So, in November 1921 I set out for Berlin and was soon listening to lectures by Wolfgang Köhler and Max Wertheimer and attending Lewin's seminars. Wertheimer was a short, intense man. He gave his lectures in one of the larger rooms of the university and was very popular with the young intellectuals of Berlin. It was always amusing and interesting to listen to him. He had a unique style of talking as of writing. He operated by fits and starts in a way that produced the impression that his ideas were fresh and pungent. One felt that this little man with the walrus mustache really believed what he was saying and that it must be something new since it made him so excited. One of the most enjoyable seminars I ever attended was one of his on the blind spot. There was a small group of ten or fifteen students; each of us, after making some observations of his own on the blind spot, had to suggest hypotheses to explain what he had observed. Then he had to test his hypotheses by deriving consequences from them. We had to check them then and there and make new observations to see whether they would confirm the hypotheses. It was a remarkable demonstration of the hypothetico-deductive method and at the same time of gestalt laws, because the way the blind spot appears is mainly determined by gestalt principles and not by experience. We do not see what we have "learned" to see but what fits best.

Köhler, a younger man than Wertheimer, held the position that in America would be department chairman. He had a princely appearance and his lectures were fascinating and full of information, but he was not easy for an outsider like me to get to know. A good friend of mine told me that when he talked with Köhler he always felt that he himself was a chimpanzee, the animal about which Köhler had written a famous book. He had actually begun his academic life in physics and wrote a book on what he called *The Physical Gestalten* (1920) in which he tried to show that the chasm between physical and mental reality is not as wide as is generally believed, and that both follow structural gestalt laws.

There was, of course, a connection between the Graz School and Berlin. For one thing, the Berlin gestalt psychologists recognized Christian von Ehrenfels as one of their precursors, and he had been a student of Meinong; also Wertheimer was said to have attended lectures by Ehrenfels at the University of Prague. I naturally found myself comparing the Berlin group—and here I mean Wertheimer and Köhler—with Graz's Meinong and Benussi. Both groups were concerned with super-elementary structures, the so-called "gestalten." Benussi and the Berliners had high regard for each other in spite of the fact that they differed in their theories about these organized units and also in their emotional attitudes toward their theories. The Berliners always seemed to be engaged in a sort of holy war against nonbelievers and were much more belligerent than the Graz group. They were fervid partisans of all the ideas that had to do with configurations, with every kind of super-unit or totality. For them the very thought of attempting to derive these noble whole-qualities from despicable elements or pieces was unspeakably sinful, a clear sign of deplorable and corrupt thinking. Certainly, gestalt theory as I knew it at that time in Europe was mainly shaped by its opposition to elementarism, but later in America, the opposition to behaviorism was more important.

They saw G. E. Müller as the principal advocate of a theory built on elements, bits, and crumbs. I remember a session at the Psychological Congress that met in Bonn in 1927 when a discussion developed between Müller and Köhler. There was this white-haired old paladin of German psychology with a reputation almost equal to that of Wilhelm Wundt himself, presenting his case in a dignified and courteous way. Köhler replied, and I felt embarrassed by his sharp sarcasm. And Bühler, professor in Vienna, who had written about a form of gestalt psychology that differed from that of the Berliners in some of his theoretical assumptions, was equally despised.

I also attended a series of Kurt Lewin's seminars. I was soon in close contact with him, and we remained good friends until he died 25 years later when we were both living in America, at that time both in Massachusetts where we visited back and forth with our families. I showed him some of my attempts to deal with the causal structure of the environment insofar as it is relevant to perception and cognition. He suggested that we get together once a week for discussions at his house, but this did not work out, since then, as in later years, he was already overburdened with his work and all sorts of other commitments.

An ever present problem during this time in Berlin was, of course, the necessity of earning my keep once the money from my father's books was used up. I do not remember all the different ways I tried. For a few months I tutored a little boy in Latin; one time I substituted for an acquaintance who had a job testing apprentices; and for a time I worked as an electrician for Lewin's brother, who owned a company that installed burglar alarms, sometimes in plush homes in the west end, at other times in big wholesale establishments in the inner city.

I loved diving into this ever-changing stream of life in the big city and felt that I was gradually learning to understand and to talk to all these different kinds of people. When I spoke with them, I had the feeling that I lived; when I talked with psychologists, it was to speak about life but not to live it in the same way. The atmosphere was somehow real and stimulating. There was always a kind of intoxication that vibrated softly underneath.

During this time I was also trying to think through psychological problems, developing some of the ideas in my thesis further, and in 1922 and 1923 I wrote the paper that was published as "Ding und Medium" (1926; in English, "Thing and Medium," published in 1959). Lewin thought that there were interesting ideas in it and helped me get it into print. He also asked me whether I would care to go with him to a small gathering in Erlangen, mainly philosophers, who discussed such problems. He was sure that they would be interested in the questions I examined in the paper. The group included Rudolf Carnap and Hans Reichenbach, neither of whom was as yet well known. I especially remember Carnap's talk. At that time he was enthusiastic about the symbolic logic of Bertrand Russell and Alfred North Whitehead and proceeded to explicate the statement "one and one make two." Before he finished he had covered two blackboards with symbols. I wondered how many blackboards he would have needed for the addition involved in a simple grocery order, and I learned from his example that it is not always profitable to dig all the way down to core concepts. In the course of the meetings I gave a talk on my ideas about certain problems of cognition, and the discussion afterwards strengthened my feeling that it was worthwhile to develop them further.

After having spent three years in North Germany, I decided to go back to Graz, but with little idea of what I would do next. I stopped off in Vienna to visit with a bachelor second cousin who lived with two maiden aunts. He took me for a walk and said something that brought about a profound change in my immediate outlook and probably influenced my whole future. He offered me a small monthly allowance, enough so that I was no longer under constant pressure to earn my sustenance. I spent the next months in Florence, then was back in Graz, facing the fact that my years of wandering were over. I was 30 years old and for the first time began to think seriously of settling into a life career. I realized that my talents in writing and painting were too slight and unreliable to provide me with a solid foundation and that in the last years my interest in psychology had grown stronger and more persistent. I felt confident that my ideas, both in perception and in interpersonal relations, held promise of future development, though most of them were still embryonic. Not the least factor was Lewin's continuing interest in my "Thing and Medium." Once, after I had left Berlin, he wrote that he had treated it extensively in his seminar.

I decided to look for a position as a university assistant, roughly the equivalent of an American assistant professorship. By the spring of 1927 several offers had materialized, and I was soon settled into a position as assistant to William Stern at the University of Hamburg. An important factor in my choosing that position was the fact that Stern, Heinz Werner, and Ernst Cassirer were important figures there and would give me an opportunity to learn new aspects of psychology.

As I got to know Stern, I realized that he was a complicated sort of man behind a simple front. In talking to him I always felt that there was something lacking, the kind of warm person-to-person feeling that was so strongly present when I talked, for instance, with Werner or even with Cassirer, though I knew Cassirer much less. Yet I never doubted that Stern was an imposing thinker who had somehow a vision of the whole area of psychology. He stands as one of the founders in several fields of psychology, in child psychology, in the psychology of individual differences and testing, in legal psychology, and others. He was the first to suggest the use of the intelligence quotient. And he was also the very subtle observer of psychological states and processes, which has made him seem akin to the more recent existentialists or phenomenalists in some of his writings. His psychology even had a place for the troublesome problem of intentionality or representation, which was familiar to me from Meinong but which is often pushed under the rug or not perceived at all.

There was a profound difference between the views of Stern and those of the gestalt psychologists, though as far as I know they did not indulge in open polemics. The Berliners were the monists; they preferred a belief in the essential quality of physical and psychical events, while Stern's philosophy was based on a profound dualism, the difference between "person" and "thing."

Comparing Stern with Meinong, I would have to concede that Stern's thinking did not show Meinong's logical precision; and comparing him with the Berlin gestalt psychologists, one feels that his theories are not as firmly anchored in experimental results or in striking demonstrations. On the other hand, I would think it quite possible that in fifty or a hundred years psychology in general will show more similarities to Stern's basic ideas than to those of Meinong or the gestalt psychologists.

The departments of philosophy and psychology used some of the same rooms, and I often met Cassirer there when I visited his lectures and seminars. He was also an impressive person with the eyes of a poet and a magnificent way of lecturing. His memory was phenomenal, and he could quote long passages from Kant or Plato without using the text. Looking back now, I feel that this contact with Cassirer, slight though it was, played a part in my gradual development. It served to bring some of Meinong's ideas down from their monastic heights into a more human atmosphere, and at the same time helped me understand Lewin's theoretical position—not surprising, since Lewin had taken a course with Cassirer in his student days and had written, "Scarcely a year passes when I do not have specific reason to acknowledge the help which Cassirer's views on the nature of science and research offered" (Marrow, 1969, p. 9).

And there was Heinz Werner. When I think of him, I always have a picture of his bemused grin and his twinkling eyes before me. He was a thoroughly humane person with a warm sincerity that was very engaging. I read his classic book on developmental psychology right away and was especially impressed by his wonderful collection of examples of primitive thought. From our first meeting I felt close to him and enjoyed frequent visits with him in Hamburg and later in America, until his death in 1964. There was also a very bright graduate student who will appear in later pages of this account, Martin Scheerer.

Of the other members of the Hamburg Institute I especially want to mention Dr. Martha Muchow, a tall, heavily built woman with a sensitive and imaginative mind. She published interesting papers based on observations of children. She was an utterly decent person, the best type of North German. She committed suicide soon after the Nazis took over the institute.

My work at the university was to give lectures and seminars to students who intended to become teachers, and it led me to think about interpersonal relations of the classroom. I collected materials from students about incidents in their own early school life but soon realized, as I had with my observations of anger ten years earlier, that I lacked a network of clear concepts that would enable me to make these descriptions of concrete cases fully meaningful.

At one point it struck me that names for personality traits are often related to interpersonal behavior. I tried to analyze examples of personality descriptions but did not get very far. Long after, I came to the conviction that one would have better success by proceeding in the opposite direction: in other words, one will get a better idea of the meaning of trait names if one already has a theory of interpersonal behavior.

One pleasant event of the Hamburg years was a gathering in Rostock in the spring of 1928. All my life, wherever I have been, I have tried to get people together for discussions, and in Hamburg I suggested to Werner that we have a meeting with Lewin somewhere between Berlin and Hamburg. Werner liked the idea, so I wrote to Lewin. He was all for it and characteristically thought at once of a larger gathering. In the end he took care of the arrangements, and this is how the Rostock meeting came about. Wertheimer and Köhler came with Lewin from Berlin, A. Michotte from Louvain, Edgar Rubin from Copenhagen, with David and Rose Katz our hosts in Rostock. They were all gestalt psychologists or in sympathy with the ideas of the gestalt group. It was Rubin who first discussed in detail the importance of the difference between figure and ground in perception. Katz had investigated color phenomena including "color constancy." Michotte was known in later years for his study of the perception of causality. Certainly this was not what I had in mind when I suggested a cozy little meeting with Werner and Lewin, but it was an interesting and friendly get-together.

In the spring of 1930 came an evening when the psychologists and philosophers celebrated the election of Cassirer as rector of the university, an honorary office filled each year by vote of the faculty. It was at this affair that again something happened to change the course of my life. Stern asked me whether I would like to go to America, and without a moment's hesitation I said, "Yes." He explained that Kurt Koffka, who was at Smith College in Northampton, Massachusetts, was looking for someone to do research related to the education of deaf children at a school in the same city.

Stern and I assumed that my acceptance of his suggestion would mean a relatively short interruption of my Hamburg life, but what happened was far different. First, may I add that my quick decision was probably influenced by the fact that there had been a time in my boyhood when my father thought of moving his family to America. This was after the San Francisco earthquake and fire, when he thought that there would be endless opportunities there for an architect. All of us were reading books about America, "the land of limitless possibilities." In the end the plan was dropped because of my mother. She had grown up in Vienna, and

Graz, four hours away by train, already meant exile that she found hard to bear.

On August 22, 1930, I sailed and stayed a few days in New York with a feeling of exhilaration that I was actually in the fabled land about which I had read as a boy. I soon went to Northampton. Koffka was not there— the school for the deaf opened earlier in the fall than the college—but he had written me the name of one of his assistants, also connected with the school, whom he had asked to find an apartment for me and who could introduce me to the setting in which I was to work, a Miss Moore.

Smith College was one of a group of colleges for women in the Northeast known as the Seven Sisters. Its president was William Allan Neilson, a Scot, who had come to Smith College from a professorship at Harvard. He had made important contributions to the field of English literature and above all was a man of great warmth with a quick, puckish sense of humor, an outspoken liberal, and a firm believer in America as the country where beyond any other he knew, each person had the opportunity to reach the level in life to which his own abilities entitled him. As the tenth year of his presidency approached, a fund was raised to establish in his honor what was then probably unknown and is still probably rare in an undergraduate college, a chair for research. The gestalt psychologist Kurt Koffka was the first occupant of this "Neilson Chair," and it was during his five-year tenure that I joined his staff, principally to work in the research department of The Clarke School for the Deaf. This school, situated on a hill near the college, was the first major school to teach deaf children to communicate by speech and lipreading instead of finger spelling and signs. The latter, though they are more easily mastered, usually have their own grammatical structure and leave the deaf person outside the life of his own family and community. I may mention that a man who played an important part in developing the "oral" method used at The Clarke School was the Scottish phonetician Alexander Graham Bell, better known of course for his invention of the telephone. He was a member of the board of trustees of the School, for some years its president, as Neilson was when I came to Northampton.

With the plan to bring an internationally known psychologist for a five-year appointment as the first Neilson Professor, it was hoped that he would play a part, at least, in the psychological division of a research department that was being planned at the School. As all this was happening, Miss Moore, soon to be known to me as Grace, was attending nearby Mt.

Holyoke College and was an occasional visitor to the School. Her elder sister was deaf and had been educated there; and her mother, who had trained there as a teacher, at first only with the idea of teaching her own child, was nationally known among educators of the deaf. Grace graduated from Mt. Holyoke with a major in psychology that had even included special readings in what was available in gestalt psychology, just as the plan was under way for Koffka's appointment. She was promised a place in his laboratory with a hope on the part of both school and college that she would be able to interest him in the projected research department at the school.

When Koffka arrived, he visited the school with Grace and agreed to supervise the work of the psychological division of the research department, but stipulated that someone more advanced than she then was must be found to head the division on a day-to-day basis. At that time there were more positions than "takers" in the field of psychology in the United States, which meant that after a general search Koffka appealed to Stern and I was offered the position, two years after Koffka's appointment to the Neilson Chair. Grace, during that time, had been at the school, working for a master's degree before Koffka arrived and after he came making experiments with deaf children under his guidance and attending his Smith College seminar.

This meant that Grace was able to tell me a great deal about this new setting into which I had come, and her earlier acquaintance with gestalt literature and her time with Koffka's group gave us a common base for discussing the work that was going on and making plans for the next step. Our talks soon began to deal with subjects beyond the immediate scene. We talked about our past lives, our expectations and hopes for the future, and found that we agreed in many respects, surprisingly when one considers that we had grown up in what might be called completely different worlds, even speaking different languages. It did not take us long to know that we were in love, and in spite of the shock that was experienced by the school and understandably by Grace's family, we were married at the beginning of the Christmas vacation of my first year in America. My father had died in the meantime, so there was less concern among my relations. The general comment was that this could only happen in America.

In addition to our work at The Clarke School, Grace and I were members of Koffka's laboratory and attended his weekly seminar. He was a complex, intense person. He came from a family of Berlin lawyers and was a great Anglophile, admiring everything that reminded him of England. He had had an English "nanny" as a little boy and had studied at the University of Edinburgh. Whenever possible, he favored a British pronunciation over the American—he called his work place the la*bora*tory, not the *lab*oratory. He was a generous man, always giving credit to others for their contributions, however small, and had a touching admiration, a real hero worship, for Wertheimer and Köhler, with him the cofounders of the Berlin gestalt psychology.

Members of the Psychology Department of the college and some of their advanced students, as well as a scattering of people from nearby colleges, attended the weekly seminar. It was a pleasant, relaxed gathering. Koffka sat at the head of a long table in the laboratory, puffing on his pipe, packing and packing again the tobacco in its bowl. Discussions centered on the wholly or partially gestalt-oriented literature of the time, including Tolman's *Purposive Behavior in Animals and Men* (1932), Lewin's work, Köhler's, and much else. Discussions often became heated. Koffka, as I remember, accepted criticism from points of view that differed from his own except when he felt that an unfair argument was made against Köhler or Wertheimer.

The year that I came to Northampton, two new members of the laboratory staff were Tamara Dembo and Genia Hanfmann. Both had been children in Russia and had fled with their families to Germany during the upheavals at the end of World War I. I had known Tamara in Berlin when she was a student of Lewin writing her dissertation on experiments she made about anger. Genia's doctorate was taken with W. Peters in Jena.

Aside from the professional stimulation of the seminar meetings, it was through them that we came to know members of the college Psychology Department. They included Harold Israel, a Ph.D. with Boring from Harvard, therefore inheriting the German Wundtian tradition to which gestalt psychology was directly opposed, and J. J. Gibson, who was to become known for his work in perception. During the years of the seminar Gibson was often opposed to positions that Koffka took, but always in his own friendly fashion. Among the graduate assistants who took master's degrees in the department were Elsa Siipola who was to become Mrs. Israel and after a doctorate at Yale remained in the department until her retirement. In the group a year or two later was Eleanor Jack, who also went to Yale for a doctorate. She married Gibson and has recently retired from Cornell.

When I look back over my life what seems most obvious is that it is made up of two parts, the first of 34 years belonging to Europe and the second of more than 50 years to America. Since the first years of one's life seem to have greater weight than the later ones, these two parts seem to be of almost equal length when I measure them in subjective time. Every so often I have thought about the effect that this break into two parts may have had on my life. Did I experience what is now called culture shock as I moved from the first half to the second? I doubt it, since the transition was made so easy for me, first because I right away found Grace, whose ways seemed so familiar and congenial to me, and also because so many of our acquaintances at Smith College, even from the beginning, had also come from Europe. And, of course, with the Hitler era, we began to meet more and more people from that same background. Then, I believe that I sympathized with many features of American life because of my father's democratic tendencies.

Nevertheless, it is certainly true that during my first years in the new life I sometimes felt a certain unfamiliar lassitude and a lack of inspiration. I always thought that the reason was the fact that I had to use a different language from my German mother tongue and that I so often had to grope for the right words. I remember sitting in my office and trying to force myself to think up new experiments and somehow my brain refused to work. After a bit I decided to fill these ebb tides with something that I could work at without having to have new ideas so I started to learn statistics, which was still largely unknown in Europe—nobody in Berlin or Hamburg, as I remember, was familiar with it.

In the summer of 1932 we went to Europe to give Grace and my relatives a chance to get acquainted with each other, and at the end of the summer we attended a meeting of the International Psychological Congress in Copenhagen. The old tensions between Berlin and Vienna were still strong, and I remember one interesting evening when the Vienna assistants had asked me, who stood more or less outside the two groups but had friends in both, whether I could arrange a meeting with the Berlin group, especially with Köhler, whom they were extremely interested to meet. Grace and I set up a late evening gathering at one of the many Copenhagen night clubs. As I remember Otto Lauenstein and H. von Restorf from Berlin were there and Egon Brunswik, Else Frenkel, and Paul Lazarsfeld from Vienna. I have a vivid picture of how we were sitting at a table chatting as we waited for Köhler and his wife. They came in, stood for a moment looking at us before they sat down, and Köhler said, "Well, did you expect me to have horns?" There followed a good conversation, and we were sure that the Bühlers never heard of this clandestine affair.

During this summer the world was becoming more aware of the Nazi movement. Hitler suffered a couple of defeats, and people were saying that he would never recover. Unfortunately these predictions were wrong, and in less than a year he had taken over the German government. Lewin was at the end of a term as visiting professor at Stanford when the Nazis came to power. He followed his plan of returning to Germany by way of Japan and Russia, where he had speaking engagements. However, he was one of those who saw the handwriting on the wall and telegraphed several friends in this country to ask whether they know of any positions that were available. The telegram included the understandable code sentence, "Gertiland now impossible." (Gerti was the name of his wife.) But in a letter that he had already written from the train as he crossed Siberia, he said, "The idea of emigration is harder to bear than I had ever imagined."

The first omens seemed bad, but nobody dreamed how bad the situation was to become. Everyone knows the history of the next years. Köhler was in some ways one of the heroes of the period. As a pure "Aryan," professor at the major university of Berlin, and a member of the Prussian Academy, he could easily have weathered the Nazi years. At first he stayed to help his colleagues in their struggle to protect their historical "freedom to learn and to teach." Lewin wrote to me from Amsterdam in May 1933 that Köhler was the most upright of all German professors. It is probably no exaggeration to say that he risked his life by a letter that he wrote for a newspaper. He began by praising the Nazis for some of their innovations, then went on to criticize them for depriving the universities of their traditional liberties. Someone sent Koffka a copy of this letter, and he was deeply disturbed. How could his admired friend, Köhler, have acknowledged publicly that there was anything good in what the Nazis were doing? It was only gradually that we learned it was extraordinarily brave for anyone to criticize the regime, even in a letter that also praised it. In the end Köhler had to realize that it was a hopeless battle, and he left Germany for the United States. He spent his first American years at Swarthmore College.

To mention a few of the others who were best known to us: Wertheimer was soon established at the New School for Social Research in New York, which was founded to help make places for the arrivals of those years. Lewin soon obtained the backing of Lawrence K. Frank of the Laura Spellman Rockefeller Foundation and the General Education Board and was at Cornell, then at the Iowa Child Welfare Research Station; then after a time in Washington during the war, he was invited to

MIT. Stern was dismissed from Hamburg and spent his last years at Duke University. Werner ended up at Clark University, and Egon Brunswik went to Berkeley where he had visited earlier. Else Frenkel came to New York where she and Egon were married, visiting us soon after in Northampton.

Koffka, when his five years as Neilson Professor ended in 1933, became a member of the Psychology Department, where he remained teaching, completing his book *Principles of Gestalt Psychology* (1935), and continuing experimental work.

During these years when Köhler or Wertheimer came to Northampton to visit the Koffkas, we were often invited to join their gatherings and watched with great interest and pleasure the interaction between Koffka and the guest of the occasion. In spite of agreement on principles that made the collaboration of this brilliant trio so successful, there were also differences that meant that each had made his own contribution to their joint product. Wertheimer was the temperamental and inspired artist, Köhler the somewhat reserved physicist, thinking very much in spatial terms, and Koffka the highly verbal logician who tried to bring everything into a total system. As we saw them together, we had the impression that Köhler and Wertheimer did not have as great an admiration for Koffka as he for them. Nevertheless, it may easily be that his *Principles of Gestalt Psychology* will stand as the major production of that gifted group.

Koffka, as a liberal and a firm Anglophile from his youth, followed each step as the European drama unfolded, increasingly concerned as war began in the summer of 1939. It seemed ironic that he died the day before Pearl Harbor, which was followed by America's entrance into the war.

In the fall of 1933, when Lewin was at Cornell, he wrote me suggesting that we try to get a group of "younger psychologists interested in our things" together for some discussions. This led to the first meeting of the group that came to be known as the Topological Psychologists. It was held in Northampton in Koffka's laboratory and included mostly people who had become acquainted with Lewin during stays in Berlin. For later meetings Lawrence K. Frank stepped in, arranging for other participants to create interesting exchanges with the core group. I remember especially the year that he brought Edward Tolman to debate with Koffka, Köhler, and Lewin, and another meeting to which Margaret Mead and Gregory Bateson were invited. Lewin, from the beginning of his life in this country, had drawn students and postdoctoral fellows who were to become leaders in the years to come. Grace and I came to know many of the outstanding American psychologists as we attended the meetings as often as we could until the final one some years after Lewin's death in 1947.

I should go back to our work at The Clarke School. Koffka remained director of our research, but once Grace had completed the studies she began with him before I came, he left us very much to follow our own inclinations, standing ready for consultation when we needed advice. Over the next years we worked on a series of problems that appeared as "Studies in the Psychology of the Deaf" (1940, 1941). Along with these formal studies were insights that contributed to my continuing interest in interpersonal relations. Indeed, one may say that deafness, because it affects means of communication, is eminently a social handicap as compared with blindness, which is more directly a handicap in relation to physical space.

My duties at The Clarke School and at Smith College, where I had soon begun teaching a seminar in psychological experimentation, left me time to work after hours on the more abstract problems that continued to concern me. I published an article "Environmental Determinants of Psychological Theories" (1939), which deals with a number of theories in terms of differences in the ways in which they organize their data, with the distinction between proximal and distal stimuli playing an important role in specifying these differences. It is evident that this paper grew out of "Thing and Medium," written ten years earlier. And I realize now that it also deals with the role of *attribution* in psychological theories, something that would be presented more explicitly in the book that I was to publish almost twenty years later.

In 1936 we acquired a little farm near a Vermont village and found ourselves neighbors of the New York philosophers Ernest Nagel and Sidney Hook. Then came the war years, which we spent mostly in Northampton, having given up the farm as too expensive for us at that time. One pleasant event of those years was a visit with Lewin to the laboratory of Adelbert Ames in Hanover, New Hampshire. Ames had discovered a defect in vision called aniseikonia and, with Rockefeller support, established an eye clinic near Dartmouth College. I found Ames's experiments highly pertinent to the distinction between distal and proximal stimuli that had been part of my own thinking. I could not agree with some of Ames's theory, which leaned heavily on Helmholtz's ideas about the role of experience, but I cannot help feeling that his experiments should occupy a central place in "ecological" treatments of perception. They certainly demolish any theory that would contend that we always see distal objects in their true shapes.

During this time my interest was coming to center more and more on questions related to interpersonal relations, and I was very much aware of the fact that the starting points for theorizing in this area were all around me. Everybody has his not-yet-systematized thoughts about other people, his concepts about love and power, benefit and harm, and when I say everybody, I do not exclude rat psychologists. But how to grasp all that systematically? When I read nonscientific literature—novels, stories, plays—I often ask myself right away, "What do these expressions of ordinary language really imply? How do they relate to each other? Do they form a system in which each term has a defined place?" I soon saw that topology as it had been developed by Lewin did not help much with the description of processes going on between persons: it is often a question of dealing with two or more interacting life spaces at the same time, not with the single life that topology describes. But the success of Lewin's topology in representing action stimulated me anew to search for a conceptual tool that could be equally useful in clearing up the concepts whose apparent opaqueness was bothering me.

I did not abandon what I had learned from Lewin and Cassirer, that in order to make progress in science one has to find some systematic way of representing one's material. In the search for such a tool I drove to New Haven through one autumn to attend Clark Hull's weekly seminar at Yale to see whether something of his approach would help me with what I was trying to do. Hull's name is now almost forgotten except for a small circle of older psychologists. In the 1930's and 1940's he was one of the most influential teachers. Every respectable psychologist who wanted to be taken seriously had to speak in terms of his concepts of drive reduction, goal responses, and so on. It is very hard to believe now, but at that time there were many who thought that Hull would be the American Newton of psychology. For a time there was a loose connection between Hull and Lewin. In spite of differences in the content of what they thought of as psychology, they found common ground in their emphasis on the importance of using theory as a starting point in attacking a problem—Hull in what he called his hypothetico-deductive method and Lewin in his less formal maxim that "nothing is as practical as a good theory."

It was in the hope that I might be able to use some of Hull's ideas for the representation I needed for my thinking about interpersonal relations that I made these trips, but I soon realized that the empirical base of his rat experiments was too meager and derived from a too simplistic theory to deal with the rich give-and-take of everyday human experience. Today one has difficulty remembering the degree to which the laboratory rat once dominated American psychology, when even such a humane and thoughtful man as Edward Tolman dedicated his book on the behavior of animals and men to the white rat. I returned to the arduous work of clearing up the simple common-sense concepts that we use in thinking about people and their relations to each other. I did not yet have a definite plan to write a book dealing with these subjects. I just wanted to make my own thinking more definite and precise, and to sharpen the mental tools that I had to use. I spent long years explicating the meaning of words used to refer to everyday experiences and in analyzing the content of short stories, fables, novels, and plays, always trying to translate the content into concepts that could fit into a larger network of concepts.

Henry Murray's book on *Explorations in Personality* came out in 1938, and it seemed to let in a ray of true life compared with the rat experiments of the day. I soon was able to show that eight of Murray's needs could be seen as a connected system. In the end I realized that I could not use his concepts as such in spite of the fact that they were based on good observations and not on abstract speculations. First, he failed to suspect that there were systematic connections between them; and second, he stuck to the simple paradigm of a single entity, the person, and some kind of force in the person. It is better to use another paradigm, namely a schema with two or more entities and some kind of relation between them. Finally, I worked out a system of notation for myself that makes the relations between concepts more obvious, and I used it for a number of years, though it does not allow for predictions as Lewin's topology does. There is a brief description of it at the end of *The Psychology of Interpersonal Relations* (1958).

It was only gradually that I came to a firmer understanding of the direction in which I had to proceed and began to use new experiences as steps in that direction. At first I was conscious of it only in a limited sense. The 1944 paper entitled "An Experimental Study of Apparent Behavior," which I wrote with Marianne Simmel, then my student at Smith College, belongs to this period in which I was working toward a goal of which I was very much aware but had not yet fully defined. This study is based on descriptions made by groups of subjects of a short moving picture in which three simple geometric figures, a large triangle, a smaller triangle, and a circle, are seen to move about a field.

The principal result of the analyses of the moving picture descriptions was that movements—behavior if you like—of even simple, unchanging forms can produce a compelling impression of interpersonal events and attitudes. That same year my ideas began to take shape further in a paper entitled "Social Perception and Phenomenal Causality" (1944), in which I suggested that Wertheimer's unit-forming factors (similarity, proximity, etc.) may not only be "unit-forming" but often serve to produce the impression of causality as well. That would mean, for instance, that two phenomena that are similar are more likely to be seen as connected by a causal relation than two that are dissimilar: one is easily led to attribute a bad deed to a person who himself is considered bad. These ideas led me to the formulation of the balance hypothesis in a paper entitled "Attitudes and Cognitive Organization" (1946). I began to think, again in gestalt terms, of a general tendency to prefer orderly and consistent arrangements to those that are less orderly and that can less easily be perceived as units.

I may mention that on the way to this point I found Spinoza's *Ethics* a help. It is a truly remarkable book and has two features that were especially relevant to my gropings. First, it tries to represent its subject matter in a systematic way; and second, among other topics, it deals with interpersonal relations in a number of propositions that fitted in with my own "commonsense" approach.

During World War II, I became more and more involved in teaching at Smith College. This, along with what had become part-time work at The Clarke School, took up most of my time and energy during the academic year, and the summer vacations did not give me enough time to deal with the ideas that I was gradually developing. Somehow my brain does not seem to be a very efficient organ. It generates some acceptable products, but only after periods of leisurely dreaming and inactive somnolence. I am not a person of great energy, and the thinking that goes on in the head always seems to be without my personal participation. Nietzsche's words that one should say "It thinks" not "I think" seem very much to fit my case and the life I was leading did not seem to give "it" much opportunity. I became more and more discouraged.

Gradually during this time I came to the idea of writing a book on interpersonal relations, but if I was to do that I needed more unbroken stretches of free time. To get this I would need some sort of grant, and after a few trials it became clear that none of the foundations would accept a proposal for the kind of "conceptual research" that I wanted time to deal with. This was a period of tension and anxiety for me, but several events changed the picture. We spent the summer of 1946 on Martha's Vineyard in a small house with an open garage where I worked in the fresh ocean air, a good change from my big third floor study. We had a number of visitors that summer, including the Lewins and later Rudy Arnheim, a friend from my Berlin days who was deep in studies of art based to a large extent on gestalt psychological ideas. But most important, as regards my immediate situation and difficulties, was a visit from Elisabeth Koffka. She knew what I was trying to do and had an immediate answer for my problem. I remain deeply grateful to her for suggesting it. She said that I should apply for a Guggenheim Fellowship. Köhler knew my work, he was on the board, and she was sure that he would back my application.

I went back to Northampton in a hopeful mood and sent in the application. Then came another development. Roger Barker, whom we had known for some years from the Lewin meetings, was at nearby Clark University as G. Stanley Hall Professor of Psychology, and we often met with the Barkers for dinner someplace between Worcester and Northampton. On one of these occasions he came up with an unexpected question: would we consider moving to Kansas? He had been offered the chairmanship at the University of Kansas and would like to go if he could get some of his friends, by which he meant people of the Lewin group, to go with him. We realized right away that this could give me what I needed after the years at Smith College, an opportunity to teach graduate students with whom I could develop my own thoughts as well as present the basic ideas of the field. I accepted right away, as casually as I had decided at the celebration in Hamburg to come to America.

In Kansas we especially enjoyed the pleasant atmosphere of our relatively small Psychology Department. Those of us who had been associated with Lewin (and our wives) had known each other for some years, at least from meetings of the "Topologists." Roger Barker, with a doctorate from Stanford, and Herbert Wright from Duke University had been postdoctoral fellows in Lewin's Iowa group. They soon selected a small town near Lawrence and moved there to pioneer a study of "psychological ecology," which attempts to describe the psychologically relevant features of the environments in which people live. One of the younger men who was already in the department, Anthony Smith, chose to throw in his lot with the newcomers and was soon a good friend.

Martin Scheerer, whom I had known when he was still a student at Hamburg, joined us the next year. He had been a student of Stern and Cassirer and was intimately familiar with gestalt psychology. His Hamburg thesis (Scheerer, 1931) was an interesting critique of gestalt theories from the Hamburg point of view, which stressed Stern's personalism and Cassirer's neo-Kantianism. Martin was a very welcome connection with my European past. He was a close friend until his sudden death in the fall of 1961.

In 1949 another friend from the Topological meetings, Alfred Baldwin, joined us. He had been a graduate student at Harvard when Lewin was visiting professor there a few years earlier. And two years after that Beatrice and Erik Wright came. They had been graduate students with Lewin in Iowa when Roger and Herbert were postdoctoral fellows. Beatrice had worked with Roger on a monograph about psychological aspects of physical handicap while Erik added an M.D. and a medical residency to his Iowa Ph.D. He remained a warm friend to our family and to many, and a tower of strength in the University and community until his unbelievably sudden death in the spring of 1981.

Another aspect of our life in Kansas was our friendship with members of the psychoanalytically oriented Menninger Foundation in Topeka. David Rapaport was someone we had met years before, when he attended a meeting of Koffka's seminar, and we were soon friends, getting together with him and Sybille Escalona every few weeks for discussions. The parents of Bille, as she was known, had been friends of the Lewins in Berlin, and she had spent her first years in this country with the Lewin family in Iowa.

We also came to know George Klein and his wife, Bessie, a gifted artist. I think of George as one of the psychologists who most completely understood the different aspects of my thinking. Incidentally, he played an important part later in arranging the publication both of my book on interpersonal relations and of a series of papers, going back to "Ding und Medium" in its English translation.

As the Menninger Foundation psychologists whom we knew when we were first in Kansas moved on to centers elsewhere, others came who became friends. I think especially of Gardner and Lois Murphy; Gardner the warm, wise, and effective person whose broad interests had made him a major figure in several important fields of psychology, and Lois a creative pioneer in child psychology who began a study on which Grace worked for several years.

During my first year in Kansas the Guggenheim fellowship allowed me to devote my whole time to thinking and writing what I was becoming more certain would be a book on interpersonal relations. As I have told, I had collected a formidable mass of examples that seemed relevant to a study of events involving two or more persons. These events were described in commonsense language, and I felt they had to be mulled over and meditated on. Always what kept me going was the strong conviction that these simple commonsense words did not represent a mass of chaotic, unrelated meanings but that in spite of the many different kinds of relations among them there must be some sort of system of which they are parts, even though it was not quite visible at first glance.

I have mentioned that I soon found that topology was not very helpful in solving my problem of describing events involving two or more people, but I have the feeling that it stayed with me as a model for the kind of thing I wanted to do. I cannot say that I intended to produce a general "theory of interpersonal relations"; what I was trying to do first was to elucidate the excellent commonsense descriptions of behavior by bringing some sort of conceptual clarity to them. One way of studying the commonsense concepts that I found taking shape was to line them up and look at each one in the light of others. The poet Donne has said, "No man is an island"—so one can also say of the concepts dealing with interpersonal relations, "They are not islands; *they show their full meaning only in interaction with others.*" There is a complicated network, a system hidden in these seemingly "simple" concepts that is a wonderful instrument for capturing the subtle meanings of human happenings and states.

For example, when I want to get a clearer idea of the concept of "ought," I am not satisfied with just steeping myself in thoughts about this word "ought" as such. I try to make some mental experiments to get an idea of what I mean when I use this word. What consequences does it have when I think, "He ought to do x—but he does not do it"? And then what are the relations between "ought" and the possibility concepts? Can one say, "He ought to do x," when x is impossible for him to do? I asked myself such questions in order to get some understanding of the unformulated theories about human behavior that I was convinced are latent in the words of our everyday lives. And to look forward in my account, I may add that in the first chapter of the book that appeared ten years later, I tried to explain these attempts to understand the deeper meanings of simple language, and as one example I used an analysis of words referring to interpersonal relations in one of the simple fables that was part of my working materials.

All this is part of what I was doing during that first year in Kansas when the Guggenheim freed me of ordinary work obligations, but in the fall of 1948, when I began teaching, the book was still not finished. One boost came when Alfred Baldwin began reading rough drafts of chapters of the still unnamed volume. He had them mimeographed and sent copies to a few people who might be interested. Then one summer Sidney and Ann Hook, friends from our Vermont days, stopped on a trip west. Sidney and I, of course, talked about the progress of my work and my discouragement about getting it into the final form in which I would want it to appear. Sidney, knowing more about these things than I did from the vantage point of his New York life, suggested what had never occurred to me, that since I had had one Guggenheim Fellowship, it would be a simple matter to get a second to complete the work that was under way from the first—so that is what I did. And, by this time, other foundations were more open to my nonexperimental approach, and I was able to get funding for an assistant to help with the final preparation of the chapters that were to form the book. Here I had incredible good fortune: Beatrice Wright, who, like Grace, was not allowed to teach because of nepotism rulings and who was not yet deep in her own book, agreed to work with me on a half-time basis for a year. With her help the task came to an end and in 1958 Wiley published *The Psychology of Interpersonal Relations*.

As the book became known, there were invitations to visit other departments. In the spring of 1959 I taught at Cornell. Then after a year at home in Kansas we were at the University of Oslo for a year, I on a Fulbright Fellowship, and Grace on one from the National Institute of Mental Health. We were able to visit the Heider family home in the country near Graz that first summer and see relatives who gathered there, including the cousin whose allowance had been a turning point in my fortunes so many years before. And there was another meeting of the International Congress of Psychology at which we were again with friends from both sides of the ocean.

In 1965 I received the American Psychological Association's Distinguished Scientific Award and was especially pleased because our old friend, James Gibson, who had the task of presenting the awards that year, spoke of my "trailblazing thoughts about the fundamentals of perception" and said that I had shown "long ago the puzzle of the relation of things to their stimuli." I took that to mean that he had at least partly accepted the contention in "Thing and Medium" that it is important for psychology to consider the "ecological" conditions.

I continued teaching until 1966 when I reached Kansas's then mandatory retirement age of 70. I had enjoyed teaching and my years of contact with graduate students whose master's theses and doctoral dissertations developed ideas with which I had been working for so long. Here I especially want to mention Nehemiah Jordan, whose dissertation dealt with "balance theory" and who has continued in his own energetic way to explore basic psychological and now philosophical ideas over the years. But in spite of the satisfaction of teaching I was glad to be free to devote myself to the ideas that had come to me since the book appeared.

All through the years I have been making notes about problems that I am trying to think through. I always have a little sheet of paper and a pencil stub in my pocket during the day and by my bed at night so as to be able to jot down the thoughts that come to me. Otherwise they often seem to fade away and get lost. Once preserved in this way, they were safe, and I have expanded them, classified them to some extent, and copied them into notebooks. Actually the book on interpersonal relations grew out of such notes, which I finally got time to put together properly. With the book completed I began a new collection. Some of these have appeared in papers that I wrote over the next years and many more repose in a row of perhaps fifteen large loose-leaf notebooks that stand on a shelf in my Lawrence study. I have, of course, found real satisfaction in the fact that some of my ideas about interpersonal relations, so far chiefly those about balance and attribution, have proved useful to others, and I may add that I have been a little surprised that the thing-medium distinction has not been picked up in current studies of perception, but that may still come.

With this chapter completed and a longer version that I could not resist writing for my three sons and psychologist friends, I shall turn back to those volumes of notes and see what I can do to make them more comprehensible than they are in their original form. And in the meantime, I take great pleasure in knowing that Marijana Benesh-Weiner, wife of Bernard Weiner, professor of psychology at UCLA, became interested in the notes and decided that they should be printed. She did the long and laborious task of editing them and Volume I, entitled *Methods, Principles, and Philosophy of Science* has already appeared, with five more volumes to follow.

Selected Publications by Fritz Heider

(1926). Ding und Medium. *Symposion, 1*, 109–157.
(1930). Die Leistung des Wahrnehmungssystems. *Zeitschrift für Psychologie, 114*, 371–419.
(1939). Environmental determinants of psychological theories. *Psychological Review, 46*, 383–410.
(with G. M. Heider) (1940). Studies in the psychology of the deaf. *Psychological Monographs, 52*(1), 1–153.
(with G. M. Heider) (1941). Studies in the psychology of the deaf. *Psychological Monographs, 55*(5), 1–158.
(1944). Social perception and phenomenal causality. *Psychological Review, 51*, 358–374.
(with M. Simmel) (1944). An experimental study of apparent behavior. *American Journal of Psychology, 57*, 243–259.
(1946). Attitudes and cognitive organization. *Journal of Psychology, 21*, 107–112.
(1958). *The psychology of interpersonal relations*. New York: Wiley.
(1959a). On perception and event structure, and the psychological environment. *Psychological Issues, 1*(3), 1–123.
(1959b). On Lewin's method and theory. *Journal of Social Issues*, Suppl. 13.
(1960). The gestalt theory of motivation. In M. R. Jones (Ed.), *The Nebraska Symposium on Motivation* (pp. 145–172). Lincoln: University of Nebraska Press.
(1970). Gestalt theory: Early history and reminiscences. *Journal of the History of the Behavioral Sciences, 6*(2), 131–139.

Other Publications Cited

Koffka, K. (1935). *Principles of gestalt psychology*. New York: Harcourt Brace.
Köhler, W. (1920). *Die physischen Gestalten in Ruhe und im stationären Zustand*. Braunschweig.
Marrow, A. (1969). *The practical theorist: The life and work of Kurt Lewin*. New York: Basic Books.
Meinong, A. (1906). Ueber die Erfahrungsgrundlagen unseres Wissens. Sonderheft der *Zeitschrift für den physikalischen und chemischen Unterricht*, Heft 6.

Murray, H. A. (1938). *Explorations in personality*. New York: Oxford University Press.

Russell, B. (1948). *Human knowledge*. New York: Simon and Schuster.

Scheerer, M. (1931). *Die Lehre von der Gestalt*. Berlin: de Gruyter.

Tolman, E. C. (1932). *Purposive behavior in animals and men*. New York: Century.

Leo M. Hurvich

Dorothea Jameson

Leo M. Hurvich and Dorothea Jameson

How does a freshman know what his life's work is to be? Yet there it was below a classmate's picture in the class album: "Intended Occupation, Museum Curator." Leo's own career thoughts were polarized only negatively. He knew only that he was not headed for medical school, which was surely his parents' hope, although rarely mentioned and even then never hard pressed.

Leo's college start was a wobbly one. His admission was delayed until late in the summer of 1928, and since it had simply never occurred to him as a good student growing up in nearby Chelsea—a small working-class suburb of Boston—that he would go to some college other than Harvard, he had applied nowhere else. The wait was an uneasy one. Once admitted and finished with registration, he stopped by to see his assigned freshman advisor, a geologist named Kirk Bryan. Their exchange in capsule form: Had Leo's father gone to college? No. What was his occupation? Painter and paperhanger. Why didn't Leo follow in his footsteps? Leo was dumbfounded and doesn't remember what he said, but he is sure there was an element of truculence in his reply. They never met again, and it's safe to say that Professor Bryan never knew that when Leo graduated, it was with high honors and election to Phi Beta Kappa.

Leo's very first day in school was also a traumatic one. He was born on September 11, 1910, the second of two boys in another Boston suburb, Malden. On his sixth birthday, primed by his parents for the delights of schooling, he started school. When the very first class ended he was caught whistling exuberantly in the cloakroom as he was putting on his coat to leave for home and made to "stay after school." He returned home in tears, disgraced. From this lowest of lows there was nowhere to go but up, and his memories of school thereafter are on the whole pleasant ones. But he has never forgotten two male teachers in grade school who on separate occasions each mistreated one awkward and difficult youngster who surely must have been what we now recognize as dyslexic. And in high school, a mathematics teacher, again a male, bore down mercilessly on a female student who simply could not get the hang of geometry. It took some of the enjoyment out of this, for Leo, most exciting subject.

Leo's parents had come to the United States in the early 1900's from Eastern Europe and were married in Boston. His father grew up in Vilnius in Russian Poland, and his mother in a not too distant village across the "border" in Russian Lithuania. They came from large families, and Leo got to know most of his aunts and uncles and cousins, those in the States and those who had moved to Paris. But he never met either set of grandparents, who were alive as he was growing up; he knew them only through photographs. His parents were alike in many ways. They had little formal education, were bright, warm, had a good sense of humor, liked people, and held strong social and political views. His father had been a youthful, mischievous rebel. He was fun loving and relaxed, liked to play cards, particularly pinochle, and was a nature lover: birds, dogs, plants. His mother, who had grown up in a hostile village environment, tended to be more serious and frowned on some of his father's "frivolities." Among these was the small copper still with which, during Prohibition, he distilled driblets of vodka from potato mash for his pre-supper shot. She found this operation disconcerting, especially on one occasion when there was a minor "explosion" in the bathtub. He earned what could be called a "decent living," and when his trade slackened off, he supplemented his earnings by peddling fruit and vegetables in the Greater Boston area. His language facility was a big help here.

Leo's parents moved to Chelsea before his first birthday, and when his brother Maurice was about five years old—Leo has no memory of him whatsoever—he was burned to death playing with firecrackers. Leo was two and a half years old and effectively became an only child and then some. He was no doubt spoiled, but his strongest memories are of an excessive protectiveness on his mother's part and a constant monitoring of any activity that implied bodily harm. He was physically very active and could roller skate to exhaustion on the concrete sidewalks, for example, but was never given a bicycle, which would have taken him into the streets.

His parents had gone to "night school" and learned to read and write English, and as with all upwardly mobile immigrant parents, schooling was a top priority. It seemed to be a given that Leo was to do well in school, be on his good behavior, study hard, play the violin, etc. Some of his grade school teachers can be fairly characterized as eccentric, but as he looks back at them they were all well educated and committed to standards and goals of excellence that he picked up long before he got to college. As is so often the case, they and many of his high school teachers were better teachers by far than the young instructors who confronted, or nervously turned their back on, the class in college. He enjoyed languages, history, and mathematics, but had little science in high school. Nor was he a bookworm as a youngster. His reading was limited to books assigned in school and "boys books" he took out of the library. There were, of course, the usual hack items that circulated among his peers. If nothing else, they concentrated one's attention. He read and reread parts of a three-volume encyclopedia, given him as a child, until it fell apart. Later he was given a set of the Harvard Classics but confesses here that he never made it through the entire Five-Foot Shelf despite Charles W. Eliot's endorsements.

During all his school years in Chelsea he and his parents (and occasionally a relative) lived in a three-story tenement complex with two facing U-like elements which housed eighteen families of different ethnic backgrounds. This odd-shaped set of buildings meant linked porches (an Armenian family lived next to them for fourteen years), and facing porches (across which he "spoke" for many years with a deaf mute, the older brother of one of his schoolmates, in a sign language). The housing complex stood kitty-corner to the massive grammar school he attended — the grounds and structure covered a full city block—and it was abutted by a small park on one side, and on the other by an imposing Congregational Church. There were dozens of younger and older children of neighbors as well as cousins in Chelsea and Malden as playmates. Leo attended summer school sessions in the church, where he learned basket weaving and chair caning and joined in rousing renditions of "Onward Christian Soldiers." He joined the YMCA for swimming pool activities and basketball teams in the winter and in the summer went to Revere Beach, some three or so miles from Chelsea, with his male friends. They knew precisely where the girls from their school congregated.

Leo saw all the famous actors of the Yiddish theater with his parents and, as he grew up, went into Boston for pre-Broadway tryouts, Boston Pops concerts, and Boston Symphony Orchestra concerts. He recalls attending a childhood performance of Yehudi Menuhin in Symphony Hall, intended, of course, to inspire him. But neither that concert nor the efforts of three violin teachers—the last, a French horn player(!) at the New England Conservatory of Music—helped him get beyond the high school orchestra. Grade school and high school drama roles and even a later post–World War II one were fun but always only a minor diversion. He went to the movies frequently and, oddly, usually by himself. Maybe one could cry more openly seeing Lillian Gish carried away on the ice floes if one were alone, or give way to fantasy more easily when Louise Brooks appeared on the scene.

Unlike his closest friends and acquaintances, Leo grew up in a context dominated by his parents' overriding interest in and commitment to socialism. His mother's village environment was a backward one where she had been taught to read Yiddish, for example, on the sly by an older woman. His father, who literally walked off a railroad station platform and into the woods to escape the tsar's draft and had, as a child, been exposed to the conventional male upbringing and gone to Hebrew school— he knew the cat-o'-nine-tails well—was contemptuous of institutional religious doctrine and openly critical of the "hypocrites" surrounding them. His father would occasionally buttress his attitudes by quoting biblical passages in Hebrew or Russian and then translate them into English before dissecting them. Leo never knew either of his parents to set foot in a synagogue. He did, but only to satisfy his curiosity. Leo was left, unfortunately, with some major cultural gaps to fill in later, but he has had no reason to question the rightness of his parents' judgments in religious matters then or now.

When he was in high school, Leo helped his father during the summer months and acquired some proficiency in paperhanging. However unwittingly, his "freshman advisor" had touched a sensitive spot. Leo recalls being sent to pay his father's union dues at the AFL business office on Washington Street in Boston and has vivid recollections of brick throwing near their house in Chelsea when the Walton Shoe Factory nearby was on strike. He can still see the scabs being shielded by police with drawn guns, as well as the scared young daughter of a neighbor who was driven home daily in the telephone company's automobile when she was scabbing as an operator.

His parents belonged to the Workmen's Circle, and the Labor Lyceum building in Bellingham Square, which was a quarter of a mile up the street from where they lived, was the focal point for the socialists' gatherings—serious and social. Leo attended countless Sunday morning business meetings in a large auditorium and listened to the right- and left-wingers mutually demolish each other's positions under the stern gaze of a large portrait of Karl Marx that hung behind the chairman's podium. The content was often way beyond him, but the charged scenes stay with him. There were also social functions, poetry readings, and visiting lecturers. He attended the Volkschule to learn to read and write Yiddish and to study Jewish cultural history. (Years later Gordon Allport asked him if he had any interest in teaching a psychology course in an educational program being offered by a local socialist group. Leo was agreeable and found himself teaching an elementary course in the very same Labor Lyceum building where he had spent many youthful hours.)

This was social and political indoctrination by observation and osmosis. But these unthinking beginnings found later support in lots of reading, particularly the reading he did for course papers in college. He remembers spending countless days in the Business School library "researching" several of them. He will, of course, be accused of reading selectively, but after the 1929 Wall Street crash and a debate on the merits of socialism versus capitalism in his section meeting of Taussig's economics course was resolved by a 19 to 1 vote in favor of socialism, he had all the support he needed! But this is getting ahead of the story.

Having walked out on his official freshman advisor, Leo was essentially on his own. (Would he have become a geologist had his advisor been the least bit sympathetic?) But with the concentration-distribution requirements in place at Harvard in his freshman year, his course choices were restricted mainly to alternatives (e.g., a science among sciences, etc.), and he took elementary Greek as his one free elective. This was the smallest of his classes, probably eight or so students, but beyond a nod he did not get to interact with any of them. Leo was a commuter, and by and large commuters lived in a world apart from the students in the freshman dormitories and upper classmen who lived in the Yard. The commuters generally congregated in Phillips Brooks House where they socialized, discussed course work, argued, and ate lunches brought from home. Leo occasionally joined this group but more often lunched at crowded local restaurants like the Georgian or Hazens in Harvard Square.

Leo was on tuition scholarships for most of his undergraduate years, but with finances always tight he took on part-time jobs available in the University. He helped with registration procedures, ushered at football games, worked on the "dog carts" carrying water and equipment for the athletic teams, and later proctored exams. Extracurricular activities were out of the question. He made no new close friendships during his undergraduate days and continued to see his old high school chums. There was a freshman physical educational requirement, and most of his friendships at Harvard were made on the basketball court and lacrosse field. He played in the goal in lacrosse and by his senior year got so skillful and cocky that he played without any padding and even without a mask. This was foolhardy to say the least. But like a youthful stint setting up duck pins that flew wildly in the air in a bowling alley and electing to play catcher in sandlot baseball, he sees this behavior as an overreaction to his overprotection in physical matters as a child.

Harvard boasted a lot of "greats" when Leo was an undergraduate, and he faithfully took notes in the large lecture courses they gave. He has no way of knowing what ultimate impact the "greats" had on his subsequent career. Interactions and events in small section classes with largely unknown Ph.D. candidates who were the instructors have left more readily accessible memories. But there is little question that Harvard introduced him into a new world, both intellectual and physical. It is epitomized by the contrast between the beautiful, comfortable Farnsworth reading room in Widener Library and the small leftist library in the Chelsea Labor Lyceum.

It seemed natural when it came to choosing a major that the Department of Social Ethics was his niche. His introduction to it was Richard Cabot's course in social ethics. (Cabot was a wealthy Boston Brahmin, an eminent cardiologist, a philanthropist, and Professor of Social Ethics.) In addition to the usual lectures and weekly section meetings, this course was distinguished by periodic field trips to nearby social institutions. Visits to the "insane asylum" at Tewksbury and to the Charlestown State Prison have left Leo with images of the inmates and physical facilities that no book reading could ever convey. The executions of Sacco and Vanzetti in the State Prison only two years prior to the visit there and President Lowell's role in the case were very much live issues for Leo at the time.

Harvard's individual tutorial system had been established, and though he remembers his tutors well, their efforts left little trace on him. This is in contrast to Pitirim Sorokin, who came in 1930 to head the new Sociology Department. Sorokin's background (he had been a member of the Kerensky government during the Russian revolution and was banished by the Bolsheviks), his strong opinions delivered in a heavy Russian accent, and his iconoclasm created quite a stir. But of all Leo's sociology courses, the most memorable was a small one with Thomas Nixon Carver, an economist. Carver's conservative, anti-environmentalist views stirred strong reactions from many of the students, but he welcomed give and take exchanges in class as he argued not so much that might makes right but that it would prevail in any event. He now seems wiser than when he seemed to enjoy egging on the youthful idealists.

Leo was sailing along smoothly and blandly as a sociology major until Gordon Allport appeared on the scene in 1930 as an assistant professor in psychology. Leo signed up for his social psychology course in which Gordon used his brother Floyd Allport's text. It was in this small class that Leo suddenly became aware of the individual and something called the "reflex arc." He was instantly hooked. In the following year Allport suggested that he undertake a review and critique of Vilfredo Pareto's 1916 "Trattato di sociologica generale" for his senior honors thesis. It was then available in a two-volume translation from the Italian into French by Bosanquet, and Leo read French with ease. Allport was especially concerned with Pareto's analysis of social action into its rational and irrational aspects, and Leo's thesis sought to put this into its psychological context. Allport urged him to publish his undergraduate thesis, but he was not convinced that his demonstration that Pareto's "residues and derivations" were essentially the psychologists' "instincts and rationalizations" warranted publication. Unless his memory tricks him, he believes that shortly thereafter William McDougall published a paper making precisely that point.

In addition to Allport's social psychology course Leo's only other undergraduate psychology course was Henry A. Murray's abnormal psychology. It was here that he was introduced to Freud, witnessed Murray's hypnosis of a student who dramatically carried out a post-hypnotic suggestion, studied the list of Needs, all carefully arrayed in separate folders on the shelves of the clinic library, and served as an undergraduate subject in the development of what he believes turned into the Thematic Apperception Test. Murray has written of himself that he was not much of a teacher. Leo enters a demurrer here. Donald MacKinnon, who spelled Murray as lecturer, might have been more systematic and extensive in his coverage, but Murray had the style and the flair which his periodic stutter served only to enhance.

There had never been any doubt that Leo would return to graduate school to work with Allport following his graduation and summer job in 1932. He no longer remembers whether that was the summer he assisted in a hat store, drove an ice cream delivery truck or chauffered a businessman and worked in a fireworks store. (It was not the summer he sold produce from a horse-drawn wagon; that was 1929.) After his undergraduate degree, it was obvious that commuting was wasteful of time and energy, and it was just as obvious that he needed to get away from his parents' home. They had by that time moved to a section of Boston called Mattapan, and he resolved to move to Cambridge. Most of his graduate school years were spent in Perkins Hall, where he had several roommates from different disciplines. Oscar Handlin was among them, and Leo saw him and his wife Mary frequently in later years when they became affiliated with the History Department. He also got a little taste of dormitory life and learned to play tennis on the courts of Jarvis Field, which lay behind Perkins Hall and is now the site of the Graduate Center. But it was his year there in 1933–34 with Alfred H. Holway that had the greatest impact on his life and career, though that part of the story comes later.

Allport wanted Leo to get the departmental requirements out of the way as quickly as possible so that he might move on to a research project, and they did start a small joint study in Leo's first year (1932–33). Each of them rated the same subjects on a set of traits following an interview that lasted precisely five minutes. Their judgments were to be evaluated against the results of a more extensive study. Not surprisingly there was little agreement between Allport and Leo. Allport summarized the project with the statement that the ratings were more revealing of each of the interviewers than of the interviewees.

To get the preliminary exams behind him—his only two psychology courses to that point having been social and abnormal—Allport advised that he take one of Boring's systematic courses, statistics, and Carroll Pratt's Psychology 9. At one point during a conference Allport asked Leo how the psychophysics course with Carroll Pratt was coming along. Leo was more than baffled. He was having a thoroughly enjoyable time in Pratt's aesthetics course, with its emphasis on music and its meaning, and psychophysics seemed to play no role in it whatsoever. When the smoke cleared away it turned out that Allport had intended that Leo sign up for Psychology 11 (psychophysics) instead of 9 (aesthetics) but had never used a descriptive term in their conversation. Nor was Leo particularly surprised that when he joined other students to discuss possible questions that might appear on the upcoming preliminary exams, he drew complete blanks, even though he was by then immersed in an animal behavior course and Boring's history of psychology. He anticipated no "courtesy passes," so he postponed the exams for that year and took and passed the prelims in his second year.

Among the younger instructors when Leo arrived were John Volkmann, Dwight Chapman, Merle Elliot, and Hadley Cantril; a number of young instructors came thereafter for short periods, only to roll off to make room for replacements. The department was weak in learning, but efforts to bolster this part of the curriculum never seemed to take. Beebe-Center was the workhorse of the department as far as course teaching was concerned. His sensory lectures were based heavily on Troland's volumes, and in those days before photocopying, he spent many hours working up new material from journal articles that he studied and assiduously made notes on in Robbins Library. His other courses were in what was then called "higher mental processes" and "P and U" (pleasantness and unpleasantness). He remained on the staff for years as a lecturer, and rumor had it that, independently wealthy, he was not salaried.

Boring's courses always had an element of pretentiousness. He seemed bent on making the material appear deeper and more abstruse than it was. In contrast to the instructor whose role it was to elucidate the text, the professor, he once wrote Leo, should presuppose and transcend it. "University Hall," he wrote, "does not expect me to be a good teacher." Leo learned early on that Boring was more aggrieved to have a historical error pointed out in his book *The History of Experimental Psychology* than he was satisfied to have the datum set right. Leo then kept his errata list to himself, particularly after his experience in Boring's history seminar, where he refused to accept Leo's report that Helmholtz, in an 1852 paper, had rejected Young's three-component color vision theory (Hurvich and Jameson, 1949). In another of Boring's seminars Leo stirred up a lot of commotion and annoyance by presenting a paper on the color vision of the rat, only to conclude that rats had none, thus confounding the expectation he had apparently set up in his listeners!

Elek Ludvigh was the most intriguing of the graduate student group that included, among others, Smitty Stevens, Eddie Newman, Nathan E. Cohen, Jerome D. Frank and Douglas McGregor. Elek was a huge fellow, brilliant and erudite, who spoke with a Texas accent—or so it sounded to Leo's inexperienced ear. He was working on a thesis with Beebe-Center in Pleasantness and Unpleasantness when Leo first met him. This seemed puzzling, since Elek appeared to be expert in matters visual. And indeed, immediately after receiving his degree in 1934, he became an instructor in ophthalmology in the Howe Laboratories associated with the Massachusetts General Hospital. It was there that Leo watched him and Eugene McCarthy (a colorful, chain-smoking, nonstop sardonic commentator and former assistant to Troland) make what became the standard measures of the selective absorption of the human eye media (Ludvigh and McCarthy, 1938). These data continue to be reproduced in the visual literature along with recent determinations. Their agreement with the more recent measurements is astonishing. In Boring's seminar on the dimensions of consciousness, there was an unforgettable, embarrassing silence when Ludvigh introduced his paper by citing Troland's earlier use of the dimensions-of-consciousness concept, presumably original with Boring. Some 30 years later Leo learned that Boring, hearing of Troland's death on the West Coast in the summer of 1932, had told Ludvigh, whose thesis work on a visual problem with Troland was essentially completed, that he would need a new thesis problem. Elek went on to do distinguished work in vision and was affiliated with the Kresge Eye Institute in Detroit for many years.

The weekly department colloquium brought a wide variety of speakers. Leo recalls how upsetting William Ernest Hocking was when he came upstairs from the Philosophy Department to tell the psychologists that laws of behavior were beyond them: individuals were perverse and would upset any prediction made about their behavior. B. F. Skinner gave an arrogant presentation in which he hailed the displacement of the sensory materials in the new 1934 Murchison Handbook to the back of the volume. This was the right direction, he said, and if all went well, they would not find a place in later volumes. It's an ironic twist that finds Skinner's operant technique to be so important in measuring the sensory discriminative capacities of animals. Hallowell Davis came with a lot of equipment and demonstrated alpha rhythm behavior, and Dwight Chapman, later to be chairman of Psychology at Vassar, gave the department its first account of the newest in statistics, the analysis of variance. Selig Hecht made a dramatic presentation of his photochemical theory of vision that accounted for a large body of data and dominated the field for a long time. His photochemical theories, which generated so much interest, are now outdated, but his experiment with Shlaer and Pirenne on the number of physical quanta necessary to excite a visual sensation is still regarded as the classic work (Hecht, Shlaer, and Pirenne, 1942).

There was also the occasion when L. J. Henderson, distinguished biochemist, first director of the Society of Fellows, and recognized to be an important behind-the-scenes force at Harvard, was hoist by his own petard. Henderson, who at this time had a new found interest, namely Pareto, gave a highly laudatory account of his work. When a certain graduate student ventured to ask Professor Henderson about Pareto's loose and nonrigorous use of his basic concepts, Henderson chose to demolish the upstart critic with a series of prosecutorial questions. When the student had admitted to having written no books, no monographs—not even a journal paper—Henderson proceeded to the coup de grace: "Young man, just what have you ever written?" When the answer "A thesis on Pareto" came back, the bomb burst. If looks could kill, Leo would not be penning this autobiographical account. Henderson had violated the first principle of cross examination taught to all aspiring lawyers: never ask a question the answer to which you don't already know.

Science came into being for Leo with Al Holway's arrival on the scene from Massachusetts State College in 1933. He was five or so years older than Leo, married, and already had a B.S. and M.A. in psychology. Alice, his wife, had a nursing job back in her native Northampton and did not come down to Cambridge immediately. When he came to Harvard to study with Boring, Al was already committed to and deeply involved with problems of sensation and perception. He had been collaborating on issues of sensory quality with Michael Zigler of Wellesley College, whom he had gotten to know in Amherst, and they had already undertaken some collaborative experimental work. Al and Leo joined forces immediately. Leo had been on the local scene and was knowledgeable about it, he was single, bright (as Al saw him), had no strongly fixed course, interacted more easily with people than Al did—in short an ideal teammate from Al's point of view. In turn, Al's goal-directedness, his knowledge, his constant probing and criticism, and the excitement he created about turning the field on its head with novel theories and experiments captured Leo completely. His heterodox views moved in the direction of assuming chemical changes in nervous tissue, and the present-day developments in neurochemistry, neurotransmitters, etc., would have been right up his alley. Aside from his psychological interests, Al read widely in the classical literature and was a devotee of the detective story. Like Leo, he was an avid moviegoer.

Leo had the unhappy task of telling Allport that his interests had shifted into sensory psychology. He was unable to face Allport in his office, so he confronted him on the top floor of Emerson Hall and told Allport of his plans. Allport drew himself up, tilted his head back to look down his nose at Leo and, his voice dripping with scorn, said, "Oh, so you're going to become a weight lifter!" Douglas McGregor, incidentally, took the opposite course. Using some of Troland's apparatus, he did his thesis on a visual problem and, when it was completed, moved into social psychology under Allport's aegis.

Leo began to work more intensively than he ever had before. Al saw a communality among all the senses and was motivated to supply data that were "wanted and wanting" in the sensory discrimination literature. The two of them got up early in the morning and experimented before classes got underway, studied for the prelims and language exams afternoons and evenings, and while Al was assisting Boring in an introductory course, they spent many nights setting up demonstrations for Boring's use the following day. Leo spent the summers of 1934 and 1935 with Holway in Amherst and joined in experiments with Mike Zigler, who was there some of the time.

When Alice came to Cambridge, the Holways moved into an apartment on Everett Street, a stone's throw from Perkins Hall, and there Al and Leo did a taste experiment using the then novel method of single stimuli that provided the Weber function for gustation for sodium chloride. This was a "wanted and wanting" function. During this time Leo also audited a number of physics courses. These included basic physics, thermodynamics and Theodore Lyman's laboratory course in optics.

Karl Lashley had come to Harvard as a research professor in the fall of 1935 and brought with him Donald Hebb and Douglas E. Smith from Chicago. Frank Beach was also in Lashley's laboratory at this time. Al and Leo took his physiological psychology course, and Leo can only agree with what others have said. Lashley clearly disliked classroom lecturing, and since neither Al nor Leo worked in his laboratories, they never had the benefit of what was by all reports his excellent teaching in informal discussions. Leo often ate dinner with Hebb and Smith in a restaurant on Massachusetts Avenue where the talk was mostly social and the meals constantly punctuated by Hebb and Smith passing a small hand-held chessboard between them. Leo developed a warm regard for and excellent rapport with Hebb, which lasted over the years even though their meetings were infrequent.

Among the many psychologists Leo met over the years, the one he most admired and whose writings he read most closely was Wolfgang Köhler. At the time Köhler gave the William James lectures in 1934 (Köhler, 1938), Leo was in the graduate seminar he also offered. This set the tone for all the later meetings with Köhler. There was an intimate threesome with him and Pratt at an Eastern Psychological Association meeting in

Atlantic City, the occasion when Köhler chaired a session at a Bryn Mawr EPA meeting where Leo gave his first paper, two separate occasions in the late 1950's when Leo was invited to be an examiner in the honors program at Swarthmore, and the last time when Köhler came to New York University to give a graduate seminar. It was then that he expressed his pleasure that Dorothea and Leo were familiar enough with Ewald Hering's work to have translated his *Grundzüge der Lehre vom Lichtsinne* (Hering, 1920).

In 1935 Boring was on leave, and Leonard Carmichael was invited to teach introductory psychology at Harvard and Radcliffe. Leo was his assigned assistant and at his request collected and prepared the demonstrational material for each of his lectures. Not trusting Harvard's equipment (or his assigned assistant), Carmichael regularly drove up from Brown in his convertible with his own demonstrational equipment. On every occasion the equipment had to be toted between his car and Emerson D and back again. All this despite the many hours that had gone into setting up the "local" show. Carmichael's pomposity only served to reinforce Leo's negativity. Leo's later assistantship for B. F. Skinner in a summer school course has left less of a mark. He doesn't even recall grading blue books for Skinner. But he does remember that Skinner demonstrated a phonograph record in which patterns of vowels played at near threshold levels sounded like speech, and one could get "projective" verbal responses from a listener.

Al maintained his contacts with Mike Zigler at Wellesley throughout his collaboration with Leo and, attracted by William Crozier's analysis of the chemical senses and his quantitative analysis of tropistic behavior, began also to see more and more of Crozier at the biology laboratories. Boring's historical and systematic interests had taken him away from a serious research program, and Al and Leo were pretty much on their own when the issue of thesis research had to be faced. They collaborated closely on each other's problems, which were concerned with kinesthetic and visual sensitivity, respectively. Al's thesis dealt with the form and behavior of the Weber-Function for lifted weights over a very large stimulus range and was related to Crozier's notions of the way the activity of the tension receptors underlay the geotropic behavior of the rat on the inclined plane.

Leo's own thesis was motivated by his interest in vision. Boring's history had drawn him there in the first place, and his fascination with the "flight of colors" phenomenon that he first viewed in a closet in Perkins Hall, where a bare-bulb fixture fastened to a pull chain provided a simple apparatus to generate these temporally varying color patterns, was a strong reinforcer. Al and Leo had also gone down to New York City to visit Hecht and his assistant Simon Shlaer. (It was then that Leo bought his three-volume set of Helmholtz' *Physiological Optics* in a small Amsterdam Avenue bookstore.) Leo studied the way variations in intensity and area affected the discrimination of brightness. Ralph Gerbrands, a superb machinist, and safety valve who gave a sympathetic ear to generations of graduate students, gave Leo an indispensable hand with his light boxes and shutters. Both theses involved interpretations in accord with then-accepted views of activated numbers of receptors, and both theses provided data for what later came to be called "Crozier's Law," namely, that the magnitude of the root-mean-square deviation of the stimulus increment tended to vary directly with the magnitude of the stimulus increment itself.

In their theses both Al and Leo were faced with resolving a seeming contradiction in the way sensitivity varied. It increased as "area" increased and decreased as intensity increased. Yet in both cases the total excitation might be said to increase. As Leo recalls their many discussions, they both hit upon the solution together. It came as a flash when they got to a simple physical analogy of trying to fill a bucket with water as the well from which it was drawn was depleted. But there is no question that Al formalized the analysis and developed what he called the "principle of neural availability." It was too late to incorporate this model into their theses, but they published their two papers signed jointly using this explanatory principle.

Holway had become a part-time assistant in Psychology at Wellesley College in his last year of graduate work at Harvard, a post he held until 1942, and he worked as a research assistant to Crozier in the biological laboratories from 1936 to 1939. Leo recalls no outside job offers at this time but was given an assistantship in the Psychology Department. He attended his first American Psychological Association meeting at Dartmouth in the fall of 1936, returned to Cambridge to an office in Boylston Hall, and remembers mostly assisting Smitty Stevens in the experimental laboratory course. Smitty has pointed out that he didn't enjoy teaching, and Leo got more experience than he was entitled to.

In the following year (1937) Leo was still not placeable. This came as no surprise. He recalls making an automobile trip with Richard L. Schanck, the social psychologist, who had done the first "private" and "public" opinion attitude studies, when he went on a personal job hunt as his assistant professorship at Harvard was coming to an end. They made a number of stops at various colleges on their drive down the East Coast to Washington, back through West Virginia and Ohio, through Pennsylvania, and made an overnight stop at Floyd Allport's home in Syracuse before returning to Cambridge. Dick was deeply absorbed with social/political issues and analyses and was a stimulating lecturer to boot (Gordon Allport chided him for lecturing without notes!). And yet he had difficulty getting placed. There was also a similar trip with Morgan Upton, who was one of the many assistant professors purged by President Conant in the late 1930's despite many years of service. Upton was one of the most engaging and delightful persons Leo got to know at Harvard. Carroll Pratt fell into the same category, and Leo also has the warmest memories of him.

Jobs were scarce. But it had never occurred to Leo that he had a special problem: he was a Jew. Harvard College might have designated Jews on its academic roles by a discreet asterisk, it might even have instructed new non-alumni sports coaches brought in from the "outside" in 1931 to use Jews sparingly, but Leo didn't learn these facts until years later. He had grown up personally untouched by anti-Semitism, although fully aware of his parents' encounters with it in tsarist Russia. The dawn came with a letter from the chairman of the Psychology Department at the University of Vermont, John T. Metcalf, who opined that Leo wouldn't "fit into the community" there. Mike Zigler later showed Leo a letter that Boring had sent him describing Leo as a "likable Jew." Taken at face value that was a plus, since he had always thought Boring didn't like him. In any event, he was appointed an instructor and tutor at Harvard and Radcliffe. In the earlier phases of this position he was assigned individual tutees plus introductory psychology sections and an assistantship in experimental psychology. Later he taught a course in sensation that Troland had once taught. The individualized tutorial system was rapidly collapsing at this time with President Conant's negative attitude towards it, and the tutorial groups began to increase in size, reaching classroom status towards the end of Leo's teaching stint in 1940.

The junior faculty at this time included Edward and Sarah Anderson from Illinois, Roger Barker from Stanford, Irvin Child from Yale, Clifford Morgan from Rochester, and Robert White from Murray's group. Leo spent a good deal of time with Irv, who left after a two-year stint to return to Yale. Morgan never ceased to amaze Leo. He seemed prepared to hold forth on any issue, whether he was knowledgeable or not. Leo saw

Lashley at department meetings during those years, and for a long time was puzzled at Murray's failure to appear at them. Leo also knew personally of Allport's resentment of Stevens and witnessed the developing clash of interests between them. But he has little to add to Hebb's characterization of Lashley as a "foreign body in the Harvard department" nor to the descriptions that Allport, Stevens, and others have given of their differences.

It was through Holway's association with Crozier that Leo got to know him in the late 1930's. It was not hard to see why Crozier attracted so many psychologists whose interests lay in areas now labeled "neurobiology" or "neuropsychology." His labs hummed with activity, and there was a daily afternoon tea that sparkled with banter and serious discussions among a group of people with common interests and different backgrounds. (It was there that Leo remembers first meeting the statistician Charlie Windsor, the psychologist-turned-physiologist Kelly Upton, Gregory Pincus, and George Wald. Wald was a new arrival from Hecht's laboratory to the Biology Department and definitely not affiliated with Crozier's group, which took a dim view of strictly photochemical accounts of the visual process.) Crozier himself was perpetually "charged." He would delight in taking a visitor through a pile of graphs to spell out a research problem that was nearing completion, but there were occasions when it got overpowering and he sailed on, even though the visitor was obviously lost. Crozier nonetheless made a lasting impact on Leo with his emphasis on the lawfulness of behavior, the lawfulness of the variability of behavior, the necessity for collecting data that were homogeneous with respect to the variable of interest, his emphasis on central neural determinants, and his studies showing the effects of bodily temperature variation on animal behavior and the genetic determination of tropistic behaviors.

In the summer if 1938 Leo got west not only of the Hudson but, for the first time, of the Mississippi River as well. A. F. Rawdon-Smith had come from Cambridge University to work with Stevens on auditory problems. He and his wife Patricia were eager to see the United States before returning to England, and this appealed to a native who had never seen them, so Leo traded his Model A roadster for a touring car, and they drove across the country with stops at most of the national parks. The Rawdon-Smiths' anticipated contact with a British friend at one of the major movie studios in Hollywood didn't materialize, to Leo's disappointment, but he recalls spending a night in Santa Barbara at the home of another of their friends where he got his first insight into how the "other side" lives. On their way back East they stopped to visit Elmer Culler's laboratories at the University of Illinois, then Rawdon-Smith dropped off in Rochester to collaborate with researchers in Carmichael's laboratory. Patricia and Leo drove on to Boston, and she returned to England from there. It wasn't until 1946 that Leo got to see the deep South with Mason Haire on a motor trip that preceded the APA meetings at the University of Pennsylvania.

Jerry Bruner has aptly described the 1938 Emerson Hall scene after he, Bill Prentice, Dorwin Cartwright, Mason Haire, John Harding, Alfred Baldwin, Jack Levine, and Don McGranahan arrived there as graduate students. Leo was still assisting Smitty Stevens in the experimental psychology course, and both Doc Cartwright and Al Baldwin were assigned to assist him. He might have complained to Smitty about having too many lab reports to read; he no longer remembers. Bruner has painted an interesting descriptive account of Smitty's manner and style and concludes by saying "he was not everybody's dish, but he was a superb comrade in arms." He surely was not Holway's dish, nor was Holway Smitty's. At the root of this was a competition for Boring's attention and support. Leo spent a good deal of time with Smitty but never reached the point where he wanted to suggest a collaboration with him. Leo's allegiance to Holway was obvious, and Smitty never proposed that Leo join him in his work.

What Bruner fails to emphasize in his characterization of Smitty was that his early missionary background and training dominated his entire outlook. Smitty was forever proselytizing. During morning breaks between classes there was one year when a group of graduate students and instructors was recruited to drive out to play at the Fresh Pond Golf Course for relaxation—but also to be coached by Smitty. There were assemblies that went into Boston's Chinatown, where everyone was instructed in the proper use of chopsticks. There were the billiard sessions and in later years the short ski program. This carried over into his scientific life, where he never stopped trying to recruit and convert. Once Smitty had "adopted" Bill Sheldon, it took a strong will not to be swept up by somatotyping and its "virtues." The scaling work took place long after Leo was gone, but he can sense the intensity of that movement from the numerous literature reports. It was, incidentally, Ewald Hering who challenged Fechner's logarithmic relationship between body and mind in a paper published in 1876, while explicitly spelling out the rule that equal stimulus ratios generate equal sensation ratios. Smitty chose to ignore

Hering's unheralded anticipation, but it was Smitty's powerful pitch that brought recognition of its validity.

What with his teaching obligations, a variety of newly acquired interests like jazz and the visual arts, dating, and joining the Harvard Teachers Union, which Gordon Allport had called to his attention, Leo's own research was limited to a study with a Radcliffe honors student on the latency of after-images and another with a Harvard undergraduate on the range of apprehension (attention). It was during this period that Holway, despite his multiple professional ties, undertook his work with Boring on the problems of size constancy and the moon illusion. These experiments were all done in the corridors or on the roof of the biological laboratory building. The size-constancy experiments could get under way only after midnight, by which time it was assumed that even the most dedicated biological researcher had given up for the night, and the moon-illusion experiments, of course, only at the moon's pleasure. The size-constancy experiments involved multiple projectors, mounting wooden frames throughout long corridor lengths, mounting of sheets, measuring adjusted light images throughout the night with a meter stick, arranging masking cloths for cue reduction, etc. The moon-illusion experiments were in many ways even more time-consuming and tiring, since the equipment had to be hauled up onto and down from the roof. In terms of sheer physical labor, they are among the most arduous Leo ever participated in. He joined in numerous informal discussions as the experiments progressed, but when Holway proposed to Boring that Leo join them as a coauthor on the publications coming out of these studies, Boring told him that he (Boring) had arranged for only Al's assistance and that Leo was Al's problem.

After much debate about whether war would or would not break out—a good deal of the debate took place in the Hayes Bickford cafeteria on the Square in the wee hours of the morning with the widest variety of night owls—Jerry Bruner and Leo decided to go to Europe in the summer of 1939. Leo has never regretted the trip—the people he met, the places he saw, the novel experiences, all are now a part of him. But in some absolute sense, in retrospect, it has to have been a foolish decision. However much fun it was to punt on the Cam, to see and visit with psychologists at Cambridge University and in the English countryside, to wander around London, Paris, Milan, Venice, and the south of France, people were leaving these vacation spots in droves in anticipation of the beginning of a war and they were right. He made it back to the States in late

October with Boring very much disturbed that his introductory psychology course had been lacking one of its assistants.

Leo's three-year instructorship was coming to an end in the summer of 1940, and job pickings were still lean. One offer came from Western Reserve where he was assured by the dean that one Jew had already been hired in the History Department and that he had turned out quite well. Holway had in the meantime (1939) joined the Division of Research at the Harvard Graduate School of Business Administration across the river, working with Ross McFarland whose interests were primarily in aviation psychology. McFarland's laboratory, which was affiliated with the Fatigue Laboratory, was about to undertake a major study of visual fatigue. Leo eagerly accepted the offer of a research assistantship and remained at the Business School for the next seven years.

His first project there was to extend the after-image latency problem to conditions of oxygen deprivation. Thereafter a vast variety of visual tasks and capacities were evaluated in a search for indices of visual fatigue. The net upshot was that no reliable and reproducible indices could be established. There seemed to be no task whose difficulty could not be surmounted by an observer willing to put forth some "extra effort." The Business School published a volume summarizing this research effort (McFarland, Holway, and Hurvich, 1942).

As the decade of the 1940's got under way and various governmental agencies began seeking out the services of psychologists, the laboratory became involved with testing and evaluating the performance of airplane pilot candidates. Soon thereafter a study of visual range and height finders was undertaken with support from the Office of Scientific Research and Development (OSRD).

The research program was carried out both in the field and in the laboratory. The "laboratory" included the roof of Morgan Hall at the Business School, and the "field" the one-mile straightaway narrow-gauge railroad track adjoining the airport in East Boston, as well as local lakes where distance sensitivities were measured across water surfaces. Holway still held his part-time appointment at Wellesley, and rooms and attic space there were used for measures of stereo-acuity. There was much traveling between Boston and Wellesley, and Leo first met Dorothea in the Wellesley laboratories. Two recent Clark University Ph.D.'s were affiliated with this research, Bertram Warren and Jorma Niven. Ellsworth Cook, also from Clark, was assigned to the research group by the Navy.

Leo had a high selective service number and received a research deferment after the United States entered World War II. His attempt to join the Navy failed because his right eye is myopic—his left is hyperopic—a condition that (to Julian Hochberg's continuing amazement) never prevented Leo from having stereoscopic vision. When he attempted to join the Army in response to a call for researchers in what must have seemed like a more attractive position, he was turned down because he already was in research.

During the Fatigue Lab period Leo was assigned temporarily to a group working out of Princeton to check the performance of range and height finders in a cold climate. This involved spending a short time in the National Bureau of Standards in Washington to learn the practicalities of heat measurements with thermocouples, and a short time at the Frankford Arsenal in Philadelphia to install thermocouples in the four 12-foot instruments that were then sent on to Camp Churchill in Hudson Bay, Canada. There, as a civilian with a small Army detachment, Leo checked out the instruments on those few occasions when the blowing snow let up enough to expose a target to range upon. The most enjoyable aspect of this experience was the Princeton stay, working with Merrill Flood's group of mathematicians and statisticians. There, Leo again met sparkling, witty Charlie Windsor, whom he had last seen in Crozier's lab, and he had the pleasure of getting to know John Tukey, whose office he shared briefly.

Leo's Canadian experience was just long enough for him to get to appreciate the tensions between enlisted men (with whom he preferred to fraternize) and their officers. He also got just enough contact with the army at Frankford Arsenal to experience how frustrating their administrative foul-ups could be. The height finders required helium "charges" in order to reduce index-of-refraction errors to a minimum. Helium came in cylindrical tanks. The catch-22 in the situation was the Army's requirement that they receive empty helium tanks before delivering full ones. This requirement was difficult to meet. After weeks of negotiating a simultaneous exchange, two GI's appeared with a full tank of helium and casually drove off without the empty tank, unaware, no doubt, of the carefully negotiated agreement.

Dorothea was born at home, in Newton, Massachusetts, around midnight between November 16 and 17, 1920, the middle child of five. Although the event was celebrated throughout her childhood on November 17, the official records were resolved in favor of a legal but uncelebrated birthdate of November 16. The two different dates seemed somehow to dilute her identity and possibly had some superficial relevance later to her wish to retain her original surname to identify her with her work, without regard for the legalisms attendant on acquiring a spouse. In the family order, she followed an older brother and sister, and she was followed by two more brothers, one in July of 1922, and the youngest in May of 1924.

It was a lively household, where friends were always welcome, rules were few enough to be observed more often than enforced, and only unpleasant squabbles were strictly forbidden and met with banishment from the scene. Although her father was trained both in electrical engineering and law, it was her mother who taught her to repair frayed electrical cords, patch bicycle tires, and to use carpentry tools as well as a sewing machine. The "learn-how-so-you-can-do-it-yourself" attitude that characterized her environment was not unusual during the Depression years of her childhood and adolescence, but the gender neutrality of the "how-to" learning apparently was unusual. It proved useful later, both at home and in the laboratory. Also of value were the shared toys: trains that accumulated track, switches, tunnels, and cars with each succeeding Christmas; erector sets of increasing complexity and flexibility, sleds and skis that moved from one sibling to the next as height exceeded or caught up to length. In the family growing up, what one learned and did was very much more a function of age, strength, and individual preference than it was influenced by whether one happened to be a brother or sister.

In the small private schools that she attended, on the other hand, there were only girls. Despite this social distortion, the education was, in retrospect, good. It was classical, with early introduction of French and Latin, and western philosophy and theology, along with mathematics and laboratory science courses. The latter must have been taught well, because they are remembered as fun experiences in discovery and puzzle-solving. Neither family nor school seems to have fostered the prevailing cultural dichotomies between "men's work" and "women's work," and because of a naturally skeptic (and stubborn) character, Dorothea has not yet accepted the point of view that genetically-determined sex-related differences make women less likely to be interested in quantitative, analytical science than are men. Her first instruction in this presumed dichotomy occurred in a College Board examination room, when an unknown but pleasant young fellow examinee whispered: "You're in the wrong room, this is chemistry."

On the day of the September 1938 hurricane, a damaging storm that took the Boston area and New England coast by unpleasant surprise, she entered Wellesley College. She had not planned to continue her education in a non-coeducational setting, nor had she intended to attend college in her home state. During her junior year in high school she had decided to apply to Berkeley. Early in May of that year, however, her mother suffered a ruptured appendix and died less than 48 hours after emergency surgery. This sudden loss of an intensely admired and deeply loved parent (her parents' marriage had broken up years before) was a severe emotional blow, and left her with a hitherto unrecognized need for proximity to her siblings. So, rather than heading for California, she followed her sister to Wellesley, where Marie was entering her senior year as a mathematics major. It was, in retrospect, a good choice.

Her plan on entering Wellesley was to concentrate in chemistry, go on to medical school, and become a bone surgeon. Her interest in bone repair had started at age ten when a bad fall resulted in chipped shoulder bones that required a complexly designed adjustable metal contraption rather than a simple cast during the extended healing period. The career plans changed for two reasons: one intellectual, one historical. An introduction to physiological and experimental psychology convinced her that brains were both more interesting and more important than bones; and medical school was a forfeit to World War II and her involvement in wartime research on stereoscopic vision that was motivated by the need for improving stereoscopic rangefinders (made obsolete, of course, by the development of radar).

Dorothea's first psychology course was taken during her freshman year, mostly because it was the sole introductory course open to freshmen only by permission, hence promising something special. After taking the course, she never figured out the rationale for that restriction. It did open the way for an early experimental lab course, followed by a series of individual experimental courses. By the end of her sophomore year, when she was invited to join the honors program in chemistry, she was already addicted to psychophysics as a way to study a part of the nervous system and perhaps, ultimately, the brain; and chemistry, physics (especially optics and acoustics), and biology gradually became secondary to psychophysics and physiological psychology. Edna Heidbredder, whose senior seminar she remembers with respect and satisfaction, was doing research on concept formation, and although Dorothea participated in some of the studies, they did not capture her in the way that the functional relations that one could measure in the laboratory did.

The psychophysical experiments Dorothea tried on her own might yield negative results, but they always seemed to hold out more promise at the outset. One negative result she still remembers came from an attempt to determine how auditory thresholds vary with bodily posture. The experiment was based on a rather vague notion that since blood circulation is modified by posture, and oxygen supply to the brain is dependent on blood circulation, then cellular response in central sensory areas might be subject to postural changes, and this should be revealed by small but systematic changes in threshold. Many of her friends had their "volunteer" time on the tilt-table, and all showed the expected systematic variations in blood pressure and pulse rate, but the only function that could be fit to the pure-tone threshold variations was a low-frequency sine wave of insignificant amplitude.

Michael Zigler, who spent his career at Wellesley after a Ph.D. with Titchener, was in charge of the psychophysics laboratories, and had as research collaborator and course and lab assistant a young man named Alfred Holway, a recent Ph.D. with E. G. Boring at Harvard, thus also in the Titchener tradition. Professor Zigler, who soon became "Mike" even in those days of greater formality, was a genial, avuncular sort of person who encouraged independence in the students, but also maintained an effective "open door" policy and generously dispensed advice, information, and above all encouragement. Mike Zigler was also responsible for encouraging his students to make the effort to return to original sources and willingly shared with them his many hand-written translated extracts from classic studies published in German. Dorothea liked languages, read French literature with pleasure (and sought out French film showings) by the time she entered college, and at Wellesley learned German well enough to handle scientific material with some ease. But it was Zigler's example, and his expressed conviction that important ideas are best understood in their originators' own words, that remained with her.

Holway was the more important influence in the laboratory: laying out the skeleton of a problem on the blackboard, outlining the steps to test an idea experimentally, anticipating the results and conclusions, and then, when all participants were confidently ready to set up the apparatus and collect the data, calling a halt to reverse the process, demanding that we now demonstrate, if possible, why it was all wrong. Some of our own former students would recognize this process.

By the end of her junior year at Wellesley, Dorothea had finished with the assortment of summer jobs that had taught her an assortment of things, useful and otherwise, in preceding years. Although always thin ("underweight" by the height/weight tables that used to be taken seriously by school health departments), she had learned how to raise a heavy tray overhead and balance it on one hand; she had developed a healthy skepticism for market forecasts in the library of the Babson Institute while working for an economist studying the Great Crash of 1929; and she had acquired a deciphering skill while tracking down obscure references for a Victorian scholar whose handwritten notes had become totally illegible to the professor's aging eyes and nearly so to Dorothea's young ones.

In the summer following her junior year, she did full-time lab work on a variety of issues related to visual acuities involved in distance judgments. Al Holway had been dividing his time between the Wellesley lab in Pendleton Hall and the Fatigue Lab (later the laboratory of physiology) located at the Harvard Business School. The year was 1941, and although we were not to be officially at war until December 7 of that year, the process of diverting research facilities and personnel to issues of military importance was well under way. The Harvard-Wellesley research effort was carried on under the auspices of the National Defense Research Committee (NDRC), which had been founded in 1940 and in June of 1941 broadened to include the Office of Scientific Research and Development (OSRD). Her own involvement in that research was not to end until the war ended. Much of her time was spent in the lab during the 1941–42 academic year, and very nearly all of it (there and with rangefinders on the flat roof of Harvard Business School's Morgan Hall) for the next few years after June of 1942 when she received her A.B. degree. Wellesley's Pendleton Hall had one very large laboratory room on the top floor and, adjoining that room, an access hatch to a long catwalk that extended many yards through the center of the slope-roof attic space. Although with neither heat for winter nor ventilation for summer, this space would hardly pass muster under current guidelines for animal experimentation, the long, straight catwalk was ideal for experiments concerned with distance functions, and reams of data were cranked out during many uncomfortable hours.

All of the studies were initially motivated by the need for measures of practical import to the use of different types of visual rangefinders, but a number of them raised questions of more basic interest. One problem of real concern was that stereoscopic range judgments in the field could become erratic and unreliable, even though on repeated standard tests the rangefinder operators showed no such variation in distance acuity. The Wellesley group started by looking for differences in individual variability for judgments based only on binocular disparities (as in the range instruments) and for judgments in a situation essentially like that of the standard Howard Dolman test, in which one of two comparison objects actually moves toward or away from the observer. Under the laboratory conditions, they found no significant differences in day-to-day variability for the two situations, but the distance functions themselves are not the same. Samuel Fernberger of the University of Pennsylvania, and a regular visiting representative of OSRD, was convinced that both the Wellesley results and the Howard Dolman test must be based on changes in retinal image size with increasing or decreasing object distance, but the group was dubious about size variation as the single determinant of apparent distance variation. To find out, they eliminated one possible distance cue after another. Only when ways were devised to keep angular size constant as an object changed distance, when only one eye was used to eliminate binocular disparity, and when the moving object was made a collimated light beam, did the discrimination judgments degenerate to guessing behavior at all distances. The group then determined distance discrimination functions for each cue allowed to operate separately, and also in different combinations, and finally looked at the way that the sensitivities combined. The result was startlingly simple. One could obtain quantitatively identical distance sensitivity functions by measuring discriminability with all cues operating simultaneously, as in everyday binocular viewing, or by arithmetically adding the individually measured sensitivities for each identified cue allowed to operate in the absence of the others.

An effect somewhat akin to this kind of cue additivity has shown up again recently in our studies (with D. Varner and Ken Knoblauch) of temporal and spatial luminance and chromaticity modulation sensitivities (Varner, Jameson, and Hurvich, 1984). Linear algebraic additivity of cue sensitivities has recently also been found by Barbara Dosher and George Sperling in studies of perceived 3-D structure. The Wellesley lab's distance sensitivity studies of the 1940's could not be published at the time, and when finally such OSRD reports were declassified, the original authors were dispersed and involved in other problems. Only a brief note that we published in the *Journal of the Optical Society of America* in 1959 summarizes the main findings in the readily available visual literature (Jameson and Hurvich, 1959a).

There was a great deal of commuting in both directions between the Wellesley and Harvard labs, and it was during this period that Dorothea and Leo first met and became friends and coworkers.

Dorothea was also getting to meet a larger circle of people in vision and technically related fields. One visit she remembers was to the aniseikonia lab at Dartmouth, where she discussed distortions in depth perception with Adelbert Ames, Jr., learned from Kenneth Ogle in the lab that her own two eyes showed no difference in optical magnification, and saw the original versions of the various distorted rooms that subsequently became "musts" for illustration of compelling perceptual illusions and, broadened, served as foundation stone for the theoretical development of transactional psychology. She met a young Edwin Land at his fledgling Polaroid company in Cambridge while looking into vector screens that retain plane of polarization for viewing disparate projected images without requiring color differences for the two eyes. This casual encounter might well have receded beyond memory retrieval had she not, in later years, had repeated occasions to try to clarify one or another of Land's dramatically orchestrated color demonstrations for a nonspecialized, curious, bewildered or bewitched colleague.

Through her sister, Dorothea met a number of young electronics researchers from MIT, where Marie worked for a while, and then from the Radio Research Lab at Harvard. The two sisters shared apartments, first in the town of Wellesley and then at the beginning of Concord Avenue just off Harvard Square. There was a stream of drop-in friends and casual meals at which the menu depended on the available supply of ration-stamps, but there was no cross-lab shop talk at these social interactions: it was not until the war ended that Dorothea knew anything about radar, or that the reason "icicles" were suddenly not available as Christmas tree decorations was that they were needed for "jamming."

When the war was over and all our OSRD reports were in, including the design for a portable rangefinder based on three distance cues (Holway, Jameson, and Hurvich, 1945), the dean of the Harvard Business School thought an attempt should be made to relate the various laboratories that had sprung up to the general aims of the school, as the original Fatigue Lab had been. Dorothea, Leo, and Al Holway individually sampled courses on a variety of topics. We learned the case-method of teaching and emerged somewhat better informed about matters of production, marketing, management, and finance. With Ernst Wolf (later of the Retina Foundation) we did experiments on the effects on dark-adaptation of exposure to daylight that had different extents of shortwave spectral light screened out (a question of importance in aviation at the time and, more recently, to the role of shortwave light exposure as possibly contributing to retinal pathology). In a field survey, we learned how poorly designed most lighting installations were in factories, offices, libraries, and department stores (Tiffany's in New York was a notable exception) and did some laboratory performance and preference studies that were sensible but not very exciting (Holway and Jameson, 1947).

In July of 1947, Al, Leo, and Dorothea moved to Rochester, New York, to do research in color in Ralph Evans's newly formed Color Control Division at Kodak. During that first year, Holway suffered a severe breakdown, was moved to Massachusetts where his wife, Alice, had close family, and died soon after of injuries from a two-story fall from the window of his hospital room.

Our first year at Rochester was hardly productive of any scholarly accomplishments. The building that was to house our lab was still in the early stages of construction when we arrived, and with two other psychologists from Evans's group (Sidney Newhall and Robert Burnham), along with a half dozen or so additional Kodak people in technical aspects of film and film processing, both from Kodak outposts in the United States and from European countries, we went into a series of intensive technical courses related to color film and its processing and quality control. At the end of this unanticipated educational experience, we knew about H&D curves, film nonlinearities, how to make (and not make) dye-transfer prints, and, most relevant for our own interests, who the "Standard Observer" was. "It" was, of course, the average set of color-mixture data for numerous observers in two different British laboratories, smoothed, transformed, and corrected, combined with a similarly smoothed and corrected average photopic luminosity function that had been standardized earlier for photometry. This Standard Observer, with all traces of interindividual and measurement variability ignored in its many decimal places of precise values, tyrannized any and all attempts to model the color vision mechanism. (Selig Hecht had been forced to compute an additional triplex of hypothetical spectral sensitivity curves, indistinguishable by eye from the ones he first proposed, so that his photochemical theory of color vision would be a precise transformation of the Standard Observer.)

Even after the courses were finished (and exams passed!), only a section of the new Kodak building was habitable. It was months later that any lab space was usable, and still more months before the spectral apparatus that we had designed with Holway in sketch form was delivered. Holway never saw it, and in the first version that was delivered, the three vertical wedges that were intended to vary the intensity of the short, middle, and longwave regions of the spectrum independently were, to our dismay, locked in position rather than adjustable as we had requested. Anyone who has made the transition from working with an individual skilled instrument maker "of the old school" to interacting with a series of managerial and supervisory people organized for industrial manufacturing, where sketches and design discussions move to professional blueprints, materials design, and division of production between optical and mechanical elements, might have predicted this dismaying first outcome. While we continued to wait for this apparatus, we found ways to use projectors, filters, microscope stages, and tripods to get some experiments under way.

Ralph Evans had asked us to join his group at Kodak because his own previous experience had convinced him that the way colored slides, movie film, or prints looked was not adequately predictable on physical and chemical principles, and he set about to learn all he could about visual color perception. He also (when we knew him, with the assistance of a sensitive and talented photographer, Jeannette Klute) illustrated phenomena that he read or heard about and others that he discovered on his own by superlative slides photographed in the studio laboratory; to this he devoted a few uninterruptible hours each afternoon. He was certain that his color control division required experimental perception psychologists as well as dye chemists, physicists, and engineers. Lectures based on his photographic evidence had also convinced Kodak's management at the time that perceptual research was a valid part of Evans's enterprise. Our own interest was in understanding how the visual system functions to account for the observable phenomena, and Evans left it up to us to inform him about what we were working on and, when the data were in, to give him a documented report. It was an ideal working relationship, and frequently Ralph found in these papers answers to questions that he had been bothered by and that had some practical relevance to studio photography, color film, slide projection (and the projector light source), and the very large perceptual differences between colored slides and color prints. Different kinds of psychological questions, such as color memory and preference, tended to be handled by Sidney Newhall and Robert Burn-ham, who had preceded our arrival in Rochester.

Research in color vision was not, at the time, a major theme, in either the psychological or the physiological literature, particularly in the United States. The basic theory was pretty much accepted as having been stated by Thomas Young and confirmed by Helmholtz. The emphasis was on quantification and standardization, particularly of the receptor functions assumed to have a direct quality coding into red, green, and blue sensations. Selig Hecht, the biologist, had published his photochemical theory, and the major misgiving about his model (apart from how precisely it agreed with the standardized color-mixture curves) was that Hecht's postulated three curves were excessively broad and broadly overlapping throughout the spectrum (Hecht, 1930). In Sweden, the neurophysiologist Ragnar Granit had interpreted his recordings of single nerve-fiber responses to spectral lights in a variety of species as direct read-outs of cone spectral sensitivities and, by manipulating conditions, had also come up with a set of functions for the cat which found its way into many textbooks to illustrate Granit's (1947) "Dominator/Modulator" model. (A broad spectral curve recorded from some fibers was the "dominator.") The cat curves were also coded as red, green, and blue, sometimes with an additional function added in dashed line for yellow. The major misgiving about his single fiber results when measured directly in species other than cat was that, unlike Hecht whose spectral curves were deemed too broad, Granit's curves were too narrow to be convincing as cone pigment absorption distributions. In England, the physicist W. S. Stiles had published his three psychophysical curves for increment thresholds, and at first also described them as the red, green, and blue functions of Young's theory. In Stiles's case, the misgivings were his own, because his continued experiments were suggesting that the data might be more complex than their original interpretation, as indeed they turned out to be. It was many years later that the "five or possibly seven" curves that Stiles later published and labeled with the neutral designation "pi mechanisms" were analyzed and interpreted (Stiles, 1978).

But in the late 1940's, when we began to work in color, the main emphasis in research (most of it published in the *Journal of the Optical Society of America*) was on standardization, and the reductionist search for mechanism was related primarily to a search for the quantitative spectral characteristics of the assumed three classes of cones in the retina. Some years would still have to pass before new techniques would permit cone pigment absorptions to be measured directly (Dartnall, 1972), and it was not until the 1980's that a sizable body of microspectro-photometric measures on individual cones in monkey and human retina were published to specify the visual pigments. Our own tendency was also toward physiological reductionism, but with a difference from the prevailing esprit.

We were not, at the outset, wedded to any particular theory of color vision. We were committed to experiments that yielded quantitative relations, which was scientifically respectable. But we also wanted to get a firm handle on a range of qualitative experiences that, for us, constituted the essence of color vision. To the scientifically self-conscious, dominant establishment, "subjective" criteria other than "same/different" or "yes/no" were, at best, on the fringe of respectability. Nonetheless, we persisted in using whatever criterion response seemed appropriate to the question we were asking, and published several series of papers in *JOSA* in which the functional relations were based on judgments that included "white/non-white" (Hurvich and Jameson, 1951a, 1951b; Jameson and Hurvich, 1951a), "same hue/different hue" for different intensities (Jameson and Hurvich, 1951b), "same brightness/different brightness" for different hues (Hurvich and Jameson, 1954), as well as experiments that could reasonably be limited to the acceptable identity/non-identity critiera (Hurvich and Jameson, 1953; Jameson and Hurvich, 1953). When we wanted to repeat the well-known Binocular Yellow experiment that Selig Hecht had done to "settle" the issue of whether yellow was a centrally generated hue synthesized from red and green sensations, it seemed to us that the logic of his demonstration required that the lights to be presented to the two separate eyes must be selected on the basis of their uniquely red and uniquely green qualities. For a yellow-red mixed centrally with a yellow-green to give binocular yellow seemed less than decisive. When we did the experiment using Hecht's light stimuli we reproduced his result, and when we did it using light stimuli based on our logically required "subjective" criteria, we did not. The mixture of red and green lights looks white or gray, and not yellow, unless the lights are yellowish when seen separately (Hurvich and Jameson, 1951c).

Our experimental results were leading us progressively further from the generally accepted Young-Helmholtz view of a color-vision mechanism constituted of private-line red, green, and blue messages delivered to the visual cortex from sets of retinal cones similarly coded as red, green, and blue. (We were recently more appalled than amused to read in a commentary published by an eminent biochemical geneticist in a 1986 issue of *Science* that the erstwhile dogma is "in" again with the newly-discovered genes for the cone pigments; genes the discoverers have also labeled "red," "green," and "blue.")

When we finally decided that Ewald Hering's concept of paired, opponent processes as a quality-coded mechanism for color vision made more sense of the phenomena, that it could be quantified experimentally, and that, with a minimal set of simple relational hypotheses, a quantitative account could be given, in opponent-process terms, of many of the relevant threshold, matching, and discrimination data, more psychologists began to be interested in our work, and even some neurophysiologists (Jameson and Hurvich, 1955, 1956; Hurvich and Jameson, 1955). Ragnar Granit, for example, dispatched a note from Stockholm to say that he had run across "yellow modulators" in some of his records. But for many visual scientists already interested in color, we had crossed the truth-heresy barrier. Gordon Walls stopped by our laboratory in Rochester on a visit from Berkeley to straighten us out after an unsuccessful attempt via the mails. We found Walls charming and, unlike his no-holds-barred letters and published critical comments, a gentle person. L. C. Thomson, from London, made a train stop in Rochester on his way to South Bend, Indiana, to deliver a lecture at Notre Dame. He was not gentle but, in typical British debating style, attempted to lecture us on the three-variable nature of color vision and the sin of denying the red-green-blue trinity. After some verbal sparring and blackboard arithmetic, we were found not guilty of the mathematical error if not absolved of the sin, and ended a delightful evening by showing Thomson a Great Lake (Ontario) in the moonlight. (He had learned in school, but had not quite believed, that the great fresh water lakes were large enough so that one could not see across to Canada.)

We were living by then in a modest house in Irondequoit, a suburb of Rochester. It was close to Kodak in terms of commuting distance, but in a rural setting that interposed a mile of dirt road from the RFD mailbox, and was surrounded by a large tract of undeveloped rolling hills opposite us, a mostly oak woods on the ridges behind us, and Rochester's beautiful Durand-Eastman Park to one side. After the first unsettled year in Rochester, during which we made more round trip drives to Boston (sometimes separately, sometimes together) than made any sense, we had decided to extend and seal our working partnership, and we were married in October of 1948. The Boston trips were less frequent thereafter, but we continued to return for holidays and vacations to stay either with Leo's mother and father in Mattapan, or Dorothea's brother Paul and his family in Wellesley. The Jamesons' father had died from a cerebral hemorrhage in 1943. In the same year Paul had married Alba Bernardi, who was a Wellesley student and resident of the town, before serving in the Pacific with the Naval Air Force, and on his return, he and Alba settled in Wellesley to start his law practice and raise their two daughters. We were warmly and affectionately welcomed to the extended Bernardi family, and through many years now our closeness with Paul and Alba has continued and increased with shared social and environmental concerns, overlapping intellectual interests, passion for books, and, for the two males at least, an ongoing competition for "turns" in reading aloud some choice passage that must immediately be shared. (If not predictable, it is at least not surprising that when we returned to academia, most of our summer writing and other portable work would be done on an isolated high dune, not far from Boston and Wellesley, and with a view out to the Atlantic, across which we can't quite see Portugal.)

Back in Rochester, our friendships developed mostly in university circles. Ruth Adams, now in English at Dartmouth, arrived at the University of Rochester with a fresh Radcliffe Ph.D. shortly after our move to Kodak, and was responsible for our hearing "New Critics," old authors, and young poets at lecture series sponsored by the University's lively English Department. (Ruth went on to become dean of Douglass College, the women's division of Rutgers, then president of Wellesley during the hectic 1960's and 1970's before moving to the relative calm of Hanover as Dartmouth made the co-ed transition.) There were other good friends in the History Department and in the Rochester Symphony, which progressively improved during our stay there under Eric Leinsdorf's direction.

We were pretty regular attendees at the Psychology Department's weekly colloquia and had frequent, open-invitation, informal parties at our home that were mostly attended by the psychology graduate students. These gatherings were started at the initiative of Eddie Kemp, who was doing auditory research in the department and who shared with us an enthusiasm for jazz. Our collection of 78 rpm great (and not so great) recordings added zest to long and serious discussions about the variety of thesis experiments that the students were involved in. The group included Norman and Vivianne Harway, specializing in clinical and developmental disabilities, for many years now at the University of Pittsburgh, who with their two daughters have been lifetime friends. Vic Laties, whose ophthalmologist brother Alan was later to be part of our vision group at Pennsylvania, was a "regular" at these gatherings, as was Bernie Weiss; both Vic and Bernie are now back at Rochester after some years at Johns Hopkins. Bernie Harleston, who was working in learning, is now president of City College in New York and is also (with his wife Marie) a friend from his Rochester graduate student days. As a matter of social history, it was Bernie who was refused counter service because of his color at the Washington, D.C., hotel where APA met in the 1950's, after which APA refused to convene again in the nation's capital until that city could guarantee the rights of all APA members.

Racial segregation was not the only evil besetting Washington and the country in the 1950's. The Cold War was on. By 1953 more than 50,000 U.S. troops had perished in the Korean "police action" (the euphemism to avoid constitutional issues inherent in its undeclared-war status); attorneys-general in the states were vying with the U.S. Attorney-General to build longer lists of "subversive organizations" to which our citizen dissidents might belong or might have belonged; and Senator Joseph McCarthy was getting more headlines than his counterpart on the House Un-American Activities Committee in the infamous hearings where "friendly" informers were thanked by the chairman for listing names of present and former friends and acquaintances who held or once held suspect views or memberships, or where "balky" witnesses were held up to calumny and/or cited for their contempt, depending on which constitutional amendment they quoted for their right of refusal to testify. Many careers were at best interrupted or at worst destroyed during these McCarthy years, and we were lucky that the Kodak organization turned out to be more independent (or less frightened?) than many of our prestigious academic institutions, so that our own scientific careers were not derailed at this time.

Leo has already sketched his early socialist interests and background. During the late 1930's and early 1940's, he was also active in the Harvard Teachers' Union. It was affiliated with the AFL and initially was concerned with tenure, promotion, and economic issues at Harvard. It gradually established broader relations with the outside community—for example, on school issues, child labor legislation, industrial problems, etc. Through the Teachers' Union he got to know dozens of individuals, some casually and some who have become life-long friends, among them Paul Sweezy, the Marxist economist and co-editor of *Monthly Review*. As secretary, and later as vice president during the presidency of F. O. Matthiessen, Leo saw a good deal of him. The membership of the Union reached about 200 at its peak, and the distribution covered the political spectrum, but with a definite left skew. In the 1940's Leo also became active in and an officer of the Boston-Cambridge branch of the American Association of Scientific Workers. This group sought to increase the political and social awareness of scientists and to promote the education of the public in scientific matters. Among the local senior members were Kirtley Mather, Harlow Shapley, and Bart Bok. There were regional meetings, and Leo first met Harry Grundfest, the neurophysiologist, and Melba Phillips, the physicist, in New York City, and Robert Hodes, the physiologist, in Philadelphia. There was an occasional visit from an international figure, and Leo chaired a memorable session in Harvard's Emerson D where the famous British crystallographer J. D. Bernal gave a brilliant talk. This progressive group also had a left skew.

On the day that Leo answered his summons to appear before the House Un-American Activities Committee, one newspaper lead read "Kodak Psychologist Balks." When we returned to Rochester from Washington, Kodak's management wanted, and got, our personal assurance that neither of us was planning the violent overthrow of the U.S. government, and we returned to our research.

Robert Boynton had joined the University Psychology Department after finishing his Ph.D. at Brown with Lorrin Riggs, and eventually formed Rochester's Center for Visual Science, a major vision center that has continued to thrive after Bob's move to San Diego, first under the direction of John Lott Brown, until he returned to administration as president of the South Florida University system, and currently under the leadership of Walter Makous. Numerous U.S. and overseas vision scientists continued to visit Rochester and our laboratory during the 1950's. The Europeans included W. D. Wright from London, who had contributed one of the sets of color-mixture data that went into the standardized colorimetry system; M. A. Bouman from the Netherlands Institute for Perception, who was pressing his analysis of discrimination measures as controlled by quantal stimulus variations; J. ten Doesschate, from Utrecht, who had done some collaborative work with Bouman in addition to his ophthalmological research in the Donders setting and tradition; and, shortly before we left Rochester to move to Manhattan, William Rushton from Cambridge.

Rushton did not visit the lab, but spent the weekend with us at our home after delivering a lecture at the university on his early estimates of human visual pigments by reflection densitometry. William told us that he had recently given up his electrophysiological studies of individual neurons in recognition of, in his view, the likelihood that it would be Alan Hodgkin who would do the breakthrough research there. His own current aim was to explain color vision by measuring, for the first time, the characteristics of the cone pigments. It was his first venture into the color terrain, and he wanted to talk of nothing else. There ensued a marathon weekend-long tutorial, broken only briefly for Dorothea when Leo mercifully led William off through the woods to talk while she had her silent morning quota of black coffee that customarily coaxed her brain into a functioning state. We have continued to interact with some of the vision people whom we first met in Rochester, as well as many other European scientists that we came to know later at international meetings held in many different countries.

The first international meeting we attended was in Paris in 1958, after we had overcome the passport difficulties that some U.S. citizens were still experiencing at that time. In addition to Leonard Boudin's excellent legal assistance, we had the unsolicited assistance of Henri Piéron, grand old man of French psychology, who was unwilling to let the political climate in any country interfere with the symposium he had arranged under the auspices of the International Congress of Scientific Unions. It was with real pleasure that we agreed, about six years later, to Yves Galifret's request that we translate into English Piéron's monograph on visual flicker (Piéron, 1964). Galifret was a former student and junior colleague of Piéron who knew that, although some of Piéron's writings had been translated into English, he cherished the idea that this particular work achieve the wider recognition that only an English publication would make possible. Although Piéron died before its publication, he did see proofs of our translated version, and Galifret reported he was pleased.

As our theoretical papers began to attract increasing attention both here and abroad and invited papers were solicited for meetings in various places, Kodak's interest in our work was diminishing apace. They had agreed to give up their monopoly on color processing in a legal action resolved by a consent decree, and Ralph Evans's Color Technology Division was being selectively and drastically cut back. Research papers to be submitted for publication were regularly routed through the company's administrative headquarters, where the State Street legal office routinely prescreened such papers for potential patent applications. We learned from Ralph that a vice president was beginning to ask questions—such as, what does a theory of anomalous color vision have to do with color film? (Hurvich and Jameson, 1956). Ralph had always been supportive of our research, sometimes found it useful in relation to practical issues that he himself had been concerned with, and had made it clear that it was his job to justify the various activities of his Division to the company's top management.

We were quite willing to stand behind the quality of our research, but had little to say (seriously) for our enterprise in terms of Kodak's profit-and-loss sheets. (This did not deter Leo, at a farewell luncheon, from summarizing our ten years in Rochester by laying down our reprints in sequence on his left as he read titles and year, and company reports on his right as he read the regularly increasing profit figures for each succeeding year. One of the middle-management people present was too convulsed with laughter to deliver his own ceremonial farewell words.) Sidney Newhall was nearing retirement age, and Bob Burnham moved into another Kodak project unrelated to vision. Sylvester Guth, whom we knew from the Inter-Society Color Council, invited us to continue our research at the General Electric Laboratories at Nela Park, and we considered this offer seriously enough to visit Cleveland.

At about this time, Hans-Lukas Teuber, who was doing research at the New York University Medical School, stopped overnight with us. Soon thereafter, he called to arrange a visit to NYU and an interview with Stuart Cook who was head of the Psychology Department there. At the time, Howard Kendler chaired the undergraduate department at the University Heights campus, and a retirement was anticipated in the parallel chair at Washington Square. In due course, Leo accepted an appointment as undergraduate chairman in Washington Square College and as director of the graduate experimental program, also located at Washington Square. Dorothea was appointed Research Scientist, not a unique status in NYU's large and heterogeneous department. We moved into living quarters in Washington Mews, which the University seemed to have agreed upon as a Psychology Department resource at that time. An outstanding advantage was the close promixity of the Mews to both lab and office, but also, although quiet (closed to automobile traffic), it was centered in all the Greenwich Village activity; close to restaurants, shops, jazz clubs, off-Broadway theatre, and downtown galleries. Spur of the moment dinners or post-colloquium gatherings were so easily and casually arranged that colleagues quickly became friends, and social events were easily "sandwiched" in between lecture preparations, grant applications, and the other familiar extra-hours activities common to academics.

Leo was giving lecture courses (some on material that he hadn't thought much about for some years), and Dorothea took primary responsibility for setting up the lab and getting their research program under way again. Eastman Kodak had generously provided a loan of the specialized optical apparatus that we had been using in Rochester. After a period during which only a small part of it could be squeezed into the available lab space (we had innocently, and foolishly, assumed that adequate lab space would have been arranged), we eventually acquired a large laboratory area with adjoining office space in NYU's Main Building on the Square. To avoid confusion between the undergraduate psychology lab and our own, we posted a sign that read "Psychonomic Laboratory." The Psychonomic Society was newly formed; we published a paper in the first issue of its journal and seem to have had the first, and possibly only, Psychonomic Laboratory.

Our research in Rochester had initially been motivated by the problem of color adaptation, with the aim of understanding the mechanism and establishing the lawful psychophysical functions as a basis both for checking the mechanism implications and for predicting the perceptual changes. Our first experiments were addressed to that part of the mechanism involved in color matching. Any color text that touched on this topic stated that three-variable color matches, once established, are invariant with changes in chromatic adaptation, but none cited references for the experimental evidence on which the assertion was based. We did the experiment, verified the accepted dogma, and filed the data and report. (No doubt others had also checked this, and like us, had seen no point in taking up journal space with a confirmation of an already accepted result.) It is an interesting experiment to observe, because the color changes are so remarkable, but are identical for the two physically different sides of the bipartite field that have been visually matched. What the result makes clear is that the retinal receptor mechanisms involved in color matching for standard photopic foveal conditions consist of no more than three independent variables, and that the relative sensitivity changes in the three cone types do not involve any significant nonlinearities for these conditions. There are important nonlinearities, and they are relevant for the perceived color changes but not for the matches, which do not depend on the balance of cone sensitivities among the three types, but only on the equivalence of each type on each side of the matching field. It is an important starting point for understanding chromatic adaptation.

A series of experiments followed that were concerned with the psychophysical specification of white, data that were required to establish a photopic base state that would leave the system in a neutral state of chromatic balance among the various color processing mechanisms. These were followed by studies of threshold and suprathreshold spectral sensitivity functions for various states of color adaptation. And in a report not delivered at an international meeting at Teddington, England, in 1957 (the passport problems mentioned earlier had not yet been resolved at the time) but that was published in the proceedings, we reported the results of color-matching experiments in which color adaptation was controlled independently in the two eyes (Hurvich and Jameson, 1958). These experiments gave clear evidence, in "objective" stimulus terms, of the nonlinearities that could be deduced from "subjective" appearance studies that had already been reported by Dean Judd and Harry Helson. The generality was a dependence of perceived hue on intensity for non-neutral adaptation states that has been named the "Helson-Judd Effect." Our conclusion was that the mechanism involved both linear sensitivity changes (probably at the cone level) following a simple coefficient law originally proposed by von Kries in the 1890's, and a postreceptoral process of incremental, rather than multiplicative, character, equivalent to a baseline shift, and probably occurring at the level of opponent mechanisms (whether retinal or more central). It was our notion that the postreceptoral processes were responsible for many of the systematic changes that can be demonstrated, and measured, in simultaneous contrast situations that involve spatial interactions and in successive contrast or after-effect situations that involve temporal interactions.

Our experimental cancellation experiments and quantitative development of the opponent process theory of color vision, published in a series of Optical Society papers in 1955 and 1956, were summarized, at Donald Hebb's invitation, in a *Psychological Review* paper in 1957 (Hurvich and Jameson, 1957). These studies, and the quantitative theoretical model, had given us a systematic framework in which to analyze adaptation and contrast data and phenomena. The laboratory experiments that we undertook at NYU were concerned with these issues, and, as in the past, we used a variety of experimental methods: threshold discriminations, scales of hue, brightness, and saturation, and matches for brightness or hue as well as complete color matches. And the experiments involved a variety of conditions that influence adaptive state and/or spatial and temporal interactions (Jameson and Hurvich, 1959b, 1960, 1961a, 1961b).

During this period, Edwin Land had startled many by his dramatic demonstrations that, from our point of view, illustrated phenomena long known but usually presented in their familiar context of discourse. Land presented them as new discoveries that challenged the views of scientists from Newton on and implied that they undermined the whole technological enterprise of colorimetry. Textbook publishers who continue to "colorize" the standard chromaticity diagram as if it were intended to represent color qualities, rather than stimulus proportions for color matches, are perpetuating a kind of misunderstanding of colorimetry that Land, and other physicists, seem to have been miseducated into. Since the appearance phenomena of contrast and adaptation are not accompanied by alteration in color matches, chromaticity diagrams used in colorimetry are, to say the least, an unreliable guide to perceived hues and saturations. But Land's showmanship and orchestration of his very effective demonstrations attracted more attention and produced more bewilderment than a variety of sober assessments and explications (including some of our own) were able immediately to counter.

Other developments were occurring at the time that were more significant for psychology. There was a great deal of activity in physiological psychology, and it was during this period that a new section of physiological psychology was formed in the APA. (Dorothea had wanted, when leaving Rochester, to go into visual electrophysiology, but Leo thought it would dilute their psychophysical program and interrupt the progress they were making.) Teuber's group at Bellevue provided an intellectual center focused on human brain function, and because of our overlapping interests, we had considerable interaction with colleagues and graduate students there, as well as with Teuber's frequent visitors from both the United States and European countries. The big issues at the time were centered on localization of brain function and a reexamination of the nature-nurture dichotomy. At the same time, orthodox views of visual physiology were requiring drastic revision. With Floyd Ratliff, Keffer Hartline, who had gone from frog to limulus as the simpler preparation to study elementary excitatory events in the visual system, had found his simple excitatory preparation to be a gold mine of lateral inhibition, and border contrast phenomena like Mach Bands changed from a curious subjective effect to a phenomenal demonstration of visual physiology. In Venezuela, the Swedish physiologist Gunnar Svaetichin, attempting to record from single fish cones with the microelectrode he had developed with Ragnar Granit shortly before the outbreak of World War II, found instead the graded potential responses that changed polarity with change in wavelength (Svaetichin, 1956). And the Japanese physiologist T. Tomita demonstrated conclusively that, although Svaetichin's responses (which came to be known as S-potentials) must be postreceptoral, the photoreceptors in vertebrate eyes respond to light by hyperpolarizing, always considered to be a physiological manifestation of "inhibition" rather than "excitation."

Ernst Mach would not have been surprised at Hartline and Ratliff's findings of lateral interaction, although he could not have predicted their detailed manifestation, and Ewald Hering would not have been surprised at Svaetichin's finding of opposite responses to wavelengths that look red versus green or yellow versus blue, although he also could not have predicted their detailed manifestation. All these developments in retinal electrophysiology, after the initial skepticism, stimulated a surge of related physiological experiments, and also a surge of interest in the work of those whose theoretical approach was compatible with the new look in visual physiology. This certainly included our own work, and our own initial wariness about Svaetichin's findings quickly proved unfounded, partly during an unannounced visit from Gunnar to our NYU lab, and soon thereafter at a meeting at the Instituto Venezolano Investigaciones Científicas (IVIC) lab outside Caracas. On this occasion, the whole symposium group, including Russell DeValois, who had just begun his studies of color mechanisms in the lateral geniculate nucleus of the monkey (DeValois, 1965), was treated to a flawless demonstration experiment that left no doubt in anyone's mind either about Svaetichin's experimental skills or about the validity of the physiological responses that he was reporting.

With the laboratory assistance now of graduate students in NYU's experimental program, we were developing a body of data and a theoretical analysis of temporal and spatial interactions and their influence on adaptation phenomena. In addition to individual experimental reports, two significant analytical papers were published in the *Journal of the Optical Society* in 1959 and 1961 (Jameson and Hurvich, 1959b, 1961b). Scaling data were important to our analyses, since we were interested in direct appearance measures as well as indices such as asymmetric haploscopic matches (each eye independently adapted) and discrimination measures from which suprathreshold appearance changes could be deduced. The component qualities of color could be readily partitioned in percentage scaling procedures, and there were reliable ways to validate the percentage scales.

At about the same time, Smitty Stevens was launching his campaign "To Honor Fechner and Repeal His Law" by substituting the magnitude scale for the jnd scale (Stevens, 1961). Once we had demonstrated to our own satisfaction that haploscopic brightness matches for one dark-adapted and one bright-adapted eye were well predicted from magnitude scaling data for the same two conditions, we included magnitude scales for brightness in our psychophysical method kit. It was an interesting co-incidence that our own paper on "Complexities of Perceived Brightness" (Jameson and Hurvich, 1961a), which showed, by both matching and magnitude scaling methods, that there are systematic departures from brightness constancy with change in illumination, included as its most controversial finding the data showing that, in the presence of lighter sur-roundings, dark surfaces get blacker with increasing illumination. Stevens reached the same conclusion from his magnitude scales for different con-ditions, and our two independent papers were published in the same vol-ume of *Science* in closely succeeding issues.

Another development in psychology during this period was the ap-pearance on the scene of mathematical psychology. Three people who fig-ured prominently in this development were Robert Bush, Duncan Luce, and Eugene Galanter, all of whom we knew from psychological meetings and through mutual friends. Bush had been brought to the University of Pennsylvania to rebuild that department. Galanter was already there (al-though he was soon to leave), and Bush brought Luce as one of his first new appointments in math psych. and Richard Solomon from Harvard to strengthen the learning area, Philip Teitelbaum also from Harvard in physiological, and, with our recommendation, Jack Nachmias from Swarthmore in perception. The Pennsylvania department was attracting considerable attention, and it was not easy to ignore a wire from Bush in the late summer of 1961 that said, in effect, the department wanted us there and please talk before saying no. There had been other offers, but we liked NYU, we liked Manhattan, and our work was going well. We would probably have said no without further ado had Luke Teuber not decided to go to MIT to convert their psychology program into a depart-ment. Like us, Luke also liked both NYU and Manhattan, as well as the home in Dobbs Ferry where he and Marianne had extended their famous hospitality to so many colleagues from all parts of the world. We have always been convinced that had Stuart Cook who headed the NYU department felt more strongly about physiological and experimental psychology, Teuber, we, and shortly thereafter Howard Kendler would not have left at that time. But in the fall of 1962, we moved to Philadelphia. Charles Cofer, who had come to NYU from Maryland after our arrival, was also to leave before too long, despite his own attachment to the university and its surroundings.

Perhaps we should note here some very good students at NYU, who all went into different problem areas: Barbara Wilson, who finished an important thesis on brightness and spectral sensitivity just before we left, stayed in the New York area and became involved in sensory impairment problems with children. Others, like John McLaughlin, now at the University of Delaware, finished their degrees in learning. Robert Keston, who did a nice analytical thesis on the Bidwell pulsative afterimage (a temporal phenomenon in which the afterimage hue is perceived with no prior visibility of the primary hue), went into an applied area and has not, as far as we know, continued in research.

The Pennsylvania department was intellectually exciting, and David Krantz, now at Columbia, who was our first graduate student there, was a pleasure to have as a student and later as a colleague and friend. David was in the math psych program, but found color vision an attractive substantive area in which to apply his considerable mathematical talent. Indeed, most of our Pennsylvania students continued in academia and in research. One, Dean Yager, now director of research at the State University of New York College of Optometry in New York, did a thorough study of color vision in goldfish with us. At NYU we had gotten a small grant from the National Science Foundation to do a feasibility study of color vision in fish, mostly because of the lack of behavioral data comprehensive and precise enough for satisfactory comparison with the physiological findings in fish retina. The results were sufficiently encouraging to continue such studies, and Dean was anxious to continue to work with fish after an undergraduate experiment that he had done at Harvard. The first measures of photopigment absorptions for single cones in the fish retina had just been made and published in *Science*, so, despite the variability of these first measures, Dean was able to develop a theoretical model for goldfish color vision that did not require cone sensitivity distributions based exclusively on deductions from psychophysical functions.

During our third year at Pennsylvania, Leo took the sabbatical that would have been available at that time had we not moved, and during that year, we both spent some time in Svaetichin's lab in Venezuela. (It was a little more difficult for Dorothea to arrange, since she continued on a research appointment with salary from research grants. This did not preclude her from lecturing in the proseminar or conducting seminars, but it did overextend her working day. Her New England upbringing would not have permitted anything less than a normal full day on research since her salary came fully from research funds.) The time with Svaetichin was too short to complete all of the experimental work on fish retina that we had laid out before arriving at the lab, but we did get some useful information about the behavior of horizontal cells under conditions that were as systematically controlled as they would be in a psychophysical laboratory. It was somewhat difficult for Gunnar, who brimmed with ideas for testing the physiological effects of one or another drug, and our psychophysics-bred insistence on systematic experiments might well have interfered with some important new discovery, but our host was tolerant and friendly throughout.

With the help of our phoneless summer cottage on Cape Cod, we finished the translation of Hering that we had been doing in rough note form for some years, and also a small book on *The Perception of Brightness and Darkness* (Hurvich and Jameson, 1966), as well as most of the papers that continued to come out of the lab program (Jameson and Hurvich, 1964, 1968, 1972; Jameson, 1970, 1972; Hurvich and Jameson, 1974a). The isolated dune has also been an ideal site for final thesis drafts, where hours of concentrated revision seem both less arduous and less traumatic after an early morning walk along Thoreau's great outer beach and a cold dip in the open Atlantic. Joseph Cohen, who had one of these thesis visits before beginning his academic career at Mount Holyoke, was city born, bred, and educated. A clear starry night, with no light pollution except from a distant fishing boat or two, was so novel that he spent most of the night on the deck with binoculars studying the Milky Way.

There was little of nature's stimulation during the academic year, but much of the intellectual, cultural, and social varieties. At Pennsylvania in the pre-brown-bag-lunch era of the early 1960's, faculty club lunches were frequent and included a mix of the senior people along with the more recent arrivals to the department. The discussions, in typical fashion, moved from broadly scientific to psychological to social and political issues of the day. Weekly colloquia were regularly attended by almost all the faculty and graduate students, and parties at one or another faculty home followed the post-colloquium dinners. In addition to these departmental interactions, the university had one of the first neuroscience groups in the Institute for Neurological Science founded by Louis B. Flexner; we, as well as other psychologists, were members of this institute. James Sprague and Eliot Stellar had turns as director, and there were regular interdisciplinary Institute seminars in the medical school.

The roster of influential psychologists at Pennsylvania at the time and during the span of our more than twenty-five years there is long, and so also is the list of similarly influential Ph.D.s from the department. To mention only one, Robert Rescorla, after essentially taking over Dick Solomon's mantle in learning theory, has returned from Yale to Penn where he is just finishing a stint as very effective chairman. We shall not name all the members of the Penn faculty with whom we have had interesting and important intellectual as well as social interactions. The list is too long. Obviously as time went on the department grew in numbers, and unfortunately spread out into several separate buildings. Many things have changed. Get-togethers for faculty luncheons are more apt to be conferences for center-grant proposals or committee meetings, whether departmental or university. Fortunately the excellence of the faculty and their research output has not changed.

During the years at Penn, we also continued our interactions with psychologist friends in Manhattan. With Stanley Schachter of Columbia and his wife Sophia, we spent many Saturday afternoons doing gallery walks in Manhattan and catching up on the social psychology of obesity, smoking, and more recently, the stock market. Julian Hochberg and his wife, Virginia Brooks, had become close friends while we were at Kodak and they at Cornell, and visits were periodically exchanged between Rochester and Ithaca. With them we discussed everything from perception to politics, and the disagreements, particularly with Julie, were part of the spice. The Hochbergs moved to NYU after we went to Philadelphia, and Julie then went to Columbia after Bob Bush had gone there to chair the department. (Bush left Pennsylvania shortly after bringing Henry Gleitman to take over the chairmanship there, and Henry was followed by a series of rotating chairmen from within the department. The style changed from one to the next, but the quality and spirit of the department remained high.) The Hochberg/Hurvich friendship continued, as did the zestful discussions, sometimes in Philadelphia or Truro, more often in Manhattan.

The 1960's and 1970's are also recorded in a boxful of buttons, recently unearthed, souvenirs of the various protest and peace marches that we joined in various cities during the turbulent Vietnam era. This was also a time of increasing committee activity for both of us, both within the university and in our various professional societies. Problems of color vision spill over beyond perception into groups specifically concerned with technology, standardization, neuroscience, ophthalmology, optics, and, these days, computer science, and each organization brings its own demands for special activities from its willing if not eager members.

In the early 1970's, Leo took a sabbatical leave at Columbia, where he had planned, among other things, to collaborate with Clarence Graham in order to clarify some seemingly paradoxical results that Clarence had published on color blindness. Unfortunately, Graham died before Leo's year at Columbia began. Leo's additional plan was to begin drafting a book on color vision. Dorothea knew that the book Leo had in mind was not her own top priority, so she agreed to offer advice, criticism, and some editorial assistance, but not coauthorship. Instead, she stayed on in the lab during that year to finish some ongoing experiments for which their current grant support had not yet run out. They had acquired a "pad" in the Village by then and met there or in Philadelphia on weekends.

In the mid-1970's Dorothea decided that she was ready for a self-supported leave, which she spent as visiting scholar at Columbia, mostly in their libraries, as well as in the galleries and libraries of New York's major museums. She really wanted freedom from full-time commitment to a planned research program, the stimulation of a different environment, and the expanded vista of the fine arts side of the perception area, which continued to compel her intellectual interest (Jameson and Hurvich, 1975). She was also tired of treating all extra-laboratory university commitments as add-ons to her research activities, and she had come increasingly to sense her second-class status within the Pennsylvania faculty. Despite a change in 1974 from research to tenured professorship, an accumulation of small things seemed to have reached a critical mass, and at the end of her leave year she decided to resign from Pennsylvania, teach individual courses on an adjunct basis at Columbia, and return to Philadelphia to continue the lab experiments with Leo on non-teaching days. She found the arrangement more satisfactory than did Leo, and he would probably not have forgiven her had she not, a year or so later, accepted Eliot Stellar's offer, as provost, of a special professorship back at Pennsylvania. As University Professor, she is able to choose the courses and departments in which she wants to teach and do research, without having to cut through the usual administrative red tape. This has been a good experience.

In 1981–82 we spent a year at the Center for Advanced Study in the Behavioral Sciences in Stanford, California, where we had a first-rate intellectual experience with the other fellows and the director, Gardner Lindzey, caught up on much reading, and finished some papers. Dorothea amassed a collection of notes and chapter drafts for what will ultimately be a book on art and visual perception (Jameson, 1985b).

The recent period in psychology has been marked by an increasing emphasis on cognitive psychology everywhere, and we have a new graduate program in neuroscience at Pennsylvania. Elsewhere, there has been a proliferation of degree-granting vision centers. In the current academic job market, there is not much call for students trained broadly in psychology and specializing in visual perception and psychophysics.

The area of color vision seems always to have been one in which there are recurrent bursts of excitement among those in both related and unrelated fields. These bursts usually center on a newly discovered, or more often rediscovered, phenomenon. The excitement wanes as the phenomenon is demystified by scientific scrutiny. We have already mentioned Edwin Land's demonstrations in this context.

Another phenomenon, which was more robust as a new finding, was the McCollough Effect, a directionally contingent effect that produces weak, but long-lasting afterimage hues on black and white gratings of appropriate orientation. The effect also involves temporal sequencing of the stimulus patterns that generate the aftereffects. In a study with D. Varner, a graduate student of the 1980's, we found that the long-lasting characteristic was generated by the temporal sequencing, even without oriented patterns. It is yet another finding that points to the need for both receptoral and postreceptoral mechanisms to account for visual adaptation (Jameson, Hurvich, and Varner, 1979). This concept seems finally to be taking hold among vision researchers, but not without a temporary fallback to the receptoral von Kries Law that is so convenient for programming "color constancy" into computerized devices. There is no objection to useful devices, but it does not further progress in understanding perception to represent an easily programmed device as based on the human model, which is, in fact, richer and more complex.

We also continue to study issues of color blindness and color anomalies (Hurvich, 1972; Hurvich and Jameson, 1974b; Jameson, Hurvich, and

Varner, 1982). Here too our early work made it clear that the simple division into "color blind" dichromats and "color weak" anomalous trichromats was inadequate to describe the variety of diagnostic types that we encountered. So too was the nearly universal attribution of all color vision abnormalities exclusively to the cones and their photopigments. A two-level hypothesis to account for the color vision abnormalities was the substance of the paper on the theory of anomalous color vision to which the Kodak vice president had taken exception back in 1956. For some time now, serious researchers in the area of color vision have accepted the concept of opponency as essential to color processing by the visual system (Hurvich, 1981, 1985; Jameson, 1985a). Nevertheless, the oversimplified view of color vision abnormalities, which really stemmed from the obsolete coded-receptor theory, resisted reexamination until relatively recently. There are still detailed questions of mechanism to be explored, including the etiology of acquired color deficiencies that accompany visual disease processes and the losses that occur as a result of brain trauma. These, as well as the congenital phenomena, continue to occupy us in the laboratory and on the theoretical "drawing board."

Leo, although declared Emeritus in 1979, has continued research as actively as ever (even though there are now fewer psychology graduate students in vision) and also continues as program director for the university's interdepartmental vision training grant supported by the National Eye Institute, now in its eleventh year. Dorothea continues her teaching and research and, like many other senior women professors, wonders how many more committees there can possibly be that need female representation. The one major change has been a trade of the New York pad mentioned earlier for one close to the psychology lab building in Philadelphia, and of the Philadelphia townhouse for a Manhattan apartment.

Selected Publications by Leo M. Hurvich and Dorothea Jameson

McFarland, R. A., Holway, A. H., & Hurvich. (1942). *Studies of visual fatigue*. Boston, MA: Graduate School of Business Administration, Harvard University.
Holway, A. H., Jameson, & Hurvich. (1945). *A new stereoscopic rangefinder based on three distance-cues*. Boston, MA: Graduate School of Business Administration, Harvard University.

Holway, A. H., & Jameson. (1947). *Good lighting for people at work in reading rooms and offices.* Boston, MA: Graduate School of Business Administration, Harvard University.

Hurvich & Jameson. (1949). Helmholtz and the three-color theory: An historical note. *American Journal of Psychology, 62,* 111–114.

Hurvich & Jameson. (1951a). A psychophysical study of white: 1. Neutral adaptation. *Journal of the Optical Society of America, 41,* 521–527.

Jameson & Hurvich. (1951a). A psychophysical study of white: 2. Area and duration as variants. *Journal of the Optical Society of America, 41,* 528–536.

Hurvich & Jameson. (1951b). A psychophysical study of white: 3. Adaptation as variant. *Journal of the Optical Society of America, 41,* 787–801.

Jameson & Hurvich. (1951b). Use of spectral hue-invariant loci for the specification of white stimuli. *Journal of Experimental Psychology, 41,* 455–463.

Hurvich & Jameson. (1951c). The binocular fusion of yellow in relation to color theories. *Science, 114,* 199–202.

Hurvich & Jameson. (1953). Spectral sensitivity of the fovea: 1. Neutral adaptation. *Journal of the Optical Society of America, 43,* 485–494.

Jameson & Hurvich. (1953). Spectral sensitivity of the fovea: 2. Dependence on chromatic adaptation. *Journal of the Optical Society of America, 43,* 552–559.

Hurvich & Jameson. (1954). Spectral sensitivity of the fovea: 3. Heterochromatic brightness and chromatic adaptation. *Journal of the Optical Society of America, 44,* 215–222.

Jameson & Hurvich. (1955). Some quantitative aspects of an opponent-colors theory: 1. Chromatic responses and spectral saturation. *Journal of the Optical Society of America, 45,* 546–552.

Hurvich & Jameson. (1955). Some quantitative aspects of an opponent-colors theory: 2. Brightness, saturation and hue in normal and dichromatic vision. *Journal of the Optical Society of America, 45,* 602–616.

Jameson & Hurvich. (1956). Some quantitative aspects of an opponent-colors theory: 3. Changes in brightness, saturation and hue with chromatic adaptation. *Journal of the Optical Society of America, 46,* 405–415.

Hurvich & Jameson. (1956). Theoretical analysis of anomalous trichromatic color vision. *Journal of the Optical Society of America, 46,* 1075–1089.

Hurvich & Jameson. (1957). An opponent-process theory of color vision. *Psychological Review, 64,* 384–404.

Hurvich & Jameson. (1958). Further development of a quantified opponent-colours theory. In *Visual Problems of Colour* (Vol. 2, pp. 691–723). London: Her Majesty's Stationery Office.

Jameson & Hurvich. (1959a). Note on factors influencing the relation between stereoscopic acuity and observation distance. *Journal of the Optical Society of America, 49,* 639.

Jameson & Hurvich. (1959b). Perceived color and its dependence on focal, surrounding and preceding stimulus variables. *Journal of the Optical Society of America, 49,* 890–898.

Jameson & Hurvich. (1960). Perceived color, induction effects, and opponent-response mechanisms. *Journal of General Physiology, 43* (6), 63–80 (Suppl.).

Jameson & Hurvich. (1961a). Complexities of perceived brightness. *Science, 133*, 174–179.

Jameson & Hurvich. (1961b). Opponent chromatic induction: Experimental evaluation and theoretical account. *Journal of the Optical Society of America, 51*, 46–53.

Jameson & Hurvich. (1964). Theory of brightness and color contrast in human vision. *Vision Research, 4*, 135–154.

Hurvich & Jameson. (1966). *The perception of brightness and darkness*. Boston: Allyn & Bacon.

Jameson & Hurvich. (1968). Opponent-response functions related to measured cone photopigments. *Journal of the Optical Society of America, 58*, 429–430.

Jameson. (1970). Brightness scales and their interpretation. In M. Richter (Ed.), *AIC "Color 69" Stockholm* (pp. 377–385). Göttingen: Musterschmidt.

Jameson. (1972). Theoretical issues of color vision. In D. Jameson & L. M. Hurvich (Eds.), *Handbook of sensory physiology: Vol. VII/4. Visual psychophysics* (pp. 381–412). Berlin: Springer Verlag.

Jameson & Hurvich. (1972). Color adaptation: Sensitivity, contrast, after-images. In D. Jameson & L. M. Hurvich (Eds.), *Handbook of sensory physiology: Vol. VII/4, Visual psychophysics* (pp. 568–581). Berlin: Springer Verlag.

Hurvich. (1972). Color vision deficiencies. In D. Jameson & L. M. Hurvich (Eds.), *Handbook of sensory physiology. Vol. VII/4. Visual psychophysics* (pp. 586–624). Berlin: Springer Verlag.

Hurvich & Jameson. (1974a). Opponent processes as a model of neural organization. *American Psychologist, 29*, 88–102.

Hurvich & Jameson. (1974b). Evaluation of single pigment shifts in anomalous color vision. In *Modern problems in ophthalmology* (Vol. 13, pp. 200–209). Basel: S. Karger.

Jameson & Hurvich. (1975). From contrast to assimilation: In art and in the eye. *Leonardo, 8*, 125–131.

Jameson, Hurvich, & Varner, D. (1979). Receptoral and post-receptoral visual processes in recovery from chromatic adaptation. *Proceedings of the National Academy of Science, 74*, 3034–3038

Hurvich. (1981). *Color vision*. Sunderland, MA: Sinauer.

Jameson, Hurvich, & Varner, D. (1982). Discrimination mechanisms in color deficient systems. In G. Verriest (Ed.), *Colour vision deficiencies* (Vol. 6, pp. 295–301). Bristol, England: Adam Hilger.

Varner, D., Jameson, & Hurvich. (1984). Temporal sensitivities related to color theory. *Journal of the Optical Society of America A, 1*, 474–481.

Hurvich. (1985). Opponent-colours theory. In D. Ottoson & S. Zeki (Eds.), *Central and peripheral mechanisms of colour vision* (pp. 61–82). London: MacMillan.

Jameson. (1985a). Opponent colors theory in the light of physiological findings. In D. Ottoson & S. Zeki (Eds.), *Central and peripheral mechanisms of colour vision* (pp. 83–102). London: MacMillan.

Jameson. (1985b). Seeing: By art and by design. *Transactions of American Philosophical Society, 75*, (Part 6), 68–78.

Other Publications Cited

Dartnall, H. J. A. (Ed.) (1972). *Handbook of sensory physiology: Vol. VII/1. Photochemistry of vision*. New York: Springer Verlag.

DeValois, R. L. (1965). Analysis and coding of color vision in the primate visual system. *Cold Spring Harbor Symposium on Quantitative Biology, 30,* 567–579.

Granit, R. (1947). *Sensory mechanisms of the retina*. London: Oxford University Press.

Hecht, S. (1930). The development of Thomas Young's theory of color vision. *Journal of the Optical Society of America, 20,* 231–270.

Hecht, S., Shlaer, S., & Pirenne, M. H. (1942). Energy, quanta, and vision. *Journal of General Physiology, 25,* 819–840.

Hering, E. (1920). *Grundzüge der Lehre von Lichtsinn*. Berlin: Springer Verlag. Translated by Hurvich & Jameson. (1964). *Outlines of a theory of the light sense*. Cambridge, MA: Harvard University Press.

Köhler, W. (1938). *The place of value in a world of facts*. New York: Liveright.

Ludvigh, E., & McCarthy, E. F. (1938). Absorption of visible light by the refractive media of the eye. *Archives of Ophthalmology, 20,* 37–51.

Piéron, H. (1964). La vision en lumière intermittente. Paris: Monographes Françaises de Psychologie No. 8. Centre National de la Recherche Scientifique. Translated by Hurvich & Jameson. (1965). Vision in intermittent light. In W. D. Neff (Ed.), *Contributions to sensory physiology* (Vol. 1, pp. 179–264). New York: Academic Press.

Stevens, S. S. (1961). To honor Fechner and repeal his law. *Science, 133,* 80–86.

Stiles, W. S. (1978). *Mechanisms of colour vision*. London: Academic Press.

Svaetichin, G. (1956). Spectral response curves of single cones. *Acta Physiologica Scandinavica, 39* (Supplement 134), 17–46.

Bärbel Inhelder

Bärbel Inhelder

1913–1932

I was born in German-speaking Switzerland, in St. Gall, which, though a small town, was open to the world with its excellent theater, its orchestra, and its commercial college. I was fortunate in having a good start in life as a child desired and loved by generous, cultivated parents. My father, a zoologist, taught natural sciences, and my mother, a gifted writer, was much occupied with literature. In temperament they were very different: my father, calm and serene, was called Humanus by his colleagues and pupils, and combined great natural goodness with Kantian morality. Our friends from abroad regarded him as the prototypical Swiss who, like his forefathers for many generations, followed the liberal traditions of his country. My mother by contrast was lively, even brilliant during her good periods, which alternated, alas, with periods of depression. Her receptiveness of mind and her sense of humor reflected the youthful years she had spent in Berlin at the turn of the century. She maintained a voluminous correspondence, wrote a book about her mother, stories about our ancestors, as well as innumerable little plays for my young companions and myself. I was an only child and had great need of making contact with other children. Because of my choice of friends, the family called me the international child.

Of my earliest years I have hardly any recollections. I have been told that I created a language all my own, which I spoke volubly at a very early age, and rapidly proceeded to learn the language spoken by the people around me. My finest memories of the family circle date from my pre-adolescence and adolescence. During holidays in the mountains, my father took me for long walks. I remember not caring much for botanical classification but being very interested in observing animals, whose tracks I liked to follow. In the evenings, we read the Greek classics, the *Iliad*, the

I wish to thank cordially my colleagues H. and M. Sinclair for their thoughtful translation and my collaborators D. de Caprona and P. Steenken.

Odyssey, and the tragedies of Euripides. My mother led me to discover Shakespeare and, of course, the German classics. My father made me share his interest in the pre-Socratic philosophers and also explained to me, in accessible terms, the evolutionary theories of Lamarck, Darwin, and Haeckel.

Of my formal education during this period I remember the fascination with which I rediscovered some algebraic principles and the experiments we carried out in the chemistry and particularly the physics laboratory. Our young teacher was a specialist in aerodynamics and encouraged us to build model gliders. He also initiated us into the then current theories about the origins of our planet and gave us some idea of the historical changes in conceptions of causality together with a link of epistemology.

For a while I simultaneously followed private courses leading to a university entry diploma and a course at a teachers' college that provided me with a professional qualification. During this time I first came in contact with experimental psychology, which, devoid of any visible link with either theory or practice, did not retain my attention. By contrast, I loved to observe children of any age in real-life situations. Above all, I voraciously read anything that was available to me by Freud, whatever I could find on the psychology of adolescence, such as Spranger's book, and the voluminous literature on youth movements.

School at every level was marked by friendship. To a friend who was an ardent mountaineer I owe my initiation into exploring the mountains in summer as well as in winter.

Observing living beings, animals as well as children, devising experiments, living in untamed natural surroundings, and going out towards other people—these became permanent pursuits.

1932–1938

In the autumn of 1932, I set out for Geneva on a one-year trial period. Discounting a few interruptions, I have been there ever since! I was attracted not only by the venerable university founded by Jean Calvin, but also by Geneva's unique cultural climate: French on the one hand, and international on the other. Above all, Geneva was the home of the Institut Jean-Jacques Rousseau. Of high renown, the Institute was founded in 1912 by Edouard Claparède, who was professor of experimental psychology at the Faculty of Sciences in Geneva University. At the time of my arrival this was the only place in Switzerland where one could follow a

complete course in psychology, combined with either philosophy or biology.

At the Institute I soon encountered three exceptional teachers: Edouard
Claparède, Pierre Bovet, and Jean Piaget. Bovet, a humanist and educa-
tionist, was in touch with all the great educators and especially the idealists of his time. He was an enthusiastic traveler, had been received by
Mahatma Gandhi, and had invited Rabindranath Tagore to the Maison
des Petits, the Institute's experimental school. He was a pacifist as well as
a man of religious convictions and his writings were accordingly concerned with the combative instinct and with religious feelings in children.

Claparède was a particularly likeable figure, and retained into a ripe old
age his youthful curiosity about anything and everything psychological.
His bibliography presents a highly variegated picture, with titles covering
the critique of associationism, the anticipatory function of sleep, psychology, and functional education. In 1932–33 he had just finished his work
on the genesis of hypothesis (Claparède, 1933), which to this day, in my
opinion, has lost none of its topicality. With his "thinking aloud" method
he showed how trial-and-error procedures are oriented by hypothetical
implications.

This eminent scholar was also a warm-hearted man whose students
knew they were welcome in his grounds and were gladly accepted as company on his Sunday walks. Once a year, the professor, his students, and his
assistants would set off on an excursion into the mountains. I had the privilege of being frequently invited to his library, where, among many other
publications, I read the *Archives de Psychologie*, which he had founded
with Théodore Flournoy and of which I am the present editor. Claparède
also brought me along with his assistant Lambercier to the Mediterranean
coast in order to measure the size-of-the-moon illusion.

Claparède entertained close relations with all the great psychologists of
his time, among them, the Americans James Baldwin, Edward B. Titchener, John Watson, and Edwin G. Boring. He often met with Wolfgang
Köhler and many Belgian and French colleagues and also corresponded
with Sigmund Freud. The small family of psychologists in the Geneva
Institute felt itself to be part of the big international family. We worked
intensively, inspired by a sense of solidarity in the shadow of fascism
which our Spanish, Italian, German, and Austrian friends were fleeing.

Then there was Jean Piaget, who taught the history of scientific
thought at the Faculty of Sciences at the University and child psychology
at the Institute. In the early 1930's, Piaget published *The Moral Judgment*

of the Child (Piaget, 1932), in which he showed the importance of peer cooperation for the development of moral autonomy, when reciprocal respect gradually replaces unilateral deference. During his lectures on this subject, I was fascinated by the way in which Piaget showed how abstract theories such as those of Kant or Durkheim could throw light on observational data and how, inversely, these data led to a comparison of the theories.

With this book Piaget completed his cycle of works on children's reasoning and representation. He had already started on *The Origins of Intelligence in Children* (Piaget, 1936/1952), which I had the privilege of reading in manuscript in installments as it was being completed. I shall never forget the emotional shock I experienced when reading this work. Despite my youth, despite my ignorance, I realized immediately that here was a powerful theory that postulated functional continuity between biological adaptation of the hereditary core as constituted by phylogenesis and psychological adaptation via the infant's own action patterns, which leads to acts of intelligence before language appears. In the complementary work *The Construction of Reality* (Piaget, 1937/1954), with its more epistemological orientation, Piaget showed how the infant, through his gradually organizing activities, elaborates elementary forms of knowledge of object, space, time, and causality.

It was an adventure to follow lectures and seminars on the history of scientific thought, especially the progress in causal explanations of the universe, from the pre-Socratic thinkers to Galileo and Newton via the physicists of the end of the Middle Ages such as Buridan and Oresme. And how fascinating to find certain analogies between progress of thought in the child and progress of scientific thought from one period to the next. Only at the end of his life, and thanks to his collaboration with the physicist Rolando Garcia (Piaget and Garcia, 1983), did Piaget fully elaborate the relations between psychogenesis and the history of science, but already in those early days, following the French philosopher Léon Brunschvicg, he was able to study child thought with a historico-critical eye. This was heady stuff, particularly in comparison with what was being taught in other lectures on child psychology and philosophy.

Above all, Piaget gave me the impression, which was never belied, that he was engaged in a life's work. This feeling of creative work in progress, and Piaget's readiness to associate his students with his enterprise, infused us with enthusiasm.

On my twentieth birthday, Piaget suggested that I should carry out a small piece of research which later took on great importance and led to many other studies: dissolve a lump of sugar in water while the child is looking on and try to find out what the child thinks about the dissolution process and the different states of a substance. The age of children likely to be interested in such a problem ran from four to twelve. So there I was, embarking on the study of quantity conservation, which—I did not know it then—was to keep me busy for a long time. Alina Szeminska—older than I and already experimenting on numerical quantities—was a great help, and we became life-long friends. To see and to hear how one went about getting children to talk, I had to go to the University of Lausanne, where Piaget himself was still questioning children in the presence of students.

At that time, he was working on class-inclusion problems, asking children questions about a string of wooden beads, some of which were brown. After his demonstrations, Piaget would take me along to collect limnea stagnalis (fresh water snails) he had previously placed in certain ponds. He continued to check varieties of this species, which had become stable over many generations.

My study showed that between the ages of five and eleven, children change their interpretation of the dissolution of sugar. The youngest children thought that nothing was conserved, except, perhaps, just the taste of the sugar in water. With later ages, something of the sugar is thought to remain in some invisible form, but this does not mean that either its weight or its volume is conserved. Those children who are convinced of the conservation of weight and of the total volume explain the observed phenomenon in a way that is reminiscent of pre-Socratic atomism. Thus, a ten-year-old says: "The sugar is all in the water. It's in tiny bits but so small and so spread out that you cannot see them any more, but I can put them together in my head, and then I know it's got to be the same quantity of sugar."

This was the first time that we noted, coming from children, explicit expressions of some sort of reversibility, the inversion in thought of a transformation, and thus of a conservation of quantity. I was proud to see that Piaget had commented on my first publication (Inhelder, 1936) on this subject when he was invited to the tricentenary of Harvard University, and I intended to continue my research in this field for my doctoral thesis. But Piaget had a different plan: during one of our walks (most of our scientific discussions were conducted in a Socratic mode) Piaget suggested that I should design and carry out a series of experiments dealing with the quantity of matter, which might lead to a book to be written by us both. I remember the exact place and date of this proposal: it was on a sunny winter day as we were walking in the early afternoon along the Salève, the Genevan's favorite hiking mountain. I felt some regret at abandoning my project for a thesis but was excited by the idea of taking part in a major scientific enterprise. At the time, I certainly did not think this would lead to a long-lasting, fascinating collaboration.

The underlying epistemological problem was to understand how *normative facts* (i.e., principles the reasoning subject considers evident and necessary) are built up. Invariance of quantity of matter under changes of shape is such a normative fact, even when the quantity is not measurable, either objectively or in the mind of the child. The experiments were carried out with, for example, two balls of modeling clay, of which one is kneaded into the shape of a sausage. Does the sausage still contain the same amount of clay as the unchanged ball? For a typical 4-to-5-year-old, the quantity of clay has increased, because the sausage is longer than the ball: when one of the balls is broken up into bits, the quantity also increases, because there are so many pieces. Alternatively, for some children the quantity is thought to be diminished, because the sausage is thinner than the ball, and the bits are so small. When the same child is interviewed two years later, he states with great conviction that there is still "just as much clay, because nothing was added and nothing taken away, and because the sausage is longer but it is also thinner, so it comes to the same thing, and you can always make it back into the same ball as before." Such arguments of identity, of compensation, of reciprocal relations, and of inversion, as well as arguments of elementary form of commutativity in the case of the ball broken into small pieces ("all you did was to put the bits in different pieces, that was there, now it's here") reveal the construction of an underlying system that Piaget tried to model as the operational system of "groupings." I remember that when Piaget was in a period of retreat, totally immersed in his formalizations and logical elaborations, he worked with even greater concentration and ardor than when he was involved in the theoretical framework of the experimental results.

Afterwards, it was always fascinating to discover with him the many ways in which the results of formal analyses on the one hand and of psychogenetic experiments on the other clarified the epistemological problems. I was particularly interested in the different physical aspects of matter and its quantification, and in the complex notion of weight, the mass of objects that can be lifted up and their density, and in the ways children represent condensation and dilatation (mercury shrinks as it gets colder, water expands when it freezes, a heated grain of popcorn expands). The same operatory structures lead at different ages to conservation judgments of quantity, of matter, weight, volume, etc., and these age differences, or *décalages* as they are called, interested me greatly.

The existence of such décalages was often used as an argument against our structuralist approach, but the process of coming to know reality, and particularly physical reality, goes with intricate interactions between the subject's construction of this reality and its multiple aspects, which the reasoning subject tries to differentiate and coordinate. Our results were published in *The Child's Construction of Quantities* (Piaget and Inhelder, 1941/1974).

In order to grasp the constructive mechanisms of reasoning, I developed and practiced what had been called the clinical, and since, the critical exploratory method. This method favored an exchange of views based on the manipulation of real objects, in contrast with the mostly verbal method of Piaget's early research. To discover the psychological reality of the child's reasoning processes as hypothesized by the theoretical models, I tried to follow the children's thinking in its meandering flow while keeping their attention focused on the crucial points of the notions and operations I was exploring. This method calls for a thorough understanding of the theories underlying the dialogues. Throughout the interview, the experimenter has to formulate hypotheses about the cognitive bases of the child's reactions (verbal or in actions on the objects) and then devise ways of immediately checking these hypotheses in the experimental situation. In conservation experiments the children are constantly encouraged (in a quasi-Socratic dialogue) to provide arguments which they would certainly not invent on their own, but which in the interaction become focal points of reflection.

The validity of the results is essentially a function of their convergence: each theme is studied via a considerable number of different experiments which complement one another and which often had to be published in more than one volume.

During the six years when I was first a student and then a voluntary research assistant, I was at liberty to choose from a number of study-courses apart from genetic and experimental psychology and to follow my own interests. André Rey let me take part in his consultations for children with problems. He had a particular talent for inventing diagnostic tests. During a leave of absence, when he went to Lashley's laboratory at Harvard, he entrusted Edith Meyer and myself with the responsibility for his consultation bureau, which was linked to the University. Richard Meili, a student of Köhler's, introduced me to gestalt theory, and I was captivated by its aesthetic aspects; but I could not share his enthusiasm for the methods of factorial analysis, and I confess that I am still very skeptical about their value in psychology. I was admitted to the School of Medicine to follow courses on the physiology of the nervous system and on clinical neurology. And I particularly admired the lectures the specialist in evolution theories, Eugène Guyenot, gave in the Department of Science.

The Institut Rousseau was attached to the Department of Philosophy in the Faculté des Lettres, which meant that to obtain a doctorate one had to pass several exams in philosophy. At the time I was already deeply involved in Piagetian genetic epistemology, which may explain the vivid memories I retain of my astonished delight in Plato's theses as well as my understanding of the Aristotelian universe and my admiration of Kant. The works of Schopenhauer and Nietzsche were relegated as reading material for the holidays. Bergson's work left me with ambivalent feelings, Höffding was stimulating, and it was not till later on that the use of classical logic became important to me.

In those days there was a night-train to Paris, which enabled me to attend lectures by Léon Brunschvicg whose work (and particularly his book *L'expérience humaine et la causalité physique*, 1922) made a lasting impression on me. I also had the privilege of attending Henri Wallon's presentations, who with his team examined clinical cases and discussed them before an audience of students. I remember visiting Henri Piéron in his laboratory, which was then located in the attic of the Sorbonne, and conversing several times with Pierre Janet, a most kind-hearted man. I keep vivid and joyful memories of this period and of the welcoming attitude of the masters of French psychology. In 1937 I attended for the first time the International Congress of Psychology, held in Paris, and I don't think I ever missed one for the next 30 years. At this congress, I had the pleasure of meeting Albert Michotte, who to the end of his life offered me a fatherly affection, and Karl and Charlotte Bühler of Vienna. The masters of the gestalt school had already fled Germany at that time, thus leaving psychology in Europe diminished.

Compared with the curricula of psychology students nowadays, my studies certainly failed to cover many important topics, but on the other hand I was in a position to follow my personal interests and take part in what was still the unfolding of a young discipline. My father, wise man, foresaw that if I were to stay in Geneva, Piaget would continue to propose new themes for me to research, which would result in co-authored books and not in a doctoral thesis. Thus, I went back to St. Gall.

1938–1943

When I had finished my exams for a Ph.D., as well as the research on the conservation of physical quantities, it was high time to start my thesis. My interests, at that point, were in two directions: practical and theoretical. On the one hand, I wanted to take the hypothesis of operatory structures out of its theoretically circumscribed domain and show that all behavior, normal or pathological, should be studied from the point of view of the mechanisms of its development and not only as a finished product. I hypothesized that delays or deviations in development could be shown to be the result of delays or fixations of the elaboration of operations or their groupings. On the other hand, the usual tests seemed inadequate for the determination of mentally handicapped children's cognitive poten tialities; in particular, the then current tests seemed incapable of differentiating between endogenous and socio-affective retardations.

Armed with my knowledge of psychogenetic models and methods, which I had developed in the research I had just finished, I examined a considerable number of mentally handicapped children and a few adults in specialized schools and institutions. Some of them I managed to see again several years later. It was fascinating to analyze the similarities and differences between them and the normal child. I found that the more heavily handicapped children remained at a pre-operatory stage and reasoned like my young normal subjects, whereas the less handicapped reached certain elementary operations, such as those underlying the conservation of the quantity of matter. The least handicapped achieved conservation of weight, but remained incapable of dealing with volume, which requires a clear dissociation between geometric voluminosity and dynamic physical volume, and is close to the kind of reasoning that belongs to the formal stage. The handicapped subjects show curious oscillations in their arguments, giving justifications that in normal children do not occur together, but belong to different levels of reasoning. A detailed analysis of the equilibration process made it possible to discern a certain viscosity of thought that seems to be characteristic of mental retardation.

My book *The Diagnosis of Reasoning in the Mentally Retarded* (Inhelder, 1943/1968), translated into several languages, gives a detailed account of my methods and my system of interpretation.

Before I had finished my thesis, the Minister of Education of my canton asked me to create a psychological service for educational purposes: its first task was to find, throughout the canton, even in the isolated villages, those children who were in need of special education. "Listen to everybody, do what you think is right, I will back you up." And so I set out by train, on bicycle, on foot. I visited one school after another, armed with the tools of my trade: lumps of sugar (a rationed commodity in those days), play-dough, a small kitchen scale, and lots of hypotheses. I fondly remember an expedition to the smallest school of the canton (five children only), huddled at the foot of the mountain on the banks of a lake. The village was only accessible by boat and had the historic name of Quinten, close to its siblings Quarten and Terzen. My tasks were—at least in the beginning—social and administrative, as well as psychological. I spoke with parents, with teachers, with local authorities, and with private persons who made it financially possible for children to go to institutions far from home. My work provided excellent schooling in practical sociology. I was no doubt not really ready for such responsibilities, and the fact that the service rapidly took shape and became well known is to be credited to many factors: I was young and strong; I was interested in children and human relations in general; I had a fair amount of humor when I had to deal with the authorities; and furthermore, we all shared a common anxiety, the war at our frontiers.

During this same period I had the pleasure of teaching child psychology in a school for future nursery school teachers; my students were particularly inventive as well as artistically gifted, and it was a great joy to lead them to discover young children's representations of the world.

1943–1951

In 1943, when my doctoral thesis had been defended, I received a telephone call from Geneva: a position of "Chef de travaux" had become vacant, and I was invited to occupy it. This meant an important decision: to give up, at least temporarily, the total autonomy I had in an organization which I had created myself, in order to rejoin my academic life and participate in what Piaget generously called our common oeuvre. Piaget tried to convince me that he needed my presence to counter his tendency toward becoming a totally abstract thinker. After having been captivated for years by questions of algebraic formalization, he was at that time working on probabilistic models that were to explain perceptive mechanisms. My experience of our earlier working together and the atmosphere of mutual trust it engendered led me to accept his argument. So I returned to the source of epistemology and genetic psychology.

The 1940's and the beginning of the 1950's were years of great progress in genetic epistemology and its structuralist methods. Piaget was ambitiously working on the creation of an epistemology based on experimental disciplines, and this required a constant link with genetic psychology. Epistemology is concerned with the validity of knowledge and its normative problems, whereas psychology, in this context, functions as its corresponding experimental science. The study of the development of knowledge allows verification of classical epistemological hypotheses and can suggest new hypothetical constructions. On the psychological side, the aim was to bring to light underlying structures common to the different categories and concepts of knowledge, such as space, time, and causality; numerical, spatial and physical quantities; etc.

When I returned to Geneva, Piaget asked me to continue the study of children's spontaneous geometry (begun with Alina Szeminska, before her fateful return to Poland) and to study the development of spatial representation; at the same time he wanted me to start working on children's notions of probability and chance. In *The Child's Conception of Space* (Piaget and Inhelder, 1948/1956)—which remains one of my favorite books—we tried to clarify the development of spatial concepts. Does it follow the historical sequence, starting with intuitions resembling Euclidian axioms, and continue with notions of projective geometry and topology, or is the order more like the order inherent in their formalization? The experiments I designed with the help of my students showed that topological relations of contiguity, separation, and envelopment are more elementary as representations, closer to sensorimotor exploratory actions, than Euclidian and projective structures, into which the topological relations are slowly integrated over a period of representations resembling affine and plane similarity geometry. In *The Child's Conception of Geometry* (Piaget, Inhelder, and Szeminska, 1948/1960) the experiments were designed to help children understand the invariability of the length of straight lines, of surface, and of volumes in many circumstances, and to create situations so that they discovered themselves the necessity for a common measuring device. The various situations were all very simple:

for example, we asked the children to construct towers of equal height placed at different levels from the ground with a screen between them, which did not stop the youngest children from thinking that they could transport the height of the first tower "in their eyes" (in a kind of visual transposition). Another example in this series of experiments is the study of natural coordinates, where children were asked to imagine the position of a liquid in bottles held in various positions.

During this period Piaget no longer interviewed children himself, but he was present when I gave demonstrations for my students, and occasionally intervened to ask the children pertinent questions. I remember very vividly one of those occasions when I interviewed a child in his presence after I had been glued to the radio with some friends outside Geneva during a whole night (it was D day in Normandy); the passage from war to child psychology with only a bicycle ride in between remains an emotional memory.

The study of *The Origin of the Idea of Chance* (Piaget and Inhelder, 1951/1975) (suggested by a statistician) was designed to throw light on whether chance is an intuitive notion that appears early in life—children are, after all, often confronted with unpredictable events—or whether it is necessary for this notion and the probabilistic reasoning linked with it to be constructed within a framework of operations, particularly of combinatory operations. One of the many experiments carried out with young children seems a good example of Cournot's definition of chance: interference between two independent causal series. We presented children with a rectangular open box that could be seesawed on a central support and that contained on one side white and on the other red beads held in place at the start by a wooden partition. After the partition was taken away, the box was seesawed several times, so that the beads began to mingle. Children were asked to predict the position of the red and the white beads after one, a few, or many sways, and to make drawings representing the movements of the beads.

Two results, I thought, were most interesting. Children between four and seven persisted in their belief (even after having observed many pivotings) that the mixture of red and white beads was only a momentary phenomenon and that in the end the beads would all return to their proper (i.e., initial) position. Slightly older children imagined a kind of *chassé-croisé*: the red beads will end up on the side of the box where the white ones were in the beginning, and vice versa. Around the age of eleven, the children imagined a perfect system of permutations from left to right, without taking into account the inevitable interference between the trajectories of the individual beads. Only beyond this age did they understand that the mixture between red and white was an irreversible phenomenon and that each state was a particular case among all the different possible combinations in flagrant opposition to the reversibility of logical operations. Clearly the notion of chance or disorder is not a primitive intuition, but is, quite the contrary, built on early notions of logical "order."

Later, I tried out these various tasks relating to notions of chance and probability with psychotic subjects, both children and adolescents: these subjects had a tenacious belief in their magical interpretations, and those preadolescents who were capable of combinatorial reasoning manifested anxiety and refused to admit probability.

The 1940's (with publication dates between 1941 and 1951) were devoted to developmental studies born out of epistemological problems. Piaget wanted us to concentrate on the study of the mental construction of invariants as well as on their application and attribution to spatio-temporal and physical realities. To orient ourselves in action and in thought within our environment, we need the environment to show a certain consistency based on regularities in nature. But to discover these regularities, we need a consistency or logic of action and thought, whose developmental laws were to be studied in the different areas of the child's knowledge. The invariants proved to be symptomatic of the existence of operatory systems, which are structures that cannot be observed as such. The structuralist approach, as a method of study, led to an understanding of the epistemic subject, that is, of what is most general in the behavior of subjects who are in a period of provisional completion of a hierarchical structural system into which individual developmental features can be inserted.

I have often been asked what my collaboration was like with the great Piaget. Though we continued to cooperate closely, our collaboration changed over the years, depending on the themes that were being considered, on our respective availability, and also, I think, on my own development. During the period I just sketched, it was Piaget who formulated the epistemological problems and I who, either on my own or with some advanced students, proposed the experiments. I was very fortunate in that I could discuss these matters on our weekly walks and in almost daily telephone conversations. Once all the observational and experimental data were assembled, I wrote detailed reports on each experiment and subsequently we decided together on the outline of a book. At this time, every single chapter was written twice: Piaget wrote a first draft as if it were the final version (he did not like preliminary notes or sketches), and I commented on the whole chapter, and if necessary, carried out complementary research. Piaget then wrote the final version. Later on, I worked more autonomously. As we became overwhelmed by the ever-increasing amount of experimental data, it was no longer possible to rewrite everything. Much later still, there came the anxiety of not being able to complete the common work. Since I myself had benefited from the very early introduction into research, we let an increasing number of beginning students participate in our work under the guidance of our research assistants. This meant that for the start of each academic year a program of research, which would be integrated later, had to be prepared.

Apart from our effective collaboration, I had also sometimes the rare joy of being present at the birth of new ideas. Piaget often needed a (not necessarily competent) listener, since he felt that his ideas became clearer when he explained them to somebody else. I remember with excitement a hike along a glacier at sundown, both of us proceeding with the slow gait of the mountaineer, when Piaget developed his central ideas of what was to become the three volumes of the *Introduction à l'Epistémologie Génétique*. The work appeared in 1950 and was the crowning achievement of this period.

In 1946 I was appointed lecturer and in 1948 professor. It was in 1948 that the Institute was transformed into a University School with the right to deliver M.A. and Ph.D. degrees. In addition to Piaget, there were at the time only three professors of psychology, and I tried to teach many subjects that had not formed part of my own studies: learning theories, psychoanalysis, ethology, and social and cultural psychology, trying to bring to the fore the contributions of these disciplines to our knowledge of cognitive development. And since teaching is an excellent way of learning, the bounds of my knowledge kept widening. I always enjoyed teaching at university level, especially for advanced students.

1951–1960

The 1950's and early 1960's were a particularly enriching period for me, in both science and human relationships. As regards research, this is when I started personally new research programs. After years of studying various concepts and structures of thought, I started to investigate how children and adolescents begin to construct an experimental approach to the acquisition of knowledge—what at the time I called "experimental attitudes" (Inhelder, 1954). I was lucky to work with a particularly enthusiastic group of students—most of whom later became university professors.

One of the questions we asked was how the method called *ceteris paribus* (all other things being equal) was discovered. J. Rutschman, A. Weil-Sandler, and I designed an experiment in which the subjects were asked to determine the various factors that make metal rods more or less flexible (length, thickness, shape of section, kind of metal). The results of a series of experiments of this kind were highly promising, and in the corridors of the Institute one could hear excited discussions about how we had discovered a new stage: formal thought is not achieved before the age of fifteen or so!

At the end of the academic year I took, as usual, all the protocols of the experiments we had carried out, loaded them on the back of a mule to carry them up the mountains, and analyzed them in an Alpine meadow. Later during that summer, Piaget went to live in a neighboring chalet to work on his formal models derived from Klein's group and from lattices. As we explained in the preface to our book *The Growth of Logical Thinking from Childhood to Adolescence* (1955/1958), while one of us was engaged in an empirical study of the transition in thinking from childhood to adolescence, the other worked out the analytic tools needed to interpret these results. It was after we had compared notes and were making final interpretations that we saw the striking convergence between the empirical and the analytic results. This prompted us to collaborate once again, but in a new way. Though readers of the book in its final form may find it difficult to believe the total absence of prior agreement before our respective enterprises were started, I can assure them of the strict truth of this account.

In the autumn of 1955, Piaget finally succeeded in carrying out a project he had long cherished: he set up an international Center for Genetic Epistemology, thanks to the financial support of first the Rockefeller Foundation and then the Ford Foundation and the Swiss National Fund for Scientific Research. At last he had created this interdisciplinary circle that he had been aiming at for so many years. He soon proved to be as skillful and talented in interviewing scientists of various disciplines in order to find shared answers to basic epistemological problems as he had been in dealing with children. The Center saw the rise of scientists and thinkers, mathematicians, logicians, physicists, and of course psychologists (such as L. Apostel, F. Bresson, P. Greco, J. B. Grize, A. Jonckheere,

S. Papert) who were to influence the international epistemological scene, and Piaget was lucky enough to be supported and informed by people well aware of the most recent developments in their disciplines.

Each fall, for 25 years, a new theme of research was put forward. Monday mornings experimental methods and ways of interpreting the results were discussed, and, of special importance, each summer a particularly important symposium was held at which experts of different countries were convened to discuss the thesis "defended" by the Genevans. Contributions by scientists such as the logician W. V. O. Quine from Harvard, the mathematician W. E. Beth from Amsterdam, and the physicist L. Rosenfeld from Copenhagen had a profound influence on our ways of thinking.

The resulting work was published in the 37 volumes of the *Etudes d'Epistémologie Génétique*. At the end of each symposium, a dinner was held in some hostelry out in the country, and Piaget showed us another side of his character: as one of us remarked, he behaved as a country squire towards his extended family, greeting each individual participant with some pleasant, often humorous remark. The atmosphere of the Center thus also favored the growth of friendship, such as the scientific and human bonds that came to link François Bresson and myself over 30 years.

During this period I became increasingly involved in questions of mental development and was encouraged in this direction by Dr. G. R. Hargreaves, then chief of the Division for Mental Health of WHO. In four consecutive years from 1953 to 1956, Hargreaves organized symposia of two weeks each, in which specialists in various aspects of psychobiological development in childhood took part. Presentations and discussions were lively and of high quality, as was to be expected of a group that counted among its regular members Konrad Lorenz, Grey Walter, Margaret Mead, Jean Piaget, and John Bowlby, and among its invited participants Erik Erikson, Julian Huxley, and others. Four symposia were not too many for mutual understanding to develop between specialists with very different backgrounds. I vividly remember the occasion when I presented a paper on a series of experimental results showing that children interpreted certain phenomena in different ways according to their developmental level and that progress proceeded into different directions: one which was called logico-mathematical abstraction and the other physical abstraction. Lorenz took me aside after my talk and said "I always thought Piaget was one of those boring empiricists, and now I discover that he is not so far removed from Kant . . ." Later on he asked Piaget himself directly: "Are you an empiricist or an apriorist?"

Apart from epistemological problems, the group also discussed two fundamental notions of genetic psychology: the notion of stages and that of equilibrium. The discussions led us to clarify our conceptions and terminology. The stage-concept is based on postulated structures that underlie observable behavior. Their development follows an invariable sequence; they integrate one in the other without, however, being strictly age-linked, since the subject's modes of interaction with the physical and social universe play their part in it. As regards the concept of equilibrium, Piaget presented a precirculated paper to elicit reactions and realized that L. von Bertalanffy interpreted this term in the way he himself intended it, as a "steady state in an open system," but that for many others the term evoked ideas of a state of tranquillity or rest. This led Piaget to insist on equilibration as a process of maximal activity inherent in the different mechanisms of compensation.

Jim Tanner, a physical anthropologist from London, and I had the pleasant task of editing the proceedings of the four meetings, and, as we said in our foreword: "As editors we have seen at first hand the growth of mutual comprehension amongst our group. . . . We have watched the gradual and painless assimilation by each member from year to year of ideas and attitudes at first foreign and perhaps even uncongenial to him.
. . . The experiment of this International Study Group has, we believe, given us a glimpse of what might become a general pattern for maintaining those precious and precarious possessions: wide horizon and flexible minds" (Tanner and Inhelder, 1956–60).

In 1955 as well, I was able to set up a symposium for French-speaking psychologists on the subject of stages in psychology. At this meeting, René Zazzo, a follower of Henri Wallon, and I had the opportunity to carry on a lively discussion on our masters' apparent or real differences.

During the second WHO meeting, in 1954, Dr. Rolf Struthers of the Rockefeller Foundation offered me a four-month study period in the United States. It was perhaps not the most propitious time for encouraging international contacts among psychologists: the McCarthy era did not encourage us to believe in the freedom of academic research, though it heightened solidarity among researchers. After my arrival I soon saw that the Genevan studies (apart from the very earliest) were hardly known (there had been no translations for almost twenty years) and, in any case, were thought to be too complex. But I was surprised to be immediately invited to talk about my research at Cornell, Stanford, and the University of California at both Berkeley and Los Angeles. I was privileged to meet some of the best-known personalities in American psychology, and, after my return to Europe, my students were highly interested in what I could tell them about these personal contacts.

Proverbial American hospitality opened the doors for me to observe on-going research. During the first luncheon-meeting in the Rockefeller Building with its breathtaking view of the city, the program of my visits, lectures, and trips was worked out in detail. During my stay, I hardly lived in hotel rooms but was put up in charming guest or children's rooms by my colleagues. From one of these rooms, I had a magnificent view of the Golden Gate Bridge. The very first day a publisher in New York gave me the keys to his wonderful little house in Greenwich Village ("Perhaps you will find a cat and a poet") to live there while he himself went to Europe. At the time, he intended to publish all Piaget's works in English, but he ended up by becoming a psychologist.

Since my main interest was mental development, I wanted to learn about longitudinal studies. At the time, such studies and nearly all of developmental psychology were carried out in para-university institutes. Everywhere I was given access to observational data and test results that often stretched over a period of twenty years or more. In the institute attached to Yale University, research from a psychoanalytical point of view on the origins of personality was conducted under Ernest Kris and René Spitz, in collaboration with Kaethe Wolf. This was after Arnold Gesell had retired, not without some bitterness. The research that interested me most was that of Sibylle Escalona, though her observations were not strictly speaking longitudinal: she later published her remarkable analyses in *The Roots of Individuality* (1968).

It is not altogether easy, but always illuminating, to speak about one's research to colleagues who are using a different approach. I came to the United States just before the cognitive revolution in psychology broke out. Our Genevan environment was certainly not a closed community, and since the end of the war I had had many occasions to talk about our work and to discuss it with colleagues in other European universities. But my American experience was different. I had been brought up in the tradition of European philosophy and psychology, and I found myself for the first time confronted with a very different way of thinking, behaviorism and its roots in empiricism.

At Berkeley, discussions were mostly with researchers who were already close to our ideas. I remember my talks with David Kretch, at that time well known in social psychology, and was surprised to realize that he was also the Krechevsky who had written " 'Hypotheses' in rats" and, with Egon Brunswik, a highly original thinker and cultured, aristocratic personality. I was particularly impressed by the admirable lectures of Edward Tolman, both a most distinguished man and the dominant figure in American psychology, indeed one of the few psychologists who had a comprehensive theory at that time.

At Harvard I had many lively conversations with Edwin G. Boring, who asked me to send him gossip from Europe for *Contemporary Psychology* and who sent me many of his well-known single-spaced post cards. Gordon Allport invited me to the Faculty Club and ordered its famous "horsebeef," to see whether I had any prejudice in the matter, and interviewed me in detail about current trends in German psychology with which he had been quite familiar in the past. Fred Skinner spent an entire day conditioning his famous pigeons for my benefit, and in him I discovered a widely cultured personality, a reader of Proust and an ever-courteous and attentive listener, in spite of our widely opposed views on psychology as a science. We were happy indeed to receive him some years later in Geneva.

But my most essential scientific encounter was with Jerome Bruner. Bruner was involved in a far-reaching transformation of the problems of cognitive psychology, and I was privileged to be allowed to read the first chapters of his *A Study of Thinking* (1956). I was struck by the convergence of our interests and became aware of the enormous complexity of the questions that preoccupied us both. It seemed as if we were close to a breakthrough in cognitive psychology, and it was exciting to find that George Miller, when he spoke at the international congress in Montreal about the heuristics of intuition, was working along similar lines. My encounter with Bruner was the beginning of a long friendship and led to discussions which have gone uninterrupted for many years, though our perspectives are often very different.

This account of my first contact with the United States would be incomplete if I did not mention the many sights of this vast country, whose impressive land and seascapes fed my love of nature.

On my return from the United States, I was eager to undertake longitudinal studies in order to improve our understanding of developmental mechanisms and, especially, to clarify the transitions from one level to the next. It is clear that any conception of development in stages, with periods of construction and periods of completion characterized by internal structures, has to come to terms with the contradiction between theories of perfect continuity and theories of clear discontinuity. Our longitudinal studies suggest that the contradiction is more apparent than real: it seems that, in the development of cognitive structures, phases of continuity alternate with phases of discontinuity, in the sense that during periods of continuous development there is greater dependence of the newly acquired behaviors on already mastered behavior than during periods of discontinuity. During the formation period of a reasoning structure characteristic of stage A, each new procedure appears to depend on already elaborated procedures. But once a structure B is completed, new possibilities open up, and the resulting behaviors are much less closely linked to the formation processes of the structure in question. In this sense it is possible to think in terms of discontinuity. The developing subjects themselves are, of course, completely unaware of these processes. When, a long time afterwards, they came to visit me, they were so astonished at their own responses to the questions put to them that they would never have believed they could have reasoned as they did, had I not been able to show them the films in which they appeared.

Meanwhile, Piaget had been invited to spend a few months at the Institute for Advanced Study at Princeton. At the same time, he proposed that we should work together on the development of the elementary logical structures of classes and relations. For several years we had felt the need for detailed studies on this subject: in our previous research we had studied logical reasoning underlying spatial notions as well as ideas of chance and probability, but had not carried out direct research on the growth of logical structures themselves. Maybe that is what we should have started with, but all too often it is only at the completion of a series of investigations that the original problems become clear and amenable to analysis.

During a few weeks of happy vacation spent, as usual, in the mountains, I analyzed the result of some preliminary research carried out with my assistants so as to be able to judge whether our initial approach appeared appropriate. Piaget returned to Geneva reassured. Extensive research was started immediately, and after many studies with over 2,000 subjects were completed (the interpretation gave rise to many lengthy discussions), the convergence of results brought the conviction that we had indeed been able to capture developmental processes. Starting with very young children and observing their protological behavior when they "put things together," we were able to map the progress of children's thinking towards class inclusion and the mastery of logical quantification.

One of the main conclusions of this research is worth mentioning: we observed a close link between the development of the logical operations of classification and seriation and that of the spatio-temporal operations. The early forms of classification appeared to be characterized by an indifferentiation between these two modes of reasoning: very young children begin by putting objects together in figural collections (in a line, a square, or a circle) so that their collection provides a kind of spatial envelope for itself, as an image of the extension of the class. This way of "putting together what goes well together" indicates clearly that the origins of logical operations are not to be sought in the gradual mastery of verbal concepts, but in the most general forms of assembling (for classification) or ordering (for seriation) as applied to continuous as well as to discrete objects (Inhelder and Piaget 1959/1964).

My first American contacts were followed by many others, some of which resulted in publications that marked the beginning of the American "cognitive revolution." I participated in a meeting held in 1959 in Cape Cod, where I was the only woman among an Olympian group of scientists: physicists such as Francis Freeman and Jerrold Zacharias, mathematicians, biologists, psychologists, and educators who were all preoccupied with curriculum reform in the post-Sputnik era. Bruner's report on this meeting (1960) became an internationally known document, translated into nineteen languages. I was intrigued and pleased to see that famous scientists thought about educational problems and wondered how children's and adolescents' creativity could be stimulated and their cognitive development accelerated. My own point of view was that creativity is not so much a question of developmental rhythm as of the existence of necessary paths along which each stopping place is also a starting place for the next part of the journey; this idea was better understood by the biologists than by the others. From a biological point of view there is nothing strange in the idea that in the child there are interconnected systems of interpretation of reality that follow one another developmentally and that constitute the basis for further acquisitions.

Some of the most memorable exchanges of views occurred with the "committee in intellective processes," of which Roger Brown and his colleagues had made me the "auxiliary informal European member." The first meeting held under the auspices of the Social Science Research

Council took place in April 1960 in Dedham, Massachusetts, on the theme "Thought in the young child (with particular attention to the work of Jean Piaget)." With some apprehension, I gave my paper on "some aspects of Piaget's approach to cognition" (Inhelder, 1962) and was amused to see that the organizers were reassured after the event—they also must have been worried! Roger Brown reported that, after a long period of incomprehension, "computer simulation, psycholinguistics, curriculum reform, and mathematical models altered our notion of the scientific enterprise in such a way as to cause us to see Piaget as a very modern psychologist. To see that he was, in fact, the great psychologist of cognitive development." The discussion never lost sight of the main issues and remained focused in a critical but open spirit on the relations between theory and facts.

A later conference on European research in cognitive development was held north of Oslo in 1962 and made it possible for me to present the first results of our research on mental images (Inhelder, 1965). During a weekend in Bergen we jumped over the Midsummer Night bonfires with our Eastern European colleagues, in particular with A. V. Zaporozhets, H. Papoušek, and A. Szeminska.

1960–1968

In retrospect, the years 1960–68 appear to me to have been particularly full of new ideas, research, and publications. I collaborated with Piaget in two research projects that gave rise to voluminous books on mental images and memory. In addition, we published a small volume on *The Psychology of the Child* (1966/1969), which was a joy to write and which gave an overview of genetic research. It was translated into seventeen languages, probably because it presented a useful synthesis and, to some extent, the conclusions of our already completed research.

About this book, I remember that we were in the mountains in the Valais when Piaget was asked by his French colleague Paul Fraisse, who was in Italy on the other side of the mountains, to prepare a congress. Since Piaget never could stop writing, he went to see Fraisse with a big packet of pages in his pocket. Fraisse immediately wanted to know what Piaget was writing, and Piaget answered, with a good smile, that I had written the first draft of a new book, and that he was pleased for once to simply play the role of the scribe.

If so many things were done in this period, it seems to me that it was first because Piaget felt an extraordinary creative urge, which pervaded all our work, but also because a new generation of researchers (Hermina Sinclair, Pierre Mounoud, and Elsa Schmid-Kitsikis, among others) took part in the projects. In contrast with other institutes where protocols of research are from the outset given a definite form, we proposed to start with only the general themes, and the details were worked out in a group. Each Tuesday morning we got together for discussions in my office. Each collaborator was free to take considerable initiative in the research being carried out, to follow personal ideas on how to treat the theme, and to discuss (and criticize!) what the others were doing. This way of working meant that during those years I had to be totally available for the planned research and at the disposal of the researchers; so I decided to delay for a while my own projects, which may have profited from a longer period of gestation.

We were interested in studying *Mental Imagery in the Child* (Piaget and Inhelder, 1966/1971) for two reasons. On the one hand, Piaget had just finished his extensive research on perception and was now interested in studying mental images as phenomena that do not directly derive from perception but are linked to mental operations. On the other hand, we were interested in mental imagery as a form of symbolization different from language, but one that can, like language, serve both communication and memory. My interest was in the latter aspect of imagery—that is, its function—whereas Piaget wanted to study the epistemological problem of the genesis of imagery, especially whether it could be independent of mental operations or obeys their developmental structuration. It was striking to observe how young children encountered conservation difficulties in attempting an apparently simple task such as imagining the lateral displacement to the right of a cardboard square that adjoins an identical one placed below it: young children tend to make drawings in which the right but lateral straight line formed by the two squares in the position they were presented in is conserved, and the top square, whose displacement they were asked to imagine, is represented as a thinnish rectangle. Clearly, such drawings reflect their as yet preoperational level of cognitive development. At a higher level of development, mental images appear to be strongly structured by the conceptualizations that are typical of concrete operations. Our conclusion was that the symbolic representations that occur when subjects are asked to imagine the transformation of one state into another may prefigure the operations, but are not, by themselves, a sufficient basis for the construction of these operations.

Research on memory already had a long history when we started our own studies on *Memory and Intelligence* (Piaget and Inhelder, with the collaboration of H. Sinclair, 1968/1973). Our approach was different from most previous works, except that of Sir Frederick Bartlett: our research was, in a sense, a continuation of his work on memory schemata. In contrast to the behaviorist tradition, we were interested in the internal mechanisms that direct the transformations occurring between stimulus and response, especially, of course, from the developmental point of view. On several occasions my presentations of our first findings caused great astonishment among specialists in memory studies. I remember one such occasion when I gave a talk in the psychology laboratory of MIT: not only was there a dog (accompanying his blind master) who barked at each of my unusual propositions, but I could clearly see the astonishment on the faces of my audience, especially that of Lukas Teuber, when I spoke about improvement rather than degradation of recall in our young subjects. At Stanford similar astonishment prevailed, but Karl Pribram was delighted with this new direction in the study of the mechanisms that underlie the modification of memories.

In our view, the progressive and consistent modifications in reasoning we had noted in function of age in our former research pointed to the existence of laws of internal transformations, and we supposed that these also played their part in memory performance. Memory, and memory images in particular, are usually considered to be copies of reality, and memories are supposed to stay intact or to deteriorate according to the complexity of the situation and the passage of time. The code which underlies what are called the processes of encoding and decoding is thought to remain the same. If this were so, it would seem impossible for memories to improve with time. If, however, the code itself changes during development, recall, seen as an interpretation rather than a reproduction of what was not only perceived but also conceived, can improve with time.

Our results confirmed the latter hypothesis: the mnemonic organization proved to be dependent on developmental changes in cognitive structures. We had, however, no intention of equating memory with intelligence as a whole. In our view, memory in the broad sense is the apprehension of all that has been experienced or acquired in the past, whereas memory in the strict sense is limited to the evocation of particular past events, based on mental images and other semiotic representations. This distinction corresponds to that of *scheme* as a general structure of actions and operations, and *schema* as a simplified image of the result of a particular action.

During this period, my teaching in Geneva took on new dimensions. Thanks to the arrival there as professor of psychiatry of Julian de Ajuriaguerra, who was deeply interested in genetic psychology, it was possible to integrate our theoretically oriented research into studies concerning the diagnosis of dysphasic and psychotic children. This gave me the occasion to initiate my students into a method that combines two different orientations: one where the researcher studies individual subjects keeping in mind a theoretical problem of genetic epistemology and psychology, and one where the psychologist or psychiatrist studies an individual human being in order to understand his or her specific potentialities and difficulties.

The University of Aix-Marseille, now the University of Provence, set up a laboratory of genetic psychology in the 1960's. For several years I regularly went there to teach Piagetian theory and method to an enthusiastic group of psychologists. This enabled me to meet with the more expansive children of this region and to stay in a wonderful house in the middle of a pine forest, with the evocative name of "Bibemus." In 1964, this University awarded doctorates honoris causa to both Piaget and myself.

During these years, I traveled widely, giving lectures east all the way to Japan and west to Brazil. The Moscow Congress in 1966 was a memorable event. I met Alexandr Luria again and also Aleksei Leontiev, both fervent admirers of Lev Semionvich Vygotsky, who were preparing a complete edition of Vygotsky's works and were delighted that it was once again possible to pursue cognitive psychology. The Congress coincided with Piaget's seventieth birthday, on August 9, when he gave the main lecture of the Congress, which was followed by a standing ovation.

In the autumn of 1961, Jerome Bruner invited me to come to the Center for Cognitive Studies, which he had set up at Harvard. Because in Geneva there was as yet no sabbatical leave, I could only go for four months, but this period was rich in professional and personal contacts. For the first time, I felt that I was among peers, whereas in Geneva I was surrounded by either masters or pupils. Jerry, who felt like a "rebellious son" towards the father-figure of Piaget, gave vent to his disagreements with Piaget in discussions with me, especially concerning the problems of conservation. Bruner's fascinating personality, his fierce interests (sometimes also ephemeral), and his infectious enthusiasm are well-known among his friends. George Miller's more skeptical outlook made him an excellent critic of some manuscripts I asked him to read. In return he gave me the volume he wrote in collaboration with Eugene Galanter and Karl Pribram, *Plans and the Structure of Behavior* (1960). Only later did I appreciate the great value of this gift and the importance it would have for my work.

Roger Brown, who at that time was still at MIT, was writing *A First Language* (1973) and proved to be one of the researchers who had a deep understanding of Piaget's ideas. In his delicate way, he made me understand the situation of the East Coast intellectuals; and he became a faithful friend. Lukas Teuber, though working in very different fields from ours since he was a neuropsychologist, was nevertheless interested in introducing Geneva-style psychogenetic studies in his laboratory.

Many meetings provided occasions of hearing the best specialists in a great variety of fields. I also remember with pleasure our luncheon talks and the lively and refreshing discussions with graduate students. Throughout my stay, I was honored more than I deserved, but the most impressive and unexpected homage came from the undergraduate students, who, after a lecture given specially for them, gave me a standing ovation. Though I was sorry to leave Harvard, it was a great joy to return to Geneva. Piaget, being recognized as a VIP, was allowed to greet me on the apron at the airport, while members of our team were watching behind the windows of the building. Piaget told me that up until the last moment he had been afraid I would choose to remain in the United States for good.

1968–83

This new period was one of intense work, but at the same time other events had a lasting effect on life in the university. Our students and assistants in Geneva experienced the events of May 1968 as a period of awareness on several levels, and this feeling was transferred to us as their teachers and brought about changes in our research programs. In September, a group of my assistants spent two weeks in the south of France to prepare the practical work for our laboratory, and they invited me to join them for the purpose of working out conclusions. The first thing I saw on arrival was a big banner with the slogan: "The epistemic subject shall not pass; welcome to the psychological subject."

In 1968 I received a letter from Harvard University announcing my election as a professor at Radcliffe College. I was told that a woman professor would provide a role model for their students. I was touched and honored to be chosen by the committee; but I felt at the time that I should pursue my scientific work in the cultural context of Geneva.

Learning, in my view, is essentially a matter of development. With the help of Magali Bovet, my work at Harvard was mainly directed towards explaining to my American colleagues the Genevan theories and methods of study pertaining to problems of conservation, and to compare our ways of interviewing subjects as well as our conception of learning with theirs. Certain procedures were elaborated in collaboration, and were subsequently used for studies carried out in Geneva and at Harvard. But since the two groups started from different epistemological premises, their research took different directions. For Bruner, progress in knowledge rests mainly on progress of representational systems (enactive, iconic, symbolic); for us, progress in knowledge results mainly from the interaction of conceptual schemes and their application to reality. We hypothesize that the interaction of conceptual schemes of different levels of elaboration can create disequilibria that lead to conflicts and contradictions, which in turn engender regulatory processes tending towards higher level equilibria. In this perspective, we tried to understand the transition from one level to the next and to clarify the connections between various operatory systems, each following its own rhythm of development.

This new direction of research led to methods that differ from the "clinical method" used previously, which allowed us quasi-naturalistic, though controlled, observations of behavior without introducing propositions that could lead to modification of behavior. By contrast, modification was the main goal of our new methods, by which we tried to compress into a few learning sessions progress that would take far longer in spontaneous development, in order to gain insight into the functional processes that could explain the importance and nature of changes in behavior when they occurred. These studies occupied me for several years, and I was fortunate to have as one of my co-workers Hermina Sinclair, who had used learning methods to study the links between the mastery of certain comparative terms (*longer*, *shorter*) and the development of the operations of seriation, as well as of Magali Bovet, who was writing a thesis on unschooled children in Algeria. The first experiments of the learning studies took place while mental imagery and memory were still the main themes of research. As time went on learning studies become more and more important.

The results led us to establish several types of relations between schemes (without integration, incomplete integration leading to some curious compromises, and complete compensations between different schemes) and to establish connections between different operatory systems of the same level of elaboration. Here we observed notable progress in the domain of the concepts that were the theme of learning sessions as well as in a connected, but not "exercised," domain: this effect appears to be due to the dynamic character of the processes at work. Development was thus accelerated, but after comparison with the results of many previous, non-learning studies, its course was not seen to be modified. The degree of acceleration was closely linked to the initial level of development as indicated by pretests. Consequently, it seemed that acquisitions limited to a specific domain are of little interest for the progress of knowledge: what is important is to learn to understand. This research also made it possible to define our epistemological premises more precisely: all progress in knowledge and all learning are in a sense a constructive reconstruction of what is known already, and only an interactionist and constructivist epistemology can account for such cognitive phenomena which result in genuine new knowledge.

The book *Learning and the Development of Cognition* (Inhelder, Sinclair, and Bovet, 1974), in which we related our experiments, was likely to interest English-language readers, and Susan Wedgwood acted as a devoted translator, rendering the chapters into English as soon as they were written. As a result the English edition appeared at the same time as the French. The learning experiments and the methods we used gave rise to multiple replication studies, and were implemented in the context of the education of underprivileged schoolchildren.

After our research on learning was completed, the Swiss neurophysiologist Alexander von Muralt asked me to direct a research program in the Ivory Coast which aimed at the evaluation of the possible effects of malnutrition on intellectual development in the early years of life, with the collaboration of physicians, dieticians, and agronomists from Europe and from Africa (Dasen, Inhelder, Lavallée, and Retschitzki, 1978; Inhelder, 1982a). Though well aware of the complexity of such research, we felt that this was an opportunity to contribute, if only in the long run, to the improvement of the living conditions of the population and to observe at first hand the sensorimotor development of infants living in a very different cultural environment from our own.

During the pilot studies which laid a foundation for a comparison between Baoulé and European infants, we found that, in contrast with the usual tests for infants, the experiments Piaget had imagined (with a very different aim in view) when he was observing his own children made it easy to capture the attention of the Baoulé infants and showed the similarity of their behavior to European infants.

In our main study my co-workers stayed for eighteen months in isolated villages; we studied 23 couples of Baoulé children, matched by age, of which one was nutritionally quasi-normal and the other moderately ill nourished. All 46 infants belonged to the same community. The comparisons showed that moderate malnutrition, though not having a severe effect, does have a marginal effect on psychological development. The effect varies according to age, and the level of development is evidenced by a number of manifestations, including a slightly slower appearance of certain behaviors (in general, one or two months, never more than four) while the structures of knowledge and their succession remain the same.

My stay in the Ivory Coast was also an enriching human experience. I was received by the chief of each village, always an elder, who considered me an aged chief, and I submitted gladly to all the rites of welcome as well as to the rites of departure. It was necessary to ask permission to leave, to "ask for the road," and after that I waited a long time, until each chief came to me and put a lamb in my arms.

Another research project concerned the study of strategies of problem solving. Though this research grew out of my earlier research on learning, it was also a new beginning, and in a way, it meant a break with the past. The work on learning had already led from a macro- to a micro-analysis, which was to play a big part in the studies on problem solving. These studies are also, to some extent, a prolongation of Piaget's studies with his own children, as described in *The Origins of Intelligence*, though he all too soon gave up this type of research. From another point of view, the new studies were linked to my constant interest in the functional aspects of children's experimental approaches. My 1954 paper represents in a sense the beginning of a focus on psychological processes rather than structures. What was new in the problem-solving studies compared to our work in the past was the study of the procedural and pragmatic aspect of behavior, the transition from "knowing that" to "knowing how," from the epistemic to the psychological subject: how does the subject plan his actions in order to resolve a practical problem? This is a different question from the one that was predominant in our earlier work, which was essentially: how does the subject understand reality? My encounter and later collaboration with Guy Cellérier, who brought us his excellent knowledge of artificial intelligence, was of great help in the theoretical grounding of the research. I thus realized that there was still a long way to go from epistemological constructivism to psychological constructivism.

After working with the group of young psychologists in the research on adolescents, and with others who had taken part in the African studies,

I had the pleasure of being able to work with several new graduate students—E. Ackermann-Valladao, A. Blanchet, A. Boder, D. de Caprona, A. Karmiloff-Smith, H. Kilcher-Hagedorn, J. Montangero, M. Robert, and J. Weiss (see Inhelder et al., 1976)—who in their enthusiasm carried me along toward new horizons. They had all started their studies in the late 1960's and were interested in concrete situations, in which a particular subject uses his know-how in a particular context, rather than in the study of abstract general structures. Perhaps I was more aware than they were of the underlying continuity with our past work, and of the danger of falling into either an obsolete mentalism or a subjective intuitionism. These dangers were inherent in the risk involved in starting something new, and during the many years that were devoted to this research we came to see that the micro-analyses were not only fertile in themselves, but helped to clarify the macro-genesis. Indeed, the analysis of the subject's procedures and their planning not only leads to an understanding of what the subjects actually do, but also gives insight into their general systems of interpretation, as it can be observed through the meanings and representations they attach to objects and to their own actions. Our new research paradigm (Inhelder, 1983) also brought to the fore the control functions and evaluation modes of subjects struggling with a problem (which were already foreshadowed in the learning research). The research also touched upon questions of entailment logic, in which Piaget became interested in his later years when he endeavored to render his logical framework more concrete by deriving it from a very general logic of actions and meanings. In this period, when we no longer had the time to work together, Piaget's and my own preoccupations converged, maybe because of a certain zeitgeist, which led us to write a last paper together: "Procedures and structures" (Inhelder and Piaget, 1980; Inhelder, 1983).

In 1971, Piaget retired at the age of 75 and the chair he occupied was made into two professorships, one in genetic and experimental psychology and one in epistemology. I was appointed to the first and my colleague Guy Cellérier to the second. As is all too easy to imagine, it was impossible to be a successor to Piaget in all his activities; even to have the responsibility of the course in genetic psychology was a heavy load. Yet I felt I knew this discipline from the inside, and several collaborators with good knowledge of what was being done in Europe as well as in the States helped me direct the laboratories.

In the 1970's I was also given several doctorates honoris causa: by Temple University in Philadelphia (1970), where the Piaget Society was taking shape; by Smith College (1975) with its tradition of higher education for women; by René Descartes University in Paris (1974), where the ceremony took place in the solemn atmosphere of the Grand Amphitheatre of the Sorbonne; and by the University of Parana in Brazil (1979), a country where Piaget-inspired research has made great strides. I was particularly honored to be appointed foreign member of the American Academy of Arts and Sciences in 1976 and to receive the "Academico de Merito" of the Academica delle Scienze di Roma in 1979. Further interest in the work we had done was shown by the Italian psychologists and educators when the Catholic University of Milan granted me a doctorate honoris causa in 1987, followed in 1989 by the universities of Coimbra and Madrid.

Meanwhile, I had become the president of the Swiss Society of Psychology and of the Association des Psychologues de Langue Française. I was also the first woman to be elected to the Swiss Society of Human Sciences and the Swiss National Fund for Scientific Research—let us not forget that it took Swiss women a very long time to get the right to vote.

In 1976, Piaget's collaborators decided to celebrate his eightieth birthday in a worthy manner: by a ceremony that was joyful as well as scientifically memorable. Since "le Patron" did not have a doctorate in psychology, but in zoology, this seemed to be the perfect occasion to select a jury worthy of the candidate to examine Piaget's main theses as they were set out in his recent work, *The Equilibration of Cognitive Structures* (1975/ 1985). This make-believe thesis defense brought to Geneva a number of famous scientists (I. Prigogine, P. Weiss, C. Nowinsky, H. von Foerster) and Piaget's close collaborators. Piaget cheerfully kept going all day, answering questions and explaining his theses, and at the end he presented "additional theses" which went beyond his central concept of equilibration. The discussions on the occasion of the simulated defense were published in a work called *Epistémologie génétique et Equilibration: Hommage à Piaget* (Inhelder, Garcia, and Vonèche, eds., 1977).

In 1974 I was able to create a foundation called "Archives Jean Piaget." Whoever has had the pleasure of being invited to Piaget's study, where the mass of books, documents, and research protocols looked like geographical layers shaken up by an earthquake, can understand the need for such an undertaking. On the one hand, it was necessary to put at the disposal of researchers Piaget's complete works and their many translations, together with as large as possible a collection of books and papers inspired by Piaget's research. On the other hand, I was thinking of the future, and

I planned annual advanced courses with a two-fold function: informing young researchers and bringing together several highly regarded persons who were close to Piaget's conceptions but pursued their own original studies. I was very pleased that people such as Herbert Simon and Heinz von Foerster were ready to spend a week in Geneva to explain and discuss their theories.

In the month of June 1980, Piaget was still able to participate at the twenty-fifth Symposium of the Centre d'Epistémologie Génétique. He died in September. I heard the news just before I had to give a paper in Bern, and I felt that in a Piagetian spirit research should go on; Piaget's friends and collaborators who were present all agreed with me. The next year a conference in his honor was held in Geneva and united many scientists, who, like Piaget, felt the need for interdisciplinary programs (Inhelder, dir., 1982).

When I retired in 1983 (after having received a doctorate in my own country, in Fribourg, in 1981, the Award of the American Association for Research in Child Development, also in 1981), I had more time to take care of the Archives Jean Piaget and to look after the publication of Piaget's posthumous work. The two volumes, *Psychogénèse et Histoire des Sciences* (1983) and *Vers une Logique des Significations* (1987) were written in collaboration with Rolando Garcia, an Argentinian physicist who had often contributed to the published studies of the Centre International d'Epistémologie Génétique and who had a remarkably cordial and fruitful relationship with Piaget till the end, founded on a reciprocal exchange of scientific ideas. I was present at many of their discussions, and Rolando Garcia became one of my closest friends.

Since my main desire was to continue Piaget's oeuvre, and to relate it to new trends in research, I organized seven advanced courses, of which the last one was entitled *Piaget Today* in 1985 (Inhelder, de Caprona, and Cornu-Wells, eds., 1987). Piaget's profound originality, which for a long time was an obstacle to his work's becoming known and appreciated, lies in the fact that it is situated at the crossroads of several disciplines. It continues to elicit new ideas and further research, and perhaps its future lies more in epistemology, whatever direction the further development of genetic psychology may take.

To work together in a common enterprise is certainly not an easy task, especially not when one collaborates with a thinker as powerful as Piaget; but during my work with Piaget I came to know above all the sunny side of his personality, the joys of creating something new, and the love of the beauties and mysteries of nature we shared. "Chic métier" was one of his frequent sayings about our profession. A common enterprise means also that one has many friends of different generations and that is, of course, something very precious for this "international" child who was an only child. When I left Geneva University, a meeting was organized around the theme "Procedures and Structures," which turned out to be more of a celebration of my birthday than of my retirement, and an occasion for my friends to give me presents in the form of new ideas based, as they affirmed, on my own research.

Selected Publications by Bärbel Inhelder

(1936). Observations sur le principe de conservation dans la physique de l'enfant. *Cahiers de pédagogie expérimentale et de psychologie de l'enfant,* 9, 1–16.

(with J. Piaget) (1941/1974). *Le développement des quantités chez l'enfant.* Paris: Delachaux & Niestlé, 1941. (English transl · *The child's construction of quantities.* London: Routledge, 1974.)

(1943/1968). *Le diagnostic du raisonnement chez les débiles mentaux.* Thèse, Université de Genève. Neuchâtel: Delachaux et Niestlé, 1943. (English transl.: *The diagnosis of reasoning in the mentally retarded.* New York: J. Day, 1968.)

(with J. Piaget) (1948/1956). *La représentation de l'espace chez l'enfant.* Paris: Presses Universitaires de France, 1948. (English transl.: *The child's conception of space.* London: Routledge, 1956.)

(with J. Piaget & A. Szeminska) (1948/1960). *La géométrie spontanée de l'enfant.* Paris: Presses Universitaires de France, 1948. (English transl.: *The child's conception of geometry.* London: Routledge, 1960.)

(with J. Piaget) (1951/1975). *La genèse de l'idée de hasard chez l'enfant.* Paris: Presses Universitaires de France, 1951. (English transl.: *The origin of the idea of chance in children.* London: Routledge, 1975.)

(1954). Les attitudes expérimentales de l'enfant et de l'adolescent. *Bulletin de psychologie,* 7 (5), 272–282.

(with J. Piaget) (1955/1958). *De la logique de l'enfant à la logique de l'adolescent.* Paris: Presses Universitaires de France, 1955. (English transl.: *The growth of logical thinking from childhood to adolescence.* London: Routledge, 1958.)

(with J. M. Tanner, Eds.) (1956–60). *Discussions on child development, Vols. 1–4.* London: Tavistock.

(with J. Piaget) (1959/1964). *La genèse des structures logiques élémentaires.* Neuchâtel, Paris: Delachaux & Niestlé, 1959. (English transl.: *The early growth of logic in the child.* London: Routledge, 1964.)

(1962). Some aspects of Piaget's genetic approach to cognition. In W. Kessen (Ed.), *Thought in the young child: Monographs of the Society for Research in Child Development*, 27 (serial no. 83, pp. 19–34).

(1965). Operational thought and symbolic imagery. In P. H. Mussen (Ed.), *European research in cognitive development: Monographs of the Society for Research in Child Development*, 30 (serial no. 100, pp. 4–18).

(with J. Piaget) (1966/1971). *L'image mentale chez l'enfant*. Paris: Presses Universitaires de France, 1966. (English transl.: *Mental imagery in the child*. London: Routledge, 1971.)

(with J. Piaget) (1966/1969). *La psychologie de l'enfant*. Paris: Presses Universitaires de France, 1966. (English transl.: *The psychology of the child*. London: Routledge, 1969.)

(with J. Piaget in collaboration with H. Sinclair) (1968/1973). *Mémoire et intelligence*. Paris: Presses Universitaires de France, 1968. (English transl.: *Memory and intelligence*. London: Routledge, 1973.)

(with H. Sinclair & M. Bovet) (1974). *Apprentissage et structures de la connaissance*. Paris: Presses Universitaires de France, 1974. (English transl.: *Learning and the development of cognition*. Cambridge, MA: Harvard University Press, 1974.)

(with E. Ackermann-Valladao, A. Blanchet, A. Karmiloff-Smith, H. Kilcher-Hagedorn, J. Montangero, & M. Robert) (1976). Des structures cognitives aux procédures de découverte. *Archives de psychologie*, 44 (no. 171), 57–72.

(with R. Garcia & J. Vonèche, Eds.) (1977). *Epistémologie génétique et équilibration: Hommage à Jean Piaget*. Neuchâtel, Paris: Delachaux et Niestlé.

(with P. R. Dasen, M. Lavallée, & J. Retschitzki) (1978). Naissance de l'intelligence chez l'enfant baoulé de Côte d'Ivoire. Berne: H. Huber.

(with J. Piaget) (1980). Procedures and structures. In D. R. Olson (Ed.), *The social foundations of language and thought*. New York: Norton.

(1982a). Early cognitive development and malnutrition. In R. V. Garcia and J. C. Escudero (Eds.), *Drought and man: Vol. 2. The constant catastrophe: malnutrition, famines and drought* (pp. 24–29). Oxford: Pergamon Press.

(1982b). (Dir.) Hommage à Jean Piaget. *Archives de psychologie*, 50 (no. 192).

(1983). On generating procedures and structuring knowledge. In R. Groner, M. Groner, & W. F. Bischof (Eds.), *Methods of heuristics* (pp. 131–139). Hillsdale, NJ: Erlbaum.

(with D. de Caprona & A. Cornu-Wells, Eds.) (1987). *Piaget today*. Hillsdale, NJ: Erlbaum.

Other Publications Cited

Brown, R. (1973). *A first language*. Cambridge, MA: Harvard University Press.

Bruner, J. S. (1960). *The process of education*. Cambridge, MA: Harvard University Press.

Bruner, J. S., Goodnow, G. G., & Hustin, G. A. (1956). *A study of thinking*. New York: Wiley.

Brunschvicg, L. (1922). *L'expérience humaine et la causalité physique*. Paris: Alcan.

Claparède, E. (1933). La genèse de l'hypothèse. *Archives de psychologie*, 24, 1–155.

Escalona, S. (1968). *The roots of individuality*. Chicago: Aldine.

Krechevsky, I. (1932). "Hypotheses" in rats. *Psychology Review*, *39*, 516–532.

Miller, G., Galanter, E., & Pribram, K. (1960). *Plans and the structure of behavior*. New York: Holt.

Piaget, J. (1932). *Le jugement moral chez l'enfant*. Paris: Alcan. (English transl.: *The moral judgment of the child*. London: Kegan Paul.)

Piaget, J. (1936/1952). *La naissance de l'intelligence chez l'enfant*. Neuchâtel, Paris: Delachaux & Niestlé, 1936. (English transl.: *The origins of intelligence in children*. New York: International Universities Press, 1952.)

Piaget, J. (1937/1954). *La construction du réel chez l'enfant*. Neuchâtel, Paris: Delachaux & Niestlé, 1937. (English transl.: *The construction of reality in the child*. New York: Basic Books, 1954.)

Piaget, J. (1950). *Introduction à l'épistémologie génétique* (3 vols.). Paris: Presses Universitaires de France.

Piaget, J. (1975/1985). *L'équilibration des structures cognitives*. Paris: Presses Universitaires de France, 1975. (English transl.: *The equilibration of cognitive structures*. Chicago: University of Chicago Press, 1985.)

Piaget, J., & Garcia, R. (1983). *Psychogenèse et histoire de sciences*. Paris: Flammarion.

Piaget, J., & Garcia, R. (1987). *Vers une logique des significations*. Geneva: Murionde.

R. Duncan Luce

A scientific autobiography is, I suppose, a chronicle of the intellectual highlights of a scientist's career, the persons, places, and events that went along with them, and some attempt to suggest how one thing led to another. Presumably, the last interests a reader most—how did an idea, an experiment, or a theorem arise? Yet it is this for which one is least able to provide an account. I have never read an autobiography, short or long, that gave me any real sense of the intellectual flow; nor as I sit down to contemplate my own intellectual history do I sense that flow very well. The actual work is too slow, too detailed, and too convoluted to be recounted as such. I believe I see some recurrent themes and intellectual convictions which probably have marked what I have done, but little of that seems causal. Therefore, I shall not attempt to impose much of a logic on my development beyond some grouping into themes and some mention of convictions.

I begin with the steps that led me into psychology. Next, I describe my research themes, giving little attention to the where, when, and with whom. The following section provides the actual chronology, citing professional highlights and the intellectually important events and people. Finally, I close with some musings about several general matters that strike me as important.

A draft of my autobiography was circulated in the early 1970's to a few people who figured large in it. For their helpful criticisms and comments, which I have in most cases used, I would like to thank Eugene H. Galanter, Henry Gleitman, David M. Green, the late Francis W. Irwin, Cynthia N. Luce, and Patrick Suppes. The present account is an abridged, lightly edited, and updated version of a chapter in T. S. Krawiec (Ed.), (1978), *The Psychologists, Vol. 3* (Brandon, VT: Clinical Psychology Publishing Company). Permission to use the original material has been generously granted by the editor and the publisher. My thanks to my wife, Carolyn A. Scheer, for suggestions and criticisms of this version.

Undergraduate and Graduate School

My parents, although both college educated and my father trained as a dentist, were hardly intellectuals, and as a child I never aspired to be one. As a teenager in Scranton, Pennsylvania, I preferred painting landscapes and still lifes to science or mathematics, and I applied to college with some reluctance, even though my high school record made it an obvious thing to do. When I arrived at MIT in 1942, I opted for aeronautical engineering, mainly because of a romantic fascination with airplanes and flying. That passion did not die easily, as evidenced by the fact that during one summer in Palo Alto, at age 39, I obtained my private license and a year later bought a light plane. After a few years, an increasing awareness of the risks and a wife who did not like the noisiness of a light plane led me to give it up.

I soon discovered that engineering, at least as then taught, was not very congenial to me, but physical theory and mathematics were fascinating, even if difficult. By the summer of 1943 I was in the Navy V-12 program—the snobbery of the Navy being such that its officers, even during a major war whose outcome in 1943 still seemed uncertain, must have college degrees—and so I was no longer free to transfer out of engineering. That had to await graduate school. In 1945 I graduated and was elected to both the honorary engineering society, Tau Beta Pi, and to the scientific one, Sigma Xi.

Following Midshipman School at Notre Dame, during the summer when the war ended, I spent a brief, intense period in the Catapult and Arresting Gear School at the Philadelphia Navy Yard, as did all V-12 aeronautical engineers that year. I was then assigned as a catapult officer to the USS *Kearsarge*, which was receiving her final fitting out at the Brooklyn Navy Yard. In the isolation of her shakedown cruise, I decided on applied mathematics rather than physics and in 1946 returned to MIT as a graduate student in the Department of Mathematics.

As well as I can recall, I rejected physics on two grounds: its heavy involvement in weapons applications and its high level of formal development. I felt then that there must be other fields in which one could contribute in more peaceful ways and have the excitement of working in more virgin terrain. Just which field was not clear to me. At first I knew little of psychology, and economics seemed the more obvious choice. Indeed, I recall some early and feeble attempts to write down economic equations, but chance ultimately led me to concentrate on psychology.

The actual start of my career in psychology was, in a sense, sharply defined. One afternoon, Albert Perry, a graduate student in electrical engineering at MIT, and I were modifying a military surplus radio into what then passed for high-fidelity equipment, when my roommate William Blitzer returned from Leon Festinger's class in social psychology. He described to us some of the combinatorial problems they faced in dealing with social networks. Soon Perry and I were busy trying to translate these into questions about matrices, and a few days later Blitzer introduced us, with some theorems in hand, to Festinger. By the end of the summer we had a paper ready for submission, and another paper on the same topic followed shortly.

Although I didn't know it for sure, I was hooked. Still, the problem of a thesis remained—no one in the Department of Mathematics was interested in social networks, and at the time MIT did not have a psychology department. The nearest mathematical topic was cybernetics, but I had not attracted Norbert Weiner's notice. For reasons not wholly clear to me, a young algebraist named I. S. Cohen was assigned as my advisor on the then very unapplied topic of semigroups. At the time, it seemed a deflection. Some twenty years later, at a cocktail party, I ran into W. T. Martin, who had been chairman of the Mathematics Department at the time; and, to my surprise, he brought up the events surrounding my thesis, volunteering that the department had erred in not letting me pursue my psychological interests. Perhaps so, but probably not, since I later made considerable use of just this type of mathematics in working on the theory of measurement.

As work progressed on the thesis, a significant career decision had to be faced. Should I attempt the standard academic route in mathematics, largely suppressing my interest in applications to the social sciences, or should I attempt a major commitment to psychology or some other social science? My taste was for applied mathematics, in spite of a pure mathematics thesis; and I was convinced that I would not become a very distinguished pure mathematician. But knowing little about psychology, I was not at all sure how to go about entering the field, and being rather shy, I was not especially adept at finding out.

It was all resolved by an accidental social meeting. Oliver Strauss, an M.D. working in the Research Laboratory of Electronics (RLE), who had some association with Alex Bavelas's Small Groups Laboratory, appeared at the Beacon Hill apartment I shared with Louis Osborne (a physicist later much involved with accelerators at MIT and Harvard) and Alan J.

Perlis (a well-known computer scientist, now at Yale). I had earlier met Bavelas through Festinger, just before Festinger and the Center for Group Dynamics moved to the University of Michigan following Kurt Lewin's death, and I had done a little work for him. Strauss and I talked about my interests, and he soon arranged a position for me as Bavelas's captive mathematician. So a major career decision was reached through some blend of ignorance, predisposition, and chance; I expect these are the usual ingredients—only the mix varies.

During the next seven years I often questioned whether I had not made a foolish, irreversible decision. At that time departments of psychology hired statisticians, but not mathematicians with absolutely no psychological qualifications who aspired to do psychological theory. I had taken no courses in either psychology or statistics—few of the former and quite possibly none of the latter were then available at MIT—even as I picked up some statistics in self-defense, I was convinced that I did not want that to be my major teaching role. So the initial stages of the career were rocky, and I was often apprehensive.

Research Themes

Aside from a few minor excursions, my research can be grouped into four general topics: group interactions (including game theory), probabilistic choice theory, psychophysics (including response times), and the foundations of measurement. The first preceded and is rather independent of the other three, which have been closely interlocked both temporally and intellectually.

Group Interactions and Game Theory

The work first stimulated by Festinger continued during my three years with MIT's Small Groups Laboratory. The main psychological idea was that many working groups have imposed upon them a communication structure which presumably affects their ability to carry out tasks. To study this in its simplest form, Bavelas had groups of five subjects sit around a table partitioned into wedges; they passed notes to one another through slots in the center core. Any network could be imposed simply by closing the appropriate slots. The highly stylized notes provided a permanent, if clumsy, record of the communications. A number of empirical papers, including two long technical reports that were never rewritten into journal articles, were the output. But even though we wrote a great deal and presented much data, I don't think we learned very much about communication in small groups.

In part through the skeptical questioning of some of the superb group of psychologists then being collected in MIT's new Lincoln Laboratory, initially located just down the hall in the "temporary" Building 20 (still heavily used) in which we were housed, I gradually began to realize both that the graph theoretic models were not relating in any important way to the data we were collecting and that the data themselves were not inherently very interesting. As a result, I became receptive to better approaches and during my last year at MIT began to study game theory as a possible model for some kinds of interactions. At least there were actors who made choices, not the propertyless nodes of the digraphs, as well as some communication among the participants.

My knowledge of game theory deepened after I moved to Columbia University in 1953. Howard Raiffa, then of the Department of Mathematical Statistics, and I agreed to write a short summary report on game theory designed primarily for social scientists. That short report evolved into the 600-page book *Games and Decisions* (1957), which remained in print for nearly 30 years; a reprint is forthcoming from Dover.

Before its publication, however, my interest in game theory and, indeed, in the whole area of modeling processes of social interaction had waned. I concluded that despite the obvious great importance of such interactions, neither our experimental nor our mathematical techniques were adequate to the problem. My view is little changed. The fact that a problem is important does not make it tractable, and a scientist can be foolish to hammer at it as if it were. Furthermore, I had also begun to be tempted by other research topics in individual psychology.

Probabilistic Choice Theory

The shift of focus began during 1954-55 when I was, for the first time, a Fellow at the Center for Advanced Study in the Behavioral Sciences (CASBS), Stanford, California. I had become fascinated with the von Neumann–Morgenstern theory of expected utility, with the Weber-Fechner problem of psychophysical scaling, and with their relation, if any. This started an interplay between algebraic and probabilistic approaches to choice and between utility and psychophysical scaling which has dominated my intellectual life.

On returning to Columbia in late 1955, I divided my time between work on *Games and Decisions* and on the development of what I called the choice axiom—the assertion that choice probabilities behave like conditional probabilities from a much larger set of alternatives. That name was ill chosen, and I knew it at the time, because the "axiom of choice" exists in mathematics and is of much greater significance. The dilemma was that I could not think of a suitable alternative term for the intended interpretation: choice. I recall neither where the idea came from nor when I first wrote the axiom down, but probably it was during the winter of 1956–57. By the spring of 1957 a 100-page, red-covered mimeographed technical report had been distributed to some interested people. That summer a number of them met in a mathematical psychology workshop at Stanford, and the "red menace" was a major focus of discussion, including some controversy between Patrick Suppes and me. One consequence was the beginning of our friendship. I rewrote the manuscript during the next academic year with an eye to publication as a psychometric monograph, but Gordon Ierardi of John Wiley & Sons, who had published *Games and Decisions*, requested it, even though he knew that its sale would be marginal. It appeared under the title *Individual Choice Behavior* (*ICB*) (1959b) with, not by accident, a bright red jacket. The book had four main chapters: the axiom and some of its direct consequences, followed by applications to psychophysics, learning, and utility theory.

The psychophysical models led to numerical results very close to those of Case V Thurstonian models, which encouraged me to explore them further. However, after some years of effort, I concluded that, except possibly as approximations in certain cases, this approach had not resulted in satisfactory psychophysical models. So I abandoned it, returning to psychophysics only some years later.

The work on learning in *ICB* was suggested by the linear operator models of Bush and Mosteller (1955). The choice axiom led naturally to nonlinear models that have the mathematically happy feature of being commutative, but thereby totally lacking the psychologically needed property of suppressing the distant past. Interest in it, along with other operator models for learning, waned.

The chapter on utility in *ICB* led to the curious prediction that probability of choice between certain gambles should vary as a step, rather than a continuous, function of the event probability. Elizabeth Shipley and I ran an appropriate experiment and found supporting, though not conclusive, evidence. The experiment has never been replicated, and it remains an isolated fragment that seems not to have affected any later developments.

The coup de grace for choice theory (and many related approaches) was provided by Krantz (1964) and Tversky and Russo (1969), who showed that any (binary) choice model in which the choice probabilities can be expressed as a fixed function of scale values on the two alternatives is equivalent to several simple properties of the choice probabilities. A number of experiments, ranging from color perception to preference, carefully designed to maximize the possibility of difficulties, showed that these properties can be violated, and so models of this type cannot be generally correct.

The most interesting long-term consequence of *ICB* was Tversky's (1972) generalization known as choice by elimination, which explicitly takes into account that alternatives possess structure. The choice axiom is the special case in which there is no such structure.

Psychophysics, 1954–1963

My interest in psychophysics derives, in part, from the fact that mathematics has, from the start, played a significant role in the development of this field. I had been dimly aware of this from meetings at MIT in the late 1940's and early 1950's in which information theory applications to psychology generally and psychophysics in particular were all the rage. Indeed, one of my first activities at Columbia was a long paper on information theory and its applications in psychology (Luce, 1960). But not until the year at CASBS, under the wise tutelage of Albert Hastorf, did I begin to delve carefully in psychophysical theory. Starting at the headwaters of the subject, I studied the Weber-Fechner problem, and two papers resulted.

One, with Ward Edwards (Luce and Edwards, 1958), pointed out the fact, surprising to me, that Fechner's derivation—the one usually presented in texts—of his "law" from Weber's law was technically incorrect and that for any Weber function other than Weber's law, this method would have led to the wrong answer. The proper method is to solve Abel's functional equation. A small literature has resulted, which is summarized in Falmagne (1985). The second paper introduced what amounts to an algebraic approximation to the probabilities used by Fechner, but that is more appropriately discussed under measurement.

During the period from 1956 through 1961, when I was greatly preoccupied with choice models, much of what I did in psychophysics had to do with them. But not entirely. While at Harvard (1957–59), I spent a fair amount of time with the late S. S. Stevens—one either spent a fair amount of time with Smitty or none at all, for his intellectual style, although intense and persistent, was leisurely and was often intermixed with skiing in one way or another. In his firm way, he ground my nose into two sets of data: those collected some years earlier in support of neural quantum theory, the idea that the mental representation of stimuli is discrete rather than continuous, and those he had recently been collecting using magnitude estimates and cross modality matches. His classic paper "On the Psychophysical Law" (Stevens, 1957) had just appeared.

Although I was not really happy with the way either body of data had been collected, I eventually became convinced that any psychophysical theory worthy of the name had to account naturally for both sets of data. In particular, it slowly became clear to me that neither my choice models nor the theory of signal detectability, with which I had familiarized myself at Columbia, were satisfactory. I also found the theory of signal detectability wanting in another, extremely important respect: it did not generalize in a satisfactory way beyond two stimuli except as Thurstone's discriminal dispersions. Among other things, neither model predicted the limits on information transmitted in absolute identification experiments (Miller, 1956), which seemed to me another key psychophysical phenomenon requiring a natural account.

Before leaving Harvard, I wrote "On the Possible Psychophysical Laws" (1959a), an obvious takeoff on Stevens's title. As my paper really concerned dimensional analysis, it belongs in the section on measurement, but as its impact really was in psychophysics, I discuss it here. Although widely referenced, criticized, and reprinted, I fear that it has rarely been understood. The fault is mine, for although the writing seems clear locally, it is misleading globally. In truth, it says nothing whatsoever about the form of psychophysical laws, but only explains why, except for power laws, laws should be formulated in terms of dimensionless signal and response variables. However, this point is made most obliquely, and many have interpreted the paper as saying that Stevens's results on the psychophysical function were, somehow, mathematically foreordained, which is not true.

During the first half of my ten years at the University of Pennsylvania (1959–69), my psychophysical work centered on the last gasps of the choice models, already discussed, the two topics stimulated by Stevens (neural quantum and magnitude estimation data), and reaction times. The two Stevens topics, like thorns, were hard to ignore.

Neural quantum theory (Békésy, 1930; Stevens, Morgan, and Volkman,

1941) and the theory of signal detectability (Green and Swets, 1966) are completely inconsistent in their formulation of threshold phenomena. Supporters of each theory had data they interpreted as rejecting the other view. My attack on the problem was two-pronged. First, I attempted to demonstrate that ROC data (plots of the probability of saying a signal was present when it was present versus the probability of saying it was present when it was not), which had been interpreted as devastating evidence against the threshold idea, really only clearly rejected what has come to be known as high thresholds, not low ones. A tricky debate ensued as to whether or not ROC data, especially those collected using rating scale methods, also reject the low threshold model. Krantz (1969) gave the matter its most careful discussion. What seems to be evident now is that although the two-state model is wrong, no reasonable amount of ROC data can distinguish between a few states and a continuum.

The second prong of the attack was to see whether response biases, whose existence had been so clearly demonstrated by ROC plots, could account for the difficulties some experimenters had in replicating the neural quantum results. There could be no doubt that enormous biasing effects were possible; nevertheless, tantalizing hints of discrete underlying structure showed through in studies of W. D. Larkin and D. A. Norman, then graduate students. Perhaps the most difficult data for the continuous theories to encompass are the piece-wise linear ROC curves obtained using two-alternative, forced-choice procedures and different payoff matrices. Data to test some choice models, collected by Shipley in W. P. Tanner's laboratory, showed that subjects failed to discriminate signal frequency when they reported no signal present. This made sense from a threshold point of view (with appropriate response bias), but not from that of the theory of signal detectability. W. A. Lindner, working under the direction of James Egan, replicated the study and got exactly the opposite results. I have no idea why there was the difference, especially since both Lindner and Shipley are careful experimenters. I do not believe it can be attributed to experimenter bias on Shipley's part, because the issue had not even been formulated at the time her experiment was performed.

To this day, I believe that the question whether or not signal representations are discrete remains unresolved. Most psychophysicists have been convinced not, but I am not convinced their reasons are adequate to that conclusion.

Stevens's second thorn was the inability of any of the discrimination theories—those, as he used to say, that "process noise" or, as we who have worked on them said, are "local in character"—to encompass magnitude estimation and absolute identification data when the range of signals is sufficiently large. To know how deep that thorn went, I had to examine two features of the data that Stevens typically ignored: the mean response of individual subjects and the variability of the individual responses about the mean value.

Suchsoon Mo and I ran an experiment collecting weight-lifting data, resulting in four main findings. (1) Many of the mean magnitude functions exhibited systematic deviations from power functions; in the case of loudness some deviations have been as large as 5 dB. This has been repeatedly replicated. (2) The "exponents," although averaging to values near those reported by Stevens, exhibited considerable variation, from 0.15 to 0.34 for loudness versus physical energy. Again, this seems typical of later data, except that the top of the range is more like 0.6. (3) The typical distribution of responses, which is sharply peaked and has high tails, was not really fit well by any of the familiar distributions we tried. (4) The variability of the responses was appreciably greater than that obtained using discrimination techniques, such as a two-signal absolute identification design.

It was not clear to me where to go next with magnitude estimation; I dropped it for nearly a decade until a better theory led to a better understanding, new predictions, and additional experiments.

Response time is not always thought of as part of psychophysics, but it is an integral part of any decision process. Any psychophysical theory, such as signal detection and choice theory, that fails to account for the time it takes the subject to respond is surely incomplete. The mere fact that response times form a continuous random variable warmly recommends their close examination, because each observation is potentially a richer source of information than is the typical binary choice data. (For references to reaction time papers, see the bibliography of my book *Response Times* [RT] [1986].)

My first foray into reaction times, which occurred in the mid-1950's with Lee S. Christie, made two points. The first, well known to mathematicians and statisticians, but then apparently overlooked by psychologists, was that certain familiar integral transforms take the distribution of the sum of independent random variables into the product of the transforms of the separate distributions. This fact can be exploited, as was later demonstrated by W. J. McGill (1973) and by Green and Luce in several papers, including the general theory one, Luce and Green (1972). The second was to remark that it is not very easy to distinguish between serial and parallel systems using overall time. At the time this did not attract much attention, but in the 1970's James Townsend carried out a great deal of research on the issue, confirming in considerable detail that serial systems can mimic locally independent parallel ones but not the converse.

Work resumed when Eugene Galanter and I interested a student, Joan Gay Snodgrass, in the area. The key idea in our approach was to apply information feedback and payoffs to reaction times, just as to choices, to find out how malleable the reaction times are. We had two initial questions: could the subject be made to track a narrow band of payoffs over a range of times, and to what degree could we reduce the variability by narrowing the band? The results showed that subjects could indeed track the band, but that the variability was a U-shaped function suggesting there is a natural reaction time and that the band is tracked by the subjects' introducing, in some fashion, delays that add to the variability. We also found that although the variability could be made as small as a 25-msec interquartile range, there was no advantage in using a band payoff much narrower than 20 msec. In later work and using a somewhat different procedure, A. B. Kristofferson reduced the estimate of variability even more, to as little as about 10 msec.

Perhaps the most perplexing thing in these data was the form of the distribution of reaction times. In contrast to the rather rounded mode often reported, usually from less careful experiments and frequently from data averaged over subjects, we found very peaked distributions. Attempts to fit them to various well-known distribution functions were not very successful.

I am now convinced that any data, like these, based on strong signals are incapable of telling us much about the psychological decision process because its duration is too brief relative to other delays in the system, such as sensory transduction, neural transit times, muscle innervation, and so on. Weak signals are another matter.

A student of this same era, Robert T. Ollman, became interested in the speed-accuracy trade-off problem and developed and tested the fast-guess model, which was also independently developed by John Yellott, Jr. I was never taken by it conceptually and later worked out an alternative model with David M. Green. We provided data that showed the fast-guess model does not, by itself, account for responses to weak signals. I suspect that the fast-guess model may well be correct, or approximately so, when the experimenter drives the subject beyond the range of his ordinary decision mechanisms; it is behavior of last resort, in despair of complying with the instructions. Data of Richard Swensson and Ward Edwards strongly supported the idea of fast guesses, but with the new wrinkle that there are prolonged runs in the fast-guess mode alternating with runs in the attention mode. Also Donald Blough presented beautiful discrimination data for pigeons that clearly exhibited fast guessing.

Psychophysics, 1964–1981: Collaboration with David M. Green

By 1963 my work in psychophysics had lost direction. I had abandoned the choice models; my efforts at deciding whether or not there is anything to neural quantum theory were indecisive; the variability of magnitude estimates was not much understood; and I had failed to incorporate response times successfully into any model. Moreover, I lacked an overall theoretical scheme in which I had any faith. The way out of this unhappy state was totally unclear, and in all honesty, I clumsily backed into my next attack on psychophysics without knowing where I was going.

The so-called method of free response, in which the signals to be detected are presented according to some haphazard temporal schedule with the subject free to respond whenever a signal seems to have occurred, appealed to me as being a far better idealization of natural detection problems than are the usual psychophysical procedures that delineate brief time periods during which a signal may or may not appear. However, the method of analysis then used, of treating the detection process as a sequence of fixed-interval yes-no decisions, did not appeal at all. The data consist of two interlaced time series—that of signal presentations and that of the responses—and the theoretical problem is to understand the probabilistic structure of the response series and its relation to the signal one. This has to do with continuous stochastic processes, not discrete ones.

I worked out an idealized two-state, continuous-time model in which each signal presentation had some fixed probability of activating the detect state and the background had a temporally random (Poisson) tendency to do the same. David Green, who had come to the University of Pennsylvania, became interested in the model, and we decided to try to test it. After a bit, we began to realize we were being plagued by the fact that, under a Poisson schedule, the signals tend to occur in bursts (because the most probable time between two signals is zero), and so a second and even a third signal could occur before the response to the first could have been completed. At first we attempted to model what might be going on, but the mathematical problems compounded until we decided it was better to change the experiment. Basically, there were two possibilities. One was to focus directly on the problem of how two temporally close signals interfere with each other; this, unbeknownst to us at the time, was the fruitful path followed by A. T. Welford, leading to his "single-channel" hypothesis (Section 5.4 of *RT*). The other, which we followed, was simply to rid ourselves of the interaction.

We wanted a design for which the onset of a signal is totally unpredictable while not having a second signal intervene before the response. This led us to a simple reaction-time design with random (i.e., exponentially distributed) foreperiods and weak signals. We also found the modeling to be much simpler if we used response terminated signals rather than ones of fixed duration. We worked out the two-state model, with the occurrence of states governed by one Poisson process before signal onset and by a different one, with a larger parameter, during its presentation. In essence, the problem for the subject was to decide when the parameter of the process had changed value. A somewhat unusual data analysis, outlined in Section 3.2.4 of *RT*, showed the simplest model to be wrong and suggested the next approach.

This postulates that neural pulse rate serves as a surrogate for signal intensity, and the task for the brain is to estimate the local rate from small samples. Clearly, the greater the number of interpulse observations, the better the estimate. Equally clearly, larger samples from a single channel mean slower response times. The latter dictated some parallel acquisition from statistically independent channels. Our focus on rate estimates led to two distinct models: counting ones, in which the sample time is fixed, and timing ones, in which the sample size is fixed (Luce and Green, 1972). The former had been previously studied, but not the latter, which interested us because of their automatic account of the inverse relation between reaction times and signal intensity (the weaker the signal, the slower the pulse rate and hence the slower the decision time). However, they also led to the prediction that the yes-no ROC curves (in z-scores) should approximate straight lines with slopes considerably greater than one, unlike any data of the time. We were led to an auditory experiment, reported in Green and Luce (1973), which involved response deadlines. When the deadline applied to all trials, the ROC slopes were, as usual, less than one, agreeing with the counting model. Applied just to signal trials, however, the deadline led to slopes greater than one, agreeing with the timing model. Subsequently, Brian Wandell, a graduate student of mine at the University of California at Irvine, confirmed the finding in vision.

Further research with Wandell provided evidence that subjects aggregate information across neural channels by averaging rather than taking the maximum time. Further, Green and I observed that if timing is the natural mode of operation and assuming that the short duration signals of the usual psychophysical experiment invite counting, then one feature of laboratory training, leading to stable behavior, is reprogramming from timing to counting. Such reprogramming is slow.

One remarkable fact, not yet mentioned, is that all of our detection studies of acoustic intensity near threshold led to estimates of the Poisson rate parameter that grew approximately as a power function of intensity, with the exponent varying from 0.15 to 0.60 over subjects and averaging somewhere near, but below, 0.3. Stevens (1957) had shown this directly for the entire stimulus range by plotting average magnitude estimates versus signal intensity, and we found it to be true for individual subjects, especially if mean ratios of successive magnitude estimates are plotted against the corresponding signal ratios. This law (Stevens's law) seems to describe a central tendency of the transformation of acoustic intensity into the pulse trains that enter into sensory decisions.

Although the timing model gave a natural account of reaction times to weak signals, it was quickly shown not to be fully correct. As I mentioned earlier, the empirical distributions tend to be so peaked at the mode as compared to the rate of decay in their tails that it is impossible to fit them by any of the classic distributions, including those that arise from timing models. Stephen Burbeck, then a graduate student at Irvine, became challenged by this problem and came up with a plausible solution (Section 4.4 of *RT*). Reactions to weak signals are assumed to be triggered by a race between two independent processes, one having to do with perceived jumps or changes in the signal intensity, which is called a "change detector," and the other having to do with changed levels of activity, which is called a "level detector." The difference is that the change detector is sensitive to abrupt changes in the derivative of the wave form, whereas the level detector compares averages computed over successive periods of time. Functionally, the difference is that a change detector, when triggered, is fast; but, should it miss the change, as is possible with weak signals, it fails. The level detector is fundamentally more reliable, but at the expense of being much slower.

A particular transformation of the data known as the hazard function, first urged by McGill (1963) for use with response time data, is ideal for testing such a model because the hazard function of a race among several independent processes is simply the sum of the hazard functions of those processes. Reasonably strong evidence in favor of such dual detection was found. My guess is that the timing model, which is normally used for signal identification, is drawn into play in the pure detection situation and serves as the slower level detector. That results in the relatively long tails to the distribution. The basic change detector, which searches for rapid changes in the waveform, yields the highly peaked mode that is observed.

On my arrival at Harvard in 1976, Green and I gave a seminar on the use of time measures in psychophysics and later, from time to time, I gave it alone. Gradually, I learned more of the extensive literature, and my notes began to impose some structure on the material. In 1979, when thinking about what to do on my 1980–81 sabbatical, I decided to try to put it all together in a book, which became *Response Times*, completed in late 1984. During 1982–84 a number of seminars at the AT&T Bell Laboratories, organized by Saul Sternberg, critiqued drafts of chapters and led to substantial changes. The book is mostly a survey, with some original analyses and a plausible organization of a sprawling literature; it has received relatively kind reviews.

Another line of inquiry sparked by Green's and my neural model was into the global psychophysics of magnitude estimation and absolute identification. In our 1972 paper, we suggested that the pulse rates estimated from the sum of a fixed sample of interpulse times could serve to account for both experiments: the estimated rate multiplied by a constant being the number emitted in magnitude estimation, and the estimated rate being a Thurstonian random variable underlying the categorization asked for in absolute identification.

We quickly demonstrated that, in this simple form, both hypotheses are wrong. To improve the fit of the model to data, we next considered an "attention" hypothesis of the following sort: if a signal falls within an attention band, which we estimated to be about 10–15 dB wide for loudness, decisions are assumed to be based on a sample of interpulse intervals that is close to an order-of-magnitude larger than when the signal falls outside the band. This means that the standard deviation of the resulting estimates is smaller by a factor of about 3 (approximately $=\sqrt{10}$) when the signal is in the band than when it is outside it. Not only does this hypothesis seem to account for some anomalies in the magnitude estimation data, but it provides a natural account for the asymptotic form of the function relating information transmitted to number of signals in absolute identification (Miller, 1956) and to the form of the cumulative d' measure reported by Braida and Durlach (1972).

Increasingly, we became aware of the fact that both in magnitude estimation and in absolute identification there are very pronounced sequential effects. To ignore them is misleading. For example, in absolute identification, if one looks at the matrix of correlations between successive responses as a function of the signal pairs, it is found that roughly the same correlation obtains along the diagonals running from upper left to lower right. In other words, the correlation varies systematically with signal difference (measured in dB), being about 0.8 to 0.9 when the signal is repeated and dropping to zero or possibly a negative value when they are widely separated.

A second phenomenon is that the ratio of the standard deviation to the mean response to a signal as a function of the dB separation between that signal and the preceding one is decidedly V-shaped. Responses to a signal that is repeated are less variable than when the preceding signal is more distant.

A small theoretical and experimental literature has developed around these problems, but no really satisfactory model seems yet to have resulted. From the point of view of experimentalists, the situation is (or should be) deeply frustrating, because we do not know how to gain real control of the sources of these sequential effects. As a result, it is virtually impossible to draw any firm conclusions from the variability in magnitude estimation and absolute identification since any estimate of it is so thoroughly contaminated by sequential effects as to be meaningless. Much the same problem exists in using distributions of response times, as is summarized in Section 6.6 of *RT*. I am not sure how widely this dilemma about global psychophysical methods is fully appreciated.

At this point I found myself not working actively with an experimental group, and I lacked any new idea, so I stopped working on the problem.

Measurement, 1955–1972

For specific references, both to my work and that of others, in measurement, see the bibliographies of the three volumes of the *Foundations of Measurement* (*FM*) (Krantz, Luce, Suppes, and Tversky, 1971, 1989).

In contrast to my work on choice behavior and psychophysics, where the models are probabilistic, that in the foundations of measurement is algebraic. My training strongly favored this approach, and I have always found algebra more aesthetic than analysis; however, such models are usually difficult to relate satisfactorily to experiments. I suspect that the best way to look at them is as descriptions of some central tendency of a process that is best thought of as probabilistic. When the latter is quite complex or ill understood, however, it may be best to begin with just the central tendency.

My first paper (1956) in the area was devoted to an axiomatization of an algebraic concept of threshold called "semiorders." The axioms were a natural, and surprisingly simple, generalization of those for a linear order, the main difference being that the indifference relation is not transitive. Important later elaborations were made by Peter C. Fishburn and Fred S. Roberts.

The next contribution did not appear until my joint paper with John W. Tukey (1964), which was the lead paper in the newly founded (see below) *Journal of Mathematical Psychology*. That research began in the summer of 1961 at an informal seminar held in Tukey's study at CASBS, where he proposed that measurement additive over components might serve for the social sciences in a way analogous to that served by extensive measurement (e.g., additive over a combining operation) for the physical ones. We axiomatized it. Given the later, much simpler and more revealing proofs of E. Holman and David H. Krantz (*FM I*, chapter 6) that neatly relate additive conjoint measurements to extensive measurement, it is surprising how tortured our first proofs were.

My next efforts concerned more realistic idealizations in which solvability is assumed only locally, both for the conjoint case and, with A. A. J. Marley, for the extensive one, including the bounded case (e.g., relativistic velocity). Krantz followed this up by producing a very useful local version of Hölder's theorem, which is one of the basic theorems employed in *FM I*. Improved versions of both the above papers are included in *FM I*.

During the early and middle 1960's, Patrick Suppes and I participated in and organized a number of conferences where questions in the theory of measurement were frequently discussed. In spite of his chapter with J. Zinnes (Suppes and Zinnes, 1963), we increasingly felt the need for a systematic presentation and integration of the materials on measurement, which spanned a wide range of disciplines including economics, management science, mathematics, operations research, philosophy of science, physics, psychology, and statistics. As we outlined a book that could do this, we became acutely aware of areas in which we had not made contributions and were not especially expert. These topics were nicely covered by two brilliant and industrious young men, David H. Krantz and Amos Tversky. I had known Krantz from the time he was a graduate student at the University of Pennsylvania, where he worked with my friends and colleagues Leo Hurvich and Dorothea Jameson, and I had met Tversky, who was working on a dissertation under the late Clyde Coombs on finite conjoint measurement. We invited them to join the project. Our initial outline suggested a book of some twenty chapters, and so it has remained, despite the fact that early on it fissioned into two volumes and, in 1987, into three. (The additional two introductions raised the chapter count to 22, and some of the topics also changed over the years.) We titled it *Foundations of Measurement*. Although I had expected the work to be completed within a few years of the first volume, it was not finished until the end of 1987. The delay is discussed below.

Much of Volume I was completed during 1966–67, when I was again a Fellow at CASBS. A major task was to find the least number of mathematical results that describe basic algebraic structures which have additive numerical representations and from which we could derive all of the results in the additive theory of measurement. Ultimately, we showed that three theorems would do (*FM I*, chapter 2). This meant, however, that virtually every result in the literature had to be reproved to fit into our scheme; in the process of doing that, we uncovered some new results and improved many other theorems. My eight measurement papers during the late 1960's and early 1970's arose from this effort. Our hope was that by integrating and systematizing the results this way, we would make it easier for others to build new structures and better integrations. That has happened.

Chapter 10 on dimensional analysis was particularly troublesome. Dimensional analysis is a method whereby physicists, engineers, and biologists often can arrive at the form of a physical law simply by knowing exactly which variables are relevant—of course, that is a great deal to know. Since I first encountered the method in graduate school, it has fascinated and perplexed me. Although useful, the subject seemed conceptually slippery. Read carefully the introductory chapter to any book on the subject, and you soon realize that something mysterious is going on; only when you get to the applications does it begin to make sense. During that year at CASBS three long sessions of a Stanford-Berkeley seminar on measurement were devoted to Robert Causey's dissertation on physical similarity, which is a major aspect of dimensional analysis. Part of the reason these sessions ran long was my inability to understand exactly what was involved in the concept of dimensional invariance. During the following year Causey's paper was published, and we corresponded at length about it, until I finally got straight what I found objectionable.

Although part of the problem had been clarified, I came to realize, as I was drafting Chapter 10 in Rio de Janeiro, that there remained a major, apparently unremarked, lacuna. No one ever provided a serious reason why physical scales (e.g., mass, length, time, velocity, etc.), which arise from the theory of extensive measurement, should have anything to do with the representations of physical quantities discussed in dimensional analysis. The latter structure was axiomatic in character, and no one had ever showed how to construct it from the former, although everyone obviously believed such a construction to be possible. So I undertook the task.

There were two keys to the construction. First, one must assume that, in addition to extensive structures, there are conjoint ones, written as products, and that some physical quantities, although not all, are measured both extensively and conjointly. Second, in physics, these two kinds of measures are always related by power transformations. I found a reasonably neat qualitative way of characterizing that transformation by what I called laws of similitude and of exchange, which relate the conjoint and extensive structures. Subsequent generalizations, involving a qualitative notion of the distribution of a measurement structure on a component of a conjoint one, have greatly improved those results (1978a, 1988, *FM III*, chapters 20 and 22).

It has always struck me as an odd curiosity of history that although some physical scales obviously have an internal additive structure and some a multiplicative decomposition into other scales (e.g., length is additive, and momentum is the product of mass and velocity), philosophers of physics during the latter part of the last century and the first half of this one axiomatized only the additive aspect. Their failure to axiomatize the multiplicative decomposition was not for lack of technical power (O. Hölder, who axiomatized extensive operators, was an accomplished mathematician) but apparently lack of motivation to do so. Not until behavioral scientists, who for their own reasons, axiomatized additive conjoint measurement was the other half of physical measurement properly formalized. With that done, it became possible to provide a natural account of dimensional analysis.

Measurement, 1973–1988: Collaboration with Louis Narens

I break the discussion of measurement not at the time I left Irvine for
Harvard, but at the time I began to collaborate with a brilliant younger
colleague Louis Narens, who received his training under the late Abraham Robinson, the founder of nonstandard analysis. This collaboration,
which still continues, has been one of the most fruitful of my career. I feel
fortunate to have been able to work with someone whose mind is a marvelous mixture of creativeness, fantasy, philosophical demandingness, and
mathematical power. Through his impact, I have done better work than
I had done earlier. Some is summarized in Narens (1985) and some in
chapters 19, 20, and 22 of *FM III*.

Most work on measurement, to this point, focused on structures with
additive or averaging representations. The exceptions to this statement
were isolated, and we understood little about the full range of qualitative
structures with non-additive representations. The first question we tack-
led was to find fairly general conditions under which a general (non-
associative) operation can be represented uniquely by some numerical operation other than +. It turned out that the solution to this problem pretty
much provided the solution to the general question of representing a conjoint structure in terms of some function of scales on its two components.
Our results, however, left it unclear how the different representations of
the same structure relate to one another. For example, in the classical additive measures of physics, we do not simply say that a unique representation is singled out once a unit is assigned, but rather that the set of all
representations forms a ratio scale in the sense that any two are related by
a multiplicative constant. We could not say, at the time, how the several
representations of non-associative operations were related.

After coming to Harvard in 1976, I encountered a maverick graduate
student Michael A. Cohen, whose mathematical skills were just what was
needed for these measurement problems. In a term paper for my seminar
on measurement he came up with the, to me, surprising result that the
family of transformations relating the representations was in fact very
simple—namely, isomorphic to some subgroup of the positive numbers
under multiplication. At first I didn't believe it, especially since the proof
he turned in was, like his personal style, disheveled, but eventually I became convinced and put him in touch with Narens, who had also been
working on the problem. Narens's approach was directed at seeing what
happens when you impose a property to the effect that the family of transformations is rich in the same sense that a ratio scale is. Put another way,

no element is distinguishable from the others solely by its behavior, a property called homogeneity. Coupling that restriction with Cohen's result led to a remarkably simple characterization of non-associative, ratio scale representations, one that I believe may prove useful in psychological theorizing. It was only fully worked out in Luce and Narens (1985) and further generalized in Luce (1988).

During our July 1980 collaboration, Narens became obsessed with the question of classifying the scale types of all measurement structures that can be represented by real numerical systems. He arrived at a partial solution, which included in it some of the ingredients for the general solution. That was achieved in 1984 by Theodore Alper, who became aware of the problem during my measurement seminar, in his senior mathematics thesis under the guidance of his advisor, Andrew Gleason.

Independent of that, Narens and I classified a broad class of structures with operations, and we worked out much of the theory for the two distinct types of structures that can arise—generalizing additive and averaging representations. In particular, this led to an interesting generalization of subjective expected utility that seems capable of dealing with several of the empirical difficulties that have been encountered.

Subsequently, Narens and I have pursued and solved a number of related questions, including what to make of the fact that there are a number of different notions of commensurability of measurement scales when an operation exists; how to generalize such concepts of commensurability when there is no operation; and what in that case is the generalization of the Cohen and Narens result about homogeneous operations. It turns out that in the homogeneous case, the situation is ever so much neater than we had any reason to expect, with everything fitting together in a beautiful fashion. Closely related is the general definition of distribution that is needed to put these structures together in a fashion suitable for dimensional analysis. Again, the result is very neat, but this is not the place to attempt a detailed exposition.

I was also able to establish that the elusive idea of dimensional invariance is just a special case of a general notion of meaningfulness, much like the one that arose in nineteenth century geometry and that S. S. Stevens (1951) raised in asking about how statistical practice should be affected by the scale type of the measure. Everyone who has thought about this at all agrees that we do not fully understand why we demand such invariance. Intuitively, one would like to say that something is meaningful in a structure provided it can be defined in terms of the primitives of that structure.

The problem is to formulate, in a philosophically well justified fashion, what exactly is meant by that. This, as one might expect, has turned out to be extremely elusive. For the past four or five years Narens has worked very hard on the problem, and he has many interesting results forming a large book manuscript, but the core problem remains unresolved as I revise (March 1988).

What exactly are measurement models good for? In my APA Distinguished Scientific Award address (Luce, 1972), I argued that even within psychophysics there is no evidence that we can construct a system of variables and measures comparable to that of physics. The main difficulty is that while (approximate) power relations abound, the exponents seem to vary considerably from subject to subject. If not that use, then what? I later (Luce, 1985) pointed out that the successful applications of the measurement models to psychophysical problems can best be described as formalizing the structural relations involved in some central tendency of the sensory transducer. They permit us an economical characterization of the average information reduction effected by the transducer as revealed in the various trade-offs among stimulus variables that yield, on average, the same internal representation. Krantz (1972) has also argued forcefully that measurement methods are a means to begin to get basic relations among variables as well as to measure them. Falmagne (1985) illustrates this for psychophysical models. Increasingly, however, as we have uncovered the generalizations mentioned above, I have come to believe that the major significance is to lay out, as completely as we can, the possibilities for numerical measurement. This provides a chart for the behavioral and biological sciences of what is potentially possible by way of one-dimensional measurement and, in particular, of adjoining new ratio scale measures to the structure of units developed by the physical sciences. Whether we will be able to take advantage of the opportunities that are now understood remains to be seen—it is far too early to make a judgment—but at least we now know that additive operations are definitely not the end-all of measurement.

Persons, Places, and Events

MIT, 1950–1953

Within six months of my joining Bavelas's Small Groups Laboratory at MIT, he left to work on a classified project for the State Department and turned the management of the laboratory over to Lee S. Christie and me. I was hardly qualified for a position of leadership in a psychology laboratory, and that had unfortunate consequences. I neither trusted my judgment sufficiently to oppose the momentum of the group on an expensive subproject, nor could I face squarely the weaknesses of our research. The subproject, well underway when I joined the laboratory, was to build a special purpose computer—of relays, tubes, and tape—to "automate" Bavelas's card-passing experiments. By its very design, it was less flexible than his partitioned tables and cards and, of course, orders of magnitude more expensive. Worse still, it was plagued with technical problems, and despite the heroic efforts of the late Josiah Macy Jr. and the technicians under his direction, it was never completed. After being exposed to it and being privately persuaded that it was worthless, I ignored it, feeling too insecure to try to terminate the brainchild of Bavelas, Oliver Strauss, J. C. R. Licklider, and Jerome Weisner (then associate director of the Research Laboratory for Electronics and later President of MIT). It was aptly named "Octopus."

Probably the most important intellectual experiences for me during this period were two groups of seminars. One was a regular luncheon meeting in RLE involving various groups interested in behavioral and information-theoretic projects. The other, and more interesting one, was evening sessions of hardheaded Cambridge psychologists, which meetings were called the Pretzel Twist. I learned a good deal of psychology informally from what has turned out to have been a quite illustrious list of tutors, including Bert F. Green, J. C. R. Licklider, William J. McGill, George A. Miller, Walter A. Rosenblith, and Warren Torgerson, among others.

Columbia University, 1953–1957

In the winter of 1952–53, I began to accept fully that the Group Networks Laboratory was going to fold and that another position was imperative. In the spring of 1953, I received an offer from the Department of Mathematics at the Stevens Institute of Technology, but that was not my intended route, and Hoboken repelled me as a place to live. At the last minute, Paul F. Lazarsfeld of the Department of Sociology of Columbia University hired me as managing director of the Behavioral Models Project, which was charged with preparing expository documents on models relevant to the social sciences, although research was not entirely precluded.

Our small group was housed in one of the imposing brownstone houses on 118th Street. We shared an ugly, dirty-green apartment with Fred Iklé, who largely ignored us and later ended up as a high official in the Department of Defense. We were mostly left in isolation except for occasional directives from Lazarsfeld, sometimes gruffly communicated by the official director of the project, Herbert Solomon. Those members of the group that I remember best are Sidney Morgenbesser, now professor of philosophy at Columbia, who while clearly brilliant was most reluctant to write; Ernest Adams, now professor of philosophy at Berkeley; and James Coleman, a former chemical engineer who was then a graduate student in sociology and is now a professor of sociology at Chicago, famous for, among other things, his report on educational interventions for culturally deprived groups.

Lazarsfeld, who was involved in founding the Center for Advanced Study in the Behavioral Sciences at Stanford, attended its opening year, 1954–55, and he arranged for me to be invited. His was a European view of the academic hierarchy: the more junior fellows should learn from the senior ones by assisting them. Fortunately, director Ralph Tyler and the Center board vetoed the idea of two classes of fellows, and the precedent has been maintained that each fellow decides exactly what he or she will do, a wise decision.

The year at the Center was productive, including the drafting of portions of *Games and Decisions*. Much of the rest of that book was completed the next year when I was back at Columbia, and Howard Raiffa was at the Center. I have always felt that we would never have written it had we been together, because it would have been too easy to talk.

My last two years at Columbia were brightened considerably by numerous weekend discussions with Eugene Galanter, then an assistant professor at the University of Pennsylvania. He was an ebullient, outspoken Young Turk who outraged many experimentalists (who tend to be a rather conservative lot). But Galanter's quick, reactive mind was impressive to many others, including me. Although our styles were very different, we each found the other's company agreeable and intellectually stimulating. He systematically tutored me in psychophysics, and he first introduced me to Stevens's work. I taught him something of the mathematics I was developoing for *ICB*. There is no doubt that our dialogues affected that book, were influential in my deciding to go to Pennsylvania, and continued to influence my work into the middle 1960's.

At some point, either just before or after leaving Columbia, I was invited to participate in the exclusive Eastern under-40 Psychological Round Table. In a sense I took this to be a semi-official anointment of me as psychologist in lieu of a Ph.D. in the field.

Harvard University, 1957–1959

I went to Harvard on a five-year appointment as lecturer on social relations, but stayed only two years. Frederick Mosteller, of the Departments of Social Relations and Statistics, arranged the position. Aside from teaching jointly with him in his undergraduate statistics course and working with a group of junior faculty on a methodology course, my contacts with members of the department were marginal. Most of my intellectual activity was with students, including the late Merrill Carlsmith, Bernard Cohen, Saul Sternberg, and Wayne Wickelgren; with Elizabeth Shipley, a research assistant introduced to me by Galanter and later my Ph.D. student; with S. S. Stevens of the Department of Psychology; and with Robert R. Bush and Galanter, with whom I had a small grant from the American Philosophical Society, which permitted us to meet frequently on weekends.

In addition to Stevens's other influences, which I discussed above, he toiled over my writing. English was a continuing problem for me as a child and as an adult. I found it difficult to master: spelling plagued me and still does to a degree, although it is now alleviated by an automated spelling checker; my vocabulary remains modest; I am unable to this day to pronounce a new word on sight; and compositions of only a few paragraphs were hideously hard work and the results mostly absurd. A high school English teacher warned me that if my compositions did not improve, I would fail in college; MIT did immediately place me in a remedial composition class, and I was often marked down for poor writing.

As an undergraduate, I eventually came to accept the importance of written communication and became increasingly sensitive to the elegance of such authors as Bertrand Russell. As a graduate student, I tried more and more to write, often writing up lecture notes with some care. Over the years, I have slowly improved, helped in part by trying to analyze the writings of authors such as George A. Miller and in part by careful editing and rewriting by Stevens, to whom I shall always be indebted. I try to repay them by now and then rewriting passages of students' and colleagues' manuscripts.

At Harvard, there began a most satisfactory funding relationship with the National Science Foundation (NSF), which, except for my three years at the Institute for Advanced Study, has been continuous. One of the joys of dealing with NSF has been the flexibility permitted the researcher. I rarely see where I am going beyond the next study, and, depending on what ideas arise and what opportunities present themselves, I shift about, pursuing leads where they take me, sometimes returning to old themes after years and sometimes starting new ones. One needs a sympathetic agency to understand the nature of such unprogrammed research.

University of Pennsylvania, 1959–1969

In 1956 and 1957 the chairmanship at the University of Pennsylvania Department of Psychology became open. On a train ride from New York to Cambridge to visit me, Bush and Galanter hatched the implausible— given that Bush was not a mainstream psychologist—idea of proposing him. Surprisingly he was made chairman in 1958, and I joined the department a year later as professor.

For the first time in my career, I held a senior position, one with considerable local influence because of my close advisory role to Bush. I found some features of academic politics to my taste, but never sufficiently appetizing to lead me seriously to consider the chairman-dean-provost-president route, or any segment of it except for once being a rotating chairman (see below). I enjoy the private and policy aspects of helping to run a department or a school, especially one in a new growth phase, but I detest the unrelenting routines and public performances required of most official administrative positions.

Aside from helping to reconstruct the department, which effort we always viewed as quite successful, the main joint activity carried out with Bush and Galanter was the three-volume *Handbook of Mathematical Psychology* (*HBMP*) (Luce, Bush, and Galanter, 1963–65a) and the associated two volumes of *Readings in Mathematical Psychology* (Luce, Bush, and Galanter, 1963–65b). During this same period, I was involved in two other activities also designed to foster mathematical psychology. First, several of us active in the area (R. C. Atkinson, R. R. Bush, C. H. Coombs, W. K. Estes, W. J. McGill, G. A. Miller, P. Suppes, and I) founded the *Journal of Mathematical Psychology*. We did this largely as a response to our difficulties in finding suitable outlets for our articles. None of the usual psychological journals were terribly happy with our articles, either because they included too much mathematics or because of our different and, to them, unacceptable analyses of data.

The second arose when the Social Science Research Council (SSRC) terminated its Committee on Mathematical Social Science. A number of us—Bush, Estes, Coombs, Suppes, and myself—felt that the summer training activities and workshops supported by SSRC had been extremely effective and should not only be continued but expanded, especially in social sciences other than economics and psychology. We persuaded NSF to fund the project (at a level of about $250,000 per year) with CASBS having fiscal responsibility and the newly created Mathematical Social Science Board having intellectual responsibility. Later, responsibility was transferred to the National Research Council (NRC) of the National Academy of Sciences (NAS). I was closely associated with this board over the years, as a member and twice as its chairman. Eventually this program was terminated, being seen as too elitist, in favor of ordinary peer-reviewed proposals, but that has not worked well. In my opinion, this has been a significant loss for mathematical social science because much in the way of energy and direction was achieved at these summer institutes. One recommendation of an NRC report (Gerstein, Luce, Smelser, and Sperlich, 1988) on prospects for the behavioral and social sciences is that such activities, in a variety of areas, be resumed, but with evaluation handled separately from individual research grants.

In 1963 I was elected to membership in the Society of Experimental Psychologists—the national, more elderly, and far more staid counterpart of the Psychological Round Table—and in 1966 to the Boston-based American Academy of Arts and Sciences.

Except for *HBMP*, the collaboration I had anticipated with Bush and Galanter never worked out. Bush was caught up in his administrative position, and in any event the overlap of our intellectual interests was not really large. After Bush resigned as chairman in 1964, my relationship with him waned, for we then had neither politics nor research in common, and there was little else that bound us. I did not see him often in the ensuing seven years, during which time his health deteriorated leading to his untimely death in 1971.

Work with Galanter continued, especially jointly with students, but it never evolved into the working relationship I had hoped it might. Because I am convinced that collaborations between theorists and experimentalists are important, I will expound on some of the problems involved in my final section.

One person with whom throughout my ten years at Pennsylvania I maintained a steady, largely luncheon-based friendship was the late Francis W. Irwin. He was a splendid example of a gentleman and scholar, of

the sort one reads about in turn-of-the-century novels but does not expect
to know. Many of our lunches included other people as well; I especially
recall those with the exceedingly knowledgeable Richard L. Solomon and
the vivacious biologist Vincent Dethier, who were collaborating on the
difficult question of whether or not a fly can be conditioned operantly. It
was a question perfectly suited to Irwin's analytic approach.

Shortly after Galanter left Pennsylvania, David M. Green arrived. We
ran our first free-response detection experiment just before he moved to
the University of California at San Diego. This collaboration was productive and nearly ideal for about fifteen years, quite capable of with-
standing the vicissitudes of many changes in location.

Another important relationship, that with Patrick Suppes, deepened
about this same time. We had known one another for some time and had
already collaborated on a chapter for *HBMP* and on two articles for the
Encyclopedia of the Social Sciences, but our planning and work on *FM*
drew us closer and we became personal friends. One reason I elected to
spend my 1966–67 sabbatical as an NSF Senior Postdoctoral Fellow at
CASBS, aside from its inherent quiet, beauty, and good general intellectual stimulation, was to be able to collaborate more closely with Suppes
on questions of measurement. Among other things, together with Ernest
Adams, we set up a joint Stanford-Berkeley seminar on measurement
which met regularly throughout the year.

The most frustrating thing about collaborating with Suppes is trying to
get him to spend time on your problem, rather than one of a dozen others
he is also involved in. His mind is as quick as any I know, his memory prodigious, and his breadth of interest staggering. It includes everything I have
worked on and at least twice as much again: logic, philosophy of physics,
learning, computer-assisted instruction, perception, semantics, and more.
Moreover, for many years he ran a very large research establishment at
Stanford, at times numbering more than 100 people; he has maintained
worldwide speaking, administrative, and research commitments; and he
founded and has led a substantial company, Computer Curriculum Corporation, which sells computer-based learning systems to elementary and
high schools. I have never understood how he has withstood the onslaughts
on his time and energy and maintained, into his mid-sixties, a youthful intensity and a jovial curiosity about all ideas. In any event, one has to be de-
vious or persistent or both to get his attention. As *FM I* neared final form
and certain parts required his concentration, I simply moved in with him
and his wife for three weeks until the work was done.

Bush was succeeded as chairman by Henry Gleitman. Although they differed greatly in style and research interests, I continued serving in an advisory role much like the one I had with Bush. Gleitman was very influental in arranging that I be honored the year following my Center stay by being made Benjamin Franklin Professor of Psychology, one of their six University Professors at the time. Since a named chair was in many ways ideal for me, especially with its minimal teaching obligations, it may seem odd that after spending the next year on leave, I left Pennsylvania in 1968. To account for this, I must bring in a personal matter. I do not believe one's personal life belongs in an intellectual history unless there is a direct connection; here there is.

My first marriage, to Gay Gaer Luce—known to many psychologists for her expository work on sleep, dreams, and biological rhythms—ended in divorce in 1967. Shortly thereafter I married Cynthia Newby. A number of my professional decisions after that were seriously, and quite reasonably, influenced by her preferences, which include a passion for mild climates and artistic people, some distaste for the more pretentious elements of the academic establishment, and a strong aversion to large, noisy, cold, and smoggy cities. Philadelphia was anathema to her. Brazil, where she had lived for several years before our marriage, was most satisfying. I agreed to try Brazil for a year to see how I reacted to it, and we spent 1968–69 in Rio de Janeiro, which although both large and noisy is mild; where we lived was free of smog because of ocean breezes and was relatively quiet because our apartment was at the end of a dead-end street. I was an Organization of American States Visiting Professor at the Universidad Católica de Rio de Janeiro, a guest of Aroldo Rodrigues, a social psychologist trained at UCLA. Although I responded to some of the appeal of Brazil, I could never live there permanently. One reason was that I found it nearly impossible to pick up Portuguese—my difficulties with languages date back to early childhood when, in a private grammar school, I was virtually unable to learn French and had difficulties with English. Another problem was that no one there was really interested in the sort of work that I do.

The Institute for Advanced Study, 1969–1972

Shortly before I left for Brazil, Carl Kaysen, then recently appointed director of the Institute for Advanced Study, Princeton, N.J., inquired about my joining their faculty. Although the conditions—a visiting appointment for two years with his personal assurance that it would become permanent once some political problems were overcome—would not normally have been acceptable to me, in many ways the Institute seemed an agreeable compromise between my needs and those of my wife, and so I leapt at his proposition. It turned out to be a form of purgatory. There was strenuous political opposition, mounted primarily by the mathematicians and later joined by the humanists, against Kaysen, against the social sciences, and against me in particular. The battle between Kaysen and the faculty erupted in the public press the year after I left when he attempted to force the appointment of a social scientist against a majority of permanent faculty; it was an ugly atmosphere, and it resulted ultimately in collecting a social science faculty far more humanist than scientific in orientation.

In spite of my enormous discomfort and frustration at my situation, I was able to complete work on *FM I*, to write a number of papers, and to maintain the research program with David Green. Moreover, I had enjoyable intellectual contacts with various social scientists who spent a year during that time—among them Robert Audley, Peter Fishburn, Tarow Indow, W. J. M. Levelt, David Rumelhart, and John Yellott Jr. Especially valuable to me were several informal seminars I ran on measurement and on information processing for psychologists in the area, which included the superb group at Bell Laboratories.

While at the Institute I received two very major honors: in 1970 one of the three annual Distinguished Scientific Awards of the American Psychological Association and in 1972 election to the NAS. Both led to new responsibilities. The APA subsequently appointed me to the Scientific Awards Committee for the period 1971–74. And the NAS almost immediately asked me to become a member of the fifteen-person Executive Committee of the newly formed Assembly of the Behavioral and Social Sciences (ABASS) of the NRC.

As my third year at the Institute began, I finally accepted fully that permanency would be possible, if at all, only after a bruising battle. Moreover, although this may be a matter of sour grapes, I began to doubt whether the atmosphere would ever prove congenial to me. So I began to explore alternatives, especially ones in mild climates. Yellott, who had moved to the University of California at Irvine (UCI), arranged an attractive offer in the School of Social Sciences which I accepted.

University of California at Irvine, 1972–1975

The UCI campus was founded only in 1966, and the School of Social Sciences was the brainchild of its first dean James March, who favored both interdisciplinary opportunities for social science research and mathematical approaches to such problems, both of which are congenial to me. As a result of his initial direction, the School is composed of people who tend to have one or both of these traits; and, in an effort to promote unusual interactions, it was not then subdivided into departments. The School was controversial at UCI because of various factors—including the intellectual style of some faculty members, a strong intention not to mimic traditional structures, and the fact that much of its approach is not very appealing to average quality undergraduates—and so it was under some attack by the rest on campus. Furthermore, it had its own self-doubts. It was then in a period of unresolved crisis. After some political exploration, I concluded that shy of becoming dean there was little I could do to alter its path in the short run. In the ensuing years, it has gradually matured (if for no other reason than the aging of its initially very young faculty).

Aside from personal matters, by far the most important event of my experience at UCI was meeting Louis Narens, then an assistant professor. As a person, he can be unusual and, to some, he is disconcertingly intellectual and all-too-often oblique if not obscure. My experience is that, more often than not, the obscurities are ultimately transformed into remarkable theoretical insights. Working with him for the past twelve years has been the single most rewarding intellectual experience of my life. At times it has been taxing, for his standards are higher than most of us aspire to, but the rewards of discovery (outlined earlier) have been very great.

The period of UCI involved two outstandingly important personal events. First, in the fall just before I moved to California, my mother died, and my father, then 90, could not manage for long on his own. With surprisingly good spirits and adjustment for someone who seemed very set in his ways, he moved with us to California. He became my responsibility until his death in 1978. Second, in the fall of 1974 my second marriage, which had for some time been pretty ragged, collapsed. This was especially hard on my father and sad for me because Cynthia insisted on moving our daughter Aurora back to Brazil.

Once David Green, who had moved from San Diego to Harvard in 1973, became aware of my changed circumstance, he convinced his colleagues to recommend my appointment, which was approved. I accepted, and I made the unusual decision to come in January of 1976 because at my father's age a delay of six months could matter greatly. He accepted the change, though not happily, because he had found a congenial social life in his hotel in Laguna Beach, and the coldness, both of people and climate, in the Northeast, while familiar, did not please him.

In that last year in California I made a number of friends and found life at Irvine far more agreeable than it had been, so it was with some feeling of ambivalence that I left.

Harvard University, 1976–1988

Cambridge had always been a magnet for me, and I came very close to moving to Harvard in 1966. I did not accept that offer for two reasons, both of which now seem most inadequate. The one was that I had just moved in Philadelphia. The other was the incredibly aloof attitude of both the department members and the administration—something often said of Harvard. When the dean knowingly offered me $500 less than my Pennsylvania salary, I said to myself, "Who needs this?" So, there I was, a decade later, moving to Harvard, the department nearly as aloof as before but the dean, Henry Rosovsky, far more persuasive, among other things awarding me one of the IBM Alfred North Whitehead chairs. (Only later did I discover it was a five-year "folding chair," and for a couple of years in the early 1980's I was, as it were, without a seat until honored with the Victor S. Thomas Professorship of Psychology.)

Life in the department has been a mixed experience. Perhaps the most uncomfortable aspect was the gradual collapse of my collaboration with David Green. It was, no doubt, placed under considerable strain by Green's becoming chairman in 1978 for three years, which (no matter how efficient an administrator one is—and he is an exceedingly accomplished one) is a very consuming burden; by the tragic, agonizing illness and death of his first wife; and by my becoming chairman in 1981. But probably the most telling reasons were shifting intellectual interests and frustrations with the work. Had the phenomena proved more tractable, who knows? Another factor, no doubt, was my increasing attention to other matters: measurement theory, the NAS and NRC, and my book *Response Times*.

As was remarked earlier, *FM II* long remained unfinished while numerous other projects were completed—which, of course, was part of the problem. Four authors, each seriously over-committed and no one of them really feeling priority to complete it, is a recipe for delay. Another part of the problem was Krantz's view that nearly everything we had written could be appreciably improved, either in exposition or in substance or both. The problem was to effect the revisions. In an effort to overcome this dam, I took a leave of absence in 1984–85 to be at the AT&T Bell Laboratories, where he then was. Progress was made, especially on the chapters concerning the latest work on non-additive structures and scale types, but not as much as I had hoped for. Little progress was made during the next year, but in the fall of 1987 I returned for a third time as Fellow at CASBS, and Suppes and I forced completion of the project.

The National Academy of Sciences / National Research Council, 1972–1988

In 1976, after three years as a member, I became chairman of ABASS. Few of my activities—chairing meetings sometimes involving touchy problems and people, evaluating proposed projects, reading and criticizing draft reports, and appearing six times a year at meetings of the NRC Governing Board to defend ourselves from attacks by "hardheaded" engineers and physical scientists—are worth relating in any detail except for one observation. Once the hardheaded enter into areas of social implications of technology, which is true for most important NRC reports, a surprising number stop being rigorous and become quite softheaded. Suffice it to say that under the talented, if sometimes imperious, direction of David Goslin, its executive director, ABASS prospered and became a widely respected part of the NRC. My tenure with ABASS was climaxed in 1979 by one of the warmest send-off parties I've seen.

Probably the most exciting part of my chairmanship was two trips to the Soviet Union. The first, in 1976, was to Moscow, leading a group of about a dozen psychologists and half as many spouses to establish a seminar series in experimental psychology. Only two seminars occurred, one at UCI in 1978 on physiological psychology and the other the next year, on mathematical models of decision making, chaired by William K. Estes, in Tbilisi, Soviet Georgia. Both were nearly canceled over Soviet attempts to deviate from the agreement we had carefully and painstakingly crafted to avoid just such difficulties. In the case of the Irvine meeting they cabled us announcing last minute changes in several delegates, which was their all-too-common practice at the time. The NAS reply was simple: the group agreed upon or no meeting. The meeting was, in fact, relatively successful. For the Tbilisi meeting, two of our scientists were permanent resident non-citizens of the United States. We had raised this possibility in 1976 and, with considerable reluctance, the Soviets agreed to language permitting a few. Their clear preference was to restrict participants to citizens. They objected to one, a prominent Israeli citizen, but eventually a solution was found, and he received a visa. This meeting, while personally interesting because Soviet Georgia, being almost Mediterranean in quality, is so utterly different from Soviet Russia, was judged pretty much a failure by our delegation. The Soviets had little of interest to offer and seemed excessively reluctant to provide us with any real details of their work. The rest of the series was terminated when the NAS stopped all group arrangements with the Soviet Union as long as Sakharov was held in exile. He has been released, but the current NAS policy is to hold seminars only in fields where there is obvious parity in the level of research expertise; psychology is not one.

After that I was not terribly active for the NRC except for participating in the overall quality control of reports carried out by the Academy's Report Review Committee (RRC). Ultimately I began to wonder if my impression of being a capable committee chairman was all a private delusion, but that fear was dispelled when in 1983 I was appointed co-chair, with Neil J. Smelser, of the Committee on Basic Research in the Behavioral and Social Sciences. This standing committee had just accepted the tricky task of preparing an appraisal and outlook for basic research in these sciences. That report was released in March 1988, after a year of revisions (Gerstein, Luce, Smelser, and Sperlich, 1988). I am much too close to it to evaluate it dispassionately.

In addition to these NRC activities, I have served in various capacities in the NAS as chair of the Psychology Section and then chair of the Class of Behavioral and Social Sciences. These tasks are not especially important or exciting, but they do tend to get one involved in other committees: Nominating, Structure of the Academy, Bylaws, and the RRC. Beyond a doubt, the intellectually most interesting of these is the RRC, which is the oversight committee of Academy members who coordinate the reviews of important, controversial reports.

University of California, Irvine, 1988–

The academic year 1987–88 saw my third fellowship at the Center for Advanced Study in the Behaviorial Sciences, where Narens and I had organized a special project on measurement. It involved Jean-Claude Falmagne, Kenneth Manders, and de facto Mark Machina, an economist from the San Diego campus of the University of California much interested in utility theory, as well as numerous visitors for brief periods.

In November, Narens raised the question of submitting my name to UCI for the annual campus-wide Distinguished Professorship. I was willing for the following reason. When Green had introduced the Research and Training Group (RTG) structure in the department at Harvard, I had not recognized the profound effect it was going to have on resource allocation, and I erred in not creating an explicit RTG in mathematical psychology. Coupled with the fact that our small cadre of assistant professors was gradually being reduced, there was little opportunity to strengthen my areas of interest, and so I was contemplating early retirement and retreating to our country place in New Hampshire. The UCI plan, which as it unfolded involved the creation of an Irvine Research Unit (IRU) in Mathematical Behavioral Science and a 10-year period of faculty and student growth, seemed far more attractive than actual retirement. In January I was told that I would receive the Distinguished Professorship, and after a few months of the usual processing it was effected, the IRU was approved, and I was made director of it. At that point I did take early retirement from Harvard, but the next five to ten years promise not to be idle.

Musings

As the first draft of this spilled out of my typewriter (many years ago), it included a number of asides prompted by something in the research or the chronology. Some were brief enough that I have let them stand. Others I decided to excise and bring together, sometimes in expanded form, into this final section. Each is an isolated fragment, not related to the others.

Teaching

Since I have spent most of my adult life in university settings with professorial titles, I cannot but be a teacher in some sense. But certainly not a TEACHER; rather, a RESEARCHER-teacher. To the extent feasible, I prefer to blur the roles. I am more at home in an advanced seminar or working individually with students than teaching a large lecture class. Since I do not get my kicks on the lecture platform, I do as little lecturing to large groups as possible, mostly only at invited talks devoted to my research. In recent years I came to violate this rule to the extent of giving a Harvard CORE course called Sound and Hearing. This was one of the basic science offerings, and it tended to be populated by students not in the sciences who, left to their own devices, would stay as far from science as possible. They didn't like it, and I refused to make it a "gut" course. It was fun for neither them nor me.

My greatest contribution to teaching is not as a classroom lecturer, but as an author. Howard Raiffa and I have "taught" tens of thousands about elementary game theory, and some of my other books—especially *HBMP*, the previously mentioned *Contemporary Developments in Mathematical Psychology* (Krantz, Atkinson, Luce, and Suppes, 1974), *FM*, *RT*, and the new edition of the *Stevens' Handbook of Experimental Psychology* (Atkinson, Herrnstein, Lindzey, and Luce, 1988)—and many expository articles were designed in part to instruct students and peers.

Collaboration of Experimentalists and Theorists

An applied mathematician doing psychological theory is always in danger of losing contact with empirical reality, and one must continually force oneself to consider the testability as well as the depth and generality of ideas. Otherwise, one is likely to become a pure mathematician of indifferent quality. One possible solution is also to run experiments. This solution is often urged by one's experimental colleagues; for example, Stevens was vociferous about it. This is fine when the equipment and data collection are both simple—and I have had students and assistants run several such studies—but it is a strenuous strategy when the experimental techniques and apparatus are complex. Although there are exceptions (in vision, Floyd Ratliff and Edward Pugh are two examples), one is likely to stop doing theory and become a second-rate experimentalist. My feeling in such cases is that, as in physics, theorist and experimenter should collaborate closely. This can happen only if the theorist understands well the problems facing the experimenter who, on his or her part, must understand well the language of the theory; they should complement, not compete. Of course, this does not mean that the theorist should have no ideas for experiments or the experimenter none for theories—quite the contrary—but that each should work out the details of what he or she does best and, presumably, finds most congenial.

If such collaborations are really desirable, why do so few exist in psychology? Perhaps the major reason is that only recently, and then in only a few areas of psychology, is the equipment becoming so complex as to warrant it. In any event, for me at least, it seemed clear that auditory psychophysics had achieved such a level of complexity that I did not want to run my own laboratory.

Statistical versus Scientific Inferences

Psychology is one of the heavier consumers of statistics. Presumably the reason is that psychologists have become convinced that they are greatly aided in making correct scientific inferences by casting their decision making into the framework of statistical inference. In my view we have witnessed a form of mass deception of the sort typified by the story of the emperor with no clothes.

Statistical inference techniques are good for what they were developed for, mostly making decisions about the probable success of agriculture, industrial, and drug interventions, but they are not especially appropriate to scientific inference which, in the final analysis, is trying to model what is going on, not merely to decide if one variable affects another. What has happened is that many psychologists have forced themselves into thinking in a way dictated by inferential statistics, not by the problems they really wish or should wish to solve. The real question rarely is whether a correlation differs significantly, but usually slightly, from zero (such a conclusion is so weak and so unsurprising to be mostly of little interest), but whether it deviates from unity by an amount that could be explained by errors of measurement, including nonlinearities in the scales used. Similarly, one rarely cares whether there is a significant interaction term; one wants to know whether by suitable transformations it is possible or not to get rid of it altogether (e.g., it cannot be removed when the data are crossed). The demonstration of an interaction is hardly a result to be proud of, since it simply means that we still do not understand the nature and composition of the independent factors that underlie the dependent variable.

Model builders find inferential statistics of remarkably limited value. In part, this is because the statistics for most models have not been worked out; to do so is usually hard work, and by the time it might be completed, interest in the model is likely to have vanished. A second reason is that often model builders are trying to select between models or classes of models, and they much prefer to try to ascertain where they differ maximally and to exploit this experimentally. This is not easy to do, but when done it is usually far more convincing than a fancy statistical test.

Let me make clear several things I am not saying when I question the use of statistical inferences in scientific work. First, I do not mean to suggest that model builders should ignore basic probability theory and the theory of stochastic processes; quite the contrary, they must know this material well. Second, my objection is only to a part of statistics; in particular, it does not apply to the area devoted to the estimation of parameters. This is an area of great use to psychologists, and increasingly statisticians have emphasized it over inference. And third, I do not want to imply that psychologists should become less quantitative and systematic in the handling of data. I would urge more careful analyses of data, especially ones in which the attempt is to reveal the mathematical structure to be found in the data.

Computers: A Personal Scientific Dilemma

My career has pretty much coincided with the introduction and later widespread availability of digital computers, and I have been repeatedly urged to involve myself deeply with them on the grounds that computers will or should be a theorist's main tool. I have resisted, thereby probably branding myself a scientific conservative, if not a reactionary. To discuss my position, let me list some of the ways a computer can play a role in psychology and how I have related to each.

1. To compute. I am delighted with the power the computer gives us. Much of what Green and I did would not have been possible without such aid.

2. To simulate. For many stochastic processes that arise in psychology, there are no analytic expressions for statistical quantities of interest. One may then try to estimate these quantities by simulating the process. Although I have used simulations, most recently in *RT*, it is with reluctance. The method is cumbersome and can be expensive when sufficiently many parameters are involved; one can be easily misled because of sampling variability; and one always fears that some interesting region of the parameter space was missed.

3. To control experiments. The use of a modest-sized, on-line computer to control stimulus presentations, provide information feedback, and record responses is a godsend for any laboratory which is largely electronic rather than mechanical. Care is needed, however, to avoid complex designs we are incapable of analyzing.

4. To process words, as I am now doing. Marvelous! It has eliminated for me almost all of the frustrations I once had with typewriters, revisions, and secretaries. And that can only improve. To be sure, there are new frustrations, like hard-disk crashes.

5. To teach. All sorts of teaching now involves computers, particularly when there are standard routines to be mastered as in elementary math-

ematics and statistics. In general this strikes me as a good thing. Systematic efforts toward better computer-assisted instruction, involving contingencies that depend on the progress of the student, have the potential for altering significantly the labor distribution in the teaching profession.

6. As a model of the brain. This is not really a use of the computer as such, but an attempt to conclude that the brain must be organized much as a computer or a computer program is. For a time, attempts were made to equate the binary language of the computer with the binary pulses of the central nervous system. This is basically wrong. The presence or absence of synchronized pulses carries information in a computer, whereas it is almost certain that temporal patterns of pulses carry it in the brain and so the brain is far more of an analog device than a digital one. Also, the physiological evidence suggests that information is not stored in the brain in single locations, but somehow is more diffusely represented.

Another argument centers around concepts of universal machines and all computable functions. There might be something to this were one willing to accept the present basis of mathematics as the ultimate one, in which case the brain must indeed operate within those limits. But wouldn't it be odd, if as of now, all basic mathematical concepts were in hand and all that remained was to elaborate them? But if some mathematical concepts are not yet developed, those appropriate to brain function may be among the missing, which convinces me that we psychologists should study the brain and behavior, not the computer. In the process some genius may invent—albeit, sloppily at first—some new mathematics which, conceivably, might lead to better computers.

7. To formulate psychological theories. Here is the focus of my dilemma. The proposal is that interesting psychological phenomena—language production, comprehension, perception of complex patterns and arrays such as pages of print, problem solving, concept formation, theorem proving, game playing, etc.—are processes far too complex to state in any ordinary mathematical fashion, but they can be embodied as computer programs. The test of a theory so formulated ranges anywhere from its abilty to solve problems that some human beings can solve (artificial intelligence) to far more detailed comparisons of step-by-step protocols.

With the advent of considerable computer power and much hard work, this approach is increasingly being more fully realized. As this section was written, Allen Newell was giving the 1987 William James Lectures at Harvard University, describing over the course of eight well-attended lectures both the philosophy and the realization of his current version of a universal psychological theory, called SOAR. He argued that this is the effective mode of encoding psychological theories—that computer programs, designed as knowledge systems, are replacing mathematics as the language of theory.

Two aspects of this approach have, all along, disturbed me sufficiently so that I have been unwilling to undertake the labor of pursuing it in my work. The first was the difficulty its proponents initially had in articulating clearly the psychological principles underlying the programs they write. I can no longer, however, make this charge, for Newell spent considerable time on such principles and on how he has arrived at them from a consideration of a wide range of empirical data. Still there is a problem. The principles are very general and correspondingly nonspecific in specific situations. Their realization seems not uniquely determined by the situation but to rest heavily on the intuitions of the person formulating the program. The second, closely related, point concerns the number of untested assumptions, functions, decision rules, and the like that, together, form a program. I know from my own work as well as from that of others how difficult isolating and testing simple, well-articulated principles and assumptions can be. A chastening example is the elaborate set of studies sparked by Sternberg's (1969) attempt to decide whether searches of short-term memory are self-terminating or exhaustive. If such limited, apparently sharply formulated questions cannot be decided readily, how can we possibly test large complexes of such ideas strung together as a program?

Newell argues that the great mass of psychological data so constrain the theory that the problem is simply one of finding something that works, not to worry about whether it is correct. I find this somewhat unpersuasive, since the theory seems to be little more than a great "kludge" of numerous small theories, all structured in a similar fashion, but individually no more overdetermined than has been any previous, well-specified theory. If no systematic tests are possible on the components that make up the program, then is this psychological theory or artificial intelligence? The latter is fine, but it does not happen to be my area of interest. Newell clearly feels it is decidedly a psychological theory.

So, despite some fear that I am missing a major intellectual development, rather than avoiding a fad, I have elected the more conservative, more plodding route. The problems I can tackle are not so glamorous to the average person, and the building and testing of ideas is slower, but I have some limited hope that a fragment or two will survive as a permanent part of psychology. I am not as optimistic about any attempt I might make at writing a program for something really complex.

Mathematics in Psychology

When asked my profession by strangers, I usually say "psychologist" or "mathematician" and only rarely "mathematical psychologist." When young I did, but experience made me wary. Too often I have been told in no uncertain terms that mathematics has nothing whatsoever to do with psychology or been skeptically asked to explain the connection. For a while, I had hoped the question meant an open mind, and I would try to discuss the matter. At first I used to illustrate applications by example, but we always bogged down in technical detail—usually both experimental and mathematical. That failure led me to try some form of the clever-question gambit. For example, to the wife of one physicist, I agreed to try to answer her question if she would explain to me why mathematics had anything to do with physics. I fear that the cleverness of my strategy escaped her notice for, to her, the prima facie evidence seemed a sufficient answer. Another tack I have tried is to ask if all factually correct things one might say about a person are independent of one another, and then to suggest that the study of how one set of statements can be deduced from a set of other statements, taken as primitives, was in fact mathematics. At best this tends to draw a sympathetic, but pained, expression and at worst the more or less explicit suggestion that I belong under the care of a good (presumably clinical) psychologist.

Nonetheless, there are two serious questions lurking near the surface. First, has mathematics as yet played a serious role in the development of any areas of psychology? Second, is it conceivable that the mathematics we now know, molded as it has been by the development of physical science, is especially appropriate to psychological problems?

At the risk of offending some colleagues, aside from the special use of statistics in much psychological research, I believe that there are only three areas where mathematical modeling can be shown to have had a profound impact: the study of sensation and perception, psychological testing, and patterns of preferences. In the sensory area, the modeling appears to be cumulative, to have led to empirical discoveries, and to be essential to the ongoing life of the subject. In testing, modeling appears to be essential in handling the masses of data involved, and while I have my doubts about how deeply it gets at questions such as what intelligence is, there can be no doubt about its social significance. Psychological testing is the one large-scale technology spawned by psychology, and it is more mathematized than most people realize. Studies of preference and motivation have resulted in a number of careful mathematical analyses (of which I have contributed several) followed by ingenious experimental studies that show difficulties. I believe the latter is an example of the initial interplay between theory and data that tends to sharpen both and also helps to accumulate a body of solid empirical findings that make it increasingly difficult to formulate a theory that cannot be rejected out of hand. This stage precedes the one where we begin to feel we have a good first approximation to a correct theory.

In learning, hundreds of papers studying and testing stochastic operator and Markov models have, in my opinion, come to very little. True, models can be set up that give surprisingly accurate descriptions of certain sets of experimental data, but this seems to have provided us with little depth of insight into the learning process—witness the inability of modelers to account well for certain basic phenomena such as the effects of partial reinforcement and reversal learning or to predict the outcomes of new experiments. In the 1970's work shifted away from such models and experiments towards more schematic formulations of information processing and memory in which mathematics plays a decidedly auxiliary role. Recently, however, the modeling has become active and some developments are promising.

One difficulty in much psychological modeling is in separating the theory of the human being from the boundary conditions that model the context (experiment) in which the person is placed. This separation is characteristic of all physical theory and pretty much accounts for the different use of the words "theory" and "model" in science (though not philosophy); it has not been very characteristic of most mathematical work in psychology. To the degree it is achieved, one begins to see both cumulative improvements in the theory and the ability to predict new experiments; to the degree it is not achieved, one sees only models of specific experiments in which the role of the person and that of the experimental design are not clearly separable. One area where such a separation is made very clearly is the modeling of the past ten years concerning schedules of reinforcement (Herrnstein, 1982).

I suspect that much of our problem in using mathematics effectively arises from the state of conceptualization in psychology rather than from the appropriateness of mathematics in formulating psychological theory. But there does remain the haunting fear that the existing mathematics is not, in fact, particularly suited to the problems of psychology. Consider, for example, the representation of uncertainty in decision making. I can never get over the feeling that the attempt to cast it into probabilistic terms is misguided; intuitively, I sense that, however human beings handle uncertainty, their calculus is different from probability. Or take memory and learning: can it be that the troubles we have had have to do with the fact that memories seem to be diffusely represented in the brain and so may not be very amenable to our usual set theoretic formulations? Recent work of the connectionist school is pursuing an alternative approach.

Perhaps only rarely—psychophysics may be the prime example—is the existing mathematics well suited to the phenomenon; in other areas we may have to become involved in the creation of new sorts of mathematics. If, as I believe, this is the case, our time perspective had better be a long one, for we await a latterday Newton.

Selected Publications by R. Duncan Luce

(1956). Semiorders and a theory of utility discrimination. *Econometrica*, *24*, 178–191.

(with H. Raiffa) (1957). *Games and decisions: Introduction and critical survey*. New York: Wiley.

(with W. Edwards) (1958). The derivation of subjective scales from just noticeable differences. *Psychological Review*, *65*, 222–237.

(1959a). On the possible psychophysical laws. *Psychological Review*, *66*, 81–95. (Reprinted in R. D. Luce, R. R. Bush, & E. Galanter [Eds.], *Readings in mathematical psychology* [Vol. 1, pp. 69–83]. New York: Wiley, 1963; and in Bobbs-Merrill Reprint Series.)

(1959b). *Individual choice behavior: A theoretical analysis*. New York: Wiley.

(1960). A survey of the theory of selective information and some of its behavioral applications. In R. D. Luce (Ed.), *Developments in mathematical psychology* (pp. 1–119). Glencoe, IL: Free Press.

(with R. R. Bush & E. Galanter, Eds.) (1963–1965a). *Handbook of mathematical psychology*, *Vols. 1–3*. New York: Wiley.

(with R. R. Bush & E. Galanter, Eds.) (1963–1965b). *Readings in mathematical psychology*, *Vols. 1–2*. New York: Wiley.

(with J. W. Tukey) (1964). Simultaneous conjoint measurement: A new type of fundamental measurement. *Journal of Mathematical Psychology*, *1*, 1–27.

(with D. H. Krantz, P. Suppes, & A. Tversky) (1971–1989). *Foundations of measurement, Vols. 1–3*. New York: Academic Press.

(1972). What sort of measurement is psychophysical measurement? *American Psychologist*, *27*, 96–106.

(with D. M. Green) (1972). A neural timing theory for response times and the psychophysics of intensity. *Psychological Review*, *79*, 14–57.

(with D. M. Green) (1973). Speed-accuracy tradeoff in auditory detection. In S.

Kornblum (Ed.), *Attention and Performance* (Vol. 4, pp. 547–659). New York: Academic Press.

(with R. C. Atkinson, D. H. Krantz, & P. Suppes, Eds.) (1974). *Contemporary developments in mathematical psychology, Vols. 1–2*. San Francisco: Freeman.

(1978a). Dimensionally invariant numerical laws correspond to meaningful qualitative relations. *Philosophy of Science*, 45, 1–16.

(1978b). A mathematician as psychologist. In T. S. Krawiec (Ed.), *The psychologists* (Vol. 3, pp. 125–165). Brandon, VT: Clinical Psychology Publishing Company.

(1985). Mathematical modeling of perceptual, learning, and cognitive processes. In S. Koch & D. E. Leary (Eds.), *A century of psychology as science* (pp. 654–677). New York: McGraw-Hill.

(with L. Narens) (1985). Classification of concatenation structures according to scale type. *Journal of Mathematical Psychology*, 29, 1–72.

(1986). *Response times*. New York: Oxford University Press.

(1988). Measurement structures with Archimedean ordered translation groups. *Order*, 4, 165–189.

(with R. C. Atkinson, R. J. Herrnstein, & G. Lindzey, Eds.) (1988). *Handbook of experimental psychology, Vols. 1–2*. New York: Wiley.

(with D. Gerstein, N. J. Smelser, & S. Sperlich) (1988). *The behavioral and social sciences: Achievements and opportunities*. Washington, DC: The National Academy of Sciences Press.

Other Publications Cited

Békséy, G. von. (1930). Über das Fechnersche Gesetz und seine Bedeutung für die Theorie der akustischen Beobachtungsfehler und die Theorie des Hörens. *Annalen der Physik*, 7, 329–359.

Braida, L. D., & Durlach, N. I. (1972). Intensity perception: 2. Resolution in one-interval paradigms. *Journal of the Acoustical Society of America*, 51, 483–502.

Bush, R. R., & Mosteller, F. (1955). *Stochastic models for learning*. New York: Wiley.

Falmagne, J. C. (1985). *Elements of psychological theory*. New York: Oxford University Press.

Green, D. M., & Swets, J. (1966). *Signal detection theory and psychophysics*. New York: Wiley. (Reprinted 1974, Huntington, NY: Krieger)

Herrnstein, R. J. (1982). Melioration as behavioral dynamism. In M. L. Commons, R. J. Herrnstein, & H. Racklin (Eds.), *Quantitative analyses of behavior: Matching and maximizing accounts* (pp. 433–458). Cambridge, MA: Ballinger.

Krantz, D. H. (1964). The scaling of small and large color differences. Unpublished doctoral dissertation, University of Pennsylvania, Philadelphia.

Krantz, D. H. (1969). Threshold theories of signal detection. *Psychological Review*, 76, 308–324.

Krantz, D. H. (1972). Measurement structures and psychological laws. *Science*, 175, 1427–1435.

McGill, W. J. (1963). Stochastic latency mechanisms. In R. D. Luce, R. R. Bush, &

E. Galanter (Eds.), *Handbook of mathematical psychology*, (Vol. 1, pp. 309–360). New York: Wiley.

Miller, G. A. (1956). The magical number seven, plus or minus two: Some limits on our capacity for processing information. *Psychological Review*, *63*, 81–97.

Narens, L. (1985). *Abstract measurement theory*. Cambridge, MA: MIT Press.

Sternberg, S. (1969). The discovery of processing stages: Extensions of Donder's method. *Acta Psychologica*, *30*, 276–315.

Stevens, S. S. (1951). Mathematics, measurement, and psychophysics. In S. S. Stevens (Ed.), *Handbook of experimental psychology* (pp. 1–49). New York: Wiley.

Stevens, S. S. (1957). On the psychophysical law. *Psychological Review*, *64*, 153–181.

Stevens, S. S., Morgan, C. T., & Volkmann, J. (1941). Theory of the neural quantum in the discrimination of loudness and pitch. *American Journal of Psychology*, *54*, 315–335.

Suppes, P., & Zinnes, J. L. (1963). Basic measurement theory. In R. D. Luce, R. R. Bush, & E. Galanter (Eds.), *Handbook of mathematical psychology* (Vol. 1, pp. 1–76). New York: Wiley.

Tversky, A. (1972). Elimination by aspects: A theory of choice. *Psychological Review*, *79*, 281–299.

Tversky, A., & Russo, J. E. (1969). Substitutability and similarity in binary choices. *Journal of Mathematical Psychology*, *6*, 1–12.

Eleanor E. Maccoby

Eleanor E. Maccoby

I was born in 1917 and grew up in Tacoma, Washington, the second daughter in a family of four girls. My parents were Midwesterners who came out to the Northwest at the time they married, in 1911. My father, Eugene Emmons, was a farm boy, an only child raised under very frugal circumstances by his grandparents. From the age of five, he was expected to do his share of the hard work—milking the cows, chopping wood, hoeing corn—and through helping the neighbors with their chores on Saturdays, he earned the money for his clothes throughout his school years. He took pride in doing well in school and worked his way through Purdue University, where he earned a degree in engineering.

My mother was one of seven children. The children nearest in age to herself were four brothers, and she grew up playing boys' games. As the only girl among the older children, however, she learned to sew and, as a teenager, made all her brothers' shirts, as well as dresses for herself, her mother, and her little sister. Her father was in charge of organizing the musical portion of the Chautauqua programs in the Midwest region. He traveled frequently, but in his time at home taught all the children to play musical instruments. The family imported the first set of Swiss bells seen in this country and made limited concert appearances in which all the family members participated as bell ringers. My mother was seventeen when her father died, and in order to help support the younger children she joined a Chautauqua group as a musician. She did her last year of high school studies in hotels and railroad stations, taking her exams by mail, and meanwhile made a collection of folk songs and spirituals. She had a beautiful contralto voice and sang a variety of classical and folk songs, accompanying herself on the guitar. For a brief period, she was teamed with William Jennings Bryan—she opened the Chautauqua program with her songs, and he followed with his "Cross of Gold" speech. She was able to go to Chicago for a period of vocal training, earning the money for lessons by singing at weddings and funerals and in her mid-twenties became the director of the glee club at Purdue. She was something of a beauty, and the family home in Lafayette became a magnet for a number of the young men attending Purdue. My father was among them. They were engaged by the time he graduated and went out West to make his fortune; he sent for her after a year's separation, and they settled down in Tacoma to work and raise their family.

My father established a small millwork business, manufacturing cabinets, doors, and windows. The business varied greatly over the years, in terms of size and prosperity; it employed about 130 people in good times, many fewer in bad times. A feature of our childhood was the annual company picnic, when there were all kinds of races and contests, including a log-rolling competition, a three-legged race, and a contest to see who could hammer large nails through a thick plank in the least time without bending the nails. As a child, I spent many Saturday mornings at my father's factory, "helping" to glaze windows with handfuls of warm putty, listening to the whine of the big lumber cutting machines, playing with wood shavings and scraps of plywood and glass. Later, I worked in the office, and learned how to read blueprints—a skill which was useful later, when as a college student I had a summer job selling unit heaters and expansion joints and had to make bids based on architects' drawings.

My parents were disappointed not to have a son, and in retrospect it seems clear that they put me in the role of the boy of the family; or perhaps they only allowed me to adopt it. I was called by a boy's nickname, and wore a short boyish haircut. My tomboyishness was generally expected and accepted in the family—except perhaps for my youngest sister, who has told me in recent years that she was acutely embarrassed to see me playing marbles on the boys' side of the school playground. I thought most girls' games were boring, although I did like jump rope and hopscotch. I loved to climb trees and slide down steep slopes, and was often scolded for being so hard on my clothes. Girls were required to wear dresses to school, and my mother made all of our clothes. I usually wore cotton print dresses with matching underpants, mostly inherited from my older sister. But the pretty dresses were soon torn and the pants covered with grass stains, and nothing ever survived to be handed on to the next sister. Until the teenage years, I don't believe I ever cared how I looked. I was allowed to wear blue jeans on weekends, and on Saturdays I sometimes went to the golf course to caddy for my father. On those occasions, I used to like to pretend to be a boy, but I don't believe the other caddies ever took me for one. When I was nine or ten, I borrowed the neighbor's St. Bernard dog and marched in the annual "Boy and dog" parade down Tacoma's main street. Until high school, I seldom had a close girlfriend. After school (when I wasn't reading) I played with my sisters or with a neighbor boy, and we invented many adventures in our large backyard. I was slightly hurt falling off our clothes line, when I tried to use it as a tightrope after reading about a similar exploit in Tarkington's *Penrod and Sam*. The long and short of all this is: in childhood I was an authentic tomboy.

My "experimental" bent was something of a joke in the family. An oft-repeated story concerned my complaint that I had been given only un-breakable dolls. Because of my reputation for being hard on clothes and toys, I possessed only soft-bodied dolls with heads made of some tough material. (My favorite was Charles, whom I scalped and buried when I was playing Indian, but then rescued and rehabilitated.) I wanted a real china doll like my sister's. My paternal grandmother, an austere lady who visited the family only occasionally, brought me a beautiful china doll for Christmas. As we were assembled on our cement-floored porch, I asked her: "Is it *really* breakable?" She said, "It certainly is." I held it out care-fully and dropped it. It broke in many pieces. I felt satisfied, and my grandmother was outraged. On another occasion, I hopped on one leg all the way home from school and several times around our block, finally fall-ing exhausted on the living room rug. When my mother asked me what I was up to, I explained that I wanted to find out how well I could manage if I had only one leg.

I learned to read at the age of four and read constantly throughout my school years. When I was old enough to ride a bicycle, I went every Sat-urday morning to the main city library, which was about two miles from our house. I would take out four to six books each week, and bring them home in my bike basket, to be read during the week and returned the next Saturday. I went on author binges, reading everything the library had by a particular author—Jules Verne, Dumas, Mark Twain, Dickens, the Brontës; later, in high school, Tolstoy, Dostoevsky, Victor Hugo, and Al-dous Huxley. I did very well in school, but do not remember being con-scious of being an exceptional student. In retrospect, I know that my par-ents were proud of my academic accomplishments, but they did not show it openly. They believed that praise spoiled children; if any of us preened ourselves in front of a mirror, we would be told "Pretty is as pretty does." Bragging was strongly discouraged.

Singing was always part of our family life. My mother gave voice lessons in our living room, and we always went caroling early on Christmas morning. I learned to play the guitar at about age eleven, and with my two nearest-age sisters, formed a trio. We began by singing some of my mother's folk songs and spirituals, but in high school switched to popular music, imitating some of the Andrews Sisters' routines and inventing some of our own. We put on occasional performances and briefly had a weekly program on the local radio station.

When I was about nine, my parents joined the Theosophical Society. Until that time, my sisters and I had been sent to several different Protestant Sunday schools, the latest being Unitarian, but none of these Christian denominations satisfied my parents, and Theosophy was a rich intellectual and spiritual world for them. The Society was established to promote the study of comparative religion and "the latent powers in man"; although the Society had no official doctrine, it emphasized the study of Eastern religions. Our family adopted a vegetarian diet, partly because we did not believe in taking the lives of our "younger brothers," but also because animal substances were thought to be inimical to some of the higher levels of spirituality we strove for. These beliefs led to confrontation with the local school board. The board adopted a requirement that children could not register for school unless they had been vaccinated for smallpox, and my mother took us all out of school rather than have the vaccine—a foreign animal substance—introduced into our bodies. My older sister and I were allowed to go on a business trip with our father while my mother brought her case to the school board. I never learned how or why she won her case. In retrospect I suspect that the fact that she was state president of the Parent Teacher Association may have had something to do with it. We returned to school without being vaccinated.

Having strong principles and acting on them was something that was taken for granted in my family. My maternal grandmother, who lived with us, had grown up in the post–Civil War years, and she was a strong believer in trying to overcome the regional antagonisms that resulted from that war. She taught us children that we must never sing such songs as "Marching Through Georgia," and I remember firmly clamping my mouth shut when this song was sung in school. Another of our family principles was never to refuse aid to people in need. I remember an occasion, when I was about eleven, when a drifter came to our back door asking for a handout. My mother gave him a meal in the kitchen, and I sat with him and asked him about his life. He showed me his membership card in the Industrial Workers of the World and told me about the revolution they believed would soon come about. I found this very exciting, and brought it up at the dinner table. My father (a Republican) said that IWW stood for "I Won't Work" and thought my mother shouldn't expose us to this kind of influence, but she insisted that one could not turn a needy person away, no matter what his political beliefs might be.

My parents' entrance into the Theosophical Society had many implications for our lives, in addition to our change of diet. Lecturers for the Society came to town, and many of them stayed at our house. I well remember the visit of Annie Besant, the English woman who had been a member of the Fabian Society in its heyday and had organized a union among women workers in England before she moved on to become a leader of the movement for Indian independence. She became international president of the Theosophical Society, headquartered in India. At the time of her visit to Tacoma, she must have been about 80, a small woman who normally spoke quietly, but whose voice filled an auditorium with wonderful resonant phrases when she occupied the speaker's podium. I admired her intensely. Another visiting lecturer was a woman who had been a lieutenant to the Pankhurst sisters in the British suffragette movement. I remember sitting at her feet before the fireplace in our house, listening to her stories about the exploits of the suffragettes—how they risked their lives to run out on the racetrack and stop the Derby, how they chalked slogans on the pavements, how they spoke from horse-drawn carts and galloped away when people began to throw cabbages at them. I found all this inspirational.

My parents joined with several other Theosophical families and bought some land on Orcas Island in the San Juan Islands in Puget Sound. They established a Theosophical summer camp, where we spent our summers from the time I was about ten. There was a communal kitchen and dining area, and individual families had their own tents (and later, cabins). During the several weeks when the camp was officially in session, there were lectures and discussion sessions, as well as music and art groups, and there would be between 80 and 120 people at the camp, most of whom came year after year. During the rest of the summer there would be smaller groups; a team of teenagers (plus adult supervisors) came during the two weeks prior to the opening of the formal camp session, to get the cabins ready for occupancy; and a group stayed on after camp to repair and close cabins. And a few people, usually including my family, stayed late enough to pick the fruit in the orchard. It was during the building of our own cottage that I first came to appreciate my father's skills. In addition to carpentry, he did all the plumbing and electric wiring, and when he needed large stones to build the chimney for our fireplace, he rigged a pulley system for hauling them up a cliff from the beach below.

It was the custom at the Theosophical summer camp for teenagers to move out of their parents' cabins. Initially they slept in a large girls' or boys' tent, or in the haystack under the stars. Later a large tepee was built, with a stone fireplace, and young people from about eleven to eighteen would take their sleeping bags there. They would talk or tell ghost stories or sing as long as anyone was still awake. Most of the young people of this age earned part of their camp fees by participating in work groups. Wood taken from the fallen trees on the camp grounds was the only source of heat during the long period when the camp had no electricity, and teenage work crews sawed and chopped the wood for cabins and the kitchen cooking. Young crews also worked in the kitchen—setting tables, washing dishes, helping with food preparation—and drove the trash truck and helped to build new cabins. As a member of the work crews I learned to lay flooring as well as to split shakes from cedar logs with a frue and nail them onto roof frames.

A strong teenage culture existed at the camp within the framework established by the adults. The adults were always nearby, and provided supervision where needed, but left the teenagers to do their own work and provide most of their own recreation. I had an active social life at the camp, in sharp contrast to my life as a loner at home. At camp, we organized our own swimming and hiking expeditions. We would build a campfire on a beach at night and swim in the ice-cold water under the stars, moving through the sparkling clouds of phosphorescent light that came from our movements in the dark water. A number of romances blossomed among the teenagers at the camp, but the experimentation with sex was very moderate by present-day standards.

The teenagers who had intellectual interests were welcomed as part of the adult discussion groups. These dealt with a variety of issues, ranging from international relations to literature to philosophy of science. Most Theosophists subscribed to a number of beliefs derived from Hinduism. They believed in reincarnation, in karma, and in a variety of occult phenomena. There were classes in astrology at the camp (some taught by my mother), and many individuals practiced daily meditation. The camp diet, of course, was vegetarian. Some of the discussion leaders and invited lecturers had a strong interest in finding scientific backing for some of the Theosophical beliefs. They introduced me to the work of the British Society for Psychical Research, and at the age of about thirteen or fourteen I read the books by Meyer, Crook, and von Schrenknotzing detailing the investigations of reported cases of psychical phenomena. As I became more versed in Theosophical doctrine, I was occasionally asked to give a talk at the camp or at one of the Theosophical lodges in the Northwest; I believe the adult members were especially pleased to have a young teenager appear as an advocate for their views, and they encouraged me in many ways.

When I entered high school, I finally developed a social life. Our school put on an operetta every year, and I enjoyed singing in these and dressing up in period costumes. I discovered the pleasures of dressing in feminine clothes, experimenting with hairdos, and being attractive to the opposite sex. I occasionally dated some of the "popular" boys whom I met in the operettas or in class. I began to play tennis, and was introduced to the local tennis club by a young man who became partly a boyfriend and partly a tennis coach. My primary peer group, however, was the little group of intellectual students who ran the debating club and put out the school newspaper. I joined this group and became one of the editors. And outside this group, I found common interests with a few other students. I remember noticing a girl carrying a copy of Darwin's *Origin of Species* under her arm as she walked down the hall. I fell into conversation with her and learned that she was reading it out of her own interest, rather than as an assignment. She told me about it with great excitement, and we began to discuss other things that we had read. We became close friends and remained so for many years.

Many of us developed intense political interests growing out of the unrest of our times. Our high school years—the early 1930's—were a time of deep economic depression. The state of Washington was a particularly active site of left-wing political thought and activity. A radical group called the Commonwealth Federation grew swiftly throughout the state and became influential within the Democratic party, electing several of its members to state and national office. As high school students we took an intense interest in possible remedies for what we saw as widespread social injustice and attended meetings of various advocacy groups. We decided to form a political youth club outside the confines of the school. Our club met in the basement room of the Theosophical Society building. The size of the group varied from about 20 to 40 and included students from the local College of Puget Sound and some unemployed youths as well as our group of high school students.

We embarked on a program of self-education. We had weekly meetings where we discussed the works of Bertrand Russell, Shaw, Laski, Marx, the Webbs, Keynes, and a number of other writers who were proposing various solutions to the economic ills of the times. In the fall of 1933 (my senior year in high school), Tacoma was visited by two German "goodwill" ships—the *Emden* and the *Karlsruhe*—staffed with young officers who spoke excellent English and whose mission was to enlist sympathy for the new National Socialist movement in Germany. We invited two of them to visit our club and debate with us. It was an intense encounter, with passions aroused as it became clear that their views of socialism were very different from ours.

A number of us joined the Young Socialist League and had a marginal role in the activities of the local Socialist party. There was much excitement over the impending visit of Norman Thomas. The more conservative elements in the community were concerned over what they viewed as the dangers of revolution, and the Tacoma City Council enacted two ordinances: one forbade the display of any red flag, and the other required that at any public meeting of three or more people an American flag at least three feet by four feet in size must be prominently displayed. These ordinances were quickly challenged by the Socialists, whose emblem was a red flag. A group of us staged a march downtown, each carrying a large American flag and each bearing a sign which said: "I am prepared to meet two friends. Are you?" In addition, telegrams were sent to the mayor and the chief of police, advising them that a red flag would be displayed at the forthcoming large meeting to be held on the occasion of Norman Thomas's visit. On that evening, Thomas marched into the packed hall, flanked by two people, one carrying an American flag, the other the Socialist red flag. No arrest occurred, and the ordinances were dead.

Most of our club members were pacifists as well as socialists. We joined with students at the University of Washington to stage a demonstration on the occasion of the Army Day parade in Seattle. The university students put a truck into the parade, covered with patriotic banners; when it reached the reviewing stand, they pulled off these banners and displayed the ones underneath: "Billions for armaments; $1.20 a week for the unemployed." The students in the truck were attacked by members of the veterans' groups marching next to them in the parade, but the students escaped into the crowd. The assignment of our Tacoma contingent was to station ourselves in the meeting hall where the marchers in the parade were to go to hear patriotic speeches. We sat on the front row of the balcony, with banners and leaflets under our coats, and when the first speaker was introduced, rolled our banners down over the edge of the balcony and showered our leaflets down onto the heads of the crowd. Veterans ran up the stairs shouting "Kill the Reds" and began to grab those of us they could identify. Several of our group were dragged down the stairs by the heels; several were arrested. As president and leader of the Tacoma group, I felt especially indignant at not being either arrested or roughed up. I realize in retrospect that I looked younger than my sixteen years and had the appearance of a well-brought-up middle-class girl—not very plausible as an enemy of society.

My friends were a skeptical lot. They scoffed at my Theosophical views. We argued about spiritualism and extrasensory perception, and I persuaded them to devote some club time to doing some experiments on ESP. We wrote to J. B. Rhine at Duke University, and he sent us a pack of the Zener cards he used in his experiments. We attempted to replicate some of his studies. We found that a "thought receiver" could do somewhat better than chance so long as the backs of the cards were visible, but when the sender and receiver were in different rooms, performance was at a chance level. When we examined the cards closely, we realized that they were quite thin, so that the pattern stamped on the faces showed through very faintly in the form of embossed patterns on the backs. I found the negative results quite sobering. I began to read Houdini and other writers who provided some insights into how magic tricks could be used to produce spiritualist phenomena. My confidence in the evidence behind Theosophical doctrine began to erode.

Where would I go to college? My father's business was in trouble, and money was scarce. It was taken for granted that I would go to the state university, with its low in-state tuitions, until I won a one-year scholarship to Reed College in Portland, Oregon. I was delighted. Reed had a reputation as an experimental school where students received a great deal of individual attention from the faculty and where intellectual values were fostered. I went there in the fall of 1934 with the highest expectations and was not disappointed. For the first time, I was given assignments that were really challenging; the library contained riches that I had never dreamed of; the teachers met with students in groups of ten and conducted discussions in which they challenged half-baked ideas. In these sessions, I found myself being pressed to be precise about what I meant in stating a position and to think carefully about what kind of evidence could be mustered in support of views that had seemed obvious until challenged.

There was a ferment of left-wing thought and action on the campus. We boycotted Japanese silk because of the Japanese invasion of China, and wore lisle stockings (nylon had not yet been invented). We raised money for a variety of causes, including struggling young labor unions. I quickly became involved in these activities, but the heart of my first-year experience at Reed was my academic work. I remained a vegetarian through the year and got rather tired of explaining to other students about my belief that one did not have the right to take animal lives for food when other food would do. They, of course, pointed out inconsistencies in my behavior: that I was wearing leather shoes, swatting mosquitoes, etc. There were a number of late-night discussions in the dorms about religion and our philosophies of life. I became aware of the range of beliefs other people held; my own began to seem no more defensible than others—indeed, *all* religious beliefs came under question.

I loved Reed. At the end of my first year, I very much wanted to return, but there was a problem about the money for tuition. I went to secretarial school during the summer, long enough to learn shorthand, and worked as a secretary for the following year while living at home. I saved enough money for the next year's tuition at Reed. During this year, I also had a part-time job as an organizer for the National Council for Prevention of War. I returned to Reed in the fall of 1936 for my sophomore year. I quickly became involved in campus activities once more, serving as secretary of the student government.

It was at this time that I took my first course in psychology. The teacher was William Griffith, known as "Monte" (from his Montana origins). He was a gargantuan figure—a former copper miner, football player, and heavyweight fighter—weighing about 300 pounds at the time I knew him. His fame as a raconteur was considerable, and visitors to Portland would seek him out for long evenings of drinking and amusing stories— one such visitor was Eugene O'Neill. As a teacher Monte was witty, Rabelaisian, and iconoclastic. He had done his graduate work with Edwin Guthrie and was a behaviorist. In my disillusioned and growingly skeptical state, his radical reductionism struck exactly the right note. I was ready to jettison the intellectual cargo that remained from Theosophy. I was intrigued by the experiments on conditioning and was interested in seeing how far conditioning principles could be applied to explain a wide range of human behaviors. The idea of operational definition came as a revelation to me. One could sweep away a whole range of troubling questions—such as the nature of an afterlife—by showing that these were questions that could not be stated in measurable terms and therefore weren't worth asking.

Monte was surrounded by a group of admiring students, and I began to spend time with a number of them, one in particular. We spent occasional evenings at Monte's house, quite literally sitting at his feet. The Monte culture was an intensely male one. His male students loved the fact that he could still beat them at handball despite his weight, and the ribald quality of his wit (especially when he had been drinking, which was often) was more appealing to male than female students. I was present primarily as the girlfriend of one of his students, but I soaked up the rather arrogant skepticism that he generated in his followers. I developed a superior and barely tolerant attitude toward my parents and abandoned my vegetarian diet. (The first hamburger tasted delicious!) And then, toward the end of the school year, I felt rootless, without purpose, insignificant; nothing seemed worth living and working for. I dropped out of school a few weeks before the end of the year. My morale recovered somewhat during the summer, and it turned out that my academic record had been good enough up to the time of my leaving school to permit retrieving credits by finishing a few papers. I found that I could transfer to the University of Washington as a junior. I was pleased to be going to Washington, in large part because I wanted to study psychology with Edwin Guthrie.

When I entered the University of Washington in the fall of 1937, my father could only manage to send me $25 a month, which had to cover food, housing, and books. I could not afford to live in the dormitories and lived off campus, sharing a tiny one-room apartment with another Tacoma girl. We cooked on a two-burner hotplate in a closet. I worked as a secretary for one of the psychology faculty members (for 40 cents an hour) to earn my tuition money, and spent nearly all my free time, including evenings, at the department. As a junior and senior, I took all the psychology courses that were available, including the graduate courses, and began to meet the small group of graduate students who served as teaching fellows. One of the graduate students was Nathan Maccoby, who had been one of Monte's proteges at Reed. We had not met there, but our common Reed background was an initial bond. Mac was an excellent tennis player and offered to help me improve my game. We began to play tennis on weekends (and have done so ever since, for 50 years). The teaching fellows shared a large office, and we would work there in the evenings. Occasionally, when we could afford it, the whole group went to a local pub for beer or, even more rarely, on a ski trip. There were beach parties or evening parties at someone's apartment, to which I sometimes brought my guitar to accompany group singing. We gradually paired off; Mac and I were married in the fall of 1938, at the beginning of my senior year. We were very poor, and lived in a converted double garage, shabbily furnished, with a little pot-bellied wood stove for heating. We could not afford a telephone nor, of course, a car. We took these conditions pretty much for granted and did not feel especially deprived, since most of our friends were in similar situations. (I do remember, though, wanting a new dress and not being able to get it because it cost $7.95.)

The Psychology Department at Washington had a dominant doctrine: Guthrie's contiguity theory of learning. Guthrie taught several courses, but taught essentially the same thing regardless of whether the course was titled Learning, Personality and Human Conflict, or Psychological Statistics. Other senior members of the department also organized their teaching around this point of view; the course I took in child psychology was a peculiar amalgam of studies of the IQ (with a hereditarian emphasis) and studies of classical conditioning of young organisms, including Watson's famous work with Little Albert. We had a formidable course in the neural basis of behavior and learned Hilgard and Marquis's book on conditioning and learning from cover to cover.

One maverick on the faculty—Ralph Gundlach—was not a Believer. He was interested in gestalt psychology and Lewinian field theory, and in social issues. He was never allowed to teach a course in either comparative psychological theories or social psychology, which were his main interests. He did manage to incorporate gestalt principles into his course on sensation and perception. He put a copy of a book by Lewin on a shelf in the graduate students' office, in the hope that some of us might read it, even though it was never assigned in a course. As far as I know, no one did. We were all thoroughly imbued with Guthrian doctrine and considered other viewpoints—what we knew about them—to be softheaded. In particular, we sneered at psychoanalytic ideas, which we considered to be hopelessly mired in assumptions about unobservable internal processes. There was a considerable flurry of excitement in the department when Skinner's book *The Behavior of Organisms* was published. One of the graduate students,

Fred Sheffield, reviewed it at length in a seminar. The book was quite controversial at Washington, mainly because of its distinction between operants and respondents, and its emphasis on reinforcement as a primary learning mechanism. We regarded Skinner's book as a major challenge to Guthrie, whose primary learning mechanism was association by contiguity, not reinforcement. Though this aspect of the book was problematic for us, its strict behaviorism was welcome. We liked the strictly S-R approach and the absence of any reliance on internal mediating processes.

During the two years at Seattle, I was primarily absorbed in psychology and in my new marriage, and was only marginally involved in political activity. However, we were enthusiastic supporters of many of the New Deal measures and did some house-to-house lobbying in favor of revising the State of Washington's tax structure in a less regressive direction. Those were the days of the United Front, when liberals, Socialists, and Communists made common cause on a number of issues. I participated in fund-raising efforts to support the Loyalist cause in Spain and knew several young men who went off to fight in the Abraham Lincoln Brigade. Ideologically, it was a confusing time. Pacifist views were difficult to reconcile with opposition to the growing fascist and Nazi movements in Europe.

The University of Washington Psychology Department had given only two Ph.D.'s in its history. It was understood that the graduate students would take a master's degree and then go elsewhere to finish their graduate work. Mac finished his M.A. work in the spring of 1939 and during the summer received an offer of an instructorship at Oregon State College in Corvallis. We decided to take it, although it would mean my foregoing the teaching fellowship at Washington that I had been offered. I would have an opportunity to take some graduate psychology courses at the University of Oregon, 40 miles from Corvallis, and Mac's nine-month salary of $1,800 was attractive. We moved to Corvallis in the fall, driving the elderly car my family had given us. I commuted to Eugene several times a week for course work. The course in gestalt psychology, given by Robert Leeper, is the one I most remember. The approach was scholarly, but so different from the way I had come to think about psychology that I found the concepts rather undigestible. At Corvallis, Mac and I built some apparatus and attempted to replicate Lynn Baker's infamous experiment on one-trial subliminal conditioning of the eyeblink response. Like others, we found that we could not reproduce the phenomenon.

We felt intellectually isolated at Corvallis and were eager to move on.

World War II had begun in Europe, and there was a sense of urgency about national affairs. We wanted to be more in the center of things. Mac applied for and got a job in the U.S. Civil Service Commission, and in the summer of 1940 we moved to Washington D.C. My B.A. in psychology did not qualify me for much in the way of interesting work, but I found a job in the State Technical Advisory Service, an office in the Social Security Board which was responsible for preparing tests for State Merit Systems. For a year and a half, I spent most of my working time writing test items. Outside working hours, I made contact with some of the folk singers in town and for a brief time had a weekly radio program on which I sang primarily children's songs. I essentially withdrew from political activity. The period between the beginning of World War II and Pearl Harbor was one of intense political disillusion. The Moscow trials of the mid-1930's had already undermined much of our optimism about the great Soviet experiment; the Nazi-Soviet pact and the Russian invasion of Finland were the coup de grace. They brought the United Front to an abrupt end.

A number of our West Coast friends came to Washington to take jobs in the expanding government agencies, and most of them stayed with us while looking for a place to live. Through them we learned about the various opportunities for psychologists that were opening up, and I heard about the organization that Rensis Likert had established in the Department of Agriculture. His Division of Program Surveys had been organized at the direction of the then-Secretary of Agriculture, Henry Wallace, to monitor the impact of federal agricultural programs on farmers at the grass roots. It had a staff of interviewers who interviewed farmers regarding their experience with federal programs and reported their complaints and suggestions to the persons responsible for the programs. After Pearl Harbor, the division expanded rapidly, becoming the survey organization utilized by many government agencies to gather information about public reactions to, and understanding of, their wartime programs. At that time, the Bureau of Agricultural Economics (with its Division of Program Surveys) and the Census Bureau were the only organizations equipped to draw nationwide probability samples of households, and so the division was the natural home for the growing volume of public opinion survey work needed by wartime agencies.

A number of academic psychologists joined the Washington staff, including Dorwin Cartwright, Angus Campbell, Robert MacLeod, Ernest Hilgard, George Katona, Jerome Bruner, Richard Crutchfield, David

Krech, James Bayton, and Robert Holt. I applied and was hired as an assistant study director. The division did a wide variety of work. Studies I worked on, first as an assistant and then as study director, included a study of fuel oil rationing for the Office of Price Administration, a series of studies on war bond purchasing for the Treasury Department, a study of returning veterans for the War Department, and a series of studies on consumer spending and saving for the Federal Reserve Board.

The scheduling of our work was tight. Studies were conducted on a ten-week cycle. During the first two weeks the interview schedule was designed and pretested at a field site with a group of experienced interviewers from the field staff. During this time, the sampling section was working with area maps to draw whatever sample of city blocks and rural areas was needed for the purposes of the study. The interviewing was done in the next two to three week period, and during this time a code was prepared for analyzing open-ended questions, and coders were trained. Then two to three weeks were used for coding, and the remainder of the time was allocated for analysis and write-up. We were equipped with state-of-the-art IBM machines, mainly counter-sorters, which allowed us to cross-tabulate a stack of punched cards by two or more variables. This seemed very high-tech at the time, and there was a certain fascination in standing in front of the counter-sorter, watching to see whether the cards were falling out according to one's hypothesis.

The war years were critical ones for professional development for both Mac and me. After serving in administrative and personnel work in the Office of Price Administration, Mac was drafted in 1942, and a year later was brought into the new experimental section of the Pentagon Research Branch, an organization formed by Carl Hovland to do psychological studies of troop morale. In our two research settings we learned how to organize and carry out large-scale studies in field settings and gained experience in applied psychological work.

At the end of the war, the Department of Agriculture wished to scale down the operations of Program Surveys, returning it to its focus on agricultural issues. Likert decided to move his organization outside of government and negotiated an arrangement with the University of Michigan whereby a core group of division personnel would establish the Survey Research Center at Michigan, some having faculty appointments in either psychology or sociology, and retaining the structure of the national field staff. During the negotiations for the shift, Donald Marquis, then chairman of the Michigan Psychology Department, came to Washington. We met, and he asked me whether I would like to work for my Ph.D. at Michigan. I was enthusiastic, and Mac too wanted to finish his graduate work. We arranged to go to Michigan, both of us to work at the Survey Research Center for as much time as possible while doing our graduate work. Likert could not move his entire operation at one time, however, and decided to keep a small office open in Washington to carry on the work for the Federal Reserve Board. I was needed for this work and remained in Washington for a year, working with George Katona on the studies of consumer finances. I moved to Ann Arbor, joining Mac there, in 1947. I thus became a graduate student eight years after completing my undergraduate work.

Graduate work in the late 1940's was a very different experience from what it became at a later time. Large numbers of people were returning to academic work from the armed forces or wartime jobs and were relatively mature. As students, we were intensely interested in the subject matter of psychology, much of which was still quite new to the intellectual world. Most of us read fairly widely. Universities were expanding and students were confident that there would be good job opportunities when they had earned their degrees. We wanted to finish quickly and worked hard to surmount the rather formidable set of hurdles that were set for Ph.D. candidates in those days. There were quite a few required courses. Prelim exams included the general section, covering most of the areas of psychology, and special exams in one's own area. Classes were large—larger than any I had been in as an undergraduate. I specialized in learning theory and studied in this area with Marquis and Edward Walker, while also taking courses in a variety of other subfields.

I was especially intrigued by a course in perception, taught by Bert Thuma. He had a gestalt orientation. I wrote my term paper on attention, and in the process of doing so, went to see Pillsbury, then an emeritus professor at Michigan, in his eighties. He had written a book on attention in 1906. I came away from my brief exploration of this topic with a sense of dissatisfaction; the phenomenon was obviously important but, I thought, poorly understood, and I filed it away as a topic I would want to come back to at a future time. My only course in personality was taught by Urie Bronfenbrenner. It was Urie's first teaching experience—he had just finished his own graduate work, and was the same age as many of his students. He has since told me that that was his most difficult teaching year. Many of his students were outspoken and skeptical, but he remembers me in particular as a thorn in the flesh, with my hard-line S-R approach and my scornful attitude toward "soft" psychology.

In Ann Arbor we once again became politically active. I had done little during the war years, except to participate in the work for desegregation. In retrospect it seems hard to believe, but Government cafeterias were racially segregated in the early 1940's. I was active in a successful move to bring about integration, both at Agriculture and at the Federal Reserve Board. In Michigan, Neil Staebler, a local business man, was leading a move to rejuvenate the state Democratic Party. We worked with him to win control of local party caucuses. By this means, the Staebler group brought about the nomination of G. Mennen ("Soapy") Williams for Governor. In working for his election—and subsequently on other state-wide issues—we became acquainted with people outside our academic sphere, including some people from the large organized labor movement in Michigan. Our primary social circle, however, was made up of people from the Survey Research Center, the Center for Group Dynamics, and faculty and students from the Psychology Department and the Program in Social Psychology. In particular, Ted and Mary Newcomb made their home a center for the social life of people from these various settings. Mac and I had bought a small house, and we too did our share of the party giving. It was a very busy time.

By the fall of 1949, Mac had finished his graduate work and was offered an excellent job at Boston University. I had finished all my work except the dissertation, and we decided to go to Boston and see whether I could locate a laboratory setting there in which I could do a dissertation experiment in absentia. When we arrived in Boston, I went to see B. F. Skinner, who received me graciously and expressed interest in the experiment on partial reinforcement that I wanted to do.

Skinner's lab was highly automated, by comparison with other labs in existence at that time. He had a large circular drum, about five feet in diameter, with nine pie-shaped compartments, each large enough to hold a pigeon. A timer turned the drum at half-hour intervals, moving a new bird into the working position. At this one position, there was a lighted disk which the pigeon could peck, and on a predetermined schedule a food compartment would open long enough to allow the bird to eat a few bites of grain. The pigeon's pecks were recorded on a moving paper tape. In running an experiment, one would put eight birds into the apparatus and leave the ninth compartment empty, so that each subject had an opportunity to work for half an hour, and after all the birds had been run, the apparatus would come to rest on the empty compartment. The mechanism was designed so as to allow the experimenter to set different reinforcement schedules for different birds in advance, and then leave to do other things (or sleep) while the subjects were being run. As it happened, shortly before I arrived, there had been a fire in the lab, and Skinner was not sure which of the relays in the apparatus were still working and which needed to be replaced. He was glad to have someone run an experiment to test out the apparatus, and I was delighted to have such a sophisticated set-up to work with. There *were* problems with the apparatus: it would occasionally skip a compartment, leaving seven records on the tape with no clue as to which subject (on which schedule) had been skipped. It proved to be necessary to be present for every session, which meant a good deal of late-night work in the basement of Memorial Hall.

I led a second, disconnected intellectual life during that dissertation year. Jerome Bruner and I had become acquainted during our wartime survey research work, and he recruited me to do some pilot work on some political surveys in the Boston area. I also served as staff to a Harvard faculty committee on the economic status of the faculty, an assignment that involved interviewing faculty members in a variety of disciplines and learning a good deal about the Harvard milieu. The committee work, as well as the work with Bruner, was centered in the Department of Social Relations. As far as I know, I was the only person who had keys to both the Psychology Department in Memorial Hall and offices in Social Relations in Emerson Hall. The two departments were at odds, and the members had virtually no contact. Social and clinical (including personality) psychology, along with social anthropology and sociology, were in Social Relations; experimental psychology, physiological psychology, and sensory and perceptual psychology were in the Psychology Department. The atmosphere of the two departments was utterly different: Psychology had few students, and had an authoritarian, restrictive, almost military style of operation. The life of the department was in the laboratories. The graduate students and post-docs tended to take on the ideology of their major professors, including a devotion to "hard science" and a rather contemptuous attitude toward the work that went on in Social Relations (which they actually knew little about). Social Relations was a relatively new department. It was overflowing with students, both graduate and undergraduate. It had a bustling, lively atmosphere, with a good deal of contention as faculty and students argued over their diverse views. Its life was in corridors and classrooms as well as in the research offices. Students were required to take work in all four of the component disciplines, and a number of courses were co-taught by faculty from different disciplines. The faculty often did not achieve their goal of integrating the diverse concepts from the several disciplines, and so the students were faced with the necessity of attempting to do this on their own. It was frustrating, but at the same time there was a sense of an exciting experiment under way.

Confronted by these two atmospheres, I was ambivalent: I still considered the concepts of learning theory to be the core concepts for psychology as a whole, capable of being applied to the entire range of human behavior, from perception to social behavior. I thought many of the ideas in the Social Relations cluster of disciplines were poorly defined and unscientific in the sense that it was difficult to make them operational for research. But I found the orthodoxy of the thinking in the Psychology Department distasteful. It seemed stultifying, narrow. I enjoyed the intellectual life of Social Relations much more. Furthermore, my experience in survey research had given me some knowledge of applied research and made it possible to combine my professional life with my interests in social issues; the work in Social Relations seemed much closer to these interests.

When my dissertation was finished and I had gone to Ann Arbor to take my final orals and to turn in my thesis, I was ready to look for a full-time job in the Boston area. I was lucky. Robert Sears had recently been brought to Harvard to establish the Laboratory of Human Development and teach the child psychology courses in Social Relations. His wife Pat Sears joined the faculty of Harvard's School of Education. Their colleagues, the anthropologists John and Beatrice Whiting, came at the same time—John to teach in the social anthropology program. They wanted to do a large-scale socialization study in which they would attempt to relate the child-rearing practices of parents to certain personality characteristics being developed in their children. They were looking for someone to run the mother-interview part of the study—to field-test an interview schedule, hire and train interviewers, devise a coding scheme and supervise the coding process, and participate in the analysis of the interview data. My background fitted these needs very well, and I was hired. (I think the Old-Boy network came into play: Sears and Marquis had been fellow faculty members at Yale, and Marquis was consulted.) I was delighted with my new job. It held promise of bringing together two themes in my life which so far had been separate: my interest in learning theory and my desire to do work which might have some fairly immediate applied value.

The Laboratory of Human Development was housed in an old frame house—Palfrey House—which had been converted to include offices, a meeting room, and an experimental room with one-way windows for observation. At the daily bag lunches, there was lively discussion of the work that various faculty people, post-docs, and graduate students were doing. The Searses and Whitings had come out of the Institute of Human Relations at Yale. At Palfrey House, they carried on the effort that had begun at Yale to operationalize Freudian concepts and state them, whenever possible, in the language of Hullian learning theory. The socialization of children was a natural problem to attack from this standpoint. The starting point was the psychoanalytic view that intrafamily experiences in infancy and early childhood were important in the formation of enduring personality characteristics. This view was entirely compatible with a learning theory approach that viewed personality as the outcome of cumulative learning experiences. Freud's instinctual needs were easily recast as Hullian drives. Parents were seen in part as stand-ins for the experimenter in an animal learning study: they determined what the child would be required to learn and administered the rewards and punishments that would cause the child to learn. In their role as teachers and controllers, parents would inevitably frustrate children. Therefore (following the work on frustration and aggression done by the Yale group of which Sears had been a part) it was inevitable that children would develop aggressive impulses toward their parents. The fate of these impulses would depend on how the parents responded. If they punished parent-directed aggression, one could expect to find the children employing the Freudian defense mechanisms and displacing or sublimating their anger or turning it toward themselves. Freudian ideas concerning such interpersonal dynamics as identification and dependency were more difficult to handle, and there were arguments over whether dependency was best conceptualized as an acquired drive or as a habit based on the parent's having become a secondary reinforcer.

We had a division of labor on the socialization study. I was responsible for the mother-interview portion of the study. A separate team conducted a doll-play session with each of the children, designed to assess their degree of identification with each of the parents, their adoption of adult roles and sex-typed behaviors, their guilt over transgressions, and their tendencies to display either aggression or dependency. This portion of the study was done primarily by the Searses; they were assisted by Harry Levin, who came to the laboratory as a post-doc at the time the study was being launched. The two research groups were under a strict injunction not to discuss individual cases with one another, so that the child measures and mother measures would remain independent. When the data had been collected and the interviews coded, different members of the research team took on portions of the analysis task and began to explore the connections between child-rearing practices as reported by the mother and the children's characteristics as revealed in the doll-play session.

Our scores were entered on IBM cards, and we had not only a counter-sorter but the newest machine—a tabulator—which could compute means, standard deviations, and even correlations, and could provide significance levels as well. These machines were primitive forerunners of our present-day computers. They were large and noisy and very limited in what statistical functions they could perform. It is difficult for anyone familiar with modern computers to imagine the excitement we all felt when we saw our tabulator ingest a pack of cards and then not only do our calculations but *print out* the results on a paper tape.

We were in the midst of the analysis when a crisis occurred. Bob Sears was offered the chairmanship of the Psychology Department at Stanford. He and Pat had both been Stanford undergraduates and were both the children of Stanford professors. They very much wanted to return, but they did not want to disrupt the completion of the study. The question was: how could the work be reorganized so that we could finish the analysis and write-up at two different locations? The agreement was that Bob Sears, Harry Levin, and I would take responsibility for writing a book on the mother-interview portion of the study, collaborating at long distance. The Searses would continue to work on the doll-play data. John Whiting would take over the direction of the laboratory, where the main focus would now be the cross-cultural work then under way. There would be copies of the mother interviews and the IBM cards at both Harvard and Stanford, and we would all be free to do whatever analysis with them we wished to do.

The departure of the Searses from Cambridge in 1953 had a number of repercussions for my professional life. Bob had been teaching the courses in child psychology in the Department of Social Relations. A replacement was needed at short notice. I had already been doing some teaching in the department: jointly with Jerry Bruner and Raymond Bauer, I was teaching a large undergraduate course in public opinion, and in addition had a graduate seminar in survey research methods. In view of my current work in the Laboratory of Human Development, I seemed a natural person to help fill the teaching gap created by Sears's departure while a search was conducted for a replacement for Sears. For the first year, George Mandler and I taught the large undergraduate course in child psychology, but after that it became my regular assignment, and no new appointment in child psychology was made.

The years following the Searses' departure were very busy ones for me. In the process of training the students in my methods seminar, I conducted a field study each year, using random samples of Cambridge households. Several of these studies yielded publishable results. The first was a study of the impact of television on the lives of children and families. TV was new in the early 1950's, and we took advantage of the fact that only about half the families in Cambridge had acquired TV sets. We located families who had television and matched to them a set of families that did not. We compared the two groups of families with respect to how the children spent their time, in an effort to discover what activities were being dropped and how family life was reorganized when children began to spend time watching TV (Maccoby, 1951, 1954). This was the first (and smallest) of several studies in which people took advantage of the newness of the medium to find reasonably well-matched samples of TV and non-TV households. An informal network of people doing work in this new field took shape and led to some long-standing personal and professional relationships (one was an enduring friendship with Hilde Himmelweit).

A second study dealt with the social control of juvenile delinquency. We identified two low-income areas in Cambridge, one of which had a high delinquency rate and the other a low rate. Our hypothesis was that in low-delinquency areas, neighborhoods would be more cohesive, meaning among other things that people would know their neighbors and recognize the neighborhood children. In consequence, we thought, if people in the low-delinquency area observed a child misbehaving, they would be more likely to talk to the child or the child's parents about it than if they lived in the high-delinquency area. These hypotheses were largely supported (Maccoby, Johnson, and Church, 1958). A third study examined the voting behavior of young first-time voters, to determine whether or not they followed the political lead of their parents. On the basis of my assumptions about the power of identification with parents, I hypothesized that the nature of the parenting style which had prevailed in the young person's family would have a bearing on the degree to which parental political attitudes would be adopted. Our findings provided some support for this view (Maccoby, Mathews, and Morton, 1954).

At the time these studies were going on, I was carrying on my part of the socialization study at the Sears-Whiting laboratory and also conducted several film studies. I was fascinated with the phenomenon of identification. Intuitively it did seem to me that there must be a process whereby people could put themselves, mentally and emotionally, into the place of another and experience vicariously what that other person was experiencing. Such a phenomenon did not fit well with the then current learning-theory models and had proved to be a difficult psychodynamic concept to translate into S-R language. Following the thinking at Palfrey House, identification was thought to provide a mechanism whereby children could take on mannerisms, attitudes, and values from their parents without direct tuition. But I thought that the phenomenon was broader than this and need not depend on the interpersonal dynamics of family life. Surely there could be fleeting "identification" with fictional characters, particularly under the special conditions of movie viewing, when viewers' own real-life identities and activities were temporarily suspended. I thought that different people, watching the same film, would identify with different characters, and that this choice ought to be predictable on the basis of joint characteristics of the viewer and the filmed character.

My first foray into this question involved showing a romantic film to individual college-age subjects and watching their eye movements during the scenes when only the male and female stars were on the screen. We not only found that viewers spent more time watching their same-sex character (as predicted), but saw that their faces often mirrored the emotions being depicted by that character (Maccoby, Wilson, and Burton, 1958). A second study involved large groups of school-aged children, who were shown a film having strong leading parts for a boy and a girl in an adventure story (we had to view many films before we found one with strong parts for both sexes!). In this study, the hypothesis was that if viewers identified more fully with the same-sex character, they would notice and remember more of that character's behavior, and that in addition, they would notice and remember more of the stimuli to which that character was responding. Post-film testing of the children concerning what they remembered from the film provided support for both hypotheses, with the proviso that children of each sex remembered more of their own-sex character *if* the actions were gender appropriate (Maccoby and Wilson, 1957). In the third study in this series I wanted to see whether there were aspects of similarity other than gender that would lead viewers to attend selectively to certain characters. I found a film in which one leading character was a lower-class gang leader and the other a middle-class boy who had enviable technical knowledge and expertise. I showed this film to children of varying social-class backgrounds and found that children attended more to the character of their own social class. There was an exception, however: working-class boys who wanted to go to college attended more to the middle-class character than to the gang leader. This finding pointed to some of the motivational complexities that underlie a viewer's choice of identificand (Maccoby and Wilson, 1957).

These studies had very little impact and have seldom been cited. Social learning theory was not yet quite on the scene, but when it appeared, was very much less cognitive than it has since become. While I saw selective attention to a model as the first step in observational learning, my studies were not seen as relevant to such learning because I did not have a behavioral measure of imitation. However, I have always seen imitative behavior as only one indication that an observer has learned something about a model's behavior.

During these years, some important changes were occurring in our family situation. We had known for some time that we were an infertile couple. We decided to adopt children. In 1952, we became acquainted with a charming 10-year-old girl—a relative of friends of ours—who had been separated from her parents some years before and was living in a state-supported boarding home. We invited her to begin spending weekends with us, and we soon became deeply attached. She came to live with us permanently. We were registered with an adoption agency and on the waiting list for an infant, but under the laws of Massachusetts, we were eligible only for an infant with a Jewish natural father and a Protestant natural mother. (I was reluctant to identify myself as a Protestant, but soon learned that in Massachusetts the word meant simply that one was neither Catholic nor Jewish.) In 1956, a seven-month-old girl of the right pedigree finally appeared. We were overjoyed, and baby Sarah became our second daughter. I dropped to a half-time work schedule when she arrived.

In the light of current attitudes about the sharing of child-care responsibilities, I have sometimes wondered why we simply took it for granted that I would be the one who would stay home in the afternoons, rather than Mac. Partly the answer is a very practical one: he was earning much more than I was, and we needed his income. But the fact is that the issue never arose—I wanted to spend more time with the children, and Mac applauded my decision. My new responsibilities did sometimes conflict, however, with the professional life I had set up. There were completed studies that needed to be written up. I had gladly accepted Ted Newcomb's offer to do most of the organizational and editorial work on the new edition of *Readings in Social Psychology* (Maccoby, Newcomb, and Hartley, 1958). I was in the midst of writing chapters for the *Patterns of Child Rearing* book (Sears, Maccoby, and Levin, 1957) and exchanging them with Bob Sears through the mails. We carried on a lengthy and intensive correspondence over aspects of the manuscript, and there were further analyses and other revisions waiting to be done. After spending the morning at the university and an afternoon and evening in baby care and other household activities, I was tired and not ready to work efficiently when the children had gone to bed. I would wake up in the middle of the night worrying about the work that was still undone. It was at this time that I formed a habit that has continued till the present time: when there is pressing work to be done, I wake up and work from 2:00 A.M. to about 4:00; it is wonderful, uninterrupted time, and I have always found I can return to peaceful sleep and get up at 7:30 or 8:00 entirely refreshed.

In 1958 Bob Sears asked whether we could take a year's leave and come out to Stanford to work on a research project that he and Wilbur Schramm had organized. We were eager to do so, and I discussed the plan with the chairman of the Social Relations Department. My appointment was a part-time lectureship, not on the tenure track. Even so, the chairman explained, it was becoming awkward for them to keep me on so long without any sort of job security; he was pleased to have me leave for a year, so that he could terminate my appointment. When I returned, the gap in my employment would allow him to start me over again as a new appointee, without any obligations. I felt all this was rather shabby, but not unexpected. There had been many ambiguous elements in my situation from the beginning, some of which stemmed from the fact that Harvard didn't seem to know what to do with a female junior faculty member. There were hints that it would be better if I did not march with the Harvard faculty at commencement—wouldn't I prefer to march with the Radcliffe faculty? (At the time this came up, I got a note from the Radcliffe administration saying that I was not eligible to play on their tennis courts, because I was a member of the *Harvard* faculty.) I could belong to the Faculty Club, but couldn't enter through the front door—there was a women's entrance at the side. I couldn't get a book out of Lamont Library—it was closed to women faculty and students; if I needed a book from there, I sent a male student for it. There were no women assistant professors, and my marginal status seemed quite natural in the male-oriented atmosphere of those times. In retrospect I wonder why I was not more resentful of all this, but I enjoyed my work and was happy with my family and felt that the male games endemic to Harvard were simply something to be tolerated. Also, I was not especially eager to become involved in the tenure battles that afflicted the lives of the assistant professors and so did not press for an on-ladder appointment.

We went to Stanford, thinking that our visit would be for a year, but we were both offered faculty appointments. We suspect this happy coincidence was mainly engineered by Bob Sears, though he never said so. There were a number of dual-appointment couples at Stanford (the Searses, the Hilgards, the Farnsworths). The rule was, however, that the two appointments could not be in the same department. Lois Stolz was retiring, and I would fill her slot, teaching courses in child psychology. Mac would join the program in communications, which was on the verge of becoming a department, and Mac would help build it. While these negotiations were going on, another major event occurred: we got a phone call from our Boston adoption agency. Miraculously, another suitable child was available, a seven-month-old boy. I flew to Boston to get him. Our family was now complete.

During the first years at Stanford I was officially working half time, and much of that time was devoted to teaching. The research and writing I managed to do had a scattered feeling. With the assistance of colleagues in Boston, we did a follow-up study of the Patterns children (Maccoby, 1961, 1962), and I wrote some review papers. I joined forces with Lucy Rau (Ferguson) in a study of the personality correlates of different patterns of intellectual abilities (Ferguson and Maccoby, 1966) and continued to search for relationships between personality and intellectual performance in a study on activity level (Maccoby, Dowley, Hagen, and Degerman, 1965). I did a little work on children's drawings (Maccoby and Bee, 1965; Maccoby, 1968a). But I felt intellectually adrift, and could not seem to find a satisfying focus for a new research program. I was undergoing an intellectual reorientation and needed to go through a fallow phase as far as research was concerned.

The research experience at Palfrey House, while enormously stimulating, had had disappointing results. We had not been able to find any connections between the characteristics of the children as revealed in their doll-play and what we learned about parents' child-rearing practices from the mother interview. I still remember a folder in my file drawer at Palfrey House. It was labeled "Where does aggression go?" and contained the tables from a lengthy exploration of the effects of punishment for aggressive behavior. From psychodynamic theory the prediction was that the children who had received unusually high levels of such punishment would have adopted defense mechanisms such as displacement, self-punitiveness, fantasy aggression—but none of these manifestations showed up in the children's doll-play performance. A further problem was that the children's characteristics were not packaged in the way that would have been predicted from identification theory. "Adult role" responses were not correlated with the measure of sex typing nor with responses that indexed guilt over transgressions, although the prediction was that they should have been if they all derived from the resolution of Oedipal conflicts. Furthermore, we could not find any connections between the severity of socialization in infancy (severity of weaning and toilet training) and any of the outcomes that might have been predicted from Freud's theory of fixations at early psychosexual stages. Overall, the yield from the study was poor, although we did believe that we had obtained some valuable insights about socialization from the mother interviews. (The fact that we were getting such poor results from our attempts to find relationships between the socialization measures and the doll-play measures was a factor underlying our decision to write a book about the mother-interview data alone.)

Why were our results so weak? Did the fault lie with having used only projective measures of the children? Had the mothers given us invalid information about their socialization practices? Obviously, our problems with the study might have been mainly methodological. But then, too, we might have been working from the wrong theory. The Searses, of course, were disappointed too. When I first came to Stanford, Bob Sears was conducting a new study with a smaller sample in which he broadened the battery of child measures and included observation of mother-child interaction and a father interview. Yet this study too failed to confirm psychoanalytic hypotheses about identification and its consequences.

It was easy enough for me to return to my earlier skepticism about psychodynamic theory, and I was not really surprised that its predictions had failed. But I was not satisfied to stay with any of the S-R theories—Guthrian, Hullian, Skinnerian—that had been the foundation of my student years. As I continued to teach courses in child psychology, I began to read more widely. I read Heinz Werner and Piaget. The publication of John

Flavell's book on Piaget in 1962 made much more of Piaget's work accessible and meaningful to me. Other influential books were Donald Hebb's *Organization of Behavior*, Roger Brown's *Words and Things*, and Donald Broadbent's *Perception and Communication*. Chomsky's review of Skinner's book on language was compelling. In retrospect, it seems clear that in shifting away from S-R psychology, I was part of the "cognitive revolution" that was gaining momentum in the field of psychology as a whole. But I did not recognize this at the time. I seldom discussed my searchings with friends and colleagues. No doubt I had some discomfort over appearing disloyal to my mentors, past and present. For whatever reason, my reorientation was mainly a private process. Except, of course, that it pervaded my teaching. I changed the name of my large introductory course from Child Psychology to Developmental Psychology and changed its content correspondingly.

What kind of reorientation was it? The idea of development began to take on more and more importance in my mind. The major themes in the then-current versions of cognitive developmental theory will be already familiar to my readers, and it is difficult to describe the sense of discovery and excitement one could feel about them in the late 1950's and early 1960's. For me, some of the compelling ideas were that learning and development were not the same thing; to view a child's development as a process of bringing items of behavior "under stimulus control," as S-R theories did, was to miss the role of the child as an active selector, processor, and organizer of what the environment had to offer. I became persuaded that children utilized only what could be processed via the child's currently available repertoire of concepts and mechanisms. If this was true, what children learned might be systematically different from what socialization agents were providing as teachers and models. In formulating a response, children drew on the information stored in memory as well as on what was available in the current environment. They organized and reorganized the information they selected for storage. While developmental change might be driven by physiological maturation to some degree, this was by no means the whole story. If development was a process of building new structures utilizing those already constructed at earlier ages, sequencing became paramount. I began to believe that the central task for developmental psychology was to understand sequences—to describe them and to explain both the regularities and the variation in the trajectories children took over time.

As these changes took root and became a fairly coherent point of view,

I felt able to organize a new line of research. With several graduate students—John Hagen, Karl Konrad, and Aimee Dorr—I embarked on a series of studies of the developmental aspects of selective perception. This work was very satisfying. It was a pleasure to be working with harder data. And I was returning to an old love. During my ten years of teaching child psychology, my favorite segment of the course—other than the segment on socialization—had been the material on perceptual development. I had tried to keep current with my reading in this field. Through reading Broadbent, I became aware that important new work was going on on the role of attention in perception, but that very little of this work was developmental. My students and I wanted to study some of the developmental aspects of selective processes in both vision and audition, and needed to develop measurement procedures that would be valid across a range of ages in both these modalities. We devised measures that allowed us to trace age changes in both the ability to attend to one message while shutting out another and the ability to divide attention and process more than one message at a time. The latter process proved to be more difficult for children. We were able to show that the ability to divide attention developed more slowly during the age range five to thirteen than the ability to select a single message from a distracting background.

We were able to rule out a number of plausible hypotheses concerning the processes that underlay the improvements in performance with age. Older children's greater facility did not rest on any greater ability to take and hold a preparatory set; it did not reflect greater ability to overcome peripheral masking; rather, in audition it was linked to increasing knowledge of language and increasing sensitivity to the sequential probabilities in strings of words (Maccoby and Konrad, 1966, 1967; Maccoby, 1967, 1969). We pinpointed an attention deficit in elderly people and found that their difficulties were not a function of inability to focus on one message while ignoring another, but rather lay in the process of dividing attention. We found that elderly people's difficulty in holding one message while reporting another did not stem merely from the fading of a memory trace, but from the active interference generated by the act of reporting the first message (Maccoby, Jones, and Konrad, 1968). In our work on selection from visual displays, we studied age changes in the ability to trade off desired information against undesired information under conditions of information overload and found indications that there might be a qualitative change in this process at about age twelve (Maccoby and Hagen, 1965; Hagen, 1967).

As this research program gathered momentum, I attended a number of conferences with people doing work on audition. I learned about some of the highly technical methods for controlling aspects of auditory messages and realized that our techniques were quite primitive. Did I want to continue working in auditory perception? If so, I needed to take at least a year off and get training in one of the labs where more advanced techniques were being used. To do this would have been quite difficult in view of my family situation. But I also had strong interests in other research areas and could not bring myself to make such a strong commitment to the selective attention work that other work would fall by the wayside. In the 1960's I was a member of a Social Science Research Council committee on socialization, and we were working on a joint book; my assignment was to review and organize the work on moral development (Maccoby, 1968b). I found this an especially interesting topic to study, since at that time there were two active streams of research on moral development, stemming from two contending points of view. Social learning theory was just coming into its own, underpinned by the remarkable work of Albert Bandura and his students on imitation and given wide currency through the publication of Bandura and Walters's book, *Social Learning and Personality Development* (1963). Lawrence Kohlberg's neo-Piagetian work was just beginning to make its mark. As I saw it, the great strength of social learning theory was its emphasis on observational learning. This emphasis took the process of learning out of its narrow S-R boundaries; to think of a child learning a bit of behavior while merely observing a model, without making the to-be-learned response or being reinforced for it, was to make learning a form of information processing. To me, this was a welcome way of thinking. So was the theory's emphasis on the relationships between the observer and the model: a child would learn more from a model who was nurturant or had powerful control. What the theory lacked, however, was any serious attention to developmental processes. From a social learning viewpoint, a child could learn virtually anything at any age, and the child's cognitive level was not seen as relevant to what could be assimilated through observational learning. Kohlberg's cognitive development theory contributed the needed emphasis on development, but I thought it gave an inadequate account of individual differences, and it seemed to leave one suspended somewhere between thought and action. In my chapter I attempted to find points of contact between the two theories and—with only moderate success—to weave them into a single account of moral development.

Another part of my activity as a member of the SSRC committee on socialization was to form a discussion group at Stanford on the topic of the differential development of male and female children. We met frequently during the period 1962–64. Our group included Roy d'Andrade (anthropology), Sanford Dornbusch (sociology), David Hamburg (psychiatry), Walter Mischel (psychology), and myself. Kohlberg became a regular member of the group during a year he spent in the Stanford area. Others (among them, Erik Erikson and Kimball Romney) joined us for occasional sessions. Debates were lively. Discussions ranged from the biological to the societal levels. While there was some mutual influence, lines of theoretical difference also became sharper, and we decided that it would be useful to articulate these themes in a joint book, for which I would serve as editor. As this book, *The Development of Sex Differences* (1966), took shape, it became clear how sharply social learning theory and cognitive developmental theory diverged in their account of the process of sex typing. Also the cross-cultural evidence pointed to more cross-cultural universality in the roles and characteristics of the two sexes than Margaret Mead had claimed. And throughout our work, difficulties were encountered when we tried to distinguish biological from social factors in the causal nexus. Finally, our attempts to produce a coherent account were plagued by weakness and gaps in the available evidence. I was especially struck by the paucity of data on differential socialization of boys and girls. The joint work with my student Mary Rothbart (Maccoby and Rothbart, 1966) was designed to help fill this gap.

In the 1960's, a national social program was undertaken, designed to improve the chances of underprivileged children to succeed in school. It quickly became clear that any gains produced by preschool programs were in danger of being lost when the children entered traditional school settings. In some locations, therefore, pilot work was undertaken to supplement the national Headstart program with a Follow Through program aimed at the first three primary grades. There were several contending viewpoints as to what kind of programs would be most effective. Some people advocated programs based on a didactic teaching and reinforcement approach; others advocated a "discovery" approach; others thought the focus should be on involving parents in the children's learning. An experiment was undertaken called Planned Variation, in which several different programs were put in place, each at several different sites. I became involved in the effort to evaluate these programs, and wrote a small book describing and comparing the several experimental educational approaches (Maccoby and Zellner, 1970). Through participating in this work, I gained a good deal of respect for the hard-working, under-paid, and dedicated people who were attempting to maintain and improve educational quality in a deteriorating political climate.

In the late 1960's, I was asked to do the chapter on attachment and de-pendency for the upcoming third edition of the *Carmichael Manual of Child Psychology* (Maccoby and Masters, 1969). I was familiar with the way "dependency" was conceptualized in the socialization work based on Hullian and Freudian conceptions. When I began work on the chapter, I assumed that "attachment" was simply another word for the same phe-nomena we had been studying all along. I read and reviewed Mary Ains-worth's book based on her observations of mother-infant relationships in Uganda and met and talked extensively with John Bowlby. He gave me pre-publication drafts of several chapters from his new book on attach-ment. Although I had previously read some ethological work (Lorenz and Tinbergen), this was the first time I had seen this point of view applied to a critical aspect of human development, and I found it very impressive. I tried to do justice to the emerging Bowlby-Ainsworth theory in my re-view chapter. In retrospect, however, I believe I continued to treat the two concepts of attachment and dependency more equivalently than was jus-tified either empirically or theoretically. Fortunately subsequent writers (e.g., Sroufe and Waters, 1977) have made the distinction clearer. In the process of preparing the review chapter, I became intrigued with the ap-parent regularities in patterns of developmental change in attachment-related behaviors, but felt that our knowledge about these patterns was limited to too narrow an age range. At that time, almost all the work on attachment (as distinct from dependency) had been done with children under two years old. In collaboration with Shirley Feldman, I undertook a short-term longitudinal study. The children in the study were observed with their mothers in the "strange situation" on three occasions: at age 2, age 2 1/2, and age 3. We were able to trace some interesting age changes in children's reactions to this situation (Maccoby and Feldman, 1972). In retrospect I realize that the strange-situation methodology was of limited applicability to children older than two; and I also believe that it was sim-plistic to try to study the continuities in attachment-related phenomena by looking for maintenance or change over this age period in behaviors that were phenotypically the same. Clearly, the subsequent work, which looks for effects of early attachment patterns on different patterns of behavior that reflect the child's coping with new developmental tasks, has been much more fruitful.

In the 1960's and early 1970's unrest swept the campuses. For me, this was déjà vu—I had thought, all through the post-war years, that students had become a passive lot, by comparison with the activism of my own student days, and the civil rights movement and the anti–Vietnam War protests seemed in some respect like a welcome return of social consciousness. (The trashing of campus buildings, however, seemed to me to be a singularly ill-chosen form of antiwar protest; I thought the most appropriate form of action was to seek political solutions for political problems, and was distressed that students had too little confidence in the political process to give this strategy much attention.) I participated as a member of a faculty-student group that went to Washington in 1970 to call upon legislators and government policy makers to protest the invasion of Cambodia. But in general I was too absorbed in my professional and family life to have much energy left for political activity. However, I was drawn more and more into the resurgent women's movement.

I had always considered myself a feminist, and had been considerably interested in the effects on families of women's increasing participation in the work force (Maccoby, 1958). But feminist issues had not been salient in my mind for many years. Despite the curious sexism of life at Harvard, I had never felt that my career had suffered from sex discrimination. Good professional opportunities had always been open for me at the crucial points in my life when I was ready for them. It was my own decision to drop to half-time work when the children were young. When they entered school, I wanted to have a three-quarter-time appointment, so that I could feel free to be home in midafternoon to meet the school bus. I thought my department at Stanford had shown remarkable flexibility in agreeing to these arrangements. I believe I may have been the first faculty member to be granted tenure in a part-time position. Also, I was given a light load of committee responsibilities when our children were young. All this made me feel well treated.

There were plenty of time pressures, of course, but I experienced few obstacles to the development of my career. We were able to recruit good live-in people to help with housework and child care. These helpers included a strapping woman from the Australian outback, a retired widow from Dublin, a charming, wispy Chinese girl from Tahiti for whom English was her fourth language, an English girl whom we met at Stanford's

overseas campus at Harlaxton, and one Stanford student who lived with
us for part of her college career and then stayed on for an extra year.
Money was not a problem—in those days, 1 1/2 academic salaries were
enough to raise children and make the mortgage payments on a comfortable campus house. I had no idea what my colleagues were earning—
Stanford salaries were a well-kept secret at that time—but it didn't occur
to me to worry about how my salary compared. I did not expect rapid increases during a period when I was on part-time appointment and was not
publishing as much as some of my more prolific colleagues. I was startled,
then, when the unrest of the times led to the discovery that I was under-
paid. It happened this way: during a wave of protest on the campus, the
students occupied the administration building where salary records were
kept. During commencement exercises that year, a group of students
stood near the gate where the academic procession marched through to
the amphitheater, calling out the salaries of selected faculty members with
commentary: "Here's good old Professor So-and-So; the university is paying him $35,000. Do you think he's worth it?" When my turn came, the
message was, "Here's the lowest paid full professor in the university. Do
you think it has anything to do with the fact that she's a woman?" It
turned out that the base salary rate on which my part-time pay was computed *was* comparatively low—a matter which the university soon rec-
tified. I was ambivalent about all this. I had never asked for a raise in all
my working life, feeling that recompense would come if my work made
me valuable enough to my employers. I did not want to get a raise simply
because I was a woman. On the other hand I was pleased and grateful that
women were being vigilant on behalf of other women and came to realize
that gender discrimination was a reality in the lives of many women. I
began to feel an obligation to give some support to their efforts.

The 1950's and early 1960's were a time when women were giving their
major priority to the domestic side of life. Relatively few women were
getting training for higher-level professional jobs. I had become accustomed to being the only woman—or one of a small minority—on committees and at conferences. There was a good deal of satisfaction in this
Queen Bee role. I enjoyed working with men. I felt I was making it in a
man's world and rightly or wrongly felt that I was accepted by my male
colleagues on my merits rather than as a token woman. I had established
some rules of thumb for myself about how to function in this world: carry
your own suitcase, pay for your own lunch, don't wear perfume during
working hours, never be overdressed—in short, don't trade upon femi-

ninity in a professional situation. At the same time, in subtle ways, I was never "one of the boys," and this too I enjoyed.

In the late 1960's and early 1970's things began to change, and many events cumulated to strengthen and maintain my interest in the women's movement. The publication of the 1966 book on sex differences led to my being asked to give papers at meetings on women's issues, and there I had my first experiences interacting in all-female groups. A new, highly competent breed of young women began to appear at conferences, and I found them stimulating to work with. Affirmative action programs developed on campuses, and as one of the few tenured women at Stanford, I found myself being appointed to a number of university committees. (A black male colleague and I were repeatedly appointed or elected to the same committees, and our encounters began to be something of a joke.) I was elected to the faculty Senate, and knew that the women on campus expected me to introduce a woman's voice to that almost all-male body. My growing visibility as a spokeswoman led to my being sought out for still further involvement. For example, a group of women graduate students from a different department came to ask my help on an issue of sexual harassment. On a number of occasions, people told me that I was a "role model" for younger women. This made me acutely uncomfortable, and I came to dislike the phrase. It seemed arrogant for anyone to display her own life as something for other people to copy. But I began to understand that women everywhere were asking themselves: is it really possible to have it all—career, family, everything? They were looking eagerly for examples of what was possible and what was not.

I became involved in ad hoc discussion groups of feminist issues with women faculty members and graduate students from a number of departments. (In 1974, I joined with them in establishing the Center for Research on Women, and, with James March, co-chaired this organization at its inception.) In the course of these activities, I became aware of some strongly contrasting viewpoints about the value of psychological research on sex differences and similarities. One school of thought held that to study sex differences only makes them more salient. From this viewpoint, it was legitimate to be frankly political in making choices about what to study and what to publish. If one had data that might be used to the disadvantage of women, the data should be quietly buried. I held a strongly contrary view. In working on the 1966 book, I had realized how thin the evidential base was for the various impassioned views about the capacities, potentials, and proper functions of the two sexes. I wanted the strong clean light of careful research and objective fact finding to be brought to bear on matters which I thought were murkier than they needed to be. I was strongly opposed to withholding data from publication out of fear over how they might be utilized. And I thought that objectivity in research was possible and desirable, though difficult when one was also an advocate.

In 1970 Carol Jacklin came to see me. Her husband had taken a job in the Bay Area, and she was looking for an academic location where she could finish her thesis and then move on to a post-doctoral appointment with a research project. We quickly found common ground in our interest in gender-related studies, and our values were also compatible. When I asked Carol about her views on the political implications of such research, her reply was a simple one: "The truth will make us free." We entered into a collaboration that spanned almost fifteen years. We began by designing a small-scale study of barrier behavior in very young children (Jacklin, Maccoby, and Dick, 1973). But we soon embarked on what turned out to be a major enterprise: assembling the material for our book *The Psychology of Sex Differences* (Maccoby and Jacklin, 1974). The SSRC group's work on the 1966 book had included a bibliographical summary, but there had not been time for our literature review to be as thorough and thoughtful as we would have wanted it to be. And of course a great deal of new work had come out in the interim. Carol and I both thought there was need for a sourcebook that would assemble and organize the existing research literature. We wanted to make the material maximally useful to those interested in developmental change and to discuss the literature in relation to the contending theoretical points of view.

The book could not fail to be controversial, considering the ideological ferment of the times. When it was published, we were flooded with phone calls from reporters who wanted us to summarize our work in a few sentences for tomorrow's edition. Usually, they had a point of view of their own and were looking for some quotes to support it. There was a contrast effect, and we came to have a high opinion of certain thoughtful, responsible journalists who wanted to present a balanced account. Our problem was to identify which ones were worth spending time with and which ones merely wanted to exploit us.

The reactions of our professional colleagues were highly varied. We had included a summary in which we listed the sex differences that we thought had been fairly firmly established. Some thought our list was too short (e.g., Block, 1976); others thought it was too long (e.g., Tiger, 1980;

and see our reply to Tiger, Maccoby and Jacklin, 1980). Some thought we were too biological, others that we weren't biological enough. Many thought we had given too little weight to socialization pressures. In the early 1970's social learning theory provided the most popular account of the acquisition of sex-typed behaviors in childhood. We explicitly questioned this theory on both empirical and theoretical grounds, arguing that although it might be adequate to explain some sex differences, it was not adequate for others. Readers seemed to assume that if imitation and reinforcement were not the whole story, we must mean that biological factors filled the gap, and this implication was anathema to many readers. Almost no one (except Walter Emmerich, in his review for *Science, 1975*) seemed to notice that we had presented a third alternative, a cognitive one. We used the term "self-socialization" to refer to the active process whereby children drew inferences concerning the gender-relevance of various roles and activities. We argued that children formed stereotypes with which they might or might not guide their own behavior, depending on cognitive developmental factors. In retrospect, I realize that our treatment of this alternative (and our own thinking about it) were not at all clear. If I were to write the book again, I would include a chapter on the social cognition of gender and the role it plays in the development of sex-typed behavior. And I would be more explicit about the fact that neither biological predispositions, socialization pressures, nor self-regulated cognitions can alone account for gender differentiation, but that the three processes are intricately interwoven. These matters are clearer now than they were in 1973, as schema theories have been developed and additional evidence has appeared, and I have tried to elaborate them in a current paper (Maccoby, 1988).

In the 1970's Carol Jacklin and I undertook a longitudinal study of gender differentiation, studying three cohorts of children from birth to age six. (There are a number of publications from this study; in addition to those cited below, several more are listed in the references to this paper.) As part of this work, we did several observational studies of parent-child interaction, and I was thus able to return to my earlier focus on socialization. I became especially interested in circular processes and mutual influence between parent and child, working from an increasingly interactionist perspective (Martin, Maccoby, Baran, and Jacklin, 1981; Maccoby and Jacklin, 1983). Through meetings and reading, I learned a good deal about both the method and substance of studying interaction from a number of colleagues, including Gerald Patterson, Mavis Hetherington,

Michael Rutter, Marian Radke-Yarrow, Jaqueline Goodnow, Diana Baumrind, and John Gottman. I embarked on the writing of a semi-popular book *Social Development* (1980), in which I attempted to place socialization processes—particularly as they occurred within the family—in the context of the sequences through which children typically progressed. The developmental changes in level of functioning, I thought, were partially the result of prior socialization efforts, but also placed limits on what parent-child interaction could be like and what effect such interaction could have. This theme also pervaded the chapter on middle childhood that I contributed to an edited volume (Maccoby, 1984a) and my presidential address to the Society for Research in Child Development (Maccoby, 1984b).

At about the time the social development book was finished, I was invited to write the chapter on parent-child interaction for the forthcoming new edition of the *Handbook of Child Psychology* (Maccoby and Martin, 1983). This enterprise, along with the writing of the social development book, provided the opportunity to reorganize my thinking about family functioning. I became increasingly convinced that the smooth functioning of any continuing relationship—including the parent-child relationship—depended on the willingness of each partner to be influenced by the other. This hypothesis led to collaboration with a graduate student on a study of reciprocal compliance (Parpal and Maccoby, 1985). I also became increasingly interested in the effects of the social and environmental conditions impinging on parents. I began to believe that parents differ from one another in terms of the amount of attention or energy they devote to the parenting function; and that when parental investment drops—due to a variety of exogenous or endogenous stresses—certain of the more benign and child-supportive elements are dropped out first, so that minimal parenting is usually coercive as well as unresponsive and neglectful. I began to think more seriously about the nature of family stressors (Maccoby, 1983) and began to teach a seminar on children and the law, jointly with Michael Wald, a colleague in the Stanford Law School. Our students have been drawn from the law school, the schools of education and medicine, and the social science departments. Over the eight years that this seminar has been taught, we have focused more and more on divorce and custodial arrangements. In so doing, we have been frustrated over the poor fit between many of the unsolved legal policy issues and the social science data that are available to be brought to bear upon them.

My intellectual life at Stanford has been greatly enriched through participation in the activities of the Center for the Study of Families, Children, and Youth (initially called the Boys' Town Center), which was established in 1974. The first director was Bob Sears, who was followed by Al Hastorf, Merrill Carlsmith, Michael Wald, and (currently) Sanford Dornbusch. A lifelong theme in my professional life has been an interest in doing work that was both interdisciplinary and policy-relevant. These twin interests are well served at the Center. With a group of Center colleagues from anthropology, sociology, and education, I have engaged in a two-year series of discussions on issues in socialization theory and research. And the Center is the locus of my current major research project: a longitudinal study of a large group of divorcing families, comparing the post-divorce functioning of families with different custodial arrangements for their children. This work is being done in collaboration with Robert Mnookin, a professor in Stanford's law school, and with Charlene Depner, a social psychologist whom we brought to the Center from the Survey Research Center of the University of Michigan.

In embarking on still another longitudinal study, I have obviously voted in favor of this complex and frustrating research design over the simpler experimental or cross-sectional studies. I have never had any doubt about the superiority of experimental designs, where one is able to assign subjects randomly to treatments, when it comes to being able to make strong causal inferences about the findings. I have used experimental designs whenever they seemed applicable to and feasible for the problem I wanted to study. But I have never been satisfied with experimental laboratory analogues when it comes to studying parent-child interaction, family stresses, etc., for I believe that the phenomena depend crucially on long-established relationships among the persons being studied. A good compromise for some kinds of studies is to use parents as experimenters—that is, to have them be the agents through whom "treatments" are applied to children. A difficulty with this approach, of course, is that the role experimentally assigned to a parent will be more startling to a child the more it differs from the parent's habitual interaction style. In other words, one can never standardize the treatment within an experimental group when parents administer it. Leaving parental behavior free to vary "naturally" is of course a way in which one can identify and categorize the natural variety of parental styles, but the effort to determine the "outcomes" of such variation through correlation with the children's concurrent characteristics is fraught with all the problems inherent in the lack of random assignment: one never knows which direction the causal arrow points, nor what other factors, associated with the parental variations one has assessed but different from them, may be responsible for the relationships one finds.

When working on issues that do not lend themselves to experimental treatment, I have several times made the extra commitments of time and effort that longitudinal studies demand, rather than relying on cross-sectional comparisons of naturally occurring groups. I have done this for two reasons. First of all, I believe that the simple description of time changes (or age-changes) in any phenomenon of childhood one wishes to study is a necessary first step in understanding the phenomenon. In addition, I believe that longitudinal designs increase the power of causal inferences about the relationship among linked processes, although one never achieves the inferential power provided by true experiments. The current work using structural modeling to unravel causal relationships in longitudinal data is intriguing, but I remain skeptical about the utility of these elaborate statistical procedures for analysis of the relatively small samples developmental psychologists usually employ.

When selecting a problem and a method for a piece of research, I have taken into account whether the work was to involve collaborating with students. It is difficult to carve out pieces of longitudinal studies that will allow students to complete and publish work within a reasonable time. One student who worked with us on the longitudinal study of gender differentiation helped with the data collection for one cohort of children, found some clear relationships between parent-child interaction and cognitive abilities, and wrote up a paper which was accepted by a journal. Unfortunately for us all, the findings didn't replicate on the next cohort of children, and the paper had to be withdrawn. This is a lesson on the pitfalls (and importance) of replication, as well as on the complexities of protecting students' careers in collaborative work.

As I look back on the satisfactions and frustrations of my life, I realize that the satisfactions have been many and the frustrations few. I have tried to function in a number of spheres—the personal, the professional, and (to a diminishing extent) the public. In the public-political sphere I feel a pervasive sense of sadness and disappointment over the drift of events in the world around me. When I was young, it seemed obvious what kinds of political, scientific, and economic achievements would constitute "progress" toward human betterment. Now it is not so obvious. And what still seems desirable no longer seems clearly doable. I realize that it is an

inevitable part of aging to become disillusioned about the solubility of social problems that once seemed to require only effort, resources, and goodwill. With experience, one comes to know how slow social change can be,
and how difficult to achieve. Public institutions—especially govern-
ments—seem less and less effective as agencies for achieving the common
good. Probably all generations of older people have felt these frustrations.
Yet it seems that in our generation, new elements have been added that
previous generations have not had to face. In my youth, we were hardly
conscious of the implications of the world population explosion; we
thought there were plenty of resources so that all the world's population
could have a good standard of living. We did not live in the shadow of
nuclear warfare or global pollution. Even after the horrors of World War
II, nations had survived, and we felt that good had triumphed over evil.
There was a sense that collectively we had been able to accomplish something of enormous importance. Now optimism has faded on all fronts.
For people of all ages, individual values seem to have gained ascendancy
over the value placed on joint effort toward joint goals.

As a private citizen living through these changes, I have tried to remain
involved. I have joined with others on boards and committees that were
designed to help with the solution of social problems. Usually I have come
away with the feeling that, much of the time, we were spinning our
wheels. Sometimes I have envied colleagues in smaller countries, where
the recommendations of a scientific commission or study group have a
chance of being acted upon. The groups that I have worked with, however, have not seemed to have much impact. National affairs these days
seem to have such a large element of media hype that it is difficult for
serious people of goodwill to see through to the heart of issues, or get
well-thought-out solutions acted upon. Perhaps it all boils down to the
fact that it's hard for a liberal to live through a period when conservative
ideology is in the ascendancy.

As far as my professional life is concerned, my retrospective feelings are
very different. I have had the good fortune to work in a strong and har-
monious department at Stanford, with close, compatible colleagues in the
developmental program. The sharing of intellectual interests and the continuing exchange of ideas with my husband has been an invaluable resource; the intellectual side of our relationship has enriched our marriage
as well as our careers. Through meetings, conferences, national committees, review groups, and professional organizations, I have come to know
a group of colleagues in my own field at other locations who have become

my closest intellectual peer group. We have visited one another's labs, given talks to one another's students, and read pre-publication drafts of one another's papers. Several of these colleagues have spent a year at the Center for Advanced Study in the Behavioral Sciences at Stanford, and this has greatly augmented the opportunities for the exchange of ideas and data. At a less direct level, I have reviewed many other people's papers for journals, and they have reviewed mine. Through all these avenues, I have felt myself to be part of a larger, cumulative scientific enterprise. While a good deal that gets published does not seem to advance our state of knowledge significantly, much of it does, and I am constantly aware how very much more we now know than when I first began to teach and write. I have observed, and participated in, some profound changes in the way we conceptualize human thought and action. Although I feel some nostalgia for the grand and simple theories of my youth, I feel we are wiser now.

Relationships with students have been a major source of professional satisfaction for me. Among the honors I have received, the one I value most is an award for excellence in teaching. I have always spent considerable amounts of time preparing for classes, and have found that the work of organizing materials for clear classroom presentation upgrades the quality of one's thinking about research (as well as being something one owes to the next generation of scholars). And of course when students rework and expand and challenge ideas from their own points of view, this is a constant intellectual refresher.

As to the private satisfactions, mine have been many, and still are. The continuing companionship of my lifelong partner and our circle of family and friends; being with our grandchildren (of whom we now have five); the weekly singing sessions with my madrigal group; foreign travel; visiting our cottage on the Northern California coast and taking long walks along the headlands or in the deep redwood forests and occasionally swimming in the surf (very cold!); giving parties; tennis on weekends; working in the garden; all these things complement a satisfying working life.

Looking back on my life and work, I know that there was not much active choosing involved at junctures that turned out to be crucial for my subsequent career. The "choice points" were mainly a matter of the right opportunities being available at the right time. Yet, if I were to replay my professional life with deliberate choices, there is very little that I would want to do differently. I would certainly want to be in the same field. It seems almost impossible to become bored with the study of human thought and behavior. There is nothing like the thrill of sitting down with a new batch of data to find out the answers to the questions one has posed. In my experience, it never palls.

Selected Publications by Eleanor E. Maccoby

(1951). Television, its impact on school children. *Public Opinion Quarterly*, *15*, 421–444.

(1954). Why children watch television. *Public Opinion Quarterly*, *18*, 239–244.

(with R. E. Matthews & A. S. Morton) (1954). Youth and political change. *Public Opinion Quarterly*, *18*, 23–29.

(with R. R. Sears & H. Levin) (1957). *Patterns of child rearing*. Evanston, IL: Row-Peterson.

(with W. C. Wilson) (1957). Identification and observational learning from films. *Journal of Abnormal and Social Psychology*, *55*, 76–87.

(1958). Effects upon children of their mothers' outside employment. In National Manpower Council, *Work in the lives of married women* (pp. 152–172). New York: Columbia University Press.

(with J. P. Johnson & R. M. Church) (1958). Community integration and the social control of juvenile delinquency. *Journal of Personality*, *14*, 38–51.

(with T. R. Newcomb & E. Hartley, Eds.) (1958). *Readings in social psychology*. New York: Henry Holt.

(with W. C. Wilson & R. V. Burton) (1958). Differential movie-viewing behavior of male and female viewers. *Journal of Personality*, *26*, 259–267.

(1961). The taking of adult roles in middle childhood. *Journal of Abnormal and Social Psychology*, *63*, 493–503.

(1962). Class differences in boys' choices of authority roles. *Sociometry*, *25* (1), 117–119.

(with H. Bee) (1965). Some speculations concerning the lag between perceiving and performing. *Child Development*, *36*, 267–377.

(with E. Dowley, J. W. Hagen, & R. Degerman) (1965). Activity level and intellectual functioning in normal preschool children. *Child Development*, *36*, 761.

(with J. Hagen) (1965). Effects of distraction upon central versus incidental recall: Developmental trends. *Journal of Experimental Child Psychology*, *2*, 280–289.

(Ed.) (1966). *The development of sex differences*. Stanford, CA: Stanford University Press.

(with L. R. Ferguson) (1966). Intrapersonal correlates of differential abilities. *Child Development*, *37* (3), 549–571.

(with K. W. Konrad) (1966). Age trends in selective listening. *Journal of Experimental Child Psychology*, *3*, 113–122.

(with M. Rothbart) (1966). Parents' differential reactions to sons and daughters. *Journal of Personality and Social Psychology*, 4, 237–243.

(1967). Selective auditory attention in children. In L. P. Lipsitt & C. C. Spiker (Eds.), *Advances in child development and behavior* (Vol. 3, pp. 99–125). New York: Academic Press.

(with K. W. Konrad) (1967). The effect of preparatory set on selective listening: Developmental trends. *Monographs of the Society for Research in Child Development*, 32 (4).

(1968a). What copying requires. *Ontario Journal of Educational Research*, 10, 163–170.

(1968b). The development of moral values and behavior. In J. A. Clausen (Ed.), *Socialization and Society* (pp. 227–269). Boston: Little, Brown.

(with T. M. Jones & K. W. Konrad) (1968). Selective listening in later life. In S. A. Chown & K. F. Reigel (Eds.), *Psychological functioning on the normal aging and senile aged: Interdisciplinary topics in gerontology* (Vol. 1, pp 56–67). Basel and New York: Karger.

(1969). The development of stimulus selection. In J. P. Hill (Ed.), *Minnesota Symposia on Child Psychology* (Vol. 3, pp. 68–96). Minneapolis: University of Minnesota Press.

(with J. C. Masters) (1969). Attachment and dependency. In P. Mussen (Ed.), *Carmichael manual of child psychology* (Vol. 3, pp. 73–158). New York: Wiley.

(with M. Zellner) (1970). *Experiments in primary education*. New York: Harcourt, Brace, Jovanovich.

(with S. S. Feldman) (1972). Mother-attachment and stranger-reactions in the third year of life. *Monographs of the Society for Research in Child Development*, 37 (1).

(with C. N. Jacklin & A. E. Dick) (1973). Barrier behavior and toy preference: Sex differences (and their absence) in the year-old child. *Child Development*, 44 (1), 196–200.

(with C. N. Jacklin) (1974). *The psychology of sex differences*. Stanford, CA: Stanford University Press.

(with C. N. Jacklin) (1978). Social behavior at 33 months in same-sex and mixed-sex dyads. *Child Development*, 49, 557–569.

(with C. Doering, C. N. Jacklin, & H. Kraemer) (1979). Concentrations of sex hormones in umbilical cord blood: Their relation to sex and birth order of infants. *Child Development*, 5, 632–642.

(1980). *Social development: Psychological growth and the parent-child relationship*. New York: Harcourt, Brace, Jovanovich.

(with C. N. Jacklin) (1980). Sex differences in aggression: A rejoinder and reprise. *Child Development*, 51, 964–980.

(with C. N. Jacklin, M. E. Snow, & M. Gahart) (1980). Sleep pattern development from 6 through 33 months. *Journal of Pediatric Psychology*, 5, 295–303.

(with J. A. Martin, K. Baran, & C. N. Jacklin) (1981). Sequential analysis of mother-child interaction at 18 months: A comparison of microanalytic methods. *Developmental Psychology*, 17, 146–157.

(1983). Social-emotional development and response to stressors. In N. Garmezy

& M. Rutter (Eds.), *Stress, coping and development: Issues and perspectives* (pp. 217–234). New York: McGraw-Hill.

(with C. N. Jacklin & C. H. Doering) (1983). Neonatal sex-steroid hormones and timidity in 6–18-month-old boys and girls. *Developmental Psychobiology, 16,* 163–168.

(with J. A. Martin) (1983). Socialization in the context of the family: Parent-child interaction. In E. M. Hetherington (Ed.), *Manual of child psychology: Vol. 4. Social development* (pp. 1–102). New York: Wiley.

(with M. E. Snow & C. N. Jacklin) (1983). Sex-of-child differences in father-child interaction at 12 months of age. *Child Development, 54,* 227–232.

(1984a). Middle childhood in the context of the family. In W. A. Collins (Ed.), *Development during middle childhood: The years from six to twelve* (pp. 184–239). Washington, DC: National Academy Press.

(1984b). Socialization and developmental change. *Child Development, 55,* 317–328.

(with M. E. Snow & C. N. Jacklin) (1984). Children's dispositions and mother-child interaction at 12 and 18 months: A short-term longitudinal study. *Developmental Psychology, 20,* 459–472.

(with J. Marcus & C. N. Jacklin) (1985). Individual differences in mood in early childhood: Their relation to gender and neonatal sex steroids. *Developmental Psychobiology, 18,* 327–340.

(with M. Parpal) (1985). Maternal responsiveness and subsequent child compliance. *Child Development, 56,* 1326–1334.

(with S. A. Gelman & P. Collman) (1986). Inferring properties from categories versus inferring categories from properties: The case of gender. *Child Development, 57,* 396–404.

(with C. N. Jacklin) (1987). Gender segregation in childhood. In H. Reese (Ed.), *Advances in child behavior and development* (Vol. 20, pp. 239–287). New York: Academic Press.

(1988). Gender as a social category. *Developmental Psychology, 24,* 755–765.

Other Publications Cited

Block, J. H. (1976). Debatable conclusions about sex differences. *Contemporary Psychology, 21,* 517–522.

Hagen, J. W. (1967). The effect of distraction on selective attention. *Child Development, 38,* 685–694.

Sroufe, L. A., & Waters, E. (1977). Attachment as an organizational construct. *Child Development, 48,* 1184–1199.

Tieger, Todd. (1980). On the biological basis of sex differences in aggression. *Child Development, 51,* 943–963.

Paul E Meehl

Paul E. Meehl

I was born January 3, 1920, in Minneapolis to Otto and Blanche Swedal; the name Meehl is my stepfather's. My ancestry is three-fourths Norwegian and one-fourth Scotch-Irish. In Norway my paternal ancestors were skilled tradesmen and schoolteachers, the maternal side were peasants. The Scotch-Irish maternal grandfather, whom I never met, was a salesman and a psychopath. My father was a bank clerk who, despite extraordinary intelligence, quit high school to help support a widowed mother and unmarried sister. He was fond and proud of me in a cool way, and I knew it. Fortunately I got his "brain" genes, because he held Admiral Rickover's view that if a man is dumb he might just as well be dead. I identified strongly with him. My mother was affectionate, nurturant, praiseful, but somewhat seductive, which led to sexual problems for me as a young adult.

Child rearing was permissive within firm limits. My parents laid down a few general rules, small in number, which to me seemed perfectly reasonable and which I therefore found easy to obey. The result has been an attitude toward the social group and toward authority figures which I consider healthy and rational, namely, it is foolish to break sensible rules imposed by persons in lawful authority over you; but given that, you are free to do your own thing and pay little attention to what other people expect, want, or approve. I believe that one reason I had such a good time both in high school and in college talking with my teachers is that I was totally devoid of rebelliousness or any chip-on-the-shoulder attitude. I had a mostly happy childhood, although my cyclothymic temperament was troublesome. "Paul, you're getting too excited," I heard often. In school I was an A student—my parents took this for granted—but with occasional "Unsatisfactory" marks in conduct, resulting from hyperactivity and a tendency to talk too much. At the same time, some of my childhood photographs look definitely depressed. I was a leader in my peer group in terms of what games to play and how. Puny and poor in sports, I suffered less from this than usual. As my father assured me, "That stuff doesn't matter, school work does. How many boys grow up to be baseball players?" I was aware of my intellectual superiority by age six or earlier. I liked school and was a "teacher's pet," but that rarely seemed to be resented by the others, for I was regularly elected president of our grade school classes.

My parental home was wholly without racial or religious prejudice, although one grandmother admitted to a slight preference for Scandinavians. My mother's *n Nurturance* and liberal Methodism led her to view such prejudices as unloving, while my father considered them stupid, ignorant, and irrational. At age seven I had an experience that, with a succinct but powerful assist from my father, gave me insight into some unsavory features of the human condition, at least in its "herd" aspect. The families in our neighborhood were mostly Scandinavian, with a few Irish, Polish, and German, but there was one Jewish family with whose son, a boy my age, I had fallen into conversation on the way to school and we became friends. We argued about the Tunney-Dempsey long count, about politics (I was a Republican, as of course every bank clerk was in the 1920's, and he was a Democrat), and he was the first boy that I knew who "didn't believe in Jesus." I had a spotty exposure to a tepid Methodist Sunday school, and I found this theological divergence interesting to argue about. One day I saw a crowd of boys gathered on the playground, and when I got up close there was a boy confronting my Jewish friend who was simply standing, looking frightened, with a bloody nose and his glasses awry. The other boy kept poking him in the shoulder, daring him to fight, which the Jewish boy obviously did not want to do. I was frightened, puzzled, and angry, and I was ashamed of myself because I wanted to do something to protect him, but I feared the group who were standing around eagerly looking for more blood and calling out "Hit him again," "Sock the dirty Jew," and the like. I must emphasize that this school had mostly children from the middle and lower-middle class; we were not in a slum nor a violent crime-ridden area, and yet here was my friend being subjected to this treatment, as far as I could discern solely because he was Jewish. Furthermore, it seemed that *all* of the group were eager for the fight, that I was a 1-in-20 deviate!

I was troubled by this episode and my own timidity (although in retrospect I realized that if I had got into the act all that would have happened was that there would have been two bloody noses instead of one).

I asked my father that evening why they did this, "What is the matter with them?" He put down his newspaper, looked at me somewhat skeptically, and said, "Paul, you mean you haven't figured out what's the matter with them yet?" I said no, I hadn't. He spoke three words, he tapped his head and said simply, "Dumb—no brains," and went back to his reading. This episode, and my father's three word diagnosis, "Dumb—no brains," carried more impact than my routine school experience that I could think, read, and speak better than my peers. I reflected on this for several days and my conclusion was yes, they were dumb. In fact, they were not just a little dumb—most of them barely had the wit to tie their own shoes or come in out of the rain. I have lived over half a century since then and have changed my views on a variety of subjects, but I must confess that I have never had occasion to revise that judgment. Needless to say, this expectation that, statistically speaking, most of the people you meet will be fair to middling stupid is one that you cannot afford to let be manifest if you want to win a popularity contest. Of course, a frenzied egalitarian could say that I have substituted an elitism of intellect for the more common snobberies of race, family, or money, a point I cheerfully concede.

In 1931 my father, who had embezzled money to play the stock market, committed suicide. Taunts by classmates showed me human cruelty, and doubtless this (plus reading history) is why my view of mankind is closer to that of Freud and Luther than of Rogers and Rousseau. My mother began having frightening "heart attacks," and life seemed precarious indeed. At age twelve or thirteen I chanced upon Karl Menninger's *The Human Mind*, which was a healing Damascus experience. "Why, these fellows have it all figured out, the workings of the mind follow scientific laws, it's like my chemistry set! My mother isn't going to die of heart failure, she's a young widow with anxiety neurosis." I decided overnight to become a psychotherapist. My father's sister, a secondary school teacher, lent me some psychology books, and I devoured Woodworth's introductory text, Angell's *Psychology*, and Starch's *Educational Psychology*, my first exposure to statistics. Freud's *Introductory Lectures* were counterbalanced by the behaviorism of George A. Dorsey's *Why We Behave Like Human Beings*. These books were lifesavers, and I have never doubted the efficacy of bibliotherapy for the right people at the right time.

At age sixteen I suffered a second object loss when my mother (who had remarried when I was fourteen) died of ether pneumonia after surgery for a brain tumor. Her physician, an internist of high reputation, had diagnosed her as having Meniere's disease and must have never rechecked her neurologically (even eye-grounds!) while her condition steadily worsened over a year's time. The neurologist we finally called in (against her will) observed a definite choked disk and correctly localized the tumor. This episode of gross medical bungling permanently immunized me from the childlike faith in physicians' omniscience that one finds among most persons, including educated ones. It has also helped me to avoid dogmatism about my own diagnostic inferences, to which I am tempted by my self-concept as a naturally gifted and well-trained clinician. After her death I lived briefly with my stepfather, then for a year with a neighbor family (so I could finish high school), and after that with my maternal grandparents who lived conveniently close to the university.

In my last year of junior high school several causal chains converged to influence my intellectual passions and my self-concept in a way that has persisted throughout my professional career. While I have published experimental research in animal learning and psychometric studies in personality assessment, I dare say most psychologists think of me primarily as a "methodologist" (cf. Meehl, 1950a, 1959a, 1967a, 1971a, 1972b, 1973a, 1978a, 1986a; Cronbach and Meehl, 1955: MacCorquodale and Meehl, 1948b; Meehl and MacCorquodale, 1951b; Meehl and Rosen, 1955). I am happier in the arm chair than in the lab, with the clinic somewhere in between! I shall therefore discuss these converging influences in some detail.

In the ninth grade there was a course called General Science which almost all the intellectually able students took because the teacher was reputed to be so stimulating. This teacher, Victor H. Smith, was of unusually high intelligence and unquestionably had the brains to be a teacher at the college level had he so chosen. He compared his attitude towards junior high teaching with that of a Jesuit priest, the old saw about if you get them when they are young they will never get the Church out of their blood. He looked upon the teaching of general science to adolescents as "already a bit too late" for counteracting the irrational and unscientific ways of thinking that they were exposed to by the peer group, in the home, and in Sunday school. While he had no appreciable interest in day-by-day political happenings (he despised politicians as a genus and used to make sarcastic asides to that effect in his lectures), he was by no means devoid of social welfare drives or values. His view was that while there were certain unavoidable characteristics of the human condition, including natural catastrophes and the inevitability of death, a large portion of all human misery was in principle remediable if people did not think so irrationally and unscientifically about practically everything. This melioristic view of improving society by teaching young people scientific habits of thought was quite common among scientifically trained "emancipated" persons in 1934, but in recent years has fallen into disrepute. I have myself become more pessimistic, as would anybody who lived through the horrors of fascism and Stalinism, not to mention the Great Depression, but I still see more merit in Smith's position than do many contemporary intellectuals (Goebbels and Robert Ley had Ph.D.'s, but they did *not* think scientifically!).

Whatever the merits of Mr. Smith's views on science and society, he managed to convey his passionate commitment in his teaching. He was not one of those teachers who believes that you can teach young people to think without teaching them any facts or principles to think about. Every day's lecture and demonstration was capped by his dictating to us (into what we called our "fact book") anywhere from one-half dozen to one dozen *facts* or *principles*, and we knew that we would be held responsible for learning all of these. Whether he was talking about weather prediction or the way American houses are constructed (he told us that the housing industry was always running at least 100 years behind the times in terms of cost, hygiene, and comfort) or the atomic theory or the effects of drugs, he would almost always add to the purely scientific content some comments about what would happen in the world if people really understood this, took it completely seriously, and applied it in their affairs. Doubtless the rebellious spirit of teenagers found this poking fun at preachers, politicians, journalists, and so on much to their liking even when it was not entirely objective. But he was not a fanatic or a cruel man, and on balance I am inclined to think that mobilizing a little bit of adolescent aggressiveness and intellectual muscle flexing did more good than harm. In any case, the dozen or so male friends that I mostly associated with at the time were all moved and shaped by this man. Among us the word "unscientific" came into everyday use and was one of the worst things you could say about anybody. Of course this theme meshed well with my father's views on stupidity.

In 1934 I read Bertrand Russell's *Our Knowledge of the External World*, my first exposure to epistemology. I cannot explain why it fascinated me, although during my analysis we spent some hours on this question with the usual scopophilic possibility, which I did not reject given my mother's tendency to seductive exhibitionism, but which never really grabbed me at the affective level. My analyst had a lot going for this interpretation (e.g., I respond to literature and music but am blind to the visual arts; as a teenager I was fond of "shadowing" people and was preoccupied with telescopes and a toy periscope with which one could look around corners).

About this time I read *A College Logic* by Alburey Castell (the "Augustine Cassell" of Skinner's *Walden Two*) and was as entranced as by Menninger and Russell. I read all the logic texts in the public library and prepared a summary of logic and scientific method which I circulated among my friends. This "Young Logician's Group" had a feeling about rationality that was as passionate as some boys of this age are about sports, politics, religion, or the Boy Scouts. In order to be *persona grata*, you had to be smart, and you had to think rationally. There was substantive variation among us in politics and religion, the group including a Roman Catholic, a Lutheran, several atheists and agnostics, some liberal Protestants ("on the way out"), and one Buddhist. Politically we ranged from Marxist—even one who was (as one could still be in 1935) an apologist for Bloody Joe Stalin—to a conservative Republican. So you could have a variety of political and religious opinions, but you had to do a respectable job defending them. An atheist who used dumb arguments would have been less acceptable to this group than a bright, articulate, highly rational Roman Catholic.

The extent to which thinking straight as such dominated or provided the social cement and furnished us with self-concepts can be illustrated by the following fact, which again I find unique in my experience when I have talked with others who belonged to adolescent male groups of this sort. We used to take long walks in the summer around Lake Nokomis or Lake Harriet and flip a coin at the beginning of the walk to decide who would be the Buddhist and who would be the agnostic or Roman Catholic, or who would be a socialist and who would be a conservative Republican. Thus you found yourself defending a position that was not your own based upon the flip of a coin, and the point was to see how good a job you could do at it.

We were never harsh with one another. It was excusable to make a mistake, although if you made too many egregious ones you would not be well accepted; but the unpardonable sin was to *refuse to recognize* that you had committed a fallacy, formal or material, when it was pointed out. A close second major sin would be to keep committing the same fallacy over and over again and having to be reminded of it. This kind of experience as a teenager, which persisted through my high school and undergraduate college days, I am afraid "spoiled" me as regards the life of the mind in academia. I had the expectation when I became a faculty member that anybody with the brains to get a Ph.D., who had taken courses in statistics and logic and the like, could be depended upon to be 95 percent rational, an expectation which was rudely upset by subsequent experience in faculty meetings and committees. While I have mellowed with age and become more tolerant of other people's frailties (as I hope they are of mine), I must confess that I have never fully recovered from the shock of realizing that one can become a college professor and not be able to think straight. This has led to a note of petulance creeping into my scholarly publications, for which I have been faulted.

The emphasis on rational argument and the ability to defend an opponent's point of view effectively meant (perhaps strangely) that intellectual one-upmanship or skill at verbal fencing, just being good at "winning the argument," were strongly disapproved of. This attitude has persisted into my adult life and old age. When I meet an academic who is an intellectual show-off—especially one for whom scholarly controversy has the character of a pissing contest—I lose interest in talking with that person. I look upon the intellect as a kind of sacred thing, and to have a conversation with the aim not of getting at the truth, clarifying one's ideas, or exploring new possibilities, but rather putting the other fellow down, showing that you are more resourceful and agile at debate, seems to me a corruption of the intellect and—speaking less melodramatically—a silly way to spend one's time.

To anticipate, not a single member of the 1938–1945 Minnesota psychology faculty engaged in this kind of vulgar gamesmanship. After I took my Ph.D. and began to move around the country and deal with professors from different academic subcultures, to find that there were quite a few who viewed an intellectual conversation like a chess game baffled and disappointed me. After all these years, I am still mildly surprised when I come across a flagrant case of it. Since I myself am intellectually resourceful and verbally fluent, and others tend to view me as "intellectually dominant" (by which, I think, they do not mean I am domineering), I am reasonably sure that my distaste for this kind of pseudo-intellectual discourse stems not from the fact that I am a loser at it, but from my belief that it's pointless, and a kind of spiritual corruption.

At age fifteen I decided to be a college professor, which troubled the high school counselor because I hadn't chosen what to profess. I said I might do psychiatry, psychology, philosophy, or statistics, but whichever it was, a professor I would be. It seemed clearly the only life for my sort of person, and he couldn't dissuade me from that conviction.

I began at the University of Minnesota in March 1938, taking premed courses so medical school would be an option; in any case I wanted to learn some physical and biological science. I persuaded R. M. Elliott, Chairman of the Psychology Department, to break the "sophomores only" rule for the general psychology course by telling him of my high school reading. I enjoyed almost every class I took and regularly managed to top the class. After a year of premed I decided I did not want to be a physician and became a psychology major, partly because I learned that academic clinical psychologists could do some therapy, and I knew I didn't want to be a full-time practitioner, of *anything*! Also, most of my premed friends, and their older brothers who were medical students, interns, or residents, did not stimulate me intellectually as much as did majors in psychology, philosophy, mathematics, and political science. I took calculus and mathematical theory of statistics (rare for psychologists in those days), partly because my physicist friends talked about partial derivatives and I wanted to know what that stuff was all about.

I received the B.A. *summa cum laude* (my advisor, D. G. Paterson, insisted on it) with a minor in biometry (another Paterson requirement). I thoroughly enjoyed my undergraduate years, including the "anonymity" which students complain about. It never occurred to me that the professors at a big university were supposed to "love me as a person" or that an institution of higher learning should "give me an identity." I would have classified such talk as immature and irrational, and I still do. I picked my friends for brains, intellectual passion, and the aspiration to think straight. My undergraduate experience solidly confirmed my teenage view that the life of the mind was fun.

The summer after graduation I loafed, except for two leisurely reading projects, Pavlov's *Conditioned Reflexes* and Hilgard and Marquis's *Conditioning and Learning*. In September 1941 I began my graduate work as a T.A. in the Psychology Department, which I found fairly enjoyable. An attack of rheumatic fever in 1942 left me with a mild mitral regurgitation, not troublesome but sufficient to keep me out of World War II. While I felt the world shouldn't put up with Hitler and Tojo, they weren't worse than Stalin, and I was unabashedly pleased to be classified 4-F, unfit for military service. As the war went on, this became a term of opprobrium, but it never bothered me in the least. "Sticks and stones . . ." was a hard childhood lesson, and I believe I have practiced the precept with 95 percent success.

In 1938 Minnesota's Psychology Department had a small faculty despite its many majors and national prestige, consisting of chairman R. M. Elliott (theoretical, biographical), D. G. Paterson (individual differences, vocational), C. Bird (abnormal, social), W. T. Heron (learning, comparative), K. E. Clark (psychometrics, attitude measurement, polling), M. A Tinker (experimental, history), K. H. Baker (laboratory, advanced general), H. P. Longstaff (personnel, advertising), and B. F. Skinner (language, theoretical). The introductory psychology course was taught by full professors. Starke Hathaway was in the Medical School but taught a course in physiological psychology. Paterson, a founder of the "student personnel" movement, was the dominant figure, giving the department a uniquely applied emphasis. The local quasi-geniuses were reputedly Hathaway and Skinner, and to be accepted as a doctoral candidate by either of them was a plum. The scholarly ethos was objective, skeptical, quantitative, and behavioristic. Hathaway and Paterson disliked theory, and the human experimental side was weak because Tinker's research was mostly "applied" (reading eye movements, illumination levels). Gestalt psychology was ignored, and Freud's theories mentioned grudgingly and skeptically. All Ph.D. candidates took certain core courses, so that a future industrial psychologist had Heron's animal course, and a Skinner advisee heard differential psychology from Paterson. We were all more broadly educated than is true of many psychology students.

In addition to formal classroom and laboratory experiences I spent a great deal of time in conversation with faculty. When graduate students complain about having insufficient contact with faculty, I wonder whether this is entirely realistic. I had no such complaints, but I was fairly aggressive in seeking professors out for conversation on topics that interested me and that I thought would interest them. I never felt that the hundreds of hours I spent in the offices of Paterson, Heron, Skinner, or Hathaway were begrudged by these eminent and busy men. I was never docile in debate or hesitant to pursue an argument down to rock-bottom disagreements about epistemology or philosophy of science, but I was free of any chip-on-the-shoulder attitude, or the desire to show up smarter than the professor. I am quite certain that these professors enjoyed their conversations with me as much as I did with them.

The Minnesota selection system, which relied heavily upon the Miller Analogies Test along with undergraduate records from first class schools around the country, but did not steer away our ablest undergraduates from taking graduate work at Minnesota, provided a peer group of the highest intellectual caliber. Among students who were T.A.'s at about the

same time I was were Kenneth MacCorquodale, Frank Barron, William
K. Estes, George Collier, Keller and Marian Breland, Norman Guttman,
Howard F. Hunt, and William Schofield, all of whose names would become well known in their specialties. Other able students did not become
as visible in the academy because they went into applied settings, among
them Brent Baxter, William A. McClelland, William E. Kendall, Kenneth
Millard, and Harold F. Rothe, who had successful careers in industry and
government.

We talked very little about current affairs, and 95 percent of our conversations were "talking shop" over both theoretical and applied subject
matter. It is tempting to fall into the old-oaken-bucket delusion in talking
about one's graduate student peers, but I do not think I deceive myself in
believing that for clinical psychologists a change has taken place over the
half century since then. There seems today to be a bimodality. The majority, since the early 1960's until very recently, were oriented to clinical
practice, having little interest in either methodology or substantive scientific questions. This was not true in the 1940's and until at least the middle 1950's, although some change was discernible by that time. Every clinical student that I knew in 1941–45 was interested both in the diagnosis
and treatment of patients and, with equal passion, in theoretical problems
of psychodynamics, learning, measurement, statistical prediction, and the
like. Are psychometric factors real? How much of Freud is translatable
into Skinnerese? Do neuroses have a genetic predisposition? Why do
Rogersian reflections "work"?

Most current discussions by philosophers of the problems of testing
psychoanalytic theory are pretty boring to me, not because I perceive them
as incorrect (although they sometimes seem a bit clinically naive), but
mainly because I heard them all 40 years ago as a graduate student. What,
if anything, is proved by the analyst's discerning that a patient's associations to a dream *seem* to "hang together" in a meaningful pattern? That
one topic probably received at least 100 hours of intense scrutiny in these
conversations during my three years of graduate work. It is not surprising
that I come across few methodological arguments pro and con psychoanalytic inference that are new to me. I remain in doubt about what to
conclude, but as to the arguments themselves, I've heard them all before.
I have written two papers on problems of inference in the psychoanalytic
session (Meehl, 1970c, 1983b), a mixed epistemological and statistical
question that has fascinated me since I was an undergraduate. I have not
made much progress in thinking it through, except to say definitely that

the evidentiary problem here is closely analogous to that in other "documentary" domains (e.g., law, history, even paleontology).

When Hathaway accepted me as a Ph.D. advisee, one of the consequences was that I was required to take my minor in the medical school. In that minor was a six-credit course taught by the world famous neuroanatomist Andrew T. Rasmussen, and I count this as the only aversive experience I had during graduate school. Psychologists were competing with medical students who had had a year of practice studying this kind of material. Psychologists were expected to get an A in the course and so far all of them had done just that, so it made one feel somewhat under the gun. I am not skillful at biological dissection, as I had already noticed when I took freshman zoology, and my severe spatial defect where three-dimensional relations were involved made the course content difficult. There were a lot of connections that didn't seem to have much sense to them, and I had the feeling that I was memorizing things that didn't cohere very well, the same sort of feeling I had when I didn't understand the (sometimes loose) balancing rules in undergraduate chemistry. So I relied on my excellent verbal memory, plus a set of flashcards developed for the lab exam which one of the medical fraternities had. I managed to get the required A grade, but there was enough anxiety associated with that course so that today, if I go into the anatomy building and get a whiff of formaline, I can still experience a little twinge of visceral anxiety.

In 1944 my good friend Howard Hunt enlisted in the Navy, and I was appointed instructor, while still working on my doctoral dissertation, to teach the introductory clinical class. I recall often skipping lunch because I was typing an outline of the lecture which I hoped would fill up the class time. As usually reported by young teachers having this experience, I never ran out of material, but I never got over the fear that I would do so.

As Hathaway's T.A. I lectured to medical students on psychometrics, graded their Mental Status cue-sheets, tested patients, and helped with MMPI research. I did some T.A.T.'s on Dr. B. C. Schiele's well-heeled private patients, which was interesting and paid well but left me wondering just how much it helped the patient. Hathaway disliked formally designated therapy supervision—"too much like psychoanalysts and social workers," he said—but if you brought up a case informally, he was helpful.

Hathaway and Hunt were doing quite a bit of hypnosis; though I did a little, I was never a skilled operator. I knew I had some resistance against it, which I didn't understand. During my analysis the best we could make of that inhibition was that the magical and irrational features of the process offended me so deeply that I could hardly believe my own suggestions! To say to a person that he won't be able to open his eyes or that his arm will move up involuntarily still strikes me—although I have seen it many times and have been hypnotized myself—as so preposterous that I don't manage to convey the required assurance. I was a moderately good subject for hypnosis myself, until at a social gathering Keller Breland suggested an analgesia of my hand which was not complete, and a post-hypnotic suggestion that it wouldn't hurt afterward (he had burned me with a smouldering match) also didn't take. Since then I have never been hypnotizable by anybody, including a couple of operators who had previously succeeded in hypnotizing me.

The academic anxiety produced by the neuroanatomy course was the only negative part of the required neuropsychiatry minor. The rest was fun. I particularly enjoyed going on the neurology rounds with A. B. Baker. Watching him or McKinley perform the neurological exam and zero in on the probable locus of a lesion was one of the few occasions in which I experienced some regret at not having gone to medical school. Strangely enough, the neurology rounds interested me as much as the psychiatry rounds. There was also at that time a widespread interest in psychological deficit psychometrics as contributing to the neurologist's assessing of the possibility of minimal organic brain damage, a subject on which Howard Hunt did his doctoral dissertation. We did about as much testing for psychological deficit in the 1940's as we did the assessment of general intelligence or of personality. Other components of the required 22 credits of the neuropsychiatry minor consisted of a reading course in neurophysiology and neuropathology with Rasmussen or one of the neurologists, regular attendance at the Grand Rounds on Saturday morning, some credit for psychological testing as part of one's externship, and the lecture courses in psychiatry and neurology taken with the medical students.

It amuses me to find psychologists who think that I was one of the "developers" of the Minnesota Multiphasic Personality Inventory, which I would be proud to be, since it is the most widely used psychological test as of this writing. But I was a high school junior at the time Hathaway and McKinley concocted the item pool, and I did not become Starke Hathaway's assistant until a year after the first mimeographed manual had appeared. While I have been author or co-author of some keys, my major contribution to this instrument was in expounding its theory and urging its actuarial interpretation. A colleague suggested that the accurate historical reconstruction would be "McKinley wanted it, Hathaway built it, and Meehl sold it." This last is an exaggeration of my role, since the encyclopedic scholarship of Grant Dahlstrom and colleagues at Chapel Hill in their handbooks and the work of my Minnesota colleague James Butcher with his annual MMPI workshops were at least as important as the lectures and papers I produced in the first decade or so after my doctorate, completed in 1945.

Because my early career and visibility and, I like to think, some of my worthwhile lasting contributions to the field involved the MMPI, it is appropriate here to say a few words about its origins. The scholarly antecedents go back to E. K. Strong, whose Vocational Interest Blank was built by "blind, empirical" item analysis of a heterogeneous pool of likes and dislikes for activities, occupations, kinds of people, and the like, with the selection of items for occupational keys being based upon an item's stable capacity to discriminate between men who were successful in a vocation and "men in general" (example: liking persons with big jaws earned you a point on the insurance salesman key) Starke Hathaway, who had taken his master's degree at Ohio and then came to Minnesota for the Ph.D. had, of course, taken Donald G. Paterson's famous course in individual differences. Hathaway was impressed with the validity of the SVIB constructed in this way, an impression strengthened by Hathaway's own skepticism of psychological theory and Paterson's "dustbowl empiricism" lectures. Hathaway's first paper on personality showed how the neuroticism scale of the Bernreuter Inventory could identify psychopaths by their supernormal ("non-neurotic") scores. The file research was suggested to him by a psychopath who, taking the Bernreuter, said, "It says 'I am easily embarrassed.' I've never been sure just what that word means." Right out of Cleckley, the lack of normal social fear! Research by Landis, Zubin, Page, and Katz at New York Psychiatric Institute revealed that many such items found on inventories built by academic, nonpracticing psychologists did not "work" in psychiatric populations. It seemed that one should not look upon the response to a verbal item on a structured personality inventory as merely a carelessly framed surrogate for what a patient would reveal in a diagnostic interview, let alone a psychotherapeutic interview of some depth conducted by a sensitive, perceptive clinician. Hathaway and McKinley conjectured that inventories such as the Bell, Bernreuter, Laird, and Heidbreder were not useful clinically partly because they were based upon the idea of obvious "face" validity for items, sometimes combined with rather crude measures of internal consistency, but also because the dimensions assessed were not clinically relevant to the diagnosis and treatment of mental patients.

Hathaway, although an academician, was in the habit of speaking somewhat scornfully of "academic psychologists," by which he meant professors of psychology who were interested in personality and built tests of this kind, but who had had little or no contact with patients suffering with full-blown mental diseases and who knew practically nothing about medicine. In the same vein, he had a distaste for what he called "captive fake clinics," that is, "clinics" under the wing of psychology departments which had no psychiatric personnel and, as he used to say, "don't deal with anybody crazy or anybody who has anything more wrong with them than a mild case of homesickness in a college freshman."

My first publication, "The Dynamics of Structured Personality Tests" (1945), was in response to a paper by Max Hutt on projective methods. I argued that structured tests like SVIB or MMPI should not be viewed as superficial approaches trusting the accuracy of "mere self-report," but were samples of verbal behavior that could be treated in a psychodynamic way (e.g., the "subtle" items on the Hy key reflect the hysteroid preference for repression and denial as defense mechanisms, never mind how objectively correct their content). This I tried to link up with the "blind empirical keying," not perhaps very successfully, by contrasting SVIB and MMPI with face-valid tests (e.g., Bell, Bernreuter). Although I now think the pure "dustbowl empiricism" keying doctrine too strong as I presented it 44 years ago, the paper made several points important at the time and is still being cited. It's an example of how something can be a half-truth worth pressing hard at a particular stage of scientific development.

There was no pressure at Minnesota to do a doctoral dissertation on the MMPI. My first thesis ideas involved the Rorschach or the T.A.T., I suppose because of my psychoanalytic interest, but it was easy for Hathaway to convince me—not by any contentiousness against projectives but by simple methodological points—that the designs were not capable of answering the interesting questions I was trying to put and, if souped up adequately, were too grandiose for a doctoral dissertation.

Hathaway and I were interested in the psychological source of "false positives" on the MMPI. Three factors had aroused my curiosity about this problem. First, I had several friends and relatives who, having taken the MMPI out of curiosity, generated quite pathological profiles. I knew these people intimately enough to be confident that while they may have had their problems in the psyche, they did not have a diagnosable mental disorder, they were not in therapy, and they were functioning academically, socially, and sexually. I had also been interested in the history of the Humm-Wadsworth Temperament Schedule (from which many of the MMPI items were borrowed); that test included a so-called "normal" component suggested by a theory of the psychiatrist Rosanoff. He conjectured that there was a sort of steadying, stabilizing, or "normalizing" component of temperament that acted on pathogenic traits of the psyche, the way we think of modifiers that protect against the development of a genetic disease. Third, I had listened to recordings of Hathaway's psychotherapy sessions with clients that Howard Hunt referred to as having a "psychiatric hypochondriasis." They weren't really hurting very much, but they thought they were, with excessive introspection and preoccupation with signs of poor mental health—a syndrome confined almost wholly to intellectuals familiar with psychological jargon.

So I embarked on a project of constructing a "normality scale" for the MMPI, proceeding according to the accepted blind empirical keying method by item analyzing the entire pool of 550 items on psychiatric patients whose MMPI's were matched individually, within a point or two scale by scale, with profiles drawn from the general file of Minnesota standardization "normals." The resulting scale I christened *N*. Studying the item content and the (sizable and consistently patterned) correlations with clinical scales and with unpublished nonclinical scales derived in a variety of ways, I became convinced that I was not measuring a "normalizing" buffer or safety component of temperament à la Rosanoff, but rather a test-taking attitude. The statistical rationale for applying such a scale had been provided in the discussion of suppressor variables in Paul Horst's *Prediction of Personal Adjustment* (1941).

After my doctorate Hathaway and I embarked on a project improving the suppressor variable, or test-taking attitude, calling people who got high scores "plus-getters" and people with low scores "defenders." We had the clinical impression that in some subjects plus-getting was downright faking at being bad, in others a cry for help, in others deviant semantical habits, and in others what has been called acquiescence. We studied various groups such as patients in a psychiatric unit under court order who obtained normal profiles and were presumably being defensive and nursing and medical students who attempted to present themselves either as mentally ill or as paragons of mental health. The items in my N-scale being culled more carefully, we finally ended up with a smaller set of items that behaved consistently in many substudies; this we called K. As in my dissertation, the relationships of K with the clinical scales and with the various trial keys that had been developed in finally choosing K allowed a coherent interpretation. The correlations were good-sized ones, holding up in normal and abnormal samples, in both sexes. Factor analysis of a half-dozen scales of suppressor type, constructed in very different ways and in different populations, yielded one large factor which accounted for all of the communal variance. We called it the *K factor*, published in Paterson's journal (Meehl and Hathaway, 1946).

We did suggest a possible psychological relationship between the K factor as a test-taking variable and the opposite poles of hysteroid and obsessional personality, and noted a mysterious relationship to education and social class which we didn't explain. But our emphasis in the original article on the K factor and in the subsequent paper with McKinley (McKinley, Hathaway, and Meehl, 1948), showing the optimal amount of statistical correction as a suppressor, focused mainly on the psychometric suppressor function. Subsequent research has made it clear that the truth about the psychological nature of this factor lies somewhere between our emphasis in the K articles and my original intent when investigating the Rosanoff notion. The K factor is not *merely* a test-taking attitude but has a somewhat broader meaning that one might characterize psychodynamically as the adequacy of repression, suppression, and denial as defenses. Most MMPI users consider a moderate amount of elevation on K as being healthy and only an extreme deviation as having pathological significance as in a hysteroid character or gross dissimulation.

Another of my early publications on the MMPI was the first "profile sorting" study in which the emphasis on the profile pattern, already generally shared in Minnesota circles, rather than doing single significance tests on scales against single formal diagnoses for which the scale was named, yielded positive results. My paper on profile analysis (Meehl, 1946), was adopted with improved "objective" profile pattern rules by one of my first doctoral candidates, Donald R. Peterson, in an impressive study (Peterson, 1954) involving patients who were diagnosed anxiety neurosis when seen but whose MMPI's appeared schizophrenic by the rough psychotic/neurotic profile rules I was then using. The MMPI, on follow-up several years later, turned out to be right more often than the psychiatrist, if we define "right" as predictive of a subsequent hospitalization with florid schizophrenia. This finding set my switches to be receptive to the concept of pseudoneurotic schizophrenia in the classic paper by Hoch and Polatin (1949).

Today, after Goldberg, Dawes, Weiner, and others have shown that linear combinations, even nonoptimally weighted, of variables can do about as well as configural approaches, most MMPI users still believe in eyeballing the configuration, whether or not they use any of the formal cookbook rules. Out of that early work of myself and Peterson, combined with the implications for profile interpretation of the clinical/actuarial comparisons (see below), and doubtless influenced by hearing my lectures on the problem in the introductory clinical psychology course, Minnesota Ph.D.s Marks and Seeman, and then Gilberstadt and Duker, developed the first "codebooks" for configural analysis of the profile generating trait symptom attributions of the patient. It remains unsettled whether Goldberg and Co.'s strong generalization that "linear composites are good enough" applies to the kind of configural taxonomy presented by these investigators and their computerized successors, Butcher, Caldwell, et al.

In my presidential address to the Midwestern Psychological Association (Meehl, 1956a) I argued strongly on philosophical, mathematical, and clinical grounds for development of "mechanical" or objective, actuarially based profile interpretations. My student Charles Halbower showed that actuarially derived attributions (based upon therapists' blind Q-sort procedures) did markedly better than experienced MMPI interpreters in describing patient's personalities, *both* in descriptive and psychodynamic aspects.

In 1951 Hathaway and I published the *Atlas for Clinical Interpretation of the MMPI*, presenting actuarial data on curve types (grouped by the numerical code he had recently invented) and case histories of patients with various codes. In the early 1950's we wasted considerable time and taxpayer money trying to compare the efficacy of a half-dozen measures of profile similarity, the results being so weak and inconsistent that we never submitted it for publication. We had not examined critically the whole notion of "overall similarity" between two personalities and concluded by wondering whether it could mean anything either clinically useful or theoretically illuminating.

My Midwestern Presidential Address led to an episode which puzzled and troubled me at the time as reflecting a serious problem in the profession. Though aware of the tension between clinical practitioners and academic experimental psychologists, I was surprised by its emotional intensity and was not skillful at defusing it. In presenting empirical data relevant to the idea of formalizing profile interpretation rather than "clinical eyeballing," I had told a couple of funny stories, employing some snide expressions about clinicians who reject objective data. Following the talk, which was well received both by scholarly clinicians and nonclinicians, I was invited for drinks in the hotel room of a distinguished experimental psychologist. There were a half-dozen of his experimental brethren along with two academic clinicians. The general flavor of the discussion was "Meehl, you sure gave those clinicians a good beating," an overinterpretation of my message which I found troublesome but let pass. The sentiment was that it was fine to see a clinical psychologist who also ran rats and knew how to take a partial derivative getting elected to a prestigious office and thereby provided with a big audience. The experimentalists had not seen my recent book on clinical and statistical prediction, but via the *anti*-actuarial arguments in that book, one of the clinicians was able to bring up the subject of the clinician's "third ear" and those kinds of inferences about the psychodynamics or historical past that it would be hard to imagine objectifying.

That there were such "pro-clinical" examples in the book came as a surprise to the experimentalists, and I was asked to illustrate this by examples. I used what to me are the most striking examples of an inferential process difficult to actuarialize and objectify, the interpretation of dreams in psychoanalysis. I had not then completed a full-scale analysis but I had some 85 couch hours with a Vienna-trained analyst, and my own therapeutic mode was strongly psychodynamic. I recounted examples from scholarly sources (e.g., Reik's *Listening with the Third Ear*) and some that I considered punchy and fascinating from my patients. The glowing warmth of the gathering cooled noticeably. A well-known experimental psychologist became suddenly hostile. He glared at me and said, "Now, come on, Meehl, how could anybody like you, with your scientific training at Minnesota, running rats and knowing math, and giving a bang-up talk like you just gave, how could *you* think there is anything to that Freudian dream shit?" I made the mistake of raising sophisticated epistemological questions, including some notions from current philosophy of science with which they seemed unfamiliar and perceived as obscurantist. It didn't degenerate into a real fight, but when I left the gathering I felt much less an honored pal of experimental psychologists than when I entered the room!

My teenage interest in logic and epistemology was focused on philosophy of science by my college freshman year, and while I did very well in science courses and found them interesting, books like Reichenbach's *Experience and Prediction* (1938) were more exciting. In 1940 Herbert Feigl, the Vienna Circle member who introduced logical positivism to English readers, joined the Minnesota faculty. Mostly self-taught, I was pleased when he said I had a better grasp of the subject than most fresh Ph.D.'s in philosophy, which shows one *can* learn about a subject without being lectured at. (Most faculty seem unable to believe this well-attested truth.) Feigl was slightly heretical among positivists because he worried about the mind/body problem, the justification of induction, and the reality of the external world. He was not a strict "operationalist" and was sympathetic to psychoanalysis. From the first class I had with him as a senior, we got along famously. After my Ph.D. we co-led a seminar in philosophical problems of psychology. In 1947 the philosopher Wilfrid Sellars came to Minnesota and a group of us began to meet one night a week at our homes to discuss epistemology. In 1953 Feigl, Sellars, and I founded the Minnesota Center for Philosophy of Science, which became the model for other such centers around the world. Eminent philosophers and scientists came to the Center for conferences, some for longer visiting professorships. The Center has been highly productive, its renowned *Minnesota Studies in Philosophy of Science* having recently published volume 12, with others in preparation. It is hardly necessary to say that my writings on methodological problems of psychology with Cronbach, MacCorquodale, Golden, and Rosen, as well as solo have been influenced by my Center connection. My papers on substantive matters (e.g., theory of schizophrenia, latent learning, taxometrics, prediction, psychoanalytic inference, psychiatric diagnosis) all show this influence clearly, whether or not I explicitly invoke philosophical concepts. The main change in my views over the years has been toward greater tolerance of "open concepts" and the recognition that what some psychologists proudly label "operational definitions" are pseudo-operational. For a short time I counted myself a Popperian, but today I am a "neo-Popperian" philosophical eclectic.

After World War II money became available for rapid expansion of psychology departments, and we decided that theoretical psychology, especially in the "soft" areas of clinical, counseling, social, and personality, was underrepresented. By 1950 we had added a group of "Young Turks" (K. E. Clark, L. Festinger, J. J. Jenkins, K. MacCorquodale, E. Rosen, W. A. Russell, S. Schachter, and myself) who could outvote our elders, although it rarely happened. There were vague anxieties which began to surface in faculty meetings, and after one somewhat stormy session in which I had played effectively a clarifier-and-compromiser role, Mike Elliott told several of the Young Turks that he was resigning as chair and "you should make Meehl chairman." At first I flatly refused, but they worked on me in a series of meetings until I capitulated. I was a Minnesota Ph.D., with feet in both applied and theoretical camps, and trusted by both old and young. I felt an obligation to hold the crew together during the transitional storm, and of course it was a prestigious job at the age of 31. Status I like, but my power motive is singularly weak. I have A's on the C.P.A. and Public Administrator keys of the SVIB—the "managerial" and "let's do this rationally" side of my nature. I was a pretty good chairman, kept the job for six years, wrote an excellent department constitution, held things together until they settled down, made some superb appointments (e.g., Gardner Lindzey, Lloyd Lofquist, Marvin Dunnette), and count my administrative stint as a worthwhile social contribution and a personal growth experience.

I quit, to everyone's dismay, because I got bored with it. Doubts I had as to my "social potency" were largely allayed. I exercised more leadership (e.g., strong urging of my views in faculty meetings) than is considered proper in these days of frenzied egalitarianism, and "lost" only one vote in six years, most votes being unanimous. I also learned two important facts: (1) bright, scientifically trained persons may become grossly irrational when issues of territory, dominance, and bonding are involved; (2) when you become alpha baboon, the communication tends to deteriorate. One knows these facts intellectually, but sitting in that chair gives a real appreciation of their power. Ethology rules the academy more than logic.

When I was a student and young faculty member, the big debate in learning theory was between Hull and Tolman and had in the 1940's converged on the phenomenon called latent learning. MacCorquodale and I published several experimental papers on that subject, some of which are still being cited. We showed, for example, that the Blodgett effect—a steep drop in time and errors following the first goalbox feeding—could be produced even when the feeding was not in the goalbox or at the end of a run, but in an extra-maze box, elevated and behind the entry box. Perhaps the Blodgett effect was attributable to a kind of "drive-conditioning," yielding a boosted Hullian drive-multiplier on differential habit strengths accumulated during the "latent" period. We also showed that rats make nearly errorless runs after prolonged free exploration of the Blodgett maze with no food reward involved. On the other hand, hungry rats who have been running the maze to goalbox food reward with culs closed will, when culs are open for the first time, enter every cul to get nearly 100 percent error scores. On the theoretical side, we published a tentative formalization of Tolman's expectancy theory, since its inexplicitness was one of the major Hullian complaints (MacCorquodale and Meehl, 1953b; 1954).

Following a conference at Indiana University (where Fred Skinner was chair), a group of us obtained a grant to spend the summer of 1950 without teaching or other responsibilities examining learning theories at Dartmouth College. Participants were W. K. Estes, S. Koch, K. MacCorquodale, C. G. Mueller, W. N. Schoenfeld, W. S. Verplanck, and myself. The book we produced, *Modern Learning Theory* (1954), was an influential work, and some think it sounded the death knell of Grand Theories in psychology. Its effect on me was marked, as I never published another rat experiment, partly because my colleague MacCorquodale became a Skinner disciple and lost interest in latent learning, but mostly because I became skeptical about the possibility of devising strong experimental tests of theories like Hull's or Tolman's. So many bright people had cooked up designs they hoped would be *experimenta crucis*, but it turned out they never quite were. I began to suspect there was something fishy about psychology and its theories. Unfortunately, my reading in philosophy of science about ad hoc postulates and auxiliary theories was not reassuring in this respect.

One traumatic event marred the time at Dartmouth and, in its long-term effects, had an adverse effect on my professional career: walking along a ledge above a stream at a place called the Flume in New Hampshire, I had a grand mal seizure. If MacCorquodale had not turned around and noticed me convulsing and pulled me back from the edge, I would not have survived. I had no history of seizures even as a small child and no epilepsy in my family. My EEG was definitely abnormal, with a focus in the right parietal area (the few seizures I had subsequently were definitely Jacksonian, beginning with a tingling numbness and twitching in the fingers in the left hand plus some nystagmus). I had an anomalous blood sugar curve and there was diabetes in my family, so the neurologist concluded that the seizure arose from a hypoglycemic influence on a focal brain lesion. I did not go on any medication at that time, and did not have another seizure for five years.

A more thorough neurological study showed only a mildly anomalous glucose tolerance curve, and the focal EEG convinced Abe Baker, the head of our Neurology Department, that while I should avoid carbohy-drate breakfasts, that was not the main problem. He put me on Dilantin, which controlled the seizures, but despite some clinical claims that Dilan-tin has negligible psychological side effects (although it can make your gums bleed), a perceptive psychiatrist colleague said that VA patients with brain injuries who were on Dilantin for long periods of time did suffer a definite side effect, a kind of dulling of affect and loss of energy or zest, though they did not become depressed. He told me that frequently the first indication of this long-term slow effect of Dilantin was observed not by the patient himself but by the wife, who would notice that he had "lost interest" in his usual hobbies of fly tying, playing golf, and the like. I am convinced that in the seven years (1955–61) when I was on Dilantin I had a definite lowering of hedonic tone and motivational level. A trial of going off Dilantin during that period resulted in another grand mal sei-zure, and then I had one during sleep, inferred from the fact that my tongue was badly chewed up in the morning. The best etiologic bet of the neurologists was a small brain scar attributable to the rheumatic fever I had had at age 22.

In 1962 my physician took me off Dilantin and put me on a new anti-convulsant which, as we subsequently learned, produces depression in a sizable minority of patients. It had that effect in my case, which was hard to put up with because it was the year I was president of the APA and had to write a presidential address, preside at meetings, deal with corre-spondence, etc. I called my former psychoanalyst (now at Hartford) who looked into the matter and recommended taking me off the new drug, whereupon my depression lifted in a couple of weeks. A depression on becoming APA president might exemplify Freud's "those wrecked by success," but since its onset was a year after my election and three weeks after the new drug, I incline to the pharmacologic interpretation. I now take an anticonvulsant (Cytadren) which has no side effects and has con-trolled the seizures for 30 years. This personal experience has given me more awareness of the problem of pharmacologic side effects than some clinicians have, especially the danger of believing negative statements arising from the fact that patients have not been observed for a long enough time period, or that minor signs of change have taken place so slowly that neither the patient nor any professional notices.

I cannot recall exactly when I became interested in the problem of clin-ical versus statistical prediction, but it was at least a decade before the pub-lication (1954) of the little book that made me somewhat famous (perhaps

I should better say, at least in clinical circles, "infamous"). I was lecturing briefly on the topic in 1944, and Arthur H. Brayfield, auditing the course, called my attention to T. R. Sarbin's classic paper (1942), which was in a sociology journal and hence unknown to me. I believe Paterson, in his individual differences class, mentioned a controversy in the 1920's between the industrial psychologists Max Freyd and Morris Viteles. Gordon Allport's monograph on personal documents appeared in 1942, and I read that monograph shortly after its appearance. It is easy to understand why someone with my psychological history should be fascinated by this question. Having undergone an intense bibliotherapeutic experience from reading Menninger, I had then studied under faculty who were skeptical about psychodynamic theories, especially those arising from clinical experience rather than from the experimental laboratory or statistical studies of clinic file data. This skepticism, which to more freewheeling psychologists appears as negativism, reflected a *methodological* more than a *substantive* stance. Paterson and Hathaway may have had an intellectual distaste for the content of Freudian ideas (including some based on personal resistances), but the main thrust of their complaint was not substantive, rather it was the lack of a trustworthy method for *testing* such conjectures from the evidentiary base provided by the psychoanalytic hour. No bright, reflective, theory-oriented student, coming to psychology from an interest in psychodynamics and exposed to this environment of first rate minds who gave it little credence—and not for silly reasons—could fail to experience intense cognitive dissonance and a strong, persistent need to resolve it.

I reread my 1954 book recently and am still of the opinion that it was an evenhanded treatment, which is what most—not all!—of the reviewers said, whether they were primarily identified with the clinical or the statistical approach to prediction. It was easy for me to be relatively fairminded about this charged topic, as I had strong identifications on both "sides." If you combine that with my interest in statistics and my epistemological interest continuing from our little group of teenage logicians, and add my exposure to some of the ablest intellects pursuing philosophy of science, you have a setup for writing a pretty good book.

In fact, I had trouble finding a publisher, and when Margaret Harding, director of the University of Minnesota Press, took it (as a favor to Psychology's chairman), she expected to lose money on it. When the book went out of print in 1973, it had gone through seven printings and sold 12,500 copies.

The reviews were uniformly favorable and some were enthusiastic, even "rave" reviews. Even those who didn't like the overall "message" said that I had *tried* hard to be evenhanded but hadn't quite succeeded. Both clinicians and anticlinicians reacted to it as a projective technique. The subtitle "A Theoretical Analysis and Review of the Evidence" shows what I was up to. Only one chapter dealt with empirical comparisons, and I did not view that chapter as the most important part of the book. Many more pages are devoted to defending the unique inferential activity of the clinician than to criticizing his predictive deficiencies. I had spent much time reflecting on clinical inference, especially during psychotherapeutic sessions, trying to get clear about just *where* the unique cognitive activities of the clinician took place and *why* it would be difficult to teach a clinically inexperienced "clerk," as I provocatively labeled the actuarial competitor, to do the same things.

The profession's reactions to this book, while I can hardly complain about their contribution to my becoming a highly visible psychologist, gave me my first real insight into the extent to which social scientists read superficially and carelessly. Perhaps this is because so much written in the "soft" areas is not conceptually precise, deep, or methodologically sophisticated, so that one gets into the habit of reading carelessly because it usually doesn't do you any harm!

An indirect derivative of that book was the "cookbooks" for MMPI interpretation discussed above, the fusion of computerization as a technology with the actuarial approach to making inferences from tests. I think motivations for resistance to its implications for a rational clinical practice are almost insurmountable. The subject no longer exercises the fascination it did for me as a young man, partly because the accumulation of the research evidence is so overwhelmingly on the actuarial side of the debate that reading it becomes rather boring, as one knows in advance how it will come out. Either the clinician will be about equal to the mechanical prediction formula or table, or (in around a third of the studies) he will be inferior. I do not see much point in showing that over and over again, since the studies currently available (over 100 in number) have shown it about clinicians of varying degrees of experience, with varying degrees of feedback opportunity to correct their errors, with various combinations of input information, making predictions over a qualitatively diverse domain of predictive tasks. Those who still resist the generalization that the human mind is not very good at this kind of thing now have the burden of proof to come up with clear and replicable studies showing the exceptions (Meehl, 1987).

In the years following publication of that book, I myself wrote some papers listing a half-dozen factors about the predictive task, subject matter, kind of data, etc., that might make the clinician superior in his success rate or, better, make a qualitative difference where the clinician would be able to come up with a prediction and there would be no actuarial method of *doing* so, accurate or otherwise. My own efforts at finding empirical examples of this superiority were confined to one of my predictively pro-clinical factors, namely, configural effects in multivariate profiles. Having MMPI protocols and MMPI experts available to me, I pursued that one, the diagnostic decision being the dichotomy between psychosis and neurosis, which is both theoretically interesting and of practical importance. It seemed a good bet for the study of configural effects in profile interpretation because one kind of psychotic patient has a different profile pattern from another kind of psychotic patient, so it seemed likely that a nonconfigural approach, such as a linear discriminant function of thirteen MMPI scales, would not capture the configural effects. Perhaps I suffered from some reaction formations, or perhaps a bit of defensiveness toward those clinicians who thought I was out to "beat up the clinician." I was hoping to find that the skilled clinical eye could discern features of the profile pattern that the statistician could not unless he went into configural effects—pairwise (Meehl, 1950c) and even perhaps higher order scale interactions.

This pro-clinical bias led to the only paper I've published in which the finding is literally incorrect, not merely not replicable but incorrect on my own data (Meehl, 1959b). I have a lame excuse in that the discriminant function job was done not by my research assistant but by one working for my colleague David T. Lykken, who had the same bias because he was interested in showing the superiority of an actuarial method that he had devised for profile interpretation. So when it turned out that the linear composite of MMPI scales did very poorly, he was willing to accept that result without careful scrutiny of the data, and so was I. It was foolish of both of us, for our different reasons, to trust a finding that showed a linear combination of scores doing as poorly as it did. Subsequently Lew Goldberg showed that even a nonoptimally weighted linear composite on that same set of data did as well as the more complicated configural rules Dahlstrom and I had developed (Meehl and Dahlstrom, 1960; Meehl,

1960a) or Lykken's "function-free actuarial box" method (Lykken, 1956). It was obvious that we were relying on a computational mistake. I cannot recall the details, but it came about from a transformation into octals for the computer, done under time pressure by a bevy of undergraduate research assistants. We should have known better.

Arguably I ought to spend more time propagandizing for the actuarial approach to clinical decisions, since the evidence is so massive and consistent. There never was any good reason to think that the clinician could do as well as an equation, unless one believes that the human mind is a good assigner of weights and consistent (reliable) applier of such weights. There are three kinds of jobs that computers still cannot do very well in comparison with the human brain: pattern recognition, language translation, and theory construction. To the extent that *some* clinical inferences have the same kind of cognitive character as these activities, we can expect the brain to do better than a computer. But almost the only such example is psychoanalytic inference from complex data, such as the analyst's knowledge of the patient's life history and previous interpretations, put together with the manifest content of a dream and the patient's free associations to it. Whereas if one is trying to forecast whether a subject will respond to one antidepressant rather than another, or will be a premature terminator of therapy in a VA clinic, or is a likely recidivist if paroled, or is a suicide risk, or is a better bet for Rational Emotive Therapy than behavior modification, or will survive in dental school, or will be washed out in flight training in the air corps—these kinds of predictions, for reasons that I set forth in 1954, are simply not predictive tasks which we should expect to be done well by an individual clinician or by a team meeting or case conference. There is a tremendous waste, involving patients' or taxpayers' dollars, as well as the human waste involved in predicting less efficiently than is mathematically possible, in current clinical practice whether in the mental health, criminal justice, or educational systems.

Clinical psychologists often say that it can't be right to diagnose and prognose actuarially because (nonpsychiatric) physicians haven't been doing it all these years, an argument which is worthless absent a showing that physicians do it better than an equation or table. Some psychologists seem unaware that both the interphysician reliability and the validity as shown by autopsy of diagnoses in organic medicine leaves much to be desired. I still hold to my original conception (Meehl, 1954, pp. 24–25 and references to the "broken leg case" in subsequent papers) that even a complex, souped up, multiply cross-validated actuarial method would make us slightly uneasy without some clinician available to take a look at the prediction with an eye to the possibility of a broken leg case. But I insist that this will not pay off unless the "last chance" clinician is highly sophisticated about the clinical actuarial problem. He has to know that true broken leg cases in psychopathology are rare, *so* rare that his departures from the actuarial prediction should be held down to a low rate, and if they increase appreciably, the long-term result will be a decrease in predictive efficiency. I am not optimistic about educating clinicians to think this way for mathematical and philosophical reasons, but the rising costs of health care may bring about a pragmatic movement, not explicitly principled, in that direction.

In the middle 1950's the Ford Foundation solicited psychologists in the social science domain to submit large grant proposals, and a group of us Minnesotans received a grant to study "the skilled clinician's description of personality, with emphasis on developing an adequate language." I was named the principal investigator, the other members of the team being Starke Hathaway, Donald Hastings (head of our Psychiatry Department), William Schofield, Bernard C. Glueck (my former analyst and analytic supervisor), and research assistant Walter B. Studdiford. Subsequently, the statistician and computer specialist Dean J. Clyde was added to the group. In the 1950's many clinicians and social psychologists were infatuated with Q-technique as an approach to the study of personality, and I must confess that this is one of those rare cases in which I fell for a fad. Only brief accounts of the project have been published (Glueck, Meehl, Schofield, and Clyde, 1964; Meehl et al., 1962; Meehl, Lykken, Schofield, and Tellegen, 1971), but I will cover it briefly because we still anticipate publishing at length.

We were troubled by the extent to which the items appearing in structured personality inventories and rating scales were drawn from a traditional and rather narrowly focused list of traits or behaviors thought to be relevant in psychopathology. Since the success of the MMPI and the SVIB were partly attributable to their deliberately diversified item content, we began by constructing an item pool as free as possible of these traditional restrictions. We did include item content from numerous rating scales in clinical use that had appeared in the literature, plus a provisional phenotypic and genotypic pool on which I had done some research (largely unpublished, but see Meehl, 1960a, p. 131). We also scanned the famous Allport-Odbert list of trait names; our group discussion eliminated, on an armchair basis of multiple criteria, most of those trait names, paying attention to Raymond B. Cattell's earlier screening of that list. We thought that even using ordinary human trait names as a source of item content was culturally stereotyped. For example, it is known that there are many more trait names in the dictionary mentioning undesirable human attributes than desirable ones. So we proceeded by what turned out to be a time-consuming and costly process that didn't yield as much as we had hoped. We gave both clinicians and intelligent, educated but not clinically trained people (e.g., professors of literature) brief episodes of randomly sampled speech or conduct from a variety of sources such as recorded interviews, social-work case histories, modern and Victorian novels, and even a random sample of episodes from the Bible. These readers were asked to write (or dictate) short paragraphs "characterizing" the sort of person who would do such-and-such and to assign a phrase or composite or disjunctive trait name. The team members were urged to concoct items from our clinical experience that could be sentences or short paragraphs for which there was no standard common language or psychiatric term available.

The initial 1,808-item pool in the Ford Project was a so-called phenotypic pool, not in the geneticist's sense, but in the sense that while it was not strictly behavior items, it was intended to be descriptive of traits summarizing first-order behavior dispositions with a minimum of theoretical inference. First, 586 items were eliminated when too many psychotherapists (after 25 interviews) said they could not make a judgment on the items because of insufficient data from the interviews. One surprising finding was how many items that dealt with rather simple and obvious aspects of the patients' behavior therapists claim to have heard nothing about. Although we did no formal statistical analysis, we were surprised that psychotherapists often learn amazingly little about overt features of the patients' sexual behavior. The lay stereotype that "shrinks like to make you talk about sex" does not seem to be true, even for psychotherapists in the broadly psychodynamic or Freudian tradition. Considerations of reliability, a crude measure of therapist effect versus true differences among patients, and an initial factor analysis combined with examination of quasiredundant content resulted in elimination of items down to a final set of 329. Factor analysis of the final pool of phenotypic items yielded 40 factors.

Unfortunately, for a variety of reasons not connected with the project, the research team dispersed geographically. Dr. Glueck, who had taken over as principal investigator when the Ford grant ran out and the project continued under NIMH support, made practical applications of the individual patients' factor profile at the Hartford Institute of Living. Starting with our results, he constructed several subpools (such as the doctor's subdeck and the nurse's subdeck), and for a period of time when he was research director at the Hartford Institute of Living, what had been rechristened the "Minnesota Hartford Personality Assay" was in routine use on the wards and in connection with research such as comparative efficacy of psychotropic drugs.

We had also constructed a genotypic pool consisting of the Murray needs and the twenty mechanisms of defense. A configural task assigned to our therapist raters was to identify the most salient Murray needs, together with the patient's preferred mechanism of defense, in turn linking this to the *salient objects* (spouse, country, or whatever). Those genotypic data have never been analyzed although they are on computer tape and as of this writing I am trying to find out whether the material is retrievable for research purposes, as there was a grave error made by someone years ago in discarding identifying information. Whatever else may be claimed for it, I think I can say that the Minnesota Hartford Personality Assay is one of the most carefully constructed sets of personal descriptors available. Despite the "unjudgeability" by therapists of items eliminated from the final MHPA instrument, the second-stage set (m = 1,222 items) was constructed with such loving care for content diversity and niceties of language that it provides a superb item source for research purposes. We were therefore surprised and disappointed when it found negligible use by clinicians and personologists.

A spinoff from the Ford Project was a theory of schizotypy as a personality syndrome, socially learned on the basis of a hereditary neurological disorder ("schizotaxia") presented in my APA presidential address (Meehl, 1962b). Today this conception is almost trite among informed persons, but it was a radical (and unacceptable) doctrine in psychological circles a quarter century ago. I am currently working on a revised formulation, but see Meehl (1972c) and Gottesman and Shields (1982). I contributed numerous "novel" schizotypal items to the Ford Pool, based on my clinical experience and the literature, and developed a schizotypal checklist for detection of the Hoch-Polatin syndrome (Meehl, 1964). Scores of clinical researchers and training directors have requested copies of the manual, but for some reason very little use of it has ever surfaced in the literature. Another spinoff of the project was a method for reducing the subjective element in interpreting psychometric factors, the "recaptured-item technique (RIT)" (Meehl, Lykken, Schofield, and Tellegen, 1971).

Whether the main results and spinoffs have warranted the Ford grant money and brain time expended I do not know, but I am inclined to doubt it. A possible exception may be my work on developing new taxometric methods, which has been my main research preoccupation in recent years (Golden and Meehl, 1978; Meehl, 1965b, 1973b, 1979, 1986b; Meehl and Golden, 1982). I consider taxometrics potentially as important as the dimensional statistics of classical psychometrics (e.g., multiple factor analysis, regression theory, and multidimensional scaling). I do not share the prejudice of American psychologists against types, taxa, and disease entities. "No types, only dimensions" was one of D. G. Paterson's favorite principles, and within the "normal" range of individual differences, it is doubtless valid as a strong best bet. But the dogma that *every* class name is merely a crude way of denoting regions in a dimensional hyperspace is not safe in the domain of psychopathology. My approach to the taxometric search problem is heterodox, as I am skeptical of cluster methods, uninterested in the usual Fisherian issues (M.L.E.?), and instead favor emphasis on numerical agreement among nonredundant estimates of the *sample* latent values ("consistency tests"). My efforts in this area have been hampered by my inadequate mathematical education, although it is better than 90 percent of psychologists and 99 percent of clinicians! There's a moral there somewhere.

My first psychotherapy patient (1942–44) was a severe obsessive-compulsive who I now think may have been schizotypal. He had a morbid fear of damaging his brain, whether by rapid or sudden motion, minor shocks, poor diet, "overwork," or emotional excitement. An ex-physics major of high IQ, he had quit college because his phobic avoidance of protracted study (brain fatigue!) led to poor grades. Orgasms being intense, he avoided sexual activity, including masturbation. He once walked up twelve stories for a dental appointment, lest the elevator acceleration damage his brain. He exemplified the fact that a severe neurosis can be more incapacitating than some psychotic conditions.

I initially treated him, doubtless unskillfully, by a mix of Rogersian and psychodynamic therapy, with no results. He had at age twelve killed a boy "accidentally" by shooting him in the head, an event whose thematic relation to the brain obsession he easily accepted with the usual lack of affect. Hathaway suggested that since he was so hypercathected on intellect and could relate to me on that basis, that was the only leverage I had, so why not use it somehow? We embarked on a series of philosophical discussions in which I challenged his complicated theories about the neurophysiology of "pure" versus "derived" pleasure and repeatedly demonstrated that, on his own premises, he was depriving himself of net pleasure more than cumulative minimal brain damage would. He was ingenious and resourceful in argument, but so was I. We enjoyed our conversations immensely. His emphasis on intellect and his need for me to perceive him as internally consistent and rational within his own premises slowly moved him into doubting the long-term rationality of his constricted way of life. I then shifted to systematic desensitization (pre-Wolpe!) and accompanied him on walks and automobile rides. He became 90 percent "cured" of the symptoms, returned to college, became a high school physics teacher, married, and twenty years later was symptom-free and functioning effectively and contentedly.

This rewarding experience as a healer using cognitive and behavioral methods contributed to my later open-mindedness to Joseph Wolpe, Albert Ellis, Aaron Beck, and the operant behavior modifiers. But at the time I remained psychodynamically oriented. I had 85 couch hours with a Vienna-trained analyst (H. S. Lippman, M.D.) and later 300 with B. C. Glueck, M.D., trained at the Columbia Psychoanalytic Clinic under Sandor Rado's aegis. With Glueck I did a couple of controls and a continuous case seminar with three psychiatrists. For several years I practiced fairly classically, enjoyed the work, and I believe benefited some of my patients. But I could not help noticing that my rare departures from classical technique were often effective, and after some contacts with Albert Ellis I increased their frequency. I was also puzzled by the rather low correlation between interpretative closure and therapeutic results. At present I would have to call myself "eclectic," although I dislike the term, because it often means pure seat-of-the-pants therapy with no attempt at theoretical integration. I still have a couch in my office and from time to time put a client on it, imposing the Fundamental Rule. Otherwise I am quite "active" (although less so than Ellis) and employ several interview tactics, including information-giving (e.g., learning theory, sex differences, primate ethology, genetics). At times I even encourage "intellectualizing" discussion of ethics, politics, and other cognitive frameworks bearing on the client's lifestyle. If asked by colleagues or sophisticated prospective patients to label my approach, I sometimes say "mixed rational-emotive and psychoanalytic." As would be expected from my Menninger experience, "understanding how the mind works" is an important element in my psy-

chotherapeutic interest, and in this respect the work is often frustrating.
I don't think we understand neurosis or its treatment well in any scientific
sense, and I have not found reading the process research on psychotherapy
illuminating.

From 1957 to 1962 I served on the American Board of Professional Psychology and still favor academic clinicians being boarded. As an examinee
(the first "non-grandfather" to be appointed) I had felt strongly about the
poor quality of the written examination, and there had been numerous
complaints. I was astonished to learn that in ten years the Board had never
researched the scoring reliability of its research exam, an essay test scored
in the usual "global" manner. Ken Clark, Ed Henry, and I (Ph.D.'s from
Ohio State and Minnesota!) insisted on a reliability study, and it turned
out that the interscorer reliability was .25 (i.e., an examinee's score depended 4 percent on his behavior and 96 percent on "chance," the random
assignment of readers). Ed Henry explained the "school solution" scoring
system used in the War College, which preserves the essay format (requiring inventive *production* rather than mere answer *selection*) but
achieves a high interrater reliability by means of a content checklist. I was
asked to build a school solution research exam, and it had a scoring reliability of .86. My prize effort was an imaginary experimental report that
contained 31 errors in design, analysis, and interpretation—some examinees only spotted two of these! We also constructed a large pool of
multiple-choice items, building each annual exam stratified by content
areas, the domain proportions being based on a questionnaire sent to recent examinees.

Soon after Clark, Henry, and I went off the Board, all this was abandoned, mainly because "too many people didn't like or understand it."
The lesson I took from this was twofold: (1) psychologists outside the lab,
clinic, or library may not think like psychologists; (2) don't invest time in
problem solving if the solution's acceptability is a matter of politics, PR,
ideology, etc., rather than scientific objectivity.

Before reading Menninger, I had intended to be a lawyer, and on the
SVIB my law interest score has equaled my psychology score in five re-
testings over 48 years. (Around age twelve I studied and mastered my father's six-volume book set on law and in junior high school became expert
on *Robert's Rules*, the school paper's typifying Meehl quote on graduation
being "I rise to a point of order." In watching baseball games I even
tended to identify with the umpire!) In the 1960's I served as an expert
witness in two notorious murder cases and audited several law school

courses. For ten years I cotaught, with a lawyer and a psychiatrist, a class in Law School. I read extensively in jurisprudence, cotaught a class in it, and felt honored when the law faculty voted unanimously to okay my teaching it alone. (Law students are great fun to teach, as are philosophers; psychologists are a poor second; medical students and psychiatry residents are boring.) I authored or coauthored several articles in law reviews, including one cited in a landmark federal case (Lessard v. Schmidt) on civil commitment (see Livermore and Meehl, 1967; Livermore, Malmquist, and Meehl, 1968; Meehl, 1970a, 1971c).

I think that in addition to the excitement of the courtroom scene, and the interesting conceptual puzzles presented, one appeal of forensic psychology to an academic is the application of the intellect in deadly earnest. One is playing chess for blood. There is a certain attraction, even if one is not strongly power oriented, in knowing that if you succeed in convincing the judge or jury on the rational merits of your evidence and arguments, things will happen accordingly, backed up by the full power of the state. This is not an admirable motive, but I believe it is a real one. More altruistically, to write a scholarly article that influences the holding of a federal judge and thereby *directly* affects literally thousands of mentally ill patients and millions of dollars of taxpayer money is a more clear and concrete contribution to society than most scientific research or classroom teaching. We hope that our scientific papers and our instruction of graduate students make some difference in the world, benefiting persons that we never see face to face; but the causal connection there is not quite as obvious as a law review paper that influences courts. In this respect, forensic psychology carries a punch to it for an academic analogous to the practice of psychotherapy.

Early attainment of tenure, good salary, and professional recognition mean that a person not insatiably driven by motives of power and prestige is free to do pretty much what he wants, given the permissive mores of the academy. Arguably this can be a disadvantage, allowing dispersal of energies rather than strong focus on long-term theme-centered research programs. I detect some ambivalence here, having the feeling "I could have made more significant contributions, had I played it right." But this is an unrealistic appraisal, because my cyclothymic temperament, low boredom tolerance, and the psychological generators of the interest pattern that got me into psychology would have made such long-term concentration psychologically impossible. Also the early death of my parents, especially my father's suicide, connected as it was with excessive ambition, generated in me a somewhat easygoing approach to productivity. This is comfortable and prophylactic, but rather close to what high-achieving academics call "laziness." Life is short, and one should enjoy it as much as possible. As long as I meet my formal professional commitments, one of the joys of academia is feeling free to pursue whatever interests me. (In ethics and politics I am a moral minimalist, contractualist, and libertarian.)

The result of these attitudes on my scholarly reading and writing was a more varied kind of output than most social scientists permit themselves or feel that they can get by with. Scanning my publication list, I come up with some pretty strange creatures. I find papers that I am proud of for their high-level conceptualization, but which few psychologists have read or even heard of. Examples: several papers on the metaphysical mind/body problem; an article with Michael Scriven in *Science* on the compatibility of science and ESP (Meehl and Scriven, 1956); a paper with Wilfrid Sellars on the philosophical concept of "emergence" (Meehl and Sellars, 1956); a paper on the relation between religion and mental health (Meehl, 1957a); a paper on the treatment of guilt feelings, delivered to the American Catholic Psychological Association (Meehl, 1960b); the article on parapsychology in the *Encyclopaedia Britannica* (Meehl, 1962a); a paper on Feigl's mind/body identity thesis, which some able philosophers have told me is one of the best they have ever read on this subject (Meehl, 1966); articles in law reviews on the insanity defense, civil commitment, relations of clinical psychology to delinquency (Livermore and Meehl, 1967; Livermore, Malmquist, and Meehl, 1968; Meehl, 1970a, 1971c); a paper with Feigl on determinism and freedom (Feigl and Meehl, 1974); two papers in a philosophy journal on the problem of distinguishing psychokinesis from precognitive telepathy (Meehl, 1978b, 1978c); an article in the *American Political Science Review* on a paradox in voting behavior, calling into question the currently fashionable econometric analyses of why people vote as they do or why it is rational to bother voting at all (Meehl, 1977); and an article on statistical procedures for estimating the completeness of the fossil record (Meehl, 1983c). I had a lot of fun writing these and would not want to have not written them, although I confess to the paranoid thought that if you publish in certain scholarly areas without the required union card, you are in danger of going unread.

In the early 1960's Dr. Robert D. Wirt organized and chaired a conference (the "Stillwater Conference") to discuss the training of clinical psychologists and particularly to raise the question of an alternative doctorate for practitioners. The only strong advocates of the Psy.D. were Hathaway, Wirt, and myself. Reflecting on the barrage of objections by which we were met, both by the academics *and*—to my surprise—by scholarly professionals from the practitioner community, led me to write a defense of the alternative doctorate (Meehl, 1965a, 1971b). I maintain that nobody has written satisfactory rejoinders to my rebuttals of the usual objections. Though this paper exerted some influence, I decided that there was no point in fighting a losing battle. While I still defend the idea of a Psy.D., I do not myself enjoy instruction with the kind of student who is likely to take it! I sometimes think there is something odd about my mind in matters of this sort. Many psychologists don't advocate anything they wouldn't want to be a part of implementing; indeed, they tend to oppose it on ideological or theoretical grounds. I have never understood this attitude, and I believe some consider me inconsistent when I strongly favor something I would prefer not to have anything to do with. The same is true for me with regard to the distinction between theoretical interest and social importance. People are shocked, especially the liberal intelligentsia that preponderate in social science, if you tell them you are not much interested in a current social problem, and they infer that means you don't have any ethical opinions regarding it. Why should this be? There are all sorts of matters that are terribly important which one does not necessarily find intellectually interesting to think, read, talk, or write about. I am sure that garbage disposal and sanitary sewage are far more important to human welfare, my own included, than mathematical taxometrics or the mind/body problem, but I do not find the technology or economics of sewage disposal an interesting subject to discuss at a cocktail party.

Among the miscellaneous papers I have written are several labeled "methodological," and while they deal with psychology as a subject matter they are mainly contributions to the philosophy of science. In 1947 Kenneth MacCorquodale and I were having a late-night conversation (while we consumed a fifth of rye whiskey) about Hull's famous intervening variable diagram and whether those so called intervening variables were truly such in Tolman's original usage. We decided there was a confusion between intervening variables and what we unfortunately labeled "hypothetical constructs"—(they were not *constructions* in the sense of Bertrand Russell, but we didn't realize that at the time)—and we arrived at a three-fold distinction between the two classes of concepts which seemed persuasive and illuminating. We expected that on awakening in the morning the glow would have gone; as it turned out, we both woke up with a mild hangover but with a persisting conviction that we had arrived at a clarification worth calling to the attention of the profession. Much of the debate between the Hullians and their opponents involved methodological questions about what kinds of concepts were acceptable in science and what kinds were not. We published a paper (1948b) that became widely cited, and disputed, "On a distinction between hypothetical constructs and intervening variables." In 1955 Lee Cronbach and I, as a result of deliberations of the APA committee on test standards, applied this distinction to the problem of psychometric validity in a paper that is considered a minor classic, "Construct validity in psychological tests."

In the early 1960's the Psychology Department heard a series of visitors in one of the "soft areas" who reported on ongoing research programs which were excessively ad hoc. Each new ad hoc hypothesis concocted to preserve a theory from falsification generated another series of experiments, some of which panned out, others not, leading to more ad hockery, and so on. These research enterprises did not appear to be converging on anything solid, and the ad hoc adjustments were multiplying as fast as the facts, so that the situation is what philosophers and historians of science would, if they use Lakatos' terminology (Lakatos, 1970, 1974; Lakatos and Musgrave, 1970), call a degenerating research program, although sufficient to publish papers and achieve academic promotion! It seemed to me that there was something radically wrong with the whole strategy, but the thing I focused on was a point about statistical significance tests arising from the fact that in the life sciences the null hypothesis is always false. I wrote a paper in *Philosophy of Science* (1967a) pointing out that improvement in precision and sampling stability in the hard sciences subjects a theory to graver danger of refutation; if the theory is strong enough to make point or range predictions, the more sensitive the design or precise the measurements, the greater the chances of detecting a discrepancy between the facts and the theory's predictions. In the soft areas of psychology, where the theory is too weak to generate predictions stronger than directional trends, as the sample size and the reliability measurements increase, the statistical power function rises, and hence the probability of refuting the null hypothesis (which is always false) approaches unity regardless of the theory's verisimilitude. I subsequently developed this line of reasoning further in a paper (1978a) which reached a wider audience among psychologists, and even in this day of easy photocopying I received 1,000 reprint requests before I quit counting. As of this writing I have in press a long paper on the problem which will appear in the Cronbach *Festschrift* (Meehl, in press a).

I have been gently needled by friendly colleagues for writing more "think pieces" than empirical studies, especially in recent years. I enjoy it more, and I'm better at it, as shown by the long-term citation rates of my work in the *Science Citation Index*. Indeed, I daresay few highly visible psychologists have publication lists so preponderantly theoretical and methodological as mine. The profession does not usually view much "armchairing" favorably. Colleagues even josh me about my being a Donald G. Paterson undergraduate advisee, and then a Starke R. Hathaway Ph.D. (both of them disliking—almost despising—"mere theory") and yet writing so many more "think pieces" than empirical studies. Ben Willerman once asked me, "Paul, you are so fascinated by Freud's theory of dream work and tell us persuasive stories from your psychoanalytic practice. Why haven't you done any experiments to test it?" To which I replied (shockingly but honestly), "Ben, it's because *I don't know how!*"

In my own defense, I should point out that the published track record is misleading in this respect, for reasons largely out of my control. During the years 1948–65 I was engaged in three major research projects which occupied thousands of hours but have led to scanty publication. One was on political behavior with political scientist Herbert McClosky, psychologist Kenneth E. Clark, and sociologist Arnold Rose. We built some good instruments and collected a large body of data which have been thoroughly analyzed and are quite fascinating. But the team members dispersed or died, and our leader McClosky (now at Berkeley) became otherwise involved, so the projected book was never written. I was also working with MacCorquodale on a large-scale study of drive and reinforcement parameters in the Skinner box, and after running a couple of thousand rats, we discovered a systematic "box effect" that confounded things so badly that the intended parametric interactions were uninterpretable. The Ford Project on personality descriptors led to a wide-coverage and finely honed instrument, and we published a factor analysis of the findings. As noted earlier, through incredible inadvertence the original raw data were apparently lost—data that were qualitatively and quantitatively unparalleled, including 248 therapist ratings after 10 or more hours of contact on 791 patients, using a phenotypic and psychodynamic item pool of the highest excellence. These three bad outcomes make one wonder whether The Cosmos intended me to stick to my armchair!

But I cannot deny that my personality also plays a role in this think-piece preponderance. My cyclothymic temperament leads me to become bored with most subject-matters after a while. There is also an element of passivity in me that perceptive clinicians come to discern but that is missed by persons who are struck by my verbal fluency and high social potency, especially in the domain of intellect. (Perhaps this is why I enjoyed psychoanalytic therapy more than RET, although the latter is more cost-effective.) At heart I am more of a knowledge-absorber, knowledge-integrator, and knowledge-transmitter than knowledge-producer. I read more widely than most psychologists and enjoy nonpsychology reading far more than the strictly "professional" stuff. For example, during my dozen years as a Lutheran, I read over 300 treatises on theology. When I was on the Law School faculty I read more books and articles on jurisprudence and the appellate decision process than any of my law colleagues had done (e.g., none of them had suffered through Roscoe Pound's six-volume *Jurisprudence*, but I did). I have enough scholarly expertise in philosophy of science to teach a graduate course in it, and my philosopher colleague Herbert Feigl once said that any time I wanted to switch fields he could write me a strong letter of recommendation as a philosophy professor. Now all this "Renaissance man" syndrome may be good or ill—the bright students rather like it for a change—but one cannot do it without sacrificing time from empirical research. I have chosen to do so, despite experiencing twinges of scientific guilt about it. (I was pleased to be officially appointed Adjunct Professor of Philosophy because that put an institutional seal of approval on my armchair doings.) Certainly it is not a safe model for a young psychologist to emulate, and I am careful to point that out to those who identify too strongly with me.

These psychodynamic and external happenstance factors are not the whole story, as they are strongly confluent with two rational considerations that (I like to think) play the main role in my preference for writing "think-pieces." The first rational consideration is that a scientist should do what he is good at, and I am better at conceptualizing than at experimenting. My synthetic-creative talents are only somewhat superior to most psychologists (cramped by the dustbowl empiricist flavor of my Minnesota training?); but my analytic powers are, I believe, exceptionally strong, and well cultivated through long association with top-caliber philosophers of science. Knowledge is advanced in several ways, and it has been my experience that there are many more psychologists who are capable of performing a clever and replicable experiment than there are high-level ideators who can create a novel concept or deeply analyze a familiar one, especially one in controversy. Living off the taxpayer, I feel it appropriate to do what I am best at, especially since (1) it's rare, and (2) I find it more fun.

The second rational consideration is more important, less narcissistic, but somewhat controversial. (For younger readers of these autobiographies, it could be morale lowering and bad career advice—but we were asked to be as frank and revelatory as seemed fitting.) By age 35 or so, I had come reluctantly to the sad conclusion that *most empirical research in psychopathology on theoretical matters is nearly worthless, that it does not prove much of anything interesting, one way or another* (as the Dartmouth Conference of 1950 had, alas, convinced me of the weakness of the "grand learning theory systems," a view that is now commonplace). This was not a snobbish dismissal of what others were doing; my research files were full of studies—both on rats and on patients—which were clearly publishable but were never written up.

Schizophrenia provides a good example. In my APA presidential address (1962b) I propounded a neurological-genetic theory of schizophrenia that was pretty heretical, especially among clinical psychologists. During the ensuing decade I took some friendly criticism from colleagues about not having published empirical research on this theory. They assumed I was content to have concocted an interesting theory (they were 60 percent correct about that) and was not even *trying* to research it. But I was. In the decade surrounding that 1962 lecture, I had a half-time R.A. and was attempting to study the schizotypal personality in several ways. We conducted numerous statistical analyses of large samples of VA hospital patient histories, built a Q-sort for the Hoch-Polatin syndrome, analyzed MMPI and checklist data on my private practice cases, studied psychosomatic and other nonpsychotic symptoms and traits in schizophrenic veterans, collected self-descriptive "good" and "bad" adjectives on schizophrenic and borderline cases, studied MMPI "test misses," identified a strong "cognitive slippage" factor in the Ford Project item pool, tried to replicate the old Worcester findings as to vestibular nystagmus, entered Roget's *Thesaurus* to locate possible schiz-related low-frequency adjectives, studied MMPI shifts on remission from a schizophrenic episode, constructed a nonpsychotic schizotype-specific MMPI key, etc. A lot of thought, time, and work went into these projects, and most were publishable, but we never published them. Why not? *Because while they were mildly interesting and largely consistent with my views, they did not strongly corroborate or refute my theory or anyone else's.*

Meanwhile, as this discouraging truth was becoming clear to me, Popper's *Logic of Scientific Discovery* had appeared in English (in 1959), and his emphases on strong tests, noninductivism, falsification, etc., were leading topics of discussion in the Minnesota Center for Philosophy of Science. I finally concluded that the whole social science tradition of testing weak theories by H_0-refutation was a methodological mistake, and I found that Popper, Lakatos, and some local statisticians agreed with me. I realized sadly that if a clinical student needed to "learn about schizophrenia" in a hurry, I would have him read and reread Bleuler's 1911 classic, then spend 100 hours talking with recent and chronic schizophrenics, then read the research on schizophrenia genetics, and finally the research on schizophrenic soft neurology. But I would *not* have him waste his precious time reading the hundreds (no, thousands) of research studies conducted by psychologists, whether psychometric or experimental. The work is usually inconclusive or trivial, sometimes both. This vast and dismal literature rarely tells us anything we didn't know (when it "refutes" clinical experience, who believes it?) and has not, in my opinion, told us anything really important about the disease nor helped appreciably to settle any of the controversies concerning it. Seeing this, I resolved not to make any more empirical efforts until I had (1) developed my theory further, (2) found a few schizotaxia indicators in the literature that show *replicably large* separations, and (3) found or invented taxometric methods capable of testing numerical point predictions from a strong genetic model. As of this writing, these three conditions have finally been met, and I am codesigner of a research project that we believe will definitely corroborate or refute my conjecture that schizophrenia is a low-probability ($p<.10$) decompensation of a soft neurological integrative disorder (schizotaxia) which is inherited as an autosomal dominant of 100 percent penetrance. We believe we can now *answer* these questions, but it has not been possible to do it until the last decade or so.

My methodological skepticism about conventional significance testing has meanwhile engendered some good think pieces about that dangerous topic (Meehl, 1967a, 1978a, in press a), and the recent literature indicates that they have begun to have an impact. My current thinking and writing are oriented to formulating a positive methodological program (I call it "neo-Lakatosian") to replace the conventional H_0-refutation strategy. If I can make even a small advance in this direction, that, plus my earlier destructive criticism of the received doctrine, will be worth a dozen or two average-quality empirical studies that I might have done instead—and that might only have added to what Lakatos called the "intellectual pollution" of the social sciences (Lakatos, 1970, p. 176n).

If I have a McDougall "master-sentiment," it is that of rationality, emphasizing *critical open-mindedness*. I have been rather little moved by desires for power, money, or helping (collective) mankind. My professional-status motive, the academicians' *n Recognition*, is fairly strong, but I think weaker than in most high achievers I know, witness my long-standing nonattendance at APA conventions, the declining of almost all speaking invitations or book-chapter opportunities, and general "nonpoliticking." (Given these attitudes and habits, it is odd that I was elected APA president, and I wouldn't stand a chance today. Publishing in both "hard" and "soft" areas, or "pure" and "applied," was important during the postwar period, witness the names Hilgard, Sears, Mowrer, Cronbach, Osgood, Miller, Hebb, Lindzey.) While critical of many societal arrangements and deeply cynical about politicians, I am not a world-improver (exception: I was a passionate and, for me, active opponent to the Vietnam War). My undergraduate socialism stemmed primarily from the (mistaken) opinion that a socialist economy would be more efficient, rather than from compassion for the poor, hatred of the rich, or the usual academic's hostility to businessmen. Voltaire said that in contemplating human affairs, those endowed with an excess of feeling are moved to weep, those with an excess of intellect, to laugh. I am clearly of the second sort.

The overarching value of being open-minded, shutting no cognitive doors, entertaining even strange possibilities (fusion of *n Cognizance* and *n Play*) I see as stemming from a combination of parental precept + reward + modeling ("one should be *fair*"), Mr. Smith's science class, early reading of authors like Bertrand Russell and science journalist Albert Edward Wiggam, and my "teenage logicians" peer group—all converging upon a genetic makeup that included high *g*, low *n Dominance*, low *n Affiliation*, and a certain kind of "passivity" (contemplation over action). While this fair-mindedness obsession, an Allportian *radix*, has helped me to make scholarly contributions, it has its bad side. Example: I spent time and money (when I hadn't much of either early in my career) learning Rorschach with Samuel Beck and Bruno Klopfer and then doing a lot of it for a while, because I wanted to be sure the Minnesota skepticism about projectives wasn't biasing me. I finally realized that the useful yield of incremental validity did not warrant regular use of these instruments, at least as administered by me. I could better have learned that early from the research literature, plus the anecdotal fact that the "masters" Beck and Klopfer, while clinically perceptive men, were in reality *not* all that impressive when interpreting blind. The plain fact is that I wasted a lot of time making sure that I was not being "intellectually unfair" about projectives.

This unity-thema of critical open-mindedness (plus more extensive reading in intellectual history than most psychologists indulge in) has sometimes made me receptive to possibilities that are strictly taboo among scientifically trained intelligentsia. ("Taboo" is not too strong a word here, my experience shows.) The ideology of scientism (as a metaphysic, an epistemology, and a group-shared faith) proscribes certain substantive concepts as well as extrascientific ways of knowing. Colleagues find me paradoxical (some would say inconsistent) here, because while I don't understand or trust unscientific ways of knowing, I do entertain substantive notions that are anathema to almost all American psychologists. Example: I am inclined to think there is something to telepathy, and if forced to bet a large sum one way or another, I would wager affirmatively. My friends invoke the "rational conservatism" of science (which, in general, I accept as a sensible *policy*) and tell me this is being too open-minded for my own good. Example: Despite its Teutonic metaphysics, Wagnerian bombast, dogmatism, and numerous factual errors, Oswald Spengler's *Decline of the West* is, I believe, a work of genius containing profound truths about culture and history and disturbingly diagnostic of our present society. Most scientific historians view Spengler as nothing more than a mystical and fascistic crank, so I was pleasantly surprised when a recent issue of *Daedalus* counted the *Decline* among the ten most important historical works of our first half century.

The most shocking heresy to which critical open-mindedness has led me is skepticism about the received doctrine of organic evolution. Students and colleagues react to my (rare) overt expressions of this view with a mixture of disbelief and amused tolerance, the flavor being, "Well, Meehl is a very bright and reflective man, so we will just have to put up with some funny ideas from him now and then." Some attribute my grave doubts about neo-Darwinism to a Lutheran upbringing—quite wrong, as my minimal childhood religious exposure was to a tepid, liberal Methodism, my parents and the clergymen I met being comfortable evolutionists. But I find it quite useless to explain to people that my objections to evolutionary theory are philosophical and scientific, not religious. I have had no denominational connection for a quarter century, and presently hold no theological opinions. I believe Kant's third great question is unanswerable, but if pressed to speculate about the untestable, I would opt for a kind of nonethical polytheism—a doctrine hardly suitable for spiritual support or edification!

An autobiography in this series is no place for polemics about a nonpsychological theory, but since my aberrant views about evolution have been a matter of some curiosity, speculation, and gossip, it is perhaps permissible to list here, without argument, my scientific objections, which are (1) the improbable "chance" origin of the genetic code, (2) the mutual dependence of DNA and complex cellular organelles ("chicken-or-egg" problem), (3) the joint teleology of structures like the vertebrate eye or the neural wiring for the bee's communicative dance, (4) the central "improving" role of random mutations when the thousands of known examples are uniformly disadvantageous or at best neutral, and (5) the absence of transitional forms in the fossil record. There has been increasing concern about these terrible conceptual and empirical difficulties among scientists in recent years (see, e.g., Denton, 1985, and references cited therein) but no real doubts as to the theory itself. Nor will there be any, because evolution is unique among scientific theories in having no imaginable scientific alternatives. Hence it will be held by educated denizens of our culture, regardless of its theoretical implausibility or empirical counterevidence. For my part, I don't believe macroevolution by accumulated random mutations ever took place, and I regret that I won't be around a thousand years hence to see whether the verdict of history vindicates me. Whether my deviant views on this question, held for some 40 years now, have significantly lowered my credibility as to other scholarly matters I do not know.

Writing this autobiography has turned out to be more fun than I had anticipated, providing an opportunity to collect my thoughts about the psychologist's enterprise and my modest role in it, and fond remembrances of persons and tasks. The pleasure is tempered by realizing the ephemerality of much of what goes on in our field, and some ambivalent regrets about how I have conducted my professional life. Although I do not see myself as a highly ambitious person and I believe that I have rarely done any work *mainly* with visions of social acclaim, like everybody I enjoy narcissistic rewards. I think the profession has delivered such ego pellets to me somewhat more than I deserve, in terms of lasting major contributions, but this is the kind of thing that the subject of an autobiography is probably not the best person to assess. I sometimes think that professional recognition came to me too early "for my own good," if that makes any sense. My work on the MMPI, latent learning, and methodological questions was becoming fairly widely cited by the time I was in my late twenties; I became chairman of one of the top psychology departments in the world at the age of 31; I was president of the Midwestern Psychological Association at 34; recipient of APA's Distinguished Scientific Contributor award at 38; and APA president at 42. Since 1968 I have enjoyed the prestigious academic title of Regents' Professor at Minnesota. I've been elected to the American Academy of Arts and Sciences and received the Bruno Klopfer Distinguished Contributor Award in personality assessment. In 1987 I was elected to the National Academy of Sciences. I have a respectable tally in the *Science Citation Index* (some articles 40 years old are still being cited) and a few in the *Humanities Citation Index*. So, as regards "professional success," I have had my share of it, and earlier in life than most. My book on prediction is considered a minor classic, although I wish it had a greater impact than it has on clinical practice, from the standpoint both of helping patients and of saving taxpayer dollars. Colleagues perceive me as having contributed to a more quantitative/ objective approach to clinical work, but I am unable to detect much impact in most clinical settings. An exception would be the actuarial (now increasingly computerized) interpretation of MMPI profiles; but even there the careful validation and empirical comparison of programs has lagged uncomfortably behind their proliferation. I have a theory of schizophrenia (currently being revised) that has received favorable attention, although my diagnostic checklist for schizotypy has not attained wide use.

An influence harder to trace, but perhaps more important in the long run than anything I have published, are the Ph.D. candidates I have turned out over the years, an average of one per year for the 42 years I have been on Minnesota's graduate faculty. I am proud to have served as advisor to such contributors as Alexander Buchwald, Dante Cicchetti, Richard Darlington, Robert Golden, Harrison Gough (my first Ph.D.!), Will Grove, Donald R. Peterson, Leonard Rorer, William Seeman, and George Welsh. As a teacher I influenced many students who were not my own doctoral candidates, such as Grant Dahlstrom, Harold Gilberstadt, Ben Kleinmuntz, David Lykken, Philip Marx, William Schofield, and Norman Sundberg. The distinguished behavior geneticist Thomas J. Bouchard, Jr., currently chair of our department, is an "academic grandson" of mine, via Harrison Gough at Berkeley.

One gratification in being a college professor is to realize that at least hundreds, sometimes thousands, of persons one has never met have been shaped, helped, and inspired by the lectures, articles, and textbooks of one's students. I have the same feeling when I reflect that there are clinical facilities scattered here and there over the world in which the care of mental patients has become more efficient because the practitioners have been influenced by my writings (however slightly!) or by academic teachers and clinic supervisors who are in the academic line of descent from Paterson through Hathaway through Meehl through Meehl's students.

I have led a secure and leisurely life with a minimum of the financial anxieties and the daily irksome episodes that are part of the human condition outside the academy. I formed a definite vocational goal to be a college professor at an early age, and I have never regretted that decision. But I have sometimes regretted the *field* I went into, because of its low yield of solid scientific intellectual satisfactions. Those branches of psychology that tend to show the most respectable properties of cumulative and quantitative science are not the ones that interest me or got me into the profession. While I have never had any illusions about being a genius or near genius, I am aware that I'm a pretty bright man, and from time to time I find myself thinking *if* I had gone into some other field, like genetics, I would have not merely had a respectably productive academic career and enjoyed myself at it, but I might have been one of those rare nongenius highbrights who makes a major scientific breakthrough. Of course, one knows the statistical odds are against that, even for people in the IQ bracket 175–190, and there is also the element of sheer luck, unless one is possessed of unusual focused persistence, which I am not. The weak (but not zero) "social worker" side of my nature required at least some degree of activity in direct, face-to-face helping, such as experienced by psychotherapists, physicians, social workers, clergymen, and lawyers.

Apart from the egocentric question of whether I could have achieved something "bigger" had I not become a clinical psychologist, there is another factor that leads me to say that despite a pleasant life, interesting companions, and more than the usual share of acclaim by one's fellows, I am at age 68 a somewhat disappointed man. I find this difficult to explain to younger colleagues and graduate students, and I think the reason is that the cognitive orientation of young people is more realistic—perhaps I should say saner—than was true when I was a student and young faculty member. The decade between the mid-1930's and the end of World War II was characterized by high optimism about the expected progress of clinical psychology, including optimism about integration of three great traditions, from the experimental laboratory, psychometrics, and psychodynamics.

When I talk to students about this "integrative optimism" prevailing among faculty and students, say, in 1941 when I entered graduate school, I get the impression that our attitude 45 years ago strikes them as terribly naive on the part of reasonably bright people. In a way it was. But think of the great books that appeared in the decade 1935–45. We had Dollard's *Criteria for the Life History*, Thurstone's *The Vectors of Mind*, Miller and Dollard's *Social Learning and Imitation*, Allport's *Personality: A Psychological Interpretation*, Murray's *Explorations in Personality*, Dollard, Doob, Miller, Mowrer, and Sears's *Frustration and Aggression*, and Hull's *Principles of Behavior*. (I have omitted the most important single book of that period—namely, Skinner's *Behavior of Organisms*—because only a few of us at Minnesota appreciated its earthshaking significance.) These "great books" of that decade were produced by first-class intellects with quite different biases and interests and little overlap in research technique, but it was possible for a person who was neither stupid nor hysteroid to see in them the signs of rapid advance and intellectually satisfying integration. Thurstone was telling us how to identify the individual differences factors of the mind; Hull was mathematicizing the laws of learning; the Yale group were translating Freudian concepts into learning theory and doing ingenious experiments to show reaction formation and displacement in the rat. While I don't suppose any of us had the crazy idea that psychology was practically on the threshold of becoming like chemistry or physics, these exciting developments did make it reasonable to think that it wouldn't be very many years before a large integrative job between the clinic, the laboratory, and the mental testing room would be accomplished.

It didn't turn out to be that way *within* the "grand theories" of the three great traditions, let alone the integration across them. We have settled for more modest theoretical aspirations, and even with that resetting of sights, the record of psychology as a cumulative quantitative science, especially in the "soft" areas, cannot be considered impressive by anyone familiar with the state and history of chemistry, physiology, or genetics. I do not want to blow up this change in the academic subculture into some sort of personal tragedy for me or my contemporaries, which it certainly was not, although I have known a few psychologists who suffered a major identity crisis, severe enough to include psychiatric symptoms, when they "lost the faith" they were reared in by their mentor, whether Skinner, Hull, Rogers, or a second-generation disciple of Freud.

Looking back, I think that one of my generation's mistakes was to take one kind of scientific theory, what may be called the "functional-dynamic," as *the* model for all science, forgetting that there are other kinds of theories in the sciences which may be labeled as "structural-compositional," theories concerning what something is made of and how its parts are arranged, and "developmental-historical" theories that narrate how some system or entity formed and grew (cf. Meehl, 1986d). Secondly, after taking the more exact physical sciences as our sole theoretical paradigm, we further thought in terms of "grand theories," theories which as my friend Paul Feyerabend says are "cosmological," in the sense that they say something about everything there is and everything that happens, whereas there are many interesting, complex, and intellectually respectable mini-theories in other sciences (e.g., the theory of capillary attraction that one learns in a high school physics course).

A person with mixed cognitive and helping needs prefers to have an intimate connection between theoretical understanding and the helping process, which I managed only in the relatively short period in which I was treating patients classically, and even then with the nagging background thought that what I found interesting and scientifically defensible didn't necessarily relate closely with how much I helped the person. I am more likely today to rely on leverage from the "relationship" and a mixture of common sense, intuition, and bits and pieces of psychodynamics than I am to proceed with some "grand strategy," as when we say, "Whatever happens, your task is to interpret," or "Whatever happens, your task is to reflect acceptingly the client's current phenomenology," or "Whatever happens, your job is to reinforce healthy responses and extinguish unhealthy ones." I am not criticizing practitioners who find it possible to live by these monolithic principles. They may be more effective than I am by doing so, even if they are not theoretically correct. Except for certain pervasive attitudes of skepticism and flexibility that I attribute to my basic science training in psychology, much of what I studied to pass my Ph.D. prelims is not closely related to what transpires in an interview. I have learned to live with that fact, but the point is that when I was a graduate student I assumed that by the time I reached my present age we would have figured it out! I am resigned to this intellectually unsatisfactory state of affairs, and today it rarely makes me uncomfortable in my work—but I am not pleased with it.

These cognitive deprivations aside, I can say that I have had a pleasant and sometimes exciting life as a psychologist. I doubt that I could, in fact, have done a better job or made more important contributions in some other field, and there are fields of science for which my talents and temperament make me totally unsuited (e.g., experimental physics). My advice to young persons (other than "pick your grandparents wisely") is to have intellectual fun, because I am convinced that being turned on by the life of the mind is the most important factor, other than brains and energy, in making even such modest contributions to a field of knowledge as I have made.

Selected Publications by Paul E. Meehl

(1946). Profile analysis of the Minnesota Multiphasic Personality Inventory in differential diagnosis. *Journal of Applied Psychology*, *30*, 517–524.

(with S. R. Hathaway) (1946). The K factor as a suppressor variable in the Minnesota Multiphasic Personality Inventory. *Journal of Applied Psychology*, *30*, 525–564.

(with K. MacCorquodale) (1948a). A further study of latent learning in the T-maze. *Journal of Comparative and Physiological Psychology*, *41*, 372–396.

(with K. MacCorquodale) (1948b). On a distinction between hypothetical constructs and intervening variables. *Psychological Review*, *55*, 95–107.

(with J. C. McKinley & S. R. Hathaway) (1948). The Minnesota Multiphasic Personality Inventory: 6. The K scale. *Journal of Consulting Psychology*, *12*, 20–31.

(with K. MacCorquodale) (1949). "Cognitive" learning in the absence of competition of incentives. *Journal of Comparative and Physiological Psychology*, *42*, 383–390.

(1950a). On the circularity of the Law of Effect. *Psychological Bulletin*, *47*, 52–75.

(1950b). A most peculiar paradox. *Philosophical Studies*, *1*, 47–48.

(1950c). Configural scoring. *Journal of Consulting Psychology*, *14*, 165–171.

(with S. R. Hathaway) (1951a). *An atlas for the clinical use of the MMPI*. Minneapolis: University of Minnesota Press.

(with S. R. Hathaway) (1951b). The Minnesota Multiphasic Personality Inventory. In *Military Clinical Psychology*, Section 9 (pp. 71–111). Washington, DC: Department of the Army, Technical Manual TM8-242.

(with K. MacCorquodale) (1951a). A failure to find the Blodgett effect, and some secondary observations on drive conditioning. *Journal of Comparative and Physiological Psychology*, *44*, 178–183.

(with K. MacCorquodale) (1951b). Some methodological comments concerning expectancy theory. *Psychological Review*, *58*, 230–233.

(with K. MacCorquodale) (1951c). On the elimination of cul entries without obvious reinforcement. *Journal of Comparative and Physiological Psychology*, *44*, 367–371.

(with K. MacCorquodale) (1953a). Drive conditioning as a factor in latent learning. *Journal of Experimental Psychology*, *45*, 20–24.

(with K. MacCorquodale) (1953b). Preliminary suggestions as to a formalization of expectancy theory. *Psychological Review*, *60*, 55–63.

(1954). *Clinical versus statistical prediction: A theoretical analysis and a review of the evidence*. Minneapolis: University of Minnesota Press.

(with W. K. Estes, S. Koch, K. MacCorquodale, C. G. Mueller, W. N. Schoenfeld, & S. Verplanck) (1954). *Modern learning theory*. New York: Appleton-Century-Crofts.

(with K. MacCorquodale) (1954). E. C. Tolman. In W. K. Estes, S. Koch, K. MacCorquodale, P. E. Meehl, C. G. Mueller, W. N. Schoenfeld, & W. S. Verplanck, *Modern learning theory* (pp. 177–266). New York: Appleton-Century-Crofts.

(with L. J. Cronbach) (1955). Construct validity in psychological tests. *Psychological Bulletin*, *52*, 281–302. Reprinted in Meehl, 1973a (pp. 3–31).

(with A. Rosen) (1955). Antecedent probability and the efficiency of psychometric signs, patterns, or cutting scores. *Psychological Bulletin*, *52*, 194–216. Reprinted in Meehl, 1973a (pp. 32–62).

(1956a). Wanted – a good cookbook. *American Psychologist*, *11*, 263–272. Reprinted in Meehl, 1973a (pp. 63–80).

(1956b). Symposium on clinical and statistical prediction (with C. C. McArthur & D. V. Tiedeman). *Journal of Counseling Psychology*, *3*, 163–173.

(with M. J. Scriven) (1956). Compatibility of science and ESP. *Science*, *123*, 14–15.

(with W. Sellars) (1956). The concept of emergence. In H. Feigl & M. Scriven (Eds.), *Minnesota studies in the philosophy of science: Vol. 1. The foundations of science and the concepts of psychology and psychoanalysis* (pp. 239–252). Minneapolis: University of Minnesota Press.

(1957a) Religion and the maintenance of mental health. In *Society's stake in mental health* (pp. 52–61). Minneapolis: University of Minnesota, Social Science Research Center.

(1957b) When shall we use our heads instead of the formula? *Journal of Counseling Psychology*, *4*, 268–273. Reprinted in Meehl, 1973a (pp. 81–89).

(1959a) Some ruminations on the validation of clinical procedures. *Canadian Journal of Psychology*, *13*, 102–128. Reprinted in Meehl, 1973a (pp. 90–116).

(1959b) A comparison of clinicians with five statistical methods of identifying MMPI profiles. *Journal of Counseling Psychology*, *6*, 102–109.

(1960a) The cognitive activity of the clinician. *American Psychologist*, *15*, 19–27. Reprinted in Meehl, 1973a (pp. 117–134).

(1960b). Treatment of guilt-feelings. In American Catholic Psychological Association: W. C. Bier and R. J. McCall (Eds.), *Three joint symposia from the ACPA-APA meetings of 1957, 1958, 1959* (pp. 34–41). New York: Fordham University.

(with W. G. Dahlstrom) (1960). Objective configural rules for discriminating psychotic from neurotic MMPI profiles. *Journal of Consulting Psychology*, *24*, 375–387.

(1962a). Parapsychology. *Encyclopedia Britannica* (Vol. 17, pp. 267–269).

(1962b). Schizotaxia, schizotypy, schizophrenia. *American Psychologist*, *17*, 827–838. Reprinted in Meehl, 1973a (pp. 135–155).

(with W. Schofield, B. C. Glueck, W. B. Studdiford, D. W. Hastings, S. R. Hathaway, & D. J. Clyde) (1962). *Minnesota-Ford Pool of phenotypic personality items, August 1962 edition*. Minneapolis: University of Minnesota.

(1964). *Manual for use with checklist of schizotypic signs* (Report No. PR-73-5). Minneapolis: University of Minnesota, Research Laboratories of the Department of Psychiatry.

(with B. C. Glueck, W. Schofield, & D. J. Clyde) (1964). The quantitative assessment of personality. *Comprehensive Psychiatry*, *5*, 15–23.

(1965a). Let's quit kidding ourselves about the training of clinical psychologists. In R. D. Wirt (Ed.), *Professional education in clinical psychology*. (mimeo; available from University of Minnesota)

(1965b). *Detecting latent clinical taxa by fallible quantitative indicators lacking an accepted criterion* (Report No. PR-65-2). Minneapolis: University of Minnesota. Research Laboratories of the Department of Psychiatry.

(1966). The compleat autocerebroscopist: A thought-experiment on Professor Feigl's mind-body identity thesis. In P. K. Feyerabend & G. Maxwell (Eds.), *Mind, matter, and method: Essays in philosophy and science in honor of Herbert Feigl* (pp. 103–180). Minneapolis: University of Minnesota Press.

(with R. M. Dawes) (1966). Mixed group validation: A method for determining the validity of diagnostic signs without using criterion groups. *Psychological Bulletin*, *66*, 63–67. Reprinted in Meehl, 1973a (pp. 156–164).

(1967a). Theory-testing in psychology and physics: A methodological paradox. *Philosophy of Science*, *34*, 103–115. Reprinted in D. E. Morrison & R. E. Henkel (Eds.), *The significance test controversy* (pp. 252–266), Chicago, Aldine, 1970.

(1967b). What can the clinician do well? In D. N. Jackson & S. Messick (Eds.), *Problems in human assessment* (pp. 594–599). New York: McGraw-Hill. Reprinted in Meehl, 1973a (pp. 163–173).

(with J. M. Livermore) (1967). The virtues of M'Naghten. *Minnesota Law Review*, *51*, 789–856.

(with J. M. Livermore & C. P. Malmquist) (1968). On the justifications for civil commitment. *University of Pennsylvania Law Review*, *117*, 75–96.

(1970a). Psychology and the criminal law. *University of Richmond Law Review*, *5*, 1–30.

(1970b). Psychological determinism and human rationality: A psychologist's reactions to Professor Karl Popper's "Of clouds and clocks." In M. Radner & S. Winokur (Eds.), *Minnesota studies in the philosophy of science: Vol. 4. Analyses of theories and methods of physics and psychology* (pp. 310–372). Minneapolis: University of Minnesota Press.

(1970c). Some methodological reflections on the difficulties of psychoanalytic research. In M. Radner & S. Winokur (Eds.), *Minnesota studies in the philosophy of science: Vol. 4. Analyses of theories and methods of physics and psychology* (pp.

403–416). Minneapolis: University of Minnesota Press. Reprinted in *Psychological Issues*, 1973, *8*, 104–115.

(1971a). High school yearbooks: A reply to Schwarz. *Journal of Abnormal Psychology*, 77, 143–148. Reprinted in Meehl, 1973a (pp. 174–181).

(1971b). A scientific, scholarly, nonresearch doctorate for clinical practitioners: Arguments pro and con. In R. R. Holt (Ed.), *New horizon for psychotherapy: Autonomy as a profession* (pp. 37–81). New York: International Universities Press.

(1971c). Law and the fireside inductions: Some reflections of a clinical psychologist. *Journal of Social Issues*, *27*, 65–100.

(with D. T. Lykken, W. Schofield, & A. Tellegen) (1971). Recaptured-item technique (RIT): A method for reducing somewhat the subjective element in factor-naming. *Journal of Experimental Research in Personality*, *5*, 171–190.

(1972a). Reactions, reflections, projections. In J. N. Butcher (Ed.), *Objective personality assessment: Changing perspectives* (pp. 131–189). New York: Academic Press.

(1972b). Second-order relevance. *American Psychologist*, *27*, 932–940.

(1972c). Specific genetic etiology, psychodynamics and therapeutic nihilism. *International Journal of Mental Health*, *1*, 10–27. Reprinted in Meehl, 1973a (pp. 182–199).

(1973a). *Psychodiagnosis: Selected papers*. Minneapolis: University of Minnesota Press.

(1973b). MAXCOV-HITMAX: A taxonomic search method for loose genetic syndromes. In P. E. Meehl, *Psychodiagnosis: Selected papers* (pp. 200–224). Minneapolis: University of Minnesota Press.

(with H. Feigl) (1974). The determinism-freedom and mind-body problems. In Paul A. Schilpp (Ed.), *The philosophy of Karl Popper* (pp. 520–559). LaSalle, IL: Open Court.

(1977). The selfish voter paradox and the thrown-away vote argument. *American Political Science Review*, *71*, 11–30.

(1978a). Theoretical risks and tabular asterisks: Sir Karl, Sir Ronald, and the slow progress of soft psychology. *Journal of Consulting and Clinical Psychology*, *46*, 806–831.

(1978b). Precognitive telepathy: 1. On the possibility of distinguishing it experimentally from psychokinesis. *NOÛS*, *12*, 235–266.

(1978c). Precognitive telepathy: 2. Some neurophysiological conjectures and metaphysical speculations. *NOÛS*, *12*, 371–395.

(with R. Golden) (1978). Testing a single dominant gene theory without an accepted criterion variable. *Annals of Human Genetics London*, *41*, 507–514.

(1979). A funny thing happened to us on the way to the latent entities. *Journal of Personality Assessment*, *43*, 563–581.

(with R. Golden) (1982). Taxometric methods. In P. Kendall & J. Butcher (Eds.), *Handbook of research methods in clinical psychology* (pp. 127–181). New York: Wiley.

(1983a). The insanity defense. *Minnesota Psychologist*, Summer, 11–17.

(1983b). Subjectivity in psychoanalytic inference: The nagging persistence of

Wilhelm Fliess's Achensee question. In J. Earman (Ed.), *Minnesota studies in the philosophy of science: Vol. 10. Testing scientific theories* (pp. 349–411). Minneapolis: University of Minnesota Press.

(1983c). Consistency tests in estimating the completeness of the fossil record: A neo-Popperian approach to statistical paleontology. In J. Earman (Ed.), *Minnesota studies in the philosophy of science: Vol. 10. Testing scientific theories* (pp. 413–473). Minneapolis: University of Minnesota Press.

(1986a). Trait language and behaviorese. In T. Thompson & M. D. Zeiler (Eds.), *Analysis and integration of behavioral units* (pp. 315–334). Hillsdale, NJ: Erlbaum.

(1986b). Diagnostic taxa as open concepts: Metatheoretical and statistical questions about reliability and construct validity in the grand strategy of nosological revision. In T. Millon & G. L. Klerman (Eds.), *Contemporary directions in psychopathology*. New York: Guilford Press.

(1986c). Causes and effects of my disturbing little book. *Journal of Personality Assessment, 50*, 370–375.

(1986d). Psychology: Does our heterogeneous subject matter have any unity? *Minnesota Psychologist*, Summer.

(1987). Theory and practice: Reflections of an academic clinician. In E. F. Bourg, R. J. Bent, J. E. Callan, N. F. Jones, J. McHolland, and G. Stricker (Eds.), *Standards and evaluation in the education and training of professional psychologists* (pp. 7–23). Norman, OK: Transcript Press.

(in press a). Why summaries of research on a psychological theory are often uninterpretable. In R. Snow & D. E. Wiley (Eds.), *Straight thinking: A volume in honor of Lee J. Cronbach*. Hillsdale, NJ: Erlbaum.

(in press b). Psychological determinism or chance: Configural cerebral autoselection as a tertium quid. In M. L. Maxwell and C. W. Savage (Eds.), *Science, mind, and psychology: Essays on Grover Maxwell's world view*. Boston: D. Reidel.

(in press c). Schizotaxia as an open concept. In A. I. Rabin and R. Zucker (Eds.), *Studying persons and lives*. New York: Springer.

Other Publications Cited

Denton, M. (1985). *Evolution: A theory in crisis*. Bethesda, MD: Adler & Adler.

Gottesman, I. I., & Shields, J. (1982). *Schizophrenia, the epigenetic puzzle*. New York: Cambridge University Press.

Hoch, P., & Polatin, P. (1949). Pseudoneurotic forms of schizophrenia. *Psychiatric Quarterly, 3*, 248–276.

Horst, P. (1941). *Prediction of personal adjustment* (Bulletin No. 48). New York: Social Science Research Council.

Lakatos, I. (1970). Falsification and the methodology of scientific research programmes. In I. Lakatos & A. Musgrave (Eds.), *Criticism and the growth of knowledge* (pp. 91–195). Cambridge, Eng.: Cambridge University Press.

Lakatos, I. (1974). The role of crucial experiments in science. *Studies in the History and Philosophy of Science, 4*, 309–325.

Lakatos, I., & Musgrave, A. (Eds.). (1970). *Criticism and the growth of knowledge.* Cambridge, Eng.: Cambridge University Press.

Lykken, D. T. (1956). A method of actuarial pattern analysis. *Psychological Bulletin, 53,* 102–107.

Peterson, D. R. (1954). The diagnosis of subclinical schizophrenia. *Journal of Consulting Psychology, 18,* 198–200.

Sarbin, T. R. (1942). A contribution to the study of actuarial and individual methods of prediction. *American Journal of Sociology, 48,* 593–602.

George A. Miller

George A. Miller

No one grows up without help, and I had a lot.

In West Virginia during the Great Depression, science was not a career possibility for me or my friends. It was not that we rejected it; we simply never thought of it. And even if I had thought of it, becoming a psychologist would have been at the bottom of my list. Fortunately for me, at every step I had close friends who helped me get on with it. But in retrospect it still seems unbelievable.

Blame it on those close friends. At my best, I am what they made of me; at my worst, I am what they allowed me to become.

The Book Salesman

On the steps of Alexander Graham Bell Hall at George Washington University—in the fall of 1937, I think—a book salesman waiting for a professor struck up a conversation with a freshman. I remember being shown a psychology text. I glanced through it, found drawings of the brain and other organs, and gave it back. I was raised by Christian Scientists, I had been trained to avoid *materia medica*, and I could recognize the devil when I saw him.

Donald A. Ramsdell

A second encounter came two years later in Tuscaloosa, Alabama, where Donald Ramsdell, the Professor of Psychology at the University of Alabama, liked to hold seminars in the comfort of his own living room.

I wasn't interested in psychology. The seminar topic was Kurt Goldstein's *The Organism*, which presupposed a grounding that I lacked. It was not Goldstein's holistic neurology that attracted me. I was there because I was interested in Katherine James; she was interested in psychology. Ramsdell surrounded himself with bright young people; he had a talent for provoking them. Never before had I heard that kind of conversation—complex arguments over points I would never have thought to question, Ramsdell's rapid deployment of richly suggestive analogies, the easy movement from warmth to heat and back again. It was the interaction, not the topic, that enchanted me. I discovered the intellectual life in Donald Ramsdell's living room.

Apparently Ramsdell saw some promise in me. Although I had taken no formal courses in psychology, when I finished a Master of Arts in the Speech Department, he offered me a job teaching sections of introductory psychology. He took $900 that was allocated for three graduate students, talked the Dean out of an extra $100, and made one instructorship for me. Katherine James had become Kitty Miller, our first child had appeared, the Depression was still a reality, and I needed the job. In the summer of 1941 I prepared: long hours passed in puzzlement over Freeman's *Physiological Psychology* and Allport's *Personality*.

According to my stepfather, if you don't feel that you're worth twice what you're being paid, you're not earning your salary. By that criterion, I probably deserved my $1,000 that year, but I learned far more than I earned. Ramsdell was fresh from his Ph.D. with E. G. Boring and S. S. Stevens at Harvard, and he used an introductory textbook by Boring, Langfeld, and Weld. Every week he lectured to 300 undergraduates on Mondays and Fridays, and I led sixteen discussion sections: five on Tuesday, six on Wednesday, five on Thursday. I hope I told them the truth. After sixteen times through the same material, I believed it.

A year of teaching introductory psychology did not make me a psychologist, but it was the only job I had. I obviously needed better training. It was decided that I should attend summer school, and in June 1942 Ramsdell shipped me off to his teachers at Harvard.

Wendell R. Garner

The bus from Birmingham arrived at dawn, an hour when Bostonians want to get wherever they are going. By the time my bags and I negotiated the subway to Harvard Square I had discovered that Northerners are a hostile lot. A policeman begrudged me Emerson Hall, where signs guided me to the chairman's office on the third floor. The place was deserted. I waited half an hour on a long bench under a skylight in the central hallway before an unimpressive, dark-haired young man with a chubby face climbed the stairs, rattled Gordon Allport's doorknob, and joined me on the bench. He, too, was a new student reporting in: Wendell Garner, fresh from Franklin and Marshall.

A janitor told us, "These people don't get in before ten in the summer." Garner suggested that we look for a room together and come back later when Emerson Hall was open for business. We found a large, sunny room we could afford on the top floor of a boarding house on Wendell Street. Later we learned that two prostitutes conducted their business downstairs, but they, the war in Europe, absent families, and all other distractions were blotted out by our cooperative obsession with psychology. I was once again a student, something I had always been good at. Wendell proved a marvelous rival, as sure that he was better than I as I was sure that I was better than he. We both memorized Woodworth's *Experimental Psychology* in the fury of our competition.

I called him Wendell that summer. Not until fall did Boring's secretary rename him Tex: the vice president then was a Texan named Garner.

Graduate school is a time for professionalization. But I did not come to think of myself as a professional psychologist. Tex and I became professionalized as military research workers, more engineers than psychologists. As the faculty we had come to study under became increasingly involved in the war, formal instruction shrank to nothing. So we educated each other, confirming my Alabama discovery that the best way to learn anything is to teach it. We not only survived, we were the better for it.

S. Smith Stevens

They did take time to teach us writing, however. Stevens told us that science is not finished until it is communicated; Boring argued that if better writing saved every reader five minutes, it should be worth five hours of an author's time. When you asked Boring to read a manuscript, he returned it with three or four typewritten pages of single-spaced comments covering everything from misspellings to his philosophy of life. Stevens, on the other hand, called you in to sit beside him at his desk while he read the paper aloud.

Smitty: "What does that mean?"

Victim: "Ah, come on, Smitty. You know what it means."

Smitty: "Of course I know what it means. But look at what it says!"

My earliest research at Harvard built more on my Alabama training as a speech scientist than on the little psychology I had managed to pick up. I spent World War II testing voice communication systems in the Psycho-

Acoustic Laboratory, which was conceived, built, and directed in the labyrinthine basement of Memorial Hall by S. S. Stevens. Smitty was a handsome and driven man, a Westerner of Mormon faith who treated his laboratory (or as much of it as would submit) as his extended family. He didn't need to be loved, but he hated to be ignored.

Work began at 8:30 A.M.—it was not uncommon for Smitty to hang around the lab entrance to berate latecomers. And it often continued late into the night, punctuated only by dinner with Smitty at the Faculty Club. The fact that you worked past midnight was no alibi for being late the next morning. It sounds hard, yet I now look back longingly on those dedicated, uninterrupted hours.

The Department of Psychology was badly polarized: the experimentalists Stevens, John G. Beebe-Center, and Edwin G. Boring on one side, the social and clinical psychologists Gordon Allport, Henry Murray, and Robert White on the other. The rivalry seemed to be between fields of psychology, but it was also a clash of personalities: Stevens and Allport disliked each other intensely. Smitty's lab gave me a salary and deferment from military service, but it isolated me from the social and clinical psychologists with whom I intended to study. And I was to remain isolated.

I once asked Allport why, since I studied the highly social process of speech communication, he refused to consider me a social psychologist. "Because you don't know any social psychology," he replied.

As the war ended, the Psychology Department split. Gordon Allport, Talcott Parsons, and Clyde Kluckhohn formed a new Department of Social Relations. The fission broadened the horizons of Harvard's social, clinical, and developmental psychologists, but it unwisely narrowed Harvard's experimental and physiological psychologists.

The Secret Thesis

After helping out here and there around the Psycho-Acoustic Lab, I was finally given a project of my own: to determine the optimal design of masking signals for spot jamming of voice communication systems. The Germans were using a five-tone "bagpipe" signal that men in the field found extremely annoying. The Signal Corps wanted us to find an even more annoying jamming signal to beam back at them.

Annoyance proved an elusive goal. Acoustic properties that people judge most annoying—high pitch, unexpected intermittency—are properties that make a signal ineffective in masking speech. I tried to persuade the military that it was not the sound of a Stuka dive bomber coming right at you that reversed peristalsis and caused loss of sphincter control. I conducted irrefutable demonstrations that optimal masking signals are better than the best nuisance signals. The war ended before my recommendations were incorporated in field equipment.

It was agreed that my long technical report on "The Optimal Design of Jamming Signals" could be submitted in lieu of a doctoral dissertation, and a date was set for my final oral examination. I foresaw two problems. As Stevens's protégé, I knew that Allport would be out to get me. And my thesis was classified Top Secret, so that only Stevens and E. B. Newman were cleared to read it. I prepared for the examination by studying Allport's book intensively, and by replotting my jamming data to look like auditory masking.

Ph.D. orals are designed to humiliate. It is the faculty's last chance to show a candidate that he still has a lot to learn. I thought I was ready for it, but they fooled me. They were so damn considerate. First, some guarded questions about the thesis, which I, fearful of breaking security and unfamiliar with the new way of plotting my data, stumbled over; Allport must have wondered whether there really was a thesis. Then Newman asked questions that he knew I could answer, but on material I had not reviewed; Allport must have wondered whether I knew anything at all. J. S. Bruner tried to help Newman find something I could answer, but by then I was rattled. Finally, it was Allport's turn. He asked quietly whether I believed in personality. I said yes, and braced myself. But he had no further questions! White and Murray asked no questions at all. They thanked me and the inquisition ended.

I withdrew to Boring's outer office to lick my wounds and await their decision. Minutes passed. How could I have done so poorly? The clock kept ticking, and I relived the shame of the examination. More minutes. What were they doing? Something was wrong. They didn't need this much time to agree that I had failed. I felt ill. Would they let me take it again? What was taking so long?

I waited 45 miserable minutes before Boring came bouncing in, saw me, and stopped dead. "Oh my," he said. "Congratulations!"

The faculty, dealing with pressing business related to the impending split, had forgotten me.

Two copies of my Top Secret thesis, properly wrapped and sealed, went on file in Widener Library. Periodically during the next decade I was informed that its classification had been reduced, but it was many years before the wrappings could come off. In 1982 I received a letter from the librarian: the library needed space and was removing duplicate copies of Ph.D. theses; did I want to purchase the copy of mine? I did. A month later I received another letter reporting that apparently my thesis had been misplaced. Fortunately, I had published the important results in the *Psychological Bulletin* in 1947.

Tex Garner and I were among the last doctorates granted by the old Department of Psychology. Tex had less trouble in his oral exam than I had with mine. But now suddenly we both were faced with the need to find jobs. One evening, after dinner at the Faculty Club, Stevens and Clifford T. Morgan had a long session in Stevens's office with the door closed. The next day Tex and I were told that he would go to Johns Hopkins with Cliff and I would stay at Harvard with Smitty.

Frederick C. Frick

In those days, Ford Frick was the president of the National League. His son Fred had been in the war and had studied Wittgenstein at Cambridge before taking his Ph.D. in psychology at Columbia. When Fred arrived at Harvard as an assistant professor, we quickly became friends. He is one of the few psychologists I know who plays golf, and he had a pass to all the baseball games. Most of all, he is fun to argue with.

Fred's credentials were in Skinnerian behaviorism and operant conditioning, about as far from my competence in speech and hearing as I could then imagine. But we found something that fascinated us both: Markov processes. The Psycho-Acoustic Lab was on the distribution list of Bell Laboratories, and as their publications arrived, Smitty would look them over and pick the ones he thought worth reading. In 1948 he routed one to me: Claude Shannon's "A Mathematical Theory of Communication." My life was never again the same. Not only did Shannon's measure of amount of information explain some results in speech perception that had puzzled me for years, but its use to measure transmission in the presence of noise and to estimate the redundancy of sequentially constrained signals introduced me to Markov processes.

I shared Shannon's beautiful theory with Fred Frick; together we tried to apply it to the description of behavior. We used Shannon's mathematical apparatus in a couple of ambitious articles on operant conditioning and called it "statistical behavioristics." The name didn't stick; "mathematical psychology" soon became the label for the kind of ideas we had in mind.

Fred and I discovered modern algebra in the course of our attempts to understand matrices of transitional probabilities. We taught a seminar together in which we baffled the graduate students with all the wonderful uses we thought we saw for logic, lattice theory, probability theory, information theory, game theory. In the fall of 1950 I took my sabbatical leave at the Institute for Advanced Study in Princeton, where I could spend all of my time pursuing those ideas and trying to think like a mathematician.

Fred and I did one study together that we never published. The idea was to introduce cyclic patterns of binary events and to see how long it took subjects to discover different regularities. Patterns that repeated in short cycles should be easier to recognize and learn than patterns with long cycles. When people knew what we were doing, however, the experiment failed. They would simply remember as much of the beginning as they could, usually six or seven events, and wait for that string to recur.

We needed to disguise the purpose of the experiment. So Ralph Gerbrands built a pinball machine for us. The magnets that controlled the path of the ball were elaborately concealed from our subjects by running the wires through a leg of the machine, under the carpet, and out to control devices in the next room. At the bottom of the board we had a row of return slots, half white and half black; the subject's task was to predict on each play whether the ball would end up in a white slot or a black one. To further disguise our purpose, each subject began with a haphazard sequence of blacks and whites, so that even if he anticipated some regularity, he would have no idea when it started. They began with 50 random trials, followed by 50 trials with a simple black-white alternation, then ended with another sequence of 50 random trials. Eight undergraduates played the game.

Results: Nobody recognized that the middle 50 trials alternated perfectly between black and white. Four subjects learned nothing: their percentage of correct predictions hovered at 50 percent throughout. The other four subjects showed a nice learning curve during the middle trials, their probability of correct prediction rising close to 1.0 by the end of the patterned segment. How could a subject predict an alternation accurately and yet not be able to report verbally that the events were alternating? The question bothered Fred so much that he finally interrupted one young man and asked, with elaborate casualness, how he was doing.

"I think I've got it," he said. "Look, when I twist the plunger to the right, it goes in the white." He demonstrated. "And if I want it to go in the black, I twist it to the left." He demonstrated. "See, right is white." He demonstrated. "And left is black." He continued to demonstrate, in perfect synchrony with the alternation. Even I knew enough Skinnerian psychology to recognize superstitious behavior. But it was complicated, life was full of things to do, and we decided to drop the project and let Ward Edwards use the pinball machine for his thesis research.

J. C. R. Licklider

In 1950 J. C. R. Licklider moved to the Massachusetts Institute of Technology. Lick was at Harvard when I arrived in 1942, and he stayed on after the war. His graduate training at the University of Rochester had been in physiological psychology, but research on military voice communication systems added a heavy overlay of experimental psychology and electrical engineering. He moved to MIT because he welcomed the challenge of building his own research team in an engineering context.

Lick was the All-American Boy—tall, blond, and good-looking, good at everything he tried. Long before I met him he had fallen in love with science and technology; he was the kind of guy you found off in a corner at a party arguing about Fourier transforms. At least it was Fourier transforms in 1950; today it is more likely to be the latest wrinkle in computer science. Extremely intelligent, intensely creative, and hopelessly generous—when you made a mistake, Lick persuaded everyone that you had just brought off the cleverest possible joke. Since I made a lot of mistakes, I lost no time in cultivating his friendship.

The occasion for assembling a group of psychologists to do human engineering at MIT was the cold war and the Distant Early Warning (DEW) line, an air defense scheme for putting radar stations across northern Canada in order to provide warning of the approach of Russian bombers. MIT realized that doing secret research for radar engineers would not attract top psychologists, so Licklider was allowed to build a doctoral program in psychology as well. The educational side of the enterprise was folded into the Department of Economics and Social Science, presumably because that was where Kurt Lewin's group had been—and where Alex Bavelas still was.

And so it happened that in 1951 Walter Rosenblith and I were invited to join Lick at MIT. Considering my severe case of Harvarditis, it still surprises me that I had the gumption to accept. Walter had some problem with his security clearance. He was eventually able to persuade the FBI that he was not a spy, but during the interim he had an opportunity to build an excellent biophysics lab of his own at MIT. My clearance was in good shape, so I went on the military payroll immediately. Fate works in funny ways.

With military money and the help of Patricia Nicely, I set up a lab to study speech perception. I wanted to apply Shannon's measure of transmitted information to input-output matrices, where the input was a spoken syllable and the output was the listener's judgment of what had been spoken. Ordinarily, the input and output would agree very closely, especially if the listener knew exactly what syllables might be spoken, but I intended to force errors by degrading the stimuli—by masking them with random noise or filtering out parts of their acoustic spectra. In that way I hoped to identify the phonetic features that had to be preserved in order to enable a listener to recognize what was said. I chose consonants because they carry most of the distinctive information in speech signals, and because articulatory phonetics prescribed a classification of consonant sounds that might or might not govern perceptual phonetics as well.

Pat Nicely compiled a three-foot shelf of notebooks filled with data, and I ground it through endless computations of bits of transmitted information. We found that masking the speech with random noise had very much the same effect as filtering out the high frequencies of the speech spectrum. The features that phoneticians had developed to describe consonant articulation turned out to be important for perception as well—consonants sharing many articulatory features are more easily confused than are consonants that are articulated very differently. And some of those features (the distinction between voiced and unvoiced consonants, for example) were much harder to mask or filter out than others (place of articulation was extremely vulnerable to distortion).

It was a large piece of work and I was proud of it, so I decided to publish it in *The Journal of the Acoustical Society of America*. I was able to make that decision because I was the associate editor of *JASA* responsible for speech and hearing. During the time I held that position I did not publish any of my own papers. Now I was resigning; I gave myself this favor as a reward for six years of hard work. And since I was rewarding myself, I did something that I would not have let other authors do: I published seventeen large and expensive tables giving all of our input-output matrices.

The phonetic generalizations supported by our studies were more comforting than surprising; they simply confirmed what any sensible person should have expected. The information theoretic measures that I used to analyze our data matrices are no longer of any interest. But the matrices themselves have been analyzed repeatedly by psychologists who have developed new and improved methods of multidimensional scaling. In the long run, my editorial self-indulgence proved more valuable than our scientific conclusions. They call it serendipity.

By this time I knew that I was a psychologist, but I didn't think of myself as merely a psychologist. I was an associate editor of *JASA*, I collaborated with electrical engineers, I was a member of a distinguished Economics Department, I was fascinated by mathematics, statistics, and linguistics. The wonderful thing about MIT is that it doesn't matter: the place is task oriented, not discipline oriented. Anyone can become whatever he needs to be in order to get the work done. At MIT Lick's identity as a psychologist was as tentative as my own.

Lick and I worked well together, probably because I had the good sense never to compete with him. Whatever he decided to do was his, and I found something else. Between us we assembled a remarkable group of young psychologists. It is true that Lick found intellectual problems much more interesting than administrative problems; his theory of administration was that it wouldn't take as long if you did it later. But he was always good-natured when we dug something out of his in-basket and did it for him.

Lick's method of hiring a secretary was to give all applicants the Miller Analogies Test. We had a string of brilliant young women who lasted about three months before resigning in violent boredom. I finally took over and hired an ordinary, quiet, young Catholic woman of slightly better than average intelligence, the seventh child in a family of twelve. When she had nothing to do, she sat waiting at her desk. Everyone adored her. She was working there years after I left.

Although Lick insisted on treating me as his peer, it was clear to MIT that he was the key man in our enterprise. In 1953 he was given tenure, at which point Dean Burchard remarked that that would be the last tenured position MIT would give to that field. Shortly afterward I was offered a tenured appointment at Harvard—E. G. Boring was retiring. Breathing heavily, I grabbed it.

Seven, More or Less

Many people who know nothing else about George Miller know about the paper "The Magical Number Seven, Plus or Minus Two: Some Limits on Our Capacity for Processing Information." I feel obliged to spend a few paragraphs telling how it happened to be written.

I was asked to prepare an invited address for the April 1955 meeting of the Eastern Psychological Association. The invitation threw me into high ambivalence. All my pride and ambition wanted to accept, but fear of embarrassing myself argued against it. Finally, fear won out. I wrote a long letter to the program chairman explaining that I was working on two totally unrelated projects at the moment: the application of information measures to absolute judgments of unidimensional magnitudes, and the use of recoding to extend the span of immediate memory. I described the two projects in some detail. The problem, I confessed, was that neither project alone was sufficient for a one-hour public lecture. I thanked him for asking me and apologized that the invitation reached me at a time when I was unable to accept.

Fortunately, I was writing to a psychologist. He replied that anyone who needed two pages to say no obviously wanted to say yes, so why didn't I reconsider. He was right, I did want to say yes. So I reconsidered. In order to provide an hour's entertainment, I had to report on both lines of work. The stylist in me refused to give two 30-minute talks having nothing to do with one another. So I asked myself whether there was *anything* in common to the two of them.

The only thing I could think of was a numerical similarity. The span of immediate memory for digits is about seven. The channel capacities that had been coming out of the studies of absolute judgments ran around 2.5 to 3 bits of information. When I suddenly realized that 2.5 bits is six alternatives, I saw how the two might be linked together. It was a superficial similarity, but it enabled me to accept the EPA's invitation. I chose a humorous title for the talk, "The Magical Number Seven, Plus or Minus Two," thinking to make it obvious that I knew this shotgun wedding of absolute judgment and immediate memory was little more than a joke. To give it a little more legitimacy, however, I threw in a third instance, the experiments at Mount Holyoke College on the discrimination of number: when haphazard patterns of dots are flashed briefly on a screen, people can estimate the number accurately up to five or six dots.

The experimental data on absolute judgments had been collected by my friends. It involved the same kind of input-output matrices that Nicely and I had used to analyze consonant perception: a predetermined set of stimuli occurred in haphazard order, and subjects attempted to identify (in absolute, not relative terms) which one of the stimuli had just occurred. The difference was that the stimuli were unidimensional magnitudes (brightnesses, pitches, loudnesses, etc.) and the responses were identifying numbers, not written syllables. All that I contributed was a uniform way of plotting their data in terms of transmitted information in order to bring out the similarities among the diverse results.

The work on short-term memory, however, was my own. In 1952 J. R. M. Hayes, then a graduate student working with Licklider, confirmed the long-known fact that the span of immediate memory changes very little for different types of test materials. The span for binary digits is only slightly greater than the span for monosyllabic words. Dick Hayes pointed out that this result confounded any attempt to characterize performance in terms of informational capacities. A span of ten binary digits is 10 bits; a span of five words is about 50 bits.

Lick had asked me how I would explain Dick's results. I was walking toward our labs in the Sloan Building one day when the answer suddenly hit me. It should be possible to increase the span of immediate memory up to at least 40 binary digits by recoding them as octal digits. With the help of Sidney Smith, a graduate student working with me at the time, we proved that recoding really did work. When I thought of it, I did not know that such binary-to-octal recoding was a standard procedure for computer operators in those days, and for precisely the reason Sid and I did it—to enlarge short-term memory. So we can't claim to have invented the idea. But we did measure it and point out its theoretical significance.

I reported these ideas in the EPA lecture and tried to make it clear that, whereas absolute judgments are limited to an invariant number of bits of information, short term memory is limited to an invariant number of chunks of information, where the bits/chunk can vary with recoding. The idea of recoding—or chunking, as most called it—became one of the standard tools of cognitive psychology in the years that followed.

I don't really understand why the paper has been so widely cited. It has some good ideas in it, but other papers I have written with equally good ideas sank from sight without a ripple. Its central message is that the human mind is limited, which may please some people for reasons of their own. The title helped, of course: the idea of a magical number with a confidence interval tickles the fancy. And it did appear at a time when many psychologists were looking for new ways to think about their science.

Edwin B. Newman

You can never go home again. The Harvard department in 1955 may have been the same one I left in 1951, but it didn't seem the same to me. I expected to resume the place I had occupied in Smitty's lab, but I was wrong. Relations were cool. Smitty had no interest in my attempts to apply information theory to psychological problems. The office he assigned me was a small, awkward space that had once served as a control room for an acoustic testing lab.

I assumed that meant Smitty was tired of supporting the whole department on his research grants; that he was kicking me out of the nest to see whether I could fly on my own. I didn't understand until years later why Smitty resented my return. Smitty's candidate for the position had been Licklider. One of those notorious ad hoc committees that Harvard convenes to advise on tenure appointments had overturned the department's recommendation and submitted my name instead.

My return to Harvard marked the end of those wonderful years when I could count on others to raise the money and provide the facilities. Thereafter I would be on my own. When my situation finally dawned on me I went to E. B. Newman, who was the chairman of the department. Eddie had a small grant that he offered to share, and together we put in for a larger one. Thus, a new and dismal dimension of the scientist's life opened to me. I was lucky to have Eddie as a guide.

We were all lucky to have Eddie. He knew a little something about everything, and he enjoyed being a resource for others. His tireless curiosity fed an enormous memory. Long before trivia buffs were nationally recognized, he would throw into a conversation the salmon run on the Columbia River in 1928, the major exports of Peru, or Hermann von Helmholtz's birthday. If you asked, he said, "I thought I might want to know that some day."

Eddie thought he might want to know so many different things that he never focussed his considerable talent on psychology. One example: he designed a complicated special-purpose computer for an experiment because he wanted to understand how buffer memories worked; when the device was built, he left the use of it to me. Eddie was the utility infielder, the man who filled in on all the odd jobs nobody else had time to learn how to do. The department functioned because of him, and he let the rest of us take the credit. He did love to talk on and on—"Eddie has no terminal facilities," Smitty would say—but that was a small price for the services he rendered.

The Psychology Department I returned to was as polarized as the one I had known as a graduate student, but now the opposing poles were S. S. Stevens and B. F. Skinner, one at each end of the Memorial Hall basement. We needed all of Eddie's talents just to hold us together. Graduate students who wanted to study operant conditioning, or who were willing to study psychophysics, were in good hands: they could join stable laboratories with on-going programs of research. Those who had other interests, and they were a variegated lot, worked with Beebe-Center, Newman, or me. In self-defense, I began to define my own turf more explicitly as the psychology of communication.

The return to discipline-oriented Harvard forced me to recognize that I had become a professional psychologist, and it made me restless. I have intellectual claustrophobia: ideas always seem greener in the other fellow's garden. Especially in the summer time.

Noam Chomsky

Walter Rosenblith told me I should meet Noam Chomsky, but it was not until September 1956 that we finally got together at a symposium on information theory held at MIT.

In order to characterize the sequential structure of communicative signals, I had followed the statistical lead that Shannon provided. In a series of discussions during the fall and winter of 1956, Noam convinced me that such a Markov model could never converge on English, that is, on all and only the grammatical strings of English words. I became persuaded when I calculated that a childhood of six to eight years is too brief for anyone to master the full set of transitional probabilities involved in generating sentences of twenty words or less. Noam eventually published a logical proof that generative systems of the Markovian type cannot generate all and only the grammatical sentences of a language that permits self-embedded constructions, that is to say, sentences of the form "The people who said *S* are here," where *S* is a sentence embedded inside a matrix sentence; *S* may, of course, have another sentence *S'* embedded inside it, and so on.

I had pushed the transitional probabilities of letters and words about as far as I could see to go and was wondering where to go next. Noam showed me that a Markov generator is simply a special case of a more powerful kind of sentence generator, which he called a phrase structure grammar. Of course, Noam formalized phrase structure grammars only to attack them. He believed that further, still more powerful transformational rules are required in order to characterize natural languages like English. These new ideas came just as I was most in need of them.

I studied Noam's lecture notes, but they were merely a sketchy and informal outline of a large work, *The Logical Structure of Linguistic Theory*, which he had completed in 1955 but which had been rejected for publication because it was too unconventional. One reviewer of the manuscript commented that Mr. Chomsky should first make himself famous, and then he could publish a book like that. Which is what Noam did—*LSLT* was finally published in 1975, by which time Noam was very famous indeed—but it was infuriating advice at the time.

As a special favor, Noam loaned me his personal copy of *LSLT*, the copy that contained all his hand-written notes and revisions. I was studying it one afternoon in my office in the basement of Memorial Hall when Eddie Newman stuck his head in. "Hey, George! Memorial Hall is on fire!"

We dashed together to the outside door and looked up to see flames rising from the clock tower. The Cambridge fire department was right across the street, but they were helpless—the water pressure was inadequate to reach the fire. We had just enough time to save our most valued possessions: Eddie grabbed the laboratory cat, and I grabbed Noam's manuscript. So encumbered, we watched from a safe distance while the fire burned down until water could reach it.

The summer of 1957 has a special place in my memory. In those days the Social Science Research Council served as a clearing house for all varieties of worthwhile projects. During the 1950's one of their projects that I became involved with was a series of summer workshops dedicated to the idea that social scientists should learn to think about their problems mathematically. The 1957 workshop was held at Stanford University. It was divided into four seminars, each devoted to a different mathematical application. I was responsible for a seminar on mathematical theories of communication. I planned to begin with a review of Markov models and their limitations, then move to the more powerful theories that I had been learning about from Noam. Since I felt shaky about the second half of that syllabus, I got permission to recruit Noam Chomsky as my assistant.

So it happened that his family and mine lived together for six weeks in a huge house on the Stanford campus—a house occupied during the academic year by the Stanford chapter of Sigma Chi. They slept in one wing of the house and we slept in another, but we shared the kitchen and living rooms. Spending long hours every day with Noam Chomsky was exciting and depressing: exciting to see his mind at work, depressing to realize that

I would never be able to think that way. I thought I knew something about proving theorems, but I was just a novice. I fumbled intuitively toward generalizations by trying to imagine what processes might be occurring. When I was able to produce a plausible conjecture, Noam would formalize it, then either disprove it or prove it and push on to further theorems. By summer's end we really understood the structural properties of finite state grammars—which is what we called Markov processes when the probabilities were stripped off and the state transitions were generalized.

We got Noam to do an experiment that summer, probably the only one ever. Oliver Lacey, one of the students, refused to accept Noam's assertion that, because they share the same phrase structure, there is no way that a speaker can use intonation to disambiguate sentences like "Flying planes can be dangerous." Oliver regarded it as an empirical claim to be verified experimentally. So we devised an experiment. Noam wrote two passages. In one, the citizens complained that the airport runway was too close; they lived in fear because flying planes can be dangerous. In the other passage, the citizens complained that the mayor should not pilot his own airplane because flying planes can be dangerous.

We asked ten people to read one passage and ten more to read the other, and we recorded their voices on magnetic tape. As they finished, Noam asked each speaker: "Does that mean that flying planes IS dangerous or flying planes ARE dangerous?" In every case the question was met with a surprised stare; no one had recognized that the sentence is ambiguous. Further questioning established that everyone had understood it appropriately while they were speaking it.

We enlisted Carol Chomsky, who had become a highly skilled tape splicer in the course of her thesis research at Harvard, to cut out all occurrences of "Flying planes can be dangerous" and splice them together in a test tape. Then we challenged the seminar (and anyone else who would listen) to tell which interpretation the speaker of each sentence had had in mind.

The results were completely random. Oliver Lacey was dismayed that nobody could draw the distinction that seemed so obvious to him. Noam was unimpressed—he had known all along how the experiment had to come out—but inwardly he must have been pleased. I was impressed by the predictive power of these ideas, and I resolved to initiate research intended to test the psychological validity of transformational generative grammar.

Carl I. Hovland

Carl Hovland was as incurably Yale as I was incurably Harvard, but he influenced me more than some of my colleagues closer to home. He was living proof that you did not have to be narrow in order to be a good experimental psychologist. I wish I had known him better. I first met him at the Psychological Round Table, then later at meetings of the Society of Experimental Psychologists. His interests in communication were different from mine, but I admired his wartime research and respected his insistence on the advantages of experimentation over correlation.

When we had time together, we talked about the latest developments in electroacoustics. Carl was a music lover. That was his excuse to build advanced high-fidelity systems, which kept him informed about electronics. He seemed to know about the theory of information as soon as I did. When I learned that Carl was using Shannon's measure to estimate the amount of information subjects received in a concept recognition experiment, I became keenly interested in his work.

In my early enthusiasm for Shannon's theory I took it as my mission to persuade psychologists that information measurement is a Good Thing. Every sign that someone agreed with me was a personal victory. What Hovland showed, of course, was that the amount of information is *not* the important variable: information coded in an affirmative statement is far more useful than the same amount of information encoded in a negative statement. Perhaps that result should have discouraged me, but I didn't see it that way. To me, it demonstrated the usefulness of information measurement: it made possible a precise comparison of the values of positive and negative statements. If good science is science you are grateful for, Carl Hovland's use of information theory was good science.

Carl was impressed by the success of SSRC's summer workshops in mathematics for social science, so he decided to organize a similar summer workshop to educate psychologists about computers. Herbert A. Simon and Allen Newell were the central figures since they, along with their students, were creating the new kind of computational psychology. Why they included me was a mystery. Maybe I was the nearest thing to a computational psychologist that they could find at the time. Or maybe Carl just liked me. In any case, I was flattered to be part of it.

The team from Carnegie Tech assembled for the summer of 1958 at the RAND Corporation in Santa Monica, along with twenty experimental psychologists who had enrolled as students. We learned about cognitive simulation, list-processing languages, the General Problem Solver (GPS), and the Experimental Perception And Memory system (EPAM). Carl and I slogged through the exercises and practice programs, but I must confess that the ideas interested me more than the actual programs. I told Herb Simon that if I understood a cognitive process well enough to simulate it, I wouldn't need to. He said that I had missed the central point of the workshop: the program *is* the theory.

Carl was always helpful, always cheerful. He was a large man, soft in speech, gentle in manner, and shy in a genial way. I promised myself to find some way to work with him again, but it was not to be.

The Center for Advanced Study in the Behavioral Sciences

On a low hill, overlooking Stanford University, the Center offers a commanding view: the campus, the town of Palo Alto—on clear days you can see the San Francisco harbor. Its redwood buildings, scattered in tiers, may have been inspired by motel architecture, but they allow a free choice between community and privacy. It is a beautiful spot to be, an ideal place to think and write, and a wonderful melting pot for social and behavioral scientists from all over the world. It is also a great blessing to the book publishing industry and an unparalleled recruiting ground for Stanford faculty.

It is not easy to generalize about the Center. Every year has a character of its own, in part by design, in part by accident of the 50 personalities who happen to find themselves assembled there. The good thing is that everyone knows it is a one-year adventure. Consequently, no one aspires to tenure, no one competes for promotion—when two people talk to one another, it is because they are interested in what they are talking about. But beyond that, every year is different. Everyone who has been there begins their comments about it with the phrase, "In my year . . ."

In my year (1958–59) three clusters formed. The social anthropologists met regularly to talk endlessly about kinship and kinship terminology. The political scientists and sociologists also had an active seminar program of their own. And there was a loose collection of us who shared a concern for language, but we interacted so intermittently on that topic that we did not deserve to be called a group.

I attended some of the seminars. More valuable was the opportunity to ask ignorant questions of leading experts in fields that I hardly knew existed. The answers were enormously helpful; I did a lot of reading that I should have done long before.

It was broadening. When I returned from my first trip to Europe, in 1955, I told my father that he should visit Europe, too. He asked why—what did they have there that he couldn't get better in Winter Haven, Florida? I tried to explain how broadening it had been. He said he was broad enough already. So, if you know what broadening means, I don't have to explain; if you don't know, I can't explain. I was a different person at the end of the year.

While all that educational catching up was going on, I still had work of my own that I was eager to pursue. I arrived in Palo Alto with a pile of technical reports and computer printouts that I had collected at the summer workshop in Santa Monica, and I was hot to argue about them with somebody. Eugene Galanter and Karl Pribram were the natural colleagues to argue with. I had gotten to know both of them fairly well during visits they had made to Harvard. Gene was interested in mathematical models, and these computer simulations seemed to be a similar but even more powerful form of modeling. So we started talking about it. At first, Karl Pribram was less interested than Gene and I were, but we forced him to participate. Karl's first marriage had just broken up; a good theoretical argument was the best psychotherapy we could offer.

As the discussion developed, we all became infected with the youthful disease of enthusiasm. The California sun baked all the New England prudence out of us, and we competed for outrageous ideas. One idea triggered another like chained explosions in our heads; some were new, but many were old insights dressed in new clothes—it was surprising how much better they looked. Our daily arguments became exciting, absorbing, heady stuff. We began to believe what we were saying. "This is so good," we said, "that we've got to write a book about it."

The result was *Plans and the Structure of Behavior*, published in 1960. It all seems pretty obvious now, but at the time it excited a lot of people. The ideas came from everywhere, but they were integrated in terms of their bearing on Newell and Simon's ideas about cognitive simulation. We distributed the responsibility for writing first drafts of different parts of our argument, but eventually everything had to pass through my typewriter, which gave it a stylistic unity. I enjoyed the writing. The book has stood up rather well because there is a bit of art in it.

I intended to carry the theoretical ideas of *Plans* into the experimental laboratory when I got back to Harvard. The centerpiece was to be the TOTE unit—*T*est whether the goal was realized, *O*perate to reduce discrepancies between the actual situation and the goal, then *T*est again, and *E*xit when the test was satisfied—which was the informational equivalent of the feedback loop that had played such an important role in theories of regulative behavior. But I was unable to take the next step.

The trouble was not that the theory was wrong, but that it was too universal. Our characterization of the TOTE was so general that it placed no significant constraints on the kinds of information processing that could occur. To say that a bit of behavior could be described by a hierarchy of TOTE units was like saying that the description could be written in ink. In that respect, therefore, TOTE units were no improvement over S-R units. Both are notational systems, and notational systems are not true or false. Theories are true or false. Notational systems are convenient or inconvenient. The real message of *Plans* is that you can think more effectively about behavior if you use TOTE notations than if you use S-R notations. But true or false hypotheses can be formulated in either notation.

Jerome S. Bruner

All the while Tex and I were graduate students, we heard stories about two young paragons who had left Harvard just before we arrived, drawn by war into more important activities. No matter how well we did, we were assured that M. Brewster Smith and Jerome S. Bruner had done better. We awaited their return at war's end in hushed respect. Both did return to Harvard, but to the new Department of Social Relations. Brewster's version of social psychology never drew him in my direction, but Jerry's version got him intimately involved with experimentalists.

Jerry's "New Look" in social psychology claimed that rock-solid psychological processes like object perception were subject to unconscious bias when a perceiver's motivation was involved. In other words, social status is so important that it permeates *every* psychological process, and any psychologist who tries to ignore it will necessarily collect very noisy data. The general reaction from the psychophysical contingent in the rump department was: (1) the claim is false, and (2) we knew it all along. Jerry is not one to back off from a debate, so I had frequent occasions to see him in action.

I have always enjoyed Jerry's nimble wit and been reassured by his confidence. We kept in touch even while I was down the river at MIT, but Jerry did not become an important person in my intellectual life until I returned to Harvard in 1955. He was a social psychologist deprived of experimental colleagues. I was an experimentalist deprived of social colleagues. The fact that Allport and Stevens disliked each other didn't mean that their students couldn't get along. Jerry and I took advantage of every opportunity to collaborate: we lunched together frequently at the Faculty Club; I attended a conference at St. Johns College, Cambridge, that Jerry and Sir Frederick Bartlett organized; we wrote a couple of papers together.

After I returned from California, in 1960, I realized that I was acutely unhappy with the narrow conception of psychology that defined the Harvard department. I had just spent a year romping wildly in the sunshine. The prospect of going back to a world bounded at one end by psychophysics and at the other by operant conditioning was simply intolerable. I decided that either Harvard would have to let me create something resembling the interactive excitement of the Stanford Center or else I was going to leave. That was a hard decision for someone suffering from Harvarditis. I needed to talk, so I took my misery to Jerry. We had him out to our house for dinner and afterward, over a bottle of either port or madeira, we've never agreed which, I described my unhappiness and outlined my dream.

I knew that he would be a sympathetic listener, and I was right. More right than I expected. Jerry had been struggling with his own feelings of dissatisfaction with his departmental colleagues. Neither of us wanted to leave Harvard, but neither of us wanted to go on as we had been. My suggestion that we try to create at Harvard a small imitation of the Center for Advanced Study in the Behavioral Sciences struck him as an ideal solution for both of us.

Jerry took charge. He arranged an appointment with McGeorge Bundy, then the Dean of the Faculty of Arts and Sciences, who gave us his blessing and a house for our new enterprise. And Jerry arranged with John Gardner for core funding from the Carnegie Corporation of New York. With surprising speed we were in business. Sometimes it pays to complain. We called our new enterprise the Harvard Center for Cognitive Studies. I asked Dean Bundy whether that title would offend anyone. "After all," I said, "Harvard University is a center for cognitive studies."

"Go ahead," he replied with a broad grin. "A little imperialism in these matters is not a bad thing."

Jerry's group at Bow Streeet had been calling themselves the Cognition Project for some time, so we had a precedent for using the term to name the Center. To me, even as late as 1960, using "cognitive" was an act of defiance. It was less outrageous for Jerry, of course; social psychologists were never swept away by behaviorism the way experimental psychologists had been. But for someone raised to respect reductionistic science, "cognitive psychology" made a definite statement. It meant that I was interested in the mind—I came out of the closet.

My principal interest during those years was to test what, following a hint we found in the writings of Edward Sapir, we called "the psychological validity" of Chomsky's transformational generative grammar. Most of the actual studies were conducted by graduate students, but they were all related by that theme. In retrospect, I realize that I was more eager to prove the claim than to disprove it, so we may have chosen our test materials with an unconscious bias. In any case, subsequent workers in psycholinguistics have drawn the appropriate distinction between a theory of grammar, which interested Chomsky, and a theory of parsing, which would govern the kinds of phenomena we were studying experimentally.

My objectivity may have been dulled a bit by my zeal to demonstrate a viable alternative to behavioristic psychology. In 1963–64 I was a Fulbright Visiting Professor at Oxford University. No sooner had I arrived in England than Larry Weiskrantz, whom I had known as a graduate student at Harvard and who was then at Cambridge, invited me to give a colloquium. I accepted, and proceeded to give the same talk I had been giving at colloquia in the United States. The first 30 minutes criticized the behaviorists for trying to apply their ideas to something as complicated as human language, and the last 30 minutes sketched the kinds of experiments we were doing to test Chomsky's structuralistic ideas.

They listened attentively and it seemed to go reasonably well. But afterward Larry came up with a puzzled frown on his face. "That was an interesting talk, George," he said, "but tell me, what was all that about behaviorism?"

I didn't understand.

"Well," he explained, "there are only three behaviorists in England, and none of them were here today."

After that I stopped wasting the first 30 minutes of my colloquium talks.

Jerry and I worked well together. Every spring we had dinner and then, over bottles of both port and madeira, we hatched our plans for the following year. I like to say that he planned for success and I planned for failure, so whatever happened we were prepared. Since we enjoyed considerable success, his plans worked out more often than mine. But neither of us should take too much credit for the Center's success. It was an idea whose time had come. We were able to bring together some remarkable young people and expose them to a few distinguished visitors; they did all the rest.

The Chairmanship

The Center worked so well, in fact, that they tapped me for chairman of the Psychology Department. That was when I learned that I possess no special administrative magic. I was willing to accept responsibility, but without authority I was helpless. It was a difficult time. Eddie Newman felt unappreciated because he had been kicked out as chairman. Neither Fred Skinner nor Smitty Stevens wanted to teach, and I had no authority to force them to. It was up to R. J. Herrnstein and me to try to look like a department.

About that time a national evaluation of psychology departments ranked our department above Michigan's. Dick Herrnstein and I congratulated each other that the two of us were better than the more than 100 tenured psychologists at Michigan. We understood how such things happen, but it was still good for a giggle.

Our situation didn't seem funny very often. I felt that my load was especially onerous. Jerry and I were teaching the big introductory course for undergraduates, Dick and I were teaching the first-year graduate proseminar, and I was trying to offer both graduate and undergraduate instruction in my own specialty. I was chairman of the Department, with all the official meetings that that entails, and still codirector of the Center, where I supervised the work of graduate students. And I spent, on the average, one day a week in Washington, mostly at the National Institutes of Health, trying to ensure continued funding for the Center and for the computer-based laboratory that Don Norman and I had created.

It doesn't always pay to complain. When I recited my oppressive list of responsibilities to Franklin Ford, dean of the Faculty of Arts and Sciences, I got no sympathy. Indeed, I got no understanding. "But I've always let you do what you wanted," he said, plaintively.

He had a point. Did I really expect the dean to protect me from myself?

One day I ran into Fred Skinner in William James Hall. I must have looked pretty bad. "Are you all right?" he asked.

"I'm exhausted," I said. And then, in a sudden burst of candor, I told him how exploited and overworked I felt. Maybe I hoped he would volunteer to help.

Fred listened with patient interest. "Yes," he said, "you are something of an empire builder, aren't you?"

That was when I decided to leave Harvard. The Center had enabled me to postpone the decision for seven years, but I finally recognized that I had to escape. Three years of working very hard to strengthen Harvard's Psychology Department cured my Harvarditis, and I departed for The Rockefeller University in New York.

That was 1967. What happened in New York is another story, some of which has been told in *Spontaneous Apprentices*, which appeared in 1977. The rest may be appropriate for still another essay someday when I have it all in better perspective.

Envoi

If someone twisted my arm to make me more self-critical, I think my response would be that I am insufficiently critical. Always have been. And it's too late now to do anything about it.

One day when I was seven or eight years old I was walking home from Kanawha School, down the long 1500–block of Virginia Street in Charleston, West Virginia. In the dirt between the sidewalk and the curb I found a small wheel that had come off some other child's toy. I cleaned it enough to see that it was an unusually nice wheel: red, with a small rubber tire. As I walked along slowly, alone, examining the wheel, it occurred to me that if I had another just like it, all I would need would be an axle and it could roll along. And if I had another pair, I could make something. I could mount them under a block of wood and make a car. To make it better I could carve the block of wood in the shape of a car. When I reached my front walk at home I was trying to remember where I had seen a small can of paint.

As I started up the walk, I looked in my hand and saw nothing there but the single wheel. Surprise etched the experience into memory.

In the 60 years since, that boy, staring dumbly at his toy wheel, has revisited me many times. Soaring imagination mocked by hard reality—who has not experienced the discrepancy? I, being insufficiently critical, have experienced it more than most.

The tendency to see what something could be more clearly than what it is has sustained me as a teacher, but I have heard it said that scientists should avoid it like poison. I wonder. Is the goal of science nothing more than the objective description of reality? I could not have remained a psychologist all these years if I were less addicted to counterfactuals.

Reality is vastly overrated. It is merely the point of origin from which everything interesting departs.

George A. Miller

George Armitage Miller was born February 3, 1920, in Charleston, West Virginia. His parents were divorced in 1927, and he and his mother returned to Charleston, where they lived with her parents while he attended public schools. He graduated from Charleston High School in 1937, then followed his mother and her second husband to Washington, D.C., where he lived with them and attended the George Washington University for one year.

When his stepfather was transferred to a regional office in Birmingham in 1938, Miller transferred to the University of Alabama. As an undergraduate he studied history and, partly to overcome adolescent shyness, became active in Blackfriars, the student drama club, where he met Katherine James—who became his wife in 1939. Interests in acting and stage production were supplemented by courses in the Speech Department, and led to a double undergraduate major in History and Speech. In 1940 he received a Bachelor of Arts degree.

The following year he was a graduate student and teaching assistant in the Speech Department at Alabama, where he took courses in phonetics, voice science, and speech pathology—courses that persuaded him that he needed to learn psychology in order to contribute to the field. In 1941 he received a Master of Arts in Speech and was awarded a fellowship to continue in Speech at the University of Iowa, but had to refuse because he was unable to afford the cost of moving his family. He was rescued from this dilemma by D. A. Ramsdell, the Professor of Psychology at Alabama, who offered him a position teaching psychology. Miller served as an instructor in psychology from 1941 to 1943.

In 1942 Miller attended summer school at Harvard, where he returned as a full-time graduate student in 1943. Although he had intended to study clinical psychology at Harvard, his knowledge of speech and hearing had prepared him for research in psychoacoustics. Consequently, during World War II he worked on military voice communications as research associate under S. S. Stevens at the Harvard Psycho-Acoustic Laboratory. At war's end, Miller submitted some of his military research on speech perception as a dissertation and received his Ph.D. in psychology from Harvard University in 1946.

At Harvard after the war, first as a research fellow in the Psycho-Acoustic Laboratory and then as an assistant professor in the Department of Psychology, Miller continued and extended his studies of speech production and perception. In 1948 C. E. Shannon's mathematical theory of communication provided conceptual tools that Miller needed in order to understand data that had accumulated during and following the war: in particular, the inverse relation between the intelligibility of a speech signal and the number of alternative signals that might have occurred instead. Shannon's measure of the amount of selective information in a message inspired a series of experiments measuring how far a listener's expectations influenced his perceptions. Miller summarized that work in 1951 in *Language and Communication*, a text that helped to establish psycholinguistics as an independent field of research in psychology.

From 1951 to 1955, as associate professor of psychology at the Massachusetts Institute of Technology, Miller continued this research on speech perception and tried to extend Shannon's measure to account for short-term memory as well. The observation that the uncertainty of a message has far less effect on a person's ability to remember it than on his ability to perceive it led Miller to propose that short-term memory is limited, not by the number of bits of information it can hold, but by the number of "chunks" into which the message is recoded. In 1956 the implications of the hypothesis that a person can retain about seven chunks in short-term memory were developed in a widely quoted (and often misquoted) paper, "The Magical Number Seven, Plus or Minus Two."

In February 1955 Miller returned to Harvard's Department of Psychology. His attempt to estimate the amount of information per word in conversational speech led him to the linguist Noam Chomsky, who showed him how the sequential predictability of speech follows from adherence to grammatical, not probabilistic, rules. The next decade was spent developing and testing the psychological implications of Chomsky's grammatical theories. Some of the ideas found expression in 1960 in *Plans and the Structure of Behavior*, a book written jointly with E. Galanter and K. Pribram. In 1960 Miller was cofounder, along with J. S. Bruner, of the Harvard Center for Cognitive Studies, and in 1964 he was appointed chairman of the Department of Psychology.

Miller visited The Rockefeller University in New York in 1967, and in 1968 decided to stay there as professor of experimental psychology. By then his research interests had shifted from syntax to lexicon, and in 1976 *Language and Perception*, written with P. N. Johnson-Laird (in large measure during a visit to the Institute for Advanced Study in 1971–72) presented a detailed hypothesis about the way lexical information is stored in a person's long-term memory. Back at Rockefeller, Miller attempted to test some aspects of the hypothesis with studies of the development of language in young children; that project was summarized in 1977 in *Spontaneous Apprentices: Children and Language*.

In 1979 Miller moved to Princeton University, where he is now James S. McDonnell Distinguished University Professor of Psychology. In 1986, in collaboration with Gilbert Harman, he established the Princeton Cognitive Science Laboratory.

He resides with his wife, Katherine James Miller, in Princeton, New Jersey. They have two grown children, Nancy Saunders and Donnally James, and two grandsons.

Selected Publications by George A. Miller

(1947). The masking of speech. *Psychological Bulletin, 44*, 105–129.

(with F. C. Frick) (1949). Statistical behavioristics and sequences of responses. *Psychological Review, 56*, 311–325.

(1951). *Language and communication*. New York: McGraw-Hill.

(with G. A. Heise & W. Lichten) (1951). The intelligibility of speech as a function of the context of the test materials. *Journal of Experimental Psychology, 41*, 329–335.

(with J. S. Bruner & L. Postman) (1954). Familiarity of letter sequences and tachistoscopic identification. *Journal of General Psychology, 50*, 129–139.

(with J. S. Bruner & C. Zimmerman) (1955). Discriminative skill and discriminative matching in perceptual recognition. *Journal of Experimental Psychology, 49*, 187–192.

(with P. E. Nicely) (1955). An analysis of perceptual confusions among some English consonants. *Journal of the Acoustical Society of America, 27*, 338–352.

(1956). The magical number seven, plus or minus two: Some limits on our capacity for processing information. *Psychological Review, 63*, 81–97.

(with N. Chomsky) (1958). Finite state languages. *Information and Control, 1*, 91–112.

(with E. Galanter & K. Pribram) (1960). *Plans and the structure of behavior*. New York: Henry Holt.

(1962). Some psychological studies of grammar. *American Psychologist, 7*, 748–762.

(with N. Chomsky) (1963). Introduction to the formal analysis of natural languages. In D. Luce, R. Bush, & E. Galanter (Eds.), *Handbook of mathematical psychology* (Vol. 2, pp. 269–321). New York: Wiley.

(with N. Chomsky) (1963). Finitary models of language users. In D. Luce, R.

Bush, & E. Galanter (Eds.), *Handbook of mathematical psychology* (Vol. 2, pp. 419–491). New York: Wiley.

(with S. Isard) (1963). Some perceptual consequences of linguistic rules. *Journal of Verbal Learning and Verbal Behavior*, 2, 217–228.

(with S. Isard) (1964). Free-recall of self-embedded English sentences. *Information and Control*, 7, 292–303.

(with K. O. McKean) (1964). Chronometric study of some relations between sentences. *Quarterly Journal of Experimental Psychology*, *16*, 297–303.

(with L. E. Marks) (1964). The role of semantic and syntactic constraints in the memorization of English sentences. *Journal of Verbal Learning and Verbal Behavior*, *3*, 1–5.

(with J. Mehler) (1964). Retroactive interference in the recall of simple sentences. *British Journal of Psychology*, *55*, 295–301.

(1965). Some preliminaries to psycholinguistics. *American Psychologist*, *20*, 15–20.

(1972). English verbs of motion: A case study in semantics and lexical memory. In A. W. Melton & E. Martin (Eds.), *Coding processes in human memory* (pp. 335–372). Washington, DC: Winston.

(with P. N. Johnson-Laird) (1976). *Language and perception*. Cambridge, MA: Harvard University Press.

(1977). *Spontaneous apprentices: Children and language*. New York: Seabury Press.

Carl Pfaffmann

Carl Pfaffmann

I was born May 27, 1913, in Brooklyn, New York. I remember very little from the early period of my infancy except one recollection of being held up to a Tiffany lamp shade over our dining room table to look at and play with the bangles so typical of that style lamp shade popular then—and even now. Why I should remember that and little else of early childhood is not of particular psychological import. It certainly did not influence my later development; I did not become a painter or an artist or even a visual scientist. I also have a strong visual memory image, from age five, of the Victory Parade up Fifth Avenue, New York, at the end of the World War I in 1918. We had seats in a second or third floor office, arranged as a grandstand to watch the parade.

My family moved from Brooklyn just over the border into Queens, to a section known as Woodhaven. Here my parents bought a two-family house, with an apartment on each floor, a garden on one side of the house, and a cottage converted to a garage in the rear. The public elementary school I attended was within walking distance in an essentially middle-class neighborhood. Just several blocks north of our house was Forest Park, still among the wooded parklands in and around New York City, which also boasted a golf course. In winter, it provided excellent sledding over and around the more hilly portions of the course. I have occasional fleeting memories of these elementary school years. Almost immediately on entering the first grade, I was moved up one half-year grade and later up another, thus advancing one full year of the elementary school curriculum.

Most important for me, as it turned out, was the arrival of the Deininger family as tenants in the second floor apartment above us. Their son, Richard, was eight to ten years older than I and an undergraduate at Brown University. As I approached college age, he would invite me to sit in on bull sessions with his college friends on vacation who attended such

institutions as Colgate, Trinity College, and New York University. Thus
I was influenced by this glimpse of college life, especially when it came to
my choice of a university. Neither of my parents had attended college, but
it was taken for granted that I and my younger sister would do so. Between elementary school and high school, I spent a couple of years in a
rapid advancement group at Lincoln Junior High and advanced another
year academically by its program. I then attended Richmond Hill High
School and graduated just after my sixteenth birthday. At first I had only
middling grades but picked up as I went along and ended with honor
grades just before graduation.

I had begun piano lessons while still in grade school, possibly stimulated by my mother's gift of "playing by ear" after hearing a melody or a
song. Although I seem to have progressed satisfactorily, she remarked, "If
you're going to go to college, ultimately you will have to help earn your
way. Piano players are a dime a dozen." She thought I might do better to
shift to the saxophone, which was in greater demand. So I began saxophone lessons while in junior high. At Richmond Hill High, I played well
enough to join the school orchestra. Its programs consisted of mostly classical music, which often didn't have parts specifically for the saxophone.
However, cello parts were sorely needed and could be provided by the saxophone by transposing the base cleft music as treble cleft. The music
teacher directing the orchestra also offered me the use of a school-owned
clarinet and recommended a former student who taught both saxophone
and clarinet. I soon became proficient enough to play regular clarinet parts
in the school orchestra. At the same time, however, I joined up with a
small jazz combo and played for hire at neighborhood dances or other
functions. I got to know other musicians and certain agents in New York
City who hired freelancers, especially during holiday season. So in the last
years of high school I was also earning funds by playing in jazz combos,
including one small group I organized called the Carltonians.

As I finished high school, Richard Deininger strongly urged that I apply to Brown University. I did so and was accepted after a series of interviews by Brown alumni in New York City. Thus I began my freshman
year just after turning sixteen. At Brown I joined the football band; I also
helped a young professor of music revive a classical orchestra for undergraduates. On concert tours, mostly to other colleges, the regular concert
was often followed by a dance, at which I also played in its dance orchestra. During summer vacation, I played in dance bands at various summer
hotels; during term, usually at weekend parties. As a graduate student, I

had a regular Saturday night job with a small four-piece combo. I even continued this musical interest at Oxford where I played in the "Bandits" dance orchestra, often at college dances of the more informal sort. The "Bandits," however, was run more as a student club than a source of income. Money received for our services went into the club kitty and was used for the purchase of music, the rental of some instruments, or even the hire of an occasional professional to fill in instrumentalist gaps—actually I had replaced the professional hired to play first sax. Ultimately, at Cambridge I gave up the dance band but did play in the classical orchestra at least for my first year as a graduate student.

But to return to chronology. During the first two years at Brown, I took a variety of required courses, including psychology in my sophomore year. Elementary psychology lectures were given by Leonard Carmichael, then a relatively young professor who had been recruited from Princeton to head and modernize the development of a psychology department at Brown upon the retirement of Edmund Delabarre, who had been trained by William James but was professor of experimental psychology as a member of the Philosophy Department. Leonard Carmichael was a very dynamic and popular lecturer. His introductory year course met on Mondays and Fridays in the largest lecture hall on the campus at that time, usually giving the same lecture three times each Monday and Friday. Discussion sections of the elementary psychology course consisted of about fifteen to twenty students each, meeting on various days of the week, and were conducted by junior faculty or graduate student assistants. The text was Warren and Carmichael's *General Psychology*, with a strong experimental, biological orientation. I also remember very well the ever-present lecture outline chalked on a large blackboard beside the podium from which Carmichael lectured. He had already been recognized as an excellent teacher and an up-and-coming academic; he went on to become dean of the faculty at the University of Rochester, then president of Tufts University, then secretary of the Smithsonian Institution in Washington, D.C.

In spite of his heavy teaching responsibilities, Carmichael conducted the graduate seminar, directed graduate students in research, and kept up an active research program of his own on fetal development of animal behavior. These latter studies involved a cesarean-type delivery of the fetus of an anesthetized cat while maintaining the fetal-maternal circulation intact. The young fetus and mother were immersed in a warm saline bath while the fetus was stimulated by touch, vision, hearing, thermal agents, and tested for reflexes and patterns of movement. After a year at

Brown, I had decided that an academic career was for me, but at first, I wasn't sure in what subject. I had had a very intriguing and interesting freshman course in history, which rather attracted me, but Carmichael's introductory psychology course ended any uncertainty as to my future.

Carmichael also personally directed the undergraduate honors program, in which individual students did research and wrote a thesis under the guidance of a faculty member. It was in one session with Carmichael that he asked what would I like to do for an Honors Thesis. By this time, I had been weaned away from my original interests in abnormal psychology, due in part to his admonition that an M.D. in psychiatry was highly desirable, if not a necessity at that time. This was before the great subsequent development of clinical psychology. Clinical psychologists were then largely involved with testing of one sort or another but had relatively little input in therapy. In any case, I didn't have the finances for medical school.

We discussed a variety of topics as possible research. At one point, Carmichael remarked that very little was known about the sense of taste compared with, say, vision or hearing. He opined that if one did a good job of research, he or she would be noticed and would also, of course, help fill a gap in knowledge. At about this time, Glen Wever and Charles Bray at the Princeton Psychology Lab had made their classic electrophysiological recordings from the cat's ear. They found that even the spoken word could be heard with only some slight distortion when the amplified electrophysiological response of the eighth nerve was fed into a loudspeaker. The higher frequency speech sounds exceeded the frequency that a single nerve fiber was capable of following. To account for their results, Wever and Bray developed the volley theory; that is, though individual nerve fibers could not follow frequencies much above 1,000 Hz, the nerve as a whole could follow 20,000 Hz or more by the alternate discharges every second, third, or fourth stimulus wave. This volley theory implied that frequency of nerve discharge was correlated with pitch of an auditory stimulus and so was contrary to the specific-place theory, which held that location on the basilar membrane determined pitch. S. S. Stevens, the psychologist, and Halowell Davis, the physiologist, were collecting data that supported location along the basilar membrane and activation of its particular cluster of nerve fibers as determining pitch discrimination. I can recall the many meetings of the American Psychological or Physiological Associations, where the opposing advocates would go over the latest evidence and argue at length about which was the correct theory of sensory pitch discrimination. The heat of the debate focused a lot of attention on this particular subject. Vision also was a popular research topic, the other senses less so, taste not at all.

In any case, with Carmichael's endorsement and prodding, I began the study of taste as an undergraduate honors project, largely in a methodological study employing, for the first time in taste, the method of *single stimuli* for determining the differential threshold, the DL. Of the psychophysical methods, only a method of constant stimuli using solutions of fixed concentration values repeatedly presented in random order were suitable for taste. Solutions were presented successively in drinking cups in a sip, spit, and rinse method. First, the standard stimulus was given, then one of five graded stimulus intensities to be judged as greater or less in intensity than the standard. The threshold was determined statistically from the percentage of greater or lesser judgments. The method of single stimuli omitted the standard and subjects rated each of the single test solutions from 1 (weakest) to 6 (strongest). Ratings of 1–3 were considered minus judgments and 4–6 as plus. Both methods yielded essentially the same thresholds and other statistical measures. I owed the specific problem to one of the junior faculty members at the time, Lester F. Beck, who subsequently went on to his own academic career at a West Coast university. I successfully completed this study, and it became my first publication (1935).

Upon graduating magna cum laude, with Honors, Phi Beta Kappa, Sigma Xi, etc., I was offered a teaching assistantship that enabled me to continue graduate studies at Brown in 1933. Meanwhile, the Department of Psychology was growing and thriving. Herbert Jasper had just arrived on the Providence scene as a clinical biopsychologist at the Bradley Home for children with behavior problems. He had done a Ph.D. in psychology at Iowa and in addition did postdoctoral work in Paris with the then still active professor of physiology Louis Lapicque. Jasper combined neurological and behavioral research methods and so had a well-equipped electrophysiological laboratory where he and Leonard Carmichael confirmed and extended Hans Berger's then new discovery of rhythmic electrical brain waves that could be recorded from the surface electrodes pasted on the outside of the human head. Since I had a good alpha brain wave rhythm, I served many times as a control subject in their experiments. In fact, I served as a laboratory assistant to Jasper over one summer vacation during which he let me also use one of his amplifiers to record nerve impulses in the frog dorsal cutaneous nerves that Adrian, Cattell, and Hoagland had described in 1931. Employing tactile and chemical solutions as stimuli, I merely confirmed their findings that touch activated large diameter nerve fibers while chemical stimuli activated smaller diameter nerve fibers judging from the magnitude of nerve impulse spikes. Thus there was a specificity of the nervous pathways when the frog skin was either touched or bathed in acid solution (Pfaffmann and Jasper, 1935).

Carmichael encouraged me to enter the competition for a Rhodes scholarship. I would not have done so on my own, though I had been involved with the freshman swimming team; I enjoyed athletic activities generally but was not a star in football or any other varsity sport. In fact, the Rhodes Scholar from my class of 1933 was Owen Walker, who was a member of the varsity football team as well as a stellar student. Although I did apply, it seemed to me a very remote likelihood that I would be accepted. By now I had the plan to seriously apply the exciting and, for that period, new technology of electrophysiology to the nerves of taste. I applied on two subsequent occasions for the Rhodes scholarship while a graduate student, at Carmichael's continued urging, and was successful in 1935 and accepted for study at Oxford. At that time, there was no formal degree program in psychology nor laboratory of experimental psychology at Oxford. Since I had had only a scattering of preparation in biological science and none in physiology per se, I opted to study physiology in the famous Sherrington School, although Sherrington himself had only just previously retired. Thus I "read," as Oxonians say, for another bachelor's degree, this time a B.A., which required two years of study and lab work with advanced standing based on my American degree. The third year of the Rhodes could be taken elsewhere, and I opted to study at Cambridge where Lord Adrian, with whom it had been my ultimate hope to work, was professor of physiology. With an Oxford B.A., it was possible to study for the Ph.D. at Cambridge with only a two-year residency requirement. By the good fortune of having a George Henry Lewis Studentship from Cambridge and support from the Theresa Rowden Fund from New College, Oxford plus a teaching assistantship in physiology labs, I was able to finance my fourth year in England. During those two years at Cambridge, since only a thesis was required, I did research full-time and wrote my thesis on the "Electrophysiology of the Taste and the Dental Nerves of the Cat."

Before being allowed to perform experiments in England on living animals, it was necessary to be licensed by the Home Office. I recall the impressive document with blue ribbon and embossed seal certifying that I could work on anesthetized cats that would be euthanized at the end of a recording session.

I had originally planned only to study the taste nerves, but I more or less stumbled onto the rich and very large nerve supply from the teeth during my dissections of the oral cavity. The nerves of the teeth were afferents of the pressure receptors in the socket of the teeth and heavily innervated by large diameter nerve fibers. Because of the rigid attachment of the nerve ending to the tooth socket and to the teeth, the pressure receptors could be activated by a very light tap on the tooth. This produced a large amplitude synchronized volley of action potentials. These volleys could be driven by a vibratory stimulus, which at high frequencies functioned according to the volley theory predictions, driven at higher frequencies that no one fiber was capable of following. So I was able to obtain evidence supporting a Weaver-Bray type volley theory that adequately described the responses of the mechanoreceptors in the tooth socket to a vibrating stimulus. In fact, I wrote two papers on this subject (1939a, 1939b). The first concerned the volley theory, using the purely mechanical stimulation with a loudspeaker crystal driving unit. The second concerned the specificity difference in impulse firing when a tooth was cracked open and irritants applied to the exposed dentyne. The dental nerves discharged a train of very small impulses rather like the pain discharges previously described in cutaneous sensory nerves.

Recording taste, on the other hand, was technically more difficult. The chorda tympani nerve from the chemoreceptors is a relatively small one, made up of medium- to small-diameter fibers that discharge asynchronously when chemicals flood the anterior tongue receptor field. In my preparations, the nerve was cut centrally to exclude the sublingual salivary gland efferent discharges. Taste stimulation was found to consist of a definite asynchronous multifiber discharge quite unlike the huge synchronous volley when tapping a tooth. In fact, it took some time before I was able to record any taste nerve activity at all, largely because the chorda had to be dissected free from the intermixed large trigeminal fibers of the lingual nerve. The taste fibers join the tongue's tactile and pain systems and ultimately distribute with them to the tongue area.

Classical psychophysics with humans had led to the view that there were four basic tastes—salty, sour, bitter, and sweet—and the prevalent physiological theory proposed that there were chemically specific receptors for each of these basic quality stimuli with which afferent nerve fibers made contact. So for the four basic receptors there were said to be four different types of nerve fibers passing to the brain. But my single cat taste fibers, when dissected from the teased-apart chorda tympani nerve and tested by flooding the tongue's receptive field with different taste solutions, did not show specificity. In fact, all single units responded to acid; many responded as well to sodium chloride plus acid, and still others responded to acid plus quinine. There was no response to sugar solutions. These results were unexpected and did not conform to any previous classification of taste stimuli or of taste qualities.

How could discrimination take place? I theorized that acid could be discriminated by the cat if all its taste fibers were stimulated en masse, but salt could be discriminated by a subset of units which responded to acid plus salt. Finally, bitter could be detected by still another subset which would react to quinine plus acid. In other words, it was the pattern of activity in all fibers concurrently active, rather than discharge only of one of the specific set of units that was responsible for taste quality. It suggested that the discriminatory processes in the brain were not as simple as the four specific fiber and receptor types hypothesized. Rather some *across-fiber pattern* seemed to be involved, which the brain somehow discriminated (Pfaffmann, 1941). My subsequent research, as well as that of many others since, showed that many taste afferents responded to more than just one of the four basic taste stimuli.

The different taste nerves, the chorda tympani from the front of the tongue, the glossopharyngeal from the back of the tongue, or the greater superficial petrosal from the roof of the mouth, each might show different relative sensitivities to the basic taste stimuli in different species (Nejad, 1986). In the macacque monkey (Sato, Ogawa, and Yamashita, 1975) there were indeed sugar-sensitive units, largely responsive only to sugar, and quinine units reacting only to quinine, whereas acid and salt units tended to react to both acid and salts but in quantitatively different amounts. The terminology of labeling of taste units by their "best stimulus" was developed by Frank (1977) to acknowledge that taste has a broad sensory "tuning," that is, that a single afferent fiber responds to more than one chemical class of taste reception, but that the "best stimulus" in some cases is uniquely sensitive to only that one of the basic four tastants.

The cat, it turned out, had not been a good prototypic taster, because it lacked sugar sensitivity, among other things. Even in the rat, recent results show that the chorda tympani receptors are less reactive to sugar compared to the glossopharyngeal and greater superficial petrosal nerves (Nejad, 1986). Other phyla among vertebrates may have unique sensitivities—for example, for amino acids. Thus the catfish (Caprio, 1980) has at least one highly specific receptor for the amino acid L-arginine, which as an adapting stimulus eliminates the response only to arginine whereas L-alanine cross adapts and eliminates the response to all amino acids except arginine. Modern theorizing is tending to focus on receptor molecular sites whose structure fits the taste molecule not in a rigid lock-and-key arrangement but in a more loose, but nevertheless specific, binding. And indeed, there are a number of experiments underway trying to identify specific blocking agents in relation to their molecular configuration. William Jakinovich (1985), one of my academic grandsons, has been working along this line to find specific blocking molecules with which to dissect the chemical character of the specific binding sites on the taste receptor.

Toward the end of my Cambridge stay, Adrian had a visit from the American scientist Detlev Bronk, then professor of biophysics and head of the Eldredge Reeves Johnson Foundation Laboratory at the University of Pennsylvania. Bronk himself had spent a postdoctoral year in England, some of it with Adrian at Cambridge, and they had published together on recordings from single motor units (Adrian and Bronk, 1929). Bronk suggested that I write him when I had finished my thesis. That was in 1939, just before the outbreak of World War II. In fact, I returned to the United States on the last normal trans-Atlantic crossing of the famous French liner *Normandy*, after which it was converted to a troop transport.

Bronk offered me a postdoctoral position at the Johnson Foundation at the University of Pennsylvania, which at that time was one of the premier laboratories for neuroelectrophysiology in the United States. H. Keffer Hartline, Frank Brink, and Martin Larrabee were in their youthful prime. Clarence H. Graham, visual sensory psychologist, and then Graham's student Lorrin A. Riggs had worked with Hartline several years before, so that a psychophysiology niche had been made in that mainly biophysical laboratory. I did not work on taste, but rather on a series of projects suggested by Bronk, such as the effect of physical pressure stimulation of bare nerve fibers, also conduction of the nerve impulse in the medullated single nerve fiber and its relation to the internodal and nodal currents. Since my Brown B.S. and M.A. were in psychology and my Oxford B.A. and Cambridge Ph.D. in physiology, the shape of my future career was unclear.

I had visited the continent on vacations as a student at Oxford and Cambridge and, indeed, had taken a summer course for foreigners at the University of Freiburg and made three trips to Poland to visit my fiancée,

Hortense Louise Brooks, an American whom I first met as a fellow student at Oxford whose family lived in Poland. Her father, a mining engineer, was president of Giesche Company, a subsidiary of the Anaconda Copper Company. He and many of the staff from the United States were operating the very rich and productive zinc and coal mines as well as a number of other ancillary activities in Poland that had been built up by the original Giesche Company. As a result of the post–World War I resettlement, these mine properties straddling the Polish-German frontier were cut in half and some of the underground mine galleries were blocked off beneath the border with concrete walls. So from my travels on the continent, and particularly in visits to Poland, I saw firsthand the growing Nazi propaganda and military preparations. My letters home, particularly those to Carmichael, were judged as alarmist, I recall. Indeed, relatively few people in the United States seemed to appreciate the scope of the rising Nazi menace. The Munich settlement only delayed the start of World War II, but it did give the British and the Allies opportunity for further preparation. It allowed me to complete my last year at Cambridge and to write my thesis for the Ph.D., subsequently published in three papers (1939a, 1939b, 1941).

The Nazis invaded Poland on September 1, 1939, and World War II had begun. The United States, of course, did not immediately respond, except to begin to build up its own forces and armaments and a program of support for the Allies, Britain and France. Because of my experiences in Europe and my concerns about what was happening, I jumped at the chance to join a summer research team led by Ross McFarland, a psychologist at the Harvard Business School and its Fatigue Laboratory. He was to lead a project during the summer of 1940 on aircraft pilot selection at the Pensacola Naval Air Station. This was then the main Navy pilot training base as well as training school for Naval flight surgeons. Our research protocol included a wide variety of physiological measures, among them the then recently discovered Berger brain waves, psychomotor performance tests, tests of sensory-motor skills and perception, paper-and-pencil questionnaires, and psychological tests. These were to be administered to the incoming classes of Naval air cadets that summer. The results of our tests were to be filed and correlated later for their relationship, if any, with the success or failure in flight training. Meanwhile, most of us on the project were invited to apply for a commission in the hospital corps of the U.S. Navy. I was so commissioned as lieutenant, junior grade USNR in 1940, but on inactive status because we had completed our summer's work. Some of the senior Naval flight surgeons most interested in the selection process were to oversee the analysis of the data, along with McFarland and several other statistically sophisticated members of the research team.

During my postdoctoral year at the Johnson Foundation, I received the offer of an academic position from the Psychology Department at Brown University, then chaired by Walter S. Hunter. My task would be to teach the experimental and physiological psychology undergraduate laboratory courses, plus graduate seminars on sensory processes and physiological psychology. The psychology department, except for Harold Schlosberg, had had nearly a full turnover of staff with Hunter's arrival. He brought a number of other distinguished faculty from Clark, including Clarence Graham, the visual psychophysiologist, and Joseph McV. Hunt, the personality and social psychologist. Donald B. Lindsley, physiological psychologist and EEG expert, was director of the EEG laboratory at Bradley Home, with a joint appointment at Brown. The department staff in research had a strongly experimental-physiological focus, but with good coverage of social psychology, personality, abnormal psychology, testing, and measurement.

My tenure at Brown, however, was brief because the attack on Pearl Harbor occurred in 1941, and by 1942 I had been called to active duty at the Naval Aviation Selection Board of Philadelphia. By then the predictive efficiency of the Biographical Inventory and other paper-and-pencil tests of the Pensacola trial run in 1940 had been validated and were in active use. After about a year at the Selection Board I was transferred to the Philadelphia Navy Yard and attached to the Initial Flight Training Unit, which gave the fledgling naval cadets their first ten hours of flight experience in propeller planes. Student aviators learned takeoffs and landing in a standardized flight pattern around one of the auxiliary air fields. After soloing they went off to more advanced training.

It was at the auxiliary field near Camden, New Jersey, that I was able to carry out an experiment on depth perception during landings with the enthusiastic cooperation of the flight instructors. They volunteered to be subjects by wearing special goggles that occluded their binocular overlapping visual fields by opaque masking tapes over the nasal portions of their flight goggles. These goggles permitted unobstructed full view of their right and left monocular visual fields, each pair of goggles having been fitted to each pilot individually. One pilot served as subject while a copilot was along in case of an emergency. In fact, there were none in executing the simple training exercise "shooting the circle," which entailed touching the airplane's wheels to the ground within a white circle marked out on the landing strip. There had been much debate as to the need of the binocular cues in flight. Actually the pilots tended to level off too high in attempting to hit the circle but the remainder of the flight pattern was unaffected. However, after a few practice landings the pilots soon learned to compensate for their modified vision and to hit the circle. So the influence of the loss of binocular stereoscopic vision was demonstrated until the pilots learned to compensate for the loss of stereopsis. This study was published in the *American Journal of Psychology* after the war (1948).

Other duty assignments at other stations included the Naval Air Gunners Training School at Hollywood, Florida, duty at the Naval Aviation Psychology Laboratory at Pensacola, and finally at the Naval Medical Research Center in Bethesda, Maryland, from which I was detached from active duty in the autumn of 1945 with the rank of commander, USNR. I returned to Brown University to take up my interrupted academic career now with the rank of assistant professor under Walter S. Hunter as chairman of the department.

Not only were the other faculty members returning from wartime service but so were most of the graduate students. Some, like Richard Solomon and Eliot Stellar, had done wartime service in personnel selection and training and human engineering. We all were anxious to begin again our interrupted careers. One of the returning veterans was John K. Bare, who developed an interest in the well-known work of psychobiologist Curt Richter (1943). Richter's concept of behavioral homeostasis as reflected in the enhanced salt appetite for sodium chloride following dietary salt deprivation or after adrenalectomy (surgical removal of the adrenal glands) had attracted considerable attention. Adrenalectomy eliminates the hormone aldosterone and leads to excessive salt excretion in the urine, which could be fatal without replacement therapy.

Normal white rats show a preference for mild salt solutions (0.02 M) over distilled water in a two-bottle preference test, whereas adrenalectomized rats show the preference at a much weaker concentration. Richter (1939) theorized that the adrenalectomized rat has a lowered salt taste threshold, that is, is more sensitive to the taste of salt. My taste recording method seemed to provide the means for a direct test of Richter's hypothesis. So John Bare joined me in doing just this. In fact his thesis not only included taste nerve recordings but also a more systematic examination of preference behavior over a wider range of concentrations of salt than had previously been examined. Not only was the preference threshold decreased, but at all suprapreference threshold concentrations as well, intake of salt solution was greater in the adrenalectomized animal than in the normal. However, the salt preference peaked at about the same value of 0.1 to 0.2 M for both normals and adrenalectomized and then declined with increasing concentrations. At every concentration adrenalectomized rats took more salt solution than did the normals. However, we found that the electrophysiologically measured taste threshold was the same for both normal and adrenalectomized rats, at a value about 0.001–0.003 M, about the concentration at which the adrenalectomized animal first showed the salt preference in a two-bottle preference test. Thus the normals could physiologically taste the salt but did not show a preference. The salt-needy took the weak salt solution as soon as they could taste it. Thus a more central motivational change was induced by the adrenalectomy (Pfaffmann and Bare, 1950).

A number of other investigators used other behavioral measurements to assess the thresholds of salt and other substances such as sucrose or other sugars and nutrients, the effect of changes in behavioral methods such as using one-bottle sequential preference tests, multiple presentations of all concentrations at once to group-housed animals, conditioned aversion thresholds versus preference behavior, effect of denervating the tongue taste nerves, the effect of preloading with stomach intubation, the effect of esophagostomy on such preferences, etc. Thus the study of taste preferences and feeding behavior generally became a hot topic and many studies were carried out and are still being carried out on related issues including clinically relevant studies in humans.

In 1948 I received a call from Keffer Hartline, then at Johns Hopkins, that one of his graduate students, Lloyd M. Beidler, was interested in the chemical senses. Would I show him my preparation and methods of recording from the chorda tympani nerve? By this time we had given up on the cat and were recording from rats and were performing behavioral tests with them in an effort to relate their sensory functions with various taste preferences and aversions.

Lloyd and I now recall as amusing his and his wife's embarrassment at turning up in rough-and-ready hiking clothes at our first encounter, their luggage having been mislaid on their bus trip from Baltimore to Providence. In the laboratory, Lloyd was impressed by the multifiber response of the rats' chorda tympani to salts and acids, which is much more vigorous than those of the insect and frog nerve preparations he had been trying. The rat's chorda tympani response to sugar or quinine is not so impressive as that to electrolytes. After returning to his laboratory at Johns Hopkins, Lloyd not only recorded from the chorda tympani and other nerves, but made an important additional technical improvement, the use of an electronic summation and chart recorder (Beidler, 1953). This gave a permanent record as well as a quantitative measure of amount of neural activity. This improved recording method was adopted almost immediately by workers in taste electrophysiology. His theory of taste stimulation (Beidler, 1954) provided a significant biophysical model for the rapidly developing field of chemosensory function sparked in good measure by a coterie of our students. He and I have continued as the best of friends over the years, as well as coworkers in science.

I owed another warm and valuable scientific friendship to our common interest in taste, that with the late Yngve Zotterman of Stockholm. He had been an early collaborator of Adrian's at Cambridge, mostly on touch, pain, and temperature sensitivity, including one early recording of taste. He returned to the study of taste in the 1940's. Notable was his and Diamant's (1959) first recording from a human chorda during otological operations performed under general anesthesia (Diamant, Funakoshi, Strom, and Zotterman, 1963). At a later time, I arranged for one of my students, Bruce Oakley, to join Zotterman for a year's postgraduate work to devise psychophysical measures that might be made on the patient before and after an operation that essentially transected the chorda tympani nerves. This work permitted a direct comparison of psychophysical measures of human taste with sensory neurophysiology. Since that time operative procedures have been modified by the use of local anesthesia, which blocks all nerve function and prevents such recordings.

Another long personal friendship that I treasure was that with Zoran Bujas, long-time professor of psychology at the University of Zagreb, Yugoslavia. He had been a student of Henri Piéron of Paris and had carried out most of the more modern quantitative psychophysical studies of human taste function, especially the so-called "electric taste." This was first described by Sulzer in 1754; then Volta, in 1792, carried out a number of experiments and correctly explained the effect as due to the flow of current. The positive pole caused sourness, the negative an alkaline, bitter sensation. In fact, Bujas spent several months in my laboratory in the late 1960's, where we studied the electrophysiological responses of the rat's chorda tympani nerve to various parameters of anodal and cathodal currents (Bujas, Frank, and Pfaffmann, 1979). In general, there is a greater correspondence between anodal make and the discharge of impulses in the chorda and human psychophysical reports of sour taste. In more recent work using hamsters, which have more sweet sensitivity than the rat's chorda tympani field, we could correlate cathodal polarization, that is, iontophoresis of the saccharin anions with stimulation of hamsters' sugar-sweet receptors (Pfaffmann and Pritchard, 1980). Thus the taste receptors show the same specificity to electrochemical iontophoresis as they do to pure chemical stimulation. Not only did Bujas share my interest in taste, but we shared a love of sailing and cruising along the Dalmatian Coast in his *Vihor* and in New England waters in my *Isis*.

Concerning the salt appetite and its relation to taste sensitivity, little further was done comparing adrenalectomized animals with normals until Robert Contreras (1977) at Michigan State used a more sophisticated reanalysis of taste electrophysiology and salt appetite by recording the response of single taste chorda tympani units. Later, he joined my laboratory as a postdoctoral fellow, and then he and Marion Frank measured the reactivity of single taste units to salt (Contreras and Frank, 1979). Bare and I had studied only the threshold range and found the same taste input for both normals and adrenalectomized rats. Contreras (1977) and Contreras and Frank (1979) also found no threshold change between the two groups but did discover a difference in magnitude of response to suprathreshold concentrations of sodium chloride. The response to the stronger salt concentrations was found to be *less* than that of normal animals. Medium to high-intensity salt solutions produced a lesser taste response in the salt-deprived than in the normal. This further negated the hypothesis that threshold or sensory changes could be responsible for the increased salt appetite in adrenalectomy. On the other hand, the finding of a reduced suprathreshold responsiveness was congruent with the fact that the sensorially aversive higher sodium chloride concentrations were attenuated in the salt-needy animal and it thus could ingest more of the concentrations which normals would reject. This argument did not, however, clarify the underlying mechanism of salt hunger, per se, in either normal or deprived animals. The first detectable saline concentrations are the same in both groups yet the preference behavior is clearly different. Presumably some mechanism involving the central nervous system must trigger a change in motivational state that effects "the pleasures of sensation" or the more appetitive aspects of intake behavior. Indeed Alan Epstein and his colleagues have in recent years found evidence that the action of the hormones angiotensin II and aldosterone play a key role in activating the salt appetite and intake. Blocking the synthesis of angiotensin II and blockade of the aldosterone receptors in the brain can abolish the salt appetite in previously salt-needy adrenalectomized rats (Saki, Nicolaides, and Epstein, 1982).

Derek Denton's landmark 650-page book *The Hunger for Salt* was published in 1982. As director of the Howard Florey Institute in Melbourne, Australia, he and his colleagues had carried out many studies of the salt hunger in sheep and other animals. This book not only covers their own work, but gives a broad scholarly coverage of anthropological, physiological, and medical aspects of the subject for which Denton and his colleagues are known internationally. He served as host and chair of not one, but two, meetings of the International Symposia on Olfaction and Taste (ISOT) with grace and hospitality.

As a professor I enjoyed teaching, even large elementary psychology sections as well as middle-level courses and purely graduate seminars. As I progressed up the academic ladder at Brown, I was generally a participant in academic life, including one year as president of the Faculty Club, along with other academic committee appointments and involvement in campus affairs generally. Excellent graduate students came to Brown, and I had my share as they selected thesis research topics in specialized areas of research. My running mate on the faculty, so to speak, was Lorrin A. Riggs, the other sensory psychophysiologist on the Brown faculty, whose prime interest was vision. Lorrin and I became and remain close friends. Though we were of nearly the same age and in closely related subjects, using similar techniques—electrophysiological recordings of sensory processes and their related behavioral effects—there was never a hint of rivalry between us. We each had a goodly share of graduate students, research grants, and laboratory facilities. No small part of Lorrin's and my compatibility was reinforced by the fair and benign treatment of junior faculty by Walter Hunter and then Harold Schlosberg as deparmental chairman. Lorrin and I shared most of the basement of the new Hunter Laboratory of Psychology, which was built midway through my tenure at Brown and named in memory of Hunter, who did so much to carry on the growth and development of the department initiated by Leonard Carmichael. Researchers using electrophysiological techniques tend to prefer basement locations, which are well-suited for the installation of electronically shielded and sound- and vibration-proof experimental chambers.

Though my research and specialized graduate teaching related to my interest in chemoreception and behavior, that is not the whole story of my academic career. Particularly broadening was a teaching experience that occurred when Henry Wriston, then president of Brown, proposed a new program of introductory courses campuswide under the general rubric of "The Identification and Criticism of Ideas." Harold Schlosberg and I conceived of a course on two of the faces of psychology, behaviorism and psychoanalysis, structured around Pavlov and Freud (Pfaffmann and Schlosberg, 1956). Contemporary reflections of the work of these two earlier intellectual giants were evident in the work of Dollard and Miller (1950) under the influence of Clark Hull at Yale, and others like Jack Hilgard and colleagues (Hilgard, Kubie, and Primpion-Mindlin, 1952) and B. F. Skinner (1953) had written in general and broad terms about behavior. We set up a year-long course with each section limited to twenty students who opted to participate in this new program. Sections met with a single professor; everyone sat around a large circular table especially designed to provide a seminar format. A weekly laboratory period was held elsewhere, in a large room with a series of cubicles to accommodate pairs of students. The first term was led by Harold Schlosberg, who emphasized the Pavlovian approach in studies of the conditioned reflex, including experimental neuroses elicited as the animals tried to cope with difficult sensory discriminations. I agreed to handle the second semester, which began with reading Freud's original lectures on psychoanalysis (in English edition, 1952), followed by the modern behavioral extensions and reinterpretations thereof. This meant that I personally had a great deal of new reading and preparation to do, both ahead of time and during the second semester.

In addition to the Keller-Skinnerian type of operant conditioning laboratory of the first semester, we included visits to mental hospitals and clinics in the second semester. At this time Ogden Lindsley and B. F. Skinner were setting up operant behavior test rooms for selected patients at a psychiatric hospital at Wrentham, Massachusetts. In addition to field trips to observe these special laboratories where patients were subjects, we also scheduled groups of students to make the rounds with staff members of the hospital itself to see the range of disabilities that were then found in a rather typical state psychiatric institution. For most of the students this was a first time for such a visitation. If nothing else came from the course, they at least became aware of what psychopathology could be like, a very sobering experience. The course was a great success and the Psychology Department at Brown ended up hiring three additional staff members to handle the extra sessions for the increased enrollment in this program.

In 1959 I was elected to membership in the National Academy of Sciences, a signal honor which I deeply appreciated. Besides that honor, election to the Academy led to my involvement in scientific issues of broad social concern. Thus I chaired the Assembly of Behavioral and Social Sciences of NAS-NRC in its formative years and edited a report on *Basic Research and National Goals* for the House of Representatives Committee on Science and Astronautics. Ultimately, sections of social-political sciences and economics were joined with the sections of anthropology and psychology to comprise class V of Academy membership.

It was during this period that I was elected president of the Eastern Psychological Association. For my presidential address I prepared what I consider to be one of my more important papers, entitled "The Pleasures of Sensation" (1960). This related my physiological and behavioral studies of taste to the broad context of sensory affect. Jacob Steiner's photographs of newborn infants responding to sour, sweet, and bitter taste stimuli were to come later, dramatic and charming photographs that give an objective emphasis to the concept of sensory affect (Steiner, 1973). P. T. Young (1961) at Illinois had long theorized about the relative importance but neglect of the hedonic aspects of experience. Beebe-Center's book (1932) on the psychology of pleasantness and unpleasantness includes a detailed review of Engels ratings of such solutions as sucrose, quinine, salts, and acids. Striking individual differences are reliably depicted in graphs of such hedonic ratings. Sensory affect could be indicated by the striking Steiner photographs not only of neonates but also young adults blind from birth. Sensory affect seems partly an unlearned response and partly an acquired response to certain classes of stimuli, since different adult individuals may differ considerably. But in newborn animals and humans much of this is unlearned.

Judith Ganchrow, who had taken her master's degree with me at Brown, and her colleagues, Israel Lieblich and Edna Cohen, at the Department of Oral Biology-Hadassah Faculty of Dental Medicine (Ganchrow, Lieblich, and Cohen, 1981) uncovered a relationship between brain self-stimulation by electric currents from an indwelling electrode in the hypothalamus and avidity for highly preferred saccharin solutions. In these studies, animals that gave high rates of self-stimulation also showed a high intake of saccharin solutions when offered these fluids in a drinking test. That there is a hypothalamic system for taste was shown by Ralph Norgren (1979) and his co-workers; as members of my laboratory at Rockefeller, they elucidated the anatomical pathway from tractus solitarius of the medulla to a pontine taste area with further neural connections to the hypothalamus and limbic structures. Further than this, Ganchrow and her colleagues' studies have found that the tendency to ingest taste substances is in part under control of endogenous opioids. Naloxone, an opiate antagonist, markedly reduces the normal ingestion of sweet substances. Others have found that feeding rats a highly palatable sweet fluid mixture enhances the release of hypothalamic β-endorphin.

In 1960 the American Psychological Association received a grant to send selected groups of its members to visit laboratories of the Soviet Union. Neal Miller, Harold Schlosberg, and I were among those selected, and we joined up to travel together as a trio because of our friendship and similarity of interests. In Moscow, we visited the laboratories of Petr Anohkin, Aleksandr Luria, Ezras Asratyn, and Aleksei Leontiev, all located in Academy of Science laboratories or the university in Moscow. We then traveled to Leningrad to visit the famous "Towers of Silence" and to see Pavlov's old office set up as a memorial to him, with many of the last papers and memoranda on which he was working just before his death. The appellation "Towers of Silence" referred to the soundproofing of all the experimental rooms in order to eliminate distracting and interfering stimuli while the animals were being conditioned. However, most of the current behavioral and conditioning research being carried out by the Moscow group was now done at the research station outside the city.

From Leningrad the three of us traveled to Odessa for a shipboard trip on the Black Sea in order to visit the Sukhumi Primate Station and Laboratory, where research on primates included field studies of social interactions as well as physiology and the standard conditioned reflex paradigm. We traveled to Tbilisi, the capital of Georgia, in order to visit the grand old man of neurological and behavioral research Ivan Beritashvili. When we arrived he was still actively involved in the work at the research station named in his honor, the Beritashvili Institute. He had been director for many years but was then retired. We were treated with great hospitality and the camaraderie of fellow scientists. The much vaunted Georgian hospitality was the source of one of the worst hangovers I have ever experienced.

This was a time of thaw in international relations between the Soviet Union and the United States. To see this kind of interaction fall by the wayside in the intervening years, when hostility characterized the relations of the two nations, saddened most of us who had visited and known our Russian fellow scientists. I'm glad that new agreements for scientific exchanges between the U.S. National Academy of Sciences and the Academy of Sciences of the Soviet Union have now been signed, and I look forward with hope for their success. Overall, we were well impressed by the research we saw and heard about. A detailed account of this and other institutes and certain centers visited by other groups of our delegations who traveled independently of us is contained in *Some Views on Soviet Psychology* (see Miller, Pfaffmann, and Scholsberg, 1962). The most recent turn of events on a broader scale signalled by President Ronald Reagan's visit to Moscow and positive interaction with the new Soviet leader, Mikhail Gorbachev, are most promising indeed and more than I ever expected to see in my lifetime.

On leaving the Soviet Union, we stopped off at Warsaw to visit Jerzy Konorski, whose institute and laboratory were very active and whose focus seemed more consonant with our own on problems of learning and conditioning than many we had seen in the Soviet Union. Konorski had been in the United States a number of times and in fact had some support from the U.S. National Institute of Health. He had many contacts with investigators in America and western Europe. Since the time of our trip, he and many of the senior distinguished scientists we met have passed away, and a new generation is now in charge. The institute where Anohkin worked has been named in his honor. He and others are well remembered by their students and former fellow colleagues.

A big change in my career took place in 1965 when Detlev Bronk, then president of the Rockefeller Institute for Medical Research, invited me to come to the Institute as a vice-president and professor to aid in broadening the institute to university status, in particular to include biobehavioral sciences, as well as to continue my own research. This meant shifting my residence from Providence to New York City. Fortunately my children were all away at college, so that to some extent they were independent and becoming more so. In fact my daughter, who had recently graduated from Mount Holyoke College, had joined the Peace Corps and was stationed in Liberia at this time.

One task at the Rockefeller was to recruit professors. The first to join in this new effort was Neal E. Miller, whose appointment gave our program a healthy boost. Not only was he a personal friend and a valued colleague, but he was one of the most distinguished of the academic psychologists of learning and behavior, having been awarded the President's Medal of Science in 1965. Ultimately, two other distinguished psychologists, this time in the field of learning and cognition, William K. Estes and

George A. Miller, joined the faculty. In a simultaneous and parallel development, the New York Zoological Society and the Rockefeller Institute jointly invited an animal behavior group, led by Donald Griffin and Peter Marler, to join the faculty, with the Bronx Zoo agreeing to provide field station facilities for their research.

Before our arrival, Bronk had recruited a very distinguished faculty group in philosophy and logic, in mathematics, and in physics. The name of the Institute officially became The Rockefeller University in 1967, and Bronk retired in 1968, having not only extended the intellectual scope of the university but also built new accommodations, a residence for students, and a building for the administrative staff, as well as other facilities. But Bronk's imaginative, broad-ranging intellectual plan was not to last. After his retirement in 1968, the presidency of his successor, Frederick Seitz, was marked by a severe shake-up that involved termination of the academic positions in philosophy. Nearly all the philosophers left Rockefeller for positions at other well-recognized universities. Nonetheless, in spite of such perturbations, Bronk's basic idea of establishing the Graduate Program was successful and is now a distinctive feature of the current Rockefeller scene.

The biobehavioral group, however, flourished under Seitz. A grant of land and building made possible the establishment of a behavioral field station where Griffin, Marler, and then Fernando Nottebohm set up a permanent base at Millbrook, New York, a kind of second campus of the university. Neal Miller and his students continued to develop his concepts of conditioning and learning in relation to health and behavior. He, together with Bernard Brucker and a group of colleagues both at the Rockefeller and at the rehabilitation unit of the City Hospital on Roosevelt Island, as well as other students and colleagues, gave dramatic illustrations of how behavioral training techniques could improve living with physical disabilities (Miller and Brucker, 1979). One of the more dramatic was the case of a girl with high cervical spinal cord lesion who was unable to sit up when lifted up because she "blacked out" from postural hypotension whenever she sat upright even in bed. Using biofeedback methods, she was taught to raise her blood pressure voluntarily and ultimately learned to sit upright in a wheelchair and even to be taken out of the hospital by an attendant on shopping trips, visits to art galleries, and concerts.

Marler and Nottebohm extended their studies of bird song learning, particularly how the young bird learned its typical species-specific song. It seems that it had to relearn its species song but with some variance each year. A good case was made that each seasonal relearning depended on the growth of new nerve cells under the stimulation of testosterone. Undeveloped stem cells were stimulated by the hormone for new growth of neurons annually. This raised the possibility that the bird (and even the mammalian) brain had more potential for correcting defects by growth and stimulation of new brain nerve cells than previously had been thought to be the case (Nottebohm, 1985).

However, after a promising and productive several years, focus on the more cognitive aspects of psychology as reflected by the laboratories of Estes and George Miller did not fare so well. After Seitz's retirement, subsequent administrative support for additional appointments for the Miller and Estes laboratories was not forthcoming. To my great regret, both left Rockefeller, Estes to Harvard and George Miller to Princeton.

Coincidentally, but independently, a number of changes occurred at Rockefeller. The Neuroscience Institute, a kind of "think-tank" founded by Frank Schmitt at MIT, moved from Cambridge to the Rockefeller under G. M. Edelman. Two new neuroscience faculty, Torsten Wiesel and Paul Greengard, whose researches had important implications for behavior and behavioral development, were appointed. Bruce McEwen, originally trained in biochemistry and a former member of Neal Miller's lab, became head of his own laboratory of neuroendocrinology. Upon my retirement as a professor and laboratory head, my successor was Donald Pfaff, a longtime member of my laboratory of physiological psychology. His focus on hormones and behavior led him to rename it the Laboratory of Neurobiology and Behavior. The interest in and concern for behavior was focused at a more reductionist mode, drawing upon methods of molecular biology and genetic engineering. Implicit in this renaming is the adaptation of techniques and methods of neuroscience and molecular biology to the mechanisms underlying behavior at a more sophisticated level than was the case in classical physiological psychology. Rather than being a subdivision of the discipline of psychology, workers in the borderline area between behavior and neural and humeral biology tend to view themselves as members of the neuroscience community.

As reported in a recent *Neuroscience Newsletter*, experimental and physiological psychologists find themselves an ever decreasing proportion of the membership of the American Psychological Association. The Division of Physiological and Comparative in 1982 consisted of 780 members, or 1.3 percent of the total APA membership. In the same year, the Neuroscience Society's membership in Psychology, Behavioral Science, and Psychobiology totalled 1,080 members, or 13 percent. Contributions to *Neuroscience Abstracts* in 1985 that involved behavioral assessment or behavior manipulations comprised 25 percent of the entries. Thus there is a growing relationship between neuroscience and physiological psychology, especially with regard to the molecular as well as more molar aspects of neural function in the brain-behavior relation. As someone trained in both psychology and physiology way back in the 1930's, I am, of course, in accord with such current trends.

There are other aspects of my academic career that in retrospect give me a sense of accomplishment and personal satisfaction. The first and most significant is having a family of former graduate students and postdoctorals who have made contributions to our field of knowledge of chemoreception per se or as it relates to behavior. Beginning with John Bare, there are the Ph.D.'s who did their research in my laboratories at Brown and at Rockefeller and have continued to be active in the field.* In addition, there are the numerous postdoctorals who favored me with their presence. Not only were they noteworthy for uncovering and documenting new findings and ideas, but the personal relations nearly always led to a warm and mutual friendship.

Two of my students, Bruce Halpern and Max Mozell, played an important role as consultants to the NIH in preparing the way for a program of support for clinical taste and smell research centers. Of the three original centers, one is at the University of Pennsylvania, headed by James Snow, chief of otorhinolaryngology, and Richard Doty, a psychologist and psychophysicist. The second is operated jointly by the University of Connecticut Health Center at Farmington and by Yale University. Originally organized by Frank Cattalanotto of Connecticut and Linda Bartoshuk of Yale, the Center is now under the direction of Marion Frank and Bartoshuk; both are former students of mine from the Brown era. I have served on the external advisory committees of both centers and am looking forward to increasing opportunities to participate in research at the Connecticut center. The third center, organized by Max Mozell at Syracuse, New York, Upstate Medical Center focuses more on olfactory functions.

*To list them alphabetically: Preston Sargent Abbott; John Kirby Bare; Linda May Buswell Bartoshuk; Robert M. Benjamin; John Anthony Carpenter; Robert Porter Erickson; Owen R. Floody; Marion Elizabeth Frank; Gabriel Paul Frommer; Earl Clifford Hagstrom; Bruce Peter Halpern; Charles Henry Hockman; Angela M. Hyman; Robert E. Johnston; Ronald P. Larkin; Donald Huston McBurney; Norman Bruce McCutcheon; Shelton MacLeod; Donald Matthews; Gordon Rolfe Morrison; Maxwell Mark Mozell; Samuel Gilbert Nord; Bruce Oakley; Rosemary Pierrel.

Several other such centers are located in the Midwest, the Rocky Mountain area, and the West Coast.

Another activity in which I take pride is in relation to ISOT, the International Symposia on Olfaction and Taste, which I helped originate, in company with Lloyd Beidler and Yngve Zotterman. The idea for such meetings came up and was developed at an informal meeting in my lab at Brown University. The three of us, Zotterman, Beidler, and I, had just participated in an international conference on all the senses held at an MIT center just outside of Cambridge, Massachusetts. We felt that, instead of just being one of the other senses alongside of vision and audition, there was enough current research activity among our students and other laboratories to warrant a meeting devoted solely to taste and smell. Zotterman observed that the International Union of Physiology was due to hold one of its triennial meetings in Holland in 1962, and that the Wenner-Gren Foundation of Sweden had just completed a conference center in Stockholm that would be well suited for an inaugural First ISOT. To make matters easier, Zotterman had just assumed the position of secretary to the Wenner-Gren Center. So it came to pass that the first ISOT was held in 1962, with Zotterman as the host. ISOTs have been held with a truly international schedule, as follows: I Stockholm (1962), II Tokyo (1965), III New York City (1968), IV Starnberg, Germany (1971), V Melbourne (1974), VI Paris (1977), VII Noordwijkerhout, Netherlands (1980), VIII Melbourne (1983), IX Snowmass, Colorado (1985). The ISOTs became official satellite conferences of the International Congress of Physiological Sciences.

Like so many other sensory sciences where human responses are involved, psychologists often play a key role in psychophysical measurements and hedonic as well as other scaling procedures. Where laboratory animals are involved, the application of operant methodologies as well as physiology is often important. Thus in meetings of researchers in the field of chemoreceptors, sensation and perception are an essential link between biology and behavior, between molecules and sensation, between affect and hedonics. I am proud to have played a role in the scientific and organizational developments of chemosensory science.

Selected Publications by Carl Pfaffmann

Selected from Pfaffmann's publications list of 150 references.

(1935). An experimental comparison of the method of single stimuli and the method of constant stimuli in gustation. *American Journal of Psychology*, *48*, 470–476.

(with H. H. Jasper) (1935). Sensory discharges in cutaneous nerve fibers following chemical stimulation. *Psychological Bulletin*, *32*, 565–566.

(1939a). Afferent impulses from the teeth due to pressure and noxious stimulation. *Journal of Physiology*, *97*, 207–219.

(1939b). Afferent impulses from the teeth resulting from a vibratory stimulus. *Journal of Physiology*, *97*, 220–232.

(1941). Gustatory afferent impulses. *Journal of Cellular and Comparative Physiology*, *17*, 243–258.

(1948). Aircraft landings without binocular cues: A study based upon observations made in flight. *American Journal of Psychology*, *61*, 323–334.

(with J. K. Bare) (1950). Gustatory nerve discharges in normal and adrenalectomized rats. *Journal of Comparative and Physiological Psychology*, *43*, 320–324.

(with H. Schlosberg) (1956). The identification and criticism of ideas: A new approach to the introductory course in psychology. *American Psychologist*, *11*, 78–93.

(1960). The pleasures of sensation. *Psychological Review*, *67*, 253–268.

(with N. Miller & H. Schlosberg) (1962). Aspects of psychology and psychophysiology in the U.S.S.R. In R. Bauer (Ed.), *Some views on Soviet psychology* (pp. 189–252).Washington DC: American Psychological Association.

(with Z. Bujas & M. E. Frank) (1979). Neural effects of electrical taste stimuli. *Sensory Processes*, *3*, 353–365.

(with M. E. Frank & R. Norgren) (1979). Neural mechanisms and behavioral aspects of taste. *Annual Review of Psychology*, *30*, 283–325.

(with T. Pritchard) (1980). Ion specitivity of "electric taste." In H. van der Starre (Ed.), *Olfaction and Taste 7* (pp. 175–178). Oxford: IRL Press.

(1982). Taste: A model of incentive motivation. In D. W. Pfaff (Ed.), *The physiological mechanisms of motivation* (pp. 61–97). New York: Springer-Verlag.

(1985). De gustibus: praeteritus, praesens, futurus. In D. W. Pfaff (Ed.), *Taste, olfaction, and the brain* (pp. 19–44). New York: The Rockefeller University Press.

(with M. E. Frank, T. P. Hettinger, & M. S. Herness) (1986). Evaluation of taste function by electrogustometry. In H. L. Meiselman and R. S. Rivlin (Eds.), *Clinical measurement of taste and smell* (pp. 187–199). Boston: Collmere.

Other Publications Cited

Adrian, E. D., & Bronk, D. W. (1929). The discharge of impulses in motor nerve fibers: 2. The frequency of discharge in reflex and voluntary contraction. *Journal of Physiology*, *67*, 119–151.

Beebe-Center, J. G. (1932). *The psychology of pleasantness and unpleasantness.* New York: Van Nostrand.

Beidler, L. M. (1953). Properties of chemoreceptors of tongue of rat. *Journal of Neurophysiology, 16,* 595–607.

Beidler, L. M. (1954). A theory of taste stimulation. *Journal of General Physiology, 3,* 133–139.

Caprio, J. (1980). Taste adaptation in the channel catfish, Ictalurus punctatus. In H. van der Starr (Ed.), *Olfaction and Taste, 8* (p. 210). Oxford: IRL Press.

Contreras, R. J. (1977). Changes in gustatory nerve discharges with sodium deficiency: a single unit analysis. *Brain Research, 121,* 373–378.

Contreras, R. J., & Frank, M. E. (1979). Sodium deprivation alters neural response to gustatory stimuli. *Journal of General Physiology, 73,* 569–594.

Denton, D. A. (1982). *The hunger for salt: An anthropological, physiological and medical analysis.* New York: Springer-Verlag.

Diamant, H., Funakoshi, M., Strom, L., & Zotterman, Y. (1963). Electrophysiological studies on human taste nerves. In Y. Zotterman (Ed.), *Olfaction and Taste* (Vol. 1, pp. 193–203). Oxford: Pergamon Press.

Dollard, J., & Miller, N. E. (1950). *Personality and psychotherapy.* New York: McGraw-Hill.

Frank, M. E. (1977). The distinctiveness of responses to sweet in the chorda tympani nerve. In J. M. Weiffenbach (Ed.), *Taste and Development* (pp. 25–41). (DHEW Publication No. NIH 77–1068). Washington, DC: U.S. Government Printing Office.

Freud, S. (1952). *A general introduction to psychoanalysis.* Garden City, NY: Garden City Books.

Ganchrow, J. R., Lieblich, I., & Cohen, E. (1981). Consummatory responses to taste stimuli in rats selected for high and low rates of self stimulation. *Physiology and Behavior, 27,* 971–976.

Hilgard, E. R., Kubie, L. S., & Primpion-Mindlin, E. P. (1952). *Psychoanalysis as science.* Stanford, CA: Stanford University Press.

Jakinovich, W. (1985). Stimulation of the gerbil's gustatory receptors by methyl glycopyranosides. *Chemical Senses, 10,* 591–604.

Miller, N. E., & Brucker, B. S. (1979). Learned large increases in blood pressure apparently independent of skeletal responses in patients paralyzed by spinal lesions. In N. Birbaumer and H. D. Kimmel (Eds.), *Biofeedback and self-regulation* (pp. 287–304). Hillsdale, NJ: Erlbaum.

Nejad, M. S. (1986). The neural activities of the greater superficial petrosal nerve of the rat in response to chemical stimulation of the palate. *Chemical Senses, 11,* 283–293.

Norgren, R. (1979). Taste: Central neural mechanisms of taste. In Darien-Smith (Ed.), *Handbook of physiology: Neurophysiology: Vol. 2. Sensory Processes* (2nd ed.) (pp. 1087–1128). Bethesda, MD: American Physiological Society.

Nottebohm, F. (1985). Neuronal replacement in adulthood. In Nottebohm, *Hope for a new neurology* (pp. 143–161). New York: New York Academy of Sciences.

Richter, C. P. (1939). Salt taste thresholds for normal and adrenalectomized rats. *Endocrinology, 24,* 367–371.

Richter, C. P. (1943). Total self-regulatory functions in animals and human beings. *The Harvey Lectures, 1942–43.* Series 38, 63–103.

Saki, R. R., Nicolaidis, S., & Epstein, A. N. (1982). Salt appetite is completely suppressed by interference with angiotensin II and aldosterone. *American Journal of Physiology, 251,* R762–R768.

Sato, M., Ogawa, H., & Yamashita, S. (1975). Response properties of macaque monkey chorda tympani fibers. *Journal of General Physiology, 66,* 781–810.

Skinner, B. F. (1953). *Science and human behavior.* New York: Macmillan.

Steiner, J. The gustofacial response: Observation on normal and anencephalic newborn infants. In *Fourth Symposium on Oral Sensation and Perception* (pp. 245–278). (DHEW Publication No. NIH 75–546). Washington, DC: U. S. Government Printing Office.

Young, P. T. (1961). *Motivation and emotion.* New York: Wiley.

Stanley Schachter

Born April 15, 1922, to Nathan and Anna (neé Fruchter) Schachter in Flushing (then a semirural part of Queens), New York. My parents were part of that great migration of East European Jews in the years preceding World War I. My father had been born in a Sholom Aleichem sort of town called Vasilau and my mother in a small city, then Radowitz, now Radauti. Both spots were part of the Austro-Hungarian empire, and my parents had been raised in the mishmash of German-Slavic-Jewish culture that distinguished this odd state. After World War I, the area became Romania, and after World War II, Russia.

My parents could well have been the self-made protagonists in one of those uncommon Jewish novels of the 1920's and 1930's in which the capitalists, for a change, were the heroes rather than the villains. My father, who loved to describe himself as the Vasilau town bully, raised a pair of oxen and at age thirteen, right after his bar mitzvah, sold the animals for enough money to pay his passage to America. He settled in New York, where his first job was as what he called a "cabinet maker." Since he wasn't worth a damn working with his hands, I've always assumed that meant that he worked in a furniture factory. In a year, he'd saved enough money to buy a pushcart, two pushcarts, then enough money to buy a candy store, then a laundry, two laundries, a steam laundry, lots of real estate, stocks, bonds, and by the time he died at age 82, he identified his profession as investor.

My mother, an orphan, came to America at about age seventeen. Her first and only job was as a seamstress in one of the sweatshops of the time. Just how they met, I'm unclear, but undoubtedly through some intermediary at the Czernowitz-Bukowina Society—a fraternal and burial society to which most immigrants from these areas belonged. There must have been some Rh problem, for though I was one of four children, I was the only one that survived, the others dying at birth or in infancy.

My early education was pure New York—P.S. 77 and James Monroe

High School—but when it came to college, I hadn't the vaguest idea of what to do. Everyone I knew was going to City College, and that is what a boy from the Bronx did in those days. I knew I didn't want to live at home during college and went to see our high school college counselor. She suggested three places—her favorite, the University of West Virginia (I'd expressed an interest in psychology and her husband was a professor of psychology there); Swarthmore, because it was supposed to be a nice place; and Yale, because she'd heard that it also had a good psychology department. West Virginia didn't, accept me, Swarthmore put me on a waiting list, and so I went to Yale.

Yale

For a 17-year-old boy from the Bronx, Yale in 1939 was hideous—a preppy-jock-socialite paradise not meant for the likes of me. I suppose it was what I deserved, for I went to Yale much against my father's wishes. He couldn't have cared less about higher education and wanted me to go to a one-year laundry college (no kidding) out in the Midwest and join him then in the family business.* In any case, after two years things began to pick up. Don Marquis took me on as his advisee and protégé, got me involved in his research, and I began to move more and more into the research and social world of the Institute for Human Relations. This was 1941, and the Institute, then, was a very different place from what it was before or after the war. Marquis was directing the department and, I think, the Institute. Most of the senior faculty were on leave for some war-related project, and the staff on the premises was either very old or very young. Al Lieberman and Charlie Osgood, both just finishing their degrees, seemed to do most of the teaching. Among the older members of the Institute, I remember particularly Clark Hull and Walter Miles. I lucked out with Hull. Graduate students were so few at the time that Hull decided to admit undergraduates to his seminar. I took it and was never quite the same. Hull had a teaching technique that both terrified and en-

---

*I never have understood what this intellectually driven Jewish immigrant business is all about. It wasn't true of my family, and I know very few families for which it was true. Like this generation's wave of immigrant scholars—the Orientals—I think we were forced into scholarship by a combination of ambition, opportunity, and puny build. Most of us, had we been larger, smarter, more agile, or better connected, would certainly have preferred being athletes, movie stars, millionaires, or practically anything rather than college professors or scholars who, where I grew up, had the status of public school teachers. To me, Jewish love of learning has always seemed a myth perpetrated by a few rabbis' sons who weren't good at anything much but going to school and then spending the rest of their lives writing novels about it.

chanted me, and I've borrowed the technique for my seminars. Each class had a reading assignment (never terribly much, usually a paper that Hull had written) and homework. Homework was a two-or-so-page detailed discussion, with questions and problems, of the assignment. The class proper was concerned entirely with the homework. Hull tried to teach Socratically. I do, too, but my version of Socrates tends more to resemble the way Miss Hogan used to run second grade back in P.S. 77—teach by terror. In any case, it worked and still does. I can't say that I ever became a convert, but I sure learned my *Principles of Behavior*.

The only other teacher at Yale who, like Hull, had a real impact on my style was W. K. Wimsatt, who managed to change my life with a couplet. Wimsatt, who was to become one of the luminaries of the Yale English department, earned his living back then by teaching freshman English. In high school I had been editor of the school's literary magazine. My command of adverbs, adjectives, and polysyllabic words was legendary and had made me one of the darlings of my English teachers. Determined to repeat this success at Yale, my first essay for Wimsatt was a gloriously wordy beaut, which he returned marked with a very large "D–" and a couplet of Alexander Pope's which went:

> Words are like leaves; and where they most abound,
> Much fruit of sense beneath is rarely found.

I was never the same and took the message sufficiently to heart to redo Pope's couplet to:

> Where leaves most abound,
> Fruit is seldom found.

I decided to go to graduate school in psychology at Marquis' urging. I was still too young to be drafted, and I guess Marquis wanted to be sure there was at least one body on the premises. I was assigned to be Walter Miles's research assistant, and under his calm, Quaker tutelage I became a virtuoso of the Hecht-Shlaer night vision adaptometer. When I was drafted, it was my work with Miles that determined my military career. After basic training I was assigned to the vision unit in the Aero-Medical Laboratory at Wright Field in Dayton, Ohio.

The Army

The Aero-Medical Laboratory was a militarized collection of displaced professors, Ph.D's, and would-be Ph.D's, all of whom shared two ambitions—to avoid being subjects in either the anoxia experiments or the "g" experiments (which required being strapped into a human centrifuge). Like it or not, though, we almost all took our turns, and I suspect the average IQ of the lab must have dropped five to ten points by the time the war ended. I worked with Al Chapanis and Dick Rouse on the effects of glass distortion on depth perception and on training procedures for improving night vision. It was solid, useful work, and the only flaky thing we ever got involved in was an attempt to verify the hot Russian claim at the time that one could dramatically reduce the time for night vision adaptation by stimulating other sense modalities such as smell, sound, taste, or touch. It was a hell of a lot of work that amounted to nothing (see Chapanis, Rouse, and Schachter, 1949), and I've refused to believe Russian claims about anything ever since.

I really have only one story out of my two-and-a-half years in the Army. It's the one about the corporal who goes to jail for telling a captain to go fuck himself, and it goes this way. I was on base, standing on a bus line with a bunch of other enlisted men. A captain joins the line, and everyone but me manages to look the other way or fall deeply into conversation or spot an airplane. I look at the man. He looks back and starts yelling that I should have called the line to attention; I tell him to go fuck himself and shortly find myself in the stockade for a week broken to buck private. The lesson in life to take away from this event is always to mumble when telling a captain to go fuck himself.

The war over, I decided not to go back to Yale. I had heard that Kurt Lewin had left Iowa and gone to MIT to establish the Research Center for Group Dynamics. I can't say that I knew very much about Lewin, but the idea that psychology might actually be useful in the study of social problems was, at my age, after two decades of depression, fascism, and war, hopelessly appealing. It was, on my part, a mindlessly idealistic decision, and I decided to go to MIT.

MIT and Michigan

I got out of the Army in the Spring of 1946 and went up to MIT that fall. Lewin had brought with him Dorwin Cartwright, Leon Festinger, Ronald Lippitt, and Marion Radke (Jack French joined up the following year), and these constituted the faculty of the Center. I think Morton Deutsch, Dave Emery, and Gordon Hearn were the first students at the Center and had started the previous year. The rest of us arrived that fall; besides me there were Kurt Back, Murray Horwitz, Harold Kelley, Dave

Jenkins, Al Pepitone, John Thibaut, and Ben Willerman. Since many of this group would be included in anyone's Who's Who of social psychology, I should point out that we were part of an extraordinary and, in a way, extraordinarily lucky generation of students. As far as I can tell, at that time, there was a remarkable group of graduate students at about every university in the business, and probably in every field. Thanks to the war, there was something like a four-year backlog of potential graduate students to choose from, and graduate departments could afford to be super-selective. It was also the case that just about anyone who got a degree in those years could be almost certain of getting a first-rate job. Those were the years of immense expansion of the country's university and research establishments. It was an academic seller's market if there ever was one, and one could virtually design one's job. My own first job at the University of Minnesota was fairly typical. My teaching load was one graduate seminar, subject of my choosing, which met once a week, and that was it. Research funds, secretaries, and assistants were someone else's worry, not mine. It was academic paradise, and one would needs be fairly incompetent not to have produced something worthwhile.

Back to MIT. I remember it fondly, but vaguely. We were all housed in one of those army surplus temporary buildings that covered university campuses throughout the 1940's. The students were jammed into two offices, the faculty into cubbyholes arranged around secretarial spaces, and there were a couple of makeshift seminar/laboratory rooms. It was humble and probably deserved to be so.

The attempts to educate us at MIT were friendly and vague. If I remember correctly, there were only two "real" courses—one given by Radke on Lewinian psychology, in which we read everything Lewin had written that had been translated into English, and one given by Festinger on statistics. Other than these, there were a variety of seminars on such things as group goals and locomotion, group norms and standards, and the like. The word "conceptual" was very big around MIT those days. For "real" courses we were permitted and encouraged to take course work at Harvard—which would have been fine if Harvard just then hadn't been going through its own grandiose attempt to combine sociology, anthropology, and social and personality psychology into a single Department of Social Relations. Between 1946 and 1948 it was just about impossible to hear a non-Messianic, non-pretentious word in all of Cambridge.

Most of my time at MIT was spent on my research assistantship with Festinger. Kurt Back and I worked as Leon's assistants in the Westgate study. Westgate was the name of an MIT married students' housing project, and the study was presumably concerned with the sources of housing satisfaction and dissatisfaction and I think was funded as such. It evolved into a study of social influence and communication and was the study which eventually led to Festinger's theories of communication and of social comparison processes. It was in this study that I discovered that although most of my talents as a scientist were modest, I did have one real talent—a knack for discovering things in the data. It's a knack that has been both a blessing and bugaboo. Anyone who pores over data long enough, and with enough love, is bound to find *something*. Problem is, are you going to find that same something when you pore over the next batch of data? Sometimes you do, and sometimes you don't. In any case, it's a knack that's been the source of much of my strength and of my difficulty in research.

Summers at MIT we spent differently. The grand plan for the Research Center for Group Dynamics had always involved a marriage of the theoretical, the empirical, and the practical as applied to social problems. During summers most of us worked on this marriage up at Bethel, Maine. Bethel was a prep school which in the summer rented its premises to what came to be called the National Training Laboratory in Group Development. I'm unsure of the details of funding (I think it was Office of Naval Research) and sponsorship and just who was involved, but Bethel, in memory, was a mammoth effort involving just about everyone at Group Dynamics, as well as a large contingent from Harvard and from the National Education Association. The general idea of this first Bethel seemed to be the application of the latest in social science techniques to training in group leadership. There were five or six training groups led by Ron Lippitt, Lee Bradford, Ken Benne, and others of their ilk. Training seemed to involve a lot of outlining on the blackboard, much talking out the heart, and an extraordinary amount of Moreno-inspired role playing.

Superimposed on this framework for training was a formidable research apparatus. A team of three observers was assigned to each training group. One observer used a version of the Bales Observation Schedule plus some newly devised group functions categories to code just about anything that might go on in the group. Since there were no tape recorders in those days, a second observer was asked to record the content of what went on, and finally, the third observer was in charge of "feelings" and personality—he was supposed to get at the latent content of what was going on; I suppose things like hidden agendas, concealed hostilities, and the like. Since I wasn't very good at feelings, had no idea what a group function was, but could write very rapidly, I was a content observer. In addition to this observational material, there were frequent sociometrics and innumerable questionnaires and personality inventories.

All of this went on for about two weeks, and there was a mammoth amount of data collected. I wish I could be more generous in my appraisal of this staggering research effort but in retrospect it was one monumental mess, saved from being even messier by the happy fact that way back then we didn't have video cameras, tape recorders, or computers. There were no real ideas guiding the enterprise—only the vague feeling that this was a golden opportunity and, if we just collected enough data, something had to come of it all. It was all something like today's psychophysiologist who feels that if he covers his subject with enough electrodes and feeds enough data into his computer, something has to come out. For Bethel, that something ended up as an issue of the *Journal of Social Issues* (Bradford and French, 1948) in which, among other exotic findings, it was revealed that those who spoke a lot in group meetings were more likely to be rated as productive group members than were those who didn't speak much. Someplace back in Cambridge or Ann Arbor there are trunkfuls, attics, warehouses of these data never to be analyzed, but perhaps much cherished by some archivist.

The shambles of this whole research effort just about ended the Lewinian dream for the Research Center for Group Dynamics as an applied-research-theoretical nexus for the study of group behavior. If Lewin had lived, perhaps those among us who weren't partial to "action research" would have felt less abused by the Bethel experience. Lewin died early in 1947 (before Bethel), and that spelled the end of group dynamics at MIT. I was never privy to just why this was so, but obviously MIT wasn't willing to continue supporting the Center, and for the next year, Cartwright, Festinger, French, and Lippitt made up a sort of traveling circus presenting panels on group dynamics and the new look in social psychology at a variety of universities that had expressed some interest in housing the Research Center. I think these included Chicago, Cornell, Minnesota, and Western Reserve. Berkeley and Michigan were also interested. Apparently Michigan made the best, or perhaps the only, offer, and we all moved, kit and kaboodle (whatever they are), to Ann Arbor.

I stayed at Michigan for the year it took me to finish my thesis. Didn't much care for the town, which is a sort of Palo Alto with rotten weather, and I was getting restless and eager to get out into the real world and on my own. It was too bad in a way, for Michigan at the time was unique. Don Marquis had moved from Yale and built Michigan into a psychological powerhouse. As far as social psychology went the cast was unbelievable: the whole Group Dynamics crowd was there, as well as the Survey Research Center group, which included Rensis Likert, Angus Campbell, and Daniel Katz; and among the non-Center affiliated regular department members were Ted Newcomb and Norman Meier. No matter how star-studded the cast, however, I was bent on finishing up and getting out of the place, and other than a few poker games, I played little part in the life of the department. Festinger, Back, and I were trying to finish our book on the Westgate study (Festinger, Schachter, and Back, 1950); I was hacking away at my thesis, and the only real stimulation that year came from Festinger's weekly evening seminar where those of us working with Leon (Back, Kelley, Thibaut, and I) worried about the design and interpretation of our theses and helped Leon work out the theory of communication and social influence that was to guide so much of our work.

In the spring of 1949, Minnesota offered me the lush job I've already described, my parents gave me a new Studebaker convertible as a graduation present, and in the fall of 1949, I drove to Minneapolis, top down all the way, for my first real job.

Minnesota

Of all the places that I've lived and worked, I think of Minnesota with the greatest nostalgia and affection. It's the place that represents much of my youth; it was there I was first married and divorced, and there that I broke away from my teachers and mentors and came of age scientifically. I started as an assistant professor with a joint appointment in the Department of Psychology and the Laboratory for Research in Social Relations. The Laboratory was Jack Darley's baby and creation, and was Minnesota's organizational response to the pressures of the time to unify and integrate the social sciences. Damned if I've ever understood quite why, but the 1940's and 1950's were a time when everyone seems to have decided that the boundaries delimiting the various social disciplines were artificial and a barrier to progress and that it was time to unify the social sciences. It probably started with Yale's Institute of Human Relations and in one form or another spread to Harvard, Michigan, Columbia, and Minnesota that I know of, and Lord knows how many institutions I don't know of.

Minnesota's version attempted to integrate, in this one laboratory, the activities of empirically oriented "people" psychologists (Ken Clark, briefly Charles Bird and Paul Meehl, me, and in time Leon Festinger and Harold Kelley), sociologists (at various times Elio Monachesi, Neil Gross, Arnold Rose, and Henry Riecken), economists (Andreas Papandreou), political scientists (Herbert McCloskey), educators (Ned Flanders), and philosophers (May Brodbeck). Jack Darley was the director, administrator, money raiser, and general guiding spirit of the enterprise. Those were, as I've noted, the lush years. Money was easy to get; subjects were easy to get; there were no ethical guidelines; teaching loads were light; space was available; secretaries were literate, and on and on—a golden era at Minnesota, which in time ruined the place. Things were so good at Minnesota that anyone who could make it, made it. And, attractive as Minnesota was, it was no non-Minnesotan's Utopia: the weather was appalling. My first year there it got above ten degrees above zero only three times during January. Probably I misremember, but it felt that way. Sooner or later, anyone who could left for his dream place. Kelley went to UCLA and his beloved California, and I to Columbia and my beloved New York City. Festinger went off to Stanford; McCloskey to Berkeley; Gardner Lindzey, between stopovers at Texas, gave Harvard one last try; and Papandreou eventually went off to Greece. I suppose that of us all, Papandreou had the most of what it takes to make it, for his father was in the Premier business and was desperately eager for his boy to go into the Premier business—almost as eager as my father had been for me to go into the laundry business.

My first few years at Minnesota were essentially "make-work" years. I was busy enough, but in essence I spent two to three years repeating some aspect of the Westgate study or of my thesis. This was a process that reached its culmination in 1952–53 when I managed to repeat my thesis in seven different countries. Dan Katz had convinced the Ford Foundation to support the Organization for Comparative Social Research, a group organized by the Institute of Social Research in Oslo to promote cross-cultural research and training in social psychology throughout Western Europe. Its members were social scientists from universities and research institutions in Belgium, England, France, Germany, Holland, Norway, and Sweden. They had decided that they would like to do a laboratory experiment (a relatively new development in social psychology at the time and almost untried in Europe) and that they would like to study the effects of threat on rejection of deviates. My thesis (Schachter, 1951) had been concerned with deviation and rejection; there was some feeling that, unlike Americans, Europeans wouldn't reject deviates, and, courtesy of Senator Fulbright, I was invited over to help develop and supervise an experiment that was to be replicated in these seven countries. The study is reported in Schachter et al., (1954). In essence, deviates were rejected in all countries but those in which the manipulation of one of the independent variables didn't work.

I returned to Minnesota late in 1953 and started a series of case studies of social isolation that led eventually to my studies of affiliation. Meanwhile, Festinger had left Michigan and come to Minnesota, and Henry Riecken had joined the Sociology Department. Leon was just starting to work on dissonance theory; somehow the millenial movement ideas came up, we read in the newspaper that Marion Keech was predicting the end of the world on December 21, 1954, and with very few second thoughts the three of us dropped just about everything else and were off to Chicago to join a group that was predicting salvation by flying saucer and the end of the earth as we knew it. It was four months of insanity and, I suppose, fun that we wrote up in a book called *When Prophecy Fails* (Festinger, Riecken, and Schachter, 1956). It was an amusement, but it did take us three months of full-time work to write the thing. Had we had but one table, with honest-to-God, real numbers, we would have had a nifty three-page article. As it is, sooner or later, someone will turn the damn thing into a TV series.

The millenium having failed once more to make it, I returned to serious work and finally struck off on my own—still essentially playing with the ideas in the Westgate book (though I didn't think so at the time)—but off at last on a program of work that felt totally my own. These were the experiments on affiliation that got me into birth order and eventually into emotion and that were published as the book *The Psychology of Affiliation* (Schachter, 1959). In these experiments we manipulated anxiety (by threatening subjects with painful electrical shocks in one condition and with only mild, tickly shocks in the other) and measured the impact of the manipulation on the subject's desire to be alone or with other subjects. There were, of course, qualifications and complications but, in essence, these studies demonstrated that the more anxious the subjects, the more they wanted to be with other people. (This tendency was particularly marked for first-born and only children—a finding which we were able to generalize to an astonishing variety of behaviors such as fighter pilot effectiveness, alcoholism, vulnerability to psychotherapy, and so on.)

Before getting into where these studies led, I must confess that I took advantage of the affiliation studies to bring myself closer to the finer things in life—if that's an appropriate way of describing professional recognition and prestige. I was in my mid-thirties and beginning to feel abused, unrecognized, and put upon. No matter what my opinion of myself, it didn't seem to be widely shared, and whether I liked it or not, I think that I was generally considered Festinger's boy. We'd worked together for so long and coauthored so many papers and books. Leon is a formidable persona; he was my senior, had been my teacher, and his name came before mine alphabetically. It was inevitable that I was in his shadow, and to break out of this mold, I deliberately decided on Madison Avenue tactics and entered a contest. I submitted the *Affiliation* book to the AAAS Social-Psychological Prize competition. I won, and though I haven't lived happily ever after, it made a difference. It was as if once a scientific counterpart of Good Housekeeping had given its seal of approval, I was on my way to becoming a scientific household name—invited to give speeches, send chapters, take part in symposia, consider job offers, and all the rest of the professional dross so important to young academics. It's a tactic I recommend to young scientists who covet recognition—go and win a contest.

Worrying through the meaning of the results of the affiliation studies got me on a new tack that in the long run led to my work on obesity, nicotine addiction, and appetitive-addictive pathologies generally. It seemed to me that the findings of the affiliation experiments could be interpreted as an indication that the emotions were as vulnerable to social influence as were the opinions and abilities (see Festinger, 1954). This, of course, was simply a point of view, not even a hypothesis, and to begin testing its implications, I took advantage of an old study by the Spanish endocrinologist Marañon (1924) in which he manipulated the physiological correlates of emotion by injecting his patients with adrenaline.

In these days of ethical guidelines and review committees, I don't think that there's a prayer that we'd be able to do the experiment we did then. In any case, Jerry Singer and I injected (or, rather, had an M.D. inject) student subjects with adrenaline or with a saline placebo, both of which we identified to the subjects as a vitamin supplement. Then, with Bibb Latané as stooge, we manipulated situations designed to make subjects euphoric in one set of conditions and angry in another set. The results of this first experiment (see Schachter and Singer, 1962) suggested that the emotions should be considered a joint function of physiological and cognitive-situational determinants. The data were encouraging enough so that we undertook a series of experiments (Schachter and Wheeler, 1962; Latané and Schachter, 1962; Singer, 1963) which, I think, pretty well established the usefulness of this formulation. My next fifteen years of work were largely concerned with exploring the implications of this formulation.

To start, at the same time that we had been demonstrating that we could manipulate the intensity of emotional states such as anxiety by jazzing up the level of sympathetic nervous system arousal via the exogenous administration of adrenaline, David Lykken at Minnesota had been doing his rather marvelous Ph.D. thesis on anxiety and criminal psychopathy (Lykken, 1957). In essence, he had demonstrated in a variety of ways that psychopaths were relatively anxiety free. One of his demonstrations had shown that psychopaths were incapable of learning anxiety-mediated avoidance behavior. With both bodies of work going on simultaneously, it was inevitable that it would occur to someone to replicate Lykken's work with subjects who had been injected with adrenaline. Working in the Minnesota state prison at Stillwater, Bibb Latané and I did just this. Using Lykken's apparatus, we replicated his study of avoidance learning, comparing the performance of subjects who had been injected with adrenaline with the performance of these same subjects when injected with placebo. It worked as we had hoped. Psychopaths with a saline placebo behaved just as Lykken's original subjects had. They failed to learn to avoid shock. With an adrenaline injection, they learned.

This was pretty heady stuff and trying to pick apart what it was all about occupied my first few years at Columbia, to which I went in 1961 as a professor in the new Department of Social Psychology.

Columbia

Columbia was different. First, unlike any other place at which I had worked or studied, the university played small part in anything but my research life. I was a bachelor again. I lived in Greenwich Village, in what my landlord called a garden apartment and my father called a basement. I was pleased with the university, but I adored the city.

Second, the university was conspicuously on its way downhill. The physical plant, a magnificent McKim-designed campus, was aging, and there didn't seem to be the money or the will to paint or patch. Its great names, too, were still there, but they were aging, and no one much was in evidence to paint, patch, or replace them either. The place seemed demoralized and drifting. Incidentally, Columbia was hardly alone at the

time in this state of semi-anomie. Senator McCarthy and the House Un-American Activities Committee had been at work, a few years earlier, protecting the country from the "Commies" and in the process debilitating the intellectual and aesthetic life of the country. Intellectuals were increasingly suspect; research was increasingly suspect; money was harder to get, and the Golden Age of universities seemed over.

Finally, the Psychology Department was a shambles. It, too, had had its great days when James McKeen Cattell and then Woodworth and Columbia colleagues such as Thorndike, Dewey, and Boas (who, for a while, taught statistics in the Psychology Department) had dominated American social science, but the department seemed to have fallen victim to religion. Somehow, I never learned how or why, the Skinnerians had obtained a foothold and, like Jesuits, had simply taken over. The department was a pigeon and eyeball department with not only no interest in, but an open antagonism to, personality, clinical, social—in fact any branch of human psychology that wasn't devoted to the demonstration that humans could be shaped as easily as pigeons.

Undoubtedly, it was this atmosphere that led Otto Klineberg, with the open encouragement of the administration and the other social science departments, particularly sociology, at Columbia, to break away and form a separate Department of Social Psychology. This was the department to which I came, and in its beginning, it consisted of Klineberg, Dick Christie, Bill McGuire, and me, all sharing, with a secretary, Klineberg's office in the Psychology Department. Within a few months, we had our own quite nice quarters and laboratory space on the top floor of a building that overlooked both Broadway and the campus. Klineberg left for a professorship at the Sorbonne, and Bibb Latané joined us.

McGuire did attitude change, I did group dynamics, Christie personality theory and measurement, and Latané animal social. It was entirely a graduate department, and though our students didn't get much of that old-time religion, they did, I think, get a hell of an education in what was hot at the moment in social. In the beginning, while waiting for our new quarters and laboratories to be built, I continued with the work on criminal psychopathy that Latané and I had begun in Minnesota. Bibb and I replicated our studies of adrenaline and avoidance learning in the reformatory at Bordentown, New Jersey, and Stu Valins and I tried to do this study once more in the prison at Riker's Island in New York. The Bordentown replication had worked out just fine with one titillating new twist. We'd been able to borrow from the RCA Laboratories an experi-

mental version of one of the earliest telemetric EKG devices. With this gadget we were able to track heart rate throughout the course of the experiment. The results indicated that subjects categorized as psychopathic were remarkably more sensitive to adrenaline than were control subjects. The finding was so startling that we all felt the need to get more subjects and to try this out at least once more. For reasons I've spelled out elsewhere (Schachter, 1971)—in essence, a city lawyer concerned with the possibility of municipal liability vetoed the study—we never did get to run the study on Riker's Island, and I've been uneasy with those findings (Schachter and Latané, 1964) ever since.

I have no idea if I'm unusual, but the question of replication bugs and haunts me (Schachter, 1978). I haven't always succeeded in replicating other people's work, and other people haven't always succeeded in replicating my work. Except for my attempts in the army to replicate Russian work on night vision, I almost always have blamed myself when I don't find what others do and blamed others when they don't find what I do. This comfortable attribution of guilt has allowed me to maintain the conviction that I am working in a science, but I can get uncomfortable about the enterprise.

In any case, though the failure to continue this work at Riker's Island was a disappointment, I wasn't heartbroken. I'd had a new idea and was considerably more eager to explore this than I was to repeat myself in a new context. I had read reports of Stunkard's (1959) findings on obesity and gastric motility, and it occurred to me that in an odd way his findings were like mine. Though we'd couched our work in the language of emotion, Singer's and my experiments with adrenaline had simply demonstrated that the exogenously induced state of sympathetic arousal did not necessarily lead to a universal label. Stunkard had demonstrated that another physiological state, in this case the gastric motility associated with food deprivation, was not invariably associated with the self-description "hunger." People of normal size tended to describe themselves as feeling hungry when the gut was contracting; the obese did not. Exploring the implications of this fact occupied my next seven or eight years and provided two cycles of Columbia graduate students with theses.

This was, incidentally, quite a group of students. It included Dick Nisbett, Larry Gross, Lee Ross, Patty Pliner, and Judy Rodin, almost all of whom have gone on to active research careers and professorships at major universities. I've had numbers of other outstanding students, and I'm often asked how I account for this fact. In truth, I blame it on me and on

their good luck, just as I consider myself unbelievably lucky to have worked with Festinger when he was hot and working on social comparison processes, or Elliott Aronson equally lucky to have worked with Leon when he was hot again and working on dissonance. I've had three waves of outstanding students and in each case they coincide with a period when I was hot—the first period, my Minnesota affiliation-emotion-adrenaline period, where the students included Jerry Singer, Bibb Latané, Peter Schonbach, Ladd Wheeler, and Larry Wrightsman; next, the obesity period; and the third, my smoking–urinary pH period, where the students included Peter Herman, Lucy Friedman, Lynn Kozlowski, Brett Silverstein, and Neil Grunberg.

It's just about impossible to write of these matters without seeming pretentious and pompous, but the hell with it; these are matters worth contemplating. I don't think that my students are any brighter, bigger, smarter, or prettier than anyone else's students. I do think that they lucked out in simply being around when there was an exciting problem to contemplate and questions to which no one knew the answer until they had done the research. Research, if it's done only to get a degree or a raise or a publication or to prove that someone else is an idiot, ends up as a tedious way to make a living. Research that leads to discovery and to new facts or to very new ways of looking at very old problems is an eternal fascination and a glorious way of life. I think one learns this only by luck, by being part of the discovery process. I learned it working with Festinger when he was on; perhaps he learned it from Lewin; I think that some of my students learned it from me.

The Social Psychology Department at Columbia survived as a separate entity for about eight years. Over this period, after Klineberg left, Christie and I took turns as chairman. Several of the Skinnerians left the Psychology Department, and Bob Bush became its chairman. For one reason or another, there was sufficient turnover in the two departments so that there was less and less reason for them to remain separate. The sources of the old tensions and antagonisms simply dissipated over the years; social psychology didn't seem viable as an entity distinct from the mother science, and there were more and more pressures in both departments to amalgamate. For good or bad, I insist on a substantial chunk of the credit for the amalgamation. When Klineberg was still at Columbia, with the help of the American Jewish Committee, he had convinced the philanthropist Joseph Klingenstein to give the new department a substantial grant for the study of race relations. I'd never been much impressed with the work that social scientists had been doing on prejudice and race relations. It seemed more polemic than scientific, and I talked my fellow department members into trying a new tack—using the Klingenstein money to support one-year appointments of experimental psychologists whose work had conceivable relevance to problems of prejudice and who would be interested for a year in trying their hands at a good faith attempt at spelling out the relevance.

Among our first such appointments were Julian Hochberg and Eugene Galanter. I'd hate to be forced to an honest appraisal of their contributions to the study of race relations, but these appointments did eventually change the face of psychology at Columbia. Both Hochberg and Galanter were appealing enough to the old psychology department that eventually they hired them. This new blood, plus the personnel turnover in both departments, made amalgamation of the two departments even more feasible and desirable, and in 1969 the two were rejoined administratively and eventually physically. There have been problems, but on the whole we've lived close to happily ever after, for it was a sensible and sane move which, incidentally, was followed some years later by Harvard's decision to reunite their Social Relations and Psychology Departments.

The amalgamation of the departments had one major impact on my work. I got a kitchen and a bathroom out of the move, which made it considerably easier to work on eating behavior and, as it turned out, on smoking behavior. Peter Herman's thesis (Herman, 1974) got me into the smoking business. Our early findings (Schachter, 1968) on obesity had suggested that the obese were far more responsive to external, food-related cues than were normal subjects, whose eating behavior appeared more to be responsive to the internal, physiological cues that accompany food deprivation. Herman drew an analogy between our findings on obese and normal eaters and the differences between light and heavy smokers. As he expected, he did find that light smokers, like obese eaters, were more sensitive to external, cigarette-related cues than were heavy smokers. However, somewhat contrary to his expectations he also found that most of his subjects, whether heavy or light smokers, gave some indication of internal sensitivity; that is, the amount they smoked was related to nicotine deprivation.

These indications of regulation became an obsession of sorts. As a psychologist, and a very heavy smoker, most of what I thought I knew about smoking came either out of my background with Hull (smoking is an extraordinarily well-learned habit and to be thought about as such) or my years with the Lewinians (smoking satisfies psychological needs or tension systems). Though obviously neither of these approaches was incompatible with nicotine regulation, they also seemed to have nothing to do with it, and I devoted the next few years to an attempt to reconcile these viewpoints and facts.

The first step was an attempt to establish the strength of regulation. It had been so long since I'd done a hands-on study of my own, without the help of another living soul, that I was delighted to study regulation myself (Schachter, 1977) in a group of my smoking friends in a place called Amagansett. This is a very small town on the eastern end of Long Island, an area in which I've spent my summers ever since I moved to New York. It's on the water, and until recently, when real estate people began to take over, it has been an ideal spot to combine work and play. I met my second, and I trust last, wife there—a Miss Sophia Thalia Duckworth. We begat our only child, Elijah, there. Just about every paper and book I've written in the last 25 years, I wrote there. And increasingly, as laboratory experiments get more and more difficult to do, I've conducted field research out there (Schachter, 1977, 1982).

The study of regulation couldn't have been simpler. The Philip Morris Co., which was supporting the research, had made up cigarettes for me which were either 0.3 mg or 1.3 mg of nicotine per cigarette. They packaged them in plain white cigarette packages and in alternate weeks I distributed to my friends cartons of either high or low nicotine cigarettes. They kept track of how many they smoked, and that is all there was to the study. Almost all of the subjects smoked somewhat more of the low than of the high nicotine cigarettes—on the average 25 percent more, hardly precise titration but an indication of low-order regulation.

Worrying about a possible machinery for regulation took me to the pharmacological literature where, while struggling to comprehend the metabolism and elimination of nicotine, I stumbled upon a fact which fascinated me because there was something I could do with it. Nicotine is an alkaloid, and its rate of excretion is determined by the pH, or degree of acidity, of the urine. It is a cinch to manipulate urinary pH with innocent pharmacological agents such as bicarbonate of soda, vitamin C, grapefruit juice, and cranberry juice, and my students and I decided to find out if we could manipulate smoking behavior by manipulating urinary pH. It turned out (Schachter, Kozlowski, and Silverstein, 1977) that indeed we could, and this seminal fact led to a program of reductionistic research which kept us happy for two years.

The reductionistic question we asked was simple. Could psychological events that were presumed to affect smoking rate be explained pharmacologically? For example, going to parties and also the state of psychological stress or tension were generally reported by smokers to affect smoking rate. We were able to demonstrate that this was true and also to demonstrate that both the state of stress and attending parties acidified the urine (Silverstein, Kozlowski, and Schachter, 1977; Schachter, Silverstein, Kozlowski, Herman, and Liebling, 1977). Since these were essentially correlational studies, we were forced to unscramble causality in a study in which, in effect, we experimentally pitted the mind against the bladder (Schachter, Silverstein, and Perlick, 1977). In essence, we manipulated the state of stress under conditions in which, thanks to sodium bicarbonate, urinary pH was stabilized and under placebo conditions which permitted pH to vary with stress. The results were clear-cut. In placebo conditions, stress acidified the urine, and smoking increased with stress; in bicarbonate conditions, pH remained high in both high and low stress conditions, and smoking was unaffected by the manipulation of stress.

I have, perhaps, doted excessively (Schachter, 1980) on these particular facts and have tended to think of this work as a reductionistic tour de force. The relationship of smoking to stress has been subject to such convoluted, tortured interpretations by the behaviorists (Ferster, 1970) and by the psychoanalysts (Marcovitz, 1969) that being able to reduce this presumably complex psychological phenomenon to the pH of the urine has been an understandably perverse pleasure. In any case, these studies were my last fling for quite a while in the socio-biological arena, for these smoking studies, via a circuitous route, led back to some of my earliest work in group psychology.

It started as one of those feeble academic jokes. Much of my work on smoking had been concerned with withdrawal symptoms; the research was going on at the same time that the U.S. Public Health Service and the American Cancer Society were in the throes of their media-mediated antismoking campaigns, and I amused myself (Schachter, 1977) by speculating about the effects on divorce rate, crime rate, etc., of having an entire population simultaenously trying to quit smoking or switching to very low nicotine cigarettes. This led to an increasing fascination with aggregate variables and inevitably to a concern with aggregate numbers and with what, as a psychologist, I could do with such numbers.

To illustrate what I mean by an aggregate number, consider a number such as department store sales. Since psychologists, even social psychologists, tend to deal with individual behavior, this is not the kind of number that we're accustomed to dealing with, but it is a single number which summarizes one aspect of the behavior of an entire population. Macy's was good enough to let me have the data on the daily sales of its Manhattan department store over a two-year period. For the same two years, Paul Andreassen worked out a coding scheme for analyzing the stories on the front page of the *New York Times*. Though Paul coded just about everything, the emphasis of the coding was on instances of violence. Our assumption was that if a story about violence made the front page of the *Times*, it would certainly be featured on the television and in the other city papers, and just about everyone in the city, all 7,000,000 of us, would know about the event at the same time.

If we make the common sense assumption that media-reported instances of violence will make people just a little uneasy, perhaps slightly loath to leave the house or their immediate neighborhood, we could expect department store sales to decrease on days in which the mass media featured stories about violence. This indeed turned out to be the case (Schachter et al., 1986) and I was hooked. It wasn't that there was anything more than psychologically banal about this particular finding, but the simple fact that we were able to relate these two numbers at all enchanted me, and I searched around for other aggregate numbers—a search that quickly led to the stock market, an area of human activity which daily produces staggering quantities of such numbers.

Playing with these numbers took up about four years. Most of this time I worked with Don Hood, a mathematically inclined physiological psychologist who is a born gambler. Shortly after Don came to Columbia to teach vision and physiological psychology, he came out for a weekend to Amagansett where, on the beach, I taught him to read the stock market pages. That was all it took to hook him, and as time went on, between trading stock market tips, we began to think of the market as an arena for psychological research. Paul Andreassen and Bill Gerin were working with us at the time. Starting with the efficient market theory and the random walk hypothesis, the four of us worked our way into a program of research designed to compare and contrast economists' and psychologists' approaches to market phenomena.

Until recently, there has been general agreement among academic economists that a random walk accurately describes the pattern of successive price changes in the market, and the economists have tended to think of the random walk as one of the basic facts of the field. However, our review of the research literature, as well as our own examination of daily price changes in a variety of markets, indicated that a random walk was far from a universal. Some markets, at some times, moved randomly and at other times distinctly did not (Schachter, Gerin, Hood, and Andreassen, 1985; Hood, Andreassen, and Schachter, 1985). This fact determined our subsequent research program, which in part was an attempt to understand the conditions that determine when the market is random and when it is not.

Rather than paraphrasing, I'll quote directly from our first presentation of the basic assumptions guiding this work. "Our attempts to understand the sources of non-randomness and dependence in price change will be guided by one central, over-riding assumption: the price of a stock is more than a rationally determined number. It is an opinion, an aggregate opinion, the moment-to-moment resultant of the evaluation of the community of investors. As an opinion, stock price is subject to the same set of social pressures and cultural influences as is any other opinion such as the evaluation of a work of art, the preference for a political candidate or the popularity and spread of a fad. The explicit recognition that price is a social fact will permit us to apply much of the research and theory of opinion formation and change to stock market phenomena" (Schachter, Hood, Gerin, Andreassen, and Rennert, 1985). From this starting point we went on to study the implications of psychological notions such as dependence and arousal for a variety of investment phenomena, including the effects of tips, the effects of trend on the volume of transactions, and so on.

The price of a stock is an opinion, and I'm back where I started 40 years ago, studying communication and social influence processes in the Westgate housing project.

Selected Publications by Stanley Schachter

(with A. Chapanis & R. Rouse) (1949). The effect of inter-sensory stimulation on dark adaptation and night vision. *Journal of Experimental Psychology, 39*, 425–437.

(with L. Festinger & K. Back) (1950). *Social pressures in informal groups*. New York: Harpers.

(1951). Deviation, rejection and communication. *Journal of Abnormal and Social Psychology, 46*, 190–207.

(with J. Nuttin, C. de Monchaux, P. Maucorps, D. Osmer, H. Duijker, R. Rommetveit, & J. Israel) (1954). Cross cultural experiments on threat and rejection. *Human Relations*, 7, 403–440.

(with L. Festinger & H. Riecken) (1956). *When prophecy fails.* Minneapolis: University of Minnesota Press.

(1959). *The psychology of affiliation.* Stanford, CA: Stanford University Press.

(with B. Latané) (1962). Adrenaline and avoidance learning. *Journal of Comparative and Physiological Psychology*, 65, 369–372.

(with J. Singer) (1962). Cognitive, social and physiological determinants of emotional state. *Psychological Review*, 69, 379–399.

(with L. Wheeler) (1962). Epinephrine, chlorpromazine and amusement. *Journal of Abnormal and Social Psychology*, 65, 121–128.

(with B. Latané) (1964). Crime, cognition and the autonomic nervous system. In D. Levine (Ed.), *Nebraska symposium on motivation, 1964* (pp. 221–273). Lincoln, NE: University of Nebraska Press.

(1968). Obesity and eating. *Science, 161*, 751–756.

(1971). *Emotion, obesity and crime.* New York: Academic Press.

(1977). Nicotine regulation in heavy and light smokers. *Journal of Experimental Psychology: General, 106*, 5–12.

(with L. T. Kozlowski & B. Silverstein) (1977). Effects of urinary pH on cigarette smoking. *Journal of Experimental Psychology: General, 106*, 13–19.

(with B. Silverstein and L. T. Kozlowski) (1977). Social life, cigarette smoking and urinary pH. *Journal of Experimental Psychology: General, 106*, 20–23.

(with B. Silverstein, L. T. Kozlowski, C. P. Herman, & B. Liebling) (1977). Effects of stress on cigarette smoking and urinary pH. *Journal of Experimental Psychology: General, 106*, 24–30.

(with B. Silverstein & D. Perlick) (1977). Psychological and pharmacological explanations of smoking under stress. *Journal of Experimental Psychology: General, 106*, 31–40.

(1978). Sin and error in science. *Contemporary Psychology, 23*, 4–5.

(1980). Non-psychological explanations of behavior. In L. Festinger (Ed.), *Retrospections on social psychology.* New York: Oxford University Press.

(1982). Recidivism and self-cure of smoking and obesity. *American Psychologist, 37*, 401–406.

(with W. Gerin, D. Hood, & P. Andreassen) (1985). Was the South Sea Bubble a random walk? *Journal of Economic Behavior and Organization, 6*, 323–329.

(with D. C. Hood & P. Andreassen) (1985). Random and non-random walks on the New York Stock Exchange. *Journal of Economic Behavior and Organization, 6*, 331–338.

(with D. Hood, W. Gerin, P. Andreassen, & M. Rennert) (1985). Some causes and consequences of dependence and independence in the stock market. *Journal of Economic Behavior and Organization, 6*, 339–357.

(with D. Hood, P. B. Andreassen, & W. Gerin) (1986). Aggregate variables in psychology and economics: Dependence and the stock market. In S. Kaish & B. Gilad (Eds.), *Handbook of behavioral economics* (Vol. B, pp. 237–272). Greenwich, CT: JAI.

Other Publications Cited

Bradford, L. P., & French, J. R. P. (Eds.). (1948). The dynamics of the discussion group. *Journal of Social Issues*, *4*, no. 2.

Ferster, C. B. (1970). Comments on paper by Hunt and Matarazzo. In W. A. Hunt (Ed.), *Learning mechanisms in smoking*. Chicago: Aldine.

Festinger, L. (1954). A theory of social comparison processes. *Human Relations*, *7*, 117–140.

Herman, C. P. (1974). External and internal cues as determinants of the smoking behavior of light and heavy smokers. *Journal of Personality and Social Psychology*, *30*, 664–672.

Lykken, D. T. (1957). A study of anxiety in the sociopathic personality. *Journal of Abnormal and Social Psychology*, *55*, 6–10.

Marañon, G. (1924). Contribution à l'étude de l'action émotive de l'adrénaline. *Revue française d'Endocrinologie*, *2*, 301–325.

Marcovitz, E. (1969). On the nature of addiction to cigarettes. *Journal of the American Psychoanalytic Association*, *17*, 1074–1096.

Singer, J. (1963). Sympathetic activation, drugs and fright. *Journal of Comparative and Physiological Psychology*, *56*, 612–615.

Stunkard, A. J. (1959). Obesity and the denial of hunger. *Psychosomatic Medicine*, *21*, 281–289.

Appendix

Appendix

CONTRIBUTORS TO VOLUMES I–VII

VOLUME I, 1930
Carl Murchison, ed.
Clark University Press

J. M. Baldwin
M. W. Calkins
E. Claparède
R. Dodge
P. Janet

J. Jastrow
F. Kiesow
W. McDougall
C. E. Seashore
C. Spearman

W. Stern
C. Stumpf
H. C. Warren
T. Ziehen
H. Zwaardemaker

VOLUME II, 1932
Carl Murchison, ed.
Clark University Press

B. Bourdon
J. Drever
K. Dunlap
G. C. Ferrari
S. I. Franz

K. Groos
G. Heymans
H. Höffding
C. H. Judd
C. L. Morgan

W. B. Pillsbury
L. M. Terman
M. F. Washburn
R. S. Woodworth
R. M. Yerkes

VOLUME III, 1936
Carl Murchison, ed.
Clark University Press

J. R. Angell
F. C. Bartlett
M. Bentley
H. A. Carr
S. De Sanctis

J. Fröbes
O. Klemm
K. Marbe
G. S. Myers

E. W. Scripture
E. L. Thorndike
J. B. Watson
W. Wirth

VOLUME IV, 1952
E. G. Boring et al., eds.
Clark University Press

W. V. D. Bingham	A. Gesell	J. Piaget
E. G. Boring	C. L. Hull	H. Piéron
C. L. Burt	W. S. Hunter	C. Thomson
R. M. Elliott	D. Katz	L. L. Thurstone
A. Gemelli	A. Michotte	E. C. Tolman

VOLUME V, 1967
E. G. Boring and Gardner Lindzey, eds.
Appleton-Century-Crofts

G. W. Allport	K. Goldstein	H. A. Murray
L. Carmichael	J. P. Guilford	S. L. Pressey
K. M. Dallenbach	H. Helson	C. R. Rogers
J. F. Dashiell	W. R. Miles	B. F. Skinner
J. J. Gibson	G. Murphy	M. S. Viteles

VOLUME VI, 1974
Gardner Lindzey, ed.
Prentice-Hall

F. H. Allport	O. Klineberg	M. Mead
F. A. Beach	J. Konorski	O. H. Mowrer
R. B. Cattell	D. Krech	T. M. Newcomb
C. H. Graham	A. R. Luria	S. S. Stevens
E. R. Hilgard		

VOLUME VII, 1980
Gardner Lindzey, ed.
Freeman

A. Anastasi	F. A. Geldard	C. E. Osgood
D. E. Broadbent	E. J. Gibson	R. R. Sears
J. S. Bruner	D. O. Hebb	H. A. Simon
H. J. Eysenck	Q. McNemar	

Index of Names

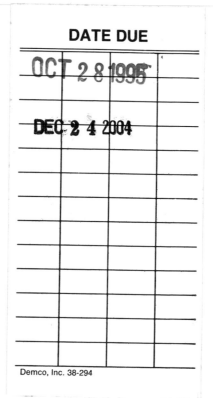